BETWEEN TWO WORLDS

BETWEEN
TWO
WORLDS

How the English *Became* Americans

Malcolm Gaskill

BASIC BOOKS

A Member of the Perseus Books Group

New York

Published by Basic Books
A Member of the Perseus Books Group

Books published by Basic Books are available at special discounts for
bulk purchases in the United States by corporations, institutions, and
other organizations. For more information, please contact the Special
Markets Department at the Perseus Books Group, 2300 Chestnut
Street, Suite 200, Philadelphia, PA 19103, or call (800) 810-4145, ext.
5000, or e-mail special.markets@perseusbooks.com.

Designed by Jack Lenzo
Set in 11 point Adobe Caslon Pro by the Perseus Books Group

Library of Congress Cataloging-in-Publication Data
Gaskill, Malcolm.
    Between two worlds : how the English became Americans /
Malcolm Gaskill.
        pages   cm
    Includes bibliographical references and index.
    ISBN 978-0-465-01111-7 (hardcover : alk. paper)—
ISBN 978-0-465-08086-1 (ebook)
    1. United States—Civilization—To 1783.   2. United States—
Civilization—English influences.   3. United States—History—
Colonial period, ca. 1600–1775.   I. Title.
    E162.G38 2014
    973—dc23
                                        2014017693

10 9 8 7 6 5 4 3 2 1

For Ed and Audrey Gaskill,
who brought me into this world

Leaving the old, both worlds at once they view,
That stand upon the threshold of the new.

—Edmund Waller, 1685

CONTENTS

PREFACE

I N THE SEVENTEENTH CENTURY more than 350,000 English people crossed the Atlantic to America. They were a mixed lot: male and female, young and old, rich and poor, rural and urban. Motives varied. There were those who fled poverty or persecution, and those who went to open trade routes or build estates, to explore and exploit. Some were coerced, including reprieved felons, prisoners of war, kidnapped children, and adolescents put into service. Frequenters of dockside inns woke up on ships that had already weighed anchor to discover they had been forced into indentured servitude. Even willing apprentices had no idea what they were getting into, though they had time to reflect later as they sweated on distant plantations. Migrants went to join relatives, to preach and proselytize, to take jobs, or to satisfy their curiosity about the New World. Some people intending to visit found themselves extending their stays, sometimes indefinitely. Others, who had resolutely forsaken England, slunk back disillusioned or ruined, homesick for the place of their birth. America was a land of promise, even a promised land; but viewed from across the ocean, amid howling wolves and prowling enemies, England could seem like a paradise lost.[1]

There was no single America. English settlements on the Atlantic seaboard stretched from Newfoundland in the north, down through Maine and New Hampshire, into Massachusetts, Connecticut, and Pennsylvania, and from there into the southern colonies of Maryland, Virginia, and the Carolinas. Bermuda and the Caribbean islands, principally Barbados and Jamaica, complete the picture. Life at a fishing station on the Avalon Peninsula of southeastern Newfoundland was very different from life in one of the ordered townships of New England, a lonely settlement of the James River, or a seething West Indian sugar field. Migrants did have one thing in common: they were no longer in England, and they had to get used to it. At best, conditions were taxing; at worst, traumatic beyond anything they had imagined while waiting for fair winds at Gravesend or Plymouth. Experience made these men and women think about the wider world, about other races and cultures, and about themselves and their native land. And their stories guided English attitudes toward America, which in turn shaped ideas about England's Atlantic identity and imperial destiny.

Experience came from adventure. The well-informed accepted the risks, or blithely dismissed them, because the prospect of change was so alluring. Youths feared missing out; ducking the challenge seemed cowardly, even effeminate. "Adventure" meant not just derring-do but also speculation. Many adventurers stayed in England, financing enterprise in America by buying company shares, sponsoring workers, or exchanging cargoes of tools and clothes for timber, furs, or fish. The success of colonization depended on both sorts of adventurers, as well as a taste for risk. Plenty of investors went bust, and many settlers died miserably. Yet even after tales of colonial disasters entered circulation, people still gambled their money on the New World and emigrated there in droves. Home may be where the heart is, as we say today, but, as Shakespeare wrote in the 1590s, it is also "where small experience grows" and a wind "scatters young men through the world."[2]

With people and materials went information and opinion. Letters from England gave instructions and asked questions; they brought news of family and national events. Letters from America put a brave face on misery, and requested supplies—and letters. Bibles and broadsheets were read to pieces in the colonies; as ships docked in Boston, men at the quayside clamored for newspapers, eager to stay in touch. While London booksellers packed barrels for the New World, English readers relished American-themed publications, from ballads to sermons, promotional literature to eyewitness reports. America became a parallel realm of existence that penetrated English life after 1600, firing imaginations and breeding possibilities. In return, visions of America were colored and clouded by migrants' perceptions of England.[3]

Adventures in America—building towns, charting rivers, fighting natives, or raising frontier families—had unforeseen consequences. For as colonists strove to leave a mark on the New World, so the New World left its mark on them. The desire to maintain integrity in oneself and in one's family, community, and society was strong, but weaker than the drift to dissolution and assimilation. Throughout the seventeenth century, "Americans" were the Indians to whom values and beliefs were exported; most colonists—described by one historian as "normal Englishmen acting normally"—called themselves "the English." The wilderness was there to be tamed, they felt, and its pagan savages reclaimed. Contact blurred boundaries, however, requiring active perpetuation of Englishness in homes, possessions, dress, communication, law, and culture. Even regional English styles and customs were exported to America. Novice settlers were ready to endanger their lives, but not their sense of themselves. Few were as incorruptible as they had hoped to be. Fears of Indians and wild creatures belonged to wider anxiety about the dilution of identity in a desert land. This anxiety was well-founded: colonists were too far from home, and too close to nature, to stay as they had been in the Old World.[4]

Whatever dreams second-generation migrants had of England, their affinity with its people had faded by comparison with their parents. White-skinned natives born in America were English in ethnicity and language, but most had only a secondhand sense of England itself. Like their transplanted parents, colonists in every foreign territory worked hard to preserve links with the Old World. They were not exceptional, if "exceptional" implies achieving uniqueness through seclusion; nor were they "Americanized," if that means having completed a fast and thorough transformation. Cultural alteration was gradual and nuanced. It emerged less from desire for change than from wanting to stay the same—a feeling more passionate than the most visceral patriotic conservatism in England. It was a yearning for transoceanic continuity and intimacy that could not, in the end, conquer feelings of estrangement. And so to the third generation in America—above all in New England—the old English became less like siblings and compatriots, and more like cousins and ancestors.[5]

Colonists of the 1690s still spoke fondly of the motherland, but the maternal instinct was weak: they craved love, but got strict parenting. To "imagine all that to be England where English men . . . doe dwell," said a Jacobean clergyman, was an idea more beloved of migrants than of English kings, who, after 1660, made distant subjects feel like peasants or slaves. But when the children rebelled, as they did long before 1776, they were revolutionary in the seventeenth-century sense only: they desired the *status quo ante*—crown patronage, not independence—and spoke a language of liberty derived from the "ancient constitution," which was not a document but an institutional memory of rights. This, too, was a striving for Englishness. If they *had* given up being freeborn subjects upon landing in America—the exceptionalist view—it is implausible that sugar magnates in Barbados in the 1650s, Chesapeake planters in the 1670s, and Boston's Puritan elite in the 1680s could have defended this privilege so fiercely against perceived abuses by the government in London. Their liberty was the prerogative to be ruled according to tradition, transcending the personal authority of the monarch.[6]

As colonists' economic fortunes improved, so the crown strove to control them. Thus constitutional nostalgia became infused with an altogether less deferential feeling: that the metropole neither valued their sacrifices nor understood their mentality. Fraternal unity, still firm, was strained. The reasons for England wanting its foreign franchises to obey—their burgeoning prosperity and alarming political self-sufficiency—highlighted the very achievements set to frustrate that ambition. Although New England, Virginia, and the West Indies did not avow to go it alone, by 1700 hard experience had imposed limits upon how much subordination was bearable. Settlers balked at compromise because their environment did not compromise, and it had changed them. Their identity was defined not only by hardship and danger but also by matters of authority—conferred, claimed, and contested—and by matters of legitimacy of power. Yet the story was not uniquely American: English people at home faced similar trials in that turbulent century.

Between Two Worlds is neither a search for the origins of the United States nor a comprehensive history of colonial America. Instead it examines a neglected dimension of the history of England: what happened to its people in America, and the effect America had on those who remained at home. Although most of the action occurs on the western side of the Atlantic, England is essential to the plot. The exceptionalist eye mainly sees America, neglecting English mentalities and events as if these were eclipsed, their influence neutralized, as migrants traded up geographically. Abundant land did make new work cultures possible, encouraging a distinctive civic identity, especially in New England's self-contained townships. And their legal means to govern, own land, and regulate labor were not simply English common law transplanted, but a unique amalgam of customs, statutes, charters, and neo-feudal mandates. More than has been recognized, however, American "innovation" used English models. The common law had *always* been flexible, and the ancient constitution was a practical resource, not an ossified code. Moreover, the realm of England was a dynamic commonwealth made up of many pocket commonwealths—9,000 parishes and 200 corporate boroughs. They all constituted an unacknowledged "monarchical republic," where amateur office-holding was widespread, and urban freemen likened themselves to citizens in classical city-states.[7]

The idea that the American wilderness made downtrodden subjects into modern men needs adjusting, then, because the progressive archetype already existed in the Old World. But there is another reason. New World prosperity and liberty for some required others to be poor, subordinated, dispossessed, and shackled. This divisive patterning also originated in England, where hierarchical obligation and discipline supported the humanistic ideal of a "golden mean" between tyranny and anarchy—the very spirit that guided New England's Puritan pioneers.[8]

We should suspend our knowledge of modern times and imagine England and European America as they once were, the former in its prime, the latter in its infancy. Even in 1700, who would have guessed that the colonies would become a global power like England? They lacked England's economic and military strength, and they had none of its social, cultural, or constitutional coherence. Even English political unrest, notably the civil wars of the 1640s, sprang not from failure and despair but from pragmatic self-reflexivity: the creative urge of those quasi-republican citizens and office-holders to confront change and pursue compromise. For them, England was an eternal presence, America a distant resource for solving economic problems, diffusing religious conflict, and extending political influence. Some still assume that the migrants abandoned England, with its outmoded structures and irksome strictures, to build a new world. In fact, with few exceptions, they set out to re-create a world felt to be vanishing at home. Landowners missed medieval feudalism, when peasants had worked manorial estates; Puritans sought to restore the church as it was before bishops corrupted it; and everyone lamented the decline in neighborliness: goodness and mercy, credit and charity. Emigration, then, was a conservative countermeasure.

My intention is not to privilege the English contribution to what were multinational and ethnically complex developments; that would simply repeat what has been called the "narrow vision of American uplift for English men" common to older works. Instead, I have taken the perspective of English migrants, focusing on their experience in what was mainly an English century of colonization. Too many American scholars still see England as backstory; too many of their colleagues across the Atlantic lose interest in the migrants as they exit the European map. The West Indies, furthermore, were cast off as British imperial history after the American Revolution. Another distortion lies in the assumed homogeneity of English colonists, whereas their differences and disputes, ambivalences and ambiguities, were striking. The book's sections—planters, saints, and warriors—are keyed to successive phases of colonization spanning three generations, yet also represent three faces of colonization which had coexisted from the start.[9]

Beneath the mythic veneer, we find authentic relationships, identities, and meanings that suggest a need to reintegrate seventeenth-century England and early America into one story. Though not without its critics, "Atlantic history" has kicked the Anglocentric imperial habit, restoring America to a broader transatlantic context, reanimating lives and minds on an intercontinental stage. At the same time, however, colonial history, though reinvigorated by postwar "new social history," has tended to focus on individual mainland colonies and communities, thus narrowing our view and restricting our understanding of the whole.[10]

Using approaches old and new, this book is a national history without boundaries, an English epic told through stories of adventure, where people speak for themselves. We encounter them in contrasting American regions (not just in New England, where Puritans continue to fog popular memory) and in England, too. In this first century of settlement, new thinking and feeling—the fruits of experience—transformed mentalities on both continents. Parallels between voyages of discovery and science fiction are apt, for all such stories feature hazardous quests, encounters with the unknown, and startling metamorphoses. England's migrants learned by trial and error what it meant to pass from one world to another. "In the beginning," the philosopher John Locke wrote in 1690, comparing primitivism with progress to stress the potential of the wilderness, "all the World was America." Yet, by Locke's day, America's white inhabitants, along with their English mercantile sponsors and imperial overlords, had already drawn America into the European sphere. And English people on both sides of the ocean had a far better sense in 1700 than in 1600 of the prizes and pitfalls of going to America, its similarities to England, and its differences.[11]

The America in which a third generation grew old was far more secure than the land their grandfathers had settled. On the mainland, there were cities, public institutions, and thriving trade. New England was more like the old England—except with higher life expectancy. Things had not looked this hopeful even thirty years earlier, when Indian wars had imperiled the English from Maine to Virginia. By 1700 the tide had turned, and fathers who straddled two worlds without fully belonging to either were quizzed by youths wondering who they were. In reply came stories of homemaking in a strange place—stories steeped in emotions: fear, anxiety, hope, relief, and rapture. The frontier had possessed souls in a way that relatives in England, or even children born in America, could barely comprehend. To retain and advance territory, adventurers had visited slaughter, dispossession, and exile upon ethnic and enslaved peoples; too rarely does the image of the English colonist as a predatory intruder (common in Irish and Native American historiography) dislodge that of the intrepid seeker after fortune or freedom in an alien, hostile world. Even so, pitiless ambition was bound up with an astonishing intensity of faith, forbearance, and courage. More than anything else, it is the quality of that courage—the quintessence of adventure—that has inspired this book.[12]

PROLOGUE
Worlds Collide

T HIS STORY BEGINS not in England or America, but in Ireland.
Captain Humphrey Gilbert, tall, imperious, and ruthlessly determined, arrived there in 1566 with orders to suppress the earls who
opposed Elizabeth I's plantations—English settlements—on their soil.
Gilbert's promotion to colonel stiffened his policies, and he began to in-
sist on unconditional surrender and to apply tactics of terror. He treated
the Irish like an inferior species, trampling their liberties and customs.
Rumor had it that the path taken by native people to his quarters, there
to abase themselves and plead, was lined with severed heads. A decade
later, his admiring younger half brother wrote that he had "never heard
nor read of any man more feared . . . amonge the Irish nation."[1]

Perhaps inspired by occult visions, Gilbert became an explorer in 1578
and began searching for "remote heathen and barbarous lands." After
some false starts, he founded a company of merchants. In 1583 he led a
fleet to Newfoundland, where, blowing a trumpet and thrusting letters patent at fishermen there, he took possession of a huge territory—
England's first major claim in the New World. High on dreams of a
greater American expedition (and lordship over a mini-England of migrant serfs), Gilbert headed south toward the Azores, where, in the dead
of night, his ship was lost in a tempest. Supposedly his last words, yelled
to a companion vessel, were: "Wee are as neere to heaven by Sea as by
lande." By this time, Gilbert's doting half-brother, himself a former soldier in Ireland, was a favored courtier. He received the bad news like a
torch placed in his hand and within months had obtained a patent—a
royal license—to obtain American lands. His name was Walter Ralegh.[2]

Ralegh, then just thirty years old, was like Gilbert in many ways:
athletic, gallant, and intellectual—a voracious reader and collector of

opinions. Among his advisers was Thomas Harriot, a young Oxford graduate, who used mathematics and astronomy to instruct Ralegh's men in navigation. He also worked on an Algonquian dictionary with two Indians who had been captured on a reconnaissance mission in 1584. The project required devising a phonetic scheme. To this expertise, Ralegh added a smart sense of public relations. One of Gilbert's close friends, Richard Hakluyt, assisted by Hakluyt's namesake cousin, was commissioned to write enticing prospectuses, while Ralegh drummed up political and financial support. He was as keen to learn from his dead brother's mistakes as he was inspired by his heroism. Gilbert's memorial in Raphael Holinshed's *Chronicles* (1587) implied hubris: the soldier who subdued the Irish had failed to master the waves. His fate chastened many adventurers, including the antiquarian William Camden. "He was taught (too late) by the devouring seas," Camden wrote, "teaching others also by his example that it is a matter of great difficulty, by the expences of a private man, to plant a Colony in farre distant Countries."[3]

Yet rewards beckoned. In the year Gilbert died, Sir George Peckham, an investor in plantations, published a book that gave the explorer a voice from beyond his watery grave. Praising Gilbert's virtue, Peckham made the case for colonization: the biblical justification, the fillip to trade, the desired affront to Spain—conquerors of southern America—and the enlarged glory of God, crown, and nation. Furthermore, the Indians, "poore Pagans . . . thirsting after christianitie," would be saved. To ignore this opportunity was sinful; but men like Ralegh and Harriot needed no persuading.[4]

In 1585 Thomas Harriot was twenty-five. A Renaissance man craving action, he was excited by Ralegh's invitation to found a colony, an outpost from which to acquire riches, either directly or by plundering Spanish fleets. As well as navigating and surveying, he was tasked with recording flora and fauna, and a draftsman named John White was recruited to assist him. White had been hired for Ralegh's initial exploratory voyage (as had Harriot), and in 1577 he had accompanied the explorer Martin Frobisher in search of a northwest passage to Asia. He had painted an Inuit man, woman, and child whom Frobisher had shipped to London as trophies. William Camden had examined them and had likened the woman's blue face-paint to the blue dye called "woad" that the ancient Britons had used for the same purpose.[5]

Elizabeth I, Raleigh's adoring "Virgin Queen," refused to let him lead the expedition, appointing instead his abrasive cousin Sir Richard

Grenville, another veteran of the Irish campaign. By the spring of 1585, the ships were ready. Ralegh issued orders, including that the Indians be respected. Three years earlier, an explorer had found South Americans "naturallie very curteous yf you doe not abuse them" (and had been thrilled by the natural world, including flightless birds called "penguins"). In July, after a chaotic two-month voyage, Grenville reached the coast of modern North Carolina. Still squabbling with Colonel Ralph Lane, who was to govern the colony, he landed his six hundred men at Roanoke, an island ten miles by three that was enclosed between a chain of smaller islands and the mainland. Earlier that year, Ralegh had been knighted, and he had received permission to name his country in the queen's honour: Virginia.[6]

The sight of cobalt shores against a bank of trees thrilled Harriot and White, flooding their senses. It was just as Arthur Barlowe, leader of the 1584 expedition, had told Ralegh: "The air smelt as sweet and strong as if we were in a fragrant flower garden." They roamed the island, testing phrases on Secotan Indians, who wondered if they were gods—it was a tempting sacrilege not to deny it.[7]

While Harriot took notes, White sketched everything he saw— a land crab, a pelican, a pineapple. Most striking were his natives, rendered in graphite and watercolor (and powdered silver and gold), inherent to a prelapsarian world. Unlike other representations, which confirmed suppositions of barbarism or monstrosity, White's natives are casually posed, engaging the viewer with stares and smiles. They regard each other and their environment; they work and play. There is abundance: cornfields, roasting fish, leather garments, and glimpses of copper. Young men look virile, women fertile; children are healthy. A girl, daughter of the chief of Pomeiooc, excitedly shows her mother a doll of an Elizabethan gentlewoman. White's Indians are industrious and ingenious, peaceable and perfectable: they are builders, toolmakers, farmers, and warriors—the kind of people with which an Englishman could do business, their home somewhere he could prosper.[8]

Harriot and White were not objective recorders: they had been told to make America appealing, and they viewed the strange through a prism of the familiar. But they were influenced as much by Roanoke as by Ralegh. To humanists for whom art and science and theology were adjacent facets of creation, life in Virginia was a beguiling cabinet of curiosities, not just a collection to gawk at; it was involving, like a hall of mirrors. Glimpsing their own reflections made adventurers ponder not

The wife of the Pomeiooc chief with her daughter, 1585. The girl's doll is clearly an English gentlewoman—a gift from Sir Walter Ralegh's explorers. This was one of a series of naturalistic watercolors painted by John White on the ill-fated Roanoke Island.

only the New World but the world that had made *them*—an absorbing education and an enchanting seduction. Had they found this primitive land, or, in some uncanny way, had it found them? The global scheme in ancient texts would have to accommodate new empirical wisdom.[9]

Not every Englishman was so moved. Ralph Lane was a vain, volatile career soldier who had cut his teeth in Ireland. Acquisitiveness and intolerance propelled him, and what was good for Irish rebels was even better for Indians. Like stubborn children or beasts, misfits in God's great chain, they would be made to obey. This mentality was shared by Lane's troops, whose genius, nurtured in the green fields of Leinster and Munster, was for violence, not diplomacy. What they built on Roanoke was a forbidding garrison, not a sympathetic commonwealth of citizen-planters. Under Lane's governance, the Old World did not so much meet the new one as collide with it.[10]

Yet for all his bluster, it was Lane who would be disciplined by Virginia, not the other way round. Thus far, Wingina, chief lord of Roanoke, had treated the English with generous equanimity only to be repaid with contempt, his people with brutality. The situation had deteriorated when Grenville returned to England for supplies and Lane took over. Wingina withheld food from his strange guests, who grew restive. Not only had they nearly exhausted their supplies of trinkets and baubles, currency for buying maize, but they had neglected to bring fishing nets and struggled to hit game birds with their muskets. Meanwhile, word spread of a plot to destroy the garrison. With increasing desperation, Lane led a party to look for a viable harbor and found one in the Chesapeake Bay; of gold and silver, there was none.[11]

The expedition limped back to Roanoke on Easter Monday 1586. They had been ambushed, they had been forced to eat their dogs, and they were empty-handed. Now they heard the rumors. Believing attack to be the best defense, on the first night of June Lane led a contingent across the sound to the sleeping village of Dasemunkepeuc. At the cry of "Christ or victory," the soldiers advanced, killing men, women, and children. Pleas for mercy in Algonquian were as unaffecting as pleas in Gaelic had been. Wingina, badly wounded, fled to the woods, but was hunted down and beheaded. The war was over, but the colony was finished. A fortnight later the legendary privateer Sir Francis Drake rescued survivors, including Lane, Harriot, and White, and they abandoned Roanoke until Grenville returned that summer. Departing again, Grenville left fifteen men to defend the fort. Their fate is unknown.[12]

Back in England, Harriot began writing an account of his year on Roanoke, a wondrous study of ethnic culture. He stressed the natives' poverty and innocence: they have cause, he noted presciently, to fear the English as well as love them. Faced with steel and gunpowder, their only tactic was to flee. Trinkets pleased them; gadgets—compasses and clocks, magnets and books—astonished them, as they seemed like divine gifts to a special people. "Conversing with us, they were brought into great doubts of their owne [God], and no small admiration of ours," related Harriot, "with earnest desire in many to learne more than we had meanes for want of perfect utterance in their language to expresse." He had been frustrated to see Indians rub themselves with his Bible, finding himself unable to explain that its power lay in the words, not the paper and bindings.[13]

Harriot's *Briefe and True Report* was published in 1588. From a defensive start, it rose to a crescendo of optimism. Harriot dismissed "slaunderous and shamefull speeches bruited abroade" by men like Grenville—whom he considered effete urbanites mad for lucre, ill-suited to the wilderness. There were less obvious riches, Harriot told investors, such as a medicinal herb that Spaniards called "tobacco." This was the boost Ralegh needed to promote his new colony. In April the previous year, John White had led a fresh cohort to America, including his pregnant daughter, Eleanor Dare. Things went wrong. An enthusiastic colonizer, White was not, however, a natural leader, and because of the events that occurred with Lane, relations were tense with the natives that White had so lovingly painted. As he saw the food stores shrink, White realized that he had no choice but to restock in England. He said farewell to his daughter and baby granddaughter, who had been born in August, the first child to English parents in America. Her name was Virginia.[14]

White's return to Virginia was prevented by war with Spain. In fact, he did not see Roanoke again until August 18, 1590, his granddaughter's third birthday. But Virginia Dare had vanished, and so had everyone else: over a hundred English men, women, and children. White's home had been ransacked, his possessions scattered. The name of a neighboring island, Croatoan, had been partially carved on a tree; but the coming hurricane season forced White to sail home, leaving the mystery unsolved—as it remains today. For all his planning and support, Ralegh had failed again. William Camden's judgment of Gilbert, that it was hard for a man to plant a distant colony, now seemed prophetic.[15]

Something remarkable did come of the venture. In 1590, the year the Roanoke experiment collapsed, Richard Hakluyt published his *Principal Navigations*, a compendium that set a course for colonization and a pattern for plantations to come. Also on sale that year was a third edition of Harriot's *Briefe and True Report*, illustrated with engravings of sublime sophistication. At Hakluyt's behest, White's watercolors had been given to an engraver named Theodor de Bry, Hakluyt's associate, who had published the new work in Frankfurt—in English, French, German, and Latin. It sold well, feeding and stimulating demand for tales of the New World. In England, the impact of de Bry's pictures with Harriot's text would endure longer than memories of Roanoke, and help to erase them. The attachment to America forged by this book was not just intellectual, political, and commercial, but also emotional.

It created a vision of the exotic and sounded a clarion call to do good overseas. De Bry made White's Indian faces more Caucasian and visually tidied settlements to European taste. But the sinuous limbs and contented expressions, an innocent conformity to nature, caused a sensation, shaping colonial ambitions for the next century.[16]

Harriot's treatise ends with a surprise: several portraits of ancient Britons. In one, a Celt stands defiantly, naked but for the iron torque around his neck and a sword belt, his body daubed and scarified. He holds a severed head, and at his feet lies another, the faces those of Elizabethan gentlemen; behind them a masted ship rides at anchor. In another, a woman's body is more richly decorated, her hair flowing; she, too, is a proud warrior—an antitype to the buttoned-up Tudor gentlewoman. The inference from these engravings was plain, as it had been to Camden studying the Inuit's face-paint. They were meant to show, as de Bry explained, "how that the Inhabitants of the great Bretannie have bin in times past as sauvage as those of Virginia"—in truth, even more so. And the moral was that Englishmen must nurture in the Indians

Theodor de Bry's engravings from 1590, based on John White's paintings, suggested that ancient Britons were pagan savages like the Roanoke Indians. But then they were civilized by the Romans, whom the English were duty-bound to emulate in America.

(and the Irish) what the Romans had given to them: law, religion, and civility. This is what Locke advised a century later: don't shy away from adventure, for the whole world was once like wild America.[17]

The exploits of Gilbert and Ralegh, Grenville and Lane, and Harriot and White established two major themes in English attitudes to America: sympathetic fascination for a pristine world and a propensity for exploitation and domination. These were like contrapuntal melodies, always together, one twisting round the cadence of the other. Empathy and antipathy consisted in paired emotions: love and hate, desire and fear, generosity and envy, tenderness and aggression, elation and misery, hope and despair. These passions stirred even in the same conflicted breast. American experience divided and transfigured colonists, forcing them to cleave to a sense of their former selves by perpetuating English ways and also to acquiesce. Yet the outcome of this strained counterpoint was always the same: slow deviation from existing sensibilities and the creation of something new, a rebirth both startling and exhilarating.

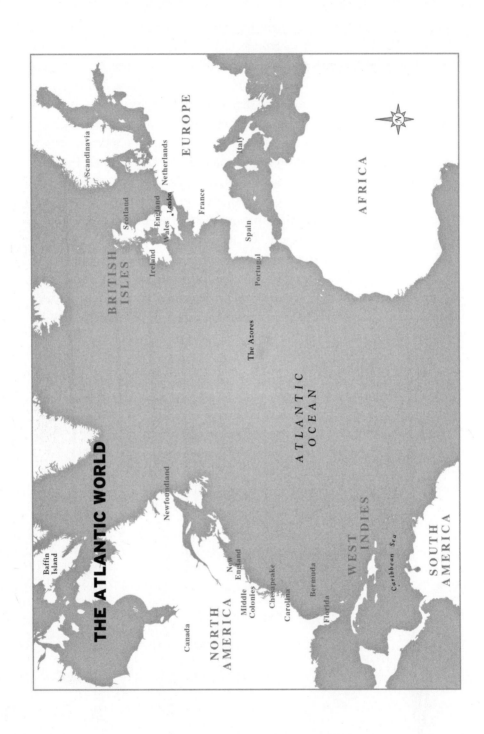

THE ATLANTIC WORLD

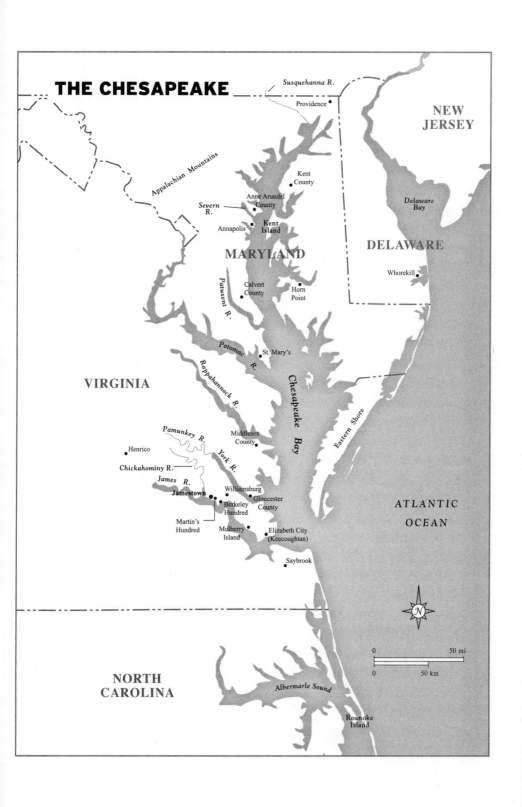

THE CHESAPEAKE

Susquehanna R.

Providence

NEW JERSEY

Appalachian Mountains

Kent County

Severn R.

Anne Arundel County

Delaware Bay

DELAWARE

Annapolis

Kent Island

MARYLAND

Whorekill

Patuxent R.

Calvert County

Horn Point

Potomac R.

St. Mary's

VIRGINIA

Rappahannock R.

Chesapeake Bay

Eastern Shore

Pamunkey R.

Middlesex County

Henrico

York R.

Chickahominy R.

Williamsburg

James R.

Jamestown

Gloucester County

ATLANTIC OCEAN

Berkeley Hundred

Martin's Hundred

Mulberry Island

Elizabeth City (Keecoughtan)

Saybrook

N

0   50 mi

0   50 km

NORTH CAROLINA

Albermarle Sound

Roanoke Island

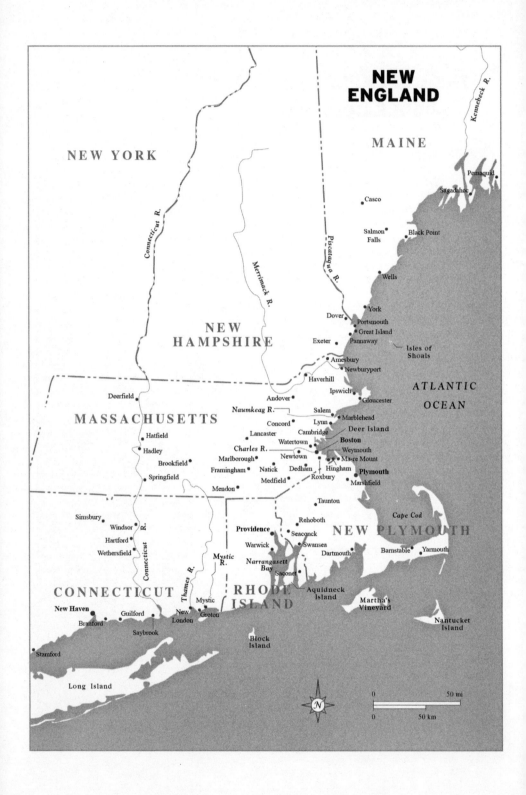

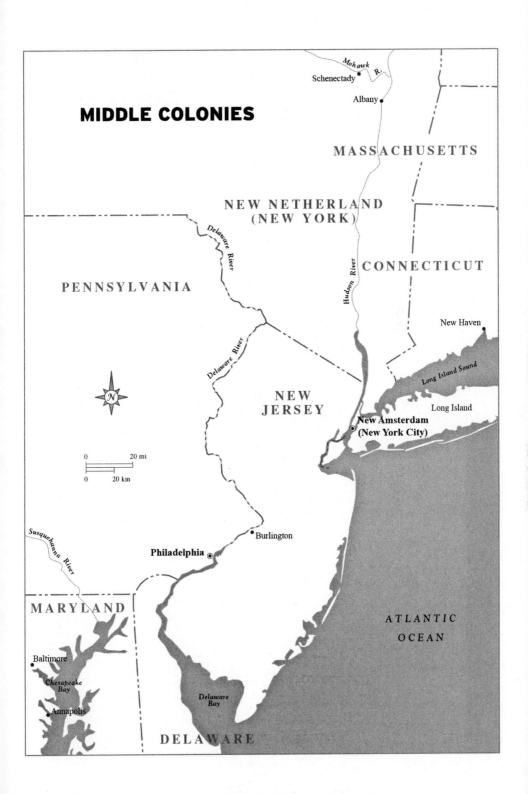

MIDDLE COLONIES

Mohawk R.
Schenectady
Albany

MASSACHUSETTS

NEW NETHERLAND
(NEW YORK)

Delaware River

CONNECTICUT

Hudson River

PENNSYLVANIA

New Haven

Delaware River

Long Island Sound

NEW
JERSEY

Long Island

New Amsterdam
(New York City)

N

0   20 mi

0   20 km

Susquehanna River

Burlington

Philadelphia

ATLANTIC
OCEAN

MARYLAND

Baltimore

Chesapeake
Bay

Annapolis

Delaware
Bay

DELAWARE

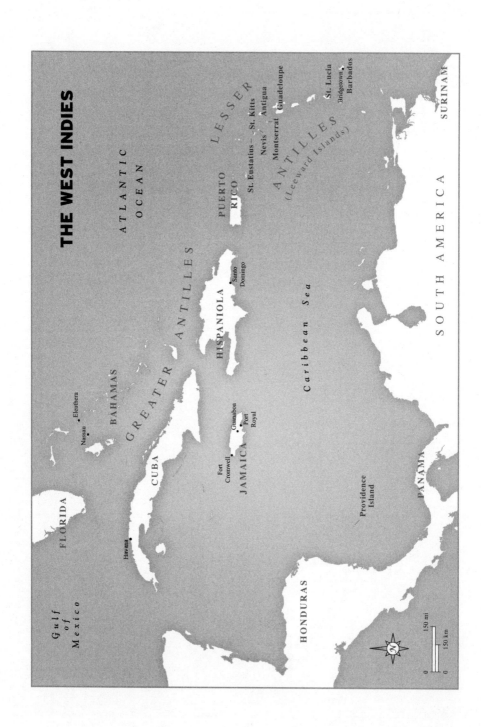

THE WEST INDIES

I
PLANTERS
1607–1640

CHAPTER 1

Brave Heroic Minds

F EW ENGLISH PEOPLE had experienced an ice storm, but on the rocky coasts of northeastern America they were common. Snow turned to freezing rain, coating everything in ice. The huddled buildings at Sagadahoc, the tip of a peninsula at the mouth of the Kennebec River, were glazed like Christmas hams. Maine winters were always bitter, but that of 1607–1608 was breathtakingly so. Colonists stayed inside as much they could, conserving energy for essential tasks like stoking fires and plugging the crevices where the wind crept in. Men kept watch on the bastion, puffing on pipes and stamping their feet. The headland's commanding views exposed it to gales that howled like Furies. From all around their fortified world, settlers peered out at a white wilderness pressed between iron-gray waters and threatening skies.[1]

Desperate to save the colony, George Popham, elderly and infirm, had handed command to Ralegh Gilbert, son of the explorer Sir Humphrey Gilbert (and Sir Walter Ralegh's nephew). But like a curse on the bloodline, the past was repeated. Gilbert, however determined, could not succeed where his forebears had failed. Fevers spread, depleting manpower, and a fire destroyed the dwindling stores. Planters who had dreamed of a new start endured the winter cheek by jowl with rough soldiers and sailors in smoky blockhouses, some reflecting that they had left comfortable lives to become paupers at the edge of the world.[2]

What *were* they were doing in Sagadahoc? The answer lies in the condition of England and the character of its people. The thoughts of men like Popham and Gilbert were shaped by divine order in the universe and the earthly stability maintained by hierarchy and tradition. But the sixteenth century had challenged old certainties. The population soared, Protestantism replaced Catholicism as the orthodox faith, and state governance infiltrated daily life. The peace of the realm depended on uneasy consensus between conservatives and reformers, landowners and tenants, masters and servants. The rhetoric of a magnificent ideology, where God was the crown's patron, made the social organism seem perpetually robust. By 1600, however, this image was projected so vigorously precisely because of the tensions and cracks it masked. Meanwhile, Englishmen searched for solutions. Their imagination and endeavors, faltering and inconspicuous at first, would over three generations produce a vast Atlantic empire.

Change in England brought opportunity as well as peril. With proper financial and logistical preparation, the New World became a plausible exit from what felt like impending chaos. The Sagadahoc enterprise was set in motion by an aristocratic entrepreneur, Sir Ferdinando Gorges, and Lord Chief Justice Sir John Popham, uncle of the ailing governor and a promoter of Irish colonization. Popham and Gorges were eager and astute, and like the earlier adventurers of the 1580s, they combined sacred duty with lust for gold and glory. Exceptional risk-takers, they were impatient with men who felt fettered by convention. In 1605 they commissioned a navigator, George Waymouth, to go to Maine, where men had described forests of oak, beech, and fir surrounding fields of strawberries and roses. Fresh water cascaded down cliffs, cod and haddock filled fishing baskets; and there was clay suitable for bricks. They had found earthly perfection, it was said, and were reluctant to leave.[3]

In 1606, Popham secured a patent, pledged a substantial investment, and began soliciting advice. On June 1 the following year, the *Gift* and the *Mary and John* set sail, and two months later their hundred or so men were eating lobsters and swapping beads for beaver skins with Indians who rowed out to greet them. Maine was all that had been promised. The sun sparkled on a perfect sea, and lush vegetation covered coastal lowlands. On August 19 the travelers landed and heard a sermon and a reading of the patent; the next day they began work on a star-shaped fort named for St. George, England's patron saint. Things went well. The palisade was raised with military precision on the Irish model, and houses built for the expedition's leaders. Plans to send a ship to England in triumph were discussed. But autumn came early, and by the time the *Mary and John* departed, the oaks were russet and gold. The winds became northerly, funneling downriver with mounting ferocity. The colonists turned up their collars and stockpiled firewood.[4]

The *Mary and John* docked at Plymouth back in England on December 1. That night, Sir Ferdinando Gorges wrote to the secretary of state, Lord Salisbury, with "greate newes of a fertill Contry, gallant Rivers, stately Harbors and a people tractable"; the only problems were elusive commodities and colonists' "pride and arrogansay, faction and privat resolution." Within two days Gorges had more for Salisbury: George Popham was pusillanimous, Ralegh Gilbert naive and headstrong. The return of the *Gift* in February 1608 brought little reassurance apart from fanciful rumors about spices and the proximity of a northwest passage. Spirits flagged among Sagadahoc's remaining forty-five men, and dreams of England replaced the summer's heady vision of Maine. Popham died, and then a relief ship brought news that his uncle, Sir John, was also dead, which "proved such a corrosive to all, as struck them with despair of future remedy." Their courage had been used up.[5]

And courage was key. In England, for a generation it had enabled men like Gorges and Popham to stake their wealth and honor on such projects. In the 1580s, the explorer Christopher Carleill had argued that everyone from prosperous merchants to "the generall sorte of people throughout all Englande" might gain from overseas investment if they raised their hearts, citing the proverb: "Nothyng venture, nothyng have." But for those actually in America, the demands were greater. Maine's colonists put faith in God, but the stamina this gave them was expended as fast as other precious resources. No Eden or Canaan, America now seemed a monument to folly, worsened by poor relations with the Indians—a legacy of George Waymouth's abduction of five Wabenakis.[6]

At last came the decision, said Gorges, "by which all our former hopes were frozen to death." When Ralegh Gilbert announced his return to England, his ragged men dismantled what they could and stowed it in the ships. Heading home, their sense of relief was tempered by shame and disappointment. Some could not accept failure. Gorges brooded, and for several years Sir John Popham's son Francis continued to send vessels to Maine. But however rich the fishing, there would be no new colony, and finally Francis Popham, too, was forced to confront his failure and loss.[7]

The repatriation of Sagadahoc's planters dismayed investors, who condemned their weakness of character. "They after a winter stay dreaming to themselves of new hopes at home," said one critic, "returned backe with the first occasion, and to justifie the suddennesse of their returne they did coyne many excuses." Colonists blamed the land, the weather, and their leadership, but never themselves, and the "base sluggishness" of a few—cowardice, by any other name—was felt to have infected men of "provident forwardnes." This was deplored, yet predictable. Classical tales that inspired champions of colonization had poltroons as well as heroes, and matched glory and grandeur with hubris and pathos. In 1624, Samuel Maverick, a traveler from Devon, arrived in Sagadahoc and surveyed it. The remains of the settlement seemed like the ruins of a lost civilization. "I found Rootes and Garden hearbs and some old Walles there," he noted elegiacally, "which shewed it to be the place where they had been."[8]

A t home, the Sagadahoc adventure was an insignificant matter, yet the problems it had addressed were critical. England was a nation of 4 million people. Royal power radiated to a landowning elite of nobility and gentry, who, as justices of the peace, upheld the law. The economy was mainly agrarian, with produce distributed through a network of market towns; there were a few cities, prominently London, supporting trade and manufacture, principally of textiles. Demography was the engine of change, for better and worse. A rapidly expanding population increased demand for food, which meant profits both for farmers able to produce surpluses and for manorial lords who exploited their estates commercially. Smallholdings were consolidated, arable land converted to pasture and orchards. Tenants, already hit by lower wages and higher prices, were squeezed out, swelling the ranks of the laboring poor. More and more young men inherited ever smaller shares of their fathers' estates—or nothing, where the custom was primogeniture. Some 200,000 textile workers suffered from falling domestic demand and rising foreign competition. Vagrancy and crime rose, as did the burden of poor relief on England's parishes. Riots against food shortages and land enclosure invoked customary liberties enshrined in the vague emotional precepts of the ancient and unwritten constitution.[9]

Most tumults, then, were deferential reminders of paternalist obligations—rights implicit in ideology and explicit in Magna Carta, a medieval agreement that the monarch's power was not absolute and arbitrary, but reciprocal and conditional. Englishmen believed themselves to be English subjects, entitled to rule by the English crown wherever they were in the world. Just as defense of custom at home followed economic change, assertion of liberties abroad went with growing interest in colonization. Forces of pull and push linked the two. The *pull* was the imagined destiny of a Protestant nation, many of whose inhabitants felt that resisting the Spanish Catholics—the dark lords of an American empire—was equivalent to resisting the Antichrist. The *push* was the corpulent, diseased commonwealth. When bodily humors were imbalanced, physicians advised letting blood; so, too, with the body politic. England could cure itself by sending its poor to plantations.

Another vivid metaphor was the hive. "We read that the Bees," observed the writer Richard Hakluyt in 1582, "when they grow to bee too many in their hives at home, are wont to bee led by their Captaines to swarme abroad, and seeke themselves a new dwelling place." The ancients knew this. Hakluyt pitied executed thieves, "superfluous people" who might have thrived in America. Throughout the 1580s he waved the colonial banner. His "Discourse on Western Planting," commissioned for Elizabeth I by her secretary, Sir Francis Walsingham, linked economic crisis and civil unrest: the report argued that by establishing a colony in Virginia, England could empty its prisons of those who, "havinge no way to be sett on worke, be either mutinous and seeke alteration in the state, or at leaste very burdensome to the common wealthe." A year earlier, Christopher Carleill had explained how the feckless lives of "our poore sorte of people" led to "the great disquiet of the better sorte," and how colonial prosperity would promote social peace. Funding such enterprises was therefore an act of Christian charity. But the queen was unmoved, and so were investors.[10]

Elizabeth had given the Roanoke venture her blessing, but no money. Her concern was not empire-building, but domestic security. Ireland and the Channel Islands were England's only overseas territories, and the English navy was small. Foreign adventures were ad hoc, limited in aims, and privately financed. Yet attracting investment was hard—witness the minutes of a Chester city council meeting from the spring of 1584. The mayor, asked by Christopher Carleill to support an American expedition, went round the table. "Every man demanded what they will adventure. . . . There were none of this Assembly that of them sellves wolde adventure eny thinge to that enterprise savinge that Mr Will[ia]m Massy saide he wolde." The assembly blamed Chester's declining fortunes, but Carleill felt the cause was timidity. He believed that men like Massy would lay the foundations for English America. Thus challenged, even the charismatic Ralegh struggled to maintain a bright façade, and failure at Roanoke brought what was left of that façade crashing down. Promoters argued that plantations would create new export markets; but Elizabethan obsessions with silver and jewels still raised expectations so high as to guarantee disappointment. A popular ballad asked:

> Have yow not hard of Florida,
> A coontré far be west?
> Wher savage pepell planted are
> By nature and by hest,
> Who in the mold fynd glysterynge gold,
> And yt for tryfels sell.

It is obvious why the conquistadors' legend of El Dorado gripped imaginations, but it is also obvious why an entrepreneur might not want to spend money looking for it.[11]

Tension between England and Spain over religion and commerce led to war in 1585. One effect of the conflict, set to last two decades, was to stimulate interest in America both as a battleground and as a locus of wealth and prestige. In 1590, Hakluyt published his *Principal Navigations*, a rationale for and summons to adventure as well as a reference work. It made America intelligible and established its author as an English Homer telling a national story. But behind the romance, skeptics asked, where was the substance? Voyages achieved little, colonial projects floundered, and royal coffers stayed shut, unless to receive loot from state-sponsored piracy.[12]

Yet the fabulousness of America also explains its tenacity as an idea. The diplomat Sir Edward Hoby jotted notes about "Norumbega," a semi-mythical northeasterly region described by Sir Humphrey Gilbert, who had heard of it from Sir Francis Drake's sailors. A place of strange beasts and precious resources, it was England's property through historical precedent and natural right. "By the law of all nations," declared Hoby, "it was ever held lawfull for a Christian to take away any thing from Infidells." This land was *res nullius*, that is, nobody's property, which might therefore belong to anyone, according to a concept of Roman law. Yet it was one thing to extend abroad the

classical *imperium* that, from early Tudor days, had united Britain ideologically, and another to claim ownership and *dominium*. The objectives
of liberty and empire were not easily reconciled, although colonization
depended on it. It took neoclassical ideals of Renaissance humanism—
civic virtue, honor, and national glory—to square the circle.[13]

In 1602, inspired by *Principal Navigations* and using Ralegh's patent,
Bartholomew Gosnold, a privateer from Suffolk, sailed to what would
become New England in search of trading posts. Among his thirty-
two-man complement was a minister, John Brereton, who recorded
the voyage. Compared to this place, he said, England was barren. He
described an island rich in grapes that had been named Martha's Vineyard, after Gosnold's mother-in-law (or possibly a deceased daughter).
An appendix, by Edward Hayes, survivor of the tempest that had killed
Gilbert, speculated that 10,000 unhappy men, women, and children
could go there, and that colonies just 200 strong might prosper—"a
matter of great consequence for the good and securitie of England."[14]

When the queen died in 1603, James VI of Scotland inherited the
realm and became James I of England. Academic, tactless, and foreign,
he was widely disliked. According to the vox populi, England, resurgent under Elizabeth—the nation's beloved "Gloriana," a popular name
for her based on a character in Edmund Spenser's *Faerie Queene*—had
made James great, not the other way round. But the king adhered to
his theories of divine right and was reluctant to play the crowd-pleasing
Protestant warrior. He made peace with Spain in 1604, dampening English spirits. Why waste funds attacking Spain when he could outsmart
her? So the justification for privateering bases disappeared; but they
were not the only kind of colony. James worried that if foreign competitors had plantations, like those he was encouraging in Ireland, it might
upset the balance of trade and demote England in the hierarchy of nations. This concern did not, however, persuade him to finance a colonization program. Like Elizabeth, James authorized adventures provided
the money came from elsewhere. His hopes of success were slim, which
was not unreasonable: so far, no adventure *had* been successful.[15]

Colonization depended on men pitting a tiny possibility against
the vast probability of failure. Among those willing to take that risk
was Lord Chief Justice Popham, the Sagadahoc adventurer. His varied
projects—plantations, land reclamation, houses of correction—were
all remedies for the malefactors "whose increase threatens the state."
Conspiracies against James, such as the Gunpowder Plot of 1605, where

Catholic plotters had almost succeeded in blowing up the English parliament building—Popham had sentenced its ringleader, a Scots-hating
mercenary named Guy Fawkes—were pressures that settling Maine
might vent. Sir Edwin Sandys, a lively and self-assured statesman,
agreed. In 1607, he frustrated royal ambitions to make England and
Scotland one kingdom, arguing that "being English we cannot be Bri-
taynes"; about foreign expansion, however, he was more sanguine. Sandys, too, had noticed the adverse ratio of paupers to usable land, and he
shared Popham's interest in draining England's fenland; he also envied
the trading prowess of European Catholic states. He became one of the
most committed champions of adventures at home and abroad, adeptly
eliding justifications for exploiting *terra incognita*, or "unknown territory," in Virginia and common land in England.[16]

Popham and Sandys understood the workings of Parliament and
the law courts, with their mix of independence and reciprocity. English institutions were imbued with feelings of popular sovereignty and
rooted in the ancient constitution. They could be exported to America,
but not tinkered with by a Scotsman, even if he was God's delegate
on earth. This frustrated the king, who took divine right seriously.
Another institution essential to English life and to the ambitions of
Popham and Sandys was the joint-stock company—a means to attract
investment and make a profit while spreading risk. These companies
wielded authority, but were accountable to both the crown and their
shareholders.[17]

The Virginia Company, comprising an eponymous London outfit
and the Plymouth Adventurers, was chartered in April 1606. Charters
had long been a means for the crown to bestow patronage, and although their promise of "free and common socage"—in effect, freehold
land tenure—was the sort of English tradition that annoyed the king, it
was vital to colonial enterprise because investors wanted real estate and
they wanted it without strings. James did, however, impose restrictions.
The Virginia Company's charter was unlike other trading patents in
that it neither transferred power nor created a corporate body; instead,
the members of a colonial council would answer to their superiors in
London, mostly private speculators under royal control. It was the Virginia Council in London to which Sir Edwin Sandys was appointed in
1607. This was a gathering of men responsible for the commercial development of 1,000 miles of the eastern seaboard of America, from Maine
to North Carolina, known as "Virginia."[18]

Plymouth received the northern sector, London the south, the two overlapping to encourage commercial competition. The Sagadahoc venture, then, was no solitary impulse by Sandys and Popham, but part of a wider project, endorsed politically and financially. In November 1606 adventurers were instructed that "the way to prosper and to Obtain good Success is make yourselves all of one mind for the Good of your Country, and your own, and to Serve and fear God." And the instruction came with a warning: plantations not raised under the aegis of heaven were doomed.[19]

The company began making preparations. All sorts of men were galvanized, from Sir Edwin Sandys to a man given five shillings by the borough of Plymouth to ride to Exeter "aboute ye virginia voyage." Tensions arose. In May 1606, Plymouth's deputy mayor was reluctant to invest in Maine unless the town would be exempt from the Virginia Council's control. Doubtless the king was dismayed that a subject might think his terms negotiable. Others smoothed Anglo-Scottish seams. Michael Drayton, a poet seeking patronage, grafted an image of Stuart kingship onto ancient English legend. His ode "To the Virginian Voyage" summoned *Britons* to America. The first stanza called on men to measure their courage:

> *You brave Heroyque mynds*
> *Worthy your Countries name,*
> *That honor still pursue*
> *Goe and subdue*
> *Whilst loytering hyndes,*
> *Lurck heere at home with shame.*

Virginia, gushed Drayton, was "earths onely paradise," a place of fertile soil, plentiful game and fish—and the obligatory gold and pearls. If you want to be really excited, he advised, read "Industrious Hackluit"—England's Homer.[20]

On December 19, 1606, three ships—*Godspeed, Discovery*, and the *Susan Constant*—left London. In command was Christopher Newport, a forty-five-year-old mariner who had recently given the king two baby crocodiles from Hispaniola. Newport's deputy, Bartholomew Gosnold, captained the *Godspeed*. There were around a hundred men, half of them gentlemen unused to adventures. One was George Percy, aged twenty-six and of a delicate constitution. His elder brother, the earl of Northumberland, had been imprisoned after the Gunpowder Plot, but he had also collected books on exploration, and these had inspired young George, who thought that he could restore the family's fortunes by trying his luck in America. Other passengers included laborers, such as carpenters, a bricklayer, a mason, and a tailor. There was also a surgeon and a drummer. Most were from southeastern England. Four were boys. The Reverend Robert Hunt, a devotee of Hakluyt, would ensure compliance with God's will.

But difficulties arose barely twenty miles into the journey. Gales held the ships off the Kent coast, and Hunt, on the *Susan Constant*, was blamed as a Jonah—mainly by men "of the greatest ranke amongst us," according to a soldier, Captain John Smith. Smith himself, suspected by Newport of plotting mutiny, was sentenced to death. Rancor and superstition, rather than Drayton's noble sentiments, colored the voyage. It was not an auspicious start to an adventure, and yet it marked the beginning of a most remarkable transformation, the seed from which would grow all of England's territories in America.[21]

The fleet reached the broad expanse of the Chesapeake Bay near the end of April 1607. John Smith—who at this time still had a death sentence hanging over his head—was not always a reliable witness, but his reports were vivid and sympathetic. He described a land of "pleasant plaine hills and fertile valleyes, one prettily crossing another & watered so conveniently with fresh brookes and springs," and marshes and plains "all overgrowne with trees & weeds, being a plaine wildernesse as God first made it." Early in May they entered a river west of the bay, three miles wide at its mouth, which they called the James. Along its banks were swamps and creeks disappearing into dark forests. The men were tormented by mosquitoes. It was humid, though no hotter than in Spain, thought Smith. Unlike most, he was a seasoned adventurer, a Lincolnshire farmer's son and former mercenary in the Mediterranean, Balkans, and Africa. Bearing a coat of arms emblazoned with three severed Turkish heads, he had been recruited by the Virginia Company after returning to England at the age of twenty-seven.[22]

Venturing deep into the country, on May 13 the adventurers anchored off a pear-shaped promontory and went ashore. They hung a sail between trees to make shade as work commenced. "Our walls were

Captain John Smith (1580–1631) was boastful, but as a pioneering adventurer and promoter of Virginia and New England he had much to boast about. Yet contrary to the dedication that accompanied this engraving, his achievements did not include "Salvages, much Civilliz'd."

rales of wood," Smith recalled, "our seats unhewed trees till we cut plankes, our Pulpit a bar of wood nailed to two neighbouring trees." At sundown, they sat around a fire roasting oysters and took shelter from the rain in an old tent. A barn-like building of lattice, grass, and mud, and houses of similar construction, later replaced the tent. So began Jamestown. Men gathered for prayers morning and evening, and heard sermons on Sundays. But charity eluded them. According to Smith, "the continuall inundations of mistaking directions, factions, and numbers of unprovided Libertines neere consumed us all, as the Israelites in the wildernesse." The colonists built defenses to keep out Indians, but they had more reason to fear one another.[23]

John Smith escaped execution. The Virginia Company's orders, opened on arrival, instead named him as a councillor with Newport and Gosnold. Newport led an expedition up the James River, accompanied by Smith, George Percy, and Gabriel Archer, a veteran of Gosnold's

1602 voyage. One, probably Archer, made a record. "The soyle is more fertill then canbe wel exprest, it is altogether Aromaticall, giving a spicy tast to the rootes of all trees, plantes and hearbs." Prospects for sugar, olives, flax, and tobacco were excellent, likewise timber, pitch, dyestuffs, furs, copper, and iron. "I know not what can be expected from wealth that either this land affordes not or may soone yeeld."[24]

Another report described people living along the river in bark-covered huts: "They goe all naked save their privityes, yet in coole weather they weare deare skinns with the hayre on loose; some have leather stockings up to their twists & sandals on their feet. Their hayre is black generally, wch they weare long on the left side tyed up on a knott. . . . Their skynn is tawny, not so borne but w[i]th dying and paynting themselves, in w[hi]ch they delight greatly." The native women, it seemed to the explorers, worked, while the men pleased themselves. Indians ate wheat, legumes, fish, fowl, and venison. They sacrificed tobacco to their gods, but watched English prayers respectfully. They were untrustworthy, yet "kind and loving . . . witty and ingenious." Newport was given a chieftain's deerskin crown. Both sides tried to communicate, though such attempts had long caused confusion. When Arthur Barlowe landed at Roanoke in 1584, he had been welcomed with the word "Wingandacoa," which he publicized as the country's name, unaware that it meant "you wear fine clothes." Two years later, Ralph Lane had thought that singing was a greeting—until arrows began falling on his group. Indian comprehension was better. John Brereton had been astonished to hear a native say, "How now, sirha, are you so saucie [bold] with my Tabacco?" The man used other phrases as well, "as if he had beene a long scholar in the language," wrote Brereton. Hopes soared that the gospel could be taught.[25]

People in England had already encountered Indians, albeit removed from their natural element. The Inuit man, woman, and child—Kalicho, Arnaq, and Nutaaq—had been admired in Bristol in 1577, when they were brought back from Baffin Island by Martin Frobisher. Kalicho had sailed his kayak on the River Avon and learned some English, but he soon died from an injury sustained during his capture. His body was dissected, and Arnaq made to watch the burial to prove the English were not cannibals. Four days later she died and was buried in the same churchyard. A nurse was hired to take her infant son to Elizabeth I, but after eight days in London, he, too, perished. In 1603, Sir Robert Cecil, the future Lord Salisbury, had arranged for a canoeing display on the Thames by "Virginians," probably Indians who had been abducted during a quest for the lost Roanoke colonists. Two years later came Waymouth's Wabenakis, whom Sir Ferdinando Gorges tried in vain to train as servants of the English in Maine.[26]

Printed accounts of American adventures imparted both wonder and horror. In 1607, as Christopher Newport's men strove to build Jamestown, a book by John Nicholl, one of sixty-seven men sent to settle Guiana, went on sale in London. They had landed on the Caribbean island of St. Lucia, where locals showed them how to cut eggs from a turtle; in return, the English gave the naked women shirts. The travelers were amazed by a symmetrical potato garden, which "made us thinke some Christians had made it." But trust broke down, forcing them to hide in what Nicholls called "a farre remote and unknowne place, amongst a cruell, barbarous and inhumane people, without hope of ever having any meanes to recover the sight of our native and deare countrey and friends." Nineteen of the travelers escaped in an Indian boat, surviving on rainwater and seabirds cured with gunpowder, from their perspective proof of God's love and the savagery of the Indians. Like papists, witches, and monsters, these exotic strangers were opposites against which to define ideals. Many English people were sensitive to this otherness, but especially those who were actually in America. And their complex emotions could swiftly turn to violent rage.[27]

On May 24, Captain Newport reached the falls of the river and erected a cross, which was inscribed with "Jacobus Rex, 1607." After proclaiming James king of Virginia and praying for success, the men turned back to Jamestown, where bad news awaited them. Two hundred Indians had attacked, killing one and injuring eleven others. The friendliness of natives upriver, it transpired, came from fear—an unheeded lesson from Roanoke twenty years earlier, when Indians had been amazed by their white visitors, and especially by their apparent immunity to disease and the absence of women in their contingent. Such puzzles still caused as much anxiety as wonder. "Paw-waws," or Indian priests, warned that more English would come and take their land—just as Indian oracles had once predicted the arrival of the Spanish, bearded men who would desecrate their icons and kill their children.[28]

Jamestown's governor, Edward Maria Wingfield, had had a close shave—almost literally—when an arrow had sliced through his beard. A soldier from Huntingdon with links to Ralph Lane, governor of

Roanoke, and Sir John Popham, Wingfield was Bartholomew Gosnold's cousin and knew Sir Ferdinando Gorges. All of these contacts
had led him to the Virginia Company. Wingfield had handpicked the
colonists and was the only investor to accompany them, making him
an adventurer in both senses. He chose Jamestown's location and initiated defensive measures he had learned in Ireland. Like Plymouth's
project in Maine, the London colony was part military trading post
and part permanent plantation. Both were confused endeavors, and
both struggled. One colonist related that Jamestown's marshy location
made the air "unwholesome and sickly"; there were no springs, he said,
"but what wee drew from a Well six or seven fathom deepe, fed by the
brackish River owzing into it." Sewage returned with the tide, and men
contracted dysentery and fever. They were constantly thirsty—modern
science has shown that this was the worst drought in seven hundred
years—and they had to finish their fort, sow corn, and make clapboard,
all while being sniped at by Indian archers.[29]

Anticipation strained nerves, especially during the long sultry nights
when every sound suggested danger. Men venturing out to collect
wood and look for food experienced a prickling sense of being watched
through the trees and tall grasses. On May 31, a gentleman staggered
back bristling with arrows, and the next day a volley fell into the enclosure. On June 4, Indians spotted a man going outside to defecate
and, taking careful aim, hit him in the head. Spurred on by fear, the
workmen completed the fort within three weeks. A triangular palisade
surrounded a one-acre plot, with one side along four hundred feet of
shoreline and cannon-mounted bulwarks at the corners. Inside, rows of
houses ran parallel to the fort walls; at the center were a storehouse and
a chapel.[30]

In July, after Newport returned to England for supplies, the colony sank into turmoil. Men were hungry and sick, and unity was impossible; the Indians were enraged by the fort—a symbol of English
dominion. In August, a man died nearly every day; on the 22nd the
loss of Bartholomew Gosnold deepened the crisis. "There were never
Englishmen left in a forreigne Countrey in such miserie as wee were in
this new discovered Virginia," wrote George Percy. "Our food was but
a small Can of Barlie sod in water to five men a day, our drinke cold
water taken out of the River, which was at a floud verie salt, at low tide
full of slime and filth." The bulwarks were unmanned, and every morning corpses were dragged out for burial, discreetly to hide declining

The Jamestown fort was both a practical necessity and a symbol of military occupation—an affront to the Indians. Many of the men who built it were veterans of the conquest of Ireland, whose first export to America was a brutal, self-justifying mentality.

numbers. In September, Indians returned a runaway boy. To Wingfield this act seemed like a possible token of trust (and proof they were not cannibals). In fact, it meant little. Intense suspicion on one side, and a haughty sense of entitlement on the other, guaranteed an Anglo-Indian future steeped in misery and bloodshed. But this was just one challenge among many for English adventurers both at home and abroad.[31]

Colonial news was old news, as several weeks separated the events and the arrival of reports. By the time Christopher Newport reached London on August 12, 1607, life in Jamestown was far worse than the descriptions found in the letters he delivered. One, addressed to Henry, Prince of Wales, dated June 22—the day Newport had sailed—celebrated the "Reall and publicke possession" of a fruitful land in his father's name. Another account, by William Brewster, a gentleman, relished "that suche a Baye, a Ryver and a land did nevar the eye of mane behould. . . . Nowe is the kinges majesty offered the moste Statlye, Rich kingedom in the world." Evidently, though, not all of Brewster's news was good. A razor had been taken to his letter, excising what was probably offending information. In any case, by the time it was read he had died from wounds sustained in an Indian raid. Newport also handed Governor Wingfield's report to the Virginia Council. The fort was built, wheat sown, and the river "so stored w[i]th Sturgion and other sweete Fishe as no mans fortune hath ever possessed the like," it said. The soil was fertile, timber plentiful—enough to make Spain panic. With investors' silver, said Wingfield, "the land would Flowe w[i]th Milke and honey."[32]

It was true, as a pamphleteer claimed, that settlers' letters praised Virginia and urged their friends to emigrate. But the news was received with skepticism as well as excitement. Arriving first in Plymouth, Newport wrote to the royal secretary, Lord Salisbury, that "the Contrie is excellent and verie Riche in gold and Copper"—a sample of the gold was on its way to London. But Salisbury received a contrasting report from an aide, Sir Walter Cope. "If we may believe either in words or letters," Cope advised, "we are fallen upon a land that promises more than the land of promise. Instead of milk we find pearl, and gold instead of honey. Thus they say, thus they write; but experience . . . teaches [us] to be of slow belief." One diplomat informed a friend that Jamestown men "write much commendations of the aire and the soile and the commodities of it; but silver and golde have they none, and they can not yet be at peace with the inhabitants of the cuntrie." He was right: Newport's ore proved worthless—reminiscent of Frobisher's 1,350 tons of "gold," which for years lay heaped outside the Tower of London.[33]

The winter of 1607–1608 that beset Popham's colonists in Maine was severe throughout the Atlantic world. Virginia was hit by the worst storms John Smith had ever seen, with easterly winds driving fog and rain, and winds from the north bringing snow and ice. Captain Newport arrived in January to find the James River frozen (like the Thames), Wingfield under arrest on a variety of charges (including hiding food and starving the colony), and barely a third of the colonists still alive. Among the replacements he brought were Francis Perkins and his son from Berkshire, who along with others hacked fish from the ice to fry. Three days later, as at Sagadahoc, fire destroyed their shelters and storehouse. On March 28 Perkins wrote to a friend in England, asking for old clothes. "Everything my son and I had was burned," he said, "except a mattress which had not yet been taken off the ship." Colonists were desperate: Perkins did not even have pen and paper to make further appeals.[34]

The fire crippled Jamestown. Greater dependence bred misunderstanding with Indians: gratitude for baubles was merely symbolic, and they were reluctant to part with corn. Little was achieved that year. Positive letters, like that of Peter Wynne to Sir John Egerton in November 1608, grew fewer. Wynne described higher ground with fresher air than at Jamestown; raw materials included pitch and soap ashes, of which samples had been dispatched. "I was not so desirious to come into this Country as I am now willing here to end my dayes," Wynne confessed, "for I find it a farr more pleasant and plentifull country than any report made menc[i]on of." Soon after his account arrived in England, Wynne died of fever in America. In England, people realized that Virginian letters might be messages from ghosts, and it grew harder to believe in the colony's vitality. Complaints were voiced that newcomers consumed more than they produced, and returning ships, according to one observer, were now "laden with nothing but bad reports and letters of discouragement."[35]

In London, the Virginia Company put out its own propaganda and censored incoming news. No one should expect miracles, was its defense, nor was it fair to compare English and Spanish achievements. The difficulties were unprecedented, but so would be the rewards for the patient and the brave. Casting aspersions on the adventure was disloyal to God and to the king who had sanctioned the project. A forty-page letter from John Smith, edited and published (without his permission), presented Jamestown as a good place to live and do business. "All our men [are] wel contented, free from mutinies, in love one with another, & as we hope in continuall peace with the Indians." But in truth, there was little love there. By the summer of 1608, Edward Maria Wingfield, freed but not reinstated, was back in England, where Virginia's reputation as a foolish investment and deathtrap had become obvious.[36]

Wingfield indicted his enemies (especially Smith) and excused himself. He denied monopolizing or hiding food: he had eaten only one roasted squirrel, which he had shared, and burying food was a good way to preserve it. His lack of a Bible did not mean he was an atheist: his books had been stolen. Even Romulus and Remus had struggled to build Rome, he observed, but Jamestown was lost to cruelty and disobedience. Above all, he had learned "to dispise ye popular verdict of ye vulgar" and to value the authority of gentlemen to safeguard liberty. Englishmen, he said, would be horrified by how casually colonists were whipped and hanged. Of course, they already knew: stories of disaster traveled fast. John Ratcliffe, Wingfield's usurper, had been assaulted by a blacksmith, who escaped execution by revealing a rebellious plot;

the ringleader, George Kendall, Sir Edwin Sandys's cousin, was shot. This was the sort of arbitrary rule associated with Catholic states. The Virginia Company denounced returnees as lying cowards, as it had the veterans of Maine. The promotional writer Robert Johnson summed up the Jamestown settlers as either "wicked Impes that put themselves a shipboord, not knowing otherwise how to live in England; or those ungratious sons that dailie vexed their fathers hearts at home, and were therefore thrust upon the voyage."[37]

Faced with waning mercantile interest, in 1609 the Virginia Council campaigned to sell shares and attract migrants. Broadsides rallied gentlemen, merchants, tradesmen, and laborers to join "an action pleasing to God, and commodious many waies to this Common-wealth." Books were commissioned. Robert Johnson's *Nova Britannia* warned that failure would cause national disgrace. Elizabeth's heroes had not been "swallowed up by dispayre, nor their hartes and spirits daunted with feare, but daily armed afresh with invincible courage and greater resolution." They had also known that foreign trade beat domestic trade. Plantations, promised Johnson, would restore England's strength, creating jobs and, as Hakluyt had argued, reviving the textile industry. At first, Virginia's rewards might be spiritual rather than material, but adventurers should focus on "reducing savage people from their blind superstition to the light of religion." Indians who lived "up and downe in troupes, like heards of Deare in a Forest," needed help—just as the "brutish poore and naked Brittans" had needed Caesar. Johnson also urged consideration of England's poor, who had been hit by an eightfold increase in the cost of renting houses and land, and so became a burden on their richer neighbors, who were required by law to support them. A derivative work by Robert Gray feared for an overcrowded nation where scarcity threatened peace. Like Johnson, Gray insisted that colonists wanted not lordship over America, but only a "residency." He dismissed worries that investors would see no return. Any hesitation would not be level-headed, he said, but fainthearted. Hoarders should be despised as men who "preferre their money before vertue, their pleasure before honour, and their sensuall securitie before heroicall adventures."[38]

In this vein the Virginia Company wrote to wealthy individuals, companies, and corporations seeking investment. In the spring of 1609, the Lord Mayor of London was asked to persuade guilds and livery companies to invest in America. A bill of adventure cost £12 10s—three or four years' wages for a laborer. In May the Merchant Taylors raised

£200 from "the poore stocke of our house." Richard Widdows, a London goldsmith, bought two bills, which made him a partner. Rather than deny every rumor, the Virginia Company injected realism. Sandys admitted to the corporation of Plymouth that Sagadahoc had failed, but only "by the Coldnes of the Clymate and other Connaturall necessities." The Chesapeake colony, however, had blossomed; perhaps, Sandys ventured, Plymouth might like to contribute a ship for the next fleet?[39]

James I asked England's clergymen to encourage the haves to invest and have-nots to emigrate. On April 25, 1609, William Symonds delivered a sermon at Southwark St. Saviour, near the Thames, arguing that God's people had a duty to colonize the New World. If they did, then, like Abraham and his descendants, they were promised Canaan. Symonds anticipated "a Virgin or Maiden Britaine, a comfortable addition to our Great Britaine," and a bulwark against Spain. Living with heathens neither hurt one's honor nor angered heaven: Was Daniel not stronger among the Gentiles? England had become a paradise after the Dark Ages, he explained, but now people swarmed like bees in summer, so that there was "very hardly roome for one man to live by another." Symonds blamed landlords who enclosed their estates, enriching themselves while turning tenant farmers into vagrants. Shopkeepers were grinding down the poor, he added, citing the example of the blacksmith, who "worketh his bones out and swelteth himself in the fire, yet for all his labour . . . hee can hardly keepe himselfe from the almes box." The destitute woman, children at her knee and breast, sewed by candlelight to feed them water gruel, "deluding the bitternes of her life with sweete songs that she singeth to a heavy heart."[40]

The Virginia Company paid for the publication of Symonds's sermon, and similar orations at St. Paul's Cross followed in May. George Benson preached that converting natives fitted the apocalyptic master plan in the Book of Revelation, while Daniel Price, chaplain to Prince Henry, praised Virginia as "the farm of Britain, as Sicily was of Rome." In the same way that the angel of Macedonia had summoned Paul, so an American angel summoned the English. In print, these sermons became stirring manifestos. The English had to understand themselves in the past—as woad-painted pagans—in order to see why they must rescue the Indians, while also recognizing their own predicament in the present to allow New World remedies to cure national ills. But terrible things were happening in Virginia, news of which was already heading back across the Atlantic.[41]

CHAPTER 2

Earth's Only Paradise

FROM JAMESTOWN'S VEXED BEGINNINGS, and the failure of Sagadahoc, would-be adventurers and investors had learned three things, and they took this knowledge with them into the next phase of pursuing their American ambitions. First, the best-laid plans went awry. They now understood that experiences of settlement would always contradict how those at home imagined it. There would be an eternal gap between the hypotheses about colonization and their actual proof on distant shores. The second and third new understandings flowed from the first: the case for colonies had to be made and remade, ingeniously and tirelessly, to sustain investment and political support; and the gap between imagination and reality would require a bridge of faith and courage. Only when faith and courage prevailed (along with investment) would English America flourish.

The greatest difficulties were money and authority, and here the crown was little help. Burdened with debt, his finances eroded by inflation, James I had few options. He would have to sell more royal land, or he would have to surrender his ancient rights over feudal estates (and the income from those estates) in return for an annual grant issued by Parliament. The former he could stomach, but the latter compromised his supremacy. He was also settling the Irish province of Ulster with Scottish and English families—another imperial project dependent on private investment and threatened by native insurrection. Nevertheless, the king remained committed to the American colony that bore his name. So he commissioned Sir Thomas Gates, a soldier knighted in the war with Spain, to save it. Once the Virginia Company had scraped together the funds and migrants to get started, Gates would be sent as deputy governor; his superior, Thomas West, Lord De La Warr, the biggest investor in Virginia, would follow when finances allowed. The king issued a new charter extending the company's liberties and giving the governor the sort of absolute control that James craved at home. Bearing this authority, Gates entered Jamestown's fort a year later, on May 10, 1610.[1]

Gates was horrified by what he found. Everything was quiet. There were breaks in the palisade, and the doors hung from their hinges. No chickens or dogs roamed the streets. Buildings were wrecked, entries gaping. The church was a shell. It appeared to Gates "rather as the ruins of some auntient [forti]fication then that any people living might now inhabit." But the men were there, sixty of them—barely a tenth of the complement from the previous autumn—lying sick in a stinking block-house. They looked like skeletons, "lamentable to behowlde," and were crying: "We are starved, we are starved!" With little hesitation, Gates relieved Governor George Percy of his command and put the men to work, but they were too weak and too few. What in the world had happened? The answer lies in the story of Jamestown's previous two years.[2]

Leading colonists likened Virginia to a womb filled with "ellimentall seedes w[hi]ch could produce as many goodly birthes . . . as of any land under the heavens." But the seeds needed fertilizing and nurturing, and failure to tend them sufficiently had been disastrous. In January 1608 Christopher Newport had delivered replacements, but then came the fire and greater dependence on England, and by summer he was asking for help. Morale and money were scarce. The Virginia Council in London felt misunderstood by crown and people; its subordinates in Jamestown felt misunderstood by the council. Obsession with Roanoke muddied the waters. The play *Eastward Ho*, by George Chapman, Ben Jonson, and John Marston, notorious for offending the king with its anti-Scottishness—had satirized the "whole Country of English" supposedly hiding in Virginia, whom the Indians loved so much that "all the treasure they have they lay at their feete." According to Captain John Smith, the council had told Newport not to come back without gold, the route to the northwest passage, or "one of the lost company of Sir Walter Rawley." What Jamestown needed were crops. The problem was partly English hierarchy: rather than thinking how best to perform a task, colonists asked who should do it, as dictated by the social order.[3]

There had been other deficiencies. Men greeting Newport's return to Jamestown in October 1608 saw something they had not seen for many months: women. In the Old World, poverty restricted marriage;

here, the problem was lack of brides. A carpenter called John Laydon was lucky: a month later he married one of the two women, which gave him a hopeful interlude as conditions worsened. Winter was coming, and there were three hundred mouths to feed. Survival depended on conciliation and gifts, such as the carved bed that Newport had given to Wahunsonacock, the *sachem*, or king, of the Powhatan tribal confederation (sometimes known as Chief Powhatan). But 1609 brought no improvement. The drought meant Indians had little food to spare, and this shortage led to theft and tension that John Smith, now governor, could not diffuse. He returned to England that autumn. In Jamestown, he was succeeded by George Percy, who detested Smith as "an ambitious, unworthy and vayneglorious fellowe." John Ratcliffe was sent up the Chickahominy River, forty miles from Jamestown, to bargain with the Powhatans. He never returned.[4]

Because of the need for food, cultural intimacy developed between English and Indian. The interaction involved exchanges more subtle than swapping hand-axes for corncobs. In December 1607, John Smith had been seized by the Paspaheghs, a Powhatan branch, while exploring the Chickahominy. He was taken to a place where people stared "as [if] he had beene a monster"—the experience of captives in England—and escorted to a large, smoky hut, where he saw what no other Englishman had seen. Wahunsonacock was seated on a platform, wearing pearls and a raccoon-skin cloak. He was attended by noblemen and women who were bedecked and painted and arranged in ranks like parishioners at worship. The king's "grave and Majesticall countenance" astounded Smith. He was filled with "admiration to see such state in a naked Savage."[5]

So far, Smith had been treated like an honored guest, but now he had his head pushed onto a clubbing block. He was saved only by the intercession of a twelve-year-old princess named Pocahontas. This may have been a ritual where Smith was symbolically killed and reborn as an Indian—representing the transformation of the thousands of English colonists to come. Smith, who assumed the execution to be real, interpreted Wahunsonacock's clemency as acquiescence to white superiority. Yet he was fascinated by the king's daughter, "not only for feature, countenance & proportion, but for wit and spirit, the only Nonpareil of his Country." And so began a chain of events leading to Pocahontas becoming a different symbol of transformation: the Christianized Indian—a living manifestation of the Roanoke girl with an English doll painted by John White.[6]

King Powhatan comands C: Smith to be flayne, his daughter Pokahontas beggs his life his thankfullnes and how he subiected 39 of their kings. reade history.

printed by James Reeve

This engraving depicts the mock execution of Captain John Smith, prisoner of Chief Wahunsoñacock, perhaps marking his symbolic death as an Englishman and his rebirth as a Powhatan Indian. His supposed savior, Pocahontas, stands to the right of the picture.

Smith studied his hosts, learned Indian phrases, and was asked *Casacunnakack, peya quagh acquintan uttasantasough?* ("In how many daies will there come hither any more English Ships?"). He judged the Powhatans to be covetous and inconstant, quick-witted and hot-tempered, with a fondness for grudges. Some were timid, some bold; most were cautious, and all *savage*. They went almost naked, although the "better sort" wore deerskin mantles like the Irish. Smith most admired their adaptation to a land where Englishmen could not even feed themselves. "They are very strong, of an able body and full of agilitie, able to endure to lie in the woods under a tree by the fire in the worst of winter, or in the weedes and grasse in Ambuscado in the Sommer." The un-English absolutism of Wahunsonacock's rule also caught Smith's eye: felons were butchered alive with mussel shells.[7]

In December 1609, John Ratcliffe, trapped by Wahunsonacock on his expedition, suffered this grisly fate. His failure to procure food meant death at Jamestown. George Percy, who had landed with silk ribbons and "sweete gloves" in his trunk, found himself living wretchedly. This was not the utopia imagined in his brother's books, but "a worlde of miseries." Everyone, he wrote, began "to feele the sharpe pricke of hunger w[hi]ch noe man trewly descrybe[s] butt he w[hi]ch hathe Tasted the bitternesse thereof." Men who stole from the storehouse were executed. All livestock was eaten, including horses. Then cats, rats, and mice became scarce. Next went shoes and leather items, boiled until tender, after which the men searched the woods for snakes and "wylde and unknowne Rootes." The Indians picked off foragers; but hunger was the colonists' master. Finally, they broke the ultimate taboo, an ironic reversal given fears of New World cannibals and necromancers. "Famin beginneinge to Looke gastely and pale in every face," Percy confessed, "notheinge was Spared to mainteyne Lyfe and to doe those things w[hi]ch seame incredible, as to digge upp deade corp[s]es outt of graves and to eate them." In at least one case, it seems, a girl who died was butchered and her brain eaten.[8]

Safe in England now, John Smith blamed poor leadership and lassitude for the "starving time." Like Percy, he told tales of vile extremity involving Indian corpses "stewed with roots and herbs." He even made a joke about a man who ate his own wife, not knowing "whether shee was better roasted, boyled or carbonado'd." The story went that Percy had the cannibal hung by the thumbs—a common torture in Europe, but alien to England—until he confessed to salting the body and throwing an unborn child into the river. It was also said that he was executed by burning, in England a punishment reserved for heretics and female traitors. Disputing Smith's accusations and Percy's excuses, Sir Thomas Gates later claimed the man had murdered his wife and invented the cannibalism story as justification, food having been found in his house. True or not, these tales made good propaganda for dissidents inside and outside the Virginia Company, and the king decided to intervene. Enter Sir Thomas Gates.[9]

Gates had left England in June 1609 in a squadron commanded by Christopher Newport and Sir George Somers, a naval hero of the type lionized in Robert Johnson's *Nova Britannia*. Why it took them nearly a year to reach Jamestown is a story for later. De La Warr, meanwhile, did not depart for another nine months. On February 21, 1610, just before De La Warr's ship set sail, the Virginia Company heard a sermon by William Crashaw. "Remember the end of this voyage is the destruction of the divels kingdome, and propagation of the Gospell," inveighed Crashaw, who asked his audience to pray for those "who have ingaged their persons, and adventured their lives to lay the first foundation, and doe now live in want of many comforts and pleasures." This "heroicall adventure" called for courage and compassion, and those who dared not go might at least honor those who did go. A good Calvinist (and Virginia investor), Crashaw preached that critics were unsanctified, drowned souls not the saved. Investment was charity, and charity denoted grace. Saints—true believers chosen by God—desired only to cover Indian bodies from shame and their souls from heaven's wrath. In return, the English would have land, so much of which in America, men said, was "wild & inhabited by none but the beasts of the fielde."[10]

Early in June 1610, an advance party from De La Warr's fleet sailing up the James River met four ships led by Sir Thomas Gates. He had abandoned Jamestown after only a month, his intended destination Newfoundland. A "heartbroken" De La Warr sent Gates back, and there heard his reasons: laziness, godlessness, and the Virginia Company's sluggish cash-flow. By the time sufficient funds had become available to send De La Warr, he explained, the colony was "worne and spent." After De La Warr's arrival, conditions at Jamestown gradually improved. The fort was rebuilt and houses weatherproofed using Indian skills. The "Laws Divine, Moral and Martiall," which Gates had introduced, were now enforced: they included military discipline and strict religious observance. De La Warr believed the former chaos had incurred divine wrath, but that God might be appeased by Indian conversions. The Indians, however, rebuffed diplomatic overtures. Wahunsonacock gave De La Warr three choices: restrict settlement to Jamestown, leave America, or expect war. De La Warr chose war.[11]

In August, Percy, now captain of Jamestown's fort, led a raid against the Paspahegh king, Wowinchopunck, and captured his wife and two children. Sailors threw the children overboard and shot them, but Percy, reeling from the violence, saved their mother, the queen. It had been expedient to respect Indian royalty, but in English minds pagan monarchs had no divine right. Colonists propagated the notion of James I as a remote but mighty sachem over native elites. Wahunsonacock guessed the cynicism of this. In a clumsy ceremony, Newport had made him a royal vassal, but a cheap crown and scarlet cloak did not bind him. The extent of English pretense was clear in the kind of treatment the Indians received at the colonists' hands in war—they dealt out mockery, brutality, and humiliation, using methods similar to those that had been used with the rebellious Irish earls. Grieving for her children, the Paspahegh queen was taken to Jamestown, where De La Warr ordered her to be burned, a sentence Percy commuted to "quicker dispatche" by the sword. The English had promised to bring liberty and light to the Indians, unlike the "black legend" of Iberian cruelty in America. "The Spaniards since their coming hither," an English historian wrote piously in the 1620s, "have behaved themselves most inhumanely towards the unarmed natives, killing them like sheep for the slaughter." But by then history had repeated itself many times.[12]

At home, few noticed the ironic nuances of such stories, and fewer still cared. Accounts of Jamestown, like the Roanoke legend, circulated as simple morality tales that brought a sense of excitement to both teller and hearer. What was happening was scornful, and people wanted to hear all about it. Obviously, Virginia was dangerous, its natives savage, yet feelings were mixed. Potential investors saw opportunity in danger, and so they became interested in the Virginia Company, which welcomed them, praising their courage and nurturing their hopes. The money that investors put into the project was never sufficient, however, and so the Virginia Company resorted to other, more desperate, measures.

A Londoner in 1612 might have heard an advertisement sung to the tune of "The Lusty Gallant," publicizing a lottery organized by the Virginia Company. Everyone was urged to join in, including women, who might improve their households with one of the excellent prizes. Naturally, the venture was not all about money:

> *It is to plant a kingdome sure,*
> *Where savadge people dwell:*
> *God will favour Christians still,*
> *And like the purpose well.*
> *Take courage then with willingnesse,*
> *Let hands and heartes agree:*
> *A braver enterprise then this,*
> *I thinke can never bee.*

People were asked to consider that England was once "a Wildernesse and savage place," and that Virginia could also be transformed. The idea, dating back to Hakluyt, that God blessed the saviors of infidels, was certainly plausible. And the publicity was sufficiently appealing to make gentlemen and artisans part with their cash.[13]

Most people bought into the lottery without examining its good causes, but for intellectuals, saving Indians did raise the question of who they were. Some speculated that the New World had been spared Noah's Great Flood because it had been uninhabited at that time, but that it had later been populated by Tartars crossing a frozen sea, or Trojans exiled by war. Linguistic traces of Latin and Greek were detected, although the ancients would have been unaware that Indians existed. Perhaps they came from the Jewish diaspora—a lost tribe of Israel; if so, their conversion might accelerate the Second Coming as foretold in the Book of Revelation. Many believed Indians to be descendants of Noah's accursed son Ham. Wherever Ham's children settled, wrote one colonist, "there beganne both the Ignorance of true godliness and a kind of bondage and slavery to be taxed one upon another." God had opened up America so the gospel could free the natives from Satan's captivity. According to Alexander Whitaker, a clergyman who arrived in Jamestown in 1611, whatever their ancestry, Indians were sons of Adam and deserved England's love.[14]

But Whitaker knew a darker reality. On August 9, 1611, he wrote to William Crashaw describing a strange journey by Sir Thomas Dale, "a warlike and resolute Captaine" who had served with Sir Thomas Gates. Dale had arrived in Jamestown on May 10, and as deputy governor and "marshall" had become a feared enforcer of Virginia Council orders. Men were to keep their clothes and houses neat, and to eat together "after the fashion of the old world." They were also to attend church, setting an example to the Indians, whom Dale distrusted. That summer, he responded to a threat from Wahunsonacock by leading soldiers up the James River. After they dug in for the night, they were assailed by ghostly noises and shapes, but scrambling from their trenches, found no one there. Disturbing visions of the Old World lay beneath impressions of the new. Later, Dale's men saw "a mad Crewe dauncinge like Anticks or our morris dancers, before whom there went a Quiockosite (or there Preist) [who] tossed smoke and flames out of a thinge like a Censer." A native guide then uncannily predicted a downpour. Such phenomena were common, said Whitaker, "all w[hi]ch things make me thinke that there be great witches amongst them and they very familiar w[i]th the divell." Even so, the Indians were a chosen people, whose days in paradise were numbered. Sodom, Whitaker noted, "was like the garden of god in the dayes of Lott."[15]

To men in Virginia, a world away from the lottery, Indians seemed intractable. Dale admitted that despite the colonists' strenuous efforts, they remained "all dead settled in ther Ignorance." In 1612, Whitaker sent the Virginia Council in London an image of an Indian god "painted upon one side of a toad-stoole, much like unto a deformed monster." Native priests, Whitaker observed, were "no other but such as our English Witches are," and worshippers fell into ecstasies, "much like to the counterfeit women in England who faine themselves bewitched, or possessed of some evill spirit." These comparisons must have struck a chord, given the witch-panic in the county of Lancashire that year. Perceptions of a satanic threat spanned the Atlantic world, as did hatred of Catholics. On November 5, 1612, the seventh anniversary of the Gunpowder Plot, Samuel Purchas, an Essex vicar, completed his survey of the globe, a celebration of Protestant patriotism. Indians, he said, summoned the devil, or *Oke*, by dancing around a fire, and carried wooden idols draped with beads (hinting at popish statuary and rosaries). A year later, Purchas became chaplain to Archbishop George Abbot, a Virginia Company investor who believed Indians to be "marvellously addicted to Witchcraft"—a charge also often leveled at superstitious papists.[16]

Reports of war further dented hopes that Indians would comply. Jamestown seemed threatened on all sides: divided, menaced by natives, undermined at home, and targeted from abroad. Sailors reported Spanish ships sizing up Virginia fortifications. The English ambassador in Madrid told of rumors, both at court and by "the ordinary and vulgar voice," that Philip III was planning to invade; colonists were advised to "live in a continual expectation of being assailed." The Spanish ambassador in London relayed these fears, erroneously informing his king that "it is not their desire to people [the land], but rather to practice piracy, for they take no women—only men." Other scraps of intelligence went to Madrid: a fanciful map of Sagadahoc (perhaps leaked), a broadside advertising Virginia, Francis Perkins's letter about the fire of 1608. Widespread fears about Spain fed settlers' paranoia and depressed confidence at home. Diplomatic channels buzzed with tales of plots, pirates, shortages, and a reviled preacher "somewhat a puritane"—a radical Protestant. News that escaping colonists had stolen a boat infuriated James I. As the Virginia Company's money ran out, so did James's patience.[17]

Sir Thomas Dale was determined to revive morale in England and America. Upon his arrival in Jamestown in 1611, he had grabbed Captain Newport by the beard and upbraided him for exaggerating the colonists' progress. A fortnight later he reported "many omissions of necessary duties" to the Virginia Council, alleging that men spent more time looking for ores than producing food. His quarrel was not with the New World. "Your purses and endevours will never open nor travel in a more acceptable and meritorious enterprize," he promised the council. "Take foure of the best kingdoms in Christendome, and put them all together: they may no way compare with this countrie." The Virginia Company exploited this optimism in their promotions, citing a wise-saw of one of Sir Humphrey Gilbert's captains: "It is not Moynes [mines] of goold & sylver w[hi]ch make a comonwealth & state to floorish." The Spanish had got it wrong: land and labor were the secret.[18]

William Crashaw's sermon, now in print, hid some flaws and made a virtue of others. The voyage, he said, was God's bridge between England and Virginia. The climate was bearable, the sun moderate: the natives' skins were no darker than if an English person were to go naked in southern England. Life was hard, but this was good: to achieve anything men should "undergoe and endure all difficulties, miseries and hardnesse that flesh and blood is able to beare." It was also noted that while some starved, others were addicted to luxury—a problem at home and abroad. Samuel Purchas mocked "Effeminate Planters" quitting Virginia "because they found not English Cities, nor such faire houses, nor at their owne wishes any of their accustomed dainties, with Feather-beds and Down-pillowes, Taverns and Ale-houses." Englishmen had forgotten courage. The promoter Robert Johnson urged the Virginia Company to emulate Henry V at Agincourt, and, like Caesar Augustus, to run the empire as a commonwealth where Indians and ordinary Englishmen were free subjects. A pamphlet by Alexander Whitaker reinforced Crashaw's idea of investment as charity for England's "hungry, naked, fatherlesse, widowes, poore men and oppressed," abused by "rich theeves." We have to wake up, one writer insisted, and deal with the "inundation of people [that] doth overflow this little island."[19]

Contemplating England inspired thoughts of America and vice versa. Don't criticize Virginia for its swamps, promoters said, when

England was blemished by the wilds of Essex, the forests of Lancashire, and Kent's fever-ridden marshes. Fears about climate were unfounded: English blood thins nicely, and sweating fortifies the body; after all, even timber needed seasoning. And don't listen to cowardly rumor-mongers, who "slovenly spit at all things, especially in company where they can find none to contradict them." A Virginia Company flyer also denounced the better sort who "lie at home, and doe gladly take all occasions to cheere themselves with the prevention of happy successe in any action of publike good." Men of good sense, the council was sure, would see "the Father of untruths" at work here. Those who declined to invest were being willfully unreasonable; they impugned their own masculinity, patriotism, and piety by surrendering to fear.[20]

More letters arrived in great houses, company halls, and council chambers nationwide. Investors, including artisans and laborers, were invited to meet the treasurer, Sir Thomas Smythe, at his mansion in the City of London. Printed share certificates were adorned with an impos-ing wax seal. Early in 1611, Smythe wrote to the Kentish town of Sand-wich, rhapsodizing about Virginia's future under De La Warr, Gates, and Dale. He listed three hundred subscribers who had pledged over half of the £30,000 required to resupply Virginia. The outcome, Smythe said, would be "a very able and strong foundation of annexing another Kingdom to this Crown." The corporation of Ipswich received the same letter in March, and in response it disbursed a "Resonable porc[i]on of monye": £100. A few days after that, a contribution was requested from the high sheriff of Leicestershire. At the end of the month, Sir Edwin Sandys sent Sandwich's mayor a reminder, which prompted an invest-ment of £25 (although a year later Sandys was still waiting to be paid).[21]

The earl of Huntingdon, Henry Hastings, made three payments of £40 between 1610 and 1613, entitling him to such land as was "recovered, planted and inhabited" in Virginia as well as a share of pearls and pre-cious metals. Samuel Macham, the publisher of Robert Johnson's *Nova Britannia*, kept Huntingdon supplied with books and news. He wrote in July 1611 to inform him that Sir Thomas Dale had arrived, and that "the voyage & plantation prospers now more & more; they want for no Corne, for they have all in abundance." At last, he said, commodities were being exported, including black walnut, sturgeon, soap ashes, and sassafras—a root much in demand as a treatment for venereal disease.[22]

De La Warr had returned to England the previous month com-plaining of scurvy and craving "the naturall Ayre of my Countrey."

Summoned to the council, he enthused about wood, hemp, minerals, and salt cod, proffering samples. Unhappy to see him back, councillors published his report to stop tongues wagging. At Jamestown, meanwhile, morale had dipped, and Dale's woes had multiplied. Lord Salisbury received a letter from him dated August 17. Dale hoped the king would extend the patent, and that criminals might be sent as laborers. Every planter complains, he said, especially about the lack of "english provisions," bemoaning his life "though haply he could not better it in England." Dale also vowed to thwart the wily Wahunsonacock, by defeat or alliance, to allow expansion into cornfields along the James River, "w[hi]ch our Companie Adventurers in England hardly believe can be here at all," and to further the search for commodities. It proved too little, too late. James granted a new charter in March 1612—recognition of failure, in that it authorized the lottery to boost company finances.[23]

The lottery was drawn over three weeks that summer. The prizes, in all worth £5,000, enthralled the ticketholders who came to St. Paul's on the last day, July 20. Some spectators, such as representatives of the livery companies, prayed they had not wasted their money. The Mercers had stumped up £50, and the Grocers had been persuaded by Sir Thomas Smythe to buy five lots at £12 10s apiece. Parish officers were also present. The vestry of St. Mary Colechurch had "agreed to adventur sixe pounde of the profitt of our churche stocke in the lottrey for the plantacion of Vergenya, and what benifitt shall hapen thereby shalbe for the good of our church." Some parishes had divided lots into shilling shares, for which the Virginia Company had issued tokens.[24]

Thomas Sharplisse, a tailor, won first prize: £1,000 worth of silver plate ceremoniously delivered to his home. The two runners-up were parish vestries. A chronicler described the lottery as "plainly carried and honestly performed," but once again, the Virginia Company was disappointed. Receipts had fallen so short that 60,000 blanks had been removed to increase the chance of finding winners. On August 3, the company clerk confessed to a friend that investments in Irish plantations were unsafe, but those in Virginia doomed. "The Last Lotteryes benefite will scars[e] pay old debts," he wrote. "There is another intended, God send better success, both to the worke and to the well willers whose adventures yeeld small or no returne." Some gamblers were left seriously out of pocket. In December, the Grocers' Company, unable to raise the £62 10s it owed, handed over a silver salt-cellar in lieu of payment.[25]

Earlier in 1612, William Symonds, the Virginia Company preacher, had published a history of the colony. Unlike Spain, whose American successes were due to the existing agrarian system and silver mining, "we chanced in a lande, even as God made it, where we found only an idle, improvident, scattered people, ignorant of the knowledge of gold or silver, or any commodities, & carelesse of any thing but fro[m] hand to mouth, but for ba[u]bles of no worth; nothing to encourage us, but what accidentally wee found nature afforded." Stirring words. But when would England succeed? How much longer could shareholders hold out for dividends? Apart from Thomas Sharplisse, now Virginia's greatest beneficiary, Englishmen would have to wait to feel America's transformative power. And when it came, it was never quite what they had expected.[26]

In the last week of July 1609, a storm scattered the fleet that was taking Sir Thomas Gates and five hundred others to Jamestown. On the flagship, the *Sea Venture*, Gates and Admiral Sir George Somers had been anticipating sight of Virginia when the winds and the waves began to gather strength. "The heavens were obscured, and made an Egyptian night of three daies perpetuall horror," wrote William Strachey, a passenger on the *Sea Venture*; "the women lamented; the hearts of the passengers failed; the experience of the sea captaines was amased; the skill of the mariners was confounded." Aged thirty-seven, Strachey had studied law in London but preferred poetry, and had squandered his inheritance within three years. He found work as a diplomatic secretary and then gambled his last few pounds on two company shares and a passage to Virginia. Now, he regretted ever bidding farewell to England: there was no one aboard who didn't.[27]

As the gales rose into a hurricane, wild pitching and hellish blackness confused Strachey's senses. Passengers clung to the ship's sides, while below, crewmen crept along its ribs, plugging leaks. As Gates rallied the men at the pumps, a wave crashed over the ship. "It strooke him from the place where hee sate," recalled Strachey, "and groveled him and all us about him on our faces, beating together with our breaths all thoughts from our bosoms, else then that wee were now sinking." By the third day the water in the hold was nine feet deep, and cannon and luggage were jettisoned. No beer or fresh water could be found, and no one slept. Admiral Somers saw a light "like a faint Starre, trembling and streaming along with a sparkeling blaze," which seamen thought a bad omen. Passengers and crew alike prepared to die. But then the skies lightened, and Somers spied land.[28]

It was not Virginia but Bermuda, an archipelago six hundred miles off the mainland, "more fearefull then an Utopian Purgatory," thought Captain John Smith, "and to all Sea-men no lesse terrible then an inchanted den of Furies and Devils." After their ordeal, though, the migrants would have gladly landed in hell itself. Somers headed for the largest island, wedging his ship between rocks, where, mercifully, the winds dropped, allowing passengers ashore. There they found not "the most dangerous, unfortunate and forlorne place in the world," recalled one passenger, Sylvester Jourdain, but "the richest, healthfullest and pleasantest they ever saw." It was tranquil and temperate—an uninhabited paradise where they feasted on boar and turtle, palm-hearts and berries. Jourdain described the peculiar tameness of the wildfowl: "A man walking in the woods with a sticke, and whistling to them, they wil come and gaze on you, so neare that you may strike and kill many of them." To those who had left lives of scarcity, this world seemed happily upside down, the peasant's fantasy of effortless plenty realized. "Truth is the daughter of Time," concluded Strachey. "Men ought not to deny every thing which is not subject to their owne sense."[29]

Sir Thomas Gates was resolved to reach Jamestown, though, and had the longboat refitted. Not everyone wanted to go. John Want, a Puritan from Strachey's hometown, Saffron Walden in Essex, believed that God had planted them in a new Eden, "freed from the government of any man." When a plot to sabotage the boat was exposed, the conspirators made explicit their craving for liberty, shorn of hierarchy and obligation. Gates reasserted his authority. In September an advance party left for Virginia and vanished. Then the men still in Bermuda built two light sailing ships, called pinnaces, made of salvaged timber and local cedar—an amalgam of old and new worlds. In May 1610 the pinnaces departed, with Gates and most of the other first Bermudans aboard. Their last act was to erect a cross, a ship's beam fixed to a stripped tree. Gates attached a shilling—the king's image—and a passage engraved in copper: "in memory of our great Deliverance." Thus the island of devils became a place of salvation.[30]

From there Gates completed his mission to relieve Jamestown, at least before he fled and had to be sent back. A few days after Lord De

La Warr was installed as governor, in June 1610, Sir George Somers wrote to Lord Salisbury describing the pitiful scenes in the fort. Four days later, Somers, "out of his worthy and valiant minde," sailed one of the pinnaces back to Bermuda to fetch food. Despite prayers for his safe return, this would be his last voyage. He died in Bermuda in November—from exhaustion, said John Smith, but others alleged it was "of a surfeit of eating of a pig." His body was shipped back to Dorset in a barrel, but his heart was buried in his strange Atlantic paradise, according to legend at his own request.[31]

Presumably the ship carrying Somers's letter to Salisbury also delivered one from William Strachey to an unknown gentlewoman, perhaps Sara Smythe, wife of the Virginia Company treasurer. Dated July 15, 1610, it detailed the Bermudan episode and was circulated, as manuscripts often were. The literary pursuits that had bankrupted Strachey and driven him to Virginia had at least admitted him to an interesting circle of writers. Among them was William Shakespeare, who may have seen Strachey's letter. Other stories in circulation included Sylvester Jourdain's account, another account by the Virginia Company, and a ballad, *Newes from Virginia*. What is certain is that by 1611, Shakespeare had written a romantic tragicomedy about a shipwreck resembling what had happened to the *Sea Venture*, Gates's flagship.[32]

The Tempest was first performed at the royal palace of Whitehall on November 1, 1611. The king surely recognized the themes of exile, discovery, and identity in the play: the same themes that were at the emotional core of colonization in real life. The monstrous Caliban embodied growing doubts about Indian virtue, in paradoxical counterpoint to Gonzalo's appreciation of his humanity. Life and art imitated each other. After two years in Virginia, Alexander Whitaker had decided to stay: like Gonzalo, he saw through a deathly, diabolic wilderness to a "place beautified by God with all the ornaments of nature, and enriched with his earthly treasures." But *The Tempest*'s turbulent world also mirrored England, Gonzalo the voice of the playwright mourning lost charity. English problems, and a determination to solve them, ensured that lessons would be learned from Maine and Jamestown and Bermuda, and that colonization would continue. Utopian dreams trumped dystopian reality.[33]

William Strachey returned to London late in 1611. He was appointed secretary at Jamestown, and the Virginia Company asked him to write a promotional history. Strachey raced John Smith into print, stealing his words, just as Smith stole from others. Strachey's "Historie of Travell into Virginia Britania" was never published: unlike Smith's work, it was too honest.³⁴ Possibly Strachey saw *The Tempest*—and saw himself reflected, his own surreal experience replayed. To godly radicals like John Want, perhaps to all the castaways, Bermuda had felt like a stage on which they were characters, with God as writer and director—a living *deus ex machina*. America, like the theater, offered both entertainment and truth. The New World was a place to be discovered, but also a place where people discovered themselves: their lives in England and their strange transformations.

CHAPTER 3

Each Man Shall Have His Share

A LAVISH MASQUE was performed at Whitehall on February 15, 1613. A day earlier, Princess Elizabeth, James I's daughter, had married Frederick V, elector palatine of the Rhineland. The marriage marked a union between Protestant states in a divided Europe. Inigo Jones designed the sets for the masque, and the script was by George Chapman, who by now had been forgiven for offending the king with the anti-Scottish elements of *Eastward Ho*. Like *Eastward Ho*, the masque reflected Chapman's interest in the New World. His audience was interested, too. John Chamberlain, a recorder of metropolitan life, commenting on the torchlight procession preceding the drama, said that "it is generally held for the best show that hath been seen for many a day." In the Great Hall, awed spectators watched as baboon-faced boys in Neapolitan suits spilled out of a golden mountain. The masquers, appearing at the summit, were dressed as feathered pagans from Virginia, whose celebration of the royal wedding accompanied their conversion to Christianity. By an extraordinary twist, another version would be staged in Whitehall three years later, this time with real Indians and a different newlywed princess.[1]

The masque, however, was nothing more than a theatrical fantasy conjuring visions of desired conformity. American reality confronted on the ground was harder to reconcile with the Jacobean worldview. The fusion of physical and metaphysical—in Bermuda's land of plenty, but more often the result of native encounters—bred paradox and unease. What emerged were not just scaled-down forecasts of civilization's impact on the wilderness, but new forms of transatlantic existence that were nuanced and multifaceted. To discover something was to be changed by it, and in unpredictable ways. English and Indian soon found their cultures rubbing off on each other, creating exchanges and reversals that in some ways brought them together, yet in others served only to highlight irreconcilable differences.

Experience complicated the idea of America. As adventurers aligned the interests of worlds old and new, and more migrants arrived and speculators got involved, so colonies were conceived as an extension of home—a place to live and work, produce and trade—and a means to contemplate England's faults and future. Inevitably, the messy facts of colonization intruded on its fictions. Ideals and imaginings became transformed by the reports of Sagadahoc's impossible winter, and of the violence and hunger in Jamestown. The Virginia Company could never have predicted how much investment, patronage, and courage it would need; nor could the colonists have predicted the extent of the challenges and risks they would face. The problems common to men in Virginia and London remained money, manpower, and management. A constant supply of food, provisions, and labor—especially skilled labor—was required to make the colony's economic infrastructure as close to England's as possible, but it was hard to sustain. Effective political and administrative control was just as elusive.

In the spring of 1614, Sir Thomas Dale, Gates's successor as Jamestown's governor, received a letter from a Virginia entrepreneur named John Rolfe. He and his wife had left England on the *Sea Venture* in 1609, and so had been marooned on the "isle of devils." Their daughter, Barmuda, born during their nine-month sojourn, lived for just a few months; William Strachey was her godfather. Sarah Rolfe, John's wife, died soon after arriving in Jamestown, and now her husband sought Dale's permission to marry Wahunsonacock's daughter, Pocahontas. A year earlier, the Powhatan princess had been kidnapped during a dispute over the Indians' retention of English prisoners and weapons, and she had been held hostage at Henrico ever since. This plantation, forty miles upriver from Jamestown, had been settled by Dale. The purpose had been to extend English territory and please the Virginia Council with a site both salubrious and useful. Named for the Prince of Wales, Henrico sat on a high neck of land. It now had three streets, a church, and workers' blockhouses, which were inhabited by what Ralph Hamor, the colony's secretary, called "the honester sort of people, as in Farmes in England." Pocahontas lodged with Alexander Whitaker, Henrico's minister, who saw in her God's purpose in calling him to Virginia. He taught her English and the rudiments of Christianity.[2]

It was one thing to civilize an Indian, however, but quite another to marry one. When Rolfe fell in love with Pocahontas, he at first felt disoriented, as if he were lost in a labyrinth, and he distrusted his own motives. Why should he love someone "whose education hath bin rude, her manners barbarous, her generation accursed, and so discrepant in all nurtriture from my selfe"? Rolfe worried that his impulses were diabolically inspired, but then decided that the Holy Spirit was testing his courage, and that the marriage would be "for the good of this plantation, for the honour of our countrie, for the glory of God, for my owne salvation, and for the converting to the true knowledge of God and Jesus Christ, an unbeleeving creature." Doubtless Rolfe was also attracted to Pocahontas, which might explain his swipes at imagined critics, "the vulgar sort who square all mens actions by the base rule of their own filthinesse."[3]

Renaming things was halfway to possessing them. When Whitaker baptized Pocahontas, she became Rebecca. The new name suggested that, like the patriarch Isaac's wife (Jacob and Esau's mother) from the Bible, she was the mother of two nations. The Indians, too, sensed power in names: "Pocahontas" was generic, concealing her real name, Matoaka. Whitaker's christening speech was not recorded, but may well have resembled something from Chapman's masque:

> Virginian Princes, ye must now renounce,
> Your superstitious worship of the Sun,
> Subject to cloudy darknings and descents;
> And of your sweet devotions turne the events
> To this our Britain Phoebus whose bright skie
> Enlighted with a Christian piety
> Is never subject to a black error's night,
> And hath already offer'd Heaven's true light
> To your darke region; which acknowledge now
> Descend, and to him all your homage vow.

We can only imagine what Pocahontas—or Matoaka, or Rebecca— thought of her new life. She had settled into English ways at Henrico, and she may even have loved John Rolfe and his countrymen. Perhaps she, too, felt like an adventurer.[4]

Dale needed Pocahontas's father to approve the marriage. Here Henry Spelman, a nineteen-year-old interpreter, was invaluable. Like

Rolfe, he was the younger son of a Norfolk gentleman and a survivor of the Bermuda hurricane. Apprenticed to Powhatan Indians, he had learned the language of his masters and was surprised by them. They had government, justice, and a social order where the "better sort" ate before the "poorer sort"—a model of English life. They married, cared for the sick, and enjoyed themselves. "When they meet at feasts or otherwise, they use sports much like to ours heare in England," Spelman later observed, "as [also] ther daunsinge, w[hi]ch is like our darbysher Hornepipe, a man first and then a woman, and so through them all, hanging all in a round." They played a game similar to soccer, too, except without the fighting common to English "football."⁵

Earlier, Spelman had plotted to seize Pocahontas; now, he would help to make her an Englishwoman. With Wahunsonacock's consent, the marriage took place at Henrico on April 5, 1614. Dale made peace with the Powhatans and was hailed as an English "king." Indian elders agreed to repel the Spanish, and they were promised red coats and medallions of James I. In June, Dale informed London that Pocahontas had "renounced publickly her countrey Idolatry" and had married Rolfe, "an English gentleman of good understanding." Wahunsonacock gave his deerskin mantle to Dale, who sent it to England.⁶

Rolfe's friend Ralph Hamor praised the union. He had captained one of the ships in 1609, and the following year had succeeded William Strachey as secretary. In May 1614, Hamor was preparing to go home, but first he wanted to see Wahunsonacock, whom Strachey described as "a goodly old man not yet shrinking, though well beaten with many cold and stormy wynters . . . of a sad aspect, round fat visag'd with gray haires." Dale granted Hamor's wish, sending him on an errand with Thomas Savage, a boy who, like Henry Spelman, had lived with natives. Such exchanges were arranged so that interpreters could be raised up, but it was easier to leave English boys with Indian tribes than vice versa: as Dale discovered, Indian offspring "are so tenderly beloved of ther paren[t]s that neyther copper nor love can drawe any from them."⁷

When Hamor and Savage arrived, Wahunsonacock demanded to know where the boy had been for the past four years: Savage, who had been entrusted to the Powhatans in 1608, had absconded on a visit to Jamestown. The chief put his hands around Hamor's throat. He was feeling for the pearls that were supposed to be worn by authorized messengers, but Hamor had forgotten them. Over a pipe of acrid tobacco, Wahunsonacock asked how married life suited his daughter, to which

Hamor haughtily replied that she "was so well content that she would not change her life to returne and live with him." Wahunsonacock laughed, saying he was glad of it. Less amusing to Wahunsonacock were Hamor's paltry gifts and a message from Dale asking to marry the chief's youngest daughter. The conference ended on a sour note, and Hamor was shown to a flea-infested hut. He chose to sleep beneath the stars and awoke to a feast of fish, crabs, and oysters. He met what appeared to be an Indian speaking perfect English: his name was William Parker, and he *was* English. Parker was a colonist but had been missing for three years. He now lived semi-naked, hunting and perhaps worshipping idols—a conversion no less extraordinary than that of Pocahontas. Hamor was shocked: an Indian could be anglicized, but the reverse was abhorrent. He forced Parker—and Savage—to return to Jamestown.[8]

John and Rebecca Rolfe lived at Varina Farms across the river from Henrico. Here Rolfe's experiments in cultivation paid off. The tobacco

Ralph Hamor visits Wahunsonacock in May 1614. The chief feels Hamor's neck for "the chaine of pearle," the agreed-upon envoy's badge. To their right stands Thomas Savage, a boy who served as an interpreter. He, and others like him, were regarded with suspicion by both sides.

exported from Jamestown was bitter; the English preferred a sweeter variety, like the kind the Spanish grew. Somehow Rolfe obtained Spanish seeds—although, for the Spanish, supplying them to foreigners was a capital crime. He cross-pollinated it with a native Virginia plant and broke the monopoly. In 1614 he sold his first four hogsheads of his "orinoco" tobacco to a London merchant: at last, the colony had a vendible commodity—the secret of thriving colonies. Yet the Virginia Company discouraged dependence on one crop, and the king was indignant that Britons should assume "the barbarous and beastly manners of the wild, godless and slavish Indians in so vile and stinking a custom." Meanwhile, tobacco's medicinal qualities were lauded. In the 1580s, Thomas Harriot had observed that Roanoke smokers were conspicuously healthy and immune to England's worst diseases. A physician noted that Indians treated infected sores with tobacco, although when smoked, "it produceth such a strange swimming, vertiginie or giddinesses like drunkennesse in the braine, with foaming at the mouth and swouning." People got used to that, and by 1615 coin-operated vending boxes were appearing in London taverns. The pipe-making industry expanded to acquire its own guild in 1619. Rolfe and Hamor were both keen smokers, as was Harriot, until his death from cancer of the nose in 1621.[9]

The impecunious Virginia Company was staring a gift-horse in the mouth. In June 1614, the company's clerk heard from its treasurer, Sir Thomas Smythe, that the plantation was "like to grow weake," as "our merchants &c want courage and heart to continue contribution unless they can see present returnes." Some luxuries reached England. The *Elizabeth* arrived from Bermuda in July with white coral, sassafras, caviar, and ambergris—a whale excretion prized as a condiment and fragrance. A month later, Captain Samuel Argall's ship, the *Treasurer*, brought skins of beaver, otter, elk, deer, and wildcat as well as fifteen tons of cedar. Success, however, lay in mass-demand commodities and in harnessing England's surplus labor to produce them. As Rolfe informed the king, "too many poore Farmors in England worke all the yere, rising early and going to bedd late, live penuriously, and much adoe to paie their Land-Lords Rent, beside a daily searching and care to feed themselves and families: what happynes might they enjoy in Virginia were men sensible of these things." Growing poverty in England certainly meant that many had little to lose. But colonists' experiences belied the utopian world promised by literary confections and Virginia Company propaganda.[10]

Instilling the right sensibility in English workers was vital if the New World was to benefit anyone, but a right sensibility was difficult to instill. Mary Frith, a Jacobean libertine whose family had decided that plantation life would do her good, liked American tobacco, but didn't think she'd like America. As her ship left Gravesend, she dove overboard and slipped into the London underworld to become the cross-dressing "Moll Cutpurse." This was an extreme reaction, but her attitude was not uncommon. Penury and promotions notwithstanding, most people had no wish to emigrate. This was unfortunate for Virginia, where the Old World imbalance of abundant labor and scarce land was reversed, and where land without labor was worthless—"the strength and prosperitie of the Colony consisting in multitudes of people," as one adventurer put it.[11]

The theory of unlimited territory appealed to everyone, though. A gentleman soldier in love with America penned this verse in 1610:

> To such as to Virginia
> Do purpose to repaire:
> And when that they shall thither come,
> Each man shall have his share.
> Day wages for the Laborer,
> And for his more content,
> A house and garden plot shall have,
> Besides t' is further ment.

Like the tame wildfowl in Bermuda, it was a fantasy come true. Men could either pay £12 10s for a share of the profits, or half of that to go to America in person. Poor migrants could pledge several years of service to a planter, merchant, or ship's captain, bound by indenture as in England. Servants and apprentices were fed, clothed, and promised "freedom dues" upon completion of their terms: land and the wherewithal to set up on their own.[12]

John Smith, who had been shunned in England by the Virginia Company, continued to champion colonization. His affections had shifted to

New England, but the point was the same. It made no sense, he said, for English laborers to pay huge rents when land in America was better and free. Nor did it make sense to support able-bodied children in England when demand for labor was so great in America. England's parishes would benefit from helping adolescents and young couples to leave. And what greater satisfaction could a man have, Smith asked, "then to tread and plant that ground hee hath purchased by the hazard of his life"? This, though, was the plan's flaw: not everyone wanted to hazard his or her life, especially in such a notoriously hazardous place.[13]

By the 1610s, enough people had been to Virginia for the dire stories to become culturally embedded. The transatlantic journey was far from being God's bridge. Crossings were slow—taking two or three months—and cramped. They were often terrifying to boot, and colonial life was then disappointing, especially to anyone who had taken the promoters at their word. The toil was ceaseless, the heat insufferable, the lodgings miserable, the food monotonous, and sickness endemic. And Virginia's difference from England rendered useless any knowledge people brought with them about social and economic order. Many who had not expected to miss England now came to appreciate its virtues. At first, the interpreter Henry Spelman found Virginia a "Good and fruitfull Country & wantes nothing save fayther Laborers to labor in the vyneyard," as he told his uncle in a letter of August 1615. If more people would come over, he added, England might think better of the colony. But soon Spelman was penniless and homesick, warning: "I feare that I shall bee utter[ly] lost in Verginia." Like many apprentices, he had left young, at the age of just fourteen, and the change in his life must have entailed a severe emotional upheaval.[14]

Too often, service abroad was imposed on the unwilling, or self-imposed by the desperate, and as a result many travelers were miserable from the start of their adventures. As he waited for his ship to depart in December 1610, Robert Evelyn wrote to his mother: "I am going to the sea, a long and dangerous vo[yage with] other men to make me to be [able] to pay my debts, and to restore my decayed estate again. . . . I beseech you if I do die that you would be good unto my poor wife and children, which, God knows, I shall leave very poor and very mean if my friends be not good unto them, for my sins have deserved these punishments and far greater at God's hands." Abigail Downing, a widow, emigrated to Virginia, where, clutching written proof that "her kindred are honest people of good fashion," she was content to work for bed and board. The emotional pain behind such decisions and family separations was profound. In 1617 Richard Ball, the son of a London tailor, was forced to go to America by his father, who had refused to support Ball's pregnant wife.[15]

Ball may have been one of the hundred people transported by the Lord Mayor of London in 1617, the cost shared with the Virginia Company. Two years later, another hundred joined them, Londoners who, according to a proponent of the scheme, "rise earely, taw and teare their flesh all the day long with hard labour . . . [yet] are scarce able to put bread in their mouths at the weekes end and cloathes on their backes at the yeares end." Paupers were chargeable to their parishes, so apprenticing them in America was a way of dispensing poor relief—a one-off payment without further cost to taxpayers. Many transportees were children, not all of whom complied, leading Sir Edwin Sandys to seek powers of enforcement; in Virginia, he hoped, strict masters would correct "ill-disposed" ways. Demand in Virginia and aversion in England encouraged child-abductors, or "spirits," to operate. In 1618, a Somerset magistrate arrested a man for trying to press women into service in Virginia and Bermuda, driving forty of them into hiding. Spirits did not solve the labor shortage, but they did allow legitimate but fickle apprentices to claim coercement. Compulsion compromised efficiency.[16]

Low productivity, insubordination, sabotage, and absenteeism taught the colonists that quality as well as quantity of labor mattered. The more a colony resembled its mother in skills, the more apt it was to thrive. By 1611, the Virginia Company was calling for every trade, from foundrymen to basket-weavers, limeburners to furriers, millwrights to "uphoulsters of feathers," as well as people who could perform basic occupations, such as brewers and bakers, smiths and sawyers. So great was the need that in 1617 Sir Thomas Smythe procured a carpenter condemned for manslaughter.[17]

And so the military trading post—the model for Roanoke, Sagadahoc, and Jamestown—morphed into a civilian plantation. At first, social distinctions were relaxed. Given the circumstances, even gentlemen had to sail and dig; those who refused sank into "a discontented melancholy [that] brings them to much sorrow, and others to much miserie," wrote Smith. Once the colony was established, hierarchy was restored, but people were connected to a structure of industries and services similar to England's. Men had to enjoy appropriate status, or confusion would reign.[18]

A decade after Jamestown's foundation in 1607, adventurers had learned that merely installing Englishmen in America was not enough; they had to identify things that made England work socially, politically, and economically and reproduce them. Peopling the land correctly was key. The Privy Council, the king's chief advisers, suggested that better bookkeeping—accounting for colonial labor and what was needed—might help. But first the Virginia Company had to improve its terms. Plots were leased to servants when indentures expired. A year's rent was waived for families in order to encourage production of food rather than tobacco. In 1618, the company offered a new package: free transport, clothes, and tools, ten shillings a week before departure, a 50 percent profit share, shorter terms, and the right to remain. Good character was a prerequisite. Felons and vagrants were cheap, but, as John Smith warned, the unvirtuous found Virginia "a misery, a ruine, a death, a hell." Ralph Rookes, transported for "incorrigible vagabondage," probably contributed little. Even appeals for ministers requested no "bad livers." In practice, however, it was hard to pick and choose, and all English types, including Moll Cutpurses, ended up in this expanding corner of the New World—the moral spectrum of the Old World transplanted.[19]

The Virginia Company kept working on its public image, aware that many people laughed at the idea of colonies as engines of progress or solutions to economic misfortunes. If conditions could not be made better, they would at least seem better. The company's ruling council would continue to manipulate opinion by attacking critics and broadcasting a positive message. But what was needed was something to capture the English imagination, and, for a while at least, they found this in a second lottery—and in Pocahontas.[20]

Sir Thomas Smythe's London home was the center of operations. As treasurer, he responded to inquiries, signed up investors and apprentices, and censored letters; many were redacted, some doubtless destroyed. In Jamestown efforts were made to intercept malicious mail. One such packet, the product of what John Rolfe called "devilish and bad mindes," was seized on the *Margaret*. Promotional tracts were commissioned to stir interest in English minds. In 1615, company secretary Ralph Hamor's account appeared, dedicated to Smythe. Hamor

claimed that migrants could now look forward to twelve acres, livestock, and "a hansome howse of some foure roomes"—a vision of a
perfect England in America, prosperous and safe. However, his observation that properties had to be "very strongly impailcd"—that is,
fortified—may have caused alarm. Moreover, his blithe justification of
the harsh legal code made more sense in Jamestown than in London,
where it seemed distinctly un-English. Hamor may have been too long
in Virginia, too distanced from English culture, to be sensitive to English thinking on either point.[21]

Of one thing Hamor was certain: John Rolfe's marriage to Pocahontas was the Virginia Company's best chance to restore its reputation. Rebecca Rolfe—to use the Indian princess's English name—gave
birth to a son, Thomas, in January 1615. Thomas personified friendship
between the two peoples. Through him, Hamor believed, "their bloud

Robert Peake's portrait of Elizabeth Watson marked her marriage to Sir
William Pope in 1615. Her mantle resembles costumes from a court masque,
with pearls arranged in an ostrich-feather design—both decorations being
symbols of the New World.

with mutuall assurance is left hereditary to their posteritie." Physical engagement with the New World, then, turned fantasies into reality, drawing the two worlds closer. In the same year, Elizabeth Watson, a Kentish heiress and daughter of a Virginia Company shareholder, also got married. She was painted, almost certainly for the occasion, and with the approval of her new husband, Sir William Pope, wearing a turban and a loose mantle embroidered with pearls. This may have been a whim of fashion—perhaps she was imitating one of Inigo Jones's masque costumes—but it was also a meaningful allegory of a fecund America. In this way, the expression of a man's desire for his bride drew inspiration from a nation's desire for America.[22]

Yet behind these heady visions lay dismal facts, and adventurers like Elizabeth Watson's father needed imagination, and even a sense of romance, to see beyond them. Once again, the Virginia Company was busy with a lottery, but this time with lower expectations. Not only had receipts been modest in 1612, but some money had yet to be recovered: the company had sued the City of London's agent for almost £3,000. The Privy Council sent the lords lieutenant—crown representatives in every county—a description of Virginia (probably written by Ralph Hamor) in February 1615, asking that gentlemen buy tickets. In March, the mayors received a similar request. Responding officials were sent registers to complete. The public response was muted. In High Wycombe, parents bought five-shilling lots for their children, but the largest purchase was just eight lots. The clerk ended his list of names

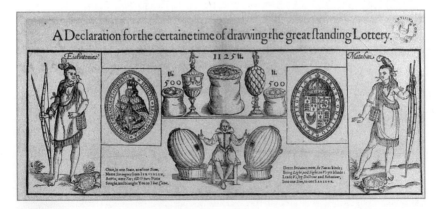

The illustration for a handbill from 1616 advertising the Virginia Company's lottery, its first prize £1,125. The Indians shown, Eiakintomino and Matahan, had been painted in London a year earlier. Note the large egg-shaped baskets from which lots were drawn.

with the deflating remark "*Possibilia spes comitatur*": "Hope depends on chance." Exeter raised £97; Richard Martyn, the Virginia Company's lawyer, thanked the city's mayor, informing him that the draw had been postponed due to "the coldness & backwardness of other places & persons in returning ther books."[23]

As preparations for the draw got under way, John and Rebecca Rolfe made arrangements to visit England. In February 1616, the Virginia Company printed an advertisement for the lottery. It depicted two Indians, Eiakintomino and Matahan, in an adaptation of a portrait made in St. James's Park the previous year. The natives were ventriloquized thus:

> *Once in one State as of one Stem,*
> *Meere Strangers from Jerusalem,*
> *As Wee were Yee, till Others Pittie*
> *Sought and brought You to That Cittie.*
> *Deere Britaines now be You as kinde;*
> *Bring Light and Sight to Us yet blinde:*
> *Leade Us by Doctrine and Behaviour,*
> *Into one Sion, to one Saviour.*

They were begging their civilized cousins to save them. A woodcut of an Indian was nothing compared to the real thing, however. A few weeks later, Sir Thomas Dale sailed home on the *Treasurer*, bringing samples of tobacco, potash, pitch, and caviar. The Rolfes came, too, together with Pocahontas's sister Matachanna and Matachanna's husband, Uttamatomakkin, whom Wahunsonacock had asked to record the sights. As their carriage trundled through the West Country that hot June, Uttamatomakkin gave up counting people. He wondered why the inhabitants of such a spacious land needed America. In London, "Lady Rebecca," wearing a high-crowned hat of white beaver and a delicate lace collar, was escorted between engagements by Sir Thomas Smythe and Lord De La Warr. She sat for a portrait, which was engraved so the image could be made widely available. John Chamberlain, who had witnessed the royal wedding of Elizabeth and Frederick in 1613, joined the crowds to glimpse this New World princess, whom he described as "the most remarquable person."[24]

Others admired how "she carried her self very civilly and lovingly to her Husband, yet she did behave her self as the Daughter of a King." John Smith wrote to Queen Anne requesting that Pocahontas be

Pocahontas in London in 1616, wearing an expensive lace collar and white beaver hat. The engraver, Simon van de Passe, did not compromise on her racial appearance, although Powhatan noblewomen probably had facial tattoos.

treated as such, or else "her present love to us and Christianitie might turne to such scorne and furie as to divert all this good to the worst of evill." An invitation to Whitehall was duly issued. Rolfe, a mere gentleman, was not invited: class had trumped race. Lady Rebecca, in expensive finery, was entertained with a masque by Ben Jonson, performed on a stage dressed by Inigo Jones. According to Smith, courtiers clamoring to meet her "had seene many English Ladies worse favoured, proportioned and behavioured." Uttamatomakkin also attracted attention, but he took umbrage at not receiving a royal present. The gift chosen by Pocahontas was reputedly a copy of the King James Bible, which she donated to the church at Heacham in Norfolk, Rolfe's birthplace. Rolfe may also have planted a mulberry tree from Virginia at Heacham Hall, a reverse symbol of English roots in America.[25]

The Rolfes prepared to return in February 1617. In their luggage they would bring £100 from the Virginia Company "for sacred use." Many now owned Pocahontas's portrait, including John Chamberlain, who, changing his mind about her, sent it to a friend. "Here is a fine picture of no fayre Lady," he sniffed, "and yet with her tricking up and high stile and titles you might thincke her and her worshipfull husband to be somebody." The engraving showed not an English aristocrat, her features made to conform, but a proud American woman. A month later, Chamberlain noted dispassionately that she had died. As her ship set sail, Pocahontas had succumbed to a respiratory illness. It was said that there was "not more sorrow for unexpected death than joy to the beholders to heare and see her make so religious and godly an end." She was buried on March 21 in St. George's church, Gravesend, and recorded as "A Virginia Lady borne." John Rolfe continued his journey, leaving the two-year-old Thomas at Plymouth to be raised by Rolfe's brother, and arrived in fog to find Jamestown busy, though people looked thin and ragged. He grieved for his wife, but took comfort from the son, whom he saw as "a brand snatched out of the fier . . . the lyving ashes of his deceased Mother." In London, the Virginia Company realized that without Pocahontas, peace with the Indians was in jeopardy. Rolfe reported that the Indians seemed "very loving"; however, they would not be loving much longer.[26]

James I's opinion of Pocahontas is not recorded. What mattered to him, apart from his creaking finances and the headache of ruling three kingdoms, was that Virginia should be stable and profitable. In November 1618 he met the new governor, thirty-year-old Sir George Yeardley. As Sir Thomas Gates's bodyguard on the *Sea Venture*, Yeardley had cut his colonial teeth in Bermuda. At dinner, the king spoke exclusively to Yeardley for over an hour, asking him "to deale gently & favourably w[i]th the Indians, and by faire means and good example of life to induce them to christianity & not tyrannize over them like the Spannyards." What the colony needed, James felt, were churches "in a decent forme & in imitation of the churches in England"; converted children should be returned to their people "as laborers into gods harvest." The king's other concern was tobacco: "Man liveth not by smoke alone," he quipped. James sanctioned production of tobacco, provided other staples were forthcoming. Before retiring, he gave Yeardley his hands to kiss, wishing him a prosperous voyage with God's blessing.[27]

Two years earlier, following Sir Thomas Dale's return to England, Yeardley, as deputy governor, had made a pact with the Chickahominy Indians to keep the colonists fed. But a patchwork of native interests meant that peace with one tribe often meant war with another. Even before the death of Pocahontas, rumors of a power struggle between Wahunsonacock and his aggressive brother Opechancanough, chief of the Pamunkeys, had reached Jamestown. Wahunsonacock died in 1618, and Opechancanough then became the Powhatan sachem. Tobacco farmers expanding into Indian territory along the James River ratcheted up the tension. One Sunday, a man who left for church ahead of his family returned to find them all dead. John Rolfe, who was to become a successful planter, reported the tragedy to London. He believed that if only colonists were more orderly and fair, "then we may truly say in Virginia, we are the most happy people in the world." That June, Governor Samuel Argall assured the Virginia Council that he had corrected "ye carelessness of ye people & lawless living." But he complained of chronic shortages. Too few replacements arrived, and those who did came too late in the season to produce more than they consumed. The pressure on food and clothing supplies only abated when, inevitably, some succumbed to the winter.[28]

Meanwhile, the Virginia Company could barely afford to send supplies. Hiring a ship for six months cost nearly £300, not including wages for a crew of twenty-two, and food for the crew and eighty passengers. Five people received 41 pounds of biscuit and four gallons of beer per day, plus 25 pounds of meat on three days of the week, as well as fish, cheese, oil, flour, and cider on the other four; oatmeal with butter was a weekly treat. The total bill for the voyage was over £850—more than a craftsman's lifetime earnings. The company's income dwindled and its capital shrank. Since 1616 it had franchised the lottery to cities such as Chester, Leicester, and Norwich, hoping that "those whom pietie or charitye perswaded not to contribute might by the possibility of gaine be induced to adventure." It was a forlorn hope. Investors had been told to expect grief as well as gain, and while this was easy for men of wealth and imagination—why else would Sir Nicholas Tufton buy a bill of adventure costing £80 in 1618, or a London gentleman risk £115 to charter a voyage?—lesser mortals needed assurances, which now were harder to make. People who "will not adventure with their purses or persons," objects of scorn to Jamestown's minister on the opposite side of the Atlantic, now seemed more prudent than cowardly.[29]

By 1619, the company was virtually bankrupt. As the stream of new investors dried up, existing ones followed the Mercers' Company, who, for several years now, had resolved to put no more money into colonial enterprises. Gradually, Sir Thomas Smythe lost the support of the London merchants whose interests he had represented so assiduously. Unlike the East India Company, the Virginia Company needed to build plantations, and from the point of view of the merchants, all of that consumed too much time and capital. They were only interested in profit. As a consequence, the company had to sell more and more land, fragmenting its territory into private plots, and this drained corporate strength and further entrenched the tobacco monoculture. Even then funding was short: between 1609 and 1619, the company raised a sum of £36,000 by selling stock, most of it before 1614; in a similar period the East India Company raised over £2 million.[30]

Sir George Yeardley arrived in Jamestown in the spring of 1619 to replace the careworn Argall as governor. In a report to Sir Edwin Sandys, the new governor described death and disorder. A soldier, for example, had recently killed another during a drunken row. The previous year, when Sandys had replaced Smythe as treasurer on the London council, he had announced reforms. These included adapting English law and administration to the conditions of Virginia and granting elites royal authority to govern according to local needs. The Great Charter, a nod to constitutional history, supplanted martial law and introduced "headrights": fifty acres of land for every migrant. An adventurer sending five apprentices now had the incentive of gaining 250 acres; a man with a wife and three children received the same. Sandys also authorized Yeardley to form an assembly comprising a council appointed in London and burgesses elected by free colonists (in England, burgesses were the parliamentary representatives of a borough). The assembly convened on July 30, 1619, in the Jamestown church, and for five days it dealt with legislation, regulation, and justice. The work was interrupted by bad weather and illness. This meeting, brief and mundane in business, contrasted with the aggressive concentrations of power aspired to in continental Europe, and yet it was entirely consistent with the self-directing habits of England's parish vestries and urban corporations. Even so, the articles drawn up by the councillors were like the blueprint for a mini-republic. They established a template for a long tradition of representative government in colonial America.[31]

The next couple of years saw patchy successes, minor miracles, and personal tragedies. Sandys reported a slight increase in population and the development of public amenities. Most plantations were reckoned to have between 30 and 100 inhabitants—a total of 670 men, 119 women, 39 "Boyes serviceable," and 57 younger children. The dregs of the Virginia Company's money, and the investments of lone entrepreneurs who had bought their land, paid for this many migrants again in the next few months: 13 ships brought 1,220 people and more than 100 cows. Twenty-odd African slaves also arrived, definite proof that English America was conceived in bondage, not liberty. From that time, in northern as well as southern colonies, slavery grew, slowly but inexorably, shaping local economies.[32]

John Pory, the new colony secretary (and the assembly's first speaker), arrived in Jamestown in April 1619. He was impressed by the potential of the land, though he found the devotion to tobacco frustrating. It was, however, understandable: with just six servants, one man had harvested a crop worth £1,000—prospects as intoxicating to colonists as they were worrying to guardians of hierarchy. "We are not the veriest beggars in the worlde," Pory wrote sardonically to a friend. "Our cowkeeper here of James citty on Sundays goes accowtered all in freshe flaming silke; and a wife of one that in England had professed the black arte (not of a scholler, but of a collier of Croydon) weares her rough bever hatt with a faire perle hatband and a silken suite." In this, she mirrored the anglicized Pocahontas. It was the sort of alteration Atlantic migrations made possible. But Pory was also struck by Virginia's high mortality rate. He saw many English people and Indians who were sick and dying that summer.[33]

Time and again, dreams died with their dreamers. In September 1620, William Tracy left Gloucestershire to lead migrants to America, including his wife, Mary; his son, Thomas; his daughter, Joyce Powell; and Joyce's husband, Nathaniel. Their destination was the Berkeley Hundred, a private Virginia plantation. The previous summer, five adventurers, including Sir George Yeardley, had arranged for a ship to be loaded with tools, weapons, food, Bibles, copies of the Book of Common Prayer, and three volumes of Arthur Dent's *Plain Man's Pathway to Heaven*. Thirty-four colonists had signed up for between three and eight years, including a cooper, a cook, a tailor, and three gentlemen. A boy named Thomas Peirse would be trained as a carpenter at his father's behest. One man received an advance so that he could recover the tools he had pawned and provide for care for his wife in his absence. At first, the Berkeley Hundred thrived. One colonist wrote that although "the seas wer trublsum[,] . . . now we are ashore wee have worke enuf to follow our daiely husbandtrie, sum to clering ground for corne and to-back[o], sum to building houses, sum to plant vines and mulberie trees." The Sabbath was kept, "vaine sportes and scandalous recreations" pro-hibited, and a day of thanksgiving observed. Their commission was to spread Christianity and to make a profit; their projects—corn, silk, vines, and tobacco—matched the diversity desired by the king.[34]

These achievements were short-lived, however. Within two years, twenty-eight of the thirty-four were dead. One man drowned, two were killed by Indians; the rest, including the budding carpenter Thomas Peirse, perished from disease. Four men already there also died. By the time the Tracys arrived late in 1620, the plantation had become a graveyard. Of the forty-five hopefuls who came with them, Indians killed six, and fourteen died from other causes. William Tracy survived for less than six months; Mary Tracy, who had been distraught as they left Bristol, and Nathaniel Powell and his pregnant wife, Joyce, were also among the dead. Thomas Tracy was the only member of his family to see England again. Their minister went home, as did two gentlemen, one on the same ship on which he had arrived.[35]

CHAPTER 4

The Vast and Furious Ocean

V IRGINIA WAS TOO YOUNG to have a clear identity, but a dozen years after the birth of Jamestown, it seemed like a place where hopes were crushed and certainties shaken. It imprinted itself upon anyone bold or foolish enough to go there, and for good or ill it affected the fortunes of investors at home. Settlers needed faith, courage, and stamina; their backers, nerve, patience, and imagination. However hard the Virginia Company sought to project a positive image, reality collided with theory in a kaleidoscopic swirl of unsettling juxtapositions, arresting parallels, and bizarre paradoxes. Experience, conveyed verbally and scripturally, fixed America in English minds as an exciting, disturbing land of untapped wealth and mortal danger. And as settlers arrived farther north, in New England, the New World also became a haven for those seeking freedom of religion—or hell-bent on defying authority, depending on one's point of view. The Pilgrim Fathers, as posterity would style them, faced problems of food and labor, authority and ethnic tensions, that were similar to the ones the Virginia colonists had encountered. But their spiritual and physical coherence threw failings elsewhere in English America into relief, enabling the Pilgrims to set new standards of colonial social and political order—an achievement made plainer once the tobacco plantations, overstretched and under-defended, were consumed by bloody catastrophe.

By the early 1620s, Virginia had four "cities"—Jamestown, Henrico, Elizabeth, and Charles—and was dotted with private plantations with names like Jordan's Journey, Archer's Hoop, and Warwick Squeak. These were gathered into "hundreds," the administrative divisions traditional in English counties. John Smyth, steward to the Berkeley family in Gloucestershire, was a partner in the tragic Berkeley

Hundred project. Early in 1621, a returning colonist arrived at Smyth's home in North Nibley bearing a letter from George Thorpe, a fellow investor from Gloucestershire who was now living in Virginia: "Notw[i]thstandinge S[i]r that you will heare many strainge reportes both of the death of o[u]r owne people and of others, yeat bee not discoraged therein for I thanke God I never had my health better in my life," Thorpe wrote. He was "p[er]swaded that more doe die here of the disease of theire minde then of theire body by havinge this countrey['s] victualles over-praised unto them in England." In other words, unreasonable expectations caused disappointment, depression, and death.[1]

Thorpe was exaggerating, but he had a point. On sale in London bookshops at this time was a Virginia Company tract declaring the colony to be "rich, spacious and well watered; temperate as for the Climate . . . abounding with all Gods naturall blessings." Livestock flourished, government and law brought order, and the settlers were "full of alacritie and cheerefulnesse." Husbandmen had arrived from Devon, ironworkers from the Midlands; deforestation for smelting and potash making, so regrettable in England, was a benefit in America. These industries, and the orchards and vineyards, absorbed idle labor and reduced imports. Yet Thorpe himself was prone to overpraising the colony, and his preference for a fermented corn-drink over English beer is suspect. But then he needed to reassure Smyth of Nibley—and not only that, but he was trying to win his wife over to the idea of coming to America. It was as well she never did. The circumstances of Thorpe's death a year later afflicted the entire colony, and would have been the end of Margaret Thorpe and her children.[2]

Virginia's double bind was that progress brought more problems, requiring the Virginia Company to keep dissembling. Early in 1620, its treasurer, Sir Edwin Sandys, had informed the earl of Huntingdon that the colony, "having been hitherto kept in a long infancy, doth now by the blessing of God beginne greatly to encrease and prosper." But that was not the whole story. Sandys subsequently received two letters from Jamestown, written days apart in June, from the former governor, Sir George Yeardley, and the secretary, John Pory. Colonists were ailing. A hundred newcomers were almost useless, "some very weake and sick, some crasey and tainted," reported Yeardley. A much-needed boatwright had died soon after landing. Pory wanted only fit, and preferably skilled, workers; he also protested that the French viticulturalist was trying "to worke miracles w[i]th his Crucifixe." Sandys heard from Captain William Weldon that migrants had no warm clothing, and had to eat flour and oil from a shared kettle. Weldon begged their patience, but the colonists were restive.[3]

Survival depended on harmony with Indians as well as support from London. Gestures went a long way. On an expedition to find a salt-making site, John Pory, accompanied by the interpreter Thomas Savage, met Namenacus, king of Patuxet. He gave Pory beaver skins and a canoe, and he "much wondered at our Bible, but more to heare it was the Law of our God." Namenacus approved of Adam and Eve's monogamy. But not every Englishman had either the chance or the inclination to be so friendly with the Indians. Godly George Thorpe's sympathy toward natives was also unusual: "There is scarce any man amongst us," he told Sandys in May 1621, "that doth soe much as afforde them a good thought in his hart, and most men w[i]th theire mouthes give them nothinge but maledictions and bitter execrations." The way to win savages for Christ, he suggested, was to civilize them with possessions, noting that they "begin more and more to affect English fassions." Indians were imperfect, but they belonged to the beauty and infinite variety of creation in America—and they were constantly, often delightfully, surprising. Thomas Dermer, a navigator, returned to Virginia in 1621 after a spell prospecting for gold farther north. He told of being shipwrecked on an island, where he was saved by an Indian named Epinew, who, to Dermer's astonishment, had lived in England. But behind the light was darkness. The farther planters moved from the forts, the more exposed and unwelcome they became. Like Thorpe, Dermer did not have long to live in this brave new world.[4]

The situation became desperate: planters had to expand to prosper, but expansion was inimical to the Indian peace on which they depended. The negative effect on the Virginia Company was marked, though still not obvious to everyone. By now it boasted investors from London fishmongers to the bailiffs of Ipswich, from the archbishop of Canterbury to the inventor of *aurum potabile*, a remedy made from gold. But like this quack-cure, much colonial enterprise was meretricious: glittering, expensive, and ineffective. Between 1619 and 1621, the company sent 42 voyages to Virginia and Bermuda, making work for nearly 4,000 people, a quarter of them sailors. The earl of Southampton paid for more than half of these ships and a third of the migrants, including 57 maidens (all spoken for by the time their ships had turned around). The earl also sent Italian glassworkers to make beads to exchange for corn and furs. Yet dividends went unpaid, and the company was £9,000 in debt. The situation worsened in 1621, when the king revoked the company's right to hold lotteries.[5]

Colonial enterprise could seem both exhausted and energized. English merchants were ever more aggressive in the Atlantic, encouraged by political confidence that trade could invigorate the nation—in a word, mercantilism. Plus, any colony that reduced its reliance on imports would be applauded. As ever, the problem was not just one of money but also of authority: weak colonial control both in America and between England and America. James liked Virginia, but not the Virginia Company, much as he hated tobacco but loved other products, above all, silk. In 1620, a treatise about silkworms by John Bonoeil, a Huguenot client of the king, was published. The eggs, he explained, do not travel well, but colonists who were interested in sericulture should strangle a calf fed on mulberry leaves. "Out of the corruption of this carcase," assured Bonoeil, "come forth abundance of Silk-wormes." To the king's annoyance, it was impossible to divert more than a few planters from tobacco. Even though only a minority truly prospered, tobacco was what they knew and did not require significant outlay of capital.[6]

Most of these colonists lived in primitive conditions, often, as at Sagadahoc, conditions worse than they had known at home. Typically, their houses had earth floors and contained unframed beds and little besides. Tools and kettles were prized, and breastplates, obsolete once Indians acquired guns, were beaten into buckets. Possessions listed at death were invariably old, including things that in England would have been discarded. Books were scarce and copied by hand. Few children reached adulthood with both parents alive—a source of emotional trauma and a communal burden. Poor diets lowered immunity and morale. Settlers complained about having only water to drink: wine was expensive, and making malt for beer arduous. Brewing colonial "wine" from boiled sassafras and liquorice was suggested.[7]

Then life grew harder. A royal proclamation against tobacco imports threatened even substantial planters, eliciting a petition from John Rolfe and others in January 1621. Tobacco was all they had, they told the king, so that "wee are plunged in soe great extremities that now remayneth neither helpe nor hope." The petitioners' rhetoric drew on the British imperial vision, natural rights, and an image of the colonist as Christian missionary, imploring the crown "either to revoke that proclamation and restore us to our ancient liberty, or otherwise to send us all home, and not to suffer the heathen to triumphe over us and saye: where is now ther god?" Even when the ban was lifted, customs stripped profits, which led to further appeals as well as smuggling. Irishmen shipped barrels from the Amazon, and a Spanish wreck was plundered in Bermuda to supply the black market.[8]

The king cared little for lives built on smoking; nor did he expect anything but blind obedience at home and abroad. No one foresaw the difficulty that would emerge from settlers' ambiguous identities and ambivalent loyalties. For now, James's attention was focused on a different kind of rebel: the Brownist, or separatist from orthodox Protestantism. During his dinner conversation with Sir George Yeardley in 1618, the king had inquired about ministers in Virginia, trusting they would always "conforme themselves to the church of England, & would in noe sorte (albeit soe farre from home) become authors of Novelty or singularity." Reading an account of this, the Virginia Company's deputy treasurer underlined the last few words and scribbled: "Note this well."[9]

By the end of 1620, however, the influx of separatists was under way, but not in Virginia. Farther up the coast, a ship called the *Mayflower* had arrived at a place passengers called "New Plymouth."

On Christmas Day 1620, Plymouth's settlers raised the frame of their first house. Two days earlier a party had left the *Mayflower* to fell trees and cut beams. The workers' hands were raw, and their clothes froze on their bodies, but they did not rest. Nor did many of them celebrate Christmas, which they saw as a pagan festival. They did allow themselves some beer as they dug postholes and hauled timber on the hillside. The site was a good one, quite unlike Jamestown. It afforded a clear view over the salt marshes and an enclosed harbor with good defenses. The cries of wolves and Indians pierced the night, but the land was otherwise deserted. Bleached bones lay scattered, signs of a pestilence that had afflicted southeastern New England for six years. The Pilgrim Fathers believed that God had cleared a space for their

Christian commonwealth. The land belonged to no one—the old idea of *res nullius*—and could be taken according to another legal principle, *vacuum domicilium*: no one lived there.[10]

A third of the *Mayflower*'s passengers came from a congregation of English religious dissenters at Leiden in the Netherlands. England had many shades of Protestant belief after the Reformation. They represented different degrees of dissatisfaction with how far the church had been purged of what was seen as Catholic idolatry. Calvinists believed that doctrine should abide by scripture, and that a church was not a house ruled by a priest or bishop but a fellowship of believers governed by Christ. Some, like the Leiden separatists, who despaired of ecclesiastical concessions to the old religion, left England. Like all Puritans, their mentality was influenced by apocalyptic predictions from the Book of Revelation. God, they said, would send holy ministers to defeat Antichrist and his popish instruments, restraining Satan for a thousand years. Christ's saints would then build a kingdom on earth, leaving predestined reprobates damned for eternity. In these last days of man, the elect should not be complacent: they must labor in the wilderness, shining light into dark corners, fighting irreligion.[11]

The story of the Pilgrim Fathers, like that of Pocahontas, has a legendary quality, and indeed the Plymouth colonists saw themselves in a temporal vista stretching back to Eden. God had made covenants with Adam and Eve, the Israelites, and the early church, but they had all fallen into error; the Reformation had offered redemption, but the revolution had stalled. The Pilgrims decided that Jerusalem would not be rebuilt in Leiden, but across the Atlantic. The world they would make there was, like Virginia, a trade-off between precept and experience, idealism and pragmatism—a myth to be defended yet adapted. An arc of purpose and meaning connected past, present, and a pristine future always just out of reach.[12]

Delivery into the Promised Land required mundane preparation. Robert Cushman, a Leiden woolcomber, at the suggestion of a London merchant named Thomas Weston, went to England to secure a grant from the Virginia Company. Having accomplished that task, he leased a ship in Canterbury. The *Mayflower* was a squat cargo vessel measuring a hundred feet by twenty-five, and had been designed for wine barrels, not families and livestock. But in July 1620, it entered the English Channel and headed for Southampton Water to rendezvous with the *Speedwell*, which was carrying the Leiden contingent. Among them was a Worcester printer's apprentice named Edward Winslow, aged twenty-two, who had fled to Holland in 1617. He described a last supper at the pastor's house, followed by anguished farewells at Delftshaven. "A flood of teares was poured out," and relatives "were not able to speake one to another for the abundance of sorrow to part." For William and Dorothy Bradford, saying goodbye was acutely painful: they were leaving a three-year-old son with other family members. Bradford, a weaver who had been exposed as a child to radical ideas in Yorkshire, and the clever, dynamic Winslow would be indispensable for the endeavor.[13]

Soon after the two ships turned westward, the *Speedwell* sprang a leak, forcing some passengers onto the *Mayflower* and others, Cushman included, to stay behind. The *Mayflower* finally left Plymouth on September 6, 1620, with 102 passengers and a crew of 30. William Bradford recalled that "after many difficulties in boisterous stormes, at length by Gods providence upon the ninth of November following, by breake of the day, we espied land." This was Cape Cod, whose strands of oak and pine from skyline to rolling white sands lifted the Pilgrims'

The Departure of the Pilgrims from Delft Haven. This mid-nineteenth-century painting, full of despair and stoicism, was the work of British artist Charles Lucy. At its center, a man—probably intended to be William Bradford— appeals to heaven for courage.

hearts. But they were a hundred miles north of their destination, and unable to round the cape owing to bad weather. Some passengers had scurvy; others had eaten mussels, which had made them sick. Their arrival outside the patent also caused discord between saints and "strangers"—ordinary adventurers who had made up the numbers when too few Leideners had volunteered, and who made up two-thirds of the ship's complement. As a result, "it was thought good," said Bradford, "there should be an association and agreement that we should combine together in . . . a civill body politicke for our better ordering and preservation."[14]

Forty-one men signed the "Mayflower Compact"—not a democratic constitution but a company contract to bind the strangers to order upon landing, a quick fix before formal authority was established. Officials were to be elected, yet even the signatories were merely pledging "Submission and Obedience"; the majority of the passengers had no say. This was liberty Old World style: not freedom to do as they pleased— the root of anarchy and apostasy—but freedom to be governed fairly in a hierarchy. The first signatory, John Carver, who had helped Robert Cushman to arrange the voyage, was made governor. Yet for the Pilgrims at least, the true leader was God: far from being democrats, they were theocrats.[15]

On the same day, November 11, William Bradford went ashore on the first boat, whose passengers, he recalled, "fell upon their knees & blessed ye God of heaven, who had brought them over ye vast & furious ocean." They saw sand dunes reminiscent of the North Sea coast, and collected juniper wood; the soil was dark and rich, the trees varied and plentiful. In the days ahead they explored the fishhook tip of Cape Cod. After a thirsty trek, sustained by hardtack biscuit and Dutch cheese, they reached a valley of tall grass and freshwater springs. The men sat, recalled Bradford, "and drunke our first New-England water with as much delight as ever we drunke in all our lives." Simple refreshment became a kind of sacrament, communion with nature for fugitives from Anglican ceremony. God's grace touched his saints in small mercies. Among the remnants of habitation they found maize, but heading back in the rain they became disoriented. Bradford stepped in a deer trap—a bent sapling with a noose "as artificially made as any Roper in England can make." Yet God guided them back to the *Mayflower*. And in mid-December, they found the safe harbor across the bay that became the site for Plymouth.[16]

As snows drifted, colonists gathered at the hearths of their simple homes. They ate whatever they could catch: an eagle "was hardly to be discerned from mutton." There was a stillbirth, and a baby that lived: his parents, William and Susanna White, named him Peregrine, meaning "traveler" or "pilgrim." Nearly half the settlers died that first winter, including Edward Winslow's wife, Elizabeth, and Dorothy Bradford, who drowned. Storms tore the reed roofs from buildings, and daub-infill fell from the frames. The *Mayflower* was tossed around like a toy. In January 1621, John Carver and William Bradford just escaped when a spark started a fire in a house where they lay sick (alongside a quantity of gunpowder).[17]

The new land was beautiful and dangerous. John Goodman and Peter Browne got lost cutting thatch and were forced to sleep rough in the snow. Arriving back, Goodman found that his shoes had to be cut from his frostbitten feet. Some despaired, including Dorothy Bradford, whose death may have been from suicide. Many worried that the wilderness would consume them. Governor Carver died in April 1621 and was replaced by William Bradford. Yet during those lean, freezing weeks, belief that God had blown the *Mayflower* to America gave survivors a unique grit. They worked whenever weather permitted— sawing, building, digging, and searching—but there was so much to do, and their means were limited. There would be no prosperity for colonists, nor returns for their investors, for years to come, which makes their courage all the more remarkable.[18]

Relations with Indians at Plymouth were, if anything, more important than in Virginia. The Pilgrims first encountered them on Cape Cod, when arrows had clattered among the advance party at breakfast. Miles Standish, their bellicose militia captain, had given chase so "that they might see wee were not afraid of them nor discouraged." He gathered the horn-tipped missiles to send home as curiosities. At New Plymouth, colonists waited apprehensively, preparing for an attack. By February 1621 they had finished a hillside fort, mounted with cannon from the *Mayflower*, where men stood guard in all kinds of weather, holding damp muskets that they knew would never fire. Then something amazing happened. A tall Indian walked into the plantation and up the main street. "Hee saluted us in English," recalled William Bradford, "and bad us well-come. . . . [He was] a man free in speech, so farre as he could express his minde, and of a seemely carriage." Fear turned to curiosity, and the settlers "questioned him of many things [as] he was the first Savage we could meete withall." His name was Samoset, and he was a Wabenaki from Maine who had learned English from fishermen. The Pilgrims draped a coat around his shoulders and laid a meal before him, including aqua vitae, biscuit, butter, cheese, pudding, and duck. He said that "Plymouth" was in fact Patuxet, whose people had been wiped out by disease. He left and returned with five Indians "of complexion like our English Gipseys," bearing skins to trade.[19]

One day a man named Squanto arrived. A Patuxet, Squanto had been abducted by a slaver and had lived with a merchant in London, where he had learned English before managing to get home. He thus had missed the epidemic among his people. While he was visiting with the Pilgrims, sixty Wampanoag warriors appeared on the hill. Squanto diffused the tense moment by arranging for Edward Winslow to meet their leader, Massasoit. With his painted face, oiled hair, and bone necklace, Massasoit struck William Bradford as "a very lustie man, in his best yeares, an able body, grave of countenance and spare of speech." Winslow gave him two knives and a copper chain and told him "that King James saluted him as his Friend and Alie." This pleased Massasoit, who tried unsuccessfully to buy Winslow's armor. Massasoit and Winslow met again soon, kissing hands and drinking toasts. A treaty was drafted, and Winslow was dispatched to the town of Pokanoket to ratify it, accompanied by Squanto. Winslow presented Massasoit with a red cotton coat, and the chief "was not a little proud to behold himselfe, and his men also to see their King so bravely attyred." The two men talked until late. Winslow was ushered to the sachem's bed—along with Massasoit's wife and two chieftains—where he was tormented by insects and "the Savages barbarous singing," with which they lulled themselves to sleep.[20]

Although some found the native presence at Plymouth irksome, the exchange of ideas and objects was animated. The natives' language was felt to be "very copious, large and difficult"; the Indians, unable to pronounce the letter "l," called Winslow "Winsnow." Like his Virginia predecessors, Winslow studied native culture. He found that the Indians respected their elders, that their justice was swift, and that their women lived like slaves. Their priests, or paw-waws, he concluded, were in league with Satan. But they were also ingenious. Squanto taught the English how to plant maize using herring as fertilizer, leading to the harvest feast of 1621—the "first Thanksgiving." That autumn, the *Fortune*, the Pilgrims' second ship, arrived, bringing "lusty young men," including William Hilton, an Anglican who had left a wife and two children in County Durham. In a letter to a kinsman, Hilton enthused about the climate, the corn and the fish, and the amity among the Pilgrims and the Indians. New Plymouth resembled England except for one thing: "We are all free-holders, the rent day doth not trouble us," he said, meaning that they were now their own men and owed nothing to any landlord. Hilton begged his family to come and join him there, and in 1623 they did. Life began to feel safer and more satisfying in Plymouth than it had been in Virginia. Edward Winslow married Susanna White, mother of Peregrine, her husband having died in the winter: the colonists' first wedding was "a civill thing" in the Dutch style. As Winslow reflected on how "few, weake and raw" they had been, and how miraculous their preservation, he was convinced "that God hath a purpose to give that Land as an inheritance to our Nation."[21]

On December 9, 1621, Robert Cushman, who had arrived on the *Fortune*, delivered a sermon on piety, industry, and charity. The selfish colonist was a "beast in the shape of a man, or rather an infernall Spirit walking amongst men." Laziness would undo them, just as "a few idle droanes spoyle the whole stocke of laborious Bees." Two days later, Edward Winslow wrote a letter to England eulogizing New Plymouth, and wishing his countrymen could be "partakers of our plentie." They caught cod and lobsters, and in the summer there were salad greens and plums; "the Countrey wanteth onely industrious men to imploy"—England's surplus. A year's experience had been invaluable. If you come, Winslow told his friend, bring a biscuit box, an iron-bound cask, a fowling gun, candle-wicks, and oily paper to cover windows. For the voyage, remember lemon juice to fend off scurvy and don't salt-cure meat.[22]

The ship carrying this letter also took Robert Cushman's sermon to be published. The land was called New England, readers learned, not just because John Smith had named it thus (in his book of 1616), but also because it resembled the motherland. The Pilgrims had built "quiet and competent dwellings," wrote Cushman, and lived spartan but spiritual lives. In Virginia, by contrast, good Englishmen had lost "the sap of grace and edge to all goodnesse, and are become mere worldlings." By failing to civilize Indians, "which are clad in skinnes and creepe in woods and holes [and] thinke their owne brutish and inhumane life the best," planters on the James River had become rather like them. But even Plymouth had its impious "strangers," whom some Pilgrims held in less esteem than they did natives. Edward Winslow's friendship with

Massasoit was based on genuine mutual respect and human understanding. As in Virginia, however, in Plymouth that peace was fragile.
The Indians, who supposed that the English had come to America because they were short of firewood, soon learned that they were envious,
authoritarian, and uncompromising in a way totally alien to indigenous
culture. Native tolerance had limits, and six hundred miles south, in
Virginia, settlers were about to learn what they were.[23]

Early in 1622, Sir Edwin Sandys, the Virginia Company treasurer,
received a letter from Elizabeth City in Virginia, one of many letters that kept him well informed. Peter Arundell, a Cornishman, acknowledged that "for me to writt unto you newes of this countrie were
to cast a few droppes of water into ye sea, you having heere such wise
and good intelligences." Life was dangerous, said Arundell, but he
promised he would "allwayes doe what I may to hide our deffects and
encourage any to the furtherance of this Christian Plantation." On
January 1, Arundell had written exultantly to John Smyth of Nibley.
"Yea, I say that any laborious honest man may in a shorte time become
ritche in this Country," he declared, adding that "these lines containe
no thing but the meere trueth." By this time, of course, Smyth knew
about the Berkeley Hundred disaster. Nor could failure elsewhere be
disguised. The Virginia Company was losing its battle, and no good
public relations could save it.[24]

The English had a grip on Virginia, but not a firm one: so many had
died or returned that the colonists were only 1,200 strong. "I like the
cuntrie well," one new settler wrote upon his arrival, as did many others; but usually they soon changed their minds. In May 1621, Captain
Thomas Nurse described Elizabeth to Sandys in terms more bleak than
Peter Arundell's. The climate was hostile, seeds had not germinated,
and cattle were scarce. "The people lyve very barely, for the most part
havinge no other foode but bread & water, and such mann[er] of meate
as they make of Mayze, which I would to God I could say they had
in any reasonable plenty." Work had no end, complained Nurse, and
death from hunger and exposure was common. The following month,
an agent of John Ferrar, the Virginia Company's deputy treasurer, requested that no more fish be sent, but suggested that honey to spread
on biscuits might lift morale.[25]

The Virginia Company decided that what colonists really needed was female company: half of the planters in Ulster, the Irish province that was being settled, were women. When there were not enough women in a colony, minds were "much dejected and ther hartes enflamed w[i]th a desire to return for England only through the wants of comforts of Marriage, without w[hi]ch God saw that Man could not live contentedlie, noe not in Paradize." The summer of 1621 brought everything from bedsteads to clay pipes, from spades to writing paper, and from fishing nets to the desired honey. There was beef, butter, and cheese; ten barrels of "good beare well hopt"; iron "tamahauks" and 30 pounds of beads for trade. Most important were the women. Mostly young and unsupported, they came from across England. Nineteen-year-old Ellen Bourn left Suffolk after her parents died. She arrived with a recommendation that she was "a sober and industrious Mayd skilfull in many workes."[26]

Political stability was sought in small things. When colonial councils, lacking the ropes and levers of authority natural in England, were unable to hold the center of power together, they policed the margins. Men were made to dress according to rank and behave decorously. Lieutenant Richard Keane received cloth for a suit and gold lace to decorate it; a woman was hired to clean the Jamestown guesthouse and do laundry. Small increments of economic progress were cheering. Early in 1622, positive reports about the manufacture of salt, glass, and iron were sent to England: Sir Edwin Sandys's brother George, who came to Virginia for four months, thought the location of the Falling Creek ironworks at Henrico was "so fitting for that purpose, as if nature had applied her selfe to the wish and direction of the Workemen." The grapes, some said, were better than in the French vineyards of the Languedoc, and tobacco was increasingly refined.[27]

Relations with the natives seemed healthy, too. Sir Francis Wyatt, who arrived with George Sandys to replace Governor Yeardley in November 1621, was delighted to find Englishmen and Indians sharing fishing boats, hunting together, and exchanging hospitality. Opechancanough, the Powhatan chief, vowed the sky would fall before the peace ended. Wyatt also found natives receptive to Christianity and was impressed by their godly advocate, George Thorpe. Thorpe had befriended Opechancanough and replaced his "hog-stye made with a few poles and stickes" with an English house. The chief was delighted, especially with the lock and key, "which hee so admired, as locking and unlocking his doore an hundred times a day, hee thought no device in all the world comparable to it." Thorpe, a Puritan humanist, had won respect.[28]

Plans were made to build colleges at Henrico and Charles for Indian and English children. Why would anyone bring children to Virginia, an English schoolmaster asked, if they risked "falling away from God to Sathan" for lack of instruction? There was a danger that the next generation would "become utterly savage." Substantial sums were raised in England: in the years 1616–1618, an order from king to bishop to archdeacon to churchwarden had led to organized parish collections. One benefactor gave £550 to transport fifty men, whose work on a dedicated plantation, overseen by the venerable Thorpe, would earn the college income. Books were donated; one minister bequeathed his entire library. Hearing of Virginia's lack of schools and churches, Patrick Copland, a Scottish chaplain to the East India Company, collected £70 from his own ship, the *Royal James*, a fund that by January 1622 had grown to over £125. Copland was also determined to emigrate. "Were there as many Devils in Virginia as there be men and trees there," he said, "thether would I goe."[29]

On April 18, 1622, Copland preached to the Virginia Company in Cheapside. For the poor to stay in England was more perilous than leaving, he said, besides which, colonists were happy, "every one busied in their Vocations, as Bees in their Hives." After seven years of peace with the Indians, moreover, the risk of mutual destruction had vanished. The legacy of Pocahontas's marriage endured, and Opechancanough was now convinced that a supreme God had punished his people for staining their children's skin—the English believed Indians were born white—thus "consecrating them to Sathan." But Copland had never been a missionary in Virginia, nor would he be; those who had been were less sanguine. George Thorpe came to realize that however much Powhatans admired English houses, they could not be won for Christ. The minister at Jamestown put it bluntly: "Till their Priests and Ancients have their throats cut, there is no hope to bring them to conversion." Then came something that changed everyone's minds forever. What Copland's congregation at St. Mary-le-Bow did not yet know was that four weeks earlier, Virginia had entered the abyss.[30]

On the night of March 21, 1622, a planter living opposite Jamestown was roused by his Indian servant, who told him that Opechancanough was about to attack. He spent the next few hours rowing up and down the river alerting people, who hurried to the stockade. Early the next

morning, twenty miles away at Berkeley Hundred, George Thorpe's
servant issued the same warning, which Thorpe dismissed. The next
hour passed normally, with Powhatan traders moving freely around
English settlements. Around eight o'clock, upon a signal, the Indians
grabbed tools or weapons and attacked whoever was nearest, mostly
people they knew. The blood-spattered Indians proceeded to the fields,
the brickworks, and the glassworks and sawmills. "Not being content
with taking away life alone," wrote Edward Waterhouse, the Virginia
Company secretary, "they fell after againe upon the dead, making as
well as they could a fresh murder, defacing, dragging and mangling the
dead carkasses into many pieces, and carrying some parts away in derision, with base and bruitish triumph." Outlying plantations suffered
the most. Eleven died at George Thorpe's house, including Thorpe,
whose corpse received "many barbarous despights and foule scornes."
The death toll at his plantation was twenty-seven; on the college lands,
seventeen. At Martin's Hundred, eighty-one died, including Thomas

Matthäus Merian's interpretation of the Indian rebellion of 1622 captures all
the spontaneity and ferocity of the attack. The deaths of so many English settlers helped to justify a more openly hostile and expansionist colonial mentality in Virginia.

Boyce and his wife and three children along with four apprentices and a maidservant; one fatally injured woman crawled to a trash-pit that became her grave. Indians also visited Henrico, killing John Berkeley, the ironmaster at Falling Creek, whose son hid in the woodland with other children. John Rolfe died at Varina Farms that year, possibly at the hands of his father-in-law's men.[31]

At least 347 men, women, and children died that day, a third of the English colonists; another 20 women were captured. The shock along the James River was seismic. According to "ancient planters," the massacre "strooke so att the life of o[u]r welfare by blood and spoile that it almost generally defaced the beauty of the whole Colony." That summer, crops went untended and surviving cattle wandered off; servants absconded. A shipbuilding project at Martin's Hundred, funded by London merchants, stalled. Dogs ate corn in the fields (and were hanged for it); colonists lived on oysters and crabs. Precious time and energy were spent on defenses; at night, Indian raiders cut down tobacco. People were afraid to leave their houses, fearing they would be burned. Supply ships came, but they refused to linger. The only option, some felt, was to go home. Without livestock, the planters said, "we shall, like a poor miserable people, be fayne to live onely upon bread & water, and that in noe plenty neither."[32]

In July, the first refugees arrived in England on the *Seaflower*, along with letters telling the same grisly story. An account received in Cambridge expressed horror mixed with gratitude to the Indian boy who had alerted Jamestown. Patrick Copland, made rector-elect of the Charles City college that month, shifted his gaze to Bermuda. Some families had to wait until Christmas to hear whether their loved ones were alive. The Virginia Company read a letter, dated August 16, "that signified extreame wantt of Corne and much bodilie sickness in the Colloney." When the *Seaflower* returned to Virginia in December, it carried a message from Virginia Company deputy treasurer John Ferrar to George Sandys and the governor, Sir Francis Wyatt, of whom nothing had been heard, describing "a generall sicknes of mynde in the whole [Virginia] Company, weake hands and feeble knees"; if this work no longer served God, said Ferrar, he would abandon it. When Sandys's report arrived in England, Edward Waterhouse rushed it into print: the colonists' only failing, he said, was to have trusted the Indians. However galvanizing the moral outrage, the blow dealt to the

Virginia Company was fatal. The king ordered men and corn to be sent to Virginia, fearing reproach to England if colonists were "driven from it by naked and cowardly Indians."[33]

The massacre was interpreted as punishment for backbiting and ingratitude. Perhaps God had let Satan inspire Powhatan paw-waws, who then persuaded their people that Englishmen would exterminate them. This analysis was self-fulfilling. According to one traveler, soon after the news reached England the colonists were ordered, presumably by the king speaking through the Virginia Company, "to take revenge by destroying with fire and sword everything of the Indians." Throughout the Atlantic world, men decided that Indians could not be trusted. In October, the Virginia Council told Sir Francis Wyatt not to give up—to do so would be "a Sinne against the dead"—and to inflict "sharpe revenge uppon the bloody miscreants, even to the measure that they intended against us, the rooting them out for being longer a people uppon the face of the Earth." By now, Sir Francis Wyatt's father in Kent had received a letter from his son referring to *fighting* during the uprising; evidently, it had not been the one-sided massacre of innocents that Waterhouse had described. In reply, George Wyatt noted that, contrary to opinion, these "Savages estrainged from al Civilitie and Religion" were brave and fought "not desperatly, but orderly." He advised treating them as a serious enemy to whom battle should be taken—advice Sir Francis would heed.[34]

As English hearts hardened, and memories of Roanoke returned, so advantages were identified. John Bonoeil, the silk promoter, invited the enslavement of Indians to advance his scheme. Edward Waterhouse also saw a chance, in that "our hands which before were tied with gentlenesse and fair usage are now set at liberty"—as when the Irish had rebelled. The "residency" was over. The best land could be now seized "by right of Warre, and law of Nations," not merely occupied. Indian corn and fishing weirs should be destroyed to cause famine, and the "savages" driven with horse and mastiff toward their tribal enemies. English America now had a glittering future. It would expand, just as Rome had grown on the heaps of its defeated enemies. George Thorpe was a martyr, declared Waterhouse, and his murderers would burn in hell. In Jamestown, George Sandys went about his work as treasurer while perfecting his translation of Ovid's *Metamorphoses*—a mythical epic describing the origins of the world, England's share of which Sandys was helping to enlarge.[35]

No migrant or investor could doubt the fragility of existence in the New World. Colonies that did not grow and prosper lasted but a short while, and usually ended in financial ruin and misery. Restraint in trade and land acquisition did not suit the questing, acquisitive spirit of Jacobean Englishmen. And yet, without diplomacy or proper defenses, inevitably expansion would jeopardize colonists' lives and enterprises, and even set colonists—an increasingly diverse lot—against each other.

CHAPTER 5

Full of Wild Beasts and Wild Men

THE 1620S BORE OUT William Camden's dictum that private men would struggle to build plantations in distant countries. James I's "plantation policy" had succeeded in Ireland mainly because of favorable cultural and logistical factors, not least proximity. Virginia was unlike this: it was far from home, and strange in so many ways, and the costs of planting were exorbitant, the risks enormous. But the problems besetting adventurers since 1607 were also political: there were irreconcilable Old World differences between the men who were involved in the endeavor. Some were radicals and others conservatives; some were conformists, others dissidents—and their desires were often incompatible. The Virginia uprising made it easier to oppress Indians, and this helped a little, in terms of binding the colonists together for a common cause. But in Virginia, and increasingly in New Plymouth and Bermuda as well, an English settler's most persistent adversary was another Englishman. Governors and investors clashed with settlers because they could be too remote to grasp the realities of America. Fellow colonists, in all their awkward variety, were just too near. These relationships bred a strained sense of contrast that both distanced settlers from England and made many long to be back there.

It was miserably cold in Virginia in February 1623. Almost a year had passed since the uprising, and planters had tried to make war on the Indians, but now the planters' arch-enemies were hunger and the cold. English raiders blown onto the Chesapeake shore spent an excruciating night there. They risked a small fire, but by morning one man was dead. As daylight exposed their position, they found their boat was leaking. A volunteer took a broken canoe to get help, paddling with his hands and feet for several hours until he reached their ship. With frostbitten

legs, the man returned that night with a rescue party—the living epit-
ome of friendship and courage. That winter produced many stories of
hardship. A colony that once had soldiers when it needed farmers now
found that it needed both. Men who had left England to grow tobacco
fought ferocious warriors in appalling conditions. They were right to
think that people at home had no idea what they were going through.[1]

E ngland had of course made much righteous lamentation for
Virginia's suffering. The Indian rebellion had satisfied an appetite
for cathartic real-life dramas, especially ones involving national honor
and God's chastisement. Within days of news arriving in England, a
ballad, "Mourning Virginia," had been registered with the Stationers'
Company. A 1622 poem by Christopher Brooke of the Virginia Company asked God if sin would now be king and "Savage men in their
Ignorance advance." A few weeks later, Brooke's friend John Donne,
the dean of St. Paul's and a self-styled "adventurer if not to Virginia,
yet for Virginia," told the company not to lose heart. Keep building
bridges, Donne counseled, not just between the Old and New Worlds,
but between humanity and "that world that shall never grow old"—the
kingdom of heaven. His sermon was read widely in England and the
colonies. The massacre also reached the stage as *A Tragedy of the Plantation of Virginia*.[2]

High-toned rhetoric, however, did not answer the question: What
should be done with Virginia? A proposal to the Virginia Company
suggested that money and men be raised to "utterly roote out thos[e]
treacherous Indians by making contynewall warre upon them." The actual response was less dramatic. Armor in the Tower of London, "unfit
and of no use for moderne service," was donated. Captain John Smith
insisted that Virginia needed a garrison. He offered to lead an army "to
inforce the Salvages to leave ther Country," or else force them into subjection, but this plan was too expensive. Most ideas involved making
dependents of the Indians: some pictured them as classical slaves, tend-
ing estates and rowing galleys. It was also argued that the king should
take over the Virginia Company.[3]

Behind the massacre's cosmic causes, of course, lay prosaic ones:
rancor, incompetence, and lax authority. Factional strife between Sir
Thomas Smythe; Sir Robert Rich, the earl of Warwick; and Sir Edwin

Sandys was debilitating. Nicholas Ferrar, John Ferrar's brother and a supporter of Sandys on behalf of smaller investors, claimed that Virginia's reputation was so poor that felons were choosing the gallows over transportation there. Desperate colonists eating a horse, he said, had wished that Smythe "were on the Mares back in the boylinge Kettle." Others blamed the settlers themselves, particularly, as in one ringing rebuke, their "owne supine negligence that lived as careles and securely there as yf they had ben in England, in scattered and stragling houses far asunder."[4]

For all England's problems—mortality crises, royal conflict with Parliament, and friction with Spain—seen from America, the motherland was stable and secure. Virginia was a vision of primeval chaos. One adventurer, John Bargrave, told Lionel Cranfield, the earl of Middlesex, that Jamestown's government had set its face against the king, proving that, as in Rome after Nero's death, "Extreame libertie" was worse than "extreame Tirranie." The governor, Sir Francis Wyatt, would do well not to treat colonists as his subjects, Bargrave continued. English and Virginia laws should be united "in naturall love & obedience," and men must dress properly. He also advocated setting up a treasury to divide tobacco dividends between public purse, private planter, English investor, and crown coffers. Because in England power was invested in land, the free-for-all in property in America resembled a *political* free-for-all. Colonists' interests, Bargrave insisted, must hinge on loyalty to the English state.[5]

Basic survival, however, mattered more than autonomy. A new arrival on the *Seaflower* wrote to his brother: "Since the massecer ther is far more dead then was by it slayne and nowe at this time a great many sick & no hopes of life. . . . So god be mercyfull unto us for he hath cast a hevy hand over us all." The *Seaflower* returned for supplies, and the colonists waited. A youth named Richard Frethorne informed his master in England that half of his shipmates had died. Their rations had been consumed by starving colonists, who, unable to digest solids, had then died themselves. Newcomers were prey to scurvy and dysentery. Frethorne asked to "be freed out of this Egipt," or at least that he receive some beef, cheese, and butter, paid for, he suggested, by parochial collections. Frethorne also begged his parents to redeem him, relating how he was working long hours for a dish of gruel and a scrap of bread. At home, he had eaten more in a day than he received here in a week. "People crie out day and night, O that they were in England without their lymbes, and would not care to loose anie lymbe to bee in England againe, yea though they beg from doore to doore," he wrote. "I know if you did but see me," he added, "you would weepe . . . the Answeare of this letter wilbee life or death to me." George Sandys warned the Virginia Company merchant John Ferrar that if the *Seaflower* did not return soon, famine would ensue. There was also sad news from Elizabeth City. After struggling to lead his people, Captain Thomas Nurse had died "very poore," having shared his meager grain-store while failing to harvest his tobacco. Sandys begged Ferrar's compassion. Nurse had sold everything to move to America. If his plantation was taken away, his widow and children would starve.[6]

Stories from Virginia in the summer of 1623 were the usual muddle of positive and negative, candor and dissimulation. Seamen reported nonedible deliveries—everything from private trunks to weapons, millstones, and furnaces—abandoned on the shore. One colonist wrote to a merchant in Devon thanking him for clothes, but wishing to God they "were turned into Meall, Oatmeall and pease." Profiteering spread amid rumors of invasion. It was said that the Spanish, furious about the tobacco trade, were planning to cut the throats of Virginia and Bermuda. Newcomers at Jamestown died in the streets and allegedly were eaten by pigs. As ever, others told it differently. John Ferrar heard of a man just back from Virginia who claimed that people "stood well in helth." Some parts were indeed recovering. Robert Bennett told his brother in London that the corn and tobacco crops were superb, and that they now had the upper hand with the Indians. Bennett described gleefully how on a diplomatic visit to the Potomac Indians, Captain William Tucker had tricked and poisoned his hosts; soon colonists would advance against the Nansemonds "to Cutt downe ther Corne and put them to the sword, god sende us vycctrie."[7]

For all the pleasure that scandalizing and satirizing Virginia gave the English, there were many, especially the unemployed, who focused on positive reports. How else to explain why migrants kept coming? Nevertheless, labor shortages remained critical. George Sandys implored Ferrar to send more servants: all his were dead, and the cost of wages such that he couldn't afford to feed his family. The colonies depended on would-be migrants seeing a chance and suppressing doubt. In 1623, a young man on the Isle of Wight, writing to his mother in Nottingham, captured the moment of embarkation for America's "hopefull and happie soile." He recommended that she read a book about "all things

Concerning Virginia . . . latelie set forth in 1622"—probably Edward Waterhouse's tract. On the ground, though, things looked bleak. In October, a damning Royal Commission report led to demands that the Virginia Company surrender its charter, which it refused to do.[8]

In January 1624, Governor Wyatt accused the Virginia Council of failing to face colonial facts. Planters were famished, and supply ships brought musty bread and stinking beer left over from previous voyages. Conscious of his father's advice, Wyatt decided that the Indians had forfeited all rights and deserved no mercy. Yet the difficulty of fighting *and* farming led planters to complain to their commanders about wasting time on a pointless war. Some weeks later, the council at Jamestown denied poisoning the Potomacs, but added that "we think it a sin againste god and man to conclude any peace w[i]th them, and thinke our selves bound to intend nothing more then their ruine and extirpac[i]on." By this time, poor Richard Frethorne was dead, and the earl of Warwick was using Frethorne's letters to discredit the leadership of the Virginia Company, and so to force James I's hand.[9]

The Virginia Company was moribund: the adventurers were listless, their ships idle, and the colonists mutinous. Privy councillors advised intervention. Governors in Jamestown blamed Sir Thomas Smythe's tyranny, as did his enemies in London. Food "full of Cobwebs and Maggots" drove men to Indian encampments; if recaptured, they were broken on the wheel. One thief was starved with his tongue nailed to a tree. "Many through these extremities," it was said, "being weery of life, digged holes in the earth and there hidd themselves till they famished." The king was sent a report by Nathaniel Butler, former governor of Bermuda, who had wintered in Virginia in 1622–1623. Colonists inhabited lonely places divided by swamps and creeks, he said, and "ther Howses are generally the worst that ever I saw, the meanest Cottages in England beinge every way equall (if not superior) with the most of the beste." The government disrespected English law, showing "not onely ignorant and enforced strayings in diver[s] particulers, but willfull and intended ones." The planters sent a rebuttal, and Wyatt dismissed Butler as a drunk—but too late. A writ of *quo warranto*—"By what authority do you rule?"—challenged the Virginia Company and upheld James's right to dissolve it. In May 1624, the charter was annulled, and a commission was appointed to run the colony.[10]

The company had fallen, but had it failed? It never delivered what it promised, and its mandate had ended. But the problems had been huge, involving issues of governance, supply, coordination, and communication. Its image management and fund-raising had been innovative and accomplished. It had made money, just not enough. It had published twenty-seven promotional books and pamphlets; 1,700 adventurers had bought shares; and it had learned lessons indispensable to future colonists in New England. Above all, the company, with the courage of its colonists underpinning its efforts—and 12,000 (over 90 percent) of them dying since 1607—had established an English bridgehead in America.[11]

In July 1624, just as the Virginia Company folded, Captain John Smith published his magnum opus on English America. Three thousand copies were printed, including a deluxe edition with maps to inspire adventurers. Its message was this: Be proud and optimistic, but don't expect too much too soon; from these modest beginnings, the colonies would flourish. Bermuda, Smith said, had had a more difficult start than Rome, Carthage, or Venice. A tract published the same year described the island as an easily defended, savage-free land where tobacco, oranges, figs, and other exotic fruits abounded—and a sugar works was planned. Yet in Bermuda, like anywhere else in the New World, "all Adams posteritie were appointed to worke for their food, and none must dreame of an absolute ease." Just how hard life could be, and how valiantly some fought for utopia, is illustrated by the experience of a minister who preached in Bermuda, Lewis Hughes.[12]

When in 1610 Sir George Somers's crew had repatriated his body, they had left behind three men who had planted corn, beans, melons, and tobacco. (They also found a quantity of ambergris allegedly worth £10,000.) Two years later, the Virginia Company sent eighty men and women, who caught more fish than they could eat. Like previous visitors, they also collected tame birds—and they found that the pigs tasted as good as English mutton. The governor built forts and raised a militia. In 1614 the company hired Lewis Hughes to preach for three years; leaving his wife in London, he arrived that spring. Hughes had been rector of St. Helen's, Bishopsgate, but was removed from his position for performing an illegal exorcism. As ever, America offered redemption for the errant. In December 1614, he wrote to friends denying that Bermuda was a land of devils. The air was superior to England's and the food plentiful. The nocturnal birds were the only downside—their songs were less sweet than those of their English cousins. "Men shall live heere in much ease without such moiling and toyling as is in England," he promised. "Come hither as it were into a new world to lead a new life."[13]

Hughes feared corruption, however. Abundance was heaven's gift, but it encouraged laziness. People boiled or roasted wildfowl instead of farming or raising livestock; some ate meat raw like beasts. God was letting the wicked destroy themselves. Hughes encouraged his friends to bring biscuits, bedding, tools, and candlesticks, but "above all things, have a care to leave their sins behind." Idle men and whorish women, he explained, lived miserably in Bermuda, "hated and loathed of all honest people, which makes them weep and sigh with teares to wish themselves in England againe." Offenders were towed around the harbor "too coole them a little." Worried that people were overeating on Cooper's Island, the governor moved them to Port Royal, where they lived in the same careless bliss, bathing in rock pools, playing on the pink sands, and dozing in woodland shade. For people who had shivered through English winters with empty stomachs, this was paradise—but one soon lost unless hardworking people arrived to develop a more civilized community.[14]

In 1615 the Virginia Company sold its interest in Bermuda to 120 of its members, who formed their own joint-stock enterprise, the Somers Isles Company—Somers Isles being the usual name for Bermuda. This territory might have refocused the rays of colonization, had chaotic land distribution not compounded the problem of a torpid workforce. Some farmers were unsure where to go; others were allocated rocky wasteland. In November 1615, Edward Dunn wrote to his Puritan patron, Sir Robert Rich, the future earl of Warwick, to ask for a specific plot. "Wee are as yet upon uncertainty," Dunn explained, a state of confusion that had prevented him from producing as much corn as he might have otherwise.[15]

Migrants kept arriving, some having read Hughes's letter in published form, but most were disappointed. High summer was stifling, mosquitoes a torment, hurricanes a terror. Houses were made of wood, mud, vines, and hair, with roofs of stripped palm leaves. Few had chimneys, so cooking was done outside; water came from a shallow well or brackish pond. Soon there were more people than Bermuda's resources could sustain. "And as they encreased," noted Hughes, "sin and disorder did also encrease, which brought the correcting hand of God." Some colonists planted more tobacco than corn, and a poorer strain than in Virginia. Others spent too much time building ships. As the wild animals disappeared, the council was forced to prohibit the killing of baby birds and turtles.[16]

Food was growing very scarce by 1615. In May 1616, a new governor, Daniel Tucker, introduced a work program to sustain the population and produce commodities. He also oversaw the division of land into defined shares. The Somers Isles Company had asked Richard Norwood, its pearl-diver (and inventor of a diving bell), to produce a map. This was sensible: he was a gifted surveyor and there were no pearls. Norwood had left England in December 1613, at the age of twenty-three, and at sea had devoted himself to God. In Bermuda, however, he broke his pledge, until Lewis Hughes arrived there. His preaching had the power to transform sinners.[17]

The dearth of food encouraged Hughes to emulate Christ. He accompanied colonists who relocated to Port Royal, and there "did pine away to skinne and bone." They lived on berries. When Hughes, whom the colonists fondly called "Mr. Lewis," grew too weak to stand, he was carried to a hillside to preach. There he accused one of the commissioners, John Mansfield, of forcing colonists to sign a declaration of independence from England. Hughes continued to speak openly of "the unlawfulnesse and evill" that was likely "to come of the rebellion" until he was banished to an island. Governor Tucker was tyrannical. Obedient colonists were fed and clothed, but dissidents were whipped, some by Tucker personally. Five men escaped to Ireland in a boat; others tried, too, but disappeared or were caught and hanged. Land was confiscated from poor men, one of whom was chained for threatening to petition the king. Lewis Hughes lived in poverty, wearing the same straw hat and shoes for three years. While the governor's mansion exhausted supplies of cedar, the church was, according to Hughes, "but a thacht Hovell which was kept so badly as when it rained there was almost no place where the people could sit drie." Tucker even heckled Hughes's sermons.[18]

After famine came plagues—first, a plague of ants (men tarred the frames where they dried figs to trap them), then worse. In 1616 a colonist informed his master that "there is hope of these Ilands, and much more would there bee if wee were ridd of our generall enemyes the ratts. . . . Much is to be feared wilbee the subversion of this plantac[i]on if you & all other woorthy minded adventurers doe not devise some course for their distruction." The governor, he added, had ordered every colonist to lay traps and poison. The rats ate the eggs and young of wild-life, increasing the shortages. When rats were found inside of fish, col-onists deduced that they were swimming between islands in their own program of colonization. People were driven half-mad. "I am not able to express the feare that was in the people," Lewis Hughes remarked, "that they should be starved when they saw that nothing that served for foode could be kept from the Rattes." A report from May 1617 said that anything could grow in the fertile soil, but because of the infestation nothing would; in the same month, however, the problem abated.[19]

The patronage of Sir Nathaniel Rich, a godly nobleman, and his cousin Sir Robert cemented the friendship of their respective clients: the embattled Hughes and Nathaniel Butler, the new governor who arrived in October 1619 (and later hastened the Virginia Company's demise). Butler's appointment was a boon to Hughes, who was contem-plating leaving. In the winter of 1617–1618, Hughes had been knocked down by winds and injured his arm, and he longed to see his wife. Sin and strife were endemic, and Hughes felt he would never win. But what had he hoped to achieve? In a letter to Sir Nathaniel, written in 1617, he mentioned his abandonment of the orthodox Book of Common Prayer. This was daring: using the liturgy of the English church was a legal ob-ligation. But the Puritan Sir Nathaniel Rich surely approved. When in 1619 Sir Robert made Butler governor, the effect was not just to curtail what some called "the time of mis-rule": rebelliously, it established Cal-vinist worship and church government in an outpost of the Anglican state. Hughes was devoted less to England than to his self-exiled flock in Bermuda. This was no New Plymouth, but had something of its dissenting spirit. Butler agreed with Hughes that Bermuda was special: his first impulse was to find where Sir George Somers's heart was bur-ied and place a marble slab there.[20]

Yet Butler's letters show that he was as shocked by Bermuda as he would be by Virginia. The problems were similar: economic disorder, internecine fighting, and contradictory orders from London. Tenants were in arrears and needed servants: as Butler's assistant put it, the working man "wearied with the labours of the daye, comeing home must beate corne, fetch water, gett and dresse his own victuales." New colonists were hopeless: women arrived pregnant, the men diseased and half-naked. The pastoral burden on Hughes was crushing. Samuel

Lang, a minister sent to help, gave interminable sermons, earning himself the nickname "Mr. Long." Butler also criticized management of the harvest in 1619, which had allowed people imprudently to gorge themselves on gruel and "huge and monstrous puddinges, everyone striveinge to have the biggest." Hurricanes in the winter of 1619–1620 blew down the watchtower and carried off a ship—to Hughes, these things were signs of God's anger at islanders' profligacy and profanity and their enmity within the Somers Isles Company.[21]

Butler worked just as hard as Hughes. In 1620 he oversaw the creation of a House of Assembly, modeled on the Virginia House of Burgesses, which met in a purpose-built statehouse. The following year he completed fortifications, built a prison, and in the English manner appointed magistrates, constables, and churchwardens (though they were not answerable to bishops or archdeacons), making the "tribes" of the colony more like parishes. Butler also introduced assize courts, which improved order but exposed the scale of crime. At the first sessions, fifty civil and twenty criminal cases were heard, including those of a man who had sodomized a boy and another who had buggered a pig. Both were hanged. Later a dead drunk from Somerset was branded a suicide by a coroner's jury and impaled at a crossroads, as was the practice in England. In October 1620, Hughes went to England to persuade the Somers Isles Company that Bermuda was verging on moral and physical collapse. Instead of receiving a sympathetic hearing, he was accused of being a Puritan enemy of the Church of England, a rebel who was alleged to have said "the Booke of Common Praier is but an olde Wifes tale."[22]

Lewis Hughes returned to Bermuda and never stopped believing that Christ's English vineyard had been transplanted there. By 1621, however, he was desperately homesick. In the autumn, Nathaniel Butler, his closest friend, left, and Hughes became one of four councillors, the House of Assembly's executive. More grief lay ahead. In August 1622 Hughes petitioned the crown to appoint a council of gentlemen to silence the "multiplicitie of voyces" in government. Prices and mortality were high; orphaned children became slaves to their dead parents' masters. In the first half of 1623, the merchant John Ferrar received letters from desperate colonists. A surgeon had been reduced to the status of a mere husbandman, an ironic reversal given faith in the New World, and begged Ferrar to send flour, oil, cheese, a frying pan, bedding, needles, and paper. Ferrar's agents were unable to collect his rents because

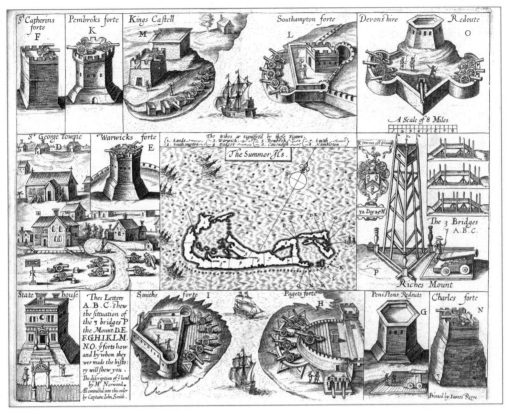

In less than twenty years, Bermuda had grown from an uninhabited "isle of devils" to a heavily defended, populous, yet turbulent colony. This engraving shows the statehouse (bottom left), home to the House of Assembly, inspired by Virginia's House of Burgesses.

people were so poor. Next came fresh infestations of worms, caterpillars, and land crabs. When the *Seaflower* arrived with supplies, men rowed out "to be mery" and, smoking in the gun-room, blew the ship up. Almost everything was lost, including sacks of precious letters.[23]

By this time, Hughes had been ejected by the company and had gone back to England forever. A stop on his salary had forced him to live "more like a slave then a Minister of Gods word"; the final straw had been a letter from his wife describing her "miserable, weake, and sicke" condition. He spent the next two years nursing her and petitioning for back-pay, struggling to cover his rent until they were evicted. Katherine Hughes died shortly afterward. In her forbearance, she, too, had been an adventurer for America and had sacrificed her life for her husband's dream.[24]

Like Virginia, Bermuda demonstrated the difficulty of managing power unsecured in footings of law, custom, and land-owner-ship—the English model. There was dissent and disorganization; some blamed an anarchic excess of freedom. To an extent, this unplanned outcome was common to all fledging colonies. Yet distance from home made deliberate acts of independence possible, even as colonists peti-tioned the crown to protect their rights. The examples of Virginia and Bermuda also showed how new challenges could lead people to forge unexpected alliances and oppositions. Tension arose not just between Englishmen and the wilderness, but also between different types of Englishmen. Antagonisms that inspired emigration, far from vanishing in America, persisted and intensified as expectations of reform and re-newal rose. The tale of Thomas Morton and his battle with New Plym-outh is a case in point.

Thirty miles north of Plymouth, a hilly spit protrudes into a wide bay, arable land known to the Indians as "Passongessit." In 1624, crown-sponsored adventurers, including Morton, arrived to obtain furs, naming the site after their leader, Richard Wollaston. The col-onists split in 1626, with Wollaston's men going to Virginia, leaving Morton to found a peculiar libertarian community. This he renamed "Ma-re Mount," punning on its coastal location and jovial atmosphere. Morton was a traditionalist: a gentleman lawyer from Staffordshire who loathed tyranny and believed in the reciprocity between crown and people implicit in the ancient constitution. An anti-Puritan, he also valued the rural festivities and Anglican ceremonies that had survived the Reformation and offended radicals. He had married a Berkshire widow in 1621, entangling himself in a lawsuit with her Puritan son, who denounced Morton in the Court of Star Chamber as "a very tur-bulent and trob) esome person to the Comon weale."[25]

Morton's arcadian experiment reacted against change in the Old World. It is hard to say what enraged the Plymouth elite more: his suc-cess in the fur trade; the selling of guns to Indians; settlers' indifference to hierarchy (they were all free "consociates"); their easy manners and tipsy conviviality; or their shameless idolatry. Quizzed by separatists about Morton, they said he read the Book of Common Prayer and the Bible, to which the separatists replied: "The booke of common prayer . . . what poore thing is that for a man to reade?" It was easy to mock 3,000 miles from the ecclesiastical courts, just as Lewis Hughes had found when he spurned the Prayer Book with impunity. Even bet-ter, ideas that were scandalous at home could be put into action so far away. In 1618, James I had rebuked Puritans by permitting sports and other recreations on Sundays. To Morton such pastimes symbolized liberty. So in May 1628 he erected an eighty-foot maypole at his settlement and organized some "harmles mirth" with singing, dancing, and drinking. Indians came to watch the revels, followed by godly troops who chopped the maypole down. "They termed it an Idoll, yea they called it the Calfe of Horeb," wrote Morton, "and stood at defiance with the place, naming it Mount Dagon, threatening to make it a woefull mount and not a merry mount." Here, then, was a vision of an iconoclastic England to come. To Plymouth's governor, William Bradford, it was "as if they had anew revived & celebrated the feasts of ye Roman Goddes Flora, or ye beastly practieses of ye madd Baccinalians."[26]

The Plymouth of 1628, by contrast, evoked a more respectable classical tradition: the republican city-state. A Dutch visitor described it thus:

> The little town stood on rising ground, separated from the sea by some twenty yards of sand. The buildings were laid out like a Roman city in miniature. Two streets crossing one another formed the town. At this meeting stood the Governor's House. Before it was an open space, the forum as one may call it, guarded by four cannon. . . . On an eminence behind the town, but within its precinct, stood the building which at once testified to the civil and religious unity of the little commonwealth, and to the constant presence of an armed foe: the public storehouse, place of worship and fort in one.

Houses were solidly built from timber on enclosed plots: the basic components of community. The colony was surrounded by a palisade, or "tun," as in ancient Teutonic settlements.[27]

This was a far cry from the rough camp of eight years earlier, lashed by gales, with not enough food and too many arriving empty-handed. Settlers had not even had fishing nets, and had relied on the Indians, straining relationships. When it was suspected, perhaps unfairly, that the go-between Squanto served no one except himself, the Wampanoag chief, Massasoit, had sent William Bradford a knife to cut off his hands and head, an invitation declined because "it was not the manner of the English." The go-between was also accused of spreading a story that the English practiced bacteriological warfare.[28]

England, too, had bred rumors. The Council for New England, the Plymouth Company's successor, decried "injurious aspersions," citing the thriving settlements that colonists refused to leave even when they

were summoned home. The settlers had no desire to deceive, insisted
the council; New England was simply an ideal destination—the golden
mean between icy Maine and sweltering Virginia. Deception, however,
was the basis of promotion, and even colonists writing home, according
to Plymouth colonist Edward Winslow, were "too prodigall in their
writing and reporting of that plenty we enjoyed." In fact, they had next
to nothing, which was obvious to newcomers, who quickly became
discouraged. Not everyone agreed with Winslow that it was better for
a man to be poor where food was free than to wander the streets of
London and be excluded from the wealth around him, "his sorrow increased by the sight of that he wanteth and cannot enjoy."[29]

When in 1623 drought threatened the harvest, the colonists prayed
for a supply ship that never arrived. A wreck was sighted and "at once
God seemed to deprive us of all future hopes," wrote Winslow. A public fast was held under a clear morning sky, and by late afternoon it
was overcast. It rained for a fortnight. "It was hard to say," Winslow
commented, "whether our withered Corne or drouping affections were
most quickned or revived."[30]

By 1624, Plymouth had 180 inhabitants, thirty-two houses, a grain
store, and plenty of cattle, pigs, and poultry. Investors gave up, but
most of the colonists—saints and strangers—stayed to repay what they
could. Eschewing dreams of enrichment, the Pilgrims carved out a
simple life more faithful to Christ than was possible in the Old World,
yet inspired by English parishes and corporations, governing themselves civilly like an Athenian *polis*. In the end, Plymouth found a way
to make money: the beaver trade, which proved, as John Smith put it,
that good men could make a commonwealth as lucrative as any Spanish
mine. Profits spoke louder than publicity. "This prosperous successe of
theirs being knowne here in England," a later treatise observed, "perswaded in many such a good oppinion of the Country that they resolved to adventure themselves and estates into those parts."[31]

"The leader of a People in a Wilderness," a Puritan historian wrote,
"had need be a Moses." That leader was William Bradford. Plymouth's
governor for over twenty years, on and off, between 1621 and 1657, Bradford lacked neither conviction nor a sense of destiny. He imagined the
saints' children proudly saying: "Our faithers were Englishmen which
came over this great ocean, and were ready to perish in this willdernes."
He drew strength from the spiritual integrity of his new Israelites,
although they were never more than a committed core. Plymouth had

its divisions, yet it survived when everyone might have starved. For all their trials, wrote another Pilgrim, "wee have enjoyed such plentie as though the windowes of heaven had beene opened unto us." Their other great providence was Indian complaisance, "whereas if God had let them loose they might easily have swallowed us up."[32]

The Virginia uprising put Plymouth on its guard and helped to justify the ruthless impositions of the militia captain, Miles Standish. When Indians sent a threatening message of arrows wrapped in snakeskin, he returned the skin filled with gunpowder. When beads were stolen on an expedition in January 1623, he forced an apology from native delegates, who, according to Edward Winslow, knelt like the English, "but in so rude and savage a manner as our men could scarce forbeare to break out in open laughter." That spring word came from a new settlement at Wessagusset, twenty-five miles north, that an attack was imminent, confirming a warning from Massasoit. A chief warrior of the Neponset, Wituwamat, had insulted Standish and mocked Europeans because "they died crying, making sowre faces more like children than men." Standish led a bogus trading mission to Wessagusset and returned with Wituwamat's severed head wrapped in linen. He was hailed as a hero, but infectious violence made some Englishmen queasy and worried the Indians. Their name for the English, meaning "coat-wearers," now became *Wotawquenange*: "cutthroats." Newcomers were taught to fear the natives, who now were blamed for every misfortune.[33]

This contempt, said Thomas Morton, became "an article of the new creede of Canaan," though not one he shared. He loved America *and* Native Americans. Arriving in June 1622, his senses had been flooded, his English sensibilities retuned. The babbling streams had lulled him, and the hummingbirds enchanted him; he gorged on lobster, and he fed his dogs goose as good as any he had ever eaten. Invalids from Virginia recovered just by breathing "the sweet aire of the shore," he said, and Ma-re Mount's springwater cured melancholy, like some medieval holy well. Morton scoffed at men who claimed that no country could be better than England: "If this Land be not rich then is the whole world poore." The humanity of the Indians, whom he got to know quite well, was superior to that of the Pilgrims, he believed—because of a natural morality indivisible from the beauty of the land. They were friendly and generous, intelligent and creative.[34]

Plymouth's ironies were legion. According to William Bradford, when the Pilgrims landed in 1620 they recoiled at the sight of "a hidious &

desolate wildernes, full of wild beasts & willd men." But Miles Standish's
deeds made it less clear who the wild men were, and where desolation
lay. Indians were baffled by the inconsistencies of the English: their rage
and affection, awe and contempt. Sharing a meal deep in Indian territory, a sachem asked Edward Winslow where he found the courage for
his adventures. "Where was true love," came the reply, "there was no
feare"; his heart "was so upright towards them that for mine owne part
I was feareles to come amongst them." Winslow's bond with Massasoit
was this love's most remarkable manifestation. Hearing that Massasoit
lay sick, possibly from typhus, Winslow hurried to Pokanoket, where
he scraped the chief's furred tongue, fed him fruit conserve, and made
pottage from strawberry leaves and sassafras to relieve his constipation.
Word spread that the English dispensed life as well as death.[35]

Perspectives shifted. Pilgrims feared men who, as Winslow said,
seemed to be made in the image of the devil rather than in the image
of God. He did not mean Indians, but the dissolute English servants.
To the polarized mentality of William Bradford, any opponent in the
wilderness was an agent of Antichrist to be destroyed. England, meanwhile, formed an impression of New England as both sink and nursery
for religious deviants: separatists, Puritans, papists, Anabaptists, and
others besides. John Smith demurred, pointing to the Pilgrims' courage
despite their "humorous ignorances" and foolish determination "to bee
severall Lords and Kings of themselves." The colony was also plagued
by division, which, as a London adventurer told Bradford in 1629, discouraged emigration, because men felt they would never get anything
done. Plymouth's most vociferous critic was Thomas Morton, who was
banished to an island (where bemused Indians fed him), then deported
in chains. As his ship passed Ma-re Mount, renamed Mount Dagon,
Morton watched it being burned to the ground, an outrage committed,
he said, so that "the habitation of the wicked should no more appeare
in Israell." In the end, "nothing did remaine, but the bare ashes as an
embleme of their cruelty."[36]

Plymouth's story in the 1620s describes an ambition that exceeded
legitimacy and compromised royal interests. But the Pilgrims were not
alone in their lese-majesty. The Prayer Book was cast aside in Bermuda,
and Virginians pleased themselves. In 1626 Parliament had to remind
the Council for New England, New Plymouth's governing body, that it
had no exclusive right to fish New England's coasts, after old Plymouth

protested. Adventuring for America, and especially being there, nurtured a sense that authority was conditional and contestable.[37]

It was a subtle shift in attitude, partly because such thoughts existed in England, too, but mostly because migrants still felt English and connected to home. Charters and patents were not flagrantly breached, and desire for limited autonomy was expressed in loyal rhetoric. William Bradford, like his nemesis Thomas Morton, was a reactionary, seeking to resurrect older, purer, even mythical versions of England that had been erased by seventeenth-century modernity. Colonists also saw English law and administration not as strictures but structures, a means to order life. And they missed them. In July 1625, David Thomson, an adventurer in New England, told his employer Thomas Howard, earl of Arundel: "Wee are lyke a bodie without a head, none to rule us, none to minister justice, infinit grievances amongst us, none to redresse, especiallie amongst the Brownists of Newplym[ou]th." Asking that the king be informed, Thomson recalled the earl's own observation that a weapon in the hands of a child or a fool was a menace. "What can be expected," reasoned Thomson, "that a rude ignorant mechanicke can doe w[i]th a sharpe sword of justice?"[38]

Camden, the antiquarian adventurer, had been proved right about private colonial enterprise—but the challenges were more than financial. Colonization was a political problem, a problem of disputed power: settlers in competition with natives, settlers with each other, and increasingly the crown with its displaced subjects. English America and the English *idea* of America were spreading and dividing, evolving into manifold forms. Promised Land, breadbasket, warehouse, elbow room, or imperial prize? The next few years would prove that the New World could be all these things; and yet the pattern refused to settle peacefully, not least because England had its own conflicts to deal with—conflicts inevitably carried across the Atlantic.

CHAPTER 6

Projects of No Fantasy

AVID THOMSON IS New Hampshire's founding father, or so it is
said. A Scot by birth, he was the Council for New England's
clerk in old Plymouth, and helped Sir Ferdinando Gorges and John
Mason, a Norfolk sea captain, establish territorial claims in northern
New England. For some years Englishmen had been catching cod from
rough coastal outposts there, but after 1620 the focus shifted to permanent settlement.

In 1623 Thomson had led fishermen and farmers to Pannaway at the
mouth of the Piscataqua River, south of Maine. It was easily defended,
with a salt marsh for grazing cattle. Ten miles offshore lay the Isles
of Shoals, barren in themselves—this is where Thomas Morton was
exiled from Ma-re Mount—yet surrounded by prime fishing waters.
Thomson's men built a palisade, a "great house" from stone, and other
buildings, but the enterprise was slow to prosper. Thomson moved his
family south to an island not far from Ma-re Mount in 1626, by which
time John Mason had installed William Hilton—the New Plymouth
man who had said "we are all free-holders, the rent day doth not trouble us"—farther up the Piscataqua River. This was a new kind of fishing
station, a plantation populated by families who built decent homes,
worshipped together, grew corn, and traded with Indians. As in Plymouth, communal sustainability ensured success. The colony became
known as Hilton's Point, leading some to believe that Hilton, rather
than Thomson, was New Hampshire's founder.[1]

The New Hampshire lives of Thomson and Hilton illustrate three
essential characteristics of English colonization. First, *determination*:
some migrants went home, especially when their colonies failed, but
others either pressed on or, like Thomson, moved somewhere more

habitable. The place he left, Pannaway, did not fail: it just took time to establish. Second, *dynamism*: the impulse behind these ventures was not rebellious escape, but lucrative interaction with the Old World. Colonists at Hilton Point sent beaver pelts to John Mason in England, and he sent men and fishing equipment. The key to William Hilton's story is not just his start in the English fishing industry but also his relationship with his brother, a London fishmonger. The Atlantic was a highway, not a hedge or a ditch. Even introspective New Plymouth did not turn its back on England: survival depended on trade. Finally, *diversity*: the proud legacies of Jamestown and Plymouth obscure an array of simultaneous American schemes undertaken by competing consortia with no single unifying vision. Attitudes toward America, the projects pursued there, and so its practical meanings as a place of adventure were multiplying and shifting. Colonies became contested sites of commercial opportunity, imperial expansion, religious freedom, and social reconstruction.[2]

By the late 1620s, the last of these traits was most apparent in Massachusetts, where English Puritans aimed to set an example to England by salvaging authority, obedience, charity, and truth from its past. The English in America were changing, inured to harsh conditions, and hyperconscious of being English in places so unlike home. But the English in England were also undergoing painful transformations of land and law, work and custom, faith and allegiance. Resistance was one response; another was nostalgia, a missionary quest for lost values that would inspire the godly migrations of the 1630s. Something of this dreamy idealism can be seen in earlier ventures—ventures a thousand miles north on the rugged island of Newfoundland.

Newfoundland's early history is suffused with determination and dynamism and hope for England's salvation. In 1610 the Society of Merchant Adventurers was chartered to colonize this island. The location had been used by generations of fishermen, but now the Merchant Adventurers would have a legally sanctioned monopoly on its resources. As in Virginia and New England, this was ownership by any other name. Sir Humphrey Gilbert had claimed Newfoundland for the crown in 1583, but his death halted plans to develop it. John Guy, a Bristol merchant, arrived at Cuper's Cove in August 1610 with

A party commanded by John Guy trades with Beothuk Indians in Trinity Bay, Newfoundland, in October 1612. The wolfskin flag with which Guy was welcomed lies on the shore, the attention of its bearers now firmly fixed on the knife he is offering.

forty men and various livestock. Over the winter they built dwellings, a storehouse, a workhouse, and a forge. Two years later, Guy established trading relations with the Beothuk Indians, who welcomed him with a fire and a white wolfskin flag. By 1613 the land had been cleared, fishing vessels completed, and America's first sawmill built. A child was born that year in March, taking the population to sixty-two, but life was demanding. Scurvy killed several people every year.[3]

There were other woes. Disputes over fishing rights flared up, because the customary rights of migratory workers were being compromised by settled communities. Then there was peril on the ocean. Merchants complained to the king about the pirates who preyed on supply ships and prevented exports from reaching their destinations. The risks of investing in Newfoundland were daunting: a single voyage might cost over £650, excluding the value of ship, the cargo, or men's lives. John Mason was commissioned to fight pirates swarming from the African coast, but the problem was too vast. Barbary privateers, or "corsairs," had cost adventurers to Newfoundland over £40,000 by 1621 and had captured over a thousand men. In that same year, Mason, who as governor of Cuper's Cove had published an effusive promotional tract for the colony, abandoned it to concentrate on New Hampshire. As with Virginia, London merchants became impatient with Newfoundland, and gentry backers failed to raise enough money to keep the company afloat. The territories and concerns of the company then became atomized in the hands of smaller, private investors.[4]

Colonization branched out, with some adventurers moving on as others arrived at the places they vacated. John Mason tired of Newfoundland, but at about the same time, in July 1621, Captain Edward Wynne landed on the same peninsula. He judged it "the beautifullest Coast and the pleasantest Sea Cant [shore] that ever mine eyes beheld . . . a very Champion Country without any Hill . . . like a pleasant Medow." He built a colony on behalf of Sir George Calvert, a grandee with Catholic sympathies who dreamed of creating a haven for those attached to the old religion. Like many Englishmen, Protestant and Catholic alike, he was troubled by change and desired a return to traditional ideals of property, piety, orderliness, and reciprocal social relations. At Christmas, Wynne's men finished their first building, a thatched house forty-four feet by fifteen, with a stone hearth in the hall. Earth from the cellar formed a rampart facing the sea. This rampart was topped with timber defenses once logging got under way in the new year. They made salt; grew wheat, barley, oats, and vegetables; and planted vines from Plymouth. Wynne reported this progress to Calvert in August 1622, praising the soil, the air, and "nights both silent and comfortable, producing nothing that can be said either horrid or hideous." The following spring, Calvert was granted a patent for what he called the province of Avalon, "in imitation of Old Avalon in Somersetshire wherein Glassenbury stands, the first fruits of Christianity in Britain." There was nothing explicitly Catholic about the plantation, but, in a striking departure from the charter granted to John Guy, in this arrangement settlers were not required to take the oath of supremacy—affirmation of the crown as the head of the Church of England.[5]

Wynne's aims were to serve Calvert, to advance God's glory, and to promote "the good of my poore distressed Countreimen." The early 1620s saw great hardship in England. Henstridge in Somerset was typical: it was depressed in trade and overcrowded, and the customs of the poor—their traditional economic rights—were abused. Fifty years earlier there had been enough farms and enough homes for the tenant-farming system to work, but the lord of the manor had felled Henstridge's forests and curtailed the use of common land for grazing and collecting wood. Sixty farms had been combined into ten estates by 1624; meanwhile, the population had increased prodigiously. In that year, Henstridge's vicar, Richard Eburne, wrote: "Truly, it is a Thing almost incredible to relate, and intolerable to behold, what a number in every towne and citie, yea in every parish and village, doe abound, which, for want of commodious and ordinary places to dwell in, doe build up Cotages by the high way side, and thrust their heads into every corner, to the grievous overcharging of the places of their abode for the present, and to the very ruine of the whole Land." Idle men committed crimes, sponged off neighbors, and tippled in alehouses, wasting their lives, whereas abroad they "might both richly increase their owne estates and notably ease and disburden ours." Anyone doubting the legitimacy of colonies was reminded that bees swarm, that Britons were savage until the Romans, Saxons, and Normans came, and that every civilization starts from nothing. "Rome it selfe," said Eburne, "was not built in one day."⁶

The Pilgrim Robert Cushman agreed: "There is such pressing and oppressing in towne and countrie . . . so as a man can hardly any where set up a trade but he shall pull downe two of his neighbours." Michael Sparke, a Puritan bookseller, likened the poor to wasps eating the commonwealth's fruit (when they should be honeybees), or slaves in Satan's galley (when they should row "the good Government of England"). Metaphors abounded. England's diseased foot was poisoning her heart; selfish men were likened to a cold hand refusing to leave a pocket and thereby stealing the body's warmth. Landlords consolidated estates, ejecting husbandmen only to rehire them more cheaply. Another Puritan warned that self-interest endangered "the valiant race of the ancient English Yeomandrie, which was one of the chiefe glories of our Nation & the principall Base and foundation of the Commonwealth." Sparke went further: unless Father England seeded the womb of the Atlantic with his poor, sin would doom the land.⁷

Richard Eburne was most inspired by Newfoundland. He had read a book about the island by Richard Whitbourne, a sea captain and veteran of the 1588 battle against the Spanish Armada. Whitbourne thought Newfoundland the ideal destination: it was almost the size of Ireland and was closer to England than any other American colony. Despite overpopulation, said Whitbourne, England lacked the courage of the Dutch, who, helped by English inertia, were forging ahead in the Antilles and the Guianas, as well as farther north in New York Bay and along the Hudson River. Emigration, he said, was "a Project of no fantasie in me, but a truth grounded upon a well-weighted experience"—although this experience did include a story about an encounter with a mermaid. His book was presented to James I in October 1619, whereafter the Privy Council urged bishops to send copies to every parish. They would be paid for by voluntary contributions. Expanded editions appeared in the 1620s—complete with Edward Wynne's enthusiastic letters—and influenced policy. In 1623 the Council for New England sought royal approval for transporting paupers, organized at the county level by lords lieutenant, and proposed that an Elizabethan statute binding poor children to apprenticeships be extended to the colonies. The king was asked to found a plantation where 3,000 people a year might receive a house and twenty acres. The scheme would be rolled out across England if trials in London were successful.[8]

Domestic reform was conceived within an expansive framework, an indication of how colonization was starting to change the way England viewed itself. In 1624, just as James I took charge of Virginia, Richard Eburne published *A Plaine Path-Way to Plantations*, promoting Newfoundland as the prime American destination for the nation. He imagined a transatlantic federation of territories inhabited by extroverted public citizens, rather than introverted fortune-seekers. Women, too fretful about their children to emigrate, were urged to try and understand that colonization was in everyone's interests: individuals, households, parishes, and the state. Eburne would make this case throughout the 1620s, speaking up for the poor, persuading Parliament and local gentry, and planning to go to Newfoundland himself (though he never did). The positive reception given to Whitbourne's book suggests that his idea appealed to men in power, many of whom favored increased responsibility on the part of the crown for the colonization of America. Jamestown, Bermuda, and Plymouth had taught them that private colonies advanced slowly, and that once they were established, they desired to govern themselves. By then their desires clashed with royal interest. Although joint-stock companies made colonial projects viable by spreading risk, sharing profits, and sparking competition, some believed that private ambition—or "privacie"—was inimical to the good of the commonwealth.[9]

A longside the idea of America as a panacea for ailing parishes, then, another was developing in the corridors of power: America as empire. In the year that Richard Eburne's book appeared, 1624, a courtier named Sir William Alexander dedicated a treatise, *An Encouragement to Colonies*, to James I's son, Charles, Prince of Wales. His plea was this: "You that are borne to rule Nations may bee the beginner of Nations, enlarging this Monarchie without bloud, and making a Conquest without wronging of others." Too many Britons saw colonization as "a strange thing, as not onely being above the courage of common men, but altogether alienated from their knowledge." To be strong, Alexander argued, a state had to resist rivals.[10]

Supreme among England's rivals was Spain. James I had long steered a middle way, especially since 1618, when the outbreak of the Thirty Years' War had pitted Europe's Protestant states against the Catholic Holy Roman Empire and its allies. The king's main problem was that his son-in-law, Frederick V, had led the Protestant Union, a military alliance, and so had been at the eye of the storm. For political balance, James sought to marry Prince Charles to a Spanish princess; the failure of this plan, called the "Spanish Match," released a wave of Hispanophobia and anti-Catholicism in the political nation. By March 1624 James had lost control of his foreign policy, and a year later he was dead. Charles's succession marked the start of a new phase of English imperialism in America—and political catastrophe at home. The civil war that began in 1642 would address fundamental questions about the locus and legitimacy of power, not just in Britain but also in England's American dominions.[11]

In the first year of Charles I's reign, a rumor circulated that the count of Gondomar, Spain's former ambassador, had seen the ghost of Sir Walter Ralegh. This harked back to 1616, when an English expedition to Venezuela had attacked a Spanish settlement, causing Gondomar to persuade James I to execute its commander, Ralegh. Now, it seemed, he was back from the dead. In 1626, the count was as shocked by England's aggression as he had been a decade earlier; Englishmen, for their part, called Spain the warmonger and warned her not to cross Charles, God's anointed sovereign. It was time, some said, to emulate Ralegh's martial qualities to win national glory. A tract dedicated to the duke of Buckingham, the royal favorite, referred to the "secret warre" between England, Spain, and Holland. The key to victory, it proposed, was not just ruling the waves but sending paupers to plantations: as the northern fishing industry contracted, for example, workers should go to Newfoundland. Mass emigration—10,000 people a year—would not only solve England's begging problem, but also create export markets and customs revenue. A venture to unlock America's potential could be funded by taxing alehouses. Samuel Purchas's five-volume study of global navigation, published in 1625–1626 and also dedicated to Buckingham, confidently cast England in an imperial role, sharpening ambition and girding a sense of entitlement.[12]

The logic was persuasive, but, like Virginia, the northern territories were already flawed. John Smith had seen them as a "barren rocky desart" from which to catch cod, and with royal approval he anglicized the "barbarous" names used by Indians and fishermen. The title "New England" marked a conceptual shift, annexing America to England in a unified dominion. However, the usual suspicions dogged colonial enterprise, pushing projects back into the realms of fantasy. In 1623, James I had encouraged the city of Exeter to invest using the Council for New England's proposals. The arguments were conventional: plantations enlarge the nation, advance religion, stimulate navigation, and supply commodities. The benefits to the depressed western counties would be huge, provided enough shares were sold. But the citizens of Exeter surmised that the best patents for coastal territory had already been snatched up; nor would they pay a proprietor rent or the crown duty. Nothing but unambiguous ownership appealed. The abiding pitfall of colonization was exposed again: reliance on private investors and companies who put themselves first and eschewed restraint, even by the king whose blessing they needed, was always problematical.[13]

Failure was an even greater deterrent. In September 1623, Robert Gorges, son of Sir Ferdinando, arrived at Wessagusset, north of Plymouth, to replace a colony that had collapsed the previous year. According to his adviser, Christopher Levett, the original settlers "went about to build Castles in the Aire" instead of fishing. The settlement was renamed Weymouth, and the new inhabitants put to work; but in the spring of 1624, beset by financial woes, Gorges admitted defeat. Some settlers returned to England; others went to Plymouth, among them William Morrell, who wrote a poem, "Nova Anglia," appealing for state sponsorship to raise "an English Kingdome from this Indian dust." Meanwhile, under Buckingham's patronage, Levett received a patent for a colony in Maine to be called "York," and the king ordered public collections for the scheme. Levett made a good start and met Indians. Their paw-waws were witches, he said, who "foretell of ill wether, and many strange things." But relations were warm and conversation lively. The Indians were puzzled about why the king had only one wife—who did his work?—and why Levett didn't beat *his* wife to make her live in America. For all Levett's advantages, the colony stagnated. Collections were paltry, and the men he left in Maine disappeared.[14]

It was a similar story in South America, where an Amazonian colony failed, diverting Sir Thomas Warner to the Caribbean Leeward Islands. He arrived on St. Kitts in January 1624 with a contingent from Suffolk. The island proved excellent for tobacco, but in September a mature crop was flattened by a hurricane. Planters blamed the hurricane on native witchcraft. No experience was wasted, though. Caribbean lessons were applied in Virginia, which remained a vexing presence in English life.[15]

Nostalgic re-creations of old England never quite worked, instead producing unpleasant ironies. Virginia seemed less like a refuge from Albion's economic crises than a stage for their reenactment. The colony grew, but with growth came complexity, competition, and social strain—all Old World exports. The English had long decried Indian witchcraft, but the first proceedings against a witch in Virginia involved an English woman. Goodwife Wright of Kecoughtan (the old name for Elizabeth City) was a midwife who foretold deaths, and, some said, caused them. In 1626, Governor Sir George Yeardley heard damning testimony that revealed Wright to be someone her neighbors both feared and relied upon in a hazardous environment.[16]

Apart from language and antipathy to Indians, settlers in Virginia rarely had much in common. Their geographical origins, recorded in court records, were diverse: a sample from February 1628 includes Durham, Worcester, Essex, Staffordshire, Cambridgeshire, and Southwark. Goodwife Wright was from Yorkshire. Furthermore, the typical first-generation farmer was an indigent tobacco planter, hungry for land. Colonists lured to America by its size, it was said, "were quickly entangled with the other extermitie, grudging to be bounded within their prospect, and jarring with their neighbours for small parcels of ground." This sounded like England, and it bred the same conflicts that caused witchcraft accusations there.[17]

Kecoughtan was famous for peaches (not witches), but elsewhere even staple food crops were neglected in favor of tobacco. Charles I inherited his father's hostility to tobacco and imposed punishing levies. Even before this, planters had protested and said they were unable to pay, in 1624 citing "the general Calmity of Famine & Scarcity, sickness, Mortality & bloody Massacre" as well as "continued Assaults & Surprizes of the incensed Enemy." The following year, Nicholas Ferrar, now an absentee Virginia landowner, heard a complaint from two servants at Martin's Hundred. They said that tobacco taxes had left them too poor to buy shoes or clothes. "We will not in dure this kind of living any longer," they declared, threatening to petition the Privy Council. Virginia still desperately needed people, and adventurers like Ferrar believed that potential migrants were deterred by stories of hardship. Virginians, some said, should enjoy the same trade terms as Englishmen anywhere else. One investor likened a crown proposal to give the colony £5,000 per annum to drawing forty ounces of blood from a weak child, then reviving him with five ounces of the same. In 1627, the king criticized Virginia commodities for their range and quantity, to which the Virginia Council replied that diversification was impossible without human resources, which had been deficient since the Indian uprising five years earlier. One family that arrived in England in 1628 became stranded between two worlds, unable to pay customs on a tobacco crop, and thus unable to sell it and return to Virginia. The crown restricted tobacco production in 1631 as harmful to the colonial economy and English manners, and further raised the import duty.[18]

Virginia had made modest advances. By 1630, the population had risen to 4,000, and it enjoyed English corn and bread—the specter of starvation had departed. Servants drank "Milke Homini"—pounded maize boiled in milk—but the "better sort" had sack, aqua vitae, and "good English beere." Masters and servants alike consumed more meat and fish than their counterparts in England; no one ate squirrels anymore. Deforestation had dried up swampland, and mortality had declined. Poverty was a fact of life (more so than in New England) and poor relief adequately organized. People enjoyed kinship and neighborliness. Defamation suits were resolved with apologies, on old church-court lines. As in England, there were more substantial houses, some brick, many timber box-framed; most men had a gun, a sword, and a mailcoat. Colonists had labored to make Jamestown commercially viable like an English manufacturing port. Cattle ruminated in lush pastures while their owners tended tobacco plantations. There was day-to-day stability, and the assembly and law courts met regularly. At Littleton, near Jamestown, George and Mary Menefie tended an orchard of apple, cherry, peach, and pear trees, as well as a garden graced with "the fruits of Holland and the roses of Provence." Virginia had become more like England; but what of its people?[19]

The 1622 massacre had toughened some and weakened others: the latter, if they could, went home, the former evolved into truculent adventurers, adapted to the environment, resentful of interference, and remote from compatriots in outlook. Yet their identity was ambiguous. A soldier named Thomas Hall was questioned at Jamestown in 1629: Was he a man or a woman? He was thought to be male, despite deformed genitals, and had been christened Thomasine at Newcastle-upon-Tyne. He dressed as a girl until puberty, then started wearing men's clothes. After fighting abroad, he became a woman again before sailing to Virginia in male attire. The court ruled that Hall was both genders and ordered him to dress as a man except for a bonnet and apron. The case illustrates the desire of insecure colonial rulers to regulate conduct, and the possibilities for personal reinvention overseas. But his case is also a metaphor for the cultural hybridization that had been caused by emigration. Thomas Hall lived between states for physical and psychological reasons; but he was also a restless, deracinated Englishman—like many, unsure who he was. America was starting to seem less like a new world than England's parallel universe, where familiarity of people and place only made the differences more startling and disturbing. Nowhere would this be truer than in Massachusetts.[20]

Virginia's first two decades suggested that English America's future belonged to small entrepreneurs such as traders, retailers, mariners, yeomen, and lesser gentry—people who were prepared to take risks (perhaps for want of choice), who would wait patiently for results, and above all, who were willing to emigrate to oversee their plantations firsthand. John Endecott was typical of this sort, a man of modest West Country origins yet "a fit instrument to begin this Wildernesse-worke," wrote the Puritan historian Edward Johnson: "of courage bold, undaunted, yet sociable and of a chearful spirit, loving and austere." In 1628 he joined a consortium of adventurers, the New England Company, and was chosen to lead fifty settlers to Massachusetts Bay to assume control of an ailing trading post at the mouth of the Naumkeag River. The Massachusetts Bay inhabitants had migrated from Cape Ann, where prosperity had also eluded them. Upon his arrival, Endecott began reorganizing Naumkeag, renamed Salem, anglicized Hebrew for "peace." In February 1629, the New England Company's governor in London, a tobacco merchant, reminded Endecott that his task was to evangelize Indians (though not to trust them—he must not forget the Virginia massacre), but that he also must find sources of timber, sturgeon, and medicines. The company issued its orders in April: uphold religion, inflict punishment, restrain youth, and defend households, "so disorders may be prevented and ill weeds nipped before they take too great a head." Recidivists should be sent home.[21]

This was the year Charles I dispensed with Parliament, which had not provided the means for him to wage war, first with Spain, then with France. So began his Personal Rule, an era of forced loans, unpopular taxes, arbitrary imprisonment, and persecution of dissenters. A combination of religious and political effrontery along with economic opportunism accelerated the colonizing schemes of Puritan noblemen such as the earl of Warwick, Sir Nathaniel Rich, and Lord Saye and Sele, who were keen to develop offshore posts of political opposition, such as Bermuda. Warwick had become governor of the Somers Isles Company for this reason in 1628. In English parishes, interest in emigration was stimulated when the bishop of London, William Laud, began cracking down on Calvinism, enforcing the Book of Common Prayer, and promoting a high-church Anglicanism that was condemned by Puritans as crypto-Catholic.[22]

Many East Anglian Puritans—or "the godly," as they called themselves—decided to emigrate to Massachusetts. They were led by John Winthrop, a Suffolk gentleman of waning fortunes. Winthrop was gaunt, austere, and courageous. He was also a New England Company member. In March 1629, the king, ignorant of the scheme's Puritan complexion, granted a charter, and the Massachusetts Bay Company was born. At a secret meeting in Cambridge, investors agreed to move their administrative apparatus to America. They had learned the first lesson taught by Virginia: absentee government constrained local

John Winthrop (1578–1649), founder of Massachusetts Bay Colony and four times its governor. A Puritan landowner from Suffolk, he dreamed of recovering England's lost social and religious values in "a city upon a hill" built in America. He stood for liberty—freedom to obey God's laws.

authority. The charter did not forbid expatriation, but this hardly meant it was permitted. Winthrop, determined to succeed, emphasized the trust absent in failed enterprises: "This whole adventure growes upon the joynt confidence we have in each others fidelity and resolucion," he said. As with the Virginia Company, adventurers were granted land free from feudal dues and would enjoy other domestic rights, this land being *vacuum domicilium* (unoccupied). It was a legal concept that Winthrop believed would give him title against all men, and of which, among English adventurers, he was particularly fond. In return for their rights, settlers were not to make ordinances "repugnant to the Lawes and Statutes of England"; they were "to continue his Ma[jes]ties Subjects and to live under his allegeance."[23]

John Winthrop was made governor in October 1629, and work gathered momentum. Much had already been done, and in short time.

Orders were placed for everything from biscuits to bricks, garters to gunpowder, and millstones to mustard seed. Jasper Churchill of Fleet Street was commissioned to make a hundred swords; a vintner would supply twelve gallons of aqua vitae; and Bibles and copies of the Book of Common Prayer were bought. The company hired a surgeon at £25 a year, plus £40 for his instruments and medicines. Richard Clayton, a thirty-four-year-old carpenter, was contracted to come with his wife, daughter, brother, sister, and brother-in-law; he put up £40, the balance to be repaid with his family's labor. A plasterer joined on condition that some of his wages go to his mother. Francis Higginson of Leicester, "a reverend grave minister," also announced his intentions. He was told to hurry and was promised a £10 bonus because he had eight children. Word spread. In February 1630, Robert Parke, a fifty-year-old farmer, wrote to John Winthrop from Lincolnshire, hoping he was not too late and asking what to bring. Recruits were chosen carefully; Parke was accepted with his two sons. Winthrop knew from John Smith's writings that dissolute colonizers made a world of anarchy. This was Virginia's second lesson. Unlike the Chesapeake, Massachusetts would be filled with families able to pay their own way.[24]

Behind the excitement of the conscientious migrants lay unease. Was it lawful? Should a man desert his family and friends? Was he betraying his country? What was the will of heaven? Robert Cushman of New Plymouth had cautioned "that whereas [the] God of old did call and summon our Fathers by predictions, dreames, visions and certaine illuminations to goe from their countries, . . . now there is no such calling to be expected." The age of miracles had passed, and decisions must come from prayer—an activity at which, fortunately, Puritans excelled. John Winthrop's "Reasons to be Considered for . . . Intended Plantation in New England," written in 1629, listed the pros and cons: Europe was sundered by war, the English church was anti-Christian, and the nation poverty-stricken. Yet the feeling lingered that he was abandoning England in extremis.[25]

Neither did people make it easy for him. The Suffolk antiquary Robert Ryece wrote in August 1629 to say that "the church and common welthe heere at home hathe more neede of your beste abyllytie in these dangerous tymes then any remote plantation, which may be performed by persons of lesser woorthe and apprehension. . . . All your kynsfolkes and most understandinge friends wyll more rejoice at your stayenge at home then to throw your selfe upon vayne hopes with many difficulties and uncertaynties." Plantations, Ryece felt, were for the young and uncouth. "How harde wyll it bee for one browghte up amonge boockes and learned men to lyve in a barbarous place where is no learnynge and lesse cyvillytie." Winthrop also received a letter from a kinswoman bereft at hearing of his intentions. But Winthrop's correspondence with his wife, Margaret, while he made plans in London, demonstrates his anguish and her devotion. Writing by candlelight in October 1629, she rejoiced at news from New England, and hoped that God would "still continu his mercy to that plantation and blesse us in our intended purpose." She went to bed wishing she "could finde in my hart to sit and talke with thee all night."[26]

The news heard by Margaret Winthrop was of an advance party to Salem led by Francis Higginson. Five ships, carrying two hundred migrants, including Higginson's wife and children and some parishioners, had arrived on June 19, 1629. With John Endecott's hundred colonists, they had "combined together into one Body Politicke under the same Governor." Higginson was amazed by his first glimpse of Cape Ann. There were great schools of mackerel, yellow flowers on the sea, and acres of dense woodland, which "made us all desirous to see our new paradise of New-England." A boat fetched strawberries, gooseberries, and roses—God's welcome basket. In Salem itself Higginson was thrilled to find sweet air, good land, cheap milk, plentiful firewood (expensive in London), large vegetables, "fat and lussious" lobsters, and abundant fish "almost beyond beleeving." His melancholy lifted, and he went about hatless in light clothes; his child's scrofula cleared up. He wrote to friends in Leicester about this Eden, begging them to come. Bring everything imaginable, he advised, "for when you are at once parted with England you shall meet neither with taverns nor alehouse, nor butchers nor grocers, nor apothecaries shops to help what things you need in the midst of the great ocean, nor when you come to land here are yet neither markets nor fairs to buy what you want." For Higginson, this was no privation: an English existence had simply been pared down to its spiritual essentials.[27]

As in Eden, though, a serpent was waiting; Winthrop's screening of passengers was imperfect. Even before their arrival, one man boasted of making a woman pregnant and mocked Puritan piety; "five beastly Sodomitical boys" were also exposed. At Salem, Higginson was accepted as minister, but the form of worship was disputed. Puritans were surer about the errors of Anglicanism than they were about what they wanted instead. Higginson remade the congregation according to a written covenant, binding the godly and dividing them from those whose status as God's elect was unproven. So began the tradition of congregational communion that would have such profound social and political consequences. Like Bermuda and Plymouth, Salem shunned the orthodox Book of Common Prayer, prompting accusations of separatism. John Endecott sent demurring councillors home—and it was he, not Miles Standish of Plymouth, who cut down Thomas Morton's maypole.[28]

Immorality and dissent seemed to the godly like divine tests or punishments, as did Salem's winters. After a season of plenty, many were reduced to digging acorns from the snow while struggling to remain optimistic. Edward Johnson wrote this: "They made shift to rub out the Winters cold by the Fire-side, having fuell enough growing at their very doores, turning down many a drop of the Bottell and burning tobacco with all the ease they could, discoursing between one while and another of the great progresse they would make after the Summers-Sun had changed the Earths white furr'd Gowne into a greene Mantell." "Distracted thoughts" got the better of some, "the Ditch between England and their now place of abode was so wide." Sickness swept the land like an avenging angel, killing Endecott's wife and disabling Francis Higginson, who died some months later.[29]

By the spring of 1630, a small fleet was anchored at Southampton; aboard the flagship, the *Arbella*, were John Winthrop and two of his sons. Winthrop wrote to his wife on March 28 saying that they were happy and had slept well, wrapped in rugs. "I must once again take my last farewell of thee in Old England," he added. "Oh, how it refresheth my heart to think that I shall yet again see thy sweet face in the land of the living!" He reminded Margaret that every Monday and Friday at five o'clock they were to think of each other and so "meet in spirit till we meet in person." At the quayside, families and friends exchanged words of love until, as Edward Johnson described, speech was strangled by sobbing. They embraced, many for the last time, and so "let fall the salt-dropping dews of vehement affection." Trusting in God, well-wishers focused on one thought: "This is the doore thou hast opened upon our earnest request, and we hope it shall never be shut: for Englands sake they are going from England to pray without ceasing for England."[30]

It is easy to see Winthrop as a closet separatist, but harder to imagine the sincerity of his love for nation and church, which, he declared in a loyal pledge, were impossible to contemplate without tears. Winthrop believed that, like the Plymouth Pilgrims, his brethren were God's instruments; unlike the Pilgrims, they were tasked with creating an exemplary England in miniature—a scion from the stock, not a new tree. Essentially, Winthrop was Sir George Calvert's opposite, the Protestant antithesis of popery. But in America he was similar: a backward-looking fugitive not from England but the seventeenth century. In this respect, both were like those arch-enemies William Bradford and Thomas Morton. Winthrop wanted to recover the primitive English church, like Calvert in Avalon. As a Puritan, he was sustained by "typology": the belief that historical events foreshadowed the future, so that the past infinitely justified the present. His life did not merely parallel that of Moses, nor his followers' lives those of covenanted Israelites: instead, present and past were divinely fused. The godly distrusted imagination, preferring the "plain style" of reason. Yet Puritanism was a mystical, emotional sensibility, and, like Catholicism, susceptible to miracles and prognostications. As a preacher in Suffolk, John Wilson, Winthrop's companion on the *Arbella*, dreamed he was in America and "sawe a Churche arise out of the earthe, which grew up & became a merveylous goodly churche."[31]

John Cotton, a friend of Wilson's from Cambridge, had traveled from Lincolnshire to deliver a final sermon to the fleet at Southampton. His text came from the Book of Samuel: "Moreover, I will appoint a place for my people Israel, and will plant them that they may dwell in a place of their own and move no more." It was not just that England was a hive fit to swarm, explained Cotton, nor that men might lawfully flee judgment. Rather, an elect congregation was being drawn to America by "a secret inclination darted by God into our hearts." To this Winthrop added his own fortifying sermon, "A Modell of Christian Charity." To manifest the Holy Spirit, they must build "a place of Co-habitation and Consorteshipp under a due forme of Goverment both civill and ecclesiasticall," united by love, mercy, and justice, to inspire their beloved England. Success, preached Winthrop, would depend on their covenant with God and each other, so "that men shall say of succeeding plantacions: the lord make it like that of New England; for wee must Consider that wee shall be as a Citty upon a Hill, the eies of all people are upon us." If they broke this covenant, they would perish.[32]

CHAPTER 7

To Clearer Light and More Liberty

JOHN WINTHROP'S ELEVEN SHIPS carried seven hundred men, women, and children; two hundred cows; sixty horses; and numerous goats. The *Arbella* and three escorts left the Isle of Wight on April 8, 1630; the rest would follow in the weeks ahead. Like war, sea voyages were monotonous and occasionally petrifying. John Winthrop kept order on the flagship, and with an eye on posterity, wrote a journal. Children devised games as the exhilaration of adventure faded. Meals of fish, pease, and stale bread were the high point of each identical day. Passengers shut their eyes against the undulating panorama of sea and sky, and thought how far from home they were or how near America. They remembered things left behind and dreamed of what awaited. Puritans read and prayed, and seasoned sailors jeered, especially when the Atlantic swell rose and dread showed. One night, clouds covered the moon and stars, and winds began ripping at the sails. Torrential rain flooded the decks, and titanic waves battered the oak walls. Possessions were hurled around, as were people who lost their grip on the ship's sides. Everyone, wrote the historian Edward Johnson, was "amased to finde such opposition in nature." Unable to eat from terror, and "hindered from cooperating with the Soule in Spirituall duties," men, women, and children were reduced to "a helplesse Condition."[1]

Many a deal with heaven was struck in those dark hours. Families huddled against bulkheads in nests of flock mattresses, bolsters, and blankets. Some curtained off private spaces, where, cupping candle-stubs, they willed the storm's retreat, imagining each fetid breath their last. Timbers creaked, infants wailed, and livestock groaned in fear. Youths traveling alone found solace in friendships of convenience; aqua vitae calmed nausea and nerves. Winthrop recorded that a maidservant

Despite promoters' attempts to reassure people that ships were like rocking cradles, the Atlantic, with its storms and pirates, terrified them. This engraving by Wenceslaus Hollar conveys well the sense of helplessness at being tossed around by implacable waves.

had "drunke so muche stronge water that she was sencelesse & had neare killed her selfe." The tempest, lasting ten days, was a disorienting ordeal, yet easy for Puritans to understand. God was as hard on ships as he was on temples, testing their resilience. The migrants became then, in Johnson's words, "the fore-runners of Christs Army." Within a month, Winthrop noted, people were inured to storm and seasickness—and had changed.[2]

The drama of the sea-crossing, and suspension between worlds, made it an obvious rite of passage. And Winthrop was right: people did change. Yet a subtler shift had taken place prior to embarkation: simply deciding to go, and beyond that, the effect of the political, religious, and economic tensions a person experienced before making that decision, had also transformed the passengers. England's stressful competitive diversity raised basic and insistent questions of governance and legitimacy, liberty and truth—as relevant to humdrum parish affairs as to debates between crown and parliament. America offered a fresh context in which to examine and perhaps solve old problems, though it did not make them irrelevant, and still less did it make them disappear. If anything, the Puritan elite felt more embattled in Massachusetts than at home, as dissent surfaced in the colony's earliest years. Beneath the rhetoric of the "city upon a hill" lay an infinitely complex and intractable society that no Christian charity could ever perfect. Discipline had to be imposed, which inevitably meant authority would be disputed, within New England as well as by England against the colonies. The ship-in-a-storm became an enduring metaphor, illustrating not just suffering and courage, but turbulence and isolation.

The *Arbella* arrived in Salem on June 12, 1630. Some passengers, unable to bear another day at sea, rowed to Cape Ann to gather strawberries. Winthrop led a party into the port, where they met John Endecott and the ailing Francis Higginson. The town was no more than a muddy road to the waterside that was flanked by wooden houses. The men "supped with a good venison pastye & good beere" and discussed the colony. Eighty of the three hundred migrants sent by the Massachusetts Bay Company had died; more were sick, and stocks were dwindling. Little had been achieved. "All things [were] so contrary to their expectation," it was said, "that now every monstrous humor began to shew it selfe." Winthrop had to think quickly: they should clear fields and build houses before winter, but they could not afford to share their food with Salem's inhabitants, especially as half the cattle had died at sea, plus almost all the horses and goats. They sailed thirty miles down the coast and entered a spacious bay on the Charles River, where a nine-year-old girl named Anne, from Saffron Walden in Essex, led elders ashore. The land, she recalled, was "very uneven, abounding in small hollows and swamps, and covered with blueberry and other bushes"—a story she was still telling in her hundredth year.[3]

The migrants called their settlement Charlestown. Clearing and building were exhausting; the food was rough and fresh water limited. But John Winthrop was disappointed only by human behavior. In mid-July he wrote to his wife: "I thinke here are some persons who never shewed so much wickednesse in England as they have doone here." Nevertheless, his faith in their holy venture was absolute. He urged Margaret to come over, bringing flour, eggs, butter, fruit, and a lockable box. The letter ended with kisses for their children, then, as a postscript, a request for axes, candles, soap, and suet. England had everything; here there was nothing.[4]

On August 23, Winthrop convened the company council, its first meeting in America. This "court of assistants"—a term borrowed from the London livery companies—was the nucleus of his godly commonwealth. It would abide by English law and royal authority, yet was sufficiently far from its source to assert itself confidently. The assistants discussed how to support the ministry and agreed to arrest Thomas Morton of Ma-re Mount. Four days later the saints assembled as a church, pledging "to walke according to the Rule of the Gospell and in all sincere Conformity to His holy Ordinances, and in mutual love and respect each to other"—a sentiment they put at the heart of civil government. Winthrop planned a settlement of farmsteads, spacious yet integrated, to avoid the disasters of Virginia, Maine, and Salem. Each family would have a "competency": land sufficient for subsistence. In September, Winthrop led settlers across the river to the Shawmut Peninsula to find better springs; he renamed it Boston after the Lincolnshire port.[5]

That summer a new settlement had begun south of Boston. It had been named Dorchester in honor of the Dorset home of its spiritual father, John White. A fire in old Dorchester, in 1613, had prompted White, the town's minister, to launch a campaign of moral renewal— the building of an English "city upon a hill." It was an ambition he extended to America. He intended to inspire and inform aspiring migrants (with a lending library containing books by Samuel Purchas and others), to support the New England Company, and to help to obtain the charter for Winthrop's fleet. In 1630 White published *The Planter's Plea*, defining a colony as a just "societie of men," a charitable cure for a state diseased by luxury and poverty. England was duty-bound to spread the gospel. Colonists should not scatter, as they had in Virginia, and they needed strong leaders and plentiful servants. Without England's framework, New England would languish. White has been called the founder of Massachusetts, though he never saw the colony to which he gave so much.[6]

Within a year, Dorchester had 140 houses, along with orchards, gardens, cornfields, and meadows, where several hundred cattle grazed. Yet the community bore out John White's dictum that "the first fashioning of a politicke body is a harder task then the ordering of that which is already framed." During the winter of 1630–1631, the town survived on grain that White sent from England. Sickness was chronic, both there and in Boston.[7]

In September 1630, John Winthrop informed his wife of the deaths of Francis Higginson and others, by which God "hath purged our corruptions, and healed the hardnesse and error of our heartes." Still Winthrop maintained that he had never been healthier or more content. Who cares for meat when there is maize, he said in November: "We are heer in a Paradice." By then, however, scurvy and fever had cut into the colony, and Winthrop worried about his wife's departure from England. Between April and December, two hundred—over a quarter of Winthrop's migrants—died. On December 22, Richard Garrett, a shoemaker from Essex, took a small boat down the coast in search of food; with him were five others, including his young daughter. A storm drove them to Cape Cod, where everyone except the girl and a frost-bitten man died. In March 1631, Thomas Dudley, deputy governor of Massachusetts, sent a letter to Lady Bridget Clinton, whose husband, Theophilus, the earl of Lincoln, was his employer and an investor in the colony; indeed, he had hosted a meeting where the Massachusetts enterprise had been planned. Dudley reported "Egyptian" levels of mortality, which he blamed on "the want of warm lodging and good diet to which Englishmen are habituated at home."[8]

Dudley also told Lady Bridget of New England's wonders. The Plymouth Pilgrims had become "a people healthful, wealthy, politic and religious," a fillip to Boston that winter. He wrote of their wholesome air, food, and spirituality and told her of Morton's ejection. Upbeat reports also reached England from Watertown, a plantation west of Boston started by Sir Richard Saltonstall, a passenger on the *Arbella*. Saltonstall's son wrote in February 1631 that "the Cuntrie abounds with good creatures needfull for sustentation of the life of man," and that there would be profits "for men that bring bodys able and minds fitted to brave the first brunts." Sir Richard recognized the hazards, too. He employed a man named John Masters to look after his family. In March, Masters wrote to his Essex patrons, the Barringtons, describing less a Puritan wilderness than a playground for leisured gentry: "The Country is very good and fitt to receive Lords and Ladies if there were more good houses, both for good land and good water, and for good Creatures to hunt and to hawke and for fowling and fisheing, and more also [for] o[u]r natures to refresh us; and if any of yo[u]rs will Come here I knowe you might have good Cheere."

Correspondents feigned bravery to encourage backers and reassure loved ones. In some letters, though, disappointment and fear went undisguised. The day after John Masters wrote, another servant, named Pond, described a different Watertown, this time to his father in Suffolk. "The cuntrey," he said, "is not as we ded expecte it." His children lay sick, prices were high, and the commodity they craved—beaver—was scarce. Only death was abundant. "I pray you remembure me as youer cheilde," Pond begged. "We do not know how longe we may subeseiste for we can not live her[e] witheought provisseyones from ould eingland."[9]

Experience varied, then, or at least varied in the way it was reported. It took a special man to call New England a paradise and really believe it. Migrants were flooding back, said Pond, and "maney more wolld a cume if thay had whare-with-all to bringe them hom[e]." Men worth £200 in England now had barely £30, and he felt like giving up. Even committed saints, observed John Smith in 1631, "make more haste to returne to Babel, as they tearmed England, than stay to enjoy the land they called Canaan." To Winthrop's disgust, some brought Babylon with them. Settlers stole and fought, gambled and deceived; one was caught selling a bogus cure for scurvy. Others were tried for denigrating authority. A youth was whipped "for uttering malicious and scandalous speeches" against the Boston court; another had his ears cut off for disrespecting Salem's church. Crusading Puritans approved the punishment. The Reverend Thomas Weld, who arrived in June 1632, particularly admired the government's intolerance of swearing.[10]

Winthrop's tendency to crush dissent rather than attempting to win consent was dangerous. He believed his mandate came from heaven, and it was a mandate that colonists cast in stark terms: as one migrant put it, they would march "to cast downe Sathan like lightening, to tread upon serpents and scorpions, to cast downe strong holds & every thing th[a]t exalteth it selfe against God." In the Old World, Winthrop's pretended power was reserved for princes; his will would not prove greater than that of 2,000 colonists, most of whom had been excluded from church membership and so, to their fury, denied political representation. Repression allowed Winthrop to focus on his vision, although harsh punishments and criticism thereof were self-perpetuating. A man was banished for "writing into England falsely and malitiously against the government & execution of Justice heere," others for threatening to contact English courts. One was disenfranchised for slandering the assistants, the best of whom "was but an Atturny"; another was fined for calling Winthrop "but a Lawyers Clerke"—a reference to his unfulfilled legal ambitions. Some migrants felt that, in their transatlantic quest for liberty, they had simply exchanged one form of tyranny for another.[11]

These were days of small beginnings. Stories flowed home, full of wonder and hope, disappointment and disaster. People back in England had to decide how much of what they heard was true, or how much hardship they could bear if they emigrated, considerations shaped by the worsening political and economic state of England, and for Puritans, persecution. Most news arrived in personal correspondence. "Here we are come into as goodly a land as ever mine eyes beheld," Thomas Weld told his old congregation at Terling in Essex. "Such groves, such trees, such a[n] aire as I am fully contented withall and desier no better while I live."[12]

Although many of the first influx in 1630 had died or returned, and the following year just 70 arrived, by 1632 the figure had risen to 400. Within two years, 2,000 were arriving annually. But life remained grueling. John Winthrop's knowledge of previous adventures proved invaluable. Aware that colonies imposed their own rules, he never apologized for hardship; neither did he or his circle raise false hopes. A tract by Francis Higginson was guaranteed to be honest and objective, free of "frothy bumbasted words."[13]

Migrant writers used the services of sympathetic London printers and booksellers, such as John Bellamy, who specialized in colonial titles. In 1634 Bellamy published an ethnology and *vade mecum* to America by William Wood, a colonist of four years' experience. "I am perswaded if many in England which are constrained to begge their bread were there," said Wood, "they would live better than many doe here that have money to buy it." But Wood was realistic. Beards froze so hard, he joked, that a man struggled to get a bottle in his mouth, although "in publike assemblies it is strange to heare a man sneeze or cough as ordinarily they doe in old England." English diseases were unknown; more twins were born; and, unlike pasty-faced Virginians, New Englanders had suntans. But Wood had missed the worst mortality, having left just as smallpox gripped eastern Massachusetts.[14]

Once the smallpox epidemic did arrive, it was the Indians who suffered the most, and this after European germs had already depleted the native population. The Massachusetts Bay Colony motto "Come Over and Help Us," snaking from a native's mouth on the company seal, acquired terrible irony. Early in 1631, a Watertown man recorded that there were but few Indians around, most having died that winter, perhaps from plague. Some colonists tried to help, unaware that they were causing the affliction. They buried corpses and gave comfort: in one wigwam, colonists grieved to find a baby sucking its dead mother's breast.[15]

With sympathy went fascination, and sometimes respect. William Wood decided that Mohawks were cannibalistic, Wabanakis alcoholic, Pequots and Narragansetts stately, Aberginians ascetic yet carefree. He described haircuts that "would torture the wits of a curious Barber to

The seal of the Massachusetts Bay Company, founded in England in 1628. The
Indian, naked but for a grass skirt, appeals to England for help—a reference to
Acts 16:9, where Paul sees a pleading Macedonian in a vision.

imitate," and scanty attire even in winter, when Indians coped better
"in a frost-paved wildernesse than the furred Citizen." The *sagamore*,
or chief, in full regalia believed he was Charles I's equal, able to "blow
downe Castles with his breath and conquer kingdomes with his conceit." Their language, Wood said, resembled Hebrew, suggesting Jewish ancestry. Their religion was base superstition, their justice limited,
their footballing skills negligible, and their sense of humor nonexistent.
If an English trader laughed, the Indian trader thought he was being cheated. Wood spoke well of native hospitality, however: disoriented colonists were entertained better by the Indians than if they had
pitched up at an inn in old England. Central to the story of Richard
Garrett's stricken party were Indian attempts to save them.[16]

John Winthrop was interested in signs that Indians might be
converted. Wood was pessimistic: progress in civility had not been
matched in religion, and natives sat blankly in church. In December
1633, Winthrop recorded the confessions of Indians dying from smallpox: they said "that the Englishe mens God was a good God & that if
they recovered they would serve him." They were touched by the fact

that Englishmen cared for them when their own people fled. On his deathbed, one chieftain, John Sagamore, entrusted his son to colonists, so that the boy "might keep closer to the English & ther God then he himself had done"; the chieftain had been converted by the Reverend John Wilson, whose name he had adopted, but had lapsed when his kinsmen threatened him over the issue. It was hard for Indians to stay changed, just as it was for colonists to stay the same. The Cambridge theologian Joseph Mede deduced that Satan had installed the Indians in the New World when Europe Christianized, and had settled there to enjoy his unique dominion. Attempts at conversion, therefore, were probably futile.[17]

Winter arrived early in 1634. In November, a storm smashed ships in the dock; then, as rain turned to snow, the harbor iced up. Plymouth was blighted by smallpox and influenza. Throughout New England, gravediggers worked long hours. Unlike at home, accumulating calamities threatened this society's extinction. That year, Ambrose Gibbons, who had been employed by John Mason and Sir Ferdinando Gorges to develop New Hampshire, had realized he was wasting his time. Investors could not understand what life was like on the Piscataqua River and how badly the plantation needed cattle, cowherds, food, and clothing. Mason had complained to Gibbons that crystalline stone sent to England was worthless; he demanded cedar and cypress instead. "I have supported, but now [am] sunke under, my burthen," replied Gibbons. "The more I thinke on this, the more is my griefe." Nor had there been unity: England's West Countrymen were culturally incompatible with Londoners.[18]

There was little amity in Massachusetts, either. One of New England's strengths, as in Ulster but not Virginia, was the migration of entire households, which were the means to a stable society and perpetual possession of land. Yet a third of settlers were young, single servants. The ideals of the "city upon a hill" faltered mainly because Boston was small; it required expansion to thrive, but expansion would threaten authority and cohesion. The town was a peninsula, useful for trade and for protecting livestock from wolves, but remote from pasture and firewood. On one hill stood a fort, on another a windmill—a contraption that terrified the Indians—and there was space to govern and worship. But by 1635 farmers had already moved their cattle and pigs to the salt marshes at Muddy River, two miles west. The court of assistants dealt with more and more disputes as the growing population pressed against available resources: as in Virginia, land quickly ran out. Boston defended its boundaries against Dorchester and Watertown, while Dorchester resisted its northern neighbor, Roxbury. Twenty miles away, a coastal settlement was founded at Marblehead in the expectation that it would merge with Salem. This it did, but not before becoming a byword for godless disorder. In July a man from an eastern plantation was tried for saying that Bay men were rogues, "and that he hoped to see all their throats cutt." So much for Winthrop's Christian charity, which already seemed like a nostalgic fantasy.[19]

Symbolic order was imposed. Winthrop, described in a report to London as "a discreete and sober man . . . wearing plaine apparell," banned "immodest fashions and also the ordinary wearing of gold and silke." He also condemned long hair in men as "prejudiciall to the Common good." But Boston's real problem was not deviance from some norm, but a social diversity that mirrored troubled England: there were Anglicans, Calvinists, sectaries, and agnostics; farmers and merchants, clergymen and artisans; respectable householders and footloose apprentices. The "great migration" was hardly a Puritan diaspora. Of 10,000 ministers in England, just seventy-six emigrated in the 1630s, a third of whom had never been censured. Political divisiveness was inherent. The elite, derided as "this absolute crue, only of the Elect, holding all (but such as themselves) reprobates and cast-awaies," believed that God had bound his wilderness people by a covenant. Although everyone attended services, congregations were not parishes where saints and sinners rubbed shoulders, as they had been in England. Congregants were admitted when they testified convincingly to possessing divine grace. Newcomers were disappointed. Susanna Bell arrived after an eight-week voyage during which she "saw nothing but the Heaven and Waters" and experienced God as never before. How much greater, then, her distress at being denied church membership: she sank into depression, doubting her election. Naturally, this self-abasement led to an invitation to join, which she resisted from a sense of unworthiness. Winthrop's fourteen-year-old son, Stephen, was admitted only after being "helde under suche Affliction of minde as he could not be brought to apprehende any comforte in God, being muche humbled & broken for his sines."[20]

Mixed reports of Massachusetts, especially the sense that it shared many of England's problems, complicated decision-making about emigration. Stephen Winthrop had no choice but to go; most of the emigrants did have a choice, though, and found it hard to make up their minds. Initially, Susanna Bell had been unmoved by her husband's entreaties to leave England: she lived a comfortable London life and did not relish the sea-passage with her young children. Her friends agreed, and only a biblical ordinance about wifely obedience, followed by her baby's death, melted her icy resolve to stay put. Suddenly, "the Lord took away all fears from my spirit," she recalled, "and I told my Husband I was willing to go with him." John Winthrop asked John White, patriarch of Dorchester, to persuade another colonist's wife to come over, aghast that she might choose poverty with her children in England over plenty in America.[21]

Fears of the voyage were very real. One man admitted that the prospect of sailing, and abandoning his family, "brought me as low as the grave." Few were soothed by William Wood's comparison of a ship to "a Cradle rocked by a carefull Mothers hand." A single story of wreck, piracy, or starvation—like that of the mariner who drank rainwater from an eviscerated corpse, "to his unspeakeable refreshment"—had more impact than a hundred safe arrivals. Tales abounded of passengers menaced by sea-monsters and witches, the latter hanged from yardarms or cast overboard. Ships felt suspended from law and obligation, like nurseries of rough justice. Primitive food and lodgings inspired mutiny. Crossings were at best uncomfortable, and passengers constantly aware that, as one writer put it, there was "but a few inches of planke betweene them and Death." Sightings of strange ships caused terror, but boredom proved a more formidable enemy than any privateer. People behaved foolishly, dangling overboard and climbing the rigging. One woman bet all her clothes she could stay awake on deck for three days and nights, but dozed off after six hours and was forced to rely on the charity of the ship's master, who paid off her debt. Desperation to arrive was intense in the final days. It was customary to nail a collection of "goodwill" money to the mast for the boy who first spied land.[22]

Accordingly, few predicted an English exodus. "We are knowne too well to the world to love the smoake of our owne chimneys so well," wrote John White, "that hopes of great advantages are not likely to draw many of us from home." Those who had not yet closed their minds to the possibility of going informed themselves about America through reading and through corresponding with people who had already gone. And they talked and prayed and meditated on the matter until they either gave up or gave in to a desire for self-realization or reinvention. America, thought Edward Winslow, was perfect for "those who desire to have themselves discovered to themselves." Others, of course, wanted only to escape pregnant lovers or unloved wives, or constables or creditors. One debt-ridden Londoner was distraught at leaving, but he realized that "my Lords desire is to imploy me for New England." His father-in-law's appeal that he reconsider for the sake of his wife and children, who were now lost in a "mournfull maze," did not dent his resolve.[23]

For Puritans, the arguments for staying and leaving were finely balanced. Early in 1633, John Cotton, Winthrop's valedictory preacher, accompanied his friend Thomas Hooker to a meeting in Surrey. There, the Reverend Henry Whitfield and other ministers tried to make them moderate their opposition to the Anglican liturgy. Whitfield failed, and instead found himself persuaded, as were his colleagues. They realized now that dissent was justified, and if God closed one door at home, he would open another overseas. Cotton was brilliantly pragmatic: "By the free preaching of the word and the actual practice of our church discipline," he argued, "we could offer a much clearer and fuller witness in another land than in the wretched and loathsome prisons of London." He and Hooker sailed in July, and four weeks later Cotton's wife gave birth to a son. His name, Seaborn, was "a remembrance of Sea-mercies from the hand of a gracious God."[24]

Once the authorities became aware of what was happening, other ministers who were ejected from their parishes for defying church canons—as Thomas Weld had been—were forbidden to leave. William Laud, now archbishop of Canterbury, chased East Anglia's Puritans with fresh vigor, blocking their exits. To the Suffolk antiquary Sir Simonds D'Ewes, Laud and his lackeys were worse than papists: they were diabolical. Good men, D'Ewes wrote in 1634, had sold estates and shipped possessions to America only to be halted at the docks. Rumors that New England was to be ruled by a royal governor—some said the colonial entrepreneur Sir Ferdinando Gorges—alarmed Puritans in America and at home. News reached Laud of a minister in the English town of Ipswich denouncing the Book of Common Prayer and promoting emigration while two ships full of debtors and Puritans were ready to sail. In December port officials were ordered to stop anyone without a license or proof of religious conformity, rogues who "live as much as they can without the reach of authoritie." Emigration became more furtive, as suggested by numerical discrepancies between passengers registered and arrivals in Boston.[25]

One fugitive was Thomas Shepard, a protégé of Thomas Weld and a fiery preacher. He had once been summoned by Laud, who, Shepard recalled, was so angry "he looked as though blood would have gushed out of his face," and accused of stirring up "a company of seditious factious Bedlams." Laud said that if Shepard ever preached again he would "everlastingly disenable" him. Friends advised Shepard to leave, but he was torn between the idea that flight caused schism and John Cotton's belief that godly emigration was a means to strengthen the communion. In October 1634, after a spell of running and hiding, he "began to listen to a call to New England." Despite a terror of the sea, he left disguised as a farmer with his pregnant wife and child. The ship was wrecked and the family driven back to England, where the child died. In April 1635, a son, John, was born, and four months later, with extraordinary courage, the Shepards tried again. They arrived in Newtown—soon to be renamed Cambridge—where he and his son would become two of the most influential divines in seventeenth-century America.[26]

Before dawn on August 15, 1635, a hurricane hit the New England coast. Trees were uprooted, houses flattened, and ships wrenched from anchor. The *James* of Bristol, which was carrying Yorkshire migrants, was blown from the Isle of Shoals and almost wrecked at Piscataqua. The Reverend Joseph Avery was sailing from new Ipswich, north of Salem, to lead the church at Marblehead. With him was his cousin Anthony Thacher, who was a tailor from Wiltshire, and their families, along with four mariners. As the women clutched distraught children, their pinnace was lifted and smashed on the shore of an island, scattering its passengers. Some climbed the rocks, only to be washed off; Thacher and his wife made it to safety. Of the Averys there was no sign, nor of Thacher's five children. Shivering beneath a fallen tree, Thacher was tormented by them "looking ru[e]fully on mee on the Rocke, there very Countinance[s] calling unto mee to helpe them." Anthony and Elizabeth Thacher, the only survivors, were rescued three days later, and with "shaking hand" and "drowned pen" Anthony sent news to relatives in England. He never recovered, blaming himself for his children's deaths when they could have lived safely in England; he was tormented by dreams of his "poore silent Lambs." The tragic island, named Thacher's Woe, became a physical reminder of the episode, which, like

Richard Garrett's story, joined the growing lore of sacrifice at the core of New England's identity.[27]

Horror and hardship made English people in New England feel special—it made them feel like New Englanders. After the decision to emigrate, this process began with the willing suspension of normal life. Property had to be sold or entrusted, debts settled, money borrowed; one man secured a passage by persuading his brother-in-law to invest in Massachusetts Bay. The Reverend John Fiske's wife was disinherited when she announced her departure, so the Fiskes had to wait for John's father to die to get to Salem. Funds permitting, all manner of clothes, tools, utensils, and foodstuffs had to be bought and loaded. Promoters issued lists, and letters home indicated things forgotten or brought in insufficient quantities: John Winthrop asked his eldest son, John, to bring spades, shovels, axes, sieves, and shoes—and a carpenter and a cooper. Men took silver, which went straight back to England to buy necessities. Ships left England packed with everything from butter, cheese, and raisins to hats, canvas, nails, and buttons. Cautious migrants traveled light, then had possessions sent once they were settled.[28]

Arrival, like departure, was a fraught business. In Boston a committee apportioned land to newcomers, usually at Muddy River. Robert Hull, a Leicestershire blacksmith, was given "a great allotment" of land there in 1636, and built a house as instructed. Hull found it hard to get settled; but as his son John, then aged eleven, later explained, God had moved them "rather to endure a voluntary exile from their native soyl & to hazard the loss of all their sweet outward comforts & relations, than to defile their Consciences." Massachusetts would be grateful: John Hull became the colony's richest man and its savior.[29]

Over a hundred people left Wiltshire between 1635 and 1638, mostly young, single servants and artisans. But a significant number of couples left for the New World, too, and there were strong ties of kinship overall. Emigrating with relatives and neighbors had the appeal of safety in numbers, but could still be nerve-racking. In the 1630s, some fifty families felt compelled to leave Norwich, seven left from Diss, and more left from towns across Norfolk: 1,350 people in all. Some godly ministers were accompanied by their flocks, as happened at Hingham, a village blighted by poverty, plague, and persecution. Beginning a five-year exodus, the Reverend Peter Hubbard led his parishioners to a place south of the Charles River, which naturally they called Hingham. Even there they conflicted with non-Puritans from the West Country who knew "Hingham" as Bear Cove and whom gradually they displaced.[30]

Lone migrants were less fortunate in this regard but could remake themselves; rogues could morph silently into blameless colonists. The opportunity to leave the past behind certainly made it easier for people to engage in adultery and bigamy. Christopher Gardiner set up home with "a known harlot," despite having wives in London and Paris; he also convinced people that he was a knight. Leaving behind a reputation, however, might be a mixed blessing. A Virginia woman who, in 1634, slandered a neighbor, saying she had seen her whipped as a whore in England, was herself censured because there was no one to substantiate the claim. One woman struggled to prove that she had been married in England; a man struggled to prove he had not. A man who had traitorously clipped silver from coins swore he had been pardoned in London, but there was no one to corroborate his story, and he was repatriated to England. Others who looked forward to starting over soon discovered flaws in themselves that prevented them from fitting in anywhere. In the mid-1630s, Barbara Rolfe was hounded out of Massachusetts, where no one would take her into service. Her father had sent her to America after she rejected "a civill and orderely course of lyfe . . . contrary to his fatherly admonitions and persuasions."[31]

Colonists became accustomed to danger—electrical storms, extreme temperatures, predators, and vermin—and acquired local knowledge. They learned how to kill wolves with fishhooks wrapped in fat, and how to render bear grease to make ointment. The testicles of a muskrat gave linen "a grateful smell." Cattle were kept away from snakeroot to keep their milk from causing "the trembles." When bread and maize were expensive, people ate fish, which was cheap, and shellfish, which was free. Children seemed to do well on the new diet.[32]

Long workdays left little time for reflection, but dreams about England exposed homesickness. A founder of Dedham, Massachusetts, missed Norwich: "The beauty of my native country," he pined, "what shall I say unto thee?" Colonists wrote more letters than they received, many scribbled in haste to catch departing ships; duplicates were sent as insurance. Then came the waiting: John Winthrop was so dismayed by his siblings' failure to reply that he thought they might be dead. Edward Howes, a London friend of Winthrop's son John, invented a magnetic device to "sympathize at a distance"—meaning perhaps to communicate across the Atlantic. A longing for home was worst among those whose early triumphs proved unsustainable. In September 1633, William Hammond of Watertown wrote to his former master Sir Simonds D'Ewes, thrilled by his "flourishing plantation" and its "wise, religious governor." But three years later D'Ewes heard that Hammond was in debt; his son, William junior, had made a desperate trip to Virginia for corn but was shipwrecked. Having lost everything, Hammond had crawled ashore on Long Island, only to be killed by "a giant-like Indian." The family's estate, John Winthrop informed D'Ewes, "is wholly overthrown."[33]

By the mid-1630s English people saw New England as a place where the rich got poor and vice versa, a topsy-turvy world of mixed appeal. Reverse migration produced well-informed critics. Thomas Morton spoke of New England "digrading and creating gentry," citing the case of a godly coffin-maker who profited from beaver to become a gentleman. Not every saint was what he seemed. A ballad referred to the "Counterfeite electe," in reality the dregs from England's prisons and houses of correction; the only law they respected was that of nature— which gave them a license for free love. (This amused one Nottingham man so much that he copied the whole thing out.) In another satire, a West Countryman arrived in new Dorchester, where he was fined for swearing and decided he preferred the old one. A spoof prayer of grace mocked the sanctimoniousness of New England's Puritans: "Wee are the Chosen Israell, thy babes, thy holye children," they reminded God at their feast, asking for every dish to be blessed, especially the custard, "for the Land of Canan flowed w[i]th mylke and honye." There was a more serious charge, too, namely, that this prayer invoked the destruction of "Antichristian" bishops.[34]

The colonists' indignation distanced them from their detractors in England. Thomas Dudley informed Lady Bridget Clinton that returnees spread "false and scandalous reports against us, affirming us to be Brownists [separatists] in religion and ill-affected to our state at home." It would be strange, he remarked, if "we should be so unlike ourselves." John White agreed: New Englanders had not disavowed England, but were like roots feeding a tree. Hostility was entrenched, however. Edward Howes informed his friend John Winthrop Jr. in 1631 that he had heard "mutteringe of a too palpable seperation of your people from our church governement." Some critics were more outspoken, such as the Dorset man who said "that all the projecters for new England Business are rebels, and those that are gon over are Idolaters, captivated, and seperatists." The Plymouth Pilgrims plainly *were* separatists, even if Edward Winslow denied it to the Privy Council in 1632.[35]

What of John Winthrop Sr.? Had earlier protestations been a sham? Intercepted letters certainly raised doubts about his people's loyalty, and when Sir Simonds D'Ewes warned him against abandoning Anglicanism, Winthrop replied: "What you may doe in E[ngland] where things are otherwise established I will not dispute, but our case heere is otherwise, being come to clearer light and more Libertye." Liberty was also stressed by Edward Trelawny, who, in a letter of 1635, described a world free of bishops, "so they come unto the land and to the Lord with new hearts and new lives, and enter into a new covenant, so to continue even to their ends. And who would not be among such a people in such a land?"[36]

One answer was the orthodox Anglican loyalist. D'Ewes received another letter from America that made Massachusetts sound like a sovereign state. It was observed that settlers, though orderly, ignored their patents, as though distance from England gave them immunity. Edward Howes in 1632 warned John Winthrop Jr. of "a thousand eyes watchinge over you to pick holes in your coats"; colonists must "endeavour in all mildnesse to doe gods worke," Howes advised, and should not, for instance, cut off dissidents' ears. Howes had met a man who called New Englanders damnable heretics who "pray for the governor before they praye for our kinge and state." This was the year that the crown began a long battle to revoke the Massachusetts Bay charter, as Charles I said, to impose "one uniforme Course of government" on the colonies. A Privy Council commission heard evidence of sedition and separatism from, among others, the bigamist Christopher Gardiner, who had been unmasked as an agent for Sir Ferdinando Gorges and deported. But whatever anyone said about New England, old England was no paradise either. "The commission of all things heare do decline very much," Sir Richard Saltonstall wrote in 1632, having returned to England from Watertown after one of his daughters fell sick. "The Court is very jealous of the Cuntrie, the Law is full of oppression and bribery, and the Church of superstitions."[37]

To complicate matters, scathing criticism came from within. The court of assistants heard in 1634 that John Endecott had cut the cross from the English flag as "a superstitious thinge & a relique of Antichriste," that is, the papacy. The episode caused concern in the colony that in England this would be seen as an act of rebellion. Endecott's unauthorized act of iconoclasm exposed dissent toward Winthrop's oligarchy, although, as Israel Stoughton of new Dorchester told his brother, a minister in England, most men supported neither the assistants nor Endecott, mainly because they were reluctant "to abuse theire Christian liberty" and make enemies in the process. Thus the *quo warranto* proceedings recently begun in London against Massachusetts were paralleled in the colony itself: Endecott and his supporters posed a challenge to the assistants' arbitrary rule. After grudgingly producing the patent he had concealed for so long, Winthrop was, according to Stoughton, viewed as a man who "had too much forgott & overshott himselfe." Now the way was open to the development of representation and accountability, although Endecott had "bred some evill blood in our body."[38]

Israel Stoughton's letters were seized in a 1635 raid on his London home, and his brother was put under surveillance. In the same year, the Ipswich minister who had encouraged emigration was imprisoned. Fresh rumors of royal plans to control Massachusetts were heard in London, and efforts were redoubled "for the Restraint of disorderly transporting [of] His Ma[jes]t[y]s Subjects." Reports of Frenchmen and Turks invading New England caused consternation among English Puritans. Margaret Winthrop, who had arrived in Boston late in 1631, received letters begging for information; a friend, Muriel Gurdon, wrote from Suffolk in 1636 saying that although accounts by returning colonists varied, on balance her husband "rathar thinke[s] he hath a calling to suffar hear then to remove himselfe." Puritans at home criticized their leaders' flight. "Oh the heavy condition of this land," lamented Gurdon, "that doe parte with such as should hav ben the pilars to uphowld it." England groaned. That year saw increased checks on conformity; a drought that stunted wheat, followed by a downpour that flattened it; and a plague epidemic in London. The king's ministers, a correspondent informed John Winthrop in March 1637, "are more lik[e] tyrants then civil men."[39]

So people kept coming. In March 1638 Archbishop Laud received a report of "incredible numbers of persons of very good abillities" selling up. Parishes were apparently threatened by loss of skills, grain, silver, and poor-relief contributions. The authorities were ambivalent. Informed about some returning Puritans, "their faith not being answerable to their zeal," Laud regretted that England was not rid of them forever. Religious nonconformity, however, was not tolerated in either America or England. The Privy Council ordered port officials to keep meticulous passenger lists, and the Star Chamber decreed that they needed licenses. Even so, migrants slipped through the net. A summons of 1638 to a couple from Maldon in Essex, for absenteeism from church, ends with a note: "Gone to New England." Emigrating Puritans radicalized as the danger to true religion grew, and so arrived in America with more steel than their predecessors.[40]

The journey to America was a voyage of discovery that taught every migrant about the Old World as well as the new one, and who he or she was in relation to both. No two people felt quite the same, and differences of opinion could be marked. In the summer of 1638, a traveler named John Josselyn arrived in Maine after an eleven-week voyage during which he ate "sea-hog" ("tasts like rusty Bacon or hung Beef"), saw a sailor whipped for stealing lemons, and watched in awe as Puritans threw back fish caught on the Sabbath. Some passengers died from smallpox. Josselyn's impression of the American coast was underwhelming: "a meer Wilderness." To Puritans, by contrast, the land was beautiful because of what it represented. In the same year, an ironmonger named John Wiswall arrived in New England from Lancashire and wrote in praise of the order there that was vanishing from England. "Truely sir, I Like it very well," Wiswall wrote, and so would any godly man once he saw how magistrates and ministers cooperated to punish sinners and reward the virtuous. A like-minded newcomer was Thomas Tillam, a Catholic turned Puritan, who wrote:

> Methinks I hear the Lambe of God thus speake:
> Come my deare little flocke, who for my sake
> Have lefte your Country, dearest friends and goods
> And hazarded your lives o'th raginge floods,
> Posses this Country, free from all anoye;
> Heare I'le bee with you, heare you shall Injoye
> My Sabbaths, sacraments, my minestrye
> And ordinances in their puritye.

Tillam ended cautiously: "Beware of Sathans wylye baites / Hee lurkes amonge yow." Within a few years he realized the truth of this, as did others, and returned to England.[41]

CHAPTER 8

In Darkness and the Shadow of Death

NEW ENGLAND PERVADES the cultural memory of early America, but to England it was not the most significant Atlantic destination. More than half of the English migrants went to the West Indies, and three-quarters of the rest to the Chesapeake; only one in ten ended up farther north. It was common knowledge that southern colonies were riskier, yet to England's youth, risk meant not just danger but opportunity. In the spring of 1638, the year that John Wiswall and Thomas Tillam arrived in Massachusetts, Thomas Rous left England for the Caribbean island of Barbados in an overcrowded, poorly provisioned ship. A third of the 350 passengers, mostly apprentices, fell sick, probably with smallpox. Rous recorded that every day another two or three went over the side, eighty in all by the time they arrived. Thus spared, and brimming with providential hope, Rous began repaying God with his labor.[1]

The world Rous entered became another variant of the colonial experience, full of fear and awe, fortune and pain. At a time when Charles I's forced loans were alienating England's gentry, and his government of Scotland was in disarray, the West Indies, together with new and expanding colonies in New England and the Chesapeake, further indicated a loosening of traditional ties, the redistribution of authority, and a chance for the legitimacy of power to be questioned and defended and asserted afresh. By the mid-1630s, Massachusetts, unable either to silence its detractors or to prevent the disaffected from setting up for themselves in Connecticut, faced political crisis. The question of how to effect God's will remained unanswered.

Virginia, too, had new troubles. Virginians resented their new neighbors in Maryland, who, like the Newfoundlanders, were reactionary in politics and religion. In the colonies, as in England, lines between liberty and tyranny, loyalty and rebellion, did not demarcate fixed ideologies, but were axes around which opposing interests revolved. Investors and planters grappled for commercial supremacy, and the king engaged enemies at home and abroad as his three kingdoms edged closer to civil war. Before then, however, New England's colonists would be embroiled in their own brutal war with the Pequot nation, marking another phase of their transformation between two worlds: the one they knew but had left, and one in which they lived but which they had yet to master. And nowhere was the contrast between old and new sharper than in the Caribbean. The economic success of the islands would draw them closer to England, but at the same time, they became frighteningly alien to England in their social and political organization.

After a decade of settlement, Barbados's 170 square miles already supported 10,000 English colonists, and competition for land was fierce. Migrants also found it extremely difficult to make a living from tobacco, the staple crop, owing to its inferiority to the Virginia leaf. Seven years later Rous owned just sixty acres—less than a tenth of a square mile—yet his ambition coincided with an economic revolution in the Caribbean, a shift to that other pillar of seventeenth-century consumerism: sugar.

English planters took advantage of conflict between Dutch and Portuguese producers in Brazil in the 1640s to grab a slice of the market. Funded by adventurers in London, they cleared land and built mills. The forests that had greeted migrant farmers in 1625 vanished as quickly as indentured servants' dreams that one day they would have their own smallholdings growing tobacco, ginger, and cotton. Sugar triumphed, enriching those with the audacity and tenacity to grow it. Rous was one such man. By the 1680s, he and his kinsmen controlled a 657-acre plantation, with three sugar works and three hundred African slaves. The Rous family patriarchs in Barbados were like the feudal barons of old: wealthy, all-powerful, and unstoppable, and they helped to make Barbados the jewel in England's imperial crown.[2]

Before 1700, the appeal of every American territory to the individual exceeded its appeal to the state. The colonies accounted for less than 5 percent of England's national income; Barbados and the Chesapeake combined had the economic capacity of a small English county. However, whereas New England was felt to offer little to England—except competition—the West Indies showed great promise. The colonists demanded every English export, and that demand increased once planters began specializing in sugar, which made them both wealthier and less able to provide for themselves. The sugar, in turn, satisfied England's sweet tooth, and success bred success. In 1627 the West Indies had been entrusted to James Hay, earl of Carlisle, under a proprietary patent, ending the era of company control of English America—further proof, after the Virginia Company's decline, that old mercantile ways, not least insistence on quick profits, were unsuited to American conditions. The following year, the island of Nevis was settled as a sugar plantation, and Montserrat and Antigua in 1632. Gradually, a niche for the Caribbean was carved into English culture.[3]

As Thomas Warner had found in the Leeward Islands, it was wise to temper expectation with realism: the environment was so wild, an Englishman might feel totally severed from the world that formerly had sustained his identity. Apart from a lack of familiar comforts, and the stifling heat, the high winds were terrifying. The Carib Indians believed that a hurricane was a spirit visible in the moon's aura, and they warned their innocent guests, who hid in caves or pits, lashed themselves to trees, or curled up in hammocks when the storms came. A whirlwind on St. Kitts in August 1638 smashed ships and, according to the London pamphleteer John Taylor, "did puffe men up from the earth as [if] they had beene Feathers." This time witchcraft was not blamed. Rather, the storm was seen as God's judgment on uncorrected heathenism.[4]

What could be done? Slavery, Taylor suggested, was a way for indigenous people to be "happily brought to Civility and Christian Liberty"; after all, Alexander the Great had civilized those he enslaved, and the Romans had done the same for the ancient Britons. No native saw it thus; neither did most white Barbadians feel like holy conquerors. Apprentices lived like serfs, except with too few free colonists to govern them. Two brothers from the West Country had led an uprising of eight hundred servants in 1634; the rebels intended "to kill their masters and make themselves free." Despite their failure, exploitation and repression led to further protest. As in Virginia, planters learned that consent between classes required mutual obligation—a given in England, with its bonds of patronage and deference, but not here. Nor was there consensus among rulers, only factionalism, and of such complexity that even Captain John Smith, a confident analyst, was be-mused by Barbados, saying: "I cannot from so many variable relations give you any certainty for their orderly Government." In England, sta-bility consisted in minimal change: the more the future resembled the past, the better. Innovation and growth happened there anyway, but in the Caribbean the transformation was more dramatic, driven by lust for gain and consequent demand for plentiful, cheap, and tractable labor. Hence, the workforce shifted from indentured service to black chat-tel slavery, boosting profits, yet destabilizing the social base. Africans suffered from what slave traders and plantation owners called "fixed melancholy," a morose unresponsiveness that led to suicide. Punish-ments, cruel and casual, were intimidating, and the babel of languages frustrated conspiracy.[5]

England could not be re-created in the West Indies, except in se-cluded spots where the wealthier planters, such as Thomas Rous, might for a few hours calm their thoughts. The Barbados Assembly, imitating Virginia and Bermuda, was first convened in 1639; it aimed to repre-sent the interests of these planters—interests that were increasingly at variance with those of the crown and inimical to those of the slaves, whom they worked to death. A colonial aristocracy in the making, grandees and governors spouted the rhetoric of freeborn Englishmen, the customary defense against unreasonable monarchs, and one heard less often from poor whites as their numbers dwindled. This was not the varied and reflexive commonwealth where the planters had been raised. Money mattered more than charity, and depravity went un-checked. Thomas Verney arrived in Barbados in 1639 and sent his father some first impressions. Verney's greatest praise was for the food: plan-tains baked, stewed, and fried; boiled potatoes with diluted potato-juice ("mobby"); and mouth-watering pineapples. Law and religion, how-ever, were derelict, and drunkenness endemic. Walking to church one morning, Verney saw colonists lying unconscious in the road, covered in land-crabs, which could nip off fingers and toes. "Yett this," he shud-dered, "doth not att all affright them."[6]

Unlike what promoters had envisioned, the West Indies were dys-topian: hot and unhealthy, socially warped and turbulent. And what happened in Barbados would be magnified in Jamaica, an island twenty-five times bigger and destined to become a gargantuan English sugar and rum factory. As commerce waxed, noble ambitions waned, creating a Caribbean world where only the luckiest and most ruthless would succeed.

A company of Puritans backed by the earl of Warwick settled a volcanic island off Spain's Mosquito Coast in 1630. Providence, as it was known, was planned as a godly utopia like Massachusetts. In July 1631, the governor, Philip Bell, wrote to the Providence Company's treasurer, thrilled by the profusion of wildfowl and watermelons, pomegranates and pigs. The abundance, he said, suggested that "in short time through gods blessinge this yor little Spott of land will growe [into] one of ye gardens of ye world." A young minister, Lewis Morgan, likened it to Eden. He began to wonder "wheth[e]r I shall live an exile from my native soyle, & land my Contented bones in this pleasant Iseland, or else my time expired returne unto my Country." His dilemma was solved for him. Although a moral code was drawn up, tobacco cultivation restricted, and idleness anathematized, settlers fell into factions, ran up debts, and challenged the natural authority of gentlemen. Morgan became the mouthpiece of dissent, but he was soon back in London begging his masters' forgiveness.[7]

Providence's prospects had all but evaporated by 1635. Another minister wrote to Sir Thomas Barrington, apologizing that "this Island hath not better answered their honours expense & expectation," and making the now familiar colonial complaint that the governor treated men like "his absolute slaves & vassalls." Increasingly, though, planters used real slaves. This troubled the Providence Company, not on ethical grounds—they believed it proper to "keep such persons in a state of servitude during their strangeness from Christianity"—but because it spoiled their cherished image of an English Canaan, which should be covenanted, communitarian, and self-sufficient. The company also worried that a recent massacre of Indians would "redound to the blasting of our own designs"—there would be divine punishment for blood guilt. Sure enough, in 1641 the Spanish invaded Providence Island, terminating the adventure. But the failure was due not to the greed of Philip IV, but to the English inability to impose upon a wilderness a settlement where men had a stake in the land and a say in taxation and expenditure. As in Virginia and Bermuda, chaos had been met with despotism, leading to cries of liberty.[8]

Conflict over liberty and legitimacy, and ungodly ambitions for territory and trade, explain why other Puritan adventures did not go according to plan, either.

By the mid-1630s, it was clear that the Massachusetts Bay Colony would never be a city on a hill, the simple land of faith and charity that, to John Winthrop, shimmered enticingly in England's past. But it was quite like the society he had left behind: acquisitive, unfilial, restless, and fissiparous. After the "great migration" to America came the "great reshuffle," a process of coming and going, exploring and relocating, and pushing back frontiers. Growth diversified New England's topography, increasing its resemblance to home. The coastal territory between Delaware Bay and Cape Cod evoked the East Anglian lowlands, behind which rose hills like those in Dorset, Devon, and Cornwall; beyond lay wooded uplands with fertile valleys reminiscent of the Cotswolds or the Dales of Yorkshire and Derbyshire. Yet whatever comfort and confidence lay in this expansion, it also led to clashes among colonists as well as between them and the motherland.[9]

As in Virginia, in New England the initiative and energy for growth originated in old England—as, for example, when the earl of Warwick bestowed estates along the Connecticut River upon his Providence Company colleagues and others. Most investors were engaged in several projects at once, which spread risk but caused conflicts of interest, and, in America, confrontation. Settlers arriving from England often found their land already occupied by compatriots—internal migrants— and this led to brawls and skirmishes. In 1633, fighting broke out on the Kennebec River when a Providence Company shallop sailed too close to a Plymouth Company fur-trading post. The Providence adventurers were also active in New Hampshire, and in 1635, armed with Warwick's charter, moved into Connecticut.[10]

The impetus for other adventures came from within. In 1635, Peter Bulkeley, a Bedfordshire minister who had been ejected by Archbishop Laud, led sixty men, women, and children, driving cows, horses, and pigs, to prime land twenty miles northwest of Boston, where the native inhabitants had been annihilated by smallpox. The Puritan chronicler Edward Johnson described the journey:

Through unknowne woods and through watery scrampes, they discover the fitnese of the place, sometimes passing through the Thickets where their hands are forced to make way for their bodies passage and their feete clambering over the crossed Trees, which when they missed they sunke into an uncertaine bottome in water, and wade up to the knees, tumbling sometimes higher and sometimes lower. Wearied with this toile, they at the end of this meete with a scorching plaine, yet not so plaine but that the ragged Bushes scratch their legs foully, even to wearing their stockings to their bare skin.

They dried their clothes over fires and sat hunched in hillside burrows, eating roots and berries and fish. Some took heart from the belief that, like the Israelities, they should suffer before entering the Promised Land.[11]

This settling of what became Concord was just the beginning. Families from Newtown, Massachusetts, founded Hartford; Windsor and Wethersfield were the offspring of Dorchester and Watertown, respectively. One writer captured the excitement: "It may well be called, as many will have it, the Aegypt of America from its wonderful fertility, and from the overflowing of the great River Connecticott which, like Nilus, annually overfloweth the banks and thereby inricheth the Soil." Unlike Egypt, the Israelites' land of bondage, Connecticut offered freedoms denied in the Bay Colony: the franchise was extended, and non-church members admitted to public office. Hartford was born after a five-day trek in May 1636. The hundred-odd people led there from Newtown by the Puritan minister Thomas Hooker included his infirm wife, who was carried in a litter, their five children, and some former Essex parishioners. With hardship came entitlement. Hooker was no democrat, but he did believe that power lay with the people.[12]

Earlier that year another colony had been founded by Roger Williams, an associate of both Hooker and Cotton, whose freethinking made him unwelcome in Boston, Plymouth, and Salem, and may have inspired John Endecott to deface the flag. Williams advocated separatism from England *and* Massachusetts (which he said belonged to the Indians). Through a bleak winter, he fled from the authorities who wished to repatriate him to England. In spring, family and friends joined him in Narragansett Bay, the nucleus of Providence, Rhode Island. Williams, whose respect for natives matched his intolerance of moderate Puritanism, built a refuge for fugitives from Winthrop's fiefdom. Meanwhile Windsor, Connecticut, emerged from disputes at Dorchester. In April 1636, Thomas Shepard consoled Dorchester's minister, Richard Mather, with the thought that King David had accepted a prophecy that his temple would have to be completed by his son. And so it was that Increase Mather, born three years later, would one day hold New England's future in his hands.[13]

Richard Mather had arrived the previous summer, moved by "extraordinary seekings unto God" and encouraged by Cotton and

Hooker. Adopting the usual Puritan typology, his farewell at Toxteth in Lancashire was compared to Paul's departure from Ephesus, "with much sorrow, many tears being shed by those who expected to see his face no more in this world." He and his family were almost killed by the hurricane that bereaved Anthony Thacher, but prayer had brought mercy. "It was a day much to be remembered," noted Mather, "because on that day the Lord granted us as wonderful a deliverance, as I think any people had felt." Over the next few months, his old congregation begged him to return, but Dorchester loved him, too, and he loved New England. Let people say what they like, he told Toxteth, but "great was the goodnesse of our God that ever he was pleased to bring us hither." Mather expressed ideas simply and built consensus—skills much needed at Dorchester and throughout New England. By the time he became pastor, around sixty people had already left to settle Windsor.[14]

At Boston, things were even worse—"very tumultuous" was what Henry Vane, installed as governor of Massachusetts, told his father in June 1636. There were encroaching Frenchmen and treacherous Indians, he said, and "the common report is also that the patent is damned, in which regard much unsettlement is like to grow amongst ourselves and great discouragement to the whole plantation." Internal criticism was stifled: a man who called colonists rebels and traitors was made to recant. In the summer of 1637, commissioners from England canceled the Massachusetts Bay Company's franchise, although, because King's Bench—one of the principal law courts—had failed to revoke the colony's charter, all the crown could do was instruct New England's magistrates to continue to govern. England's objections had an abstract quality, but in America the difficulties were starkly real. The court at Newtown vainly resisted "great disorders growing in this Commonwealth," and it was flooded with petitions about wages and prices. Infection ravaged communities, and godly folk consoled themselves that disaster presaged the Second Coming. Thomas Shepard's best friend, dying of smallpox in 1638, murmured that "god shewed him most hideous desolations coming on the church[e]s of god in the whole world," followed by glorious days for his saints.[15]

The apocalyptic cast of American life energized the Puritans. John Cotton gave weekly sermons on the Book of Revelation, spreading an emotional "spiritism" that removed God's elect farther from unregenerate sinners. John Davenport, founder of New Haven, a fledgling colony in Connecticut, believed the colonists' duty was to renounce idolatry and "unite themselves in peculiar and visible Congregations"—completing the unfinished business of the Reformation. As Thomas Hooker put it, England had "cut the head of[f] Popery, but left the body." This vision was sharp but narrow. Exposed to New Haven's congregationalism, Thomas Lechford, an opponent of Laud's policies in England, suddenly warmed to episcopacy—rule by bishops. He appreciated the difficulty of leaving "setled government" to set up "strange government" in America. But far from banishing prelates, were colonists not installing one in every church? And how could mortals discern grace in one man and banish others? The warm glow of election in a few left the rest out in the cold—literally. Lechford saw how "the excommunicate is held out of the meeting at the doore, if he will heare, in frost, snow and raine."[16]

Liberty in America forced distinctions and set boundaries, purifying worship and elevating saints. Like Providence, Rhode Island, New Haven refined an idea gone awry, first in England and then in Boston. John Davenport had arrived painfully at the decision to emigrate, protesting that he, like other harassed ministers, was a loyal subject who had been denied "a safe and quiet abode in my deare native country." Arriving in Boston in 1637, he had moved to Quinnipiac on the north shore of Long Island Sound. On April 25, 1638, he gathered his people beneath a spreading oak, where, evoking Christ in the wilderness, he preached about New Haven's covenant, thus defining and empowering the elect. Their courage and authority, Davenport told John Winthrop, came straight from heaven and permitted them to lead lives of religious truth. Winthrop had long differentiated between "natural" and "civil" liberty: the beast's freedom to be evil and the freedom to obey God. The problem, and the cause of schism, was applying these ideals. Davenport and Winthrop both believed that liberty lay in submission to divine authority; but who was to interpret this and how?[17]

The Chesapeake settlements faced different challenges, although matters of political and religious authority and allegiance were as entwined as they were in New England—or, for that matter, old England—and as likely to cause trouble. Tensions were tied up with economic interests, too, and in Virginia, conservatism had long stymied progress. In March 1632, Sir John Harvey, the governor, informed the Privy Council that food shortages had hindered the Virginians, but that tobacco production had

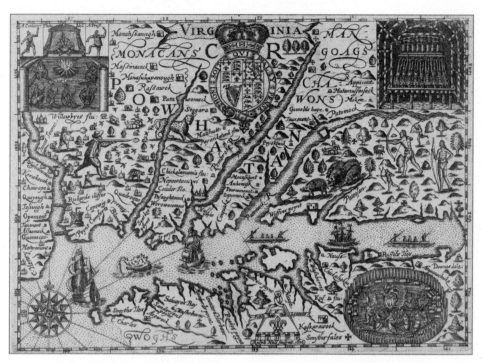

By the mid-1630s, English dominion in Virginia had spread dramatically, bringing conflict. It is unclear whether the colonists to the left and the Indians to the right are firing at wild animals or at each other. The royal crest marks the imperial claim of Charles I. Note also the native "conjuration" (top left).

been suppressed. "This stinking comodity," he said, retarded agriculture, when Virginia should be "as Sicilye to Rome, the Granarie to his Ma[je]ties Empire." Until the colony's wealth could be unlocked, such as through iron and glass manufacture, it would stay poor. Harvey complained of living beneath his station and enduring intolerable suffering.[18]

Harvey was the first of Virginia's crown governors to last more than a few years. He had ended the Indian war, which had been smoldering since 1622, and had made Jamestown a *real* town, improving buildings and public administration. Stability eluded him, however. As in the Caribbean, in Virginia the arrival of large numbers of servants, and increasingly slaves, continued to make for an imbalanced society. This insecurity was compounded by doubt about the legitimacy of government and land ownership, and exacerbated by indecision in London. Men like Harvey, a self-improving naval officer, did not command the respect here that was natural to aristocrats in England—hence his paranoia about status. As ever, the reaction was authoritarianism. For all his achievements, Harvey ran his colony as if he were commanding a ship, and he was greatly disliked. His dream "to recover a new life" for himself and Virginia went unfulfilled.[19]

Another grievance against Harvey was toleration of Catholics, who had proliferated in America. Their figurehead leader was Sir George Calvert, who had left political life in 1625 following the Spanish Match fiasco—the proposed marriage between King James I's son Charles and the daughter of Spain's Philip III—and publicly converted to Roman Catholicism. The king nevertheless made him Lord Baltimore. Two years later, Lord Baltimore finally reached Avalon, his colony in Newfoundland, where he was joined by his wife. He allowed Catholics and Protestants to worship in his house, offending the Anglican minister, who was sent back to England. Gradually, the shining sanctuary in Baltimore's mind dulled. The sea froze, the colony sickened, and Baltimore's home was turned from an ecumenical church into a hospital. "There is a sad face of winter upon all this land," he wrote to Charles I. The king insisted he come home, echoing William Camden with the remark that "new plantations . . . require much greater meanes, in managing them, than usually the power of one private subject can reach into." By the time the letter reached Avalon, however, Baltimore was already heading south. In the autumn of 1629, he arrived in Jamestown, where he refused to swear allegiance to Virginia's government and was asked to leave. Back in England, he set about obtaining a charter and sent a ship for his wife, which foundered off the coast of Ireland, drowning her. "A Man of Sorrows" and failing health, Baltimore died in April 1632. Five weeks later, his patent for Maryland was granted.[20]

Maryland was another example of that most American creation: a risky experiment, drawing on the most recent knowledge of the New World, yet following a conservative social model. The Puritans of Massachusetts Bay aimed to rebuild the primitive church, and Baltimore, like Sir Ferdinando Gorges in Maine, craved a medieval palatinate, a manorial estate traditional in faith and feudal in tenure. But ideals collided, and space was contested. Of greatest concern in Virginia was the fact that Maryland lay inside territory specified in the old charter, and even though this had been revoked, the land had been settled for a generation. Now it looked likely to be annexed and deluged with Catholics. To make matters worse, the fleet that arrived in Virginia in February 1634, naming islands after saints as they drew closer, brought a royal order for Jamestown to supply the Marylanders with livestock.[21]

English planters were not the only ones to give the newcomers a cool welcome. Thomas Cecil, an engraver and a champion of Maryland, related how Cecilius Calvert, the new Lord Baltimore, asked an Indian chief's permission to settle, only to be told "that he would not bid him goe, neither would hee bid him stay, but that he might use his owne discretion." As well as producing the colony's first map, Cecil wrote a book rejoicing in a world of rich black soil (like that at Chiswick near London) and woods free of brush perfect for hunting. Almost thirty pages were devoted to Baltimore's charter, two passages of which a reader underlined in his copy, perhaps with alarm: one referred to the adventurers as "the true and absolute Lords and Proprietories of the Countrey"; the other asserted their right to make, publish, and enact any laws necessary for the province.[22]

However worrying this was in England, where fears were mounting over Charles I's absolutism, in Virginia the threat was immediate. Three years earlier, William Claiborne, a former surveyor at Jamestown, had set up a trading post on Kent Island in the Chesapeake Bay. Dreams of an Atlantic mercantile empire sustained him in the first winter, when men fell sick and warehouses burned down. Without weapons or tools, they lived on oysters and slept in the woods on frozen ground. By the mid-1630s, however, Claiborne had made a powerful alliance with local Susquehannocks. His settlement now had houses, a fort, a windmill, and a forge. Baltimore asserted sovereignty, declaring that Claiborne could trade on the island but did not own it; this Claiborne disputed, denying the land was *hactenus inculta* ("hitherto uncultivated"), as stated in the charter. In 1635, one of Claiborne's ships was seized, resulting in a skirmish. Three of Claiborne's men died. But his resistance proved the clock could not be turned back. The colonist's taste for assemblies, elections, and justice—proclaimed in the name of freeborn Englishmen—meant that even if America had the space to live out nostalgic fantasies, its settlers would not be treated like serfs. The world had changed. Once again, Englishman had fought Englishman in America—the shape of things to come at home.[23]

Sir John Harvey, Virginia's governor, supported Baltimore. In December 1634, he informed London that Virginians would rather slaughter their cattle than sell to Marylanders, and described unrest fomented by a soldier, who "in a fury stamping cried a pox upon Maryland." Harvey's enemies alleged that a Catholic had said "they were come to plant the Catholique Religion therr," and told Protestants "to cease their bawling when they were at prayers." Harvey was charged with, among other things, exempting Marylanders from the oath of allegiance. "Many are drawn to the Romish Religion," it was said, "and Popish Preists are permitted freely to reside in Virginia." He was also accused of failing to protect planters against Indians and of calling the burgesses "Rogues and Newgate birds." Confronted in the assembly, Harvey struck a councillor on the shoulder, saying, "I arrest you on suspicion of Treason to his Majestie." Another responded: "And wee the like to you sir." Harvey's expulsion was backed by powerful London merchants who were interested in Claiborne's project. He had his revenge in 1637, when he returned as governor and seized Kent Island. Claiborne's agents were detained as "cheife incenduaries of the former seditions and mutinies"; one was executed. Other inhabitants surrendered in return for amnesty and land. Claiborne fled. He would have another chance to reclaim his property, but for now he shifted his sights to the Caribbean, where the Providence Company had commissioned him to settle an island off Honduras. This colony lasted until the early 1640s, when it went the same way as Providence, the island off Spain's Mosquito Coast, and was invaded by Spain.[24]

Colonists had numerous enemies, and rarely faced them one at a time: crown agents, religious opponents, economic competitors, foreign adventurers, and Indians. By the mid-1630s, trouble was stirring in southern New England, where a growing population pressured resources and tested native relations. The settlement at Saybrook was a prime example. Its fort stood on steep rock at the mouth of the Connecticut River—like the fort at Jamestown, it was a provocative symbol of English expansion. As ever, its proprietors, including Providence Company members, had high hopes. But the plantation was difficult to run. Farmers worried about grazing cattle on the salt marshes and who might be hiding there. Connecticut was a territory framed by cultural conflict, and, with one exception, its sponsors in England never went there. The governor, John Winthrop Jr., left after a year.[25]

In England, suspicion of Indians was played down to reassure investors and migrants. One writer cheerfully supposed that natives' "correspondency of disposition" with the English proved they had "the same Maker, the same matter, the same mould," and simply lacked art and grace. Thomas Morton, the Plymouth renegade, praised Indian gentility, wishing England's poor could live as decently as they. Keen as ever to make the Pilgrims look intolerant, he added: "Platoes Commonwealth is so much practised by these people." By contrast, seasoned colonists thought Indians dangerous, partly because they were inscrutable. All these men felt they could do was stick together and keep mastiffs for protection. Lord Baltimore also warned Marylanders against copying what one writer called Virginia's "stragling manner of dwelling"—the isolated homesteads and communities dotted along the James River.[26]

Fear bred fear. In June 1636, John Winthrop Jr. heard that the Pequot Indians "in theyr blody mynds towards the English" were about to attack in the belief that the English were themselves preparing to strike. The following month a trader was killed, inciting the Massachusetts pioneer John Endecott to raid Block Island situated off Rhode Island's coast. He and his men burned the houses and grain stores of the Western Niantic people. Endecott then sailed fifty miles west to Saybrook, where the military commander, Lion Gardiner, was incensed that Endecott had stirred up a hornet's nest in Connecticut. Defenses were strengthened and Indians demonized. From Providence, Rhode Island, Roger Williams informed Winthrop that some Pequots had boasted "that a witch amongst them will sinck the [English] pinnaces by diving under water and making holes." Williams prayed "their dreames (through the mercie of the Lord) shall vanish, and the Devil and his lying Sorceries shall be confounded." His respect for the Narragansetts helped win them as allies.[27]

The atmosphere at Saybrook crackled. When Lion Gardiner's twenty-man garrison ran out of food, a party left the fort to get maize and was showered in arrows. They fired their muskets, then fled. Two days later, men collecting hay were attacked, and one was caught as they ran to their boat. Riverside plantations were perilously exposed, and throughout October houses and haystacks were burned. Cows, detested by the Indians as a kind of advance guard of English expansion, came home from the pastures stuck with arrows. In one incident, Pequot warriors chased a pair of waterfowl hunters who were in a canoe. The men paddled frantically, but one was shot and fell overboard. The other, John Tilley from Somerset, managed to split an Indian's head with his paddle before being captured. His hands and feet were cut off and sent to the fort. The Pequots moved close enough to call to the defenders, "mocking and upbraiding them with such words as the English used when by them tortured to death."[28]

Compared to their circumstances and experiences in England, the lives of ordinary Englishmen in America were astonishing. Twenty-two-year-old Nicholas Desborough from Saffron Walden was one of Thomas Hooker's migrants to Hartford. A year later, he was a soldier participating in the most horrific colonial event since the Virginia massacre. In the spring of 1637, an Indian attack on Wethersfield, including the abduction of two girls, precipitated an expedition against the Pequots with Narragansett and Mohegan support. Rumors circulated that the devil had made Pequot warriors arrow-proof; yet, as a Boston diarist recorded, "the lord permitted not satan to hinder the penitration of the swords & bullets of the English." Where is your God now? the Indians asked tormented prisoners. The answer, Puritans believed, lay in the ensuing campaign. One of John Endecott's commanders, John Underhill, wrote a vivid account of how blood had cried to heaven for vengeance against the Pequots, who were driven from their land "by the sword of the Lord and a few feeble instruments, souldiers not accustomed to warre." Providence intervened at every turn: an arrow struck the helmet that Underhill's wife had made him wear, inspiring fresh respect for her opinions and strengthening his love for God. The Pequots, waving bloodstained clothes on poles, were likened to Satan's imps.[29]

After weeks of playing cat-and-mouse, the English advanced. On the night of May 26, a force led by Underhill and Captain John Mason surrounded a fort on the Mystic River as families slept within. Nicholas Desborough and his comrades opened fire with devastating effect, "as though the finger of God had touched both match and flint." The air was filled with screams, "but every man being bereaved of pitty fell upon the worke without compassion," Underhill wrote, "considering the bloud they had shed of our native Countrey-men and how barbarously they had dealt with them." Afterward, the English colonists exalted divine majesty and the bravery of "plebeians." A former innkeeper's servant from Chelmsford had found himself firing at natives until his ammunition ran out, whereupon he beat them with his musket. He changed that day, irrevocably, as did young Nicholas Desborough. Perhaps four hundred Pequots died in the space of an hour, mainly women, children, and the elderly. Subsequently, the warriors, who were away, were executed or sold into slavery—the final destruction of a nation.[30]

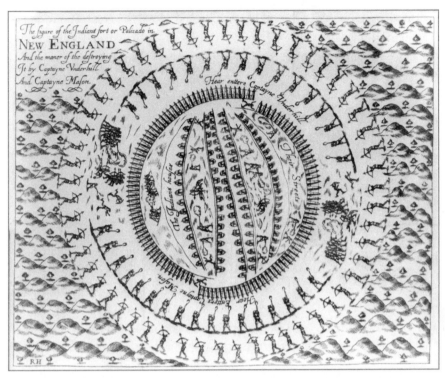

The attack on the Pequots' Mystic River fort was less dignified than this schematic illustration, from a published account by John Underhill, would have us believe. Some four hundred Indians died on that day in May 1637, mostly women, children and the elderly—"a sweet sacrifice," said one Englishman.

News spread fast. At Plymouth, William Bradford was elated. "It was a fearful sight to see them thus frying in the fire and the streams of blood quenching the same," he recalled, "and horrible was the stink and scent thereof; but the victory seemed a sweet sacrifice." This refulgent pride was not universal: Roger Williams, for one, was disgusted by the mutilation of corpses. Stories idealizing New Englanders as righteous warriors that night had the opposite effect in England, where the bloodshed suggested that something was amiss. Far from being "men of resolution that will not bee daunted by ordinarie accidents," as one apologist wrote, it seemed they had lost control. Watching Mohegans tear a Pequot limb from limb, it was suggested, would have made even a popish inquisitor flinch.[31]

Yet England's incomprehension only made frontier Puritans feel more special, and besides, the way was now cleared for expansion into the Connecticut River Valley. John Underhill was unmoved by complaints. As in the time of David, he affirmed, sometimes under God's direction a people must be exterminated. Justifications abounded. When Wesquash, a warrior traumatized at Mystic, turned Christian, his people poisoned him. "Me so big naughty Heart, me heart all one stone," he whispered to Roger Williams as he died. Wesquash is in heaven, Thomas Shepard told a friend in London: "Gloriously did the Grace of Christ shine forth in his conversion."[32]

At Boston, where God's silence was feared more than his interruptions, the war against Satan was fought on several fronts. The Bostonians countered criticism from England (where even Puritans questioned congregationalism); invoked heaven's wrath against heathens (while lionizing Christian soldiers); and silenced dissent in the so-called Antinomian controversy. At the center of the controversy was a merchant's wife named Anne Hutchinson, who, like all "Antinomians"—the term was generally pejorative—believed that faith and "free grace" alone led to salvation, making the moral law of mankind redundant. She had been chastised by the minister at Roxbury, north of Dorchester, as "a woman of haughty and fierce carriage." The daughter of a Lincolnshire clergyman, she used to travel twenty miles to hear John Cotton preach in old Boston and had joined his transplanted congregation. In America, as in England, she cared for her neighbors and attracted followers. According to her nemesis John Winthrop Sr., she believed no "sanctification"—the qualification for church membership—sufficient to prove election. Only the "inner seal of the Holy Spirit," a more exquisite blessing, would confirm it. What Boston's elders called sanctification, alleged Hutchinson, was no "covenant of grace" but a "covenant of works," a contrivance of man, not God. This was strong meat, and soon she stood accused of eighty-two separate errors.[33]

Colonists were alarmed by this toxic reprisal of old doctrinal battles. Never had Peter Bulkeley felt so alienated for "want of brotherly love." Newcomers were particularly shocked: "Oh yee New England Men and Women," implored Edward Johnson in 1636, "who hath bewitched you that you should not obey the truth?" Bewildered, he took comfort in the "soul melting" sermons of Anne Hutchinson's antagonist Thomas Shepard. The slur of witchery cast by Hutchinson's enemies stuck: as a woman, she threatened the status quo and seemed diabolically deluded. She had castigated the church as "the Whore and Strumpet of Boston, no Church of Christ," speaking treason and heresy in a single breath. The Puritan government felt it had to justify its authority and its right to impose discipline, but without seeming tyrannical or anarchic or both. Winthrop had to correct theological error while purging the Antinomians' "Indian" chaos with law and civility.[34]

Anne Hutchinson's story is only partly American, for her beliefs were formed in England. Puritanism did not fragment in the wilderness: it was already fractured and defined by stress. Godly congregations believed in autonomy, but they never agreed on the balance between personal self-regulation (which risked anarchy) and external moderation (which risked tyranny). This instability went beyond the vagaries of the Puritan mission. The society that the migrants had left behind was not solid and staid, as is often assumed, but dynamic and disintegrating, and they brought this spirit with them. It encompassed commercial ambition, fluid mobility, and a yen for debate and innovation. Attempts to preserve tradition, furthermore, led, ironically, to more innovation—especially an explicit striving in America to re-create a culture in decline at home. Ultimately, it was impossible to leave behind England's burdens: they were reconstituted in America, the main difference being that in Boston a minor dispute became a crisis of authority.[35]

Interrogated at the general court in November 1637, Hutchinson confessed to revelations—which John Cotton, her former paragon, called satanic—and predicted that the colony would fall if her warnings went unheeded. She was banished from the congregation and put under house arrest for the winter. It was an exceptionally cold winter. Boston was blasted with snowflakes the size of shillings, the bay froze, and workers lost fingers and toes to frostbite. Storms wrecked ships and people went hungry, weakening a colony already weak in spirit. John Wheelwright, Hutchinson's brother-in-law and fellow dissenter, also banished, set off for Piscataqua in New Hampshire. Hearty and resolute—reputedly his school friend Oliver Cromwell, the future Lord Protector of England, feared him at football more than any army—Wheelwright had defended Hutchinson as a pure woman. Now, in the depths of winter, he started up a community, Exeter, modeled on New Plymouth, where settlers combined "to erect and set up amongst us such government as shall be to our best discerning agreeable to the will of God."[36]

In the spring, Hutchinson, the "American Jesabel," was excommunicated. Her enemies said the excommunication broke the spell she had cast. Only Mary Dyer, a devotee, accompanied her as she exited the assembly. Who is that? a woman present asked her neighbor; the mother of the monster, came the reply. With spreading gossip came a grisly discovery: Dyer's deformed baby, secretly buried five months earlier. The story of the birth, sensationally enhanced, leaked out. The bed had shaken, maids had vomited, and the placenta had been prickly. The midwife was suspected of witchcraft. Witnesses described horns and claws on the tiny corpse; John Josselyn heard it was headless, with scales. Letters were sent to England. Dyer was "a great fomentrix of . . . horrid opinions," her child "a most hideous creat[ure]: a woman, a fish, a bird & a beast all woven together." In Suffolk, Sir Simonds D'Ewes was apprised, and a Devon magistrate wrote an account in his journal. As harbingers of catastrophe, monsters mattered.[37]

A tremor rocked ships in Boston harbor in June 1638; terrified laborers threw down their tools. "Great alterations in the Kingdomes of Europe" were predicted. Anne Hutchinson, who had moved to Aquidneck Island in Narragansett Bay, was said to have discharged a uterine growth that John Cotton described as "twenty-seven several lumps of man's seed, without any alteration or mixture of any thing from the woman." This was God's work: "For as shee had vented misshapen opinions, so shee must bring forth deformed monsters." Hutchinson had raised fourteen children far from Boston's grumbling hive, one named Mahershalalhashbaz, after one of the biblical prophet Isaiah's sons (and the longest word in the Bible). Yet the new settlement became a place of fresh disagreement. In 1642, with her husband dead and Massachusetts threatening to annex Aquidneck, Hutchinson moved her family, and three other families, to a place in New Netherland known to sailors as Hell-Gate. The Wesqueasgeek Indians, who worshipped idols, warned her to leave; but she had heard God's plan and claimed that they were "all one Indian" now. The following year, all four families, saving only a few women and children, perished in a native attack; the cattle—symbols of conquest—were burned in the houses.[38]

New English Puritanism supplied the lay-clerical authority that was also essential to order in England, but no godly consensus dawned. A decade after John Winthrop's arrival on the *Arbella*, dissent was accepted as an Antichristian spirit that could be fought but not eradicated. In 1639, a minister urged Winthrop to resist heretics with an ordinance "to hang up some before the Lord." A man was fined for calling the church covenant "a stinking Carrion and a humane invention," a woman excommunicated for criticizing Anne Hutchinson's sentence.

Sensitivity was acute. John Underhill, Mystic veteran and now governor of Dover in New Hampshire, forced the public humiliation of a separatist preacher, Hanserd Knollys, author of a deprecatory letter to England. "I have sinned in the wildernesse," Knollys confessed, "and tempted my god in the desart"; he was, he said, "a monstrous Imp" of Satan.[39]

By 1640, people in England considered seduction by the wilderness (and its monstrous outcomes) synonymous with colonial life. Tales of social and political distortion in the Caribbean, friction in the Chesapeake colonies (not least over growing popery), and factionalism in Massachusetts, not to mention the horrors of the Pequot War, made American adventures seem daring and deadly. England was discontented; but its colonial annexes, so hopeful in inception, seemed better at replicating the motherland's flaws than at emulating its good qualities. Of course, the migrants remained English, and ideas that mattered at home mattered abroad—prominently justifications for authority and meanings of liberty. Yet the experience of living in America, of hardship and danger and isolation, also cultivated an inner sense of difference and an outward defiance. In England, the New Englander's piety and pride were seen as sanctimoniousness, and visiting sailors mocked Bostonians for it. Boston, however, trusted in providence. In July 1640, the *Mary Rose*, with its jeering crew and twenty-one barrels of gunpowder, exploded in Charlestown harbor. Fiery ghosts were seen drifting over the water, lost souls with all eternity to repent their derision of God's children.[40]

Old England pitied the New England, especially its economic woes, and set up a relief fund. In return, New England pitied England for its religious backsliding and political strife. In the hot summer of 1640, as England anticipated Scottish invasion, William Hooke, a Devon preacher, instructed his American congregation not to take pleasure in the motherland's predicament; gloating, like witchcraft, was a work of the flesh. Lay aside joy at defeating the Pequots, he implored, and grieve for a divided state facing war. Think of the shattered bodies, the widows, the children sobbing for their fathers. And pray for those English brothers and sisters who, excusing New England's faults, had prayed for the colony during the Antinomian controversy. As an act of goodwill, Hooke sent his sermon to a member of Parliament, who published it in 1641. Here Londoners could read that New England's allegiance was to no other authority than that of old England. "Brethren!

Did wee not there draw in our first breath? Did not the Sunne first shine there upon our heads? Did not that Land first beare us, even that pleasant Island [which] but for sin I would say that Garden of the Lord, that Paradise?" It was an impassioned message of fraternal support to a nation on the brink of fratricide.[41]

II
SAINTS
1640–1675

CHAPTER 9

The Distracted Condition of My Dear Native Soil

T HE CIVIL WAR THAT BROKE OUT in 1642 marked a turning point in the history of England and its colonies, the start of a long phase of development where the attitudes and identities of English people across the Atlantic world were redefined by political upheaval at home. Second-generation colonists were forced to examine their consciences and allegiances to decide what being English meant and what it meant to belong physically and spiritually to America. The experience of fighting, rebelling, and experimenting in government broke conventions and created opportunities, even though discord between colonists, crown officials, and Indians became endemic. The desire to make Christian converts of natives did not abate, but it masked a more persistent desire to exploit their land; nor did it inhibit armed response when English ambitions were resisted. Commercial success bred colonial self-confidence but also fatally compromised native peoples. In due course, this grasping spirit and its achievements would also cause the English imperial state to demand the revenues and respect it needed to pursue its objectives.

C harles I made a grave error of judgment. By asserting superiority over Parliament, his father, James I, had provoked discussion of English liberties; but he had never put himself above the laws and customs of the realm. His son's take on divine right was more absolute—and antagonistic. As both regional governors and members of

Parliament (MPs), the country gentry had obstructed James, but they were actively hostile toward Charles. War was not inevitable. The realm from which so many Puritans had fled was actually more secure than anyone realized until Charles resolved to enforce his will in Scotland. The resulting war led to unpopular taxes south of the border and alliances with Scots and Irish Catholics that cast doubt on the king's loyalty to Protestant England.

Parliament in 1640 still sought only recognition of its rights and restrained the use of the royal prerogative. Within a year, however, crown intransigence had led moderates to imagine a more radical solution: England had to be governed according to its ancient constitution, preferably by a monarch, but by Parliament, should the monarch prove unfit. And so Parliament took up arms against Charles I to defend English liberty and true religion—a Protestantism based on scripture rather than the suspect ceremonialism of Archbishop Laud. Opinion was first divided, and then polarized—and upon diverse issues, from doctrinal details to exploitative rents. The quarrels of a generation erupted, shaking and shattering lives and breeding contention between English people at home and abroad.

Thomas Larkham was a chaplain in Cromwell's New Model Army, where he saw firsthand the misery of neighbors and cousins, even brothers, crossing swords. But, as he ministered to his West Country flock in the 1650s, the providence for which he was most grateful was not deliverance in battle, but escaping New Hampshire. He had emigrated in around 1640, settling at Dover on the Piscataqua River. This was the fishing ground once known as Hilton's Point—also Cochecho. It had been bought by the same aristocratic adventurers who were involved in Providence Island and Saybrook, Connecticut. Dover had been without a proper minister since the departure of George Burdett, who had given a sour report on godly New England to Laud. Hanserd Knollys, the self-confessed "monstrous imp," had assumed responsibility for the church until Larkham arrived. Subsequent conflict, like that about to sunder England, centered on disputes over the plantation's identity. Larkham renamed it Northam, after his Devon parish, to expunge associations with Robert Dover, a gentleman whose "Cotswold Olimpick games" had defended traditional pastimes against attack by Puritans. A collection of poems celebrating him had been published in 1636, and Cochecho was renamed by Burdett the following year.[1]

Knollys and Larkham clashed over Larkham's laxity regarding granted church membership. Each had a faction, and the leaders scuffled. Knollys excommunicated Larkham, who complained to magistrates. In an instance of history repeating itself as farce *before* tragedy, Knollys's men marched on Larkham's house in arms, "master K. going before the troop with a Bible upon a poles top, and he or some of his party giving forth that their side were Scots, and the other English." In other words, they had assumed the role of the Scottish Presbyterians, Calvinists who opposed episcopacy, rejected the Book of Common Prayer, and fought Charles I until October 1641. Knollys was fined for rioting and Larkham restored. On his return to London, Knollys became a parliamentarian chaplain. Larkham sailed down the Piscataqua River for the last time on November 12, 1642, overjoyed to be going home. On the same day, the king's army was halted outside London, its first major setback in twelve weeks.[2]

Other godly migrants had also had enough of America. Thomas Lechford, who was appalled by the treatment of New Haven's non-elect, now thought bishops better than rule based on "dark & uncertain interpretations" of scripture, and any monarch preferable to civil war. Like Larkham, he was poised between turbulent worlds, old and new. The choice was no longer Egypt or Canaan: both were evils. The only question was which was the lesser. Lechford sent a fond reappraisal of his homeland to a friend in Somerset in 1640 with a rebuke to New England. American "experiments of governing" meant that colonists "must hurt and spoile one another a great while before we come to such a setled Common-wealth or Church-government, as in England." The reply he received the following summer, as Parliament asserted its right to meet without royal approval, called New England "a perfect model and sampler of the state of us here at this time; for all is out of joynt both in Church and Common-wealth." Lechford reached the same conclusion as Larkham: it was better to be in a familiar land of crisis than to be in a strange land of chaos. By January 1642, he was home for what would be the last months of his life. He wrote a book against "strange government," arguing that England imported American liberty at its peril. Popular elections, he knew, meant anarchy; real liberty was the freedom to respect tradition. He cited the Larkham-Knollys spat as a cautionary tale.[3]

Lechford's book was one of thousands of tracts and pamphlets pouring off London's presses. Lurid tales of axe-murders, witches, and unnatural births were fashioned into propaganda, signs of a world turned upside down and of a providential God (and his instrument the devil) directing human deeds. Mary Dyer's deformed child was reprised for a publication entitled *Newes from New-England*, although the story was five years old. It was illustrated with a naked two-headed Elizabethan gentlewoman, a monster in lace ruffs. It was all extremely alarming, especially outside London, where people relied on rumor and were unequipped to verify the things they heard, or to gauge their significance. In America, sluggish and unreliable transatlantic communications made dispatches from England all the more frightening. Colonists heard snippets of news and filled in the blanks. Susanna Bell's husband, a minister, was in England when she learned that war had broken out. Her neighbors told her, unhelpfully, that he was in danger, and upon his return she begged him not to go back.[4]

New England's elders reacted to the fighting with concern, pity, and condescension. Had not England's sins earned this judgment? In new Dorchester, Richard Mather wept for his native Lancashire, its houses burnt and its people scattered, but he knew that punishment would come wherever "the body and bloud of Christ [was] prophanely administered to such whom the Scripture calleth dogges and swine." Others saw hope in adversity. Anne Bradstreet, daughter of Thomas Dudley, recently governor of Massachusetts, had emigrated on the *Arbella* in 1630. The war inspired her to write a poem where young America frets about Mother England's ailments. Was it, asks the child, the Norman Conquest or the Wars of the Roses that vexed her? Neither, comes the reply: a new commotion after decades of calm. Then the mother says:

> *Oh, pity me in this sad perturbation,*
> *My plundered Townes, my houses devastation,*
> *My ravisht virgins, and my young men slaine,*
> *My wealthy trading faln, my dearth of grain,*
> *The seed time's come, but Ploughman hath no hope,*
> *Because he knows not who shall inn his crop:*
> *The poore they want their pay, their children bread,*
> *Their wofull mother's tears unpitied.*

The daughter offers reassurance: blessed England will regain peace, wealth, and splendor. Letters were suffused with such feelings. Nehemiah Wallington, a London woodturner, wrote to his friend James Cole in New England, afraid he wouldn't see him again but heartened by the apparent demise of episcopacy. The Court of Star Chamber, which had censured Wallington for owning Puritan books, had also been abolished. Cole, seeing only despair, predicted "that God will force many of his out of old England to furnish New England till the Cuppe of his Indignation be overpast."[5]

Actually the reverse happened: emigration ceased and people streamed back. In part, this continued a trend: for years, about one in ten of the emigrants had found that New England was not for them and returned. Like those who came back from Virginia, the New England returnees were disparaging about the American colonies, forcing committed settlers into defensive positions. In 1643, John Winthrop Sr. was gratified by the fate of a repatriated new Dorchester youth who spoke ill of America: "cavaliers" (royalist soldiers) stole his savings. Henry Dunster, a Lancashire protégé of Richard Mather's, scolded men who arrived in New England "upon sudden undigested grounds, and saw not God leading them in their way but were carried by an unstayed spirit." They were likely to give up, he said, "upon as sleight, headlesse, unworthy reasons as they went," and like failed Virginians, they lacked courage. Others, Dunster explained, had never meant to settle and now felt the tug homeward.[6]

Many also heard the call to arms—indeed, half of New England's university-educated men came back to fight. The rest then found themselves not only defending New England but having to justify staying, just as once they had justified leaving England. New Englanders had to decide *who* they were in relation to *where* they were. As royalists ransacked his Dorchester home, the Reverend John White perhaps regretted not emigrating; but when news of the incident reached *new* Dorchester, his admirers there longed to be with him. It was a dilemma. Nathaniel Ward, minister at new Ipswich, was resolute: "We make it an Article of our American Creed," he declared, "that no man ought to forsake his owne Country, but upon extraordinary cause, and when that cause ceaseth he is bound in conscience to return if he can."[7]

The architects of America's Jerusalem disagreed. Civil war cast Winthrop in the role of his critics in 1630: from across the Atlantic, he, too, could argue that it was better to stay and build Christ's church. A joke was told in London in 1642: the devil, looking for a sect, had *faute de mieux* joined the "roundheads" (Parliament's army), the civilian Puritans having all emigrated. But soon many regiments had recruits from English America's first generation: the Puritans had come home to be parliamentarians. (A few years later, they included Winthrop's son Stephen, who insisted his return to England was temporary, but died there in 1658.) Families were divided again. Hugh Peter was Salem's minister, the scourge of the Antinomians—he had lectured Anne Hutchinson at her trial—and a tireless pioneer for New England. His appointment as an agent for Massachusetts in England in 1641 caused despondency in Salem, where his wife, Deliverance, was left to raise their infant child. When war came he served as a parliamentarian chaplain and advised senior commanders. Deliverance Peter became severely depressed and was excommunicated. She was reunited with her husband in England, but they spent little time together before he sent her back to New England, never to see her again.[8]

Lives sucked into the vortex were deranged and destroyed. The first major battle, Edgehill, was inconclusive, and was followed by negotiations into the winter of 1642–1643. When talks failed, the whole country mobilized—more than 100,000 men—to fight a series of engagements into the summer. At first, these suggested royalist superiority. Panic in London, according to reports from Oxford, where the king had set up court, had caused three hundred boxes of valuables, worth over £1 million, to be sent to New England for safety. The ship returned loaded with colonists eager to rejoin their families. Men smuggled out gold and silver coin. Old certainties evaporated. In July 1643, the twenty-five-year-old deputy governor of Maine, Thomas Gorges, wrote to his cousin, afraid of "the distracted condition of my dear Native Soyl for whose prosperity my soul prayeth & desireth an happy union between o[u]r Royall soveraigne & his Subjects." Men like Gorges were distressed by war news; they worried about what else might have happened in the time it took a letter to cross the ocean. Faith and fear sparred inside Gorges until it was unbearable. A few weeks later he arrived home in Somerset, where he became a lieutenant-colonel in a roundhead regiment and MP for Taunton—an allegiance at odds with his kinsman Sir Ferdinando, the arch-royalist he had gone to Maine to serve.[9]

According to its champions, by the early 1640s New England was a land of decency and prosperity. Edward Johnson, the Puritan historian, thought it "a second England for fertilness in so short a space that it is indeed the wonder of the world." Even the poor owned houses and ate meat, and availability of flour, butter, sugar, and apples meant that English fruit tarts had replaced pumpkin pies. At last colonists could follow recipes—"stirring up their appetites with variety of cooking," as Johnson put it. He also told of those who, loathing its strictures, had quit New England for Rhode Island and the Caribbean, craving "a thing very sweet to the palate of the flesh called liberty." What they found, wrote Johnson, was a freedom that promoted tyranny, and so they returned vowing "they would never seek to be governed by *liberty* again." Both observations were misleading. War shrank the agricultural export market on which New England's economy depended, and most New England Puritans believed they already had liberty—a yoke of liberty, explained John Davenport, "whereby you have right in all the outward priviledges of the Gospel." New Englanders were free to follow scriptural truth. John Cotton denied that their liberty equaled anarchy—Thomas Lechford's beef—and was proud of the freedom to love God and one another. The New England way, Cotton believed, averted the "disease of popular liberty," where each man was his own magistrate.[10]

A connected question was what made a true church: inclusive English parishes or exclusive American congregations? The issue was relevant at home. Some parliamentarians believed that New England's arrangements would suit England, and they invited Davenport, Cotton, and others to London. Only the banished Roger Williams went. He sought protection for Rhode Island, arguing that oppressive congregationalism would never restore the primitive church. He befriended the poet John Milton and later Oliver Cromwell. Christ taught forbearance of persecution, Williams argued, not that saints should persecute others to defend truth. This led to a spat with John Cotton, who felt that rulers must sort wheat from chaff and punish the ungodly. Williams questioned whether he should "be denied the common aire to breath in, and a civill cohabitation upon the same common earth; yea, and also without mercy and humane compassion, be exposed to winter miseries in a howling Wildernes." Cotton, he imagined, would be outraged if England expelled him for his opinions. He insisted that the problem was a transatlantic one, not a dispute between old and New England. "Is it not, in this present storm of Englands sorrows, one of the greatest Quaeries in all the Kingdom: who are the true Officers, true Commanders, true Justices, true Commissioners?"[11]

Puritan opinion ranged across a spectrum in both England and America. Samuel Gorton, an eccentric clothier who disrespected everyone except Christ, had arrived in Massachusetts during the Antinomian controversy. Like Roger Williams, he was an outspoken separatist and had been ejected from Boston and Plymouth. In 1646 he wrote about his treatment, observing that inside "pilgrims" who had fled persecution in England festered the intolerance reviled in papists, Jews, and Turks. He began with some doggerel:

> *This Story's strange, but altogether true:*
> *Old Englands Saints are banisht out of New:*
> *Oh Monstrous Art and cunning of the Devill*
> *What hidden paths he goes to spread his evill!*

In December 1642, Gorton and his followers were driven south over a vast wilderness. They waded through knee-high snow and waist-high rivers, and there were no Indians around to offer hospitality. In swamps and thickets, Gorton recalled, "we lay diverse nights together, having no victuals but what we took on our backs, and our drink as the snow afforded unto us." They settled in the salt marshes at Shawomet, which had been bought from a Narragansett sachem. It was a haven for refugees from Massachusetts and Plymouth, hence neither could stomach its existence.[12]

On the eve of the decisive battle at Newbury on September 19, 1643, English troops were also mobilizing in America. Ignoring a summons, Gorton had sent some incendiary letters, one alleging that John Winthrop's court observed "the ancient customes & sleights of Satan"; other comparisons included Herod and Judas, idolators and necromancers, Indians and dogs. He further antagonized Winthrop with his singular recognition of crown authority, by which "we should receive direction for the well ordering of us in all civill respects." When word arrived that soldiers from Massachusetts were coming, Gorton vowed to defend Shawomet. Women and children hid in woods with natives; some would die there. As the rest prepared to flee by river, they were surprised by Captain George Cooke's task force, which included Massachusetts Indians. Some settlers fled into the water; others barricaded themselves in houses. Ordering defenders to hold firm, Gorton helped his pregnant wife onto a boat sent from Roger Williams's Providence, then ran to the redoubt. After Gorton's men refused to yield to "savages," Cooke's militiamen, it was said, began assaulting women and men while Indians ransacked their homes. Witnesses from Providence were "filled with griefe at such a spectacle that the English should shed English blood"—exactly what many in England felt about their war.[13]

A truce lasted into the autumn. Boston refused to negotiate with what was "no State, or Body politique, but a few fugitives living without Law or Government," then grew impatient. The soldiers dug trenches and opened fire. As musket balls thudded into the wattle-and-daub of the redoubt, the defenders hung out the English colors "to shew our allegeance to the State of old England." This, Gorton claimed, only provoked the Massachusetts soldiers, who continued shooting until their lead and powder were exhausted. Cooke won the day and ordered the Gortonites to be killed, but reluctant soldiers sent them to Boston instead. When Gorton informed John Winthrop and his deputy, John Endecott, of his intention to appeal to England, he was told to forget it. Allowed to attend church, Gorton tried to persuade the congregation that their ministers and ordinances were "but mens inventions for shew and pomp, and no other then those silver shrines of Diana." Christ alone was the church; he was incarnate in no earthly thing. A minister tried to talk Gorton and his six co-accused out of their blasphemy, but found that, though poorly educated, "they excel the Jesuites in the art of equivocation." In court, Gorton spoke with open arms: "Yee see good people how yee are abused! Stand for your liberty." The defendants were sentenced to hard labor in shackles through the winter of 1643–1644.[14]

They were freed for their families' sake, provided they stayed away from Massachusetts, Providence, and Shawomet. The world had nowhere for them. In America, Gorton's striving to be English according to law and custom had backfired. By referring to the rebels as "Gortoneans," Boston's elders inadvertently made Indians think they were not English but some enemy nation. As Gorton explained, the Indians called his followers "Gortonoges" and the English "Wattaconoges," supposing the former to be mightier than the latter. The inference that the English civil war involved two tribes, represented at Boston and Shawomet respectively, fitted the perceived facts; so did the inference that a Gortonian majority in England would now help its emissaries defeat the Bostonians governing *ultra vires* in America. In April 1644, the Narrangansetts declared themselves subjects of Charles I, just weeks before he was trounced by Parliament's cavalry at Marston Moor.[15]

Samuel Gorton's war with Boston did not replicate the battle lines in England: neither side was obviously royalist. But it did illustrate colonial incoherence, exposing varied opinions and claims to authority. These differences, it seems, were not primarily products of American experience, however much that would shape them, but were rooted in the Old World and its ideological and theological ferments. Indians were understandably confused by these violently disputatious English-men, and may also have lost confidence in their self-righteous rhetoric. For years, promoters had justified colonization with its presumed bene-fits for native peoples: godly civility exported to blind barbarians. Inev-itably, then, friction between colonists, like England's political divide, both affected progress in conversion work and made it less certain who was civilized and who barbarous.

Edward Winslow, recently governor of Massachusetts, was in Lon-don in 1646 to defend his colony against charges of intolerance. He was astonished to see Samuel Gorton's book, and incensed by its accusation that Puritans were hostile to both the English state and American na-tives. Winslow wrote a riposte. Wilderness evangelism, he argued, was manifestly good for Indians and a fillip to the English church, which wavered at a crossroads. Thomas Lechford had argued that conversion depended on guidance by bishops, but in October 1646 episcopacy was abolished; Laud had been executed the previous year. What remained, Puritans hoped, was simple truth, and here Indian conversions offered fulfillment of an essential Christian purpose and inspiration for the fu-ture. The work would be hard. John Cotton, an enemy of inclusive con-gregations—the old Anglican model—remarked that merely preaching to Indians and "the wilde Irish" would never make them a visible church. Echoing St. Augustine, he argued that all who were *within* the house of God were not actually *of* it, and that heretics and idolaters should be barred: Catholics, sectaries, and native diabolists alike.[16]

Disagreement was inevitable. While at sea in 1643, Cotton's adver-sary Roger Williams composed *A Key into the Language of America*, a linguistic tool and ethnology. He wrote engagingly about the Mauqua-noags, who "make a delicious monstrous dish of the head and brains of their enemies." But the treatise was also a critique of hypocritical Puri-tans and their demonizing ways. "Boast not proud English of thy birth & blood," Williams cautioned. "Thy brother Indian is by birth as good." To prove it he quoted Acts 17:26, where the apostle Paul speaks of how God "hath made of one blood all nations of men for to dwell on the face of the earth." The Indians painted their bodies, but so did ancient Brit-ons. Most importantly, America was not England's opposite, framing rules of civility in the breach, but its mirror: "a cleere resemblance of the world where greedie and furious men persecute and devoure the harmless and innocent, as the wilde beasts pursue and devoure the Hinds and Roes." And how much more true this seemed during domestic wars that were set to claim 180,000 lives. For all their pride, added Williams, countless Christians had no meaningful relationship with God and were steeped in immorality:

> When Indians heare the horrid filths,
> Of Irish, English Men,
> The horrid Oaths and Murthers late,
> Thus say these Indians then:
> "We weare no Cloaths, have many Gods,
> And yet our sinnes are lesse;
> You are Barbarians, Pagans wild,
> Your Land's the Wildernesse."

New England was not Canaan: it was an annex of the old English Egypt. Since the earliest adventures, moreover, the nobility and promise of Indians invited comparison with the stunted degeneracy of the average Englishman.[17]

Missionary work was taxing, its skeptics many, and its gains appreciated more in quality than in quantity. Tales of tearful epiphanies were displayed as proof that New England's eschatological destiny was being fulfilled. A colonist who saw native mourners solemnly pray at a graveside was, he confessed to Thomas Shepard, the minister at Cambridge, humbled by their piety. Indians set good examples: reports abounded of their monogamy, sober manners, and observance of the Sabbath. The most diligent reformer was John Eliot, whose four aims were to spread the gospel, to encourage grooming among the Indians, to teach them restraint in sexual behavior, and to persuade them to lead more settled lives. He described the challenge of trying to reach remote locations. The missionaries had to carry all their food, plus much more to give to poor Indians. One Indian pressed a penny's worth of wampum, polished shells used as currency, into Eliot's hand, which moved the missionary so much that he invited the man to his house, "that I might there shew my love to him."[18]

Yet the potential for conversion had to be weighed against deteriorating relations. A war in New Netherland had caused instability and bred paranoia in New England. "We can sleep in the woods in peace without feare of the Indians," breezed Thomas Shepard. "Our feare is fallen upon them." But this was not true. In 1643, rumors swept through Connecticut of "a generall designe of ye Indians to Cutt of[f] the English"; most feared were the Narrangansetts, enemies to the colonists' Mohegan allies. Massachusetts, Connecticut, Plymouth, and New Haven joined forces, their feelings of isolation exacerbated by the "sad distractions in England," and in June 1644 war broke out with the Narragansetts. Now colonists who were worried about their loved ones in England sent anxious letters to them about their own situation, causing new worries to arise on the opposite side of the Atlantic.[19]

By this time, England's war had become one of attrition, with skirmishes and sieges and widespread hardship and dislocation. In May 1644, John Trappe, a parliamentary chaplain, and his wife wrote from Stratford-upon-Avon to a relative in Hartford, Connecticut. Although Parliament fared well, "things are as bad w[i]th us yet (for the publike) and as far from being better (for ought we see) as ever they were." Their house had been pillaged, his horse taken, and he was imprisoned. At Westminster, Trappe said, Presbyterians jostled with Independents—it was Puritans favoring a state church versus Puritans wanting only self-governing congregations. Worse, society swarmed with "Antinomians, Anabaptists & sects of all sorts." In December, Thomas Shepard, replying to a letter from Suffolk, reacted to what he called England's "sad condition" with the usual combination of sympathy and reproach. He wept for his nation, but confessed, "I have long feared a Sword to come upon that pleasant Land to make this unthankfull and evill generation understand what they would not by the voice of his Gospel." Nehemiah Wallington informed a friend in America that England was in turmoil, and for all Parliament's victories, there was little difference between the two armies in wickedness. The pastor at Rowley, Massachusetts, was told by the son of his former patron in Essex that he feared "an utter desolac[i]on and a totall destrucc[i]on."[20]

Conspiracy crossed the Atlantic. In Salem, spies who had infiltrated "a great partie for the Kinge" uncovered a plot to steal a ship—intelligence noted at Boston by the ever-wary John Endecott. The decade-old feud in Maryland between William Claiborne and Lord Baltimore flared up, with papists becoming the target they were in England. Claiborne had returned to Kent Island, claiming a mandate from England and looking for trouble. In February 1645, a swashbuckling trader named Richard Ingle, wanted in Maryland for dishonoring the king, attacked the colony's capital, St. Mary's, in his ship *Reformation*. Also pretending official authority, he ousted the governor, Leonard Calvert, thus averting Calvert's seizure of parliamentarian property. With Claiborne's probable connivance, Catholic homes were plundered, paralleling events in eastern England. Calvert, who fled to royalist Virginia, did not regain control until 1646. In London the dispute rumbled on. Thomas Cornwallis, who had captured Kent Island in 1635, sued Ingle for illegal appropriation of goods. The House of Lords, which had proposed legislation to protestantize Maryland, heard the case. A petition was received alleging that Cornwallis had stolen children in England to sow Catholic seeds in Maryland.[21]

By the mid-1640s, the defeat of royalists in England and America stood alongside the defeat of Indians by English colonists of varied

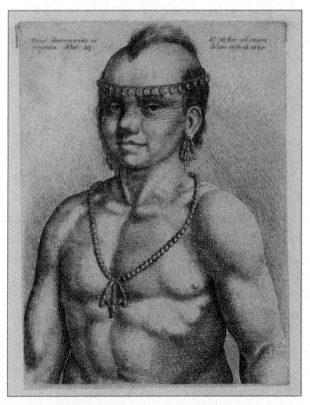

Neither savage nor fool, this Virginian Indian, as seen by Wenceslaus Hollar, exudes strength and self-assurance. And yet the circumstances of the portrait are testament to his people's plight. He is thought to have been a warrior forcibly transported to Amsterdam in 1644.

religious and political complexion. Converting Indians might not unite Englishmen, but fighting them certainly did. A few weeks before New England's Narragansett War began, the Powhatan chief in Virginia, Opechancanough, now in his nineties, had tried one last time to be rid of the English. If his 1622 revolt had intended to hobble them, it had failed: the last twenty years had seen relentless expansion. He attacked in April 1644, an outrage that parliamentary propagandists in England blamed on a royalist conspiracy. A bloody two-year war ended with Opechancanough's sordid death, Indians banned from the Jamestown peninsular, and the deportation of male prisoners over the age of eleven to an island in the Chesapeake. Charles I was declared their sovereign—just as the last royalist garrison in England surrendered.[22]

By then the Narragansett War was also over, God having "framed the hartes of the Indians to submitt." But such providential glosses concealed venality. Like the Virginians, the New England colonists had learned that such crises could advance worldly ambitions, which was why the confederation had sided with the Mohegans: they wanted to expand the beaver trade, which was vital to English interests. As Roger Williams observed, there was not a shirt or a hatchet in America that hadn't come from Europe; but in America, filthy men in smoky huts handled furs "which are after worne upon the hands of Queens and heads of Princes."[23]

B y its conclusion in the summer of 1646, the civil war had affected almost every area of English life. A ballad described a country transformed in attitudes, customs, and laws:

> *Then talke you noe moor of new Ingland,*
> *New Ingland is wher ould Ingland did stand:*
> *Newe furnishd, newe fashond,*
> *New womand, new mand;*
> *And is not ould Ingland growne newe?*

No Puritan celebrating this renewal could ignore the cost. Thousands had died, with many more maimed or scattered. The pain spread to America. When in 1643 William Hudson of Boston went to fight for Parliament, he entrusted his family to fellow church member Henry

Dawson, whose wife was in England. Over the next two years Dawson and Ann Hudson grew close. After servants reported him going to her chamber, the pair admitted sharing a bed but denied having sex. Adultery was a serious offense in Massachusetts, but for want of evidence, Dawson and Hudson were convicted only of "adulterous behaviour" and whipped. By this time William Hudson had returned. He was so sure of his wife's innocence that "he received her againe & they lived lovingly togither." He probably had doubts, but avoided playing the angry cuckold when he could mend his household instead. He also knew how lucky Ann had been: a year earlier, adulterers Mary Latham and James Britton had been hanged.[24]

In the 1640s England became more like New England; amid the disquiet caused by draconian laws, adultery became a capital crime there, too. Thomas Gorges left Maine in 1643 to be with his family in England at a time of danger, but this was not the only reason. He was fed up with America, especially the shortages, the bad winters, and the lack of news. The restrictions on church membership in Massachusetts and its Old Testament laws offended him. Adultery, he believed, was a "private sin" that was undeserving of death, which should be reserved for "national sins." By 1650, however, a "reformation of manners" was under way in England; that was the year adultery became a capital crime. The convergence of moral codes with America is striking, but so is the reluctance to apply the sanction—likewise the fact that in New England, Latham and Britton were the last adulterers to be executed. On both sides of the Atlantic, the "moral economy" softened harsh rules. This did not mean that sexual offenses were condoned, only that most people found shaming rituals more appropriate than execution. George Burdett, Thomas Larkham, and Hanserd Knollys, principals in the quarrel at Dover, were all disgraced by adultery charges.[25]

Sexual offenses assailed basic tenets of order, in New England and now also in England, where the abolition of ecclesiastical courts opened the way for active civil punishment of immorality. After twenty years of Caroline decadence, many New Englanders believed that England had some catching up to do. The Massachusetts preacher Nathaniel Ward declined to go to England to find a wife because of the offensive continental fashions favored by English women. "I have no heart to the voyage," he sniffed, "lest their nauseous shapes and the Sea should worke too sorely upon my stomach." He pitied Englishmen whose wives wore French wire-framed dresses and face-concealing capes, blaming a permissive society for such excesses. Contrasting New England's "Liberty of Conscience" (freedom from sin) with England's "Liberty of Error," he called England "nothing but a *prison* for Conscience." Unless England now took the opportunity to reform itself, the state would become a bear-pit, its church "the Devills Dancing-Schoole." In all his years in America, Ward claimed never to have heard swearing, seen a man drunk, or known more than a couple of cases of adultery.[26]

The crimes of William Plain of Guilford, Connecticut, who was executed in May 1646, began with sodomy committed in England. In America, it was alleged, he taught boys how to masturbate. John Winthrop Sr. said Plain "did insinnuate seedes of Atheism, questioninge whither there was a God &c." He was, New Haven's elders concluded, "a monster in humaine shape." England's sins had been transplanted to America and were flourishing there. The discovery of pedophiles at Boston led Winthrop to reflect that, "as people increased, so sin abounded, and especially the sin of uncleanness." And yet, he added, "the providence of God found them out." The same went for men who buggered animals—and in the New World a surprising number of them came before colonial courts. Their punishment served ideological ends, demonstrating not just heaven's expository power but the Holy Spirit's effectiveness in moving malefactors to penitence. William Hatchet of Salem, "a very stupid, idle and ill-disposed boy," apparently committed bestiality with a cow on the Sabbath, but in prison he underwent conversion. As he stood with a rope around his neck, the heifer was led out before him, upon which Hatchet "brake out into a loud and doleful complaint against himself," regretting his rejection of God's grace.[27]

Anti-Calvinists linked Puritanism with insanity, and certainly ceaseless introspection and the uncertainty of predestination exerted considerable psychological pressure. In New England, and increasingly in England, Puritan culture made sinners reflect on their conduct; it also hurt vulnerable minds, especially when its tenets were installed at the center of public life. On July 23, 1643, Anne Hett, a cooper's wife, was readmitted to Hingham's church after a year of excommunication. Instances of her "willfull Contempt of gods holy Ordinances" included blasphemy, disobedience, and attempted murder. Her problems dated back to 1637, when her fear of reprobation spiraled into desperation, causing her to drop her child down a well. Returning home, she had said she was now sure to go to hell. The child was rescued. Five years on, Hett remained "in a sad melancholic distemper near to phrensy."

She hurled another of her children, aged three, naked into a muddy creek. When the infant scrambled back, she threw it in farther, and there it stayed until rescued. Asked why she did this to her own off-spring, "she would give no other reason for it but that she did it to save it from misery," adding that her sins could not be repented. Thus, remarked John Winthrop, did Satan exploit human imperfection. He recorded other stories. For example, Dorothy Talby, who "through melancholy or spiritual delusions" killed her daughter, Difficult, was hanged. And then there was the man who leaped from a high window, crying, "Art thou come, Lord Jesus?" before vanishing into the snowy night.[28]

Anxiety about salvation—a need to know and the impossibility of knowing—was worst for New Englanders wishing to join a church. How should applicants convince existing members they were God's chosen saints? At Cambridge, Thomas Shepard kept a remarkable record of "confessions"—testimonies of grace elicited by his question-ing, in an atmosphere not coldly inquisitorial but rapturous. This was Shepard's preaching style: "close and searching, and with abundance of affection and compassion to his hearers." In contrast to his Essex hellfire, in America he became, in Edward Johnson's words, "that soule ravishing Minister," a mystical traveler across spiritual and geograph-ical planes. He was self-lacerating, especially after the death of his wife, and ruled by guilt. But his mind turned in an endless circle of joy, doubt, resolve, and joy—driven by hope and fear.[29]

Like gallows speeches, Shepard's confessions were potted life his-tories, transitions between ignorance and enlightenment, England and America. They captured experiences of emigration, not least its ag-ony and the courage with which migrants bore it. Nicholas Wyeth, a mason, related in January 1645 how his decision to leave Suffolk had caused consternation among his friends and despair in his wife. "I went through many difficulties before and when I came to sea," he said. He had sailed with his wife and two children, one of whom died at sea, in 1638. "God's hand hath been much against me," he said, perhaps because of sin, "for I have gone on formally and coldly since I came here." His failing as a Puritan was a deficit in love. Around the time he confessed, Wyeth's wife died in childbirth. He faced the tragedy like a true saint, with deference toward God and adherence to Christ. Wyeth was admitted to the church, remarried, and by 1658 had five children. He had arrived at last.[30]

All congregational churches made confession a condition for admission. In 1648 at Chelmsford, John Fiske recorded how a woman "held forth a discovery of her accursed condition in the state of nature." The best tales exaggerated before-and-after contrasts. Nicholas Wyeth's adult life, like Shepard's own, had begun in idleness and iniquity; how much greater, then, his redemption. Racial disadvantage maximized the power of testimonies, furnishing Shepard and others with what they needed to confound critics in England and America. At Dorchester, a black maid convincingly displayed "her knowledge of the Mysteries of Christ and of the work of Conversion upon her Soule." Yet it was success in Indian conversions by which the New England ministry would be judged. A young man captured during the Pequot War became a servant at Dorchester, where John Eliot taught him to read and write, and he, in turn, taught Eliot his Algonquian language. In 1649, when Edward Winslow heard his story, the youth was preparing for admission to the church.[31]

Whatever solace and strength Indians found in Christian counseling, it completed their loss of innocence. Henry Dunster told of native children happily acculturated in English homes, reluctant to resume their old lives. Most gratifying to Dunster was that they were "convinced of their sinfull and miserable Estates, and affected with the sense of Gods displeasure and the thoughts of Eternity, and will sometimes tremble and melt into teares at our opening and pressing the Word upon their consciences." The lake of brimstone was forever in view. A minister at Salem was pestered by an Indian who knew his Bible, yet kept saying, "Me are [going to hell] and walke in fire," because he struggled to really know Jesus. A maidservant, also at Salem, was observed "crying out with abundance of teares, concluding that she must burne when she die . . . and like to be miserable for ever, unlesse free Grace should prevent it." Thus Anne Hett's English madness, her weeping and gnashing of teeth, was gifted to nonwhites, a spiritual colonization to accompany the physical annexation of their land.[32]

The mid-seventeenth century demonstrated as never before the reflexivity of the old and new English worlds: it was shown in familial anguish and anxiety, shared ideas and values, reverse migration from

New England, and a motherland adopting the ways of colonial Puritans. Idealized visions of Englishness could be combative, whether in England or America, and these ideals, when backed by political power, could be subordinating to whites as well as to Indians and Africans. The events of the late 1640s and early 1650s reinforced this picture. Civil war was ignited again in the British Isles, leading England into a truly revolutionary era with profound consequences for its colonies.

CHAPTER 10

Marching Manfully On

T HE COLONIAL PARADOX was that conservative aims—restoring hierarchy on the land, rebuilding economic stability and charity, and recovering pure religious values—demanded vast creativity, motivation, investment, and thus change. Remaking England in the New World, and the retention of Englishness, were never-ending, exhausting endeavors whose achievable limits were nonetheless becoming clear by midcentury. For all the cultural confidence of the English, no singular, objective vision could be imposed. This was partly because of innate differences between Englishmen, but it was also a result of prevailing social and political conditions in America and the unnegotiable facts of its natural world.

There was no proper resistance to the wilderness. Upon an apparently blank canvas, adventurers unavoidably painted themselves into the picture, often in grotesque poses of transformation. Godless savagery surfaced in colonists as much as in the Indians, whose human nature was revealed to be uncomfortably close to that of the colonists themselves. Lines between degenerate migrants and redeemed natives were alarmingly blurred, most graphically in the juxtaposed forms of English witches and Indian saints. Nor were colonists at peace with each other, since their disputes derived from constitutional traumas at home. The Battle of Naseby in June 1645 had initiated a run of parliamentarian wins leading to overall victory the following year. Yet the future looked uncertain. Some English settlers neither wanted to come home nor could bear to stay. It was a time to weigh options as carefully as prospective emigrants once had in Caroline England.

Henry Whitfield had migrated to Connecticut in 1639. Over the next eleven years, his finances had deteriorated. By then he was nearly sixty, and he found the work and the winters unbearable. Leaving England had been difficult—he was the clergyman whom John Cotton and Thomas Hooker had persuaded to come—yet he had stolidly founded the town of Guilford, transplanting families from Surrey at his own expense. He had built a stone house to serve as a redoubt, should attacks on Saybrook spread. He was, said a fellow minister, "a soul-searching preacher" to his flock, a man who had marked his departure from Guilford in August 1650 with "tears and unspeakable lamentations." But God did not want Henry Whitfield to leave America just yet, or so it seemed. As his ship neared Cape Cod, contrary winds forced it to the island of Martha's Vineyard.[1]

Whitfield met the pastor, Thomas Mayhew, son of the namesake governor, at their small plantation. The Mayhews had a unique respect for Wampanoag rights, allowing them to convert to Christianity without swearing allegiance to England, as required in other colonies. Whitfield was introduced to an Indian preacher named Hiacoomes, whom he judged "a man of sad and sober spirit." Seven years earlier, he and Mayhew had visited Pakeponesso, a chieftain, who was so incensed over the conversion that he hit Hiacoomes in the face. "Here comes the English man," Indians mocked—meaning Hiacoomes, not Mayhew. Pakeponesso's death by lightning strike, and rampant disease among the Indians, were seen by the Indians as punishments for not stopping such conversions. Hiacoomes was defiant, his reward an English primer and a place in heaven. By the mid-1640s, his apparent immunity to disease had seduced others from what Whitfield called the paw-waws' witchcraft. An attempt to stab Hiacoomes with an arrow failed: it glanced off his eyebrow and slit the assailant's nose. Martha's Vineyard was rent by spiritual warfare, with Hiacoomes at the center of the controversy. When his baby died, he did not engage in the usual "hellish howlings" of Indians in mourning, but instead exhibited "a patient resigning of it to him that gave it." Meanwhile, Mayhew, in whose image this saintly Indian was made, persisted in his mission. In 1647 he persuaded some Wampanoags not to use "sorcery" on a sick man.[2]

Whitfield spent ten days at Martha's Vineyard probing natives' Christian understanding. He admired how Mayhew supported his family as a laborer, and observed him as he catechized native children. Arriving in Boston, en route to England, Whitfield visited John Eliot at Roxbury and heard him preach in Algonquian. Like Mayhew, Eliot had had successes: Indians kept the Sabbath, and "a great Witch" had been converted. Other evangelists were thus gratified. John Wilson had led Indian chieftains in prayer, relishing the glory of "a company of perishing, forlorne outcasts, diligently attending to the blessed word of salvation." Ignoring the onset of winter, Wilson returned to these Indians three times, helping them grasp the "wonderfull things which they never heard of before." Some questions were thorny, such as why the Indians had so long been benighted. The Englishmen skirted around the dispersal of Noah's children "because it was too difficult." One Indian wept during prayers, making his teachers cry too, and they parted, "greatly rejoicing for such sorrowing." On another visit, the Indians were taught about witchcraft; they in turn revealed that paw-waws dreamed of a great serpent, for which Puritans had an obvious demonological interpretation.[3]

Yet all ministers and converts faced the same hostility as Mayhew and Hiacoomes. Indians who came to Weymouth hell-bent on undoing Eliot's work there, though silenced by smallpox, illustrated what missionaries were up against. Nor was that the only barrier. Englishmen in England and America felt that time and money were being wasted. "They have brought the Indians into great awe," said one in 1651, "but not to any Gospell knowledge." The preachers retorted that the work would take time, like colonization itself, protesting that they were hampered by colonists' impiety. Whitfield imagined the irony of a Day of Judgment where converts were covered in God's glory as the English were plunged into "Indian darknesse." So when Indians asked John Wilson whether Englishmen were ever as ignorant as they, he replied that some were *still* that bad—no better than drunken savages. Wilson also accused critics on the other side of the Atlantic of having "more spleene then judgement," and an uncharitable blindness to the natives, who found themselves trapped between the fear of damnation and their fellows' wrath.[4]

The solution, missionaries believed, was civility in America and publicity back home. As far back as Alexander Whitaker's transformation of Pocahontas, habituation to English culture had been considered essential for understanding the gospel. So John Wilson was pleased when some Indians realized the "vanitie and pride" of wearing long hair, and when a chieftain's son donned a suit to study at Dedham. Thomas Shepard, who spent time with Indians at Nonantum, west of

Cambridge, was convinced that one native's curiosity about the Bible
had been awakened when he started wearing English clothes. Like
Wilson, Shepard was bombarded with questions. Where was Christ?
Did Satan exist before man? Could the soul escape from an iron box?
How would they know if their faith was strong enough? Accounts of
these experiences were sent to England to attract support for missionary work. A book by Shepard, published by a Puritan preacher in 1648,
was dedicated to Parliament so that the nation "might bee stirred up to
be Rejoycers in, and Advancers of, these promising beginnings."⁵

Political backing helped evangelical ventures, and the timing seemed
propitious. Henry Whitfield's dawning light banished England's
darkness as well the Indians', illuminating the transatlantic extent of
Christ's kingdom. Some years earlier, a petition had been received at
Westminster arguing that England must "endeavour to make millions
of those silly seduced Americans to heare, understand and practise the
mysterie of godlinesse." Composed by a Northamptonshire minister, it
was signed by seventy clerics in a dozen counties. Since then England
had entered a new age of religion. In 1643, Parliament made a moral
and military alliance with Scotland, the Solemn League and Covenant;
it presented a united front against popery that was applauded in New
England. Although the alliance did not last—the Scots joined the king
and were defeated in a second civil war in 1648—England would soon
be a republic, free to install Puritan government for itself. It would
also, colonists hoped, become more favorable to godly projects in the
colonies.⁶

So Thomas Shepard's stories were well received in London, inspiring
an ordinance "for the encouragement and advancement of Learning
and Piety in New England." The work was delegated to the Massachusetts agent, Edward Winslow, to whom it was supremely important.
A rabbi in Amsterdam was convinced that the Indians were exiled
descendants of Abraham, believing this conclusion was evident in remnants of the law of Moses; Henry Whitfield, who addressed his own
book to Parliament, had even heard of an encounter with circumcised
natives. A member of the Westminster Assembly of Divines wrote
that either "the Jewes did Indianize, or the Indians doe Judaize, for
surely they are alike in many, very many, remarkable particulars," adding that if the Indians *were* Jews, they must not be neglected, because
the saints' thousand-year reign during the millennium predicted by
the Book of Revelation would not begin until their redemption. New

Edward Winslow (1595–1655) arrived on the *Mayflower* and served three times as New Plymouth's governor. He also tirelessly promoted New England in London, where this portrait was painted in 1651. The letter from home he holds is signed by his "loving wife Susanna."

England might yet be Albion's final incarnation after its pagan and unreformed Christian phases, and the fulfillment of its destiny. John Eliot speculated that Indians and Englishmen were cousins: the former descendants of Noah's son Shem, the latter of Japheth.[7]

But Winslow was disappointed by a Parliament too wrapped up in its own problems to start building the new Jerusalem at home, never mind in America. Puritans had to be content with grassroots activism and benevolent schemes. In July 1649, Stephen Winthrop, by then a soldier in Suffolk, wrote proudly to his brother in Connecticut that "the conversion of the Indians with yow mak[e]s New England very famous." That year the Society for the Propagation of the Gospel in New England, or New England Company (NEC), was founded, and in October it urged English ministers to raise money for schools to free the devil's slaves. Many Indians, the company said, had already "broken their Covenant with Death, and League with Hell, by renouncing and detesting all charmes and sorceries."[8]

The NEC's charity began at home: England's poor would gain from the New World, just as Indians had gained from the old. Throughout the 1630s, communities had paid for paupers to emigrate: apprentices were entrusted to adventurers, boys were equipped for Virginia, passages to New England were paid from parish funds, and so on. In 1642, Hugh Peter and Thomas Weld had used money collected in London to transport twenty children to Boston, inspiring a man who bequeathed £120 for another twenty children. Now the operation grew. In the NEC's first year, it spent £800 sending children to New England—it was the "way of God," said Weld. Parish collections multiplied. At Earls Colne in Essex, Thomas Shepard's former home, the minister, Ralph Josselin, pledged £5 in 1651 and again in 1652—noting in his diary that it was "a loane to the lord," and then, "nay tis a debt." Josselin donated the sum of £54 11s 10d in 1653, enough to buy a small herd of cows. Gifts were also made in kind, including clothes, bedding, and Bibles, the latter much needed in Martha's Vineyard. During the 1650s, old Dorchester regularly dispatched children and families to New England.[9]

Christian love, godly reform, and poor relief converged, with a colonial dimension. Yet it did little to stop the political rancor that since the later 1640s had been dividing not the English and the Indians, nor England and America, but English people on the two Atlantic shores.

The first ship to leave New England in 1647 was engulfed by a storm. In pitch darkness, a woman burst into the captain's cabin demanding to know if he was carrying any complaints to Parliament from disaffected colonists. It was usual to suspect Jonahs—but pieces of paper? She was worrying about a warning that had been delivered in a sermon the previous November, so to appease her, a petition criticizing the regime in Boston was found and consigned to the waves. Although the winds persisted, the vessel arrived safely a fortnight later, narrowly avoiding shipwreck off the Scilly Isles. For this mercy the passengers thanked God and the hysterical woman.[10]

For all their hostility to superstition, New Englanders were rather prone to it. The Jonah petition originated in protests at Hingham against Boston's restrictions on the town's self-government, for which it was fined £100. When the marshal came to collect, the minister, Peter Hubbard, had dismissed his warrant as without royal authority, arguing that, by its patent, Massachusetts had no more authority than an English urban corporation. Hubbard was fined £20, inspiring a petition in May 1646 by Dr. Robert Child, an investor in the Company of Iron Works, accusing Boston of arbitrary rule contrary to English law. In a sense, then, Puritans were being lumped together with the king from whom they had fled. New England, complained Child, had no settled government through which most people could enjoy "Lives, Liberties and Estates according to our due Naturall rights as Free-born subjects of the English nation." Decent men at Hingham and elsewhere were being denied the right to vote or hold office, yet were being taxed. Given the fact that so many had been "banished from our native home and enforced to lay our bones in a strange wildernesse," they should at least expect to enjoy freedoms they had taken for granted in England. New England was a colony, not a republic, even if some inhabitants now called England a foreign country. This was the document that disappeared into the Atlantic that winter night. Child had been clapped in irons for sedition, and John Cotton had preached the sermon from which the woman inferred that ships carrying petitions were in peril.[11]

In April 1647, a pamphlet by Child's brother, John, an army officer, recounted the whole story, refuting the ship's providential salvation. Apparently, the jettisoned petition was a copy, leaving the original to be safely delivered. In reply, Edward Winslow, still fighting in New England's corner in London, disputed the story told by John Child, denying that Cotton had advised that petitions be sacrificed at sea. Winslow's real point, however, was that New England was unlike English shires and corporations because it had no MPs, "by reason of the vast distance of the Ocean, being three thousand miles from London." Without representation, passive acceptance of English laws made it impossible to uphold the liberty to which Englishmen were entitled. As for the people of Hingham, Winslow supposed that Satan, envying their happiness, had "cast a bone of division amongst them" to stir rebellion against their masters at Boston.[12]

This strange incident reveals how Massachusetts maintained its power and how it viewed itself by the late 1640s. Paradoxically, it was impossible for the colony's elders to defend liberty without seeming tyrannical, which then made them seem weak. Colonists cherished

England's ancient constitution, even as institutions tottered and fell. Critiques, notably from the Gortonites, reached sympathizers at home, including royalists who doubted New England's loyalty, Anglicans who accused it of separatism, and conservative Puritans who considered it a breeding ground for dangerous radicals, not a city on a hill. In November 1647, Edward Symmons, a minister of "the Ancient, Orderly and True Church of England," wrote a pamphlet skewering the crown's migrant enemies. For all their cries of persecution, he said, they had actually left from pride. During the wars, many returned "to help forward the destruction of their native soile and Country," a violent habit acquired in America. "We hear of few of the Heathens converted by them," Symmons added, "but of many masacred."[13]

Edward Winslow's spat with the dissident Samuel Gorton lingered through these years. Freed from prison in 1644, Gorton had gone to London to complain about Massachusetts, returning with the earl of Warwick's protection. Shawomet, his breakaway community, was renamed for his patron. Winslow could do little except defend the status quo and castigate Gorton. Citing various documents, he related how Gorton had polarized Roger Williams's Rhode Island community, to the extent that the two factions had armed themselves and had almost come to blows. Williams, who calmed the situation, complained to John Winthrop about Gorton's "bewitching and bemadding poor Providence." Yet the battle lines were indistinct. In 1647 Williams declared that "the foundation of civil power lies in the people," from which should arise "a government held by the free and voluntary consent of all, or the greater part, of the free inhabitants." This was not a democratic manifesto—not all inhabitants were free—but its tone contrasted sharply with Boston's pronouncements. Winslow's anti-Gortonian polemic was republished in London as *The Danger of Tolerating Levellers in a Civill State*, a title reflecting anxiety not about America but about agitators for popular sovereignty in England.[14]

Life there had been fitful since Parliament's victory. Nathaniel Barnardiston wrote from London to John Winthrop in March 1647 describing the scarcity of love and charity, for which New England was partly responsible. "This seede of pride and contention," he said, "I conceave had his first beginning in your partes; the chang[e] of the soyle hath unhappily made it more spredding here by meeting with civill discentions." Meanwhile, the Massachusetts saints were fixed on the passing of the first generation. In July, Thomas Hooker, the founder of Hartford, Connecticut, died. "Our sunne is set, our light is eclipsed, our joy is darkene[ss]," a mourner wrote to Thomas Shepard at Cambridge. "We remember now in ye dayes of our calamitie the pleasant things w[hi]ch we enjoyed in former times." Shepard was more sanguine, grateful for his American haven, "when all England and Europe are in a flame." One of Winthrop's correspondents rehearsed the reasons for going to New England, including religious reform, pursuit of liberty, and Indian evangelism, "which mercy if attained in any considerable measure will make us goe singing to our graves." Such memories were invigorating.[15]

The late 1640s brought misery to England. Trade remained disrupted, harvests failed, and prices and taxes were high; demobilization swelled an already underemployed workforce. The administrative war machine was not dismantled, and it continued to operate outside the common law. After the autocracy of the king, there was the autocracy of Parliament. A national Presbyterian church imposed rules no less irksome than its Anglican predecessor's, and many Puritans chafed for liberty to worship independently in congregational churches, as in New England. The split in English Puritanism, already visible a generation earlier, became a chasm. In religion and politics it seemed the war had solved nothing; and yet proposals for what to do next were incoherent, ranging from the radical—in effect, revolution—to the conservative—restoration of monarchy. Parliament wanted the latter, but a determined minority in the army pressed for the former.

Charles I, as uncompromising as ever, was tried and beheaded as a traitor in January 1649. His final speech echoed his political opponent, John Winthrop: the people's freedom consisted in law, advised the king, "not for having a share in Government," which was none of their concern. This was liberty Old and New World style: an obligation to obey a paternalistic ruler. England became the republic that many felt Massachusetts already was. A constitution was drawn up, and the House of Lords, the established church, and the monarchy formally abolished. The groan at Whitehall as the axe fell rippled across the Atlantic. There the king's hubris and the second civil war had been followed like an unfolding prophecy. In Boston, the silversmith John Hull considered the execution "a very solemne & strang[e] act," a work of God.[16]

The colonists' feelings were ambivalent: whatever they thought of Charles I, royal authority legitimated their charters. New England had tried not to take sides in the conflict, although its sympathies were obvious. Lapses of neutrality, as when New Plymouth seized a royalist ship and removed its coat of arms, did not help; the town also took down the inn sign at The King's Head. Allegedly, Boston's elders were dining together when news of Charles's execution arrived. According to an eyewitness, "one asked if it were good newes; another answered the best that ever came and no contradiction." On May 26, Roger Williams sent John Winthrop Jr. "high tidings" of the bloody revolution, perhaps unaware that eight weeks earlier another death had dealt Winthrop a greater blow: that of his father. John Winthrop Sr. had personified the colonization of Massachusetts, its visionary creator and guiding spirit. In August, Thomas Shepard followed him to the grave. His dying words were: "Lord I am vile, but thou art righteous."[17]

The sense of a closing era, exemplified by the deaths of Winthrop and Shepard, and that of Charles I, was reinforced by dwindling immigration. England's population, which had risen to more than 5 million—25 percent up from the year 1600—leveled off at midcentury, the high point of departures to the New World. Many English people also came to feel that, for all its faults, England was the right place to be. Edward Winslow disagreed, calling on merchants, seamen, artisans, and husbandmen to abandon it, the same advice royalists gave to roundhead rabble-rousers. Edward Johnson predicted another exodus to America, but Robert Child's assessment proved more accurate: the English "at this time are too forward to be gone [from New England], and very backward to come hither."[18]

It was different in the Chesapeake, where labor shortages led Parliament to improve terms for the transportation of servants. Many royalists left republican England in 1649 for Virginia, where loyalty to the crown had been as poorly disguised as support for Parliament had been in Massachusetts. The governor, Sir William Berkeley, publicly expressed shock at hearing about Charles, in whose household he had once lived.[19]

Henry Norwood related how he and two fellow cavaliers had fled England like "a place infected with ye plague." At first things went well. Stopping at an island, Norwood gorged on peaches and admired an Indian woman, whose son resembled the king as a boy. But then they hit a storm. It assaulted passengers "w[i]th ye fresh terrour of death," worrying even hardened mariners. As the winds subsided, they surveyed the drifting hulk, its masts gone, and soon were parched and starving. They fought over vermin. According to Norwood, a pregnant woman died after her offer of twenty shillings for a rat was declined, although the royalists managed to celebrate Christmas with a pudding made from flour-tub scrapings and dried fruit. Survivors reached an island off Virginia, where Indians fed them spit-roasted meat. At the travelers' departure, Norwood recalled, the chieftain "inclosed me in his Armes with kind Embraces not without Expressions of Sorrow to part beyond the Common rate of new acquaintance." He reached his destination, where he preserved the memory of the Indian king along-side that of a royal martyr from another world.[20]

Questions of war and revolution—liberty and tyranny, authority and anarchy—were thrashed out in America for England's sake, but they also framed uniquely colonial disputes. Exile may have made the second generation less like the mass of people at home, yet it made *some* of the former more like *some* of the latter, given, first, that their compatriots were not at peace, and second, that as English America grew, so did differences between colonists. They competed for land and power, countered dissent with orthodoxy, and detected diabolical sins in one another. The ocean divided the English in the 1640s, but not as much as politics, economics, and religion did.

The winter of 1649–1650 was biting, prompting reflection and resolution. Smallpox afflicted hundreds of New Englanders, leading godly families like John Endecott's at Salem to treat survival as a special providence. Storms lashed coastal settlements for weeks on end, and in January a ship was lost with all hands. From Roxbury John Eliot complained to Henry Whitfield that "the sharpnesse and depth of snowes this later part of winter did more [to] shut up and hinder intercourse then ever I knew in New-England." At Providence, Rhode Island, Roger Williams praised God, "who hath provided warme Lodging, Foode and Clothing, and so seasonable and Admirable an element of Fire for his poor creatures." Warding off sin, though, was harder. "I grieve that my deare Countrimen of Conecticot are so troubled with that filthy Devill of whorish practices," Williams wrote to John Winthrop Jr. He doubted that New England could ever enforce its laws as strictly as Israel had.[21]

Critics in England, of course, thought this was exactly what they *were* doing: "They punish sin as severely as the Jews did in old time," commented one, "but not with so good a warrant." England's godly republic shared some Bostonian ideals but not the will to apply them. Echoing the ballad about the countries' reversal, John Clarke, a Baptist doctor in Rhode Island, wrote to Parliament "that while old England is becoming new, New-England is becoming Old"; by "old," Clarke meant "persecuting," especially of sects like his, which in England's tolerant commonwealth were now flourishing. His ally Roger Williams believed the spirit of Christ had deserted the Massachusetts elite, who, no longer oppressed themselves, had become the oppressors. To those he criticized, however, the sectary was just another sinner: an enemy of the state, beguiled by the devil, and damned. Legislation to promote godly instruction, the "Old Deluder Satan Law," had been followed in 1648 by publication of the Massachusetts legal code, a blend of English statutes and Mosaic law. Fifteen felonies were specified, including adultery, rape, bestiality, blasphemy, and apostasy.[22]

The second crime on the list was witchcraft. No reference was made to the English statute of 1604, as would have been proper, only prohibitions in Exodus, Leviticus, and Deuteronomy. News of a major witch-hunt in East Anglia in 1645–1647 affected America; some suspects may even have fled there. Connecticut had its own panic in the late 1640s, and a healer named Margaret Jones was arrested in Charlestown. She was searched using procedures from England, and a genital teat (thought to be where she fed a familiar spirit) was found, although her neighbors failed to get a confession. As with Anne Hutchinson and Samuel Gorton, disrespect for the Boston court compounded her crime. At the hour of her execution, it was said, a tempest uprooted trees. Thomas Jones, her husband, tried to flee to Barbados, but he was refused passage. When the ship, the *Wellcome*, left Boston in calm weather, it "fell a Rollinge & continued so about 12 howers" until Jones's imprisonment broke his alleged spell.[23]

Fewer witches were indicted in New England than in England, and there were more acquittals, because magistrates insisted on proof of a satanic pact. The importance of witches, then, was largely symbolic: like religious dissenters, they were seen as demons clothed in light, and the law against them was affirmation of New England's values. As such, the idea of witchcraft gripped the minds of suspects as well as accusers. Pressured by the religious expectations of their communities and weakened by misfortune, some people actually believed themselves to be Satan's prey, coerced spiritually into joining his dark sect. Like

Margaret Jones, Alice Lake of Dorchester denied witchcraft, but admitted to being visited by the devil as she grieved for her dead child, in whose spectral form she said he appeared. She confessed that as a young unmarried woman she had tried to kill her unborn baby.[24]

The high mortality rate of 1649–1650 lasted into 1651, at first mostly afflicting children, then adults. The previous rarity of epidemic sickness in New England, remarked Edward Johnson, "cannot but speak loud in the ears of Gods people." Plagues and witches were their punishment, and the devil concentrated on people like Mary Parsons, whose defenses had been eroded by sin. Springfield, her home, was a rapidly developing frontier settlement on the Connecticut River; its original purpose had been to extend the Massachusetts beaver trade. Springfield's founder, John Pynchon, had sailed with Winthrop's fleet in 1630. He became an exporter of salt pork and a pillar of godly discipline. The town, Johnson noted, had been beset by witches, but Pynchon and others had "used much diligence, both for the finding [of] them out, and for the Lords assisting them against their witchery." Of this Pynchon had experience, having sat on the tribunal at Boston that condemned Margaret Jones.[25]

There was no better metaphor for the troubled community or colony (or, in England, state) than the house divided. Mary Parsons's household became an object lesson here when her reputation tainted her husband's. Neighbors reported accidents after dealing with Hugh Parsons, and disputes ending with threats. Most sinister was his wife's claim that she had asked him repeatedly if he were a witch and had tried to search him as he slept. He had dreams about the devil, who "came to him in ye Night at the Bed, and suckt him." Finally, she accused him of bewitching their child to death. In March 1651, Pynchon examined him, questioning thirty-five witnesses, whereafter husband and wife were sent to Boston to be tried. Mary Parsons confessed to child murder and was condemned, but she probably died in prison; Hugh Parsons's trial was delayed until May 1652, when the general court freed him. He never returned to Springfield.[26]

Dissidents at Samuel Gorton's Warwick were appalled by witch-hunting. According to an informant reporting to John Endecott, who was now governor of Massachusetts, the dissidents believed the only devils on earth to be the Bay Colony's ministers. The charge of diabolical instigation was easily reversed from accused to accuser, although whether it stuck depended on who happened to have the most power.

New England's persecution of religious sects, and their resistance, illustrates this principle well.[27]

One Sunday in July 1651, the physician John Clarke arrived at Lynn,
fifteen miles from Boston, accompanied by Obediah Holmes and John
Crandall. They were unable to attend church, Clarke later explained, because they were not members of the local congregation; instead, they held
their own service. They were interrupted by constables, whom Clarke
likened to the agents once used by bishops in England. The constables
locked them in an alehouse. Permitted to attend the evening meeting,
Clarke tried to speak, but was silenced. The next day they were taken to
Boston for trial. Governor Endecott accused them of being Baptists, to
which Clarke replied: "I am neither an Anabaptist, nor a Pedobaptist,
nor a Catabaptist." You are all those things, snapped Endecott, and you
"make all our worship a nullity." Fines were imposed. Clarke protested
that they were strangers in Massachusetts, ignorant of local customs,
and asked which law they had broken. Endecott simply said: "When you
come to the Court you shall know the Law." Clarke persisted until the
governor remarked that, strictly speaking, he deserved death.[28]

Obediah Holmes refused to pay his fine and was whipped. With
the first stroke, he felt "a spirituall manifestation of Gods presence,"
but no pain: "You have struck me as with Roses," he said as he was
untied. Spectators who shook his hand were arrested; even the surgeon
who dressed his bleeding back was summoned. Another warrant was
issued against Holmes, but he fled. In September he wrote defiantly to
Endecott that he could be called witch, adulterer, or blasphemer, "yet I
stand before the judgment of my Lord."[29]

After John Clarke published an account of the episode in 1652, the
teacher of the church at Lynn penned a rebuttal, likening Baptists to
witches, false prophets who "out of pretence of conscience bewitch souls
to death by their inchanting doctrines." Roger Williams berated the
general court for behaving as if they were constantly in crisis when they
might see that God had given them peace. They sat "drie on your safe
American Shoars," watching "the dolefull tossings of so many of Eu-
rop[e]s Nations, yea of our dearest Mother, aged England, in a Sea of
Tears and Bloud." The court replied that "persecution" was civil defense
of true religion and, however unpleasant, was better than leaving errors
uncorrected.[30]

For Williams's adversary John Cotton, this was just another clash in a
war of words spanning almost a decade. But it would be his last. Early in

December 1652, shortly after his sixty-seventh birthday, Cotton caught a chill on the Boston-Cambridge ferry and took to his bed, where, with curtains drawn, he concentrated on his devotions. A comet was sighted in Massachusetts; it was visible until noon on the 23rd, when Cotton died. His last words were an exhortation to surrender to God, after which, it was said, he "quietly breathed out his spirit into the handes of him that gave it." Mourners felt the passing of more than a man: this was the end of New England's first era, one defined by sacrifice.[31]

Survivors closed ranks. Richard Mather compared his congregation to the Apostles, "a chosen generation, a royall Preisthood, a peculiar people, called out of darknesse into marvellous light." This, too, was the leitmotif of Edward Johnson's epic *History of New-England* (1653), chronicling a saintly crusade against infidels. "Thus this poor people," Johnson wrote, "populate this howling Desert, marching manfully on (the Lord Assisting), through the greatest difficulties and sorest labours that ever any with such weak means have done." William Bradford's account of New Plymouth's first thirty years ranked the Pilgrims with the children of Israel, by which he implied not just their courage and special status, but a failure to meet expectations. The torch now had to be handed to the next generation so that *they* could complete the Reformation, whether in the old England or the new one.[32]

The comet presaging Cotton's death also warned of danger in England, including conflict with Holland and a change of government. In fact, war with Holland had broken out in July, raising fears that the Dutch would send Indians to attack English colonists. Then, in December 1653, after four years of parliamentary confusion, Oliver Cromwell dissolved Parliament and became Lord Protector, his mission to heal the nation. Like John Winthrop, Cromwell saw himself as a Moses leading his people from bondage to liberty, believing in force to advance truth. His constitution was written not by Parliament but the army, and soon he would impose regional military government. Equally worrying to some was his commitment to religious toleration, based on a conviction that God's saints were present in all churches. Puritans everywhere believed this would foment dissent and disorder. News arrived in Boston of "a Sect Called quakers . . . [who] doe much Increase, rayleing much at the Ministry And refuseing to sho[w] Any reverence to Majestrates."[33]

Alarmed by developments across the Atlantic, New Englanders appealed for "the preservation of that Liberty wherewith Christ hath made us free," fearing a new "Yoke of Bondage." In the autumn of 1654, a pamphlet blasted old England and New England alike for leaving the path of righteousness. Its author was William Aspinwall, a Winthrop migrant who resettled in Cheshire after falling out with Boston's rulers. England, he predicted, would be judged for allowing religious sects to multiply. He also warned that governments that replaced tyranny with tyranny betrayed popular trust. The only king was Christ, Aspinwall inveighed, and if England had had America's opportunities, the son of God would already have been crowned. "You are as a Beacon set on a Hill," he reminded New England, echoing John Winthrop. "Great things God hath done for you, and great things he expects from you."[34]

Aspinwall's words are a reminder not just of the reciprocal relationship between England's old and new worlds, but the multiform evolution of English loyalties and identities cutting across geographical lines. The search for God's plan exposed only the plans of men: royalists and republicans, and Puritans favoring either a state church or independent congregations. These visions did not coexist peacefully: each claimed superior authority. And in America they would do battle not only in New England, but also in Maryland, Bermuda, and especially the West Indies, where aftershocks of civil war reverberated powerfully in the 1650s.

CHAPTER 11

Devouring Caterpillars and Gnawing Worms

T HE MIDDLE DECADES of the seventeenth century saw English people separated and scattered throughout the Atlantic world. New Englanders arrived home, Catholics settled in Maryland, Bermudans came and went, and royalists took refuge in Virginia—where they could preserve their character, perhaps in denial of change, or reinvent themselves. America helped English identity take on new appearances, and behind each lay a dispute over orthodoxy and liberty, authority and legitimacy, inflected with religion. Nor was this the end of it. The ideological conflict of the 1640s would yet have some vivid and violent manifestations reflecting England's unsettled state. The Caribbean provided another stage for the drama of cultural dislocation and political turmoil; it was an exotic social wilderness where the new English republic might subdue cavaliers, who were stubbornly loyal to the monarchy, but also where a nascent imperial state could exploit transplanted subjects. The defiance of those subjects came partly from attachment to customary English freedoms, but also from personal experience of a new and challenging world.

I n the summer of 1653, Richard Ligon, a business agent, was sitting in a Southwark prison with his eyes closed. It was too dark to paint, so he conjured scenes of freedom in his mind: emerald seas, bone-white beaches, shady palms. A royalist ruined by a failed drainage scheme, he had realized after the first civil war that England had nothing left for him. "I found myself a stranger in my owne Country," he said, "and therefore resolv'd to lay hold of the first opportunity that might convoy me to any other part of the World." He chose the West Indies. But now Ligon was incarcerated for debt, and to pay his creditors, he wrote a memoir of his three years in Barbados.[1]

Ligon had sailed from London in June 1647 on the same ship as Sir Thomas Modyford, a cavalier colonel taking voluntary exile. It was unseasonably cold, with gusting winds and heavy skies, but Ligon was absorbed by the sea's wonders. There were dolphins, flying fish, and sharks—the latter mutilated by the sailors as "mercilesse Tyrants." Several weeks later, Ligon and his companions won a bet that land would be sighted before noon, and so enjoyed the expanding coastline over their winnings: hot chicken. The tall, spreading trees on Barbados suggested rich soils, and to Ligon, arriving from turmoil, they also symbolized "harmony in that Leviathan, a well governed Common-wealth." But as they docked, it was clear the island was gripped by an epidemic; indeed, bodies were stacking up so fast they had to be dumped into a bog. What may have been bubonic plague spread to the ship. A promotional work about the Caribbean that praised public health—as well as the medicinal properties of turtle meat, the sensory pleasures of pineapples, and the fertility of English women (contrary to rumor)—was found to be dangerously misleading.[2]

Slow to adapt to the heat and humidity, Ligon suffered kidney stones and treated his ailment, apparently successfully, with a West Indies remedy, dried turtle's penis dissolved in ale. Knives and locks rusted, and watches kept poor time. There were few springs, so people collected rain in ponds, where, to Ligon's disgust, Africans bathed; at Bridgetown, corpses deliquesced into the water supply. Houses had gutters leading to domestic cisterns, which were essential if homes were to become fortresses in the event of insurrection. Most buildings were of timber with low ceilings, their doors and windows facing west. This protected them from driving rain but also kept out cooling breezes. Settlers had no glass; nor did they seem inclined to make shutters. Curtains were nibbled by rats; ants got everywhere. There were no cellars because of the clay soil, so meat was hung in the rafters.[3]

Ligon's actual job in Barbados is unknown—possibly plantation manager—but his avocation was cookery. His attempts to make pastry from cassava failed until an Indian showed him how to refine flour. He was pleased with his venison pasties and enjoyed tropical drinks, such as orange squash and pineapple wine—which was preferable to "kill devil," hooch made from sugar scum. Slaves were fed plantains eked out with roasted corncobs and land-crabs. White servants received meat from diseased cattle, slaves the heads and entrails; dead horses the slaves had whole, noted Ligon, "and that they thought a high feast, with which never poor soules were more contented." At sundown planters gathered at riverside taverns, where they ate fish, fried or marinated in vinegar and spices.[4]

Everywhere he went, Ligon met royalists. The West Indies were advertised as a place where abundant food might revive English charity; the islands were said to be a haven for victims of "the plundering and utter ruine of their Estates by the cruelty of the Cavaleers." By 1647, however, most of the refugees were cavaliers themselves. Barbados promised to restore a gentleman's fortunes and advance ambitions that had been spiked by war and rebellion; yet it was in economic decline. Tobacco and cotton prices had fallen, and taxation further slashed profits. Like the Virginians, the planters protested that unreasonable levies were reducing both the quality of tobacco and their revenues from the crop, not least by encouraging smuggling. Another consequence was that colonists had less disposable income, which reduced their consumption of English imports. The commodity to change all this was sugar: a capital-intensive commodity but one that was endlessly in demand, and thus infinitely lucrative. Expansion here would prove to be England's most spectacular commercial venture of the 1650s, a revolution embraced by men such as Sir Thomas Modyford. He bought a share in a plantation and began work. As the prospects glittered, so the value of land and the need for cheap labor escalated. The solution was a vast workforce of indentured servants and slaves.[5]

Modyford's skill in commanding free Englishmen was not easily transferred to unfree Africans. In his first year, rebellion was narrowly averted. Ligon, who observed Modyford's efforts to establish himself, was surprised that slaves did not revolt more often. Apart from their poor diet, they slept on boards without blankets, although English servants were not treated much better—sometimes their lot was worse, as a planter had less incentive to care for a man he did not own. An apprentice's work began at 6 a.m., paused when the sun was hottest, then resumed between 1 p.m. and 6 p.m. He toiled in all weathers, slept in wet clothes, and was beaten if he complained. Shortly before Ligon returned to England, servants rose up across Barbados intending to cut their masters' throats and declare themselves freemen. As usual, the uprising was suppressed and the ringleaders executed. Blacks were systematically intimidated and kept away from weapons. Ligon pitied them and appreciated their humanity. They were happy and lively, many, he believed, as "honest, faithfull and conscionable" as any European. He tried to have a slave admitted to the church but was told this would set a dangerous precedent, Christian Africans being harder to enslave than heathens.[6]

During the civil war, Barbados had remained neutral, provocative visits by commissioners from both sides notwithstanding. Peace was preserved despite tension between parliamentarian roundheads and royalist cavaliers. As Parliament triumphed, however, so more royalists were welcomed in Barbados by the governor, Philip Bell, and some joined the colonial council. For a while, it was not polite to mention the war, but the past was stalking the islanders. In 1650, the introduction of an oath of allegiance to Bell's government sparked a backlash from James Drax, a pioneer planter, in defense of what one commentator called "the Liberty and Priviledge of free-borne English-men that are Inhabitants and free-holders of this Island." Drax and his followers were branded as rebels, "Impes of the Devill" pretending liberty when they wanted tyranny—exactly what had happened in England, according to anonymous libels. Heretics at Westminster, it was said, had murdered the monarch and "ruined the most glorious Kingdom . . . in the World." In return, parliamentarian settlers called their accusers "devouring Caterpillers and gnawing Wormes," who impoverished honest planters and drove them back to England. In May, Governor Bell, old and vulnerable to pressure from aggressive cavaliers, was made to proclaim loyalty to Charles Stuart, Charles I's exiled son, and to reinstate the Book of Common Prayer. Roundhead planters were arrested and fined. Drax, who was treated especially harshly, sailed home.[7]

England prohibited trade with the disloyal colonies of Virginia, Bermuda, and Barbados in October 1650; disobedient merchants would be punished as accessories to treason. The following month, Barbadian planters of all hues petitioned Parliament to demand treatment as "the free people of this nation." The response was a February 1651 instruction to the new governor, Lord Francis Willoughby, to defer to the English republic, and for the monarchy, the House of Lords, and the Prayer Book to be condemned. By autumn, Parliament was threatening Barbados with war and the destruction of its estates. The extreme royalist faction was thus able to pose as the reasonable ally of honest farmers. "This made most men joyn cheerfully in the putting [of] the Island in a Posture of Defence," an observer noted, "the most Moderate [party], like true English-men, resolving to sell themselves at a dear Rate by chusing to die rather then to live less Free then any of their Country-men." The looming conflict was no longer just a late clash between crown and Parliament: it was the spirit of old England in America resisting radical change at home. Militiamen prepared themselves, and Sir Thomas Modyford found himself back in command of a royalist regiment. Planters who had bruited about liberty now found their servants conscripted in its defense.[8]

A fleet commanded by thirty-six-year-old Sir George Ayscue arrived in Barbados on October 16, 1651. Aboard one ship was James Drax, who earlier that year had heard an astrologer predict that the commander would "receive prejudice by the undertaking"—that is, his mission would not go well. Now Drax would find out if the astrologer was right. Ayscue informed Willoughby that Barbados was "a Collony and Plantac[i]on w[hi]ch ought to be subordinate to and dependant uppon ye Comm[on]wealth." The commander said he trusted that bloodshed would not ensue. Nothing happened. In the second week of November, Ayscue pressed Willoughby to "submitt to ye Power and governem[en]t of your Native Countrey," upon which the assembly declared the royal right to the island and its intention to fight. So the correspondence continued, decorous but unyielding. Ayscue seized on Willoughby's reference to "his Ma[jes]t[y]s just Interest" in Barbados; he responded that the king had little to gain even "if there were such a Person as a Kinge you speake of." Ayscue hinted at a "sadd Catastrophe," and a week later his patience ran out. On the night of November 22, two hundred troops landed. Witnesses reported that defenders raised a white flag and then opened fire. The attackers returned to their ships with thirty prisoners, whose loyalty to the royalist cause, Ayscue told Willoughby, was crumbling. Willoughby assured him that his army was more resolute than ever. Each saddled the other with "blood guilt."[9]

On December 17, parliamentary soldiers, including Scottish prisoners from the previous year's Battle of Worcester—now no longer the last conflict of the civil wars—routed the royalist militia in Barbados. Sir Thomas Modyford persuaded his men to switch their allegiance to Ayscue, who landed early in January 1652. Both sides were weary from night-watches and enervated by the heat; Ayscue's men had scurvy. Still

Willoughby spoke of rights and liberty, to which, with scant restraint, Ayscue replied: "I will offer yet my endeavour to p[re]vent ye calamities and effusion of Christian bloud w[hi]ch followes a Civile Warre." Willoughby held out, by night riding between his forts, promising booty. When the two armies—3,000 royalists and 1,500 parliamentarians—finally met in battle, a tropical downpour interrupted them, as if God were tired of Englishmen fighting. Peace came on the 11th. Ayscue had won the day for Parliament. The English had thrown off "Tyrannicall Kingly power and government and are become a Republick, a Free State," trumpeted one account. Now Barbados would be part of it.[10]

What happened in the Caribbean was no quirk of circumstance, for 2,000 miles away, an army was cruising up the James River led by, among others, William Claiborne, claimant to the disputed Kent Island. In Virginia, too, royalism had combined with pride in English liberties. Sir William Berkeley positioned 1,000 soldiers around Jamestown, but he negotiated a settlement before a shot was fired. The governor was permitted to explain himself in a letter to the dead king's son, who was hailed by royalists as Charles II, before retreating from public life; law and government survived intact, though subordinate to the Commonwealth. For a while, Virginians were even allowed to keep the Anglican Prayer Book. Love of monarchy simmered beneath a conformist froth, as in Barbados. In June 1652, a Barbadian militia sergeant was charged with treason for crying out, to his platoon, "God bless our Sovereign and Hey for King Charles." The following year, the governor conceded to the Council of State in London that Barbados harbored spirits who, given a chance, would make "this little limb of the Commonwealth into a free state." Those spirits pleaded with Cromwell "that in regarde we are Englishmen . . . we may enjoy our part of liberty and freedome equal with the rest of our countrymen, and be made proportionable sharers of all those blessings w[hi]ch our good god, by you his instrument, hath bestowed on our nation."[11]

For all this sanguine rhetoric, there would be no fair shares of anything: Caribbean power and profit were increasingly concentrated in a few hands. Slave economies did not support the sort of cooperative social relationships that were universal in England; indeed, the familiar shaded spectrum of social rankings—known as "degrees" and "sorts"

of people—barely existed. Polarization nurtured self-interest. However starkly the ideological positions of the 1650s were articulated in
Barbados—and in Bermuda—allegiances were not directly transposed
from England to these New World locations. Rather, colonial versions
arose with the power to unite parliamentarians and royalists under the
ancient constitution whenever imperialist England threatened local
political and economic concerns. Creating a republic at home broadcast
the language of libertarian self-determination; yet for Cromwell, there
was only one "free state." His foreign policy therefore involved not just
thwarting Catholic Spain in and around Jamaica, but also subduing
English people throughout the Atlantic and Caribbean worlds.

In Barbados, the drift toward autocracy was exemplified by Humphrey Walrond, the leader of the royalist extremists, at whose opulent
home in "Little England" Richard Ligon was a frequent guest. Walrond was the only planter whose estate bordered the sea, which allowed
his servants and slaves to catch fish for his groaning table—no less than
an English gentleman used to "freedome, liberty and plenty" would
have expected. The best spread, however, belonged to James Drax, who,
Ligon said, lived like a prince. The first course of one memorable dinner hosted by Drax was beef done fourteen ways, followed by potato
pudding served with every meat imaginable, including a suckling pig
in a sauce of brains, claret, sage, and nutmeg. This was rounded off
with pickled oysters, caviar, neats' tongues, custards, and cheesecakes.
The wine, sherry, and brandy that were served had been imported from
England.[12]

Fortune favored the brave, for cultivating sugar was difficult. Thomas
Modyford was able to draw on accumulated experience; but when Drax
arrived in 1642 at the age of eighteen, he had been on his own, and his
first plantation failed. Consumers in England, Ligon wrote, had no
idea how much work went into making sugar: the timing of planting
and cutting the cane; considerations of storage; methods of grinding
and squeezing; the boiling, skimming, and distilling (for rum); the
cooling, curing, and potting—all learned by trial and costly error. The
risks did not end there. In 1648 a Barbadian planter described "many
who had begun and almost finished greate sugar workes, who dan-
dled themselves in their hopes, but were laid in the dust and their estates left unto strangers." Men like Drax were not just brave: they were
lucky. And their achievements were staggering. An enterprise producing modest amounts of unrefined muscovado sugar when Ligon arrived

was booming when he left three years later. The fact that in the last two years of the decade the island's exports exceeded £3 million—a hundredth of its modern value—owes much to Drax; indeed, a significant share of this money was his. Drax also led the way in the importation of slaves—another huge capital cost, albeit promising even huger returns. Barbados in 1650 had four whites for every black, but commercial logic dictated that this ratio would be reversed. Given its wealth, the allure of the Caribbean to adventurers hardly needs spelling out; likewise the state's green-eyed insistence on political obedience.[13]

A thousand miles north of Barbados lay Bermuda, puritanical in rule and religion and less lucrative, yet similar in its experiences. Conflict existed not just between royalists and parliamentarians but also between Presbyterians and Independents—another political rift that had been exported to the New World. The Presbyterians wanted a national structure of Calvinist churches; the Independents, as their name suggests, did not. By 1646 a small group of Independents had been compelled to move to the Bahamas, and this colony became the last adventure in Puritan utopianism in America. Its leader was the septuagenarian Patrick Copland, the Scottish minister whose godly aims in Virginia had ended with the 1622 massacre. "Our desire to goe out is not that wee are weary of the place," he wrote in his twentieth year in Bermuda, "but that wee are sick of the present Government." Their land was exhausted and they craved the "sweet society of saincts."[14]

A delegation took a petition to London on behalf of "the free-borne natives of this Kingdom, groaning under severall pressures inconsistent with their native priviledges," including arbitrary government, high taxes, and trade restrictions. People were poor, their tobacco not worth the boxes it was packed in. Bermuda depended on commerce with New England and Barbados: without cotton from Barbados, exchanged for meat and fish, its inhabitants would starve. Their "parliament," delegates complained, exercised "independent power over the Congregation" and legislated without regard for England. A defendant at their "assizes" who protested that he had broken no English law was told: "you have transgressed *our* Lawes, otherwise we could have no advantage against you." The following year Copland was imprisoned for his congregationalism, and in 1648 he was banished to what would become the colony of Eleuthera (Freedom), an island east of Nassau in the Bahamas.[15]

Bermuda slipped into chaos. In 1649 the governor declared for the king and fighting broke out. A deputation left for Barbados seeking a royalist alliance and weapons. A year later, a new governor assured the Somers Isles Company that he had defeated "a tumultuous, rebellious People" and their "perfidious Commanders." But now Bermuda had a new opponent: the English Council of State, which, like Independent usurpers and royalist rebels, threatened colonists' patent privileges. A petition in defense of tradition was sent to Westminster in July 1651. Bermudan identity was complex. Its loyalties were split between locality, company, and polity in England. The muddle inspired Eleuthera's return to Christian simplicity. But life was a grind there, and Copland, disillusioned and broke, returned to Bermuda, where witchcraft accusations proliferated. Suspects were searched, pricked, and put in water to see if they floated. Richard Norwood, the pearl-diver turned surveyor, helped to prosecute a man who was then executed. Norwood's wife was on a "jury of matrons" tasked with finding the devil's marks, and their own daughter was examined. As in New England, witch-trials were a barometer of disunity and instability. Hostile to radical change, Bermuda adhered to a moderate royalism that English interference made more extreme. A commission sent by Cromwell in 1653 to correct the island's disaffection was told three things by the assembly: it abided by its Jacobean patent; the regicide was "bloody, traitorous and rebellious"; and Charles II was king.[16]

This was intolerable: Cromwell would have obedience in Bermuda, as in Barbados. And he was also interested in ruling the waves. One night, the exiled earl of Norwich dreamed that the Lord Protector made himself "Emperor of the West Indies"—an idea alarming to both royalists and republicans, the former fearing his elevation above the law, the latter that England would suffer the fate of ancient Rome. The dream was not so fanciful: Cromwell *did* embrace republicanism, monarchy, and imperialism, and the West Indies *were* the destination to which, as one writer put it, "the Hand of Divine Providence seemeth at this time to be leading the English Nation." The Anglo-Dutch War of 1652–1654, fought mainly in the North Sea and the Baltic, had less to do with religion, however, than with controlling Atlantic trade routes and gathering taxes. So far, the century had seen public finances shift from a dependence on crown land to a dependence on taxation. Much of the crown land had already been sold by Elizabeth I, and these sales had diminished both the revenues from rents and the collateral available for borrowing money to fight wars. Taxation came especially from levies on commerce and consumption. But the taxes caused discontent and invited disobedience, not least in America, where excise duties—notably on Virginia and Bermuda tobacco—depressed standards of living and offended champions of self-government.[17]

Conflict between England and its colonies centered on the Navigation Act of 1651. Ostensibly, the restrictions that this legislation imposed on the colonies' foreign trade would protect the domestic economy and produce revenue to help the poor; but really it just proved that Cromwell shared Charles I's expansionist urges and had as few options for funding them. The law stipulated that colonial commerce must use English ships; that valuable exports, such as sugar, could only be exported to England; and that European imports to America should pass through English ports, where customs could be levied. Protectionism was contentious for Europeans and English colonists alike; the Navigation Act was a symbol of aggressive mercantilism. Like royalist and parliamentarian planters in Barbados, English and Dutch traders found in capitalism a more sincere fraternity than in religion or patriotism, although some Englishmen relished the assault on Dutch competition. Planters were not rebels against Albion but pragmatic adventurers sensitive to profit.[18]

Peace with Holland in 1654 allowed Cromwell to advance his "Western Design" in the Caribbean, evoking nostalgia for the Elizabethan exploits of Sir Francis Drake and Sir Walter Ralegh. The target was the Spanish island of Hispaniola, portrayed in Whitehall as a land of milk and honey, and thought to be lightly defended. It might absorb England's poor, speculated an adviser, and purge the "profane vile caterpillers" left by the wars. Remembering a proposal from 1640 for peopling Providence Island, Cromwell even suggested that New Englanders might be relocated to Hispaniola to boost the white population. Concern in Massachusetts and Connecticut about the economic slump New England was suffering, expressed in pleas to London for help, now turned to alarm. New Englanders postponed voyages lest they be diverted to the Caribbean, and the Lord Protector was warned to expect muted enthusiasm for his scheme.[19]

Cromwell's task force was led by General Robert Venables and Sir William Penn, commanders of England's land and naval forces, respectively. Their orders were to seize Hispaniola, where Philip IV allegedly had inflicted "cruelties & Inhumane practices" on Indians, and where the exclusion of English settlers was "contrary to Comon Right & Law of Nations." A fleet of warships carrying 3,000 men left Portsmouth in

December 1654. Among them were Thomas Gage, a Kentish minister appointed as Venables's chaplain. Formerly a Dominican friar in Guatemala, Gage hailed from English recusants—Catholic dissenters—but had defected to Anglicanism in 1642. On his return to England, he had struggled to recover his mother tongue. He thought of himself as an "English-American." With his specialist knowledge of the Spanish Caribbean and Hispaniola's poor defenses, it was he who had seeded the Western Design in Cromwell's mind. He also offered justifications: Caribs, enslaved by superstition, must be freed. This idea was endorsed by Edward Winslow, the New England agent and so-called friend to the Indians. Winslow became one of several administrators who were sent with the fleet to oversee post-invasion settlement.[20]

The adventure was doomed. The commanders quarreled, and soldiers who were recruited in Barbados and St. Kitts were reported to be "the very scum of scums, and meer dregs of corruption, and such upon whose endeavours it was impossible to expect a blessing." Landing in April 1655 at Santo Domingo, where Drake had once bested another king of Spain, they trudged through dense woodland in scorching heat; they had little sense of direction and hardly any water. Men drank their urine; some collapsed. When the fighting started many ran away. The Spanish gave chase, cutting down the invaders and marching prisoners to their fort "like slaves and cow-hearted villains." Some men hiding in the woods were picked off by "Maroons"—freed slaves—positioned there. The colors were lost. The army pulled back and lay on the beach for six days, eating its horses and dogs and incubating dysentery and malaria.[21]

The fleet left Hispaniola for Jamaica, four hundred miles to the west, in early May. Edward Winslow died of fever and was buried at sea with a forty-two-gun salute—a fitting tribute to a principal architect of New Plymouth and English America *tout court*. In Jamaica the Spanish garrison was captured without a fight, but this hardly made up for the ignominy of Hispaniola. In a letter to his father in Essex, Colonel Francis Barrington wrote that "o[u]r mens Spirits were so cowed that . . . wee had not the common Spirrit of Children, so metamorphosed wee were." Hundreds languished with only beans to eat. Furthermore, the Spanish still occupied western Jamaica and no one knew what to do. "Wee are not at the helme like men endued with Comon reason," said Barrington, "for wee all ly[e] at one place not endeavouring to p[ro]vide for the future." From the time of their arrival, he added, they had been so morally weak as to be hardly recognizable as Englishmen. He predicted they would be lucky if one in three of them survived; in fact, half of them died—over 1,000 men.[22]

By September Penn and Venables were back in England, where conversation buzzed about the expedition. Some said this would be the last Caribbean adventure; others questioned whether spilled Spanish blood expanded Christ's kingdom. Cromwell, chastened by God, sent the commanders to the Tower where, it was rumored, Penn cried like a child. Their few defenders invoked the Normans and Caesar, observing that God blessed conquerors in the end. At Portsmouth, where returning soldiers lay sick, it was hard to perceive a divine plan, still less in Jamaica, where the ragged victors wondered why on earth they were there. Thomas Gage, whose idea the adventure had been, died there early in 1656. The English garrison at Fort Cromwell, guarding Jamaica's main harbor, was demoralized and malnourished. A regimental audit explained why: provisions had been left out in all weathers, barrels were unlabeled, the accounts were a mess (both clerks having died), the storehouses were overrun with rats, and typically the bread that arrived "hath beene very Small with much Dust."[23]

Colonel Edward Doyley, who ordered this inspection, wrote to the committee for Jamaica that "we feare noe Enemie but hunger," adding that fresh food from New England would be welcome; dried pease, he said, were useless. Jamaica might be the centerpiece of English interests in America, Doyley advised, but without manpower and supplies, not in a hundred years. Virginia's problem recurred in the Caribbean: soldiers couldn't be planters, and planters couldn't be soldiers; you had to have both and plenty of them. Here Cromwell's relocation plans again saw the light of day. A magistrate visiting London from Cambridge, Massachusetts, was tasked with recruiting New Englanders to live in Jamaica, specifically, the rough settlement around Fort Cromwell. The inducements were free transport, good land, livestock, and various privileges. A flyer was printed at Boston, but there were few takers. John Endecott informed Cromwell that Jamaica's high mortality rate put people off; he begged that none be forced to go. In England, however, this was just what was happening. A diarist in Essex "heard they tooke up many loose wenches at London to send over to Jamaica."[24]

Promotional works about Jamaica appealed to men's personal ambition *and* sense of duty. One from 1657 promised that if only "our Countrymen would but raise up their dull spirits and seriously set themselves to plant there, they would not only exceedingly advance the Publique Interest, and benefit their Native Country, but very much advance and enrich themselves, their children and posterity." These entreaties were received both enthusiastically and skeptically. Either way, the advertisements could not compete with the scare stories passing by word of mouth. Early in 1658, Anglo-Spanish fighting in Jamaica saw slaves turn on their masters. In June the two sides slugged it out at Rio Nuevo Bay, ending with the defenders—Spanish, Africans, Indians, and Creoles—fleeing down the cliffs. Rio Nuevo was Spain's last serious attempt to retain influence in Jamaica, proof for Cromwell that God was his ally against Catholics. Jamaica still had little value in 1658, but it would soon generate wealth far beyond the capacity of Barbados, and so was a "dagger pointed at the heart of the Spanish empire."[25]

The political instability of Jamaica, Barbados, and Bermuda in the 1650s, a black mirror to England's inconstancy, was endemic in mainland colonies such as Maryland. In July 1657, William Wood was transporting flour along a creek of the Patuxent River when he found a corpse in the water. Back at John Dandy's mill, the dead man was identified as Harry Gouge, a servant whom Dandy had once struck with an axe. The coroner's jury suspected murder, and witnesses swore that as Dandy touched the corpse, it "did bleed a fresh at the said Scar in his head and at the nose"—this was how murder victims were thought to appeal to heaven for justice. Dandy fled, but upon capture he explained he had only done so because "the Government of this Province is not Settled," and because of unjust treatment "by those in Authority."[26]

However just Dandy's subsequent execution for murder may have been, in 1657 his lack of faith in Maryland's political institutions was probably sincere and certainly commonplace. In that year Cromwell made peace with Lord Baltimore, ending a two-year civil war between royalists and parliamentarians, a conflict that had seemed inevitable after Richard Ingle's Puritan rebellion of 1645–1646, or even after Baltimore's founding of Maryland a decade earlier. Baltimore had cleverly appointed a Protestant, William Stone, as governor in 1649, and had permitted freedom of faith, forbidding religious insults whether "Antenomian, Barrowist [or] Roundhead" or "Jesuited Papist." Puritans persecuted in royalist Virginia were also given sanctuary; they founded the town of Providence on the Severn River's north shore. News of

Charles I's execution, however, had the same radicalizing effect it had in Barbados, pushing moderate royalists into righteous defiance. Maryland declared Charles II the "undoubted rightfull heire" to the throne in November 1649, and the assembly swore an oath to Baltimore as absolute lord and proprietor of the province.[27]

Cromwell condemned Lord Baltimore for his alleged Catholic government and abuse of his patent, which, it was stated, was "onely for uncultivated places, such as were not Inhabited by any but Pagans." It had been illegal, moreover, for Charles I to put English subjects under the governance of another English subject. Rumors circulated that Maryland would be dischartered, and its "reduction" ordered in December 1652. Lord Baltimore resisted Maryland's reassignment to Virginia's jurisdiction, arguing that the former had been loyal to Parliament, whereas the latter had not. Maryland, he said, tolerated all faiths, besides which he knew of "no Lawes here against Recusants which reach into America." The Lord Protector, like a king, declared that all English laws applied in the colonies. But Baltimore, like many colonists, believed governance had to adapt to local conditions, and that his patent was superior to statute, because it guaranteed liberties and privileges. It worked, then, more like flexible custom or common law than like a fixed decree or set of regulations. The charter alone, Baltimore insisted, had persuaded him "to make so great an Adventure, without which he would not certainly, upon the conditions of a common Planter, have disbursed any thing upon a Plantation in America." The counterargument was that the patent was already void, and Maryland's claim over two-thirds of Virginia's best land was in "no way consistent with Equity and the Honor and publick Faith of the Kingdom." Lord Baltimore's palatinate powers, it was asserted, had been repugnant to the English nation since the reign of Henry VIII.[28]

To Boston's saints, the Catholics of Maryland, though far away, were, like sinners and sectaries, pests chewing the roots of American godliness. Thomas Allen was a Puritan divine who fled to Massachusetts in 1638 and returned to the city of Norwich in England in 1651. A passionate defender of John Eliot's mission, he had seen Indians freed from the thrall of "witches" and had heard John Cotton's "Revelations" sermons. Notes he kept lay in a drawer until 1655, when news from America jogged his memory. Using numerology, Cotton had prophesied that in this year, 1655, the Antichrist—the pope, that is—would receive a blow. If war came to New England, Cotton speculated, the aggressors would be "the Principalities from Hell, or this Beast the

Catholic church, or from the Image of this Beast." As tensions mounted in Maryland, the prophecy appeared to be coming true.[29]

On the fifth anniversary of Charles I's execution, January 30, 1654, Puritans in Providence, Maryland, had petitioned William Claiborne and other commissioners from England. They objected to Lord Baltimore's oath of allegiance as inimical to "the liberty of our Consciences as Christians and free Subjects of the Common-wealth of England." A second petition complained they were being forced to pledge themselves to "a Popish, Antichristian Government," to be "Traytors to our Country, fighters against God, and Covenant-breakers." Claiborne replied that absolute obedience to Cromwell was mandatory. In July, Governor Stone was removed, and the commissioners moved in. Catholics were barred from the assembly, and Maryland's Toleration Act was repealed. In January 1655, as Stone prepared to regain power by force, a merchant ship, the *Golden Lyon*, arrived. Its captain, Roger Heaman, learned of a planned insurrection led by "disaffected Roman Catholicks . . . not owning the Lord Protector of England &c., his power, in the least." Believing Providence to be in danger, Heaman began evacuating women and children.[30]

Providence's men armed themselves, saying they would "rather die like men than be made Slaves." With Lord Baltimore's standard flying above that of the Commonwealth, Stone's army advanced through icy weather, raiding Protestant homes and forcing the homes' occupants into the woods. Indians were encouraged to join in the violence, leaving families to beg heaven for courage. As a flotilla headed toward the *Golden Lyon*, which lay anchored near the mouth of the Severn, Heaman opened fire. This did not stop Stone's men from landing at a nearby creek and shouting: "Come ye Rogues, come ye Roundheaded Dogs." The *Golden Lyon* fired again, driving the attackers along the peninsula. After a six-mile march, Protestant defenders reached Horn Point, where they confronted Stone's army. It was Lady Day, March 25, sacred to Catholics, so Stone's soldiers cried "Hey for St Mary," while their opponents rallied to "God is our Strength." The Protestants charged, and their enemies surrendered. Some claimed that the field of what became known as the Battle of the Severn was littered with discarded rosaries. Fifty of the men in Stone's army had been killed or wounded; only two of Providence's soldiers died.[31]

Thus Antichrist was crushed in America, the saints resurgent. Complaints that some prisoners were killed in cold blood (and the rest saved

The Battle of the Severn, in March 1655, saw the English civil war transposed to Maryland. This nineteenth-century illustration shows William Stone, the colony's governor, and his men driven to the end of Horn Point by Puritan troops bearing the flag of the English Commonwealth.

by the women of Providence) were drowned out by Protestant trium-phalism. Here was compensation for Hispaniola. "God did appear wonderful in the field," exulted Leonard Strong, agent for Providence, "and in the hearts of the people." In Norwich, even before he could have heard the news, Thomas Allen expanded his notes of John Cotton's prophetic sermon and found a publisher. John Hammond, a survivor of the Battle of the Severn, was smuggled out of Maryland in disguise; like Strong and Allen, upon reaching London he clamored to get into print. This, Hammond insisted, he did not for profit, but only to tell the truth about the perfidious William Claiborne and Roger Heaman.[32]

The fighting of the civil wars was finally over, but the war of words would last many years. And England still needed to decide whether its future lay in commonwealth and independency following New England's congregational model, or if kings and bishops were, after all, indispensable to its ancient constitutional habits of mind.

CHAPTER 12

A Heap of Troubles and Confusion

B Y 1658 MANY ENGLISH PEOPLE felt adrift. Some, like Winthrop's migrants a generation earlier, reasoned that if the nation had become so unlike itself, perhaps they should remake it overseas. Its body had changed; the soul could be transplanted. Adventurers promoted the Chesapeake colonies as a cornucopia for the deprived Englishman, and not just Maryland but also Virginia, whose hard-won economic gains had brought colonial self-confidence as well as strained relations with England. Massachusetts developed similarly, although its Puritanism and loyalty to Parliament meant it would be left alone by England— at least so long as Oliver Cromwell was in power. But the future of the English state remained obscure. Cromwell, Lord Protector for five years, had been offered the crown to temper his absolutism with law; he refused, believing it to be against God's will to restore what God had destroyed. That summer, when Cromwell was stricken with pneumonia, it seemed like a metaphor for infirmity in the state. If he died, what would happen to the republic he embodied? How would it fare under his lackluster son, who was derided as "Prince Richard"?

There were those who were too impatient to find out: they had had enough of Puritan dictatorship, with its strictures and vagaries. On August 19, George Alsop, a London apprentice, was sitting in the chimney corner of a noisy tavern in Gravesend, on the south bank of the River Thames, composing a letter of farewell. England's schismatics and iconoclasts, he said, sullied all that was holy; the Book of Common Prayer had been "rent by Sacrilegious hands and made no other use of then sold to Brothel-houses to light Tobacco with." Who could bear to watch such desecration? He would rather be enslaved abroad than free at home and be so affronted.[1]

Alsop's chosen destination was Maryland. A fortnight later, as he waited on his ship, he penned two final letters. "I would fain have seen you once more in this Old World before I go into the New," he told his brother, an apprentice carpenter, hoping that he might join him or at least write. Alsop reassured his elderly father that he had heard Maryland was a land of hope and renewal, adding philosophically that it could hardly be worse than England. News had just reached Gravesend that Cromwell had died. "The death of this great Rebel (I hope) will prove an Omen to presage destruction on the rest," wished Alsop, although he himself would not wait to see the king's killers judged. "The World's in a heap of troubles and confusion," he explained, "and while they are in the midst of their changes and amazes, the best way to give them the bag is to go out of the World and leave them."[2]

Alsop's optimism about Maryland followed a surge of enthusiasm for the Chesapeake region from the late 1640s. *The Maydens of London's Brave Adventures*, a printed ballad, urged adolescent girls to change their lives in America. The food was nourishing, the weather clement, and maidservants earned three times what they did in England, gold and silver being "as plenty[ful] as New-Castle coales":

> *Then come, brave Lasses, come away,*
> *Conducted by Apollo,*
> *Although that you do go before,*
> *Your sweet-hearts they will follow.*

This was a destination for youngsters, all of whom would get land. George Alsop may have read the promotional tract *Leah and Rachel* by John Hammond, the fugitive from the Battle of the Severn, or been influenced by someone who had. Like Richard Ligon yearning for Barbados, Hammond relived his time in America in prose, a dreamy distraction from Cromwellian England. He was not glad to be home, and in less than four months had "been an eye and ear witness of more deceits and villanies . . . then I either saw or heard mention made of in Virginia in my one and twenty years abroad in those parts." How ironic, then, Hammond remarked, that Virginia and Maryland—Leah and Rachel—were slighted as "a nest of Rogues, whores, desolate and rooking persons; a place of intolerable labour, bad usage, and hard Diet." People in England regarded the settlers in Virginia like "people of another world or enemies."[3]

Hammond admitted that Virginia's reputation had suffered since the massacre, the legacy of which had been costly fortification, hand-to-mouth farming, and overreliance on tobacco. As a result, migrants had "rather cast their eyes on the Barren and freezing soyle of New England, than to joyn with such an indigent and sottish people as were reported to be in Virginia." Actually, wrote Hammond, Virginians were virtuous—unlike the charlatans who came from England to preach, all the good ministers having chosen Boston over Jamestown. People left their doors open and hung their washing on hedges, unafraid of theft. Moreover, the Chesapeake had diverse agriculture, flourishing trades, true religion, and rewards commensurate to work. New arrivals abandoned thoughts of returning to England, which, as Hammond observed, was hardly thriving. There he had met men who lived "wearisom lives in reliance of other mens charities, an uncertaine and unmanly expectation," and he failed to see how London's street-vendors survived. Having observed a peddler laden with firewood, Hammond had bought him a drink. When he heard that the peddler's bundles cost threepence a piece but rarely sold, he was nonplussed: Why wasn't this man in Virginia?[4]

Virginia's fortunes had improved after a trade embargo, imposed early in 1652 for disloyalty to Parliament, was lifted later that year. Previously, ships loaded with migrants had been detained in English ports, and merchants complained of losing £20 per day feeding them. It was a costly lesson: in the future, commerce would not be sacrificed to principle.[5]

New prospectuses appeared. One, gleaned from letters sent home, promised everything "the Englishman loves full dearly." Calling himself "the Adventurers or Planters faithfull Steward . . . from the highest Master to the meanest Servant," William Bullock stressed Virginia's labor needs and superb land. Delicious vegetables were easier to grow than in England's best gardens; meat and cereals were cheap, beer plentiful. Comparing New England and Virginia was like comparing Scotland and southern England: New Englanders were industrious and canny but lacked Virginia's commodities, chiefly tobacco and sugar. Anticipating skepticism, Bullock, like Sir Thomas Smythe forty years earlier, invited personal inquiries. Unsurprisingly, there were things to hide. When Virginia Company veteran John Ferrar saw that Bullock had mentioned the Indian rebellion of 1622 but not the one of 1644, he made a marginal note: "It's a Riddell to me he should not relate it alsoe."[6]

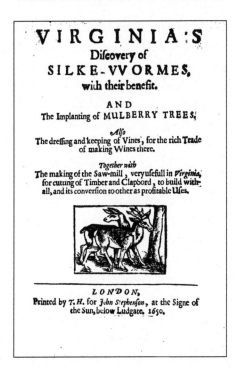

VIRGINIA:S
Diſcovery of
SILKE-VVORMES,
with their benefit.

AND
The Implanting of MULBERRY TREES,

Alſo
The dreſſing and keeping of Vines, for the rich Trade
of making Wines there.

Together with
The making of the Saw-mill, very uſefull in _Virginia_,
for cutting of Timber and Clapbord, to build withall, and its converſion to other as profitable Uſes.

LONDON,
Printed by _T. H._ for _John Stephenſon_, at the Signe of
the Sun, below Ludgate, 1650.

This mid-seventeenth-century promotional tract portrays Virginia as an un-spoiled Eden rich in opportunity for personal gain and national economic progress. Dreams of diversifying the colony's crops dated back to the reign of James I, who had hated tobacco but loved silk.

In his promotion of Virginia, a writer named Edward Williams emphasized national vigor. Postwar England was full of beggars, thieves, and levelers "who commonly like Shrubs under high and spreading Cedars imagine the spacious height of others to be the cause of their owne lownesse." Money wasted on poor relief could be spent on Atlantic adventures, he said, especially naval expansion. The old argument persisted: Virginia could absorb idle labor, create markets, and supply raw materials, especially potash and wood, to improve England's balance of payments. Virginia might become a new China or Persia supplying Europe with silk, as well as helping England resist Spain and guarding its routes to the Pacific. All classes would be provided for. Williams invited readers to "imagine the freeborne English[man] in a Countrey where he owes no Rent to any but to God and Nature." The laborer in Virginia was full of bread and optimism, whereas his English counterpart was famished and dejected, "with as little hopes of ever changing the copy of his fortune as renewing the lease of his Cottage with his Landlord."[7]

Cromwell's protection of the tobacco trade also advanced America's prosperity. Merchants complained that because competition and taxation shrank profits, planters were cutting their consignments with "poysonous and unwholesome ingredientes." A 1653 statute prohibiting tobacco cultivation in England caused uproar in Gloucestershire; its subsequent suspension then led to protest from Virginia. Importunate planters argued that "Navigac[i]on will be impaired, the Customes of this Comonwealth lessened, and the people thereof inhabiting those plantac[i]ons impoverished." Englishmen on both sides of the Atlantic were pitted against each other, leaving the state to decide whose interests also best served national interests. There were concessions, but protectionism was enforced. Virginia tobacco prices and wages rose, and more migrants were attracted to Virginia. Technical know-how promised larger yields and diversity. Edward Williams offered advice on hatching silkworms, preserving olive oil with aniseed, and cultivating and drying figs; he could also repel locusts by burning women's hair, and caterpillars by rubbing vines with bear fat or a badger's scrotum, subject to availability. Virginia also needed more sawmills of the type common in Scandinavia, and it would have them.[8]

Success stories multiplied. Francis Yeardley, the son of Virginia's former governor, wrote to John Ferrar in May 1654 enthusing about southern Virginia. He had bought land in the name of the Commonwealth of England. Indians marked the transaction by giving him a hunk of turf stuck with an arrow; in return, Yeardley promised to build the chief, who was known as "the Emperour of Roanoke," a house. Fortunes awaited the brave. Many Virginia planters accrued wealth slowly, perhaps over two generations, yet impressively. Ann Littleton's parents had arrived from Somerset in 1622 with six children and a patent for 900 acres. Five years later, her father and siblings were all dead—there is no mention of her mother—so she inherited the estate. This she expanded in the space of two marriages until her death in 1656. Her bequests, including several slaves, suggest that she lived in the manner of titled gentry in England. Thomas Willoughby, who emigrated from Kent in 1610, had spent forty years developing the 3,600-acre estate he bequeathed to his son and grandson, who, like him, married into rising families. Such tales attracted many luckless Englishmen—including George Alsop.[9]

Alsop arrived in Maryland in January 1659, thin but happy. Not only had he relieved "the pressure of a Rebellious and Traytorous

Government," but his new home was "incomparable." Deer were as numerous as cuckolds in England, the people peaceable, and "the Servants of this Province which are stigmatiz'd for Slaves by the clappermouth jaws of the vulgar in England live more like Freemen then the most Mechanick Apprentices in London." As ever, though, liberty was in the eye of the beholder. Even royalists thought Virginia and Maryland consisted of little more than unstable, scattered plantations connected by trade routes. The space where men like Alsop enjoyed freedom from tyranny, some said, was space for new tyrannies to develop. Governors from England were selfish oligarchs, men "who neither knowe the people nor their customes," wrote the promoter William Bullock, but Virginia needed government by men rooted in the land. Order also required those whom they governed to have a stake. Even wellwishers regretted the excess of "dissolute, wild, debauched, idle and nonfortuned men and women," including fugitives from justice, fleeing spouses, and runaway servants.[10]

Virginia's problems could be solved, it was said, by fighting irreligion and incivility. Indians were obstacles to stability and progress; apprentices lacked moral fiber. One problem was that young people signing on as indentured servants frequently changed their minds. One youth found his new life not to his liking, so he forged a list of goods supposedly surrendered for his release from the indenture that bound him, and presented this upon his arrival back in England. Some gave up before they began. A youth who absconded from service in Somerset to start over in Virginia got cold feet after signing a contract in Bristol and returned home, hoping that he would not be pursued. In 1657, Cromwell received a petition from Lionel Gatford, a former royalist chaplain, alleging the colony's vitiation by amoral workers, passive rulers, and poor clergy—"the very scum and off-scouring of our Nation." God came second to Mammon, and sin went unpunished: a minister convicted of attempted sodomy was merely shamed. Colonists exceeded the Indians in malice and cruelty, Gatford said; indeed, natives were treated unfairly: trespassers on English estates were burned alive. Virginians even attacked planters in Maryland. Indentured servants lived worse than dogs in England, and ships' masters blamed mistakes on witches, executing them without trial.[11]

Gatford suggested they begin by hanging "spirits," the agents supplying Virginia with miserable people, mostly abducted children—these kidnappings, he said, were a "diabolical practice" likely "to pull a curse and vengeance upon the whole Plantation." The mood on England's streets was febrile. John Hammond had decided not to persuade his faggot-seller to emigrate "for fear of the cry of 'a spirit, a spirit!'" Prosecutions bore out this fear. Christian Chacrett of London was accused in 1655 of being "one that takes upp men, woemen and children and sells them a-shipp to bee conveyed beyond the sea"; she had, it was alleged, enticed Edward Furnivall's family onto a ship bound for Virginia. Some of the trafficked children were very young: Richard Hornold was just four, and his own father was complicit in the crime. Too few magistrates took spirits seriously, however, even after an ordinance of 1645 was passed concerning them; the practice was condemned more because it degraded Virginia's workforce than for humanitarian reasons. Nor was there much sympathy for adult dupes. William Bullock condemned "lazie, simple people . . . who are persuaded by these spirits they shall goe into a place where food shall drop into their mouthes, and being thus deluded they take courage and are transported. But not finding what was promised their courage abates & their minds being dejected, their work is according; nor doth the Master studie any way how to encourage them, but with soure looks for which they care not; and being tyred with chafing himself growes carelesse, and so all comes to nothing."[12]

The solution to the problem identified by Bullock lay not in stiffer penalties but in better recordkeeping, which protected the young and the foolish as well as merchants and planters. Apart from anything else, good records stopped servants on whom an adventurer had spent considerable sums in food, clothes, and passage from claiming to have been coerced. Bristol's enrollment system led the way in the mid-1650s.[13]

Perhaps the most striking thing about Virginia in the 1650s is that it had survived, and that, for all its flaws, people still found courage to go there, and optimism to invest in it and tackle its problems. Many of the challenges would have been familiar to the Virginia Company in its heyday; but now England's insistence on orthodoxy and order, and a determination to seize resources for the state, made the Chesapeake seem more promising *and* more contentious than it had been in 1620. To obey the crown, colonies had to first resemble England in devolved government, with every man's loyalty and responsibility underwritten by a share of property and authority. Paradoxically, however, this political sophistication also meant that enfranchised planters formed clearer, more confident ideas about sharing power with England than the earlier colonists—a compromise unacceptable to Cromwell and his successors. Nowhere was this volatile situation more apparent than in New England.

O n September 3, 1658, a hurricane hit England, presaging, some said, the end of Cromwell, who died on that same destructive day. News arrived in Boston a few weeks later and was mournfully received by those who had seen the Lord Protector as an ally. John Hull heard it in February 1659, noting in his diary: "The lord give sutable affections to bewaile the loss of such choyse ones; he was one that sought the good of New England." Apprehension followed the succession of Richard Cromwell; but then, some colonists had suspected his father of ill intentions, too, especially after Barbados and Virginia were subdued, which made Massachusetts residents wonder if their colonies would be next. Prominent Bostonians were used to ruling their English outpost; they had much to lose to an intrusive Westminster government. However anglophile their hearts and minds, prosperity and power and a righteous sense of political entitlement fixed their feet in America.[14]

Boston was a thriving commercial city by the 1650s. Its manufacturing and retail trades had expanded, and its shops were well stocked all year round. The wigwams, huts, and burrows of the first settlers had been replaced by "fair and well-built houses, well furnished many of them, together with Orchards filled with goodly fruit trees and gardens with variety of flowers." So wrote Edward Johnson, who appreciated Boston's distinctly European grandeur: "The chiefe Edifice of this City-like Towne," he continued, "is crowded on the Sea-bankes and wharfed out with great industry and cost, the buildings beautifull and large, some fairely set forth with Brick, Tile, Stone and Slate and orderly placed with comly streets, whose continuall inlargement presages some sumptuous City. The wonder of this moderne Age that a few yeares should bring forth such great matters by so meane a handful." One visitor was impressed by the wide cobbled streets lined with handsome buildings "joyning one to the other as in London." From a hilltop, he surveyed the forest of masts in the bay, and to the south the spacious common, "where the Gallants a little before Sun-set walk with their Marmalet-Madams"—as in English metropolitan parks.[15]

Twenty years earlier, Boston had consisted of little more than a few houses and a couple of distinctly unfriendly inns, and New England was in a fix. The promoter's argument about markets and commodities was unpersuasive there. The colonies were self-sufficient in most essentials, and commercial shipping, its economic mainstay, offered England competition, not sustenance. New England's most precious commodity had been fur, but within a decade the Massachusetts Bay Company had exhausted its supply. Expansion in the 1630s depended on agriculture, which in turn depended on immigration. By the English civil war, however, the decline of emigration, and indeed reverse migration, suddenly meant that farmers were overproducing. Prices collapsed: a cow worth £30 went for £5. Debt rose, credit evaporated, and families faced ruin. The problem was exacerbated by the means of exchange. Barter was necessary, yet it became increasingly difficult as the value of produce plummeted. Silver was scarce—it tended to flow away from America—and wampum, the polished shells prized by Indians, was an unreliable currency. Wampum *had* worked well; but now there was too much of it and not enough beaver to sustain its worth. In Rhode Island, Roger Williams struggled to explain to Indians why their livelihoods depended on the vicissitudes of English markets.[16]

Then in the 1640s relief arrived like manna from heaven. As the sugar colonies specialized, so their need for exports from New England grew. Horses and timber were in great demand. From the mid-seventeenth century, prefabricated houses were shipped to the West Indies, where forests had been cleared for plantations and joiners were few. The biggest market was for food. A growing slave population could survive on salt cod, and its production was stimulated by England's civil wars, which in turn kept West Country fishermen away. The benefits came quickly. Boston's shipyards became busy, and cheap sugar flowed in—visitors noticed tooth decay. And European silver coin also flowed in, giving farmers the security they needed to keep producing. It felt safer to exchange produce for a medium of stable value that could be stored than an unstable one that could not. The only problem was that so much money was clipped, debased, or counterfeited, and in large denominations. A lack of change also bedeviled the colonies. Irish pennies changed hands at Jamestown; Bermuda had brass "hog shillings"; and copper tokens were used everywhere. Then there was "commodity money." In Virginia this meant tobacco, despite the inconvenience of trading with bales and barrels; bills of exchange were procured from the West Indies before tobacco could be used in transatlantic deals. Scarcity of coin in Massachusetts led the general court to declare grain legal tender.[17]

In the early 1650s, Massachusetts elected to make its own money. The decision reflected both the self-confidence and the desperation of a commercially vibrant state. No permission was sought from England; instead, its noninterventionism was assumed. Whatever sympathy Oliver Cromwell had for New England, the complexity of its politics had made taking sides or courting allies too risky. Best leave New England to its own devices, which suited colonists just fine. When John Hull was first asked to design the coinage, he refused; but the offer of a stake in their manufacture piqued his interest, so he agreed to the second proposal. His mint made shillings (bearing the image of a pine tree, similar to those on the Massachusetts seal) using silver of English quality but at three-quarters the weight of England's coins, which kept them circulating in America. John Hull took one shilling in every twenty and became rich. He bought lumber mills and land in Rhode Island, where he bred horses to send to Virginia and the Caribbean. Chesapeake planters complained that they, too, needed mints, as their lack of a currency was "a main hindrance to the advancement of . . . trades, manufactures, towns and all other things which conduce to the flourishing and happy state thereof."[18]

By midcentury, New England came to supply food not just to the West Indies, but also to Virginia, Spain, Portugal, and even, as Edward Johnson boasted, "the firtil Isle of Great Britain." "Thus hath the Lord been pleased to turn one of the most hideous, boundless and unknown Wildernesses in the world," he remarked. Most of the colonies sought to integrate their economies into the transatlantic market; but even insular townships were good at supplying themselves, and often this was enough. Agriculture at Concord, Massachusetts, was diverse and sustainable, with tillage, meadows, woodland, and waterways like England. Colonists imported clover and grass, better for grazing livestock, and weeds that protected the soil structure. In the town of Sudbury, which, like Salem and other townships, had adopted a medieval open-field system, a burgeoning population made land scarce. This situation led to the growth of commercial agriculture, consolidated estates (with an eye on commercial profit), and bitter disputes over common rights— just like what had happened in England. In the end, a faction left to settle Marlborough, which was situated ten miles away.[19]

The desire for a "competency"—enough land for comfortable independence—was also part of England's "moral economy." But in both
England and America, the impossibility of everyone getting what they
wanted wore away communal bonds. The New England town has a
mythic communitarian quality, but this came from the forms and values of rural tradition in the Old World as much as from the wilderness
exceptionalism of the new. And, as in England, it was a quality that
degraded rapidly. A generation earlier, Edward Winslow had described
New England as a place "where Religion and profit jump together";
but they were increasingly out of step. Earlier than most towns, Salem
was transformed into an economic powerhouse where mercantile clout
threatened Puritan authority. The Bostonian John Hull was a devout
man able to reconcile the two, but his city's enrichment was seen as deviation from its goals—both symptom and cause of moral decay.[20]

Wickedness abounded. On October 19, 1652, the general court ordered a fast, speaking for the first time of New England's guilt in provoking sins that flowed from its "worldly mindedness, oppression &
hardhartedness." Malefactors—rebels against God and nature—passed
through the courts, from men with long hair ("after the manner of
ruffians and barborous Indians") to sex offenders. The rape of a nine-
year-old girl at Watertown in 1654 caused revulsion; it also caused dread
at the cosmic import of such behavior. There were witches, too. And if
a hairstyle could have, in the words of one preacher, "an appearance of
evil," imagine the wrath meted out to devil-worshippers.[21]

The year 1656 saw the execution for witchcraft of Ann Hibbens, a
contentious woman from a well-to-do merchant family. She may have
been insane; her brother, Richard Bellingham, the colony's former governor, suffered from bouts of mental illness. The following year, two
women, displaying what John Hull called "a kind of raving & madness,"
caused despair among their neighbors. Some said they had committed
a secret sin, others "that Satan took advantage at a spirit of discontent
with their own Condition, as being poor & conflicting with sundry
wants." To be rich like Hull betokened saintly election; poverty, divine
disfavor. A rash of New England witch-trials in the late 1650s included
that of Elizabeth Garlick at Hartford, Connecticut, who was accused
of "familliarity with Satan, the great enemy of God & mankinde," and
of performing "workes above the course of nature," including murders. It is telling that Hartford was split ideologically, testing patience
in Boston, where elders accused warring factions of discrediting New

England's churches. John Winthrop's famous words appeared in a letter reminding Hartford that "you are a Citty whose fame hath sett you upon a hill therfore you cannot be hid."[22]

The beacon would shine brightest, many still hoped, wherever Indians were converted. This was an image of America that godly Englishmen held in their minds, imprinted by letters and tracts describing startling confessions. To the question "what is God?" Indians at Roxbury, home of their teacher John Eliot, gave answers that humbled English audiences. Manifestations of civility continued to underpin spiritual awakenings, with Indians affecting colonial customs and singing psalms to English tunes. John Endecott proudly told the president of the New England Company (NEC), the company set up to propagate the gospel, that natives could build a house precisely "after the English manner." Edward Reynolds, a London vicar, thought it a matter of "abundant thanksgivings to God to find poor Americans speking the languag[e] of Canaan, subscribing with their hand unto the Lord and sirnaming themselves by the name of Israel."[23]

Using a parliamentary grant, John Eliot had established the town of Natick, west of Roxbury, for "praying Indians." The NEC sent Bibles and other works; paper, penknives, and inkwells; clothing, tools, and seeds. One shipment included six dozen pairs of "Christall Specktacles," another tracts against swearing. Charity covered the cost. The parliamentarian army contributed £3,000 between 1649 and 1655, almost a quarter of the total for this period, the rest coming from private gifts and parish collections. In 1653 alone, Little Dunmow in Essex gave 41 shillings; at North Elmham in Norfolk, donations ranged from 2 shillings to a pound, amounting to over £10 in all; Blithing in Suffolk managed a total of £68 1s 1½d—enough for several hundred Bibles.[24]

Even so, Eliot was forever asking for more. He translated the Bible into Algonquian and, ignoring doubts about whether the Indians could be taught to read it, still less understand it, implored the NEC to send a compositor and a stock of paper. If only, said Eliot, English colonists could be as pure-hearted as the natives, who were repudiating the evil power which "the Devil and Witches use to torment the Bodies and Minds of Men." Puritan missionaries saw beyond race, making distinctions by faith alone. American pagans and ungodly Englishmen, said a Plymouth resident, were both "Indians."[25]

Results were mixed. In private, John Eliot was uncertain how much could be achieved. One of his correspondents in England agreed, calling Indian recalcitrance "a sad & strange thing." As commercial ambitions grew, so did the tensions. Eliot found Indians increasingly wary—and rightly so. The NEC sent swords and guns to the colonists so that they could defend themselves against attack by native warriors, and a dispatch from Connecticut to Massachusetts recommended that these "beastly minded and mannered Creatures" be shown neither respect nor leniency. "We cannot but conceave," the letter continued, that "it is high time to renew upon the memory of these Pagans the obliterate memorials of the English."[26]

By now Eliot was faced not just with the struggle to spread the gospel, but also a political and religious controversy between Englishmen. In a pamphlet published in October 1659, just as the army forcibly dissolved Parliament and replaced it with a "committee of safety," Eliot prayed that God would "scatter those black Clouds which do darken the mindes of God's People in England." He had not yet heard that Richard Cromwell had resigned as Lord Protector, but he knew of disunity at Westminster and the nation's crossroads in government. Swiping at the man whom royalists called "Queen Dick," and at Charles I's son, who was waiting in the wings, Eliot argued that England's godly rulers should "set the Crown of England upon the head of Christ, whose only true inheritance it is by the gift of his Father. Let him be your Law-Giver. Let him be your King!"[27]

O ne night in July 1660, an apparition hovered in the skies over Barbados. Colonists testified that an enormous man in armor removed his helmet to reveal "a very glorious Crowne upon his head, and both the Crowne, his face and body shined more bright and glorious than the finest polished gold in the world." His identity was obvious. Six weeks earlier, Charles II had arrived in London, an embodiment of the sun in splendor, amid great public celebration. News may already have reached Barbados; in the Caribbean the king's return had been expected for several months. Once again, royalism was in the ascendant throughout the Atlantic world—a world where two out of every hundred English subjects now lived in America. Their experience of subjection by a distant monarch, and of being English beyond England's boundaries, would now combine with the political complexion of their colonies before and after the Restoration to create a sharper and more strident American identity.[28]

In colonies that had been strong-armed by Cromwell, joy was unconfined. As Virginia celebrated, royalist settlers felt drawn home to greet the new dawn. John Gibbon, a plantation steward at Dividing Creek, had enjoyed a comfortable life there until, as he recalled, "at length newes arriving of the Kings restoration I was very desirous to returne to my native Country." His employer offered him a wife and a thousand acres to stay, but by March 1661 he was back in England. He was to spend the next fifty years regretting this decision. At the age of eighty-six, he wrote:

> *Once in Virginia I did dwell,*
> *Would I had ne'er bid it farewell.*

England and America both held romantic appeal for the English depending on which side of the Atlantic they were on. Puritans who had fled England, then returned for the civil war, now wished themselves in New England again. Desperate to see England's epiphany, they found themselves chasing a chimera. Others kept Albion in their hearts wherever they were. George Alsop learned of the king's return in a letter, but he did not leave Maryland. He simply prayed that Charles's name would radiate forever, and that God would give him "a hand of just Revenge to punish the murthering and rebellious Outrages of those Sons of shame and Apostacy that usurped the Throne of his Sacred Honour."[29]

God seemed ready to oblige. With the bonfires and bells and loyal cheers came restitutions and recriminations. In Gloucestershire, a minister who had come from New England was assaulted by a mob led by "a rude Cavaleer" who cried: "Yee Rogue, yee Dogg, the times are turned!" The minister was driven from his home and church, or "meeting-house," as he called it in his provocatively American way. Thomas Clark, a dissenter in Barbados, suffered even more. On the day that Charles II was proclaimed, Matthew Gray, a royalist minister, arrived drunk outside Clark's house. Clark later related how, when Gray saw him at his window, he "held up his Horse Whip, shaking at me, and said Tom, you must come no more to my Church, for now, said he, we have got a King." Boys were incited to throw stones, and "Rude People" fired guns. Clark was injured and his wife dragged out and stripped in front of her sobbing children. With vengeance came hopes that natural rights would be restored, hopes expressed by Anglicans and nonconformists alike. One Quaker wrote to the king on behalf of all West Indian colonists, pleading for protection against wicked laws that had been imposed during the Interregnum.[30]

The profitability of Barbados had surged ahead of other Caribbean colonies, increasing both planters' sense of entitlement and their anxiety that the island's prosperity would be drained off by their metropolitan masters. Another concern was the scarcity of manpower. In 1645 a naval chaplain named George Downing had enthused to his cousin John Winthrop Jr. about Barbados's African slaves—1,000 had been imported that year—who were, he wrote, "the life of the place." By 1660 there were 27,000, constituting perhaps half the total population. Not all slaves were black. Thousands of the prisoners taken in England's civil wars had been transported to Barbados—12,000 in 1646 alone—notably after the siege of Colchester. Merchants spuriously claimed that they had come voluntarily. Several thousand Irish, taken prisoner or kidnapped, were also "barbadosed," and hundreds of Scots, captured at Dunbar and Worcester in the 1650s, were sold in Massachusetts, New Hampshire, and Maine for £20 to £30 each—a reminder that even New England relied on unfree workers, be they indentured servants, Africans, Indians, or prisoners. It was even alleged that troops serving in the West Indies had been sold, both there and in Virginia.[31]

In this rapacious, largely unregulated world, the line between servant and slave was a fine one, but neither appellation suited the Englishman shipped 4,000 miles against his will. As the republic crumbled, its victims found a voice. Two royalist rebels, Marcellus Rivers and Oxenbridge Foyle, "Free-born English-men sold (uncondemned) into slavery," petitioned Parliament for themselves and seventy others in 1659. They had, they said, been sold to the "most inhumane and barbarous persons" for 1,550 pounds of sugar each; moreover, they had been kept in conditions "miserable beyond expression or Christian imagination." They were not, they maintained, the planters' property, but English subjects held arbitrarily.[32]

Rivers likened Barbados to a "disconsolate vault" where they were buried alive, longing to hear the words "Arise Free-man and walk." The petitioners asked Parliament to make their case a "touchstone by which you may discover whether English be Slaves or Freemen." Ironically, a similar cry came from the Barbadians in whose sugar mills these gentleman worked. A petition to Richard Cromwell in December 1659 asked for protection of ancient liberties and support for a representative body of freeholders to elect their governors. They craved only "to partake of those Immunityes, Priviledges & Freedoms which o[u]r Brethren of England doe or may receive." This had been promised in 1652, but not delivered. Planters in Barbados, as in Virginia, Bermuda, and Maryland, knew the political tide was turning; but their hopes were false. Charles II may have dishonored Cromwell's corpse, but he shared his enthusiasm for the Navigation Act, renewing it in 1660 and 1663. These laws were as lucrative to England as they were oppressive to colonists. Jamaica, too, may have been a conquest of the Lord Protector, but the king decided not to return it to Spain, as he had pledged, but rather, to extend his imperium over this most promising territory.[33]

New Englanders were less deceived about the Restoration. In Boston, John Hull called the king's return "a strange turne of providence" and joined a solemn fast. American Puritans prayed that their brethren overseas would be relieved of "sad distractions" and spared the designs of conservative royalists and radical Quakers. John Leverett, a Massachusetts stalwart, was in London as the colony's agent in 1660. He informed Governor John Endecott in September that a royal governor was to be sent to New England; it was just one of several rumors, another being that complaints from American Quakers had persuaded the king to grant them freedom. At the other extreme, offensive rituals were ebbing back into the English church. "The Lord keepe us and preserve his churches," prayed Leverett, "that there may not be fainting in a day of tryall." While Endecott was digesting this, a ship brought news that England was "looking sadly toward the letting in of Popery": John Hull feared they would yet copy the Israelites, who, when about to enter Canaan, were sent back to the Red Sea. During an influenza epidemic in December, Endecott petitioned the king to uphold the Bay Colony's patent, explaining why its people had come "into this vast and waste wilderness," and declaring a willingness to listen to complaints.[34]

Some New England colonies declared for the crown long before others. Rhode Island came out in October 1660, but it took Massachusetts another ten months. In the end there were feasts, volleys of shot, and cries of "God save the king" in the streets—gestures intended to persuade Charles II that Boston was not what its detractors alleged: an independent city-state in all but name. This display of affection was unconvincing, but it scarcely mattered. The harnessing of private enterprise to national goals had been piecemeal before 1660. Various commissions, committees, and councils had done little except interfere in emigration, criticize colonial charters, and advise on trade. Now, state policy would be more focused and forceful; it was the advent of a thirty-year push to impose imperial authority in America and exploit its commercial potential. Sometimes this drive lost direction and momentum, and enforcement of the Navigation Acts was patchy. But overall, the struggle was sustained, amounting to a significant departure in official attitudes from the previous era.[35]

As Boston's leaders reflected on their past and future, so a different kind of American champion offered some perspective. A merchant named Henry Gardiner, the son of an adventurer in New Hampshire, warned against painting all New Englanders as the same. He acknowledged that Boston behaved like a free state, but insisted that its inhabitants were only a fraction of a loyal population. With "good society and English Government," he suggested, New England could be the best place to live in the world. It could enlarge the king's dominions "as if all the Baltick Seas were Annexed to His Empire." Too few hands had held too much power, shunning even early pioneers. This was perhaps a failing of reason, but it was definitely a failing of kindness. New Englanders, Gardiner concluded, might learn from Turks and papists: "I could wish they had so much Charity." Love between brothers and neighbors, which had been decaying for over half a century of economic turbulence and civil war in England, had not been reborn across the Atlantic. Indeed, in its treatment of nonconformists, "the city upon a hill" appeared to have raised a flag of intolerance and persecution. In America, as at home, liberty was contingent and contested.[36]

The fall of the English republic and the return of the monarchy signaled a reversal in the reputation of the colonies. Virginia, Maryland, and Barbados, which had been punished for their royalism, now found favor for their loyalty, whereas Massachusetts would be treated with suspicion as a de facto republic that had connived at revolution and condoned regicide. Yet the identity of the American territories was also being shaped by their vexed relationship to an imperial state—a state established by Cromwell and developed by Charles II that insisted its sovereignty be respected across the Atlantic. Colonists would not easily surrender their hard-won wealth and practical autonomy. And in that truculence, expressed using the rhetoric of English liberty, they experienced a growing sense of difference from England, even as they appealed to England's most ancient and cherished constitutional values from distant plantations.

CHAPTER 13

How Is Your Beauty Become Ashes?

W HEN EDWARD JOHNSON CALLED Boston a "wonder of this
moderne Age," he might have been describing any number
of seventeenth-century transformations. State-building, scientific advances, and commercial brio were changing the world. In England constitutional events had been startling, and trade in sugar and slaves was
revolutionizing its Caribbean territories. American colonists doggedly
preserved Englishness in every part of their lives, from faith to food,
but they could not resist the influence of politics and property: they had
acquired a desire for limited self-determination and for the freedom
to enjoy the fruits of their labors without unfair taxation. From the
1660s, similarities between English people in worlds old and new often
mattered less than the fact that they were not exactly the same: the
differences rankled. Treatment of religious nonconformists, especially
Quakers, was key, because it involved the basic principles of law, morality, moderation, authority, and liberty by which societies understood
themselves. This did not mean England was more homogeneous or any
calmer than its colonies; but as one side defined itself against the other,
stereotyping was expedient and perhaps inevitable.

Complaints focused on New England. On May 31, 1660, Mary Dyer
faced Governor John Endecott in court, showing neither fear nor remorse. After supporting Anne Hutchinson in the Antinomian controversy, Dyer had settled in Rhode Island and had visited England, where
she had become a Quaker. In 1659, she had stood at the gallows wearing a noose, with fellow Quakers William Robinson and Marmaduke
Stephenson dangling beside her. At the last moment, she received a
reprieve, and then was banished. Her defiant return to Boston less than
a year later caused the mint-master, John Hull, to note in his diary: "He

must needs goe whom the divell drives." To Puritans like Hull, Quakers were anathema, epitomizing disrespect, superstition, inconstancy, and rebellion. As Endecott sentenced Dyer to death, she reminded him that as long as Massachusetts had harsh laws, God would "send others of his Servants to Witness against them." The governor, aghast at her insolence, asked if she were a prophet, to which Dyer replied that she "spake the words that the Lord spake in her." The next morning, soldiers escorted her through the streets, drums drowning out any dangerous pronouncements she might make. Perched on the ladder, her skirts knotted at her ankles, she assured the crowd on Boston Common that she was not Satan's slave and would enjoy everlasting happiness. Her face was covered, "and so, sweetly and chearfully in the Lord, she . . . dyed a faithful Martyr of Jesus Christ."[1]

An early-twentieth-century painting of the Quaker Mary Dyer being escorted to the gallows in Boston, June 1, 1660. Her execution, and the sufferings of fellow religious nonconformists, helped establish for all time the Puritans' reputation for intolerance in New England.

The author of this valediction was Edward Burrough, another Puritan who had been converted to Quakerism by its leader, George Fox. The Society of Friends, as Quakers were known, followed not religious law but mystical experiences of God in themselves and each other. Itinerant Quakers became apostles. At his execution, Marmaduke Stephenson had told spectators: "This is the day of your visitation, wherein the Lord hath visited you." Some found Quakerism at the end of a difficult journey, such as the Catholic youth who was spirited to Maryland and then abused by a Puritan master. Many Quakers were poor, yet free from worldly desire. Four years earlier, Stephenson had been a laborer in Yorkshire, "filled with the Love and Presence of the Living God" as he pushed a plough. Critics thought these communications diabolical. Quakers have a compact with Satan, the new Dorchester settler Edward Breck told his former parish in Lancashire, and "in the finest way of witchcraft & sorceries convene it over unto others."[2]

Distressed by the executions, Burrough appealed to Charles II in terms scarcely more deferential than those Mary Dyer had used to address John Endecott. The king, who reviled puffed-up Bostonians and favored toleration to rebuild a national church, decreed that persecution should end and Quakers be sent to England. In Boston, however, there would be one more hanging before the royal writ came into force. William Leddra hailed from Barbados, and, like Dyer, he had returned to Boston under a suspended death sentence. He had been whipped, his ear had been cut off, and he had been chained outside to a log in the winter of 1660–1661. Like Robinson, Stephenson, and Dyer, Leddra exhibited a patient piety that contrasted with Boston's ruthlessness. In a letter that he wrote just before he died, Leddra told his brethren not to fear: "In the power of his Meekness you shall reign over all the rage of your Enemies in the favour of God."[3]

John Endecott was accused of cruel contempt for English law. After Mary Dyer's first death sentence had been issued, her husband, William, had likened the magistrates to a bloodthirsty episcopate, and not just anti-Calvinists in the 1630s but Catholics in the 1550s. Richard Bellingham's charge against his wife, he said, echoed what "Bonner, Gardiner and ye rest of th[a]t Bloody Crew said to the poor saints in Q[ueen] Maries dayes," when bishops hunted heretics to "bring them before their thrones." Boston's intolerance was worthy of Iberia or the Orient. "What, hath not people in America the same liberty as beasts & birds have to pass the land or ayre w[i]thout examinac[i]on?" Dyer asked. If not, he suggested, England was no better than "barbarous" China. The complaint reached Westminster that Quakers' pleas for leave to appeal were being dismissed by upstarts "who would not own that England [had] anything to do with them." George Bishop, a former Cromwellian spymaster, cited a Boston minister who declared that even for trying to petition England, Quakers "should be led up Windmil-Hill, that is the Gallows in plain English, to be Hanged." Bishop, too, noted the irony that the persecuted, who once hid trembling under their beds, should have become the persecutors.[4]

Boston's defense was that it was entitled to protect itself. Quakers had been warned, but had not quelled "their impetuous frantick fury." Banishment on pain of death was a last resort, protested magistrates, like England's handling of Jesuit priests. They were not murderers: returning Quakers were suicides. As Edward Rawson, the colony secretary, insisted: "We desire their lives absent rather than their death present." The Quaker response was unbridled. The members of Boston's elite were puppets of Antichrist, punishing matters of conscience fit for God alone. On Judgment Day, predicted one, "shall your bowels be ripped open and your inside-coverings broken, and then shall your hearts be rent with perplexity." Another called the Boston leaders "Satans messengers," promising they would "have blood to drink who have shed innocent blood."[5]

George Fox offered statistics: 45 visitors to Boston had been imprisoned for a total of 307 weeks; 139 had received blows with pitch-hardened ropes; and fines totaling £318 11s had been leveled against them. Two Quaker women had been searched as witches in an examination so degrading that one of them said "she had not been so in the birth of her children." This story, which accompanied a petition to the king in 1661, also related how one Quaker had been whipped so severely that "a greate part of his body was much like unto a Jelly and his bloud hang[e]d downe as if it were in baggs."[6]

The oppression raised the question of royal authority in America. English subjects, suggested George Bishop, were free to inhabit any of England's colonies, but had no right to declare their own dominions. What chaos would ensue if they did? "Nature must be the measure of Law," opined Bishop, "not Law of Nature." It is doubtful, however, that after thirty years of habituation to its own routines, the Massachusetts Bay Colony had as much respect for English sovereignty. To many New Englanders, the substance of recriminations about Quakers was not just theological, political, and legal: it was cultural. They saw English strangers trespassing in their world, supported by others 3,000 miles away, and were affronted. Transatlantic identity was fissured by intrusion and insult. Even Bostonians sympathetic to Quakers recoiled to hear their city called "a withered branch"—the words of John Rous, a Barbadian Quaker, in a public speech. "How is thy beauty faded," he continued, "thou who was famous among the Nations for thy zeal towards God, but now thy zeal is turned in to hypocrisie."[7]

What, in general, did people in England and New England think of each other? Visitors from America were shocked by England's poverty, crime, and sin. Nor were they afraid to comment, causing the same offense John Rous had caused in Boston. The divisiveness of congregationalism bothered English parishioners, Puritans included. Richard Baxter, a Worcestershire dissenter, alerted John Eliot to the godliness hidden in the multitude: those who professed faith might be ignorant, while true saints were concealed beneath "an invincible bashfullnesse." The New Englander's pious condescension was both scorned and revered—"the ground he walks upon beloved for his sake, and the house held the better where he is." "Pride of Parts and pride of Hearts," wrote a Connecticut clergymen, eager for colonists to see themselves as others did, "pride in Apparel and Vestures, and in Gestures and in Looks; how lofty are their eyes!" "See here (by their ill measure)," said another, "the vanity of conceited men." Later in the century, a critic described even ordinary New Englanders as "very censorious and ready on all occasions to judge one another," explaining that "their Separate way makes them very high and unsociable, looking on others as mean abject creatures, who deserve their Pity rather than their Company." Their extreme biblical literalism aroused fear or amusement—for example, the size of New England's beer barrels followed stipulations in the Book of Deuteronomy.[8]

New England's image was not helped by the notorious slyness of its merchants—some thought them worse than Jews. Sharp practice was to be expected in Virginia, where colonists looked out for themselves and never paid market prices, and in Maryland, where traders ran rings around outsiders. More was hoped of Bostonians, yet still people said: "There is a New England Cheat, take heed of a New-England Cheat." Visitors were struck most by Boston's strictness. This was no tolerant entrepôt like Jamaica's Port Royal: for all its Atlantic vitality, Boston remained the fiercely beating heart of the Puritan "errand in the wilderness." The Sabbath began at sunset on Saturdays, and in taverns, strangers were chaperoned to prevent drunkenness. There were relatively few churches, and visitors could not receive Holy Communion because, like most inhabitants, they had not been accepted into congregations. Ships were searched and forbidden books burned, reminding George Fox of the days of Marian paranoia. Guests had to watch their mouths, too. In 1654, a drunk soldier named Benjamin Saucer said, "Jehova is the Devel & he knew noe god but his sworde." Arrested for blasphemy, he lay in chains for three weeks. He pleaded that he was a loyal servant of Cromwell and a "true borne subject of England . . . [and] noe inhabitant of this place," asking in vain to appeal to England. He escaped before sentencing, probably saving his life.[9]

Similar tales were heard in England. Early in Charles II's reign, a merchant named Archibald Henderson signed a petition demanding royal government in New England, complaining that Boston's government had cost him £800. Through its tyranny, "multitudes of his Ma[jes]t[ie]s Subjects have beene most unjustly and grevieously opprest contrary to y[ou]r owne Lawes of this Realm," he declared. New England had assumed, petitioners said, "the preveledge of a Free State." Henderson had arrived in Boston from Barbados in 1652, having lost part of his cargo during the conflict there, only to find the remainder preyed upon by a different English enemy. Officials made no allowance for his being "a Stranger to their Customes," complained Henderson, and subjected him to laws unauthorized by their charter. One Saturday evening a gang accused him of Sabbath-breaking and dragged him to jail. Henderson was convicted of drunkenness, made to raise bail of £300, and told that their law was different, and appeals to England forbidden. A plea to John Endecott only earned him more prison time. Meanwhile, his ship, loaded for Barbados, was blown ashore in a storm that inflicted hundreds of pounds' worth of damage.[10]

New England's merchants were probably no slyer than the merchants of any other country, and its lawmen no more officious. Yet, by midcentury, its practical loyalties had shifted, however bonded to England colonists remained on an emotional level. Robert Keayne, son of an emigrant Berkshire butcher, was a second-generation settler who had prospered by exploiting his London contacts. He had always thought of himself as an Englishman. Yet Keayne invested his wealth not in England, but in Massachusetts, the place where his godly life made most sense. He owed his civic values to the motherland; the locus for their practical application, however, was America.[11]

T he cultural hostility between the residents of old England and New England was reinforced by political strife in England itself: the crown wanted to bind its foes by legal settlement, and parliamentarians were reluctant to tolerate and forgive. Charles II pardoned all revolutionaries except those directly responsible for his father's death. Show-trials followed, including that of the Salem minister Hugh Peter, who had lobbied against the king and whose absence at the execution (due to illness) had fueled rumors that he was the masked executioner. Addressing the newly restored House of Lords, Peter declared himself to be an American missionary to England. He had been sent by God, he said, to a land "imbroyled in trouble and warre," and had come from one where he "never saw any drunke, never heard an oath, nor saw sabboth broken, nor ever heard of one beggar." He was hanged, drawn and quartered, and his head was skewered on London Bridge. Others fled to Europe and America; some joked that the only Englishman welcome in New England was a regicide. Three of Charles's judges—Edward Whalley, William Goffe, and John Dixwell—made it to America, the first two to Massachusetts, Dixwell to Connecticut via the continent. Other "military saints" also emigrated, "flying thither richly laden w[i]th the plunder of old England," according to one report. A lot of property *had* gone missing. Hugh Peter had appropriated Archbishop Laud's library, and he was questioned about the whereabouts of the entire contents of St. James's Palace.[12]

The hunt for Charles I's murderers—Whalley, Goffe, and Dixwell—began. In 1661, letters were sent to John Endecott, who replied that the Massachusetts authorities had searched diligently. Earlier that year, Endecott had told Charles II that he knelt before him in what he called the king's "Brittish Israel," adding assurances that he and his fellow migrants had left England "not upon any dissatisfaction to the constitution of the Civil State," but only to worship. However, conflicting accounts reached Whitehall. A former governor of Maine dismissed Boston's protestations of loyalty as a sham, alleging that donations for spreading the gospel were used to buy land so as to advance independence. Particularly damaging testimony came from a gentleman who had been in Boston soon after the Restoration. Upon his arrival, he said, Goffe and Whalley had been taken to Endecott, who had "embraced them, bad them welcome to New England, & wished more such good men as they would come over." Other prominent men also paid homage to these traitors, who now lived at Harvard College and were "looked upon as men dropt down from heaven." The royal warrant against them was never proclaimed, he said, or else loyalists would surely have apprehended them. Godly elders refused to condemn Hugh Peter as well.[13]

In March 1661, Captain Thomas Breedon reported to the Council for Foreign Plantations that New England's laws were either public and unjustified or secret and arbitrary. Separating freeman church members from the majority, the elect from the reprobate, he said, was as familiar a division "as Cavalleers & Roundheads was in England, and will shortly become as odious." Breedon claimed that owing to fierce disagreement, Boston's loyal proclamation to Charles II had taken a week to write, and a man falsely identified as the king himself had been arrested. New Englanders' oath of fidelity was to themselves alone, and they evaded customs, including levies on trade with Barbados and Jamaica. Breedon advised speed in "settling and establishing this Country in due obedience and subjection." Six weeks later, several reports, including Archibald Henderson's petition, were compiled in a damning indictment, which concluded that Boston was severing its ties with London. The king was urged to make the colony see that it remained part of England and must bow to the crown to survive.[14]

The belief of those who were persecuted in their own sacrifice was one area where they could not be accused of insincerity, yet pride was punctured by an equally sincere sense of inadequacy. Plymouth was forty years old in 1660. Appealing to the crown that James I's charter be upheld, settlers there compared themselves to Israelites in "a desert sowed w[i]th the seed of man & beast." Old Testament typology continued to shape their experience, from the political tussles in England to the trials of the American wilderness. In 1662, New England's wheat was shriveled by drought, attacked by fungus, and infested with caterpillars; smallpox raged. Was God punishing them for losing their way? A pious and censorious member of New Haven's church was convicted of buggery in June. As he waited to be pushed off the ladder at his hanging—a scene his daughter had foreseen in a dream—three cows, three sheep, and two pigs were slaughtered before the gallows. Having claimed that as a saint he was not afraid to die, he now fell into agonies of doubt.[15]

In the same month, a Quaker exhorted the colony to repent. "Oh New-England," she lamented, "how is your beauty become ashes, and your glory turned into shame?" Puritans knew she had a point, and they feared the younger generation was abandoning the colony's founding ideals. In response, a "half-way covenant" was allowed; it offered partial church membership to children and grandchildren of original church members, who could now be baptized without public conversion. While some considered this a means to preserving identity, others saw in it only confirmation and acceleration of cultural demise. Even Puritans in England were critical, passing remarks that angered the Boston synod.[16]

Massachusetts adopted simultaneous postures of self-regard, self-reproach, and supplication. John Hull spent much of 1662 in England as part of a deputation to meet the king; he also visited relatives (and consulted records at his wife's Northampton parish to check her age). At one royal audience, Sir Thomas Temple, Boston's first official agent, mollified Charles II by pretending that the tree on New England's coins commemorated the "royal oak," the king's hiding place after the Battle of Worcester. Charles was amused, calling his visitors "a parcel of honest dogs." For now, Boston's illicit mint was safe. The king also accepted the deputation's vow of loyalty, promising his protection provided the Bay Colony use the Book of Common Prayer and hand over the regicides. The crown had no illusions, of course, and reports of disobedience persisted. Samuel Maverick, a pioneer New Englander who had been barred from government, warned of rebellion. Like three-quarters of his people, he honored the king and desired a royal governor. Maverick suggested to the lord chancellor that a few ships full of soldiers might depose the godly oligarchy. New Englanders would "thankfully receive them as the restorers of them to Libertye from long bondage, both in Civil and in Ecclesiasticall respects."[17]

Colonial perspectives varied. New England Puritans thought their government was a middle way between popish Spanish tyranny and devilish Indian anarchy. There, and throughout America, they said, Englishmen had no wish to conquer native societies, desiring only Roman *dominium* and *imperium* (ownership and command) over land. Ideally, this power was to be secured through the establishment of miniature commonwealths, which in culture and administration, if not always in politics and religion, resembled the English parishes where their first inhabitants had started out. The problem was that so many—Anglicans and Catholics, Antinomians and sectaries, Indians and Africans, European competitors, royal ministers, and administrators, not to mention ordinary farmers, artisans, and servants outside the churches and assemblies—rejected godly "moderation" as an oppressive imbalance of power hiding behind self-serving verbiage. This was a polity that had righteously yet undeservingly assumed authority for itself. Privately, though, the members of Boston's elite doubted themselves and watched nervously for signs of God's displeasure.[18]

In the last week of January 1663, earthquakes struck New England, shaking houses, toppling chimneys, and causing panic—an omen, some said, that heaven would rock the colony to its foundations. Despite securing a royal charter the previous year, Connecticut was haunted by religious and political fear, which was manifested in a burst of witch-hunting. In May, John Higginson, a Salem minister and the son of the pioneering Francis Higginson, gave the Massachusetts election-day sermon. He reiterated the aims of the great migration, denying that saints were separatists and decrying worldliness. "New-England," he preached, "is originally a plantation of Religion, not a plantation of Trade"—and godly graybeards should drill this message into the second generation so that they might avoid the wrath of God and Charles II.[19]

That New Englanders drilled it into themselves is suggested by the popularity of "The Day of Doom," a poem scorched by hellfire. Within a year of its publication in 1662, all 1,800 copies had been sold, and many of them memorized and internalized. The author was the Dorchester preacher Michael Wigglesworth, a caricature of the woebegone Puritan, a hypochondriac who extended his morbid self-obsession to his neighbors' morals. In the 1650s, he induced a girl named Tryal Pore, who had been accused of fornication, to confess: "By this my sinn I have not only donn what I can to Poull downe Ju[d]gmente from the lord on my selve," she said, "but also apon the place where I live." Like most American Puritans, Wigglesworth had been tested by the wilderness. He had arrived in Charlestown from Lincolnshire in 1638 at the age of seven; his father moved the family to New Haven, where for a year they lived in a damp underground hovel. Food was scarce, and his father contracted scurvy and was never well. Michael was forced to abandon school and run the family farm. Tragedy followed Wigglesworth into adulthood. The stillbirth of his child and death of his wife devastated him. "Oh its a heart-cutting & astonishing stroke in its self," he told his diary. "Lord help me to bear it patie[n]tly & to p[ro]fit by it."[20]

Wigglesworth's illnesses could symbolize the debility of the body politic. A letter from his uncle in Yorkshire hoped that God would incline his family's hearts "to make a returne backe to our European England . . . [where] our Climate would better agree w[i]th yor constituc[i]on then New-England doth." Instead, following his literary success, Wigglesworth's thoughts turned to Bermuda. The island air cured English diseases, he had heard, and "many have removed from England hither only for the enjoyment of a long and healthful life." Wigglesworth sailed in September 1663. In a voyage lasting for four weeks, he caught a cold that canceled out the climatic benefits of his destination. The winter was mild, but after seven months Wigglesworth did not feel much better, and he was tired of breadless meals and "very mean" lodgings. Oppressed by May's sultriness, he cut short his stay. He arrived in New England constipated and "much puzzled to know what to make of the Lords dealings w[i]th me." His best guess was that God had wanted his congregation to appreciate him more, which once he was back, they did.[21]

In his high-minded insularity, Wigglesworth embodied much of what Charles II disliked about New England—traits of character that made the king think he should reassert English authority there, "either [by] policy or Force." Colonial governors, meanwhile, were increasingly touchy about the internal disrespect they were encountering from their own people. In March 1664, Simon Tuttle of Ipswich, Massachusetts, was tried for saying "it were better to live in turkye then heere," and "if he weare in England againe, he would soone have our laws and law makers layd neck and heeles"—that is, subjected to a public shaming ritual. Tuttle longed for a time when English warships would arrive to enforce royal will, saying, "If we cannot have the libertye the King gave us, we would winn it by the edge of the sword." Samuel Maverick's impression of public opinion was that many men felt the same way Tuttle did. Colonists resented that New England's government was "in a few sneakinge fellows hands," and, as Tuttle put it, "hopt we should have a turne . . . and have our necks from under the yoke."[22]

A Royal Commission, including Samuel Maverick as one of its members, set to work in 1664. The Boston authorities protested that they had been misrepresented—they *did* abide by the Navigation Acts.

In response they were invited to disown "seditious spirits" critical of England. In a written address to the king that October, Massachusetts conceived its enemies' lies as providential punishment; colonists desired only "to live a poor and quiet life in a corner of the world without offence to God or man," preserving charter liberties in return for fealty to the crown. The silences between these communications were agonizing. Boston was powerless to be properly defiant, yet obviously too different to make its blandishments sound convincing. In November, a comet was spotted, reminding Puritans of Joel 2:30–31: "And I will shew wonders in the heavens and in the earth, blood and fire, and pillars of smoke"—a portent that Christ was coming.[23]

The Royal Commission's report of 1665 described absurd confusion and contempt in New England. Kennebec fishermen were ungoverned, and believed "as many men may share in a Woman as they do in a Boat." New Hampshire's sawyers craved freedom from Boston. Plymouth people were poor but loyal. Connecticut, too, conformed. Rhode Island was ridiculously tolerant in religion, with "so many sub-divided Sects, they canot agree to meet together in one Place." This left Massachusetts, "the last and hardlyest perswaded to use his Ma[jes]ties name in their formes of Justice." It made its own laws, charged taxes at will, and called itself a free state; church membership was restricted, Quakers tormented, and regicides entertained.[24]

Most galling to Charles II was that his father's killers remained at large. Around this time, John Dixwell arrived in New Haven, where he called himself "James Davids." He had visited Whalley and Goffe in Massachusetts, but soon they, too, moved to New Haven, once boarding with the colony's founder, John Davenport, another time huddled in a cave. They were never caught. Dixwell, who in England was believed to be dead, lived into his eighties, exchanging sad, loving letters with his niece and her son, who begged him to go to Holland, where he would be nearer to them and as safe as he was in New England.[25]

Charles II's desire to subdue New England was no vendetta to avenge his father's murder, but part of a wider campaign to consolidate imperial authority and reap material benefits. As ever, the more worthwhile these ambitions, the more reluctant colonists throughout the Atlantic and Caribbean worlds were to give up the rewards of their sacrifices. Colonial policy became a significant part of foreign policy. The king had adopted Cromwell's pacific attitude toward the Dutch, but by 1664, pressures at court had put England back on a war footing with its Protestant neighbor. Mercantile competition was the root cause. Dutch merchants believed in free trade, but the English state believed in benefiting from the Navigation Acts. To succeed, England would have to monopolize trade routes, seize colonies, and thwart Dutch interests everywhere. The first engagement happened off the North Sea coast in June 1665, but in truth, the war had begun over a year earlier, and not in Europe, but in America.

Sir Thomas Modyford, the exiled royalist and sugar baron, was made governor of Jamaica in the spring of 1664. Hearing that England was at war with the Dutch, he assembled a regiment commanded by the corpulent Lieutenant General Edward Morgan. In July, Morgan led soldiers ashore on St. Eustatius Island, east of Puerto Rico. Dutch defenders surrendered with little resistance, but not before Morgan, much affected "by hard marching and extraordinary heat," dropped dead. The garrison was taken prisoner, and English, Scottish, and Irish settlers made to bow to Charles II. Plans to extend conquest in the region were thwarted by a disagreement between the officers and the men about the sharing of booty. Mutiny erupted before the task force even set sail. When soldiers and sailors refused to move, the only option was to return to Jamaica. A storm scattered the ships, but most of them made it back, carrying a cargo of four hundred African slaves. Morgan's replacement as commander filed a report about the expedition, describing "great confusion."[26]

There followed several actions involving Holland and France, both of which lagged behind England in America, demographically speaking. Combined, New France (situated in Maine and Canada) and New Netherland (at points around the East Coast) were home to just 8,000 colonists by 1663, compared to 58,000 in New England and the Chesapeake. America lacked the pull factor for French peasants, and the Dutch, who had it too good at home, lacked the push. The war in the Caribbean suggested a way for these rivals to claw back the advantage. In 1666, the French invaded St. Kitts with an army of slaves who had been promised freedom, plunder, and white wives; they burned sugarcane as well as houses with English inhabitants inside, inspiring the Irish servants of English colonists to rebel. Stories such as these, where national pride and courage stood out against foreign cowardice and cruelty, gratified English audiences. Spain, too, which was also increasingly eclipsed in America, clamored for more land and influence. In August, the Caribbean island of Providence, which had been recaptured from the Spanish by the buccaneer Henry Morgan (the nephew of the dead commander), was attacked by its former occupiers. After four days of fighting, the English surrendered on condition they be taken to Jamaica. Instead they were shipped to Panama, where they were enslaved; at night they were shackled in a stifling dungeon. They also suffered continual abuse about Protestantism and the king. Captivity became a salient theme in English experiences of America. But it was mercantilism—commercial aggression and state piracy keyed to global ambitions—that was to revolutionize the meaning of the West Indies.[27]

At the heart of Caribbean dreams lay Jamaica: Spain was said to be so jealous of England's possession that it wished the island would sink. Jamaica's pleasantness, however, was disputed. From the 1650s, reports were rosy, although mostly from planters needing laborers. Jamaica was healthy, they said, "it being now as strange for a man to die as formerly to live." This advertisement contrasted with impressions of the garrison, where soldiers lived in "extreame want and necessitie and almost despairing of futur[e] Subsistance and preservation." Fifty years of adventuring, however, had taught the English that a colony's value lay in its potential, and that the prizes belonged to the dauntless and far-sighted. Charles II, who had promised Jamaica to Spain in return for supporting his restoration, changed his mind, partly because of a book by a soldier named Edmund Hickeringill that was published in 1661. Hickeringill admitted that Jamaica had been "rather the Grave then the Granary" among colonies, but things were looking up. The soil was fertile and the woods full of pigs, and settlers "Naturalized to the Countrey" needed doctors less than Europeans did. Like babies, he said, young colonies thrived once they were established. A royal proclamation guaranteed that all free Englishmen could settle in Jamaica and that their children would be denizens of England. To allay fears, the governor was told to punish debauchery and enforce Anglican doctrine.[28]

By 1664, Sir Thomas Modyford, Jamaica's governor, was calling the island "a Land flowing with milk and hony," an opinion confirmed by a planter named John Style to secretary of state Lord Arlington. Style said he would gladly end his days there, blaming the island's drunks for its reputation. His mind whirred with possibilities. He wrote to farmers in England urging them to come, even though "such men are generally of the Israellites temper; they had rather sitt by there flesh potts in Egipt (though with slavery and penury) then travel into the land of canan." And yet Style hoped the crown would raise Jamaica to Barbadian levels of prestige. England was choked with paupers—imperial fodder—and the Romans would have colonized a place that was even half as good. Another writer described Jamaica as a Canaan where poor women could assist their nation—"an American blessing"—instead of becoming prostitutes. Sugar, tobacco, and other commodities made it a magnet for people on other Caribbean islands and beyond. Visitors were particularly fond of chocolate. William Hughes, addicted to this "American Nectar," recorded how hunters (and escaped slaves) survived long treks with hard, sweet lozenges—better than a Scotsman's porridge oats. Hughes consumed chocolate in different ways: dissolved in spring-water, whisked with egg, and grated into cassava porridge. "I think," he confessed, "I was never fatter in all my life."[29]

Behind the praise lay Jamaica's dark side. Thomas Modyford had arrived with several hundred planters and their slaves, marking a permanent shift in the island's economic infrastructure. Evidently, the maximal profitability of Jamaica—and Barbados, to which it was compared—depended on slavery. A sufficient number of indentured servants could not be recruited—especially not skilled apprentices—and the more blacks there were, the smaller the number of English migrants willing to share their labors. In 1664, the king granted Modyford's brother, Sir James, the privilege of sending all pardoned felons in England to Jamaica. But this was hardly a permanent solution, and so the racial imbalance gathered momentum. There were 50,000 English settlers in the Caribbean, but alongside them toiled 35,000 Africans—a number equivalent to the entire white population of New England. The Royal African Company claimed to import 6,000 slaves a year. The snag was the rise of unstable households in an insecure society. Adventurers knew the strongest colonies were those inhabited by men who owned the land they were expected to defend. The number of such men in Jamaica in comparison to the number of slaves declined so much that it was predicted that "the proportion of Blacks might in a short tyme bee such that a Rebellion of them would bee easy."[30]

Barbados had the most slaves—27,000 in 1660, compared to 26,000 whites—which explains its remarkable progress: one Whitehall adviser surmised that "the like Improvem[en]t was never made by any people under the Sonne." Another of Lord Arlington's correspondents informed him in 1665 that the colony was like a vast cultivated garden, so well stocked that no reasonable visitor could wish himself in London. Barbados was delightful, and it was dangerous. Oliver Heywood, a Lancashire minister, had two brothers who went there in the early 1660s. John, the eldest, fled a family entanglement; the youngest, Josiah, "a pretty man, flaxed hair, exceeding witty, loving natured, my mothers darling," yet a wayward drifter, followed him. Neither survived long. Still, successes attracted planters, and some did grow rich, enjoying family life, civility, and sociability in high English style. Prosperity, and the decline of the white servant, owed much to the 1661 slave code, which encouraged investment in Africans by legalizing their ownership—a model for Jamaica and all slave-owning colonies. This included Virginia, which for a generation now had been developing a concept of slavery where racial difference justified bondage.[31]

Statistics hide the impact on individuals; mundane transactions reveal more. Edward Nightingale, a Barbados merchant, exchanged 3,885 pounds of muscovado sugar in 1662 for "one negroe woman by name Phebe, together with her younge childe named Cherry and one

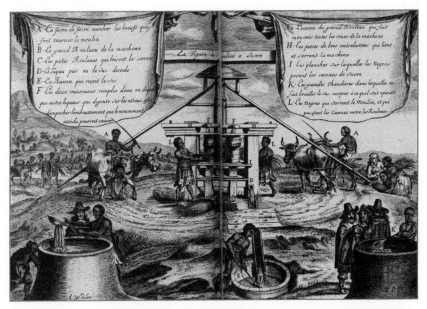

A West Indian sugar mill, c. 1665. Slaves crushed the cane to extract liquid, which was then refined in copper boilers. By the end of the seventeenth century, Jamaica and Barbados had become vast factories, producing sugar and rum that made great fortunes, yet at an appalling human cost.

breeding Sow." They were bought and sold with livestock because this was how they were viewed: as part of the land, the value of which consisted in their labor. When a planter of St. Thomas's parish bought half an estate in St. Michael's in 1668—for 500,000 pounds of muscovado—half the owner's slaves came with it. Humans became commodities. Ships from the Ivory Coast ridden with smallpox caused slavers to moan about spoiled cargoes: planters would not buy these shivering, sore-covered beasts at any price.[32]

Not every Englishman was so callous. Thomas Tryon, a vegetarian ascetic and dissenter, arrived in Barbados in 1663 to make beaver hats. He wondered how English people would feel if they were hauled off into slavery. Appalled by magnates' greed and the overseers' cruelty, he flinched to hear whips and cries of "Damn'd Doggs, Black ugly Devils, idle Sons of Ethiopian Whores." Sir Thomas Lynch, a leading planter and Sir Thomas Modyford's rival, had similar qualms. Around the time he replaced Modyford as governor of Jamaica, in 1671, Lynch gave a London publisher, Richard Blome, a bundle of notes for a book. His attitude toward slaves was paternalistic; he advised kindness to these loyal creatures "bought on ships as men Buy Horses in a Fayr." Too often, wrote Blome, men "at the height of Pleasure . . . do not consider the condition of those poor wretches, their Servants and Slaves, who are constrained to so hard a labour."[33]

Lord Francis Willoughby embodied change in the Caribbean. After his surrender to Sir George Ayscue in 1652, he was forced off Barbados, but in 1660 he was given command of the West Indies; in August 1663, the year Barbados became a crown possession, he returned as governor. Three months later he wrote to Charles II about a plague of caterpillars that was like the locusts God sent to Egypt. The caterpillars had eaten so many crops that they had impoverished Barbadian planters. Willoughby defended men whose profit margins, supply of slaves, and overseas markets were constrained by English law. As the king's delegate, however, he was obliged to curb planters' yen for self-determination. He hounded out Humphrey Walrond, the former leader of the royalist extremists on Barbados, whom he accused of inciting rebellion over taxes. Then he moved into Walrond's magnificent house—the one facing the sea, with slaves to catch fish. Willoughby was disliked and led a stressful life. He held title to Surinam, where African slaves were reputed to be "sold like Dogs and no better esteem'd" and exploited "with the severest usages for the slightest fault." Visiting there in 1665 to prepare for a Dutch invasion, Willoughby was set upon by an English settler, sustaining a head wound and losing two fingers. As he recuperated, Barbados was attacked by Admiral Michiel de Ruyter. Willoughby summoned the assembly to approve a defense budget; this occasioned a contrary petition from the speaker, Samuel Farmer, who was arrested, made to say goodbye to his wife and five children, and sent to England—a country where he knew hardly anyone.[34]

Willoughby was not alone in believing that without free trade, cheap slaves, adequate supplies, accessible land, and reliable justice, investors would shy away from Barbados and creditors would charge astronomical interest rates. Life on the island was considered so corrupt that traders claimed to have more confidence doing business in the outer reaches of the Ottoman Empire; some said just breathing its air might ruin an honest man. It was too much for Willoughby, who in August 1665, his courage spent, asked the king for leave in England. The heat inflamed islanders' bodily humors, he explained, causing them to follow their own wills rather than royal command. They were nostalgic for the Long Parliament of the 1640s, and none more so than the now exiled Samuel Farmer, "a very dangerous fellow; a great magna Charta man, and petition of right maker, the first that started upp that kind of language here." In January 1666, Willoughby's colony on St. Lucia failed, its settlers reduced from 1,500 to less than 100 within just eighteen months, owing to disease and native attacks. Willoughby had spent £50,000 on Caribbean schemes.[35]

Even now he did not give up. But like so many adventurers before him, he paid the ultimate price. In July 1666 he went to recapture St. Kitts from the French, leading the mission on a frigate named the *Hope*. After five days at sea, the fleet was blasted by a hurricane off the coast of Guadeloupe, and Willoughby was never seen again. On November 28, reports reached London, where that night the naval administrator Samuel Pepys, like all Englishmen enamored of empire, went to bed much troubled by the "ill news from Berbados."[36]

Pepys's view of America was unlike that of his grandfather's generation. At one level, the promise and perils of the New World resembled those of 1610: men like Willoughby still gambled everything and lost. But much had changed. The colonies were now larger and more numerous and diverse, and included the fantastically lucrative West Indies. Partly because of this, the English state, a strident and intolerant monarchy once more, began tightening the sinews of power between center and periphery, and raising its imperial game. Simultaneously, the settlers who made colonies valuable were being transformed, not only by the fear and discomfort of a faraway life, but also by their successes. Perspectives diverged then clashed. In London, the colonist's desire to make decisions, accrue wealth, and defend himself seemed like disloyalty. And New England's identity, a maturing sense of self-purpose forged from hardship and history and prophecy, seemed laughably pompous. This cultural distance would widen throughout the 1660s and affect English colonists from Boston to Barbados, in Puritan meetinghouses and tobacco planters' shacks and Caribbean rum-shops.

CHAPTER 14

Remembrance of an Exile in a Remote Wilderness

D EFENDING LIBERTY AND TRUE RELIGION against overmighty monarchs was a contest between versions of Englishness not confined to the civil wars. Nor was this contest confined to England. There, liberty and true religion meant different things to different people, and in the colonies often something else again. A range of faiths, from traditionalist "high church" Anglicanism to radical nonconformity, existed in England *and* America, and liberty implied government according to the customary rights upheld by English parishes and corporations—a habit of mind that migrants perpetuated. Under their charters, the English colonies were corporate bodies; yet in the New World, liberty amounted to more than this, too. For the colonists, it increasingly meant freedom to adapt common law, to legislate for local needs, to worship independently, to suppress rebellion, and to safeguard resources and trade. Loyalty to England, and affinity for its culture, stopped short of surrendering assets and authority. Central to this difference of perspective was geography: America was not England, and colonists had to attend to the practical business of living there. Two generations had found the distance from home to be a problem when one needed something, from a legal judgment or medical procedure to window panes or decent beer. But when the colonists had something to hide or protect, such as a precious commodity or an acquired political competence, it could be played to advantage. And over time, most colonies wanted less from England, and instead England wanted more from them to expand its empire of goods, territory, and global influence. Increased antagonism was inevitable.

Most settlers adapted to colonial routines, which were often similar to English ones, but emotionally and in the realm of imagination they were suspended between two worlds. At first, this feeling was exhilarating. New arrivals couldn't resist conveying it to loved ones in England. Simply heading a page "Virginia" or "Boston" was thrilling, the writer amazed to think he or she was actually there. A letter from Paschow Mooreshead to his mother from Barbados in 1674 was supposedly "writ in hast," but it said almost nothing in twenty-three lines, except that Paschow had arrived safely. Remoteness was also useful to folk in trouble. During a voyage to New England in 1672, Sarah Blacklock from Leeds confessed to murdering her illegitimate child, although women who examined her denied she had given birth, perhaps to give her another chance. Other fugitives were compromised by love for relatives in England. In the 1680s, a Virginia lighterman was identified as the thief who had stolen silver from the mayor of York twenty years earlier. As he fled to Barbados, his ship sank and he was presumed dead; but intercepted letters to his mother proved otherwise. Prosperous men moved between continents with relative ease; poorer, less mobile colonists, however, were essentially cut off from events in England that still mattered. Letters sustained a sense of transatlantic community, at least for the literate. Yet delays in the transit of people and information caused loneliness and confusion, and sheer frustration at life's complexity.[1]

Families suffered. Parents and wives fretted, and silences made them fear the worst. The woman who had a horoscope cast to learn how her son fared in Barbados was among many who sought comfort from astrologers. Dislocation strained relationships. After migrating to Massachusetts in 1638, Nehemiah Bourne, a merchant, moved his wife and children back and forth across the Atlantic for thirty years before settling in London. Bourne's absences—in 1643 to fight in the civil war—were heartbreaking separations, however hard he tried to care for his family. Responsible breadwinners sent money home or made other predeparture arrangements. Absconding fathers were traced in the colonies, although securing payments to support their families was harder there. In the 1670s, the wife and children of an Essex minister sank into poverty after his annuities stopped arriving from Barbados, and little could be done. Absent male householders could lead to domestic chaos. After Robert Parker emigrated to the Caribbean, his drunken wife beat their son, who then accused her of attempted murder.[2]

A death in the colonies could drag a family into a thicket of legal questions. Probate could take years. Wills were contested, and claimants in both worlds had to plead in far-off courts. Not all migrants settled their affairs before leaving and retained houses, farms, and estates in the land of their birth. Others inherited property in England after they had moved away—or died in America with heirs that remained in England. One wonders whether James Smith, "then leven in ould ingland," ever received the bed in which his mother died at Marblehead in 1663. Orphans lost their bearings. When Sir Thomas Lunsford and his wife perished in Virginia, their two daughters, "very younge, impotent and unable to provide for themselves," were sent home to London without clear instructions for their future.[3]

Debts were hard to call in, east to west and vice versa. Traders juggling suppliers and deliveries, cash flow and credit, or prices and profit margins while watching out for embezzlement and fraud struggled to stay ahead. Thomas Pengelly wrote vexed letters from London about shoes, which he traded for beaver and tobacco in Virginia and sugar in Barbados; but the shipments he received in return were underweight or rotten or both. Leaving behind a good reputation remained a problem. Another merchant in England succeeded in making a New England court seize beaver skins belonging to a debtor, who then procured two Londoners to plead for him; the difficulty was finding witnesses in New England to vouch for him. Settlers even had to prove their identities by writing to someone in England, who then testified to what they found in parish records. A Hertfordshire landlord's suit against a former tenant in Connecticut was settled between the Court of Chancery and the authorities in New Haven using a deposition from the defendant's brother in England.[4]

All these complications are summed up by the tale of Lawrence Littleboy, who died in Virginia in the 1650s. A plan to liquidate Littleboy's estate of £200 by exchanging tobacco in England for goods to sell in Virginia was blocked by family members in England, who claimed the deceased had outstanding debts and was not his father's sole heir. Littleboy had been sent to Virginia in the 1630s when his father died, allegedly because he had in fact fallen into "very wild & extravagant Co[u]rses." Suspecting he had been transported to block his inheritance, the executor of the Finchley estate had tried to help Littleboy fulfill his dream to return home. It was then that this poor exile fell mortally ill.[5]

Homesickness was as much a part of the colonial experience in the second generation as it had been in the first. New migrants arrived constantly and took time to adjust; some were only children, traveling alone: when she saw the boys her husband had brought over as servants, one Maryland woman asked why he had not provided "some cradles to have rocked them in." Even colonists who, by the 1660s, had spent most of their lives in America still missed the company and comforts of home. A Massachusetts colonist dedicated a book to his brother in London thus: "Though the Lord Jesus . . . hath separated us by the great Deep, yet I have you oft in remembrance, and cannot forget our alliance, and indeed love and acquaintance, that hath been between us from our childhood." Others surrendered to temptation. A New England woman who yearned to go home, but whose husband refused to let her, faked a letter informing her that she had inherited a house and must take possession in person. This sort of longing was reciprocated. In a letter to her son in New England in 1671, saying how his sisters missed him, Frances Goldsmith scribbled two anxious postscripts: "I hear ye Ingens have chalenged ye Englich into ye feld, ye Lord stand by his pepell," and a note to say that if he was cold, she would send him a periwig. Dreams, filled with anxiety and desire, connected people across the ocean. One colonist, informed that his brother had been murdered in London, reported seeing the crime in his sleep.[6]

John Winthrop Jr., the governor of Connecticut throughout the Restoration era, was not obviously homesick, but his mind was often in England while his hands were busy in America. He was a godly man, like his father, but he also believed in scientific progress and its commercial application. This led him to regard England with an ambivalence more complex than that of John Winthrop Sr. In the 1640s he established ironworks in Massachusetts; he also founded New London in Connecticut, where he set up home and built a lucrative gristmill. God's plan, it seemed, was for New England to make its own plans. Winthrop's combined religious and technical interests reflected a partial secularization of outlook. When a family died in a house fire near Hartford, he pondered two things: an undamaged providential inscription over the hearth; and whether tragedy might have been averted had the roof been made of "creek thatch," tall grass from the salt marshes, which locals preferred to straw or shingle because it retarded flame—something Winthrop had proved by experiment.[7]

Winthrop wrote to the London polymath and "intelligencer" Samuel Hartlib, an advocate of innovation to benefit the commonwealth, and from 1660 sent ideas to Henry Oldenburg, secretary of the Royal Society, which had been founded that year to advance understanding of the world. A year later, when Winthrop was in London, the society made him a Fellow. He basked in the culture of Restoration London, a world away from New London's homespun simplicity, a gentleman whose locus of activity, compared to that of most virtuosi, was rather at odds with his own sense of himself. The physical horizons of the New World were, as yet, far greater than its intellectual ones. For Winthrop, the Royal Society was not merely "the invisible college," as it was known, but the *inaccessible* college. Winthrop lamented that many of the letters he sent from America never arrived in England.[8]

He was, however, a shrewd politician, and some letters may not have arrived because they were never sent. His membership in the Royal Society eased the way to a new royal charter for Connecticut, which was granted in return for the knowledge he would send back that could be used to exploit New England. The empire of human knowledge was indivisible from imperial designs, and Winthrop knew it. He wanted to be taken seriously, but had no wish to be duped by the Royal Society, informants to a rapacious monarch, so he sent little information of practical value. Oldenburg's assurance that "even at so great a distance, you may doe that Illustrious Company great service," can be read either as flattery or a testy reminder; and in Winthrop's gratitude of "your friendly remembrance of an exile in a remote Wildernesse," there was false modesty and cunning. Winthrop was an Englishman; but the industrial and commercial development he believed in was American because this was his world.[9]

Winthrop submitted papers on tar and pitch, salt and maize, the heavens and the oceans, all read at Royal Society meetings attended by such luminaries as Robert Hooke, Christopher Wren, and Robert Boyle. Henry Oldenburg informed Boyle that Winthrop may have discovered copper; but, like many other reports, this account was never verified. For years Winthrop assured the society that he was still "very inquisitive after all sorts of minerals w[hi]ch this Wildernesse may probably affoard," but that he had been hampered by war and an unreliable post. Thus the "Commonwealth of Learning" that Winthrop was asked to build remained vague, the society's questions outnumbering the answers. What were the Indian dogs like, and how did fruit and hops fare? And might maps of "wherever the English are planted" be available soon? Oldenburg also wanted information about timber. England had to expand its navy, but was short of wood, particularly masts—an obsession of Samuel Pepys's. In 1669, it was said that 20,000 acres of England's best forests had been "cut downe and mis-spent," and fresh sources were urgently needed. Iron smelting used a lot of fuel, too, leading one Fellow to propose relocating England's ironworks to America. Connecticut had its *own* ironworks, however, and Winthrop suggested that the ships England desired might be built on his side of the Atlantic—a cannier proposition than surrendering raw materials.[10]

Winthrop prepared samples—"the productions of this wildernesse"— in 1669, after earlier consignments had failed to arrive, and asked his nephew to deliver them personally. Charles II was eager to see Winthrop's "American Curiosities." The box that arrived at the Royal Society the following year contained corncobs, oak twigs with acorns, silk-grass "cotton wool," wampum belts, a "sea-hedgehog," a deer's skull, and some oozing bark. Conveyed to Whitehall, they were examined "w[i]th no common satisfaction" by the king, who was fascinated most by a starfish caught off the New England coast. Thanking Winthrop, Henry Oldenburg said he hoped the Indians would soon become addicted to studying the natural world, along with acquiring a fondness for English piety and virtue. More parcels arrived from Connecticut. A hummingbird's nest with eggs was shown to the king, who again was intrigued. There was also an Indian bow and arrows. Books by John Eliot, including his Indian primer, were apparently sent, too, but had gone missing.[11]

Such collecting had a long history. The Guinea Company had asked merchants to send anything strange—gemstones, dried fruits, elephant skulls—in 1625. Most specimens had little use except to inspire wonder. They filled cabinets of curiosities, miniature New Worlds to possess and impress. The tusk of a narwhal, or "sea unicorn," was proudly displayed in Elizabeth I's wardrobe. The centerpiece of Sir Walter Cope's collection, amassed under James I, was an Indian canoe. The gardener John Tradescant went to Virginia in 1637 to obtain rare plants, and the following year, a visitor to his Lambeth home saw "the robe of the King of Virginia," reputedly the deerskin given by Wahunsonacock to Sir Thomas Dale in 1614. These were objects of mystery and promise. Even the fragrances were exotic, although what was described by the Royal Society as a "very odde piece of wood naturally smelling like human

Excrement" had limited appeal in a malodorous city. Thomas Povey, an administrator under Cromwell and Charles II, also built up an American gallery. He thanked his friend Lord Willoughby for curiosities from Surinam in 1655, "peices of that place w[hi]ch hath so much of your heart and your affecc[i]ons, they are therefore embraced by mee as a superstitious Lover doth ye favours of his Mistris." Humble souvenirs—a leaf or a bead or a coin—caused the same frisson: they were consecrated tokens of a new life through which to touch friends and family.[12]

Exotica could be consumed, too—sampling the foods was like a remote communion with the New World. A fondness for coconuts was mitigated by the difficulty of breaking them: Edward Hickeringill likened them to African skulls. The shells, however, could be made into cups and ornaments, polished to shine like ebony. When bananas first went on sale in London in the 1630s, they were admired as natural artworks and a perfect raw food. "Whatever alteration Mrs Housewife makes," thought Thomas Tryon, "proves improper and hurtful." But they were hard to transport, beyond their best on arrival. Pineapples, too, challenged the merchant, but they sent wealthy people into raptures. James I decided they must be what Eve had used to tempt Adam, and as such fit only for royalty. Chocolate was first sold in London in 1657, and an excise duty was soon imposed on it: anyone possessing more than six pounds was assumed to be a dealer.[13]

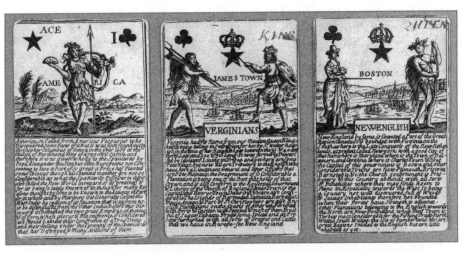

English interest in America was sustained by printed ephemera like these playing cards from the mid-1670s. The left-hand example blames Indian suffering on Spanish tyranny—the "black legend"; the one on the right mocks New England's Puritans—"Fanatickes" in search of a home.

At the other end of the social order, former luxuries were freely available by the 1670s. The retail price of sugar had halved since 1630, and Virginia tobacco that in 1619 had cost 40 shillings per pound now cost a shilling or less fifty years later. The culture of smoking had arrived. Tobacconists imported stone pipes carved by Indians; these were copies of English clay ones and favored by smokers "for their rarity, strength, handsomness and coolness." Men in English taverns, then, might drink Jamaican rum, smoke Virginia rough shag, and deal cards bearing images of the American colonies. A contemporary playing card depicted a scene of Boston accompanied by a description of New England in general: "This Country abounds with all sorts of Fantatickes, where they may finde Room to Plant."[14]

Massachusetts Puritans may have seemed fanatical to people in England, but they were also sensitive and unsteady, their outlook less optimistic and practical than John Winthrop Jr's. They believed that God sent disasters to chasten them and enemies to test them—savages, sinners, apostates, rebels, and royal officials. This was a cosmic interpretation of a temporal world filled with real dangers, and one losing moral and political integrity as it became more populous and advanced. The panic was acute and unique. Like Winthrop, Increase Mather, the youngest son of the Dorchester divine Richard Mather, was a second-generation saint, culturally part of England, yet felt a responsibility for his colony that few Englishmen had for their country.

Mather's sense of duty was bound up with his personal destiny. On her deathbed, Mather's loving mother quoted the Book of Daniel: "They that turn many to righteousness shall shine as the stars for ever and ever." That same year, 1655, the sixteen-year-old Mather had sunk into "extremity of anguish & horror in my soul" and wrote a list of his sins (which he burned). After attending Harvard he lived in England, Ireland, and Guernsey before returning to Massachusetts in 1661, vowing to rest wherever nonconformists had liberty. New England's doldrums mirrored his own. A diary entry from March 1664 read: "Very hard frost this night. Labored to imprint sermon on memory. Some brokenesse of heart in confessing sin in secret before the Lord. Grieved because of hardnesse of heart." Mather wondered whether God wanted him in America, and he despised colonists' wickedness. Bonfires celebrating deliverance from the Gunpowder Plot—a custom revived in New England—offended him, and he was "troubled at the thoughts of N.E. forsaking their first love & principles."[15]

While John Winthrop Jr. was corresponding with the Royal Society, Increase Mather was writing to England to strengthen godly ties. Puritans in both worlds sought meaning in nature, though inferences differed: comets might be astronomical phenomena, or they might be divine omens. The astrologer William Lilly received a letter from Barbados in the spring of 1665 describing a comet, which was thought to precede some enormity; its author was "very much troubled to think of what . . . is coming and like to befall most of the Nations of the Earth." Within weeks, bubonic plague was killing thousands of Londoners, news of which had rippled through New England by late summer. In New Haven, John Davenport, now in his late sixties, reflected: "Did god ever speake soe loud, and shew soe cleerly by multiplied signes . . . as he hath done to England?" Plague and war with Holland were "a double sword upon them," a connection also made by John Hull in Boston. In November a newly arrived Englishman's symptoms caused alarm at Salem. Meanwhile, New England's churches held collections "for ye relief of ye distressed by reason[n] of ye Sicknes in London."[16]

God's arrows also fell on the western side of the Atlantic. That year, diarists and correspondents recorded swarms of "flying catterpillers," mildew on crops, electrical storms, and hailstones the size of duck eggs. On the same day that a man was killed by lightning, monstrous lambs were born at Narragansett—"sad effects" linked to the previous winter's comet. Lives were claimed by disease. When in August the poet Anne Bradstreet lost her granddaughter, she released the full force of Puritan passion and love of children:

> *Farewel dear babe, my hearts too much content,*
> *Farewel sweet babe, the pleasure of mine eye,*
> *Farewel fair flower that for a space was lent,*
> *Then ta'en away unto Eternity.*
>
> *Blest babe why should I once bewail thy fate,*
> *Or sigh the dayes so soon were terminate;*
> *Sith thou art settled in an Everlasting state.*

Many times did Increase Mather fear for the life of his son, Cotton, born in 1663, on every occasion reacting with the same knotted intensity of feeling.[17]

On January 1, 1666, Roger Williams, reflecting on the plague that had "pierced the Hearts of thousands . . . of our fellow English," wrote to the town of Warwick, Rhode Island, about American complacency and God's fury. "He hath whips and Scourges for Colonies and Countries, Nations and Kingdomes," Williams warned. As predicted, New England's afflictions continued that year. At Roxbury, the Reverend Samuel Danforth kept a record: orchards were infested, wheat was "Mildewed and blasted," and the soil parched. In July, he noted, Anne Bradstreet's maid put hot ashes in a barrel and burned the house down. Seven were killed by lightning, and thirty ships snatched by a whirl-wind. Smallpox hit Boston in November, killing fifty. Early in 1667, stupefying news reached Connecticut from Barbados, passing from a merchant to John Winthrop at Hartford. The previous September, a fire in London had "utterly destroyed the greatest part of the Citty . . . [on the] Thames side not a house standing, nor Church, nor Hall [in] nine-tie parishes; S[ai]nt Pauls and the Royall Exchang[e] burn[ed down]." That glorious city, heart of the nation, was "a heape of ashes." By February, all Boston knew about it; reports had arrived from Jamaica and Nevis as well as from Connecticut.[18]

Like many others, Increase Mather blamed papists, believing the signs had been there in the comets of 1664–1665. The skies took on an apocalyptic appearance: "The smoak of that burning," wrote Mather, "caused the Sun to look as if it were turned into darkness and the Moon into blood." Another divine blamed the fire on the murder of "a pious & good King" and England's immorality. Loose-living gentry had fled to the countryside, leaving "few ruffling Gallants [to] walk the streets, few spotted Ladies to be seen at windows"; their music had been si-lenced and their wine bowls emptied, and only the poor were left. "The glory of London is now fled away like a Bird," Mather concluded, and its culture had been destroyed. Trade was in disarray: the tailor who lost the paperwork for a complicated deal between London, Boston, and Barbados was typical. The New England Company lost revenue. Only gradually did a phoenix arise from the ashes. John Winthrop's advice about fire-resistant marsh-grass arrived at the Royal Society just as Wren was busy planning and rebuilding.[19]

Some New England Puritans saw the London fire as God's punishment for royal interference in the colonial world. Despite a rumor that Charles II was too busy to worry about colonists, who could do as they pleased, men in authority knew better. In the spring of 1666, Massachusetts Governor Richard Bellingham and his magistrates received a letter from the king accusing them of obstructing the Royal Commission. They "believe that his Majesty has no jurisdiction over them," it alleged, and refused to allow appeals to English courts. Bellingham had last been in London when the row over the Quakers had erupted. Asked then by what law Boston executed these people, he had replied that it was no different from England executing Jesuits. Some had wanted Bellingham arrested, and hearing that the father of the martyred William Robinson was coming, he had left quickly. Now, in 1666, Bellingham was called back by Charles II, a summons that caused a split among his assistants. Some were compliant moderates, but the "commonwealthmen" argued—outrageously and dangerously— that although the king was sovereign, his commands might be regarded circumspectly. Bellingham, reluctant to reenter the lion's den, sided with the hard-liners and sent a written pledge of allegiance in lieu of coming in person. Questions of loyalty divided ordinary people, too. A ship's carpenter was censured at Salem in 1667 for making "seditious & dangerous speeches of a very high nature against the crowne & dignity of our Sovereigne Lord King Charles the Second."[20]

Fears that the king no longer cared about New England were fueled by gossip about his indifference toward the Dutch threat to the colony, a worry reflecting anxiety about European conflict spreading to the Atlantic and the Caribbean. Barbados feared foreign attack, yet was divided and undefended. Shortly before the arrival of Lord Willoughby, the brother of the drowned governor, in 1667, a comet had appeared, marking perhaps the disarray that Willoughby found there and presaging worse to come. The lives of Barbadian colonists were blighted. In December, William Doughty wrote to his brother in Norfolk expressing his hope that London was repenting for plague and fire; he feared that war in the West Indies would reach Barbados. God had already brought sickness, wrote Doughty, mainly "gripeing paines of the gutts." Weakened by fever, short of staples such as flour and butter, grieving for his wife and mother (who had died in his absence), and fretting about his children, he spent many hours contemplating "my nere &

deare Native Country." By January 1668, Doughty was talking about coming home.[21]

Weakness in individuals affected Barbados as a whole. To many, the privations of England's poor, which vitiated the state and justified emigration, seemed perfectly transposed. A report to Whitehall described customary exploitation of the lower orders, who "continually eat the bread of carefulness & lye down to rest with sorrow, never enjoying themselves, wifes or Children, for they can call nothing their owne, but are hired slaves to others." No one could be sure that an invasion of Barbados would be resisted, the settlers having so little worth protecting. "Judge you what heart these poor men can have . . . to expose their bodies in the way of defence," the report continued, "when as Victory should still continue them bondmen & an overthrow shall set them free." In the end, providential judgment came not as war and revolution, but as fire—a terrifying reprise of London's tragedy and a reminder that God chastised the English wherever they were in the world.[22]

The conflagration that swept through Bridgetown on April 18, 1668, was blamed on a slave taking a candle to his garret. "Ye aire seemed all of a flame . . . terrible to the spectators," wrote William Doughty, who, along with others, had fled to the woods five miles away. The fire was hard to fight because it was so close to a magazine containing 170 barrels of gunpowder, the detonation of which, Doughty said, "seemed Doomesday to us." The town was virtually destroyed. In the wreckage were eight hundred houses, plus warehouses full of sugar, tobacco, ginger, and indigo; the spoils were pillaged by slaves and apprentices. Total losses were put at £400,000. It was, wrote Doughty's business partner, "the most dismal and affecting occasion that ever offered it self from those parts." The two men, who lost their house, sent letters to London that were published. Samuel Pepys was perturbed by the news, which he heard from Sir William Penn in June. Bridgetown now expected plague, but instead it got rain—a four-day deluge in November 1669. Rivers rose between hills, inundating houses, demolishing stone buildings, and exposing human remains. "It was enough to make one think of the Resurection," remarked an observer, "for it seemed as if the Coffins did [a]wayte an Oportunity to Rise out of ye graves."[23]

William Doughty returned to England in the 1670s, as did many demobilized soldiers, who quickly fell into poverty at home. For many, neither world, old or new, afforded much comfort. Barbados had certainly lost its allure. A merchant who in 1671 recommended the island to a kinsman was told, in reply: "I feare all my friends are very averce to it, and I knowe not how to breach any such thinge to them, especially to my Wife." Barbadian representatives complained to the king that 3,000 people had left in three years. Resources were depleted, and the price of sugar had fallen, yet duties increased. In January 1673 came another fire, which destroyed thirty houses on a row named, it was noted in Boston, New England Street. Lydia Fell, a Barbados Quaker, marveled at how people had promised to repent; this, she believed, saved many homes from the flames. But they quickly forgot, leading Fell to reproach them, saying: "Ye knew that ye did lye to God, for ye still went on in the same Excess after and unto this day." Barbados, she cautioned, would do well to remember the fate of Babylon and Sodom. It was a place of sharp and deadly contrasts: a nursery of mercantile and imperial might, and a graveyard for stable governance and godliness. Thus Restoration England envisioned America.[24]

War and rebellion aside, order in England was underpinned by solid foundations of diffused central power, social reciprocity, and tradition in law and custom. In the colonies, by contrast, rapidly expanding plantations, atomized settlements, and elongated trade routes soon outgrew models of community and authority imported from the Old World. Commercial development and political disintegration were of a piece. By the 1670s Virginia presented imperial opportunities and problems similar to those of New England and the West Indies: valuable commodities, mercantile vigor, and strategically useful territory compromised by defensive vulnerability, labor shortages, indiscipline, brooding insurrection, and irksome demands from Whitehall and Westminster.

For a while, Edward Digges, a former governor of Virginia, succeeded where others had failed: in silk. His expertise belonged to knowledge promoted by Samuel Hartlib, his faith in the idea that God wanted human global dominion. Digges sent samples to the king early in the 1660s and was thanked by Thomas Povey, a member of the Council for Foreign Plantations and the Royal Society. Like John Winthrop Jr., Digges received questions and requests for minerals, plants, and animals, including muskrats, possums, and bird-eating spiders. In 1669 he was asked to write a natural history of Virginia, the society having read every available work about America. Winthrop was invited to do the same for New England in 1672; characteristically, he made an excuse. Digges never wrote his book, either, but supplied information when he could, establishing, for instance, that pipe smoke and menstruating women were both harmless to silkworms. Hartlib hoped planters would adopt silk, "unlesse you shall rather chuse to hugg your owne poverty . . . in toyling about that contemptible beggarly Indian Weed, Tobacco." This was the rhetoric that had lured so many to Virginia, and it was as misleading as ever: the silk industry idled, and Digges did better out of "E.D."—his own brand of sweet tobacco—than from his work with silk.[25]

Few had more elevated hopes for Virginia than Sir William Berkeley, a man whose vaulting intellect matched his ambition. Permitted to resign with honor in 1652, in 1660 he had returned as governor, bursting with ideas. He, too, wanted to reduce reliance on "vicious, ruinous" tobacco, even though, he admitted, it "brings more money to the Crown then all the Islands in America besides." In a tract of 1663, Berkeley recommended increasing export duties to encourage economic diversity. "Had the Dutch Virginia," he reasoned, "they would make it the Fortresse, Mart and Magazin of all the West Indies." In letters he wrote that year, Berkeley hoped the tobacco price would collapse and that men would copy him by making potash, on which he reckoned England spent £100,000 a year. He had sent home two tons of it, and if it sold, another two hundred would follow. He also sent black walnut wainscotting for rooms to be called the "Virginia Chambers"—a token of his beloved land would thus be installed in the heart of England.[26]

Berkeley criticized investors "still looking back on England," people who put into the colony only as much as they thought would benefit them. Virginians lacked communal cohesion, he said, unlike New Englanders, who "for the most part desire society." What were needed were towns to replace isolated, insecure, and indolent settlements. Such towns would not only be in the interest of planters, but in the interest of the crown, which wanted to extract resources and tax colonists efficiently. Berkeley rebuilt Jamestown, a task essential to prosperity and defense, but most settlers continued to live far from authority.[27]

Disorder was attributed to irreligion: ministers were scarce, churches remote, schools poor, sin tolerated. Many clergymen were England's dregs; the virtuous minority, who had eschewed New England's

Gifted and ambitious, Sir William Berkeley (1605–1677) governed Virginia for a total of twenty-seven years. An English royalist who disdained colonial libertarianism, he was nonetheless a loyal Virginian defending the colony he loved against external interference.

spiritual comforts, were shocked by Virginia. "There is no pious Eye nor Heart can consider the great . . . contempt of Religion there," noted one, "without resolving itself into Sighs and Teares." Parishes could be seventy miles long, and some ministers had several. Few stayed for long. Virginia needed bishops, critics insisted, to assert power top-down, not bottom-up. The colony's fatal flaw, felt Lionel Gatford, was that "the power of the Governors depends upon the favour and pleasure of the people." This was democracy, what John Winthrop Sr. once called "the meanest & worst of all formes of Goverm[en]t."[28]

England's future in Virginia may have depended on controlling the Indians, yet it seemed that colonists could not even control themselves. After a decade's retreat from Cromwellian England, the Reverend Robert Greene returned from Virginia in the 1660s. Back in England, he told the bishop of London that natives would stay unconverted "whilst so many evill and scandalous consequences attend the

Christians scatter'd manner of planting in that wildernesse." What did Indians see in the dispersed shacks of the James River? "They see Families disordered, their Children untaught, the publick Worship and Service of the great God they own neglected; neglected upon that very day which they heare call'd the Lords Day." Dishonoring the Sabbath not only perplexed the Indians, said Greene, it caused dread, as this was the day Englishmen ran riot. The solution was, first, to concentrate the population in towns; second, to set up proper parishes and dioceses; and third, to restrain the Virginia House of Burgesses, which was run by uneducated ex-servants with more money than sense.[29]

The view from England, however, contrasted with the perspective of the planters from whom Virginia's burgesses were drawn. Colonists had battled death, disease, and deprivation, not to mention the sort of isolation that made erratic communications particularly hard to bear. Writing from London to his nephew on Mulberry Island, Robert Filmer was sad to learn that all his letters of 1665–1666 had gone astray. Dismay in Virginia was, of course, greater. The enthusiasm of Alexander Moray, a Scots silk farmer, and nearly the colony's first bishop (a plan spiked by opposition), drained away between 1666 and 1668, in which time he lost several family members, his cattle and tobacco crop, and his wife, who fled back to England. By now, overproduction of tobacco was eating into profits, which, with higher taxes, meant that, like most other planters, he could barely break even. Upon his arrival in Virginia in 1671, John Rogers scribbled his wife a note describing a friend's dream, in which "thou weart come [to Virginia], but shee [the friend] cried out saying that shee had rather heare thou weart buried."[30]

Virginians felt entitled by hardship to make their own future. Many believed that English legislation had no force in a colony unless it was specifically mentioned, or even that Virginia's domestic laws (as opposed to those for trade and defense) were only valid if they had been passed in Virginia. Only the immediate concerned them—their livelihoods and safety—and most had little interest in placating Indians, whom they blamed for escalating murders and abductions. Servants at the end of their terms found that the best land had been consolidated into big estates; they were forced to venture farther into Indian territory. This, too, raised tensions. Englishmen and Indians were at war by 1666. Jamestown resolved to attack local tribes "to their utter destruction," seizing women, children, and property. Three years later, there were just 2,000 Algonquians in Virginia, compared to 24,000 when the

English arrived in 1607. The perceived native threat had vastly diminished, and when Berkeley pressed the earl of Clarendon to hike tobacco
taxes to build more forts, the danger he had in mind was a Dutch one.[31]

Virginia's other enemy was even closer to home: its laborers. Berkeley
scotched the myth that only "those of the meanest quality and corrupt-
est lives" resided there, and that "there was not one woman to thirty
men," yet he conceded that a dearth of workers held the colony back.
Patentees were given land in return for transporting apprentices. Criminals in English courts had their sentences commuted: twenty-four felons
received royal pardons in 1664 on condition that they spend seven years
in America; three years later, the Virginia planter John Pate received another twenty-one. Spirits like Robert Dutch, "a person greedy of gain,"
continued to abduct youngsters. In 1668, the chancellor of the exchequer
was asked to save a shipment of children about to leave Gravesend for
Virginia, their parents being too poor to buy them back. One trafficker
was accused of kidnapping five hundred people a year for twelve years—
no surprise, then, that a treatise on witchcraft compared those "seducing
fellows . . . who inveigle Children by their false and flattering promises"
to demons. The tale of a man who sold his wife into service in Virginia
only to suffer the same fate himself was an appetizing fantasy.[32]

Planters found transported servants to be hostile and expensive. In
the 1660s, a consignment was described as "utterly useless to this kingdom, but rather destructive in their idle course of life, whereunto they
would most willingly return upon any advantage given them to escape." Many did, and masters had to write to neighboring colonies
asking for their return. If recaptured, they had their terms extended or
were "whipped till ye blood come," although generally this made things
worse. In Virginia even decent servants rebelled. They were unable to
bear the long hours, rigid discipline, and dislocation, and they missed
the recreations and sociability they had known in England. In September 1663, youths in Gloucester County conspired, in their words,
"about a designe for their freedom" but were betrayed by a servant "out
of his honest affection to the preservation of this Country." Their trial,
steeped in the language of treason, saw the ringleaders hanged, and
a day of thanksgiving for the discovery of their plot declared. When
in 1670 Jamestown tried to ban the importation of felons, the general
court cited this rebellion as a turning point. The malefactors had not
just been slack or rude: they had "attempted at once the Subversion of
our religion, laws, libertyes, rights and p[ro]prietyes."[33]

By the early 1670s, the population of Virginia stood at 40,000, just under 1 percent of all English people in the world. Jamestown was a well-organized town with brick houses and a busy export trade. Yet its success, as in any other colony, can also be measured by comparing proposals with outcomes. In 1663 Sir William Berkeley predicted that his adopted home would become "a glorious and flourishing Country" where the population would double every twenty years, its economic fruits uniquely varied. "In one Age more," he wondered, "how great will our power, strength and reputation be in this new Western World?" In 1670, a year of high mortality, the Council for Foreign Plantations dissected his dreams, eager to understand the pros and cons. When asked how many people had died in the past seven years, Berkeley was evasive: even though new plantations were unhealthy, he said, most newcomers survived their first year, whereas formerly, it was one in five. Yet the difficulties were manifold, not least the commercial blight of the Dutch wars. In his later years Berkeley's judgment failed him, ensuring his isolation. He was not an effusive champion of Charles II's ambitions; nor did he enjoy the confidence of smaller planters, who considered him insensitive to their needs.[34]

Too many settlers felt neglected for their world to be peaceful. In December 1673, five months after Dutch raiders burned the tobacco fleet, fourteen men met at Lawne's Creek Church in Surry County to organize resistance to excessive taxes on exports. Their mentality owed much to old English ideas of commonwealth, of fairness, and of unity against landed grandees and landless laborers. Discontent focused on Berkeley. They were detected and convicted, though their fines were remitted because they were poor. As with Gloucester's unrest, the plot proved that the success of imposing English values in Virginia would always be limited by the absence—or irrelevance—of England's basic social and political structures. And the very act of trying to re-create England was an experience that bred a divergent identity. Lawne's Creek revealed colonists to be English on their own terms—terms set by tobacco and a desire for free trade. The council defended Berkeley to the king, but his support had dwindled in England and America. Within a couple of years, one councillor, Nathaniel Bacon, would break ranks, channeling planters' fears over the native animosity and their deepening suspicion—well-founded, as it turned out—that a major ethnic war was not only inevitable but necessary.[35]

In New England, too, deteriorating relations with the Indians set a course for a war of unprecedented scale. The early 1670s saw many portents of impending disaster, from royal interference in colonial affairs to wayward youth, demonic possession, and dysentery epidemics. In public and private life, Puritans joined the dots to form a pattern of divine displeasure. Their fears were justified: ahead lay English America's darkest hour.

CHAPTER 15

The Day of Trouble Is Near

THE 1670S WAS A DECADE of collisions, primarily between English and European ambitions; American prosperity and imperial covetousness; colonial heterodoxy and metropolitan orthodoxy; and Puritan values and worldly desires, including an insatiable appetite for land. Frontiers were pushed back, for instance in Carolina, in a quest driven by greed and restless curiosity about the world and all it contained. In New England, this urge would also soon collide, catastrophically, with the limits of Indian forbearance. It was a time as well of incompatible English ideals—of good local governance in tension with deference to the center; native evangelism alongside cultural subordination; reactionary social visions clouded by the reality of building plantations; the singular city upon a hill battling with a multifaceted state; and civility versus savagery, which was no longer a conflict between Indians and settlers but among the settlers themselves, whose English identity was being broken and remade in the wilderness. These antagonisms were the fruits of dramatic change in the seventeenth century, and at the core of each were seeds of liberty, authority, and identity. But not every type of seed would be viable in such a ferociously competitive environment.

In 1674, the Treaty of Westminster ended the third Anglo-Dutch War, a twenty-year struggle that colonists had followed with pity and alarm. One colonist received a letter from a relative describing England's "low condic[i]on": economic depression, poverty, and high mortality, plus the shock of the great fire and the grim audit of war. The conflict's final phase had been the most unpleasant, because it had required England to forge an alliance with Catholic France. In America contention had focused on New Netherland, which consisted of five hundred miles of fur-trading territory from Cape Cod to Delaware. Seized from the

Dutch by James, duke of York, it was reclaimed by England under the new treaty. The colony reverted to its former name, the Province of New York. New Amsterdam on Manhattan Island became the city of New York; and Long Island returned to being "Yorkshire," complete with a high sheriff and the administrative divisions (ridings) of its English namesake. Unlike England, or any other colony, New York had no representative government; the duke exercised absolute control. Dutch culture, though marginalized, was allowed to exist in a pluralistic social environment. Like the Indians, these vanquished Europeans responded with both violent resistance and quiescent adjustment to English ways.[1]

An era of concerted imperial enterprise had begun. England swaggered. "Tis evident that a Spirit of Commerce and Strength at Sea to protect it are the most certain marks of the Greatnes of Empire," wrote the diarist John Evelyn in 1674. He also believed it was evident "that whoever Commands the Ocean Commands the Trade of the World, and whoever Commands the Trade of the World Commands the Riches of the World, and whoever is Master of that Commands the World it self." The consequences of this expansive mood were obvious. Not only was fighting between European powers assured, but English state policies relating to law, government, and trade were bound to conflict with colonial interests. Officials and advisers did not think England should aspire to build an American empire for its own sake; that way of thinking had been Spain's ruin. Rather, it should invest where commerce could best be advanced, which meant in the southern regions and the West Indies. Northern colonies, principally New England, it was argued, had to be disciplined because, by trading independently with Barbados and Jamaica, "they take the bread out of our mouths, and are rather a disadvantage than advantage to us." These were the words, also from 1674, of Carew Reynell, a champion of trade tariffs and mercantilism, whose ideas were published in the transactions of the Royal Society. In peace and in war, imperial discourse merged politics, profit, and natural philosophy.[2]

The force of England's desire was exerted not just upon America but within America, and not just upon Indians and European rivals but by one Englishman against another. The Puritan vision, clouded from its earliest years, was being eclipsed by ever more varied American experiences and entrepreneurial dreams acted out along widening geographical frontiers. As adventurers reclaimed the wilderness in pursuit of gold or glory, they also succumbed to it. Henry Oldenburg told

John Winthrop Jr. in 1669 that the prospect of the colonies combining into a bloc of a million people was compromised by reports that "vast numbers of ye English are become as wild as ye Savages, and . . . remove from place to place as disorderly as ye wild Tartars." This was a conventional opinion, but it was an exaggeration and missed the point. Civility counted for little in a world where the horizons of ambition matched those of a landscape so vast and virgin that it was hard for anyone in England, with its contiguous man-made fields and lanes and hedgerows, to comprehend it.[3]

The hardiest frontiersmen went looking for a route across the Appalachians, where the serried ridges, twisting passes, and thick forest and undergrowth were uniquely daunting. In 1670, Sir William Berkeley challenged John Lederer, a German settler, to find a passage to the Indian Ocean, which the English still believed to be not far to the west. The expedition was full of wonder and peril: they found a snake with a squirrel in its belly, furious rivers, and hazardous marshes; one of their Indian guides killed a wildcat. After reaching one summit after dark, the explorers awoke to "a beautiful prospect of the Atlantick-Ocean washing the Virginian shore." Still they failed, repelled by the cold; but they tried again. This time Lederer's English companions laughed at his Indian trick of carrying flour with which to make an edible paste in the palm of his hand—laughter that subsided when their biscuits got mouldy. They were well treated by the natives they met, but shocked by the torn-off faces of three women, "wives" for a chieftain's dead son. A third expedition also came to nothing. It ended on a peak where the men toasted the king with brandy before turning back. Lederer's life was saved by an Indian who applied snakeroot to a spider-bite wound. The adventurers also learned how to "barbecue" meat. They became persuaded that hammocks—previously symbols of native indolence—were better than beds—and that the westward interior was far bigger than many had claimed.[4]

The following year, an expedition commissioned by Abraham Wood, a fur trader, reached the southern Appalachians and modern West Virginia. The men found "a curious River" resembling the Thames at Chelsea, and in their ragged, half-starved state proclaimed Charles II, firing guns and branding a tree "CR." Another venture in 1673, beset by rain and fog, discovered an enclave of "white people w[hi]ch have long beardes & whiskers and weares clothing." All but one explorer disappeared; they were probably killed by Indians. The survivor made it back by crawling through a native encampment, then running all night, sustained by huckleberries. Reports of Wood's expeditions found their way into England's state papers and the Royal Society's collections, where they might benefit the nation.[5]

America's natural environment was both absorbing and useful. John Josselyn, who lived with his brother at Black Point, Maine, between 1663 and 1671, set about examining "the Natural, Physical and Chyurgical Rarities of this New-found World." He wrote with the naive wonder of earlier adventurers about mountains, woods, valleys and lakes, hungry bears, wild turkeys (already virtually extinct), and beavers, whose dried glands were grated into wine as a tonic for pregnant women. English medicine, then, was another field to which American science might contribute. In all the colonies doctors were few and quack cures many: upon advice, one woman with a stomachache swallowed two lead bullets, and a man at Casco in Maine lost his teeth after sucking pus from his wife's breast, having previously applied rum and arsenic. Yet colonial necessity was the mother of invention. Promising remedies, some copied from the Indians, included the herb white hellebore used as an antiseptic. Things were more advanced in Boston, a city that amazed Josselyn, not just in industry and variety but censoriousness. He saw one woman, who had been convicted of sleeping with a native, wearing "an Indian cut out exactly in red cloth sewed upon her right Arm." The mercantile elite were "inexplicably covetous and proud," the clergy little better. Josselyn was more impressed by Metacom, known to the English as "King Philip," the Wampanoag sachem and son of Massasoit, whose clothes were decorated with "beads in pleasant wild works and a broad Belt of the same; his Accoutrements were valued at Twenty pounds."[6]

In English minds, America remained a world of fear and excitement, innovation and surprise, strange encounters and unexpected transformations. In September 1667, *The Storm*, an adaptation of a Jacobean comedy inspired by *The Tempest*, opened in London. In the audience was Charles II. Samuel Pepys was also there; he found the production "so-so," but liked the dance finale enough to return the following night. New World fantasies drew substance from reality. The year 1667 also saw publication of George Warren's account of his time in Surinam just before it was ceded to the Dutch. It surveyed the area's topography, climate, and flora and fauna, some of it terrifying. A leopard dragged a man from his hammock, and pigs had their teats bitten off by vampire

AMERICA.

*T'is J, in tempting diuers, for to try
By sundry meanes, t'obtaine me, caus'te them dye
And, last discouer'd, vndiscouer'd am:
For, men, to treade my Soyle, as yet, are lame.*

America personified in an engraving of 1658. Note the old colonial *canard* of
cannibalism, together with depictions of native cruelty—for example, the row
of impaled heads. The verse suggests the allure of the wilderness, with America as *femme fatale* tempting adventurers to their deaths.

bats. Scorpion stings, Warren learned, were agonizing, and toads imitated the death rattle. The popular drink "perrinoe" was made from cassava chewed by "the oldest Women and snotty Nose Children . . . with
as much Spittle as they can." In general, the natives, most of whom
were thought to be riddled with venereal disease, were cruel, treacherous, and satanic. What Surinam was good for, Warren conceded, was
growing sugar, tobacco, and cotton.[7]

Other colonies excited scientifically inclined visitors because of exports that might feed the motherland's poor. A gentleman made the
case for New World potatoes, arguing that Englishmen were happy
enough to consume Indian tobacco, which, far from nourishing them,
made "many a good Wit sottish and stupid." England could learn from

America, he said, for no nation was so barbarous that it had no good ideas. Another advocate of potatoes liked them mashed with butter; he declared them tasty, nourishing, and "provocative of bodily lust." Thomas Trapham found chocolate refreshing and good for the kidneys. The ancients, had they known of it, would have made it "serve their Deities in both Capacities of Meat and Drink."[8]

Besides explorer and naturalist, Englishmen had two other colonial archetypes in the 1670s: missionary and conqueror. Among the missionaries was the Quaker leader George Fox. His voyage across the Atlantic in 1671 was hot and cramped. The ship leaked and was chased by pirates; passengers had eaten dolphins; he was seasick; and his legs swelled. After Barbados and Jamaica, Fox and his followers braved storms to Virginia, where a drunken Bostonian shipmaster threatened to throw them overboard, unlike the Indian kings, who, Fox thought, "came very loveingly." They proceeded north into New England on "a tedious Jorney . . . through the woods & rivers & creecks & wildernesses whence it is not knowne that ever any man Rode before." Hiking by day, aching and drenched in sweat, by night they huddled by campfires, tormented by mosquitoes and terrified by the sound of wild beasts. They met fellow Quakers, English cynics, and Indians, and they held meetings in barns. The owner of some dogs that stopped barking in the travelers' presence compared them to the children of Israel. After reaching Maryland, they sailed back to England through waves like roaring mountains.[9]

Quakers also went to Carolina, a territory south of Virginia named for the king. In 1664 colonists from Barbados had been recruited to settle the jutting headland known as Cape Fear. Captain William Hilton, son of New Hampshire's founder, had explored the region and was impressed by the sweet air and the natives, who he said lacked only the "happy settlement of our English Nation." Fox was a missionary, Hilton a conqueror. Spotting the canoe of an Indian who had sniped at them, Hilton's men went ashore, smashed his belongings, and took his food. The chief abased himself, promising that the assailant would be beheaded. Hilton's commission came from the Lords Proprietor, a group of eight royalists, including Sir William Berkeley, who had been gifted with Carolina for supporting Charles's restoration. Their proprietary charter, the favored instrument of colonial control after 1660, was modeled on the medieval palatinate of Durham, creating a microcosm of devolved royal power complete with manors and baronies. Sir Robert

Harley, a royal steward and Fellow of the Royal Society, wrote that "once it be on its leggs, it wil be ye roade of trade from new england and virginia and al those northern plantations to ye western plantations in Barbados etc." The only flaw was the likelihood of ethnic friction, as the natives were "ye most warlike people in al ye world."[10]

Migrants were undeterred. "Doubtless there is no Plantation that ever the English went upon in all respects as good as this," boasted a promotion of 1666, predicting a rush of colonists from points north, south, and east. The woods and meadows, the food, and the climate were excellent; all Carolina needed was an English population. Surely no ill-starred young gentleman, the tract supposed, would "be afraid to leave his Native Soil to advance his Fortunes equal to his Blood and Spirit"; in Carolina he could found a new family dynasty. This was advertising convention, but it had something new: the promise of religious freedom. In addition, land allowances were generous: settlers would be given a hundred acres per person (including wives and children), plus another fifty for every servant or slave. Freed servants would get freedom dues of clothing, corn, and tools. If it seemed too good to be true, in these early years it was. Poor leadership, tempestuous weather, and Indian hostility caused Cape Fear to be abandoned.[11]

By 1669 the Lords Proprietor were mostly dead, disgraced, distracted (in Berkeley's case), or, after the grants were inherited by sons, disinterested. To forestall chaos, Lord Shaftesbury, one of the original eight, asked the philosopher John Locke to draw up "fundamental constitutions," an odd mix of ancient feudal hierarchy, progressive liberty of conscience, and political representation. Early in 1670, settlers arriving on the *Carolina* were welcomed by Indians who stroked their shoulders, saying, "Bony conraro Angles [good friend English]." In March passengers disembarked at Bull's Island, and from there the colony grew. Shaftesbury received hopeful dispatches about corn, cotton, ginger, potatoes, melons, and tobacco, and imagined a walled port city with civic squares. The far-flung settlements of Virginia and Maryland seemed obsolete, as did the idea of transplanting England's poor, "it being substantial men and their families that must make the plantation, which will stock the country with negroes, cattle and other necessaries." The masses, Shaftesbury felt, merely "rely and eat upon us." This notion appealed to Barbadian planters, who were desperate to counteract falling profits and provide estates for their younger sons. They did not see Carolina as an egalitarian utopia, but rather as a place to realize their

dreams of exploitation—something increasingly difficult in the Caribbean islands, where land had become scarce.[12]

Substantial men still needed indentured servants, and many indentured servants who went improved themselves after serving their terms.
Not only were they "more able to [perform] all Youthful Exercises than
in England," and their wives fertile and children ruddy-cheeked, it was
said, but they had acquired land and cattle. Some were worth several
hundred pounds, their estates growing all the time. For health, pleasure, and profit, Carolina was soon esteemed one of England's very
best colonies. A promoter described it as "this beautiful Aurora, or the
Rising Sun of America"; its cardinal quality, liberty, was rooted in land,
"the inherent Birthright of every man born into the World." There was
so much land, in fact, that something like universal male suffrage was
achieved. The allocation of wealth for a time was less stratified than it
later became—a thing that seemed wonderful to colonists and dangerous to Old World ideologues. Unsurprisingly, free planters disliked the
landowning aristocracy that was proposed by Locke's constitutions, but
were enthusiastic about entitlements. Nor did slave-owning Anglican
Barbadians live happily with dissenting yeoman farmers. The result
was cultural and political dissonance, exemplifying an acute contrast
between the rhetoric of men in London and the reality in America.[13]

D issonance existed throughout English America, but especially in
New England, where the members of the first generation, with
their lofty ideals, grew frail and wistful as the world changed around
them. In October 1668, a lame old man named Phineas Pratt wrote to
the Massachusetts general court begging relief. He had arrived in New
England in 1622 and worked as a joiner at Weymouth, surviving starvation, disease, and warring Indians. He had been "pursued," he said, "in
times of frost & snow, as a deer chased with wolves." Now, in an age of
prosperity, when "God hath added a New England to old Engl[and] &
given both to our dread Sover[ei]g[n]," Pratt sought recognition for his
part "in times of our weak beginnings." He was one of many pioneers
reflecting thus. Time was short; so many had already died. "They having done their generation-work," wrote John Josselyn, "are laid asleep
in their beds of rest till the day of doom, there and then to receive their
reward according as they have done."[14]

The winter of 1668–1669 brought dysentery and fevers. In April 1669, Richard Mather lay dying at Dorchester, attended by his son Increase, who was now charged with guiding a wayward generation. "God made him Exemplarily Faithfull, Zealous, Patient, Humble, Holy," Increase wrote of his father. "Follow him, as he followed Christ." New England needed a history full of men like Mather, as a traveler needs a compass. This year saw the publication of *New-Englands Memoriall* by Nathaniel Morton, nephew of William Bradford, upon whose manuscripts he drew. Morton regaled younger readers with the story of the *Mayflower*, reminding them how God had made "this howling Wilderness a Chamber of rest, safety and pleasantness, while the storms of his Displeasure . . . endangered the overwhelming of great States and Kingdomes." In the same vein, Roger Clap, who arrived in 1630, listed instructions for his children, whom he asked: "You have better food and raiment than was in former times; but have you better hearts than your forefathers?" Increase Mather's sadness "that in a Plantation of Religion (for such New-England was) the Generality of the Inhabitants should be in the Condition of Infidels" echoed his father's injunction to the lax parents of Dorchester: "Will you do no more for the soules of your children then Pagans & Infidels would do for the soules of theirs?"[15]

The "jeremiad" was a type of sermon known in England before 1600, but in America it found its perfect form and use. In the 1670s, the style became informed by the awareness of an inheritance squandered, the "declension," or spiritual doom, of colonial society. The first Puritans in America had sworn never to become complacent, so the realization that they had broke their godly hearts. Jeremiads, taking their name from the Book of Jeremiah in the Bible, expressed this realization as sorrow and anger. The sermons revived the tone of the reprimands to England in the 1640s and provided a commentary on moral decline. Many blamed the half-way covenant, even though between 1662 and 1675 only two-fifths of Massachusetts churches adopted the principle, and few had implemented it: congregational purity was barely diluted. Perceptions mattered, however, and the rhetoric was forbidding. There was hope in the jeremiad, optimism that charity would bring order; but it was hard to hear above the din of admonition.[16]

By the late 1660s, John Davenport was warning of heaven's rage. William Stoughton blamed "a fruitless, a faithless, a perverse Generation," apt to waste "those precious things of God in this Wilderness which were so savory and sweet unto their fathers." But it was

Samuel Danforth's filiopietistic sermon of 1670 that fixed the genre. Danforth studied the mistakes of the Israelites, asking: "How soon did they forget their Errand into the Wilderness and corrupt themselves in their own Inventions?" Similarly, he said, New England was taunting God with its pride, contention, and drunkenness. The colony had lost Richard Mather and other worthies, and the world was full of comets, earthquakes, storms, and droughts—signs of God's wrath. The most famous jeremiads—part political treatise, part epic narrative, part mythic prophecy—were preached to the elite at Boston on election days. But ordinary people, too, were scorched by their fire. At Northampton, Eleazer Mather, Increase's older brother, asked his congregation: "Men, Brethren and Fathers, You once had another Spirit, had you not? A right New-England Spirit. Oh! I should knock at your breast, and ask is the old Zeal, Love, Heavenly-mindedness that was in this Heart twenty, thirty years ago, is it there still? Are you the same men you were? Are you not strangely changed?"[17]

It was logical, as well as convenient, for Puritans to focus their anger on the Society of Friends; even outsiders noticed how they had spread. "There are none that beg in the Countrey," John Josselyn observed, "but there be Witches too many, bottle-bellied Witches amongst the Quakers, and others that produce many strange apparitions if you will believe reports." Quakers roamed the streets, advertising their sufferings and Boston's blood guilt, and settled in havens like New Dartmouth. To Puritans, they were briars in the vineyard. The Friends saw things differently. A Quaker broadside published in 1669 argued that New England was heading the way of Sodom and Gomorrah, and that its persecutions had usurped royal authority.[18]

Roger Williams collided with George Fox in Rhode Island in 1672. Williams compared Quakers first to atheists for asserting that all God was in man, then compared them to papists for their "Enthusiasmes and Infallibilityes." He framed his critique as a declaration of Protestant loyalty to the crown. In return, Fox blasted Williams's "Blasphemous Assertions" and accused Massachusetts of fratricide—its executions were worse than Cain's slaying of Abel because of the cold legality they had used in the shedding of English blood. "Did ever old England think," he asked, "that such a Company as you that fled for Religion should be the greatest Persecutors and Murderers for Religion?" Fox implored Quakers in America to trust Christ to defeat the oppressors and their master, the devil.[19]

John Oxenbridge's election sermon of 1672 chastised the second "degenerate and spurious" generation. On the one hand, this generation was seen as failing to defend its English liberties; on the other, the government of Massachusetts was itself accused of abusing liberty. In August that year, Samuel Coddington of Rhode Island wrote to Governor Richard Bellingham to berate him for attacking Quakers. The two were old friends, having migrated with John Winthrop in 1630. Despairingly, Coddington asked Bellingham what had happened to the things they had agreed upon when they were on the *Arbella*. He recommended that he return to John Foxe's *Actes and Monuments*, the chronicle of Protestant martyrdom under Mary I. "Therein you may read your own Actions and read their Ends," advised Coddington, "and you shall never find that any that persecute the People of God, as you have done (and repented not), ever were unpunished." Bellingham, the last surviving signatory to the 1629 charter, burned the letter, calling Coddington "an old sottish man." That prompted Coddington to write again in October. Bellingham did not reply, and then died early in December—it was God's way, supposed Coddington, of denying him another chance to expiate his guilt.[20]

Early in 1673, John Leverett, who had succeeded Bellingham as governor, received a letter deploring Boston's licentiousness, which the sender felt to be "much more pleasing to the Generallity of people then a strict holy course of Livinge." This was the mood which inspired jeremiads that year. Many were printed for wide consumption, with astringent titles, such as Increase Mather's *The Day of Trouble Is Near* and Urian Oakes's *New-England Pleaded With*. Oakes described "the sad Apprehension and Aboding of approaching calamities," and punishment for making "liberty" a license for libertines and levelers rather than a duty to obey government. In May 1674, Samuel Torrey, the pastor at Weymouth, called toleration the root of bondage; if New England failed to subordinate liberty to religion, it would lose both. Some days later Joshua Moodey, Portsmouth's pastor, beseeched Bostonians to put duty to their sanctified leaders first, so as to close the rifts that gratified Satan and provoked God. Another jeremiad urged imitation of Christ and repudiation of error. The devil was chained, advised Increase Mather on a day of public prayer, but it was a long chain and he walked among them. Piety and unity alone would hold him off. "If we break, we shall sink," said Mather. "If we divide we perish and are like to be an undone people."[21]

Satan advertised his presence through the sin he inspired. Communities were fractured, households in turmoil. At Stamford, Connecticut, Zachary Dibble beat his wife, and then deserted her and their child, taking everything. Some of her clothes were found in a barn, some in a swamp. The impoverished Sarah Dibble petitioned the court as "fathers of the Country, & Those that are se[n]t of God to judge for God," denying her husband's claim that she was a witch owing to "a Tett in the secret part of her body w[hi]ch was some tymes biger and some tymes lesser." An examination revealed nothing. Demonic intrusion pricked godly senses. A sermon by Thomas Walley at Plymouth compared New England's trials to those of the early Christians: "It is to be wondred at that in this time, in which the Gospel is so clearly Preached and Religion so much professed," commented Walley, "that so many should be possessed with Evil Spirits." This was more than hyperbole. Increase Mather seized on the case of Elizabeth Knapp of Groton, Connecticut, who in 1671 began weeping, laughing, shouting, and convulsing. She displayed unnatural strength, her tongue distended, and through closed lips came a voice, thought to be a demon, that reviled the pastor Samuel Willard. Was God testing New Englanders because he loved them, Mather wondered, or punishing them because he was angry? Or both?[22]

Early in 1673 in Boston, Benjamin Goad, who, like Elizabeth Knapp, was a wayward adolescent, denied buggering a horse, but based on an earlier confession he was nevertheless sentenced to death. Samuel Danforth of Roxbury, who had been appointed to preach for the occasion, recalled the "Abominable Uncleanness" that had destroyed Sodom, including the "monstrous and horrible Confusion of bestiality." Would New England now go the same way? Goad had "obtained a licentious liberty" used to corrupt society, and the church would remain polluted "until this wicked person be put away from among us." Goad was hanged, and the mare slaughtered. Like subsequent execution sermons, Danforth's text was published to amplify God's warning. Fear was vividly expressed here, even though—perhaps because—bestiality was taken less seriously than it had been forty years earlier. Goad's execution would be the last for that crime in New England.[23]

Mather's *The Day of Trouble Is Near* described Europe's descent into bloody misrule, a harbinger of American doom. New England now sounded like the world John Winthrop had escaped in 1630: its neglected piety, divided church, rife immorality, and abuse of the poor all mirrored the old England. Men took salvation for granted and cared for fortune more than faith—even the possessed Elizabeth Knapp had cried "Money, Money!" Unlike other English colonies, Mather explained, New England had been built to a religious design, whereas "now we begin to espouse a Worldly Interest, and so to chase a new God." This turn to worldliness broke the covenant; it was the same error that had doomed the kingdom of Judah. God's frowns were as plain as they had been in Jerusalem before Rome destroyed it. After earthquakes, Mather predicted, would come state-quakes: "There is a black Cloud over our heads, which begins to drop upon us," he wrote. A fast-day proclamation in the spring of 1674 listed the spread of sin, food shortages, European strife, and "the condition of our Dear native Country." All were cited as trials sent by God. But the most awful judgment looming on New England's horizon was war. The day of trouble was very near indeed.[24]

"Land! Land! hath been the idol of many in New-England," trumpeted Increase Mather, "and they that profess themselves Christians have forsaken Churches and Ordinances, and all for land and elbow-room enough in the World." This critique probably applied to Benjamin Church, a first-generation American who did not reject piety as such, but was more interested in territory and commerce. A carpenter by trade, in 1674, when he was in his mid-thirties, he bought land at Saconet, sixty miles southwest of his Plymouth home. And then he bid his wife farewell. If any typology shaped Church's life, it was not the Israelite seeking Canaan, but the questing classical hero reborn in Rhode Island, a place wilder in spirit and landscape than Massachusetts. "I was the first English Man that built upon that Neck, which was full of Indians," Church recalled. "My head and hands were full about Settling a New Plantation, where nothing was brought to; no preparation of Dwelling House, or Out-Housing or Fencing made." He brought his own livestock and cleared ground while exercising "the uttermost Caution . . . to keep myself free from offending my Indian Neighbours."[25]

Benjamin Church was not a missionary or a conqueror or even a naturalist, but something more authentically rooted in America. At Saconet, he met a squaw-sachem named Awashonks, and they became friends, possibly lovers. The tolerant society that Samuel Gorton had promoted in Rhode Island had, over thirty years, been overrun by impurer souls driven by profits in agriculture and coastal trade. As had happened to small farmers in England, Indians were pushed off the land to become a rural proletariat, and their inevitable resistance was treated as evidence of their base, uncontrollable natures. Like all Englishmen, Church saw barbarism in Indian life, but he was just as determined to expand his world through friendship as Puritans were to demonize "the other" to defend theirs.[26]

The recent history of native conversions had been checkered. Charles II, who had rechartered the NEC as the Company for the Propagation of the Gospel, was asked to authorize parish fundraising. The governor, Robert Boyle, saw the company's purpose as "the Civilyzing of those Natives . . . [and] the perswading of them to forsake their accustomed paganishe charmes & Sorceries and other Satanicall delusions." It was noticed, however, that many Indians were uncomprehending and lost interest after conversion. They abandoned their English-style coats and breeches for traditional attire and, more importantly, traded Christ for their old idols. Quakers, who taught that Christ died for Indians (and black slaves) as well as Europeans, had heard on their travels that the Holy Spirit could not dwell in nonwhites. Puritans were more concerned that Englishmen were becoming "white Indians." It was suggested that missionaries concentrate on saving colonists who, Increase Mather knew, lived remote lives, "too like the Heathen without any Instituted Ordinances."[27]

Evangelists grew fewer and less ardent. By the early 1670s, there were fourteen of John Eliot's "praying towns," for which Natick had been the template, inhabited by more than 1,000 Indians. Perhaps in these congregations they saw a last chance to preserve their collective identity. But even Eliot struggled to maintain his former optimism. He knew that the "stormy & tempestuous seed time" might never yield its harvest of saints. His mission shone brightest in the future tense: when every native was converted, a praying Indian fantasized, "Oh how happy and joyful will all your people be." Eliot celebrated news of conversions as "light and evidence to my heart that our Indians are really godly." Privately, however, he doubted that they understood his Bible. Nor did he expect to succeed without an Indian ministry; most English clergymen spurned the work as too "full of hardship [and] hard labour," and too "chargeable" (i.e., expensive). But mostly, Eliot's war was unwinnable because he required his foot soldiers—Indian converts—to commit cultural suicide.[28]

Metacom, the Wampanoag chieftain known to the English as "King Philip." This engraving from 1772, by the revolutionary hero Paul Revere, is an insulting caricature of a brave and charismatic leader who was detested and demonized by colonists in New England.

No one understood this better than "King Philip"—Metacom. In June 1674, his attendance at a service at John Cotton Jr.'s Plymouth home reflected not devotion to English governance, but resentful submission. In his heart grew a secret animus against those who threatened his land, cheated his people, and offended his shamans. Since the Pequot War of 1637, the English had assumed that if ever the Indians combined forces, they would destroy them. In the 1660s, a veteran of that conflict said it would be remembered as a comedy compared to the tragedy to come if New England didn't stop being complacent about the Indians—complacency being "the ruin of many nations."[29]

Benjamin Church, whose father had fought the Pequots, persevered despite rumors of war. He was pleased with the rich soils of Saconet and the company of Rhode Island's "Civil & obliging" colonists. Blessed with uncommon courage and energy, he built a house and reached out to Awashonks's subjects, who returned his respect. By the following spring, Church was stocking his farm and hoping to attract settlers with "a fine prospect of doing no small things." Daily reports of Metacom's designs, however, replaced hope with dread.[30]

In Boston, the threat of war was linked to turbulence in individual souls. When two servants were condemned for murdering their master in March 1675, Increase Mather gave the sermon, his theme rebellion against parents—a metaphor for the rising generation. Look around, he said, and see "the child behaving himself proudly against the Antient, and the base against the Honourable." In such things, New England had "become degenerate from the good manners of the Christian world." These homicidal youths had to die, he said, to divert God's anger from the whole colony. A week after the executions, on New Year's Day, Mather mused in his diary about whether he would still be alive a year hence. A fortnight later, his infant sons, Nathaniel and Samuel, were sick, leaving him too worried to work: "Little do children think what affection is in the Heart of the Father," wrote Mather. He begged God for their lives. That April, as the boys recovered, Mather's sermon was published to edify New England's youth. On May 4, a ship blew up in Boston harbor, killing three and injuring nine, which to Mather seemed like another sign of the times. In a sermon that same day he referred to the hanged youths, alerting New England to the coming "day of Revelation when the mystery of providence shall be opened in the sight and hearing of all the earth." When this would be, no one knew, certainly not Boston's fortunetellers, whose "Vanityes and Witchcrafts . . . are fearful transgressions in the sight of God."[31]

Everyone came to expect war, even the governor of Plymouth, Josiah Winslow, who had shrugged off warnings of Metacom's imminent attack. His mind had been changed by the murder of his informant, John Sassamon, a praying Indian, whose body had been found in a pond early in 1675. Three of Metacom's men were arrested. When one of them was brought near Sassamon's corpse, "it fell a bleeding on fresh as if it had been newly slain." The presumed murderers were hanged in the first week of June, and within three days armed Wampanoags were seen near Plymouth and the town of Swansea. By this time, Awashonks had been invited by Metacom to join his uprising. Instead, she informed Church, who assured her that Plymouth was not planning to invade Metacom's territory. Awashonks faced a dilemma. Metacom had said that if she did not join him in the attack, he would provoke the Rhode Island colonists against her. In Church's presence, she was visited by six of Metacom's warriors. They had painted faces, signifying readiness for war, and carried powder horns and bulging shot-bags. When Church asked what their bullets were for, "they scoffingly reply'd to shoot Pigeons with." He advised Awashonks to seek English protection. She assented, and Church rode to Plymouth to inform Winslow of the crisis and to obtain assurances for her people.[32]

Plymouth, though bigger and more confident than in the 1620s, now faced annihilation. Across New England, townships, farmsteads, industries, and trade routes that had been built up over two generations were threatened. Connecticut was something like an English county, with political and legal power concentrated at Saybrook and New London, respectively, and was surrounded by lesser regional centers. There were good buildings and harbors in Rhode Island, especially at Newport, which was thriving in agriculture and trade. A report of 1675 described Boston as a prosperous city of brick, stone, and timber houses, some four stories high, along with spacious meetinghouses and a busy port. It was thought to have about 1,500 households. Salem and Ipswich had about 500 households each, and Charlestown, Cambridge, and Watertown each had about 300. Around thirty other towns each had between 50 and 150 families living in them. In all, some 60,000 English people lived in New England. Routines were well established. Thomas Minor, a Connecticut farmer, recorded the rhythms of his life in the early 1670s, including the agricultural seasons, communal sociability, household economy, and so on. He reaped wheat and rye, shoed his horses, fixed his cart and his chimney, and made cider and drank too much of it. Even ordinary people ate well: sourdough bread, cheese, and oatmeal were on the menu for most. Middling folk also had roast pork with apples; eel pie in the spring; and steamed suet puddings.[33]

All this comfort, all this plenty, was in peril. At the fateful hour, the dwindling band of justified saints remembered the Gospel of St. Luke: "They did eat, they drank, they bought, they sold, they planted, they builded; but on the same day that Lot went out of Sodom, it rained fire and brimstone from heaven, and destroyed them all."[34]

III
WARRIORS
1675–1692

CHAPTER 16

Exquisite Torments and Most Inhumane Barbarities

K ING PHILIP'S WAR began with his absence. In June 1675, election time in Plymouth, Metacom—the Wampanoag sachem, otherwise known as King Philip—failed to appear before Governor Josiah Winslow with his usual tribute of two wolf's heads, thus confirming suspicions. Benjamin Church rode to Plymouth to tell Winslow of Metacom's intention to attack farmsteads at Mount Hope, Rhode Island, on June 20, the following Sunday. Settlers were permitted by the sachem to leave before their homes were ransacked. The militia mobilized, and Winslow ordered Church to find help in Rhode Island. Troops from Massachusetts joined Winslow's men at Swansea, a town between Providence and Plymouth, where, Church recorded, Indians "thirsted for English blood." For five days Swansea's seventy inhabitants hid in a stockade watching the destruction of their world: livestock were slaughtered, fences were broken, and twenty houses were razed to the ground. Elsewhere, native warriors killed colonists indiscriminately. According to Church, English corpses were subjected to "more than brutish barbarities; beheading, dismembering and mangling them, and exposing them in the most inhumane manner, which gash'd and ghostly objects struck a damp on all beholders."[1]

So began the conflict that would see New England fighting for its life in a way the early saints of Massachusetts could never have imagined. The trials of war—the defenders' unity, the commonalty of suffering—helped to shape a new colonial identity. It was a metamorphosis unique to veterans of the most brutal and desperate battles. This was for the second generation what sea crossings and scratch-building had been for the first: a hardening, defining experience. Who but they could know what it meant to face death alone? A bitter cost, however, was a deepening impression—in New England, in other colonies, and across the Atlantic—that the waves of savagery that colonists had hoped to command were washing over them.

On June 22, the council at Plymouth ordered a fast to atone for "sins whereby wee have provoked our good God soe sadly to interrupt our peace & comforts." Frantic military and diplomatic efforts were made. On the 28th, the Massachusetts secretary, Edward Rawson, sent authorities in Connecticut an account of Swansea's destruction, warning that unless the colonies joined forces, Metacom's army would fan out to harass them. English soldiers counterattacked on the peninsula two days later, driving the Indians toward Rhode Island. Their commander, William Bradford Jr., described how his men tracked their quarry over rough terrain, burning wigwams as they went. Two old men were "dispatched." Colonial authorities tried in vain to stem tribal participation. The Nipmucks were plainly hostile, and the Narragansetts, who pleaded neutrality, were suspected of aiding Metacom. At Providence, Roger Williams found that he had no rapport with the younger generation of Narragansetts, though he had been on good terms with their fathers; now, "all the fine words from the Indian Sachems to us were butt words of policie, falsehood & treachery." It was no use trying "to keepe peace with these barbarous men of Bloud who are as justly to be repelled and subdued as Wolves that assault the sheepe."[2]

Attacks multiplied throughout July, at the end of which Metacom left his miry hideout and headed north. On August 2, his Nipmuck allies ambushed a diplomatic mission outside of Brookfield, sixty miles west of Boston. Survivors took refuge in a stone farmhouse with eighty locals, mostly women and children. A soldier fetching supplies was decapitated, his head used as a football. Twenty homes were set on fire, while, it was said, the Nipmucks made the "most hideous yellings, in way of triumph." The defenders cut through the roof to beat out the flames, crying, "God is with us, and fights for us, and will deliver us out of the hands of these Heathen." The Indians laughed. The defenders held out for two days until relief arrived. Their story was rousing—two women gave birth during the siege—but also spread panic. News reached John Pynchon in Springfield, another forty miles to the west, on the 4th; seeing Brookfield's smoking ruins, a townsman had galloped back home. Pynchon wrote to the governor of Connecticut, John Winthrop, describing a people raw with fear: "How soon the Indians may be upon this town we know not," he added, pleading for troops. Winthrop assented.[3]

Although, like the Indians, the English colonists were united, they seemed unable, strategically or logistically, to cap the well of rage. Raids on English towns, and brutality on both sides, escalated in the second half of August. On the 19th, John Pynchon informed Winthrop that they had tortured and shot an Indian prisoner, commenting: "The Lord grant that so all our enemies may perish." A week later Pynchon wrote to Edward Rawson in Boston about desperate conditions in outlying plantations; Rawson in turn told Winthrop about "the whole public Interest of the English lying at stake." Letters marked "Haste! Haste!" crisscrossed the countryside, satisfying hunger for news and both allaying fears and fueling them. September deepened the despondency. Thirty miles north of Pynchon's Springfield, Deerfield was attacked, followed by Northfield the next day. In both places, an alarm sent inhabitants running to the stockade, from where they saw their town burn. Militiamen escorting wheat wagons were ambushed at Muddy Brook, and seventy of them killed there—at a site that was later renamed "Bloody Brook." John Cotton Jr. described an Indian prisoner who was hacked to death, a detail in a welter of anxiety as reports of raids and sieges came in from all directions.[4]

Increase Mather denounced the Indians for leaving stripped English corpses lying in the open like carrion. "Such also is their inhumanity," he wrote, "as that they flay of[f] the skin from their faces and heads of those they get in to their hands, and go away with the hairy Scalp." If the Indians were demonic—one "strange Enthusiastical Sagamore" was said to have communed with Satan—the English were, Mather thought, at least impious and so complicit. He had heard of an old migrant at Casco Bay who believed that God was angry at his coming to New England "for the Gospels sake," then living for years on a plantation "where was no Church nor Instituted Worship." Indians attacked Casco in September, killing the sinner, his wife, his son, his pregnant daughter-in-law, and two grandchildren; another three children were captured. On the 17th a Massachusetts council order blamed New England for inciting the Lord "to stir up many Adversaries against us, not only abroad, but also at our own doors . . . giving up many of our Brethren to the mouth of the devouring Sword."[5]

Mather described that summer as the spark that ignited a great fire. "The Lord himself seemeth to be against us, to cast us off and to put

us to shame and goeth not forth with our Armies." Remarkable providences were recorded, such as a downpour extinguishing flames in the
Brookfield redoubt. It grew harder, though, to see this war as God's test;
it was more like annihilation by degree. The English struggled to fight
Indians on their own terms: not since the earliest colonial ventures had
they seemed so poorly matched to the rigors of the wilderness. What
Rawson called the "sneaking sculking way" of the Indians, the means by
which "hideing themselves in swamps, they pick here & there," caused
disgust and terror, like the secret crimes of poisoning and witchcraft.
Colonists had yet to learn the tricks of stealth, speed, and subterfuge:
one commander reported a hail of gunfire but saw "only creeping deckt
with Fearnes and boughs." "Our English are somewhat awkward and
fearful in scouting out and spying," admitted Pynchon, "though we do
the best we can." Two of his soldiers who had been sent to fetch wood
were killed and scalped, with the assailants gone in a flash.[6]

Commanders needed to be in two places at once. On the afternoon
of October 5, John Pynchon returned to Springfield to find three people
dead, several injured, and most of the buildings smoldering. The food
stores were gone, and forty families left destitute by the destruction.
"The L[or]d will have us ly in ye dust before him," Pynchon wrote to
the Reverend John Russell at Hadley, the town he had been defending
when Springfield was attacked. Pynchon's morale was low: "I know not
how to write neither can I be able to attend any Publike service," he
confessed. "The Lord speak to my heart." When word reached Hartford, Connecticut, an official urged New England "to make war their
worke & Trade." Appeals poured into Boston from the countryside.
At Hadley the tension was unbearable. "We are in the Lords hands,"
Russell told the authorities, although he refused to believe this meant
annihilation. Pynchon sent a similar letter on October 8, observing that
God "seems to answer all our prayers by terrible things in righteousness." His people squeezed into Springfield's few remaining houses,
and without bread—the gristmill had been burnt—soldiers were restive. Pynchon feared the town might be abandoned, which would encourage the Indians and "make way for the giving up of all the towns."[7]

Reports spread contagiously in Boston and by August had reached
London. The Navy Office received an account, dated July, predicting
that the war would cause economic grief regardless of who won. By
autumn, most of the able-bodied men were in arms (many conscripted)
and horses had been requisitioned. With the men focusing on war, the

livestock became neglected, and crops lay unharvested in the fields. Colonists who had been in England in the 1640s during the English civil war had seen it all before. Towns that had taken a generation to build lay in ashes, their inhabitants dispersed. John Pynchon wrote to his son Joseph in England regarding his joining the family in America. Their house had been spared, but not Pynchon's barns, mills, and outhouses; his debtors had been ruined, he said, "so that I am really reduced to great straits." The Pynchons let Joseph decide whether to risk coming.[8]

Thrilling tales made it into print. One account sent from Boston to London described everything from the war's origins—Metacom's jealousy that his "howling Wilderness" had become towns, pastures, and orchards—to its impact on ordinary folk. "At Dorchester on a Sabbath Day," the pamphlet related, "an Indian shot at a Maid in a lone house but missed her; she with a generous courage charged and discharged a Pistol at the Indian and so wounded him." Readers got horror stories as well as adventure, the reliability of which scarcely mattered. A letter from Nathaniel Saltonstall, a Boston merchant, covering the war's first six months, appeared in December. It focused on injustice—land coveted by Metacom had been fairly acquired—and barbarism. When a Swansea man fetching corn was shot dead, his wife and son had run to the scene. "They took her, first defiled her, then skinned her Head, as also the Son, then dismist them both, who immediately died." England had known civil war, but these were nightmares from another world. Captives from the Quaker haven of Dartmouth, it was said, were flayed alive or had hands and feet cut off; women were raped and then murdered. Letters from Edward Wharton, a Salem Quaker in Boston, were also published, alleging tortures and executions by Indians "after the most horrid ways they can invent."[9]

Blood and fire became New England's leitmotifs. Mealymouthed deliberations about evangelism ceased, and despite their uses as guides and translators, praying Indians became tainted. Among the warriors who had mocked Brookfield's defenders were some who spoke English and knew the Bible. Colonists started calling them *preying* Indians, traitors who "have made Preys of much English Blood." That the savages were, after all, *savage* was less surprising, however, than the transformation of New Englanders. Once famed for their piety, in England they now seemed desperate, coarse, and ruthless. Praying Indians were interned and initially may have been glad: many colonists were ready to lynch any native they came across. Mobs demanded action. In September 1675, Boston's rulers consented to the execution of a notorious Indian by a pack of giddy amateur hangmen. An Indian friend of the condemned man came and cut a hole in his breast while he was still "half alive"; then he "sucked out his Heart-Blood." Asked the reason, he said he was gaining strength from a strong man. "Thus with the Dog-like death (good enough) of one poor Heathen," Saltonstall concluded, "was the People's Rage laid in some measure."[10]

This vile mood desecrated everything John Winthrop Sr. had held sacred. As winter frosts set in, the future looked bleak, the Indians unstoppable. "At present (if the Lord shew not mercy)," warned Edward Wharton, "they seem as if they would destroy and roul up the rest of our Nation as a burdensome and menstrous Cloth, and Cast it out of their Land."[11]

The snows were the worst anyone could recall. Men waded waist-deep, sinking into drifts, and became disoriented as the landscape lost definition. Their clothes, too thin for the biting winds, were sodden or stiff with ice; throats were dry, bellies rumbled. Postal deliveries stalled, leaving governors and families fearing the worst. "It is a humbling providence of God," noted commissioners of the United Colonies of Massachusetts, Connecticut, and Plymouth on November 12, 1675, "that putts his poore people to be meditating a matter of warre in such a season of the yeare." Yet to survive, they added, it was vital to press on. On the same day, the commander-in-chief condemned those who were leaving Springfield as "unequal, irrationall and unnaturall"; he ordered they be stopped. Towns had to hold firm.[12]

With this resolution, commissioners planned a major assault on the Narragansetts. Wait Winthrop, son of John Winthrop Jr., proposed striking while the enemy was still concentrated, rather than waiting until their dispersal in spring. Prayers in Boston early in December invoked divine help for men at the front. Increase Mather wept for war-torn New England: trade was dead, shortages imminent, smallpox and fevers spreading. "The L[or]d hath lifted up his hand ag[ains]t Boston," he told his diary; the remedy was repentance and prayer for the coming expedition. Then God would be with them. He recalled how the Tudor propagandist John Foxe had seen England's victory over the Scots in 1547 as a reward for the Protestant Reformation.[13]

Three regiments, a thousand men from each colony, had mustered in Rhode Island under Josiah Winslow's command by mid-December. On the 18th, they entered Narragansett territory, capturing grain and an Indian who became their guide. As the pale sun descended they marched toward an enemy stronghold sixteen miles away, until darkness and cold forced them to make camp. They awoke to several feet of snow, and frostbite. It was the Sabbath, but this was God's work. So they continued, passing through woodland to the Great Swamp where a stone fortress surmounted an island. Around 3 p.m., the English fired their first volley, igniting wigwams inside the palisade. As smoke billowed out, they charged, running "on the very musles of theyr guns, up to the Indeans port holes & fyred in at them, & leped over thyr brest workes & run into theyr forte." Inside they found a shambles of wounded and dead Indians, and they shot dozens more as they fled through narrow streets out into the swamp. The fighting lasted into the night. Reenacting the Pequot massacre from forty years earlier, the English burned the camp (thought to be near present-day South Kingstown, Rhode Island), producing such an inferno that it lit the army's way for three miles as it trudged back home.[14]

On the day of the battle, Governor John Leverett of Massachusetts wrote to the secretary of state, Sir Joseph Williamson, in Whitehall explaining that New England was fighting not from selfish ambition but to defend the king's rights against pagan rebels. In the same month, another Boston correspondent defended (possibly to Henry Oldenburg at the Royal Society) the conduct of a people changed by horrors unimaginable in England. Thirty people in Saco and other coastal towns in Maine had been killed, others buried up their necks "using this Sarchasm: You English since you came into this Countrey have grown exceedingly above Ground." Both Englands, wrote the correspondent, wanted the war to end, yet it would continue while Metacom lived. Readers in London, he added, would be shocked by what had happened in the "Quagmiry-Wood," but Indian blood guilt deserved it. One officer described his men's joy "to see their Enemies, who had formerly sculked behind Shrubs and Trees, now to be engaged in a fair Field," but admitted the killing was indiscriminate. Around five hundred Indian warriors died at the Great Swamp; women and children were not counted. Scores of wigwams had been destroyed with the Indians' winter supplies. Survivors would starve.[15]

The English had lost two hundred, some dead, others missing. A pamphlet in England reported that twice that number had been killed or captured since the outbreak of war, compared to nine hundred Indian dead. What the colonists were soon calling "the Great Swamp fight" was justified as a spasm of virtuous fury. Whereas the English were nobly courageous, the account claimed, the Indians acted dishonorably, with "nothing but Massacres, outrages and trecherous hostillitie." Wait Winthrop marked the event with a heroic poem, a foil to "barbarous" attacks on English towns. But similarities with enemy conduct caused unease. Some New Englanders were appalled. "I much lament that rash Cruelty of our English toward Innocent Indians," Thomas Walley informed John Cotton, who agreed. The massacre, Cotton told Increase Mather, was "Gods frowne upon the Army."[16]

The plight of the praying Indians was pitiful. Plans to exile them in Boston harbor, John Eliot protested to the Massachusetts council, would obstruct a mission ordained by God and authorized by the crown, and might prolong the war. He was ignored. In December 1675, Eliot asked the Company for the Propagation of the Gospel to help. "There be 350 soules or therabout put upon a bleake bare Iland," he wrote to Robert Boyle, "the fittest we have where th[ey] suffer hunger & could. There is neither foode nor competent fuel to be had & th[ey] are bare in clouthing." Eliot also claimed that "ungodly & unrulely youth" had murdered some Wamesit Indians. One woman, a Christian convert, saw her son killed and was herself wounded. Raising her hands to heaven, Eliot related, she cried: "Lord thou seest th[a]t we have neither done or said anything against the English th[a]t th[ey] thus deale on us." The charity that migrants hoped to cultivate in America had withered.[17]

As winter stiffened, so did leaders' determination. While the English regrouped, Metacom sought men and materiel from the Mohawks in New York. The Narragansetts moved deep into the countryside. The swamp fight had given them "so bitter a Relish of our English valour," said a colonist, "that they dreaded our neighbourhood." Behind the bluster, however, lay a ragged English army stranded in Rhode Island with nothing to eat. Men foraged for maize in the frozen fields, praying that supplies would reach them through the snows. Reinforcements arrived in January 1676, though eleven men had died en route and many had dysentery. Disease spread across New England. Boston, where the relief force had mustered, was, in Increase Mather's words, "under awfull tokens of divine displeasure." Strengthened by troops from Connecticut and a force of Mohegans, the army set off again, searching for Metacom, who was presumed to be with the Narragansetts. Despite a thaw, the pursuit was exhausting. Soldiers fought through thicket and swampland and over rocky hills, a feat that only the toughest and most determined could bear.[18]

During a steady advance across Rhode Island, the English torched Indian villages and took prisoners. Among them was a farmer named Joshua Tift, who claimed to be the sachem's slave but who many believed had, to quote Edward Rawson, "turned Indian"; some suspected him of fighting the English. Rumors about Tift, including that he had married a Wampanoag and had actively undermined Christianity, betrayed cultural insecurity yet also caused indignation—a salutary reminder to the English of who they were, however much the war blurred boundaries between savagery and civility, liberty and tyranny. Tift was hanged, drawn and quartered as a traitor to his king and his colony. But by executing him, colonists were also destroying a symbol of what they had become in the wilderness, smashing the glass in which they saw their brutalized selves reflected.[19]

Discussion of the war in London and Boston made it comprehensible as a divine drama, but conveyed little of what men endured at the front. Winslow's army was malnourished and demoralized; desertion was common. The English counterattack had carried them forty miles from any town: horses were slaughtered to avert starvation and mutiny. For a while, spirits were lifted. But in February the "hungry march" was halted and soldiers demobilized—another worry for colonists. "They are still much affraid of the Heathens," Increase Mather told his brother in Dublin, "least they should divide themselves into severall parties & burne & destroy more of the countrey & hinder the tillage of the land this year." Fatally, the disbandment of the United Colonies army coincided with Metacom's return to New England. He intended to resume the fight despite having been rebuffed by the Mohawks—a reminder that despite colonists' characterization of him as "King Philip," every tribe had its own leaders and aims.[20]

To settlers in lonely outposts, survival was the war's hard reality; the king, his governors, and Boston's saints were mere distractions. Even God seemed remote from this world of hunger, terror, and constant vigilance—of sleepless nights and traumatized children. Colonists' bravery and good luck impressed the Indians, causing one to strike his breast and declare: "The Englishmens God makes us afraid." More often, Indians taunted their enemies, as during the Pequot War. Their mocking question was: Where is your God now? "Come Lord Jesus, save this poor English man if thou canst, whom I am now about to Kill," an Indian was heard to say to a victim in the swamp. Jesus did not come, nor, some felt, was his father there either. The sense of existential isolation was greater than at any time since the English had arrived in America, and unparalleled in the Atlantic world. Metacom's death was the only objective; what lay beyond was unclear. "I see no likelihood of any Peace," Nathaniel Saltonstall wrote in a letter to England, "but much fear our Wars are far from an end."[21]

Hearing gunfire at dawn on February 10, 1676, Mary Rowlandson ran to a window and saw buildings burning. She lived in the Massachusetts frontier town of Lancaster, where she was the wife of the minister. Her husband was away in Boston appealing for military protection. Narragansett Indians, driven from their homeland but no longer resisted by an English army, had returned with Nipmuck and Wampanoag allies for food and revenge. Butchering anyone in their path, the warriors had reached the Rowlandsons' house where Mary, her three children, various family members, and several neighbors— thirty-seven people in all—were bracing themselves. Doors and windows were peppered with bullets; flax and hemp were piled around the walls and lit on fire. "Some in our House were fighting for their Lives, others wallowing in their Blood," Mary Rowlandson later recalled. She described "the House on fire over our Heads, and the bloody Heathen ready to knock us on the Head if we stirred out." In the end, the heat drove them outside, where thirteen of them were shot or hacked down, the rest taken prisoner. It was "the dolefullest day that ever mine eyes saw," wrote Mary Rowlandson. The Reverend Joseph Rowlandson returned to find smoking ruins, his wife and children gone.[22]

The tragedy was soon common knowledge. Increase Mather, worried by illness creeping through his neighborhood, lamented Lancaster's destruction and the Rowlandsons' disappearance. From Barnstable, Thomas Walley wrote to John Cotton that the news was "exceeding Sad and should greatly humble us," to which Cotton replied with a

An eighteenth-century woodcut of the attack on Lancaster in February 1676, fancifully suggesting that Mary Rowlandson defended her home with a musket. In truth, she was helpless to avoid both Indian aggression and, in captivity, exposure to native culture, however hard she clung to English civility.

copy of a letter from the Narragansetts assuring Rowlandson that "your wif & all your child is well but one dye." Here the Indians also sought to conciliate the Massachusetts government: "You know & wee know your heart great sorrowfull with crying," they wrote. Another note nailed to a tree was more defiant: "Thou English man hath provoked us to anger & wrath & we care not though we have war w[i]th thee this 21 years for . . . we have nothing but our lives to loose, but thou hast many faire houses, cattell & much Good things." The sacking of Lancaster made more colonists ask where God was. Unless he "in compassion to the English Nation in this Wildernesse wonderfully appear for our deliverance," Nathaniel Saltonstall wrote to a friend in London, "nothing could be expected but an utter Desolation."[23]

Atrocities were a medium for voicing fears and resolutions. Two young Englishmen returning from captivity in New York described how a fellow prisoner's execution had involved "cutting a hole between his Stomach and belly & pulling out his Gutts thereat." Noah Newman, a minister-turned-soldier from Rehoboth, Massachusetts, told John Cotton of a pregnant woman who was killed as she ran to a garrison house, an infant in her arms. At dawn, the colonists had found the child standing mute by its mother, a scene framed by flickering fires and fading cries. "What an emblem of the suden & dreadfull appearance of the great Judge of the world," declared Newman, "when he shall come to render vengeance to the wicked!" Violence against women was even more shocking in reverse. Word got around that two men had been brained by squaws who had cut off their genitals as souvenirs. Nathaniel Saltonstall's account of this incident, published in London, also told of a captive Englishwoman in labor whose baby was cut out and burned. It was normal, he said, for Indians to destroy their enemies "with exquisite Torments and most inhumane barbarities." They wore scalps as trophies, fingers as necklaces, and belts of skin. Some colonists tried to conceal all this from their relatives in England. Stephen Dummer of Hampshire reproached his brother-in-law in New England for failing to mention in a letter "ye Barbarous and cruell p[ro]cedings of ye Heathens." "I pray god help you and us," wrote Dummer, "to simpathize on[e] with another in our Aflictions and pray on[e] for another."[24]

Both sides behaved with extravagant cruelty. Indians tortured because martial ritual required it, the English to obtain intelligence. Captain Samuel Moseley, a leader in the massacre at the Great Swamp, interrogated a father and son, making one believe the other was dead before examining and shooting them together. English soldiers also fetishized body parts, as they had since their arrival in America and earlier in Ireland. Impaled English heads were swapped for those of the enemy. To encourage recruits to hunt Narragansetts, the Massachusetts and Connecticut governments offered thirty shillings per scalp. Nor were the English the only ones to suffer the agonies of captivity. The cries of praying Indians on Deer Island were pitiful, as were appeals by native families for lost relatives. One petition received by Boston authorities in 1676 begged that a five-year-old girl captured by the English be returned, or at least not sold out of the country as a slave.[25]

The mood in Boston grew more unsettled. In late February, Medfield, twenty miles away, was burned; a day of atonement only brought the attacks ten miles closer. Militias tracked Metacom using Indian scouts, and cavalry chased him. In March the towns of Groton, Massachusetts, and Simsbury, Connecticut, were abandoned. On the 26th, fifty-five soldiers were slaughtered in an ambush at Plymouth. Three days later, Providence, Rhode Island, was destroyed. Roger Williams's disillusionment was complete: he became a militia captain and helped sell Indians into slavery. Attacks in Connecticut led to anguished pleas for reinforcements. A summary sent to Whitehall on April 1, reported a thousand soldiers dead, a hundred miles of settled territory laid waste, and economic damage that would take two decades to repair. Several days later, the deputy governor of Massachusetts elaborated on this assessment, reiterating a commitment to defending the king's interests in America, despite the sly and unpredictable nature of the enemy. It would be easier, he imagined, to fight a major European army than a few hundred "skulking" Indians.[26]

A mild spell was followed by an unprecedented freeze, then rampant contagion. On April 5, John Winthrop Jr. died. A eulogy by fellow alchemist Benjamin Tompson called him "that most Charitable Christian, Unbiased politician and Unimitable Pyrotechnist"—meaning he had excelled in science and technology as well as in government and religion. How long, many wondered, would the soil in which Winthrop and his father rested remain English? By mid-month, most of Boston's western satellites had been overrun. Plans were made to erect a palisade around the city. Boston observed another day of atonement on the 20th, but, as before, it was followed by a devastating onslaught, this time on Sudbury, twenty miles west. Prisoners from a relief force had flesh cut from their legs and the wounds filled with hot ashes. Thus, shuddered Increase Mather, did Indians show themselves as "the perfect children of the Devill."[27]

Boston was burying three or four people every day by May—"by which things God from Heaven speaks to us," noted Mather. Other New England towns were similarly afflicted. A letter from New Haven to Connecticut's deputy governor at Hartford, dated May 2, detailed the "sorrowfull state in theise p[ar]ts . . . being und[e]r ye solemn & awfull visitac[i]on of ye hand of God by Sicknes." The letter conveyed anxiety that no news had been received for so long. It also reported the killing of a cowherd at Branford, and the consequent harsh treatment of local Indians by enraged settlers. The following day, Connecticut appeased God with new legislation against sin, while in Boston, in his election-day sermon, William Hubbard announced sorrowfully that the gospel vine that had been transplanted from England had now been uprooted. Many believed that heaven's blessing had departed, and that the war was the climax of New England's story. Benjamin Tompson had an epic poem published in Boston and London, a meditation on "New Englands hour of passion." "The mirrour of the Christian world," he mourned, "Lyes burnt to heaps in part."[28]

The summer brought victories, God being "pleased to mixe his smiles wi[i]th his frownes," as Edward Rawson put it. Indian raids met with furious counterattacks from Maine to Connecticut. Boston vainly tried negotiation, and then decided to prosecute the war as strenuously as possible. Total war demanded commitment. A colonist who sent his horse away to prevent it from being requisitioned was censured as "very prejudiciall to the common concernments of the country in this day of trouble." A poor man who refused to fight—he and his pregnant wife had sold their clothes to buy food—was imprisoned. Clerics continued to castigate sinners for provoking God, but they praised the army's courage. Morale improved with warmer weather and victories. On June 15, a bow and arrow were seen in the sky over Plymouth; it was thought to be a good omen. By the end of the month, "whereas formerly almost every week did conclude with sad tidings," rejoiced Increase Mather, "now the Lord sends us good news weekly." A fortnight later Boston held a day of thanksgiving.[29]

The turning tide coincided with the return of Benjamin Church, who had been wounded at the swamp fight. With William Bradford and others, he pursued Metacom from one hideout to another. Church contacted Awashonks and saw that her renunciation of Metacom was formalized at Plymouth. On July 1, Samuel Sewall, a Boston gentle-man, noted in his diary the recapture from the Indians of a black slave, who reported that Metacom's men were sick. A fortnight later Bradford almost captured Metacom, yet once again the Indian disappeared into the swamp. But his time was running out. Benjamin Church's men seized Metacom's wife and son on August 1, then ran back along the trail, through woodland and across rivers, lying low at night, silent and shivering. When Church encountered Indians, he either had them killed, persuaded them to change sides, or took them as prisoners. "You have now made Philip ready to dye," they told Church, "for you have made him as poor and miserable as he us'd to make the English."[30]

Finally, on the 10th, after a two-day chase, Church cornered the great sachem himself in an ambush on Rhode Island's Mount Hope peninsula, where the war had begun. Metacom was shot dead by John Alderman, a Christian Indian. When his body was dragged from the mud, he resembled "a doleful, great, naked, dirty beast," thought Church, who ordered that he should remain unburied, just as he had let English corpses rot. One of Metacom's hands was given to Alderman as a souvenir. Boston was jubilant. On August 12, Samuel Sewall made a laconic note in an almanac: "Philippus exit." To Increase Mather this was a token of God's love, the reward of prayer and lasting proof that the Indians were the devil's agents sent to frustrate the English mission in America.[31]

Shortly afterward, Benjamin Church, hero of the hour, apprehended Metacom's right-hand man, Annawon. Church offered amnesty to his warriors, but told Annawon he would be taken to Plymouth for trial. The old man respected his English adversary, even when—perhaps especially when—Church informed him of Metacom's death. In an impromptu ritual, by the light of a bright moon, Annawon admitted defeat and surrendered the sachem's regalia, including a red blanket, two powder horns, a gorget, and three belts, one of which Church described as "wrought with black and white Wompom in various figures and flowers, and pictures of many birds and beasts." Church was summoned to Boston, where glory was heaped upon him, but returning to Plymouth he was dismayed that Annawon had already been executed, still more to see his severed head displayed. Church presented the trophies to Josiah Winslow, who sent them to Charles II with a letter crediting the remarkable frontiersman and declaring Plymouth's wartime commitment to royal interests.[32]

CHAPTER 17

A People Bred Up in This Country

T HE WAR WAS for the second generation what the great migration had been for the first: a validating ordeal, an act of atonement, and a memorial to sacrifice. English colonies, some born out of antipathy to other colonies, had united against a common enemy in a show of cultural strength, and it gave them a chance to rediscover courage. A new discourse appeared, infused with anger and virtue and loss. And yet as moral ambiguities were purged, so new ones were created. Protecting civility had made Englishmen embrace savagery; they had fought fire with fire. Cruelty divided opinion between England and New England, and among New Englanders themselves. Who, furthermore, was to blame for the war? What was God punishing: native devilishness or colonial sin? Puritans had failed to live by the gospel themselves, never mind extend it to Indians. Had their defense of godly liberty led to tyranny? The Chesapeake colonies were no more immune to war and rebellion than the New England ones. Upheavals occurred there, too, and, as in New England, they recast identities and the colonies' relationship with England. Clashes between the rhetoric of imperial sovereignty and that of inalienable rights and freedoms, as well as competing definitions of loyalty, led to open conflict between Englishmen trying to make sense of themselves in the New World.[1]

In relative terms, King Philip's War was the most devastating war in American history. Over fifty New England townships had been attacked, twelve completely destroyed. In July 1676, Nathaniel Saltonstall listed the damage: at Narragansett, Patuxet, and Deerfield, no houses remained; Warwick, Providence, Swansea, Marlborough, and Grantham now had between one and three houses each. Rehoboth, Taunton, Hadley, Hatfield, Sudbury, Weymouth, and Springfield were largely ruined, "besides particular Farms and Plantations, a great Number not to be reckoned up, wholly laid waste or much damnified." With these losses, the war had cost £250,000, amounting to £21 per household in New England, more than the deputy governor of Connecticut earned per year. It would take a century for prewar incomes to recover.[2]

England had offered little aid besides parish collections, which were mere gestures. The role of the mint-master John Hull was therefore of immense significance. Hull was a rich man: his daughter's dowry when she married Samuel Sewall in February 1676 was said to be her weight in silver. But a more astonishing instance of Hull's largesse was his bankrolling of the war for the Massachusetts Bay Colony, which united the state with its mercantile elite. His accounts listed not only loans but also soldiers' wages, payments to native allies, and supplies of everything from coats and horseshoes to biscuits and tobacco. Governor Josiah Winslow of Plymouth asked for help in May 1676, explaining that they had many wounded but few surgeons. Hull supplied bandages and beds, doctors and nurses, and so New England muddled through, surviving and facing up to despoliation and death.[3]

Some 2,000 New Englanders died. Ten percent of the 5,000 males eligible for service in Massachusetts and Plymouth—the backbone of the workforce—were killed or captured. No one knows how many became invalids or were maimed, nor how many thousands of Indians were killed, dispersed, or enslaved. The emotional cost, meanwhile, was incalculable. Thomas Eames, a farmer at Framingham, was in Boston on February 1, 1676, appealing for help when Indians abducted his family and burned everything he owned. This included a thirty-four-foot house; a barn full of cereals and hay, hemp, and flax; weapons, tools, and ironware; bedding and clothing; and barrels of bacon, butter, and cheese—total value: £330 12s. His inventory of losses was headed: "Imprimis—A wife and nine children," followed by a space in the valuation column. Grief in the Massachusetts town of Seaconck overwhelmed John Kingsley, causing him to open his heart to the minister at Hartford in a letter. "I am not able to bear the sad story of our woeful day when the Lords made our wolfish heathen to be our lords," he wrote. And yet, added Kingsley, no letter could do justice to their catastrophe: Seaconck had lost its mills, animals, and carts, and people were living in squalor.[4]

Letters flew between communities, colonies, and continents. William Harris informed Sir Joseph Williamson in London in August 1676

Thomas Eames's inventory of loss, dated February 1, 1675 (i.e., 1676). Here Eames describes his property destroyed in the Indian attack on Framingham, including a house, a barn, livestock, tools, linen, and food. At the top of the list is "a wife & Nine children."

about New England's parlous state. His own son was dead, and many were in despair. Condolences multiplied. When Josiah Winslow's cousin Jonathan Winslow was killed, his widow, Ruth, was assured by her parents that this was God's will. She lived at Marshfield, Plymouth—the Winslow seat—and was fortunate that her husband left property worth nearly £100. Others were reduced to penury. Petitions and other written appeals recounted their stories: a widow begging that her son, who had been wounded at the Great Swamp, be sent home to support her;

a redeemed prisoner trying to reimburse the man who had put up his ransom; another man, who had been held captive during the planting season, unable to pay his taxes; a woman who had lost her husband and was "able to doe very little worke, save onely to attend her poore small Babes"; a trader forced to sell alcohol without a license, the war having wrecked his livelihood. New England's courts heard such tales of desperation well into the 1680s. The town of Mendon, still feeling the war's "deplorable & desolating Effects" five years after its official end, begged the Massachusetts general court for assistance, having gone beyond the limits of its strength. Thomas Eames of Framingham received two hundred acres in compensation, and the same again when he sued his Indian attackers.[5]

Captivity left a legacy of trauma and family fragmentation. Some of Thomas Eames's children survived, ending up in New Hampshire, New York, and Canada. Mary Rowlandson of Lancaster was freed in May 1676, and two of her children the following month. They had been "carried through the Jaws of so many deaths," wrote Increase Mather, "and at last brought home in peace." It was a sign that God might yet pull New England back from the abyss. Yet Rowlandson, like her colony, was utterly changed. She had tramped through snow, had slept in the open, and had seen "diabolical" rituals. The six-year-old child she clung to died, and she thought incessantly of the others "scattered up and down among the wild Beasts of the Forest." She drew strength from the Bible and from her hatred. "Little do many think," she exclaimed, "what is the savageness and bruitishness of this barbarous Enemy!"[6]

Hunger debased Rowlandson. Refusing at first to eat "filthy trash," she was soon begging a scrap of horse liver, which she cooked in embers. "But before it was half ready," she recalled, "they got half of it away from me, so that I was fain to take the rest and eat it as it was with the blood about my mouth, and yet a savoury bit it was to me." Rowlandson's rationale was that "to the hungry Soul every bitter thing is sweet"; but she might have said: "The hungry soul is a savage soul." New Englanders experienced the war as harmful exposure to the wilderness, which led people across the Atlantic to think them more "indianized" than ever. Some lived like animals, became murderers, or let their countrymen down, becoming estranged from the values that English adventurers were once so confident about instilling in the Indians. The trial of two men for betraying fellow colonists provoked disgust and shame. "God grant that by the Fire of all these Judgments," wrote the Puritan divine William Hubbard, "we may be purged from our Dross and become a more refined people." The war had certainly purged New England, but refinement was not one its obvious effects.[7]

Among the war's other psychological wounds were vanishings: some women and children had been carried off without a trace, and the fate of some men who had fought in the battles was unknown. Families waited for years, as in England's civil wars, praying and believing that someday they would return. Soldiers came back to devastated plantations to find their loved ones long gone. Stoicism supported hope, however: no sooner did troops arrive home, wrote an observer, than they "mow down their Ground, and make hay, and do other occasions necessary for their re-setling." Rebuilding was expensive, especially as many now preferred stone to wood for houses. John Thomson, a farmer and veteran, built a house at Middleborough in 1677 on the site of one that had burned down in the war: it had reinforced outer posts, brick walls from foundation to beams, and one small window on each side. Families felt safer in such homes.[8]

Others could not bear to stay and migrated farther south. This was partly due to painful memories, but it was also fear of what lay ahead that caused people to relocate. The hope that Metacom's death would bring peace disappeared. Rather than ending, the war changed shape, and Boston's joy was not universal. Although the attacks were smaller and fewer, they still took place; they simply shifted from the coastal towns to the frontier, especially Maine, where Wabenakis were resisting English expansion. Hence people in Maine drifted toward Massachusetts. "The enemy is doing mischiefe apace," wrote Richard Martyn, a New Hampshire merchant, in September 1676, referring to hostilities in northerly Wells and Casco. Houses had been gutted and people shot. Impossible demands for manpower and food had been made on Martyn's hometown, Portsmouth. In October the garrison at Black Point, Maine, stopped taking orders, started drinking, and was overrun. The same month, trembling at God's anger, the Massachusetts government published an order against sin. Colonists were told to pray that the messengers who had been sent to England for help "might find favour with his Majesty."[9]

Day and night, New Englanders who lived in towns remote from Boston felt vulnerable to attack. Even where the Indians had been decimated, they remained a chilling presence, particularly as the English frontier crept toward their places of refuge. Fear brought loathing. Racial virtue replaced religious virtue as a source of self-justification, as in Virginia after the 1622 uprising. And the second generation added something new. Samuel Nowell, a former military chaplain, was less in thrall to the pioneers—his father had arrived on the *Arbella* in 1630—than he was fiercely proud of their heirs' achievements. "You have a People bred up in this Country that have the heart of Lions," he told a Boston audience in 1678. "A tender, softly, effeminate People is a curse and misery," whereas Englishmen raised in America were hardened by danger. Were Indians the only enemy Nowell had in his sights? A royal commissioner from England thought not, and accused Nowell of "preaching up rebellion."[10]

To Nowell's friend Increase Mather, New England's salvation now seemed more distant than it had at the time of Metacom's death. Moral reformation was imperative, causing the second generation, vindicated by war, to glare at the third—"Proud, Disobedient creatures," Mather called them. One Puritan minister, in his analysis of the conflict, castigated "the rising generation that know not the god of theyr fathers but Carry proudly and harken not to the word of the Lord." Youth and irreligion triangulated with vanity. Excess in apparel had helped to uproot the gospel, thought William Hubbard: honest workers were once busy bees, not gaudy butterflies. Mather despised most those who elevated themselves above their station, such as Hannah Poland, who in March 1676 was "for her strong fashion admonished." Eight women had been fined the previous year for wearing silk hoods and "genteel garbe." That July, elders at Plymouth attributed epidemic disease to adolescent misconduct, "for which the Lord may justly be provoked to avenge the quarrel of his Covenant upon us." The disproportionate number of young lives lost to "the rage of the enemy" had been instructive.[11]

Writing to Mather about dysentery and fever at Hadley, Massachusetts, Samuel Hooker remarked: "God seemeth not to have finished his Contraversy w[i]th ye Land." Next came fire. When, in the summer of 1676, Increase Mather heard that a conflagration had destroyed the English town of Northampton, he may well have imagined Boston chastened thus. On November 26 he gave a sermon on Revelations 3:3, urging people to "hold fast and repent." At 5 a.m., he smelled smoke and saw flames. After bundling his children into the street, he ran to his study and began throwing books down the stairs, saving almost everything "through ye wonderfull & tender mercy of ye most High." Precious keepsakes were lost as fire spread: notes from his time in England, his parents' letters and papers. William Bradford's manuscript history of Plymouth, at first believed to have burned, mercifully reappeared. Most of his furniture and linens survived, as did some silver plate items, though they were melted. Eighty dwellings, several warehouses, and a meetinghouse were destroyed.[12]

Mather received letters interpreting the event. John Westgate, a former resident of New England, wrote from Harleston in Norfolk saying the fire was punishment for Boston's ingratitude to God, who had preserved it from Indian invasion. The streets were full of debauchery, said Westgate, an intolerable blot, "you being set up as a Beacon upon ye top of a mountain, being as it were a City in comparison to all other Towns." Not all blame lay with dandies and drunks. "Dear S[i]r, I pray be not offended at my plainnesse," Westgate continued, "[but] yor Fathers with much hazard, difficulty & danger went to th[a]t wildernesse . . . to set up ye pure worship of God & to enjoy libertie of their conscience." How, he asked, did tyrannical persecution of dissenters sit with this? Worshippers at Harleston had prayed for New England's deliverance, but the war's cause was obvious. Westgate had no love for Quakers or Baptists, but asked Mather why the Puritans were so offended by them, "if it be meerly for their difference from you in Judgement & practice, I cannot yet understand."[13]

Some Bostonians agreed. Richard Hutchinson wrote to London of his people's willingness "to put different Reflections upon the Murders and Spoils that have been made upon us by this Destructive War." He was pained "to remember how severe some of us have been to Dessenters, making spoil without pity." Increase Mather, unmoved, believed God's anger came from *tolerating* Quakers. The Salem Quaker Edward Wharton had heard both opinions in Boston in October 1675, when he had illicitly erected a memorial to his hanged brethren on the common. Quakers shamed their oppressors. "The Lord suffered the Heathen for a time to be a Rod in his Hand to correct thy Inhabitants," read one address to New England. Christopher Holder, a veteran of the persecution, imagined an avenging angel with one foot in Boston, the other in Plymouth. Other martyrs joined in. Samuel Gorton accused the elders of raising an idol in the wilderness, saying it was doomed just like Israel's golden calf. He hoped England would learn from what came "to pass upon a People that made a great shew and a great talk of God, Christ and Ordinances." New England was more blighted than Sodom or Egypt. Dissenters' blood, Gorton knew, cried to heaven—the sentiment inscribed on Wharton's illicit memorial.[14]

Indian deaths would also be avenged, said Gorton. Like opinions about the Quakers, opinions about the Indians varied widely. Some people thought New England had been too lax with the native population—"loosening the bridle of the Heathen." Others thought the colonists had been too severe. In London, a worried Robert Boyle, governor of the Company for the Propagation of the Gospel, wrote to United Colonies commissioners in April 1677. He received a reply dated December 20, as the postal service was still chaotic. The reply explained that the Indian diaspora had impeded expenditure of company money, and who knew when work could resume? Commissioners cited Indian aggression, but with undertones of pity. One colonist asked Increase Mather "whether o[u]r English were wholly inocent" regarding the war's causes. Similarly, settlers at Pemaquid, Maine, blamed Indian wickedness on "the perfidious & unjust dealing of som[e] English." Even Mather conceded that New England had attracted migrants "on the account of Trade and worldly Interests, by whom the Indians have been scandalized."[15]

War also hit colonies farther south. It began, as colonial disasters often did, with omens: a comet, a plague of insects, and a vast flock of pigeons not seen since the Indian uprising in the 1640s. One summer morning in 1675, a herdsmen employed by Thomas Mathew, a merchant in a frontier region of Virginia, was found dying from tomahawk wounds. His last words were "Doegs, Doegs," an accusation against the Doeg Indians of Maryland, repeated by a boy found cowering under a bed. Regiments of foot and horse chased the killers for twenty miles. Captain George Brent surrounded a cabin and, in Doeg dialect, called a conference. When the king emerged, Brent grabbed him by the scalp lock and shot him. In the ensuing skirmish, ten Indians were killed, and the king's eight-year-old son was taken prisoner. According to Mathew, the boy "lay Ten dayes in Bed, as one Dead, with Eyes and Mouth Shutt, no Breath Discern'd, but his body continuing Warm." Brent, a Catholic, thought the boy was bewitched and arranged for a clerk to baptize him, there being no minister for miles. The boy's teeth unclenched to take a spoonful of cordial—"Convincing Proofe against Infidelity."[16]

But the fighting escalated, with Doegs and Susquehannocks terrorizing Stafford County and destroying crops and herds. Soldiers were alerted throughout Virginia. Across the Potomac River, Marylanders were terrified, attacks having occurred there, too. An uneasy peace had held for thirty years, but had gradually been undermined by planters' greed and duplicity. These men dissented from Virginia's royal government, which, under the leadership of Sir William Berkeley, had used law rather than war against Indian murderers to keep the peace. But public pressure was formidable, and many began to believe that native crimes justified all-out assault by the armies of the Chesapeake. The execution of five Susquehannock chiefs in September 1675 was the final provocation. Frontier raids in January 1676 panicked the colonists, who viewed Berkeley's preservation of alliances with Indians as dilatory or disloyal. Many of those clamoring for all-out war were emancipated servants; they had been promised land in their indentures, but the colony had run out of land. They cursed the governor, hungrily eyed native territory, and took matters into their own hands. As in New England, distinctions between tribes dissolved: the enemy became "the Indians."[17]

One humid night in May, an English force approached the main encampment of the Pamunkeys, who were thought to be allies of the hostile Susquehannocks. Indians fired from the ramparts and the English charged. Many men, women, and children died; others were captured or driven into the darkness, leaving behind them the screams of those who were trapped by flames. "In the heat of the fight," reported the English commander, "we regarded not the advantage of the p[ri]sion[er]s, nor any plunder but burnt and destroyed all but what we reckon[ed] most materiall." His name was Nathaniel Bacon; he was a twenty-nine-year-old Suffolk gentleman who had been packed off to Virginia by his father two years earlier to make his way in the world. He had planted tobacco in Henrico County and had won his neighbors' respect, and his political ascent was hastened by kinship with the governor's wife. Within months, Bacon had a seat on the council. A contemporary described him as "indifferent tall butt slender, black haired and of an ominous pensive melancholly aspect." His taciturn manner hid "a most Imperious and dangerous pride of heart," until he became "Powerfull and Popular," by which time it was too late to contain him.[18]

Berkeley was in his seventy-first year, and his health and powers were waning. He was alarmed by the northern conflict, chiefly its cost. "If this warr lasts one Yeare longer," he said in the spring of 1676, "they in new England will be the poorest miserablest people of al[l] the Plantations of the English in America." Yet in Virginia his caution only intensified plebeian demands. Favor for Bacon in the assembly and throughout the James River plantations emboldened him to challenge the governor. As in Massachusetts, the crisis fed on existing anxiety about colonial status. Agents had gone to London to ask Charles II to revoke an aristocratic grant for Virginia that threatened its self-government. Concerns about defense meshed with grievances about arbitrary government and unfair taxation. In April, Bacon had been refused a commission to fight the Pamunkeys, so he formed his own expeditionary force. He had no more love for what he called the "giddy multitude" than for the "juggling parasites" of Berkeley's circle. But he was cocksure and willing, which, it was said, encouraged "the unquiet unpatient Crowd . . . to choose him for their General."[19]

Inevitably, Bacon's men were branded as "an insulting rabble who account the law their manacles"—in a word: traitors. Yet their objective was not rebellion against the crown or even the office of royal governor: they were asserting their natural rights as Englishmen. Even as they backed Bacon, they petitioned Berkeley, pleading that "wee the poore subjects are in dayly dandger of loosing our lives by the Heathen in soe much that wee are all afraid of goeing about our demesticall affaires." They wanted him to honor the paternalist rhetoric by which all English people consented to hierarchy. Bacon protested that his men were enemies of rebellion; they were Charles II's liegemen against native belligerence and inept governance, and merely protecting themselves according to "the Law of nature and nations." What else should men with "innocent and loyall intentions" do? Sir Thomas Bacon petitioned the king to show clemency to his son, arguing that his only fault was "the weakness of being over persuaded to lead the people." Proposals in England to suppress Bacon's uprising claimed that Virginia was essentially faithful, although even this looked doubtful.[20]

When on June 10 Bacon returned to Jamestown to sit in the House of Burgesses, he was arrested, and then pardoned. A fortnight later his soldiers seized the capital. In August Bacon denounced the governor for "having betrayed and sold His Ma[jes]ties Country and ye liberty of his Loyall Subjects to ye barbarous Heathen"; in turn, Berkeley accused Bacon of "being in open Rebellion against his most Sacred Ma[jes]ty." By now officials in Whitehall had received a "humble remonstrance" from the people of Virginia, "the living monuments of Calamities and greif by the losses of our Wives, children & estates." On September 26, a letter arrived in England from Bacon's wife to her sister. They had lost crops, livestock, and an overseer: "If you had been here," Elizabeth Bacon wrote, "it would have greived your heart to hear the pitiful complaints of the people, the Indians killing the people daily and the Govern[o]r not taking any notice." Virginia loved Nathaniel—"you never knew any better beloved then hee is"—but she feared he would be killed by Berkeley, if not by the Indians.[21]

Pleas, like pledges of fidelity, did not extenuate treason; neither did the rebels' excesses win them sympathy. By the time Bacon's sister-in-law read his wife's letter, three hundred troops had left their trenches around Jamestown and burned the city. This harmed Bacon's cause, as did plundering the estates of Berkeley's supporters and using their wives as human shields. More disdain stemmed from the fact that, as the poet Andrew Marvell put it, he had "proclam'd liberty to all servants and negro's"—an incitement to revolt. For this and other reasons—a lack of clear aims and the approaching army from England—Bacon's movement seemed, in Marvell's words, "an headlesse issue." Its charismatic leader was doomed. Bacon contracted dysentery and in October was evacuated to Gloucester County, where he died. He was buried secretly to prevent his corpse from being exhibited—like that of Metacom, or that other great traitor against the House of Stuart, Oliver Cromwell.[22]

The uprising collapsed. The ringleaders were arrested and twenty-three men were hanged, among them a parliamentarian veteran of the English civil war, who was, it was said, "very active in this Rebellion." Many had their property confiscated. Some of them protested innocence, including a man who said he had sat "quietly under his own roofe." Others were banished to England. Jamestown was ruined. One resident, William Sherwood, petitioned the king for compensation for his house and the debts owed him by executed rebels. Berkeley's wife, Lady Frances, set about restoring the family fortunes and ordering repairs to the mansion at Green Spring. Royal commissioners had landed with the troops. Bacon, they concluded, did "Trayterously levy Warr against us and our Government," exploiting a depraved colony without respect for God or the Navigation Acts. The rebels had prolonged the Indian war, which now could end.[23]

One commissioner, Sir John Berry, estimated in February 1677 that just 500 of 15,000 English Virginians were blameless in the rebellion; the rest, he said, were "ill Qualified as to their Obedience, and incouraged at soe remote Distance from England to cast off the Yoke and Subjugate themselves to a Forreine Power." He perceived the colonists as stubborn and hostile; blaming Bacon fooled no one. Now that the ringleader was dead, a pamphlet sarcastically predicted, England should expect to hear that Virginians were "freed from all dangers, quitted of all their fears, and in great hopes and expectation to live quietly under their own vines and enjoy the benefit of their commendable labours."[24]

Berkeley, a spent force, was removed from office, though not without protest. His resistance exposed an irony typical of English America. As Bacon's opponent, he had been an English royalist suppressing homegrown libertarians; against the commissioners he was a loyal Virginian facing down the crown and defending the colony he had served for thirty-five years. Unlike Bacon, Berkeley was someone "bred up in this Country." Embittered and determined to restore his honor, he sailed to England in May 1677, but when he arrived he was sick, and he died a few weeks later. He was buried in Middlesex, the county where he had been born early in the reign of James I, back when the commercially expansive and politically assertive Virginia to which he had contributed so much had not even existed.[25]

K ing Philip's War and Bacon's Rebellion increased English America's dependence on England, and royal ambitions to control it. Crown interest in the size of populations and industrial output, and also in religion, poverty, and crime, grew. Taxation was a major concern. The newly formed Lords of Trade and Plantations, a Privy Council committee, criticized Virginia and Maryland for allowing seamen to smuggle tobacco (in the voids between barrels), a ploy that cost the crown £10,000 to £20,000 per annum in lost revenue. But the overarching problem was the authority of colonial assemblies, which the colonies were now putting above the crown. A statesman in London received a letter from Bermuda in 1676 complaining of the "Egyptian Vassalage" imposed by councillors there, who behaved, he said, like "Rulers in our litle Israel."[26]

New England also erred. It was again noted with contempt that in Boston a Mr. Hull ran his own mint, but there was much more. An administrator named Edward Randolph returned from America in the autumn of 1676 accusing Massachusetts of gross disloyalty. "Laws made by your Majesty and your Parliament," he had learned, "obligeth in nothing but what consists with the interests of that colony." A report the following May listed Randolph's complaints: Massachusetts had formed an illegal commonwealth, ignored the Navigation Acts, made its own money, persecuted subjects for religion, and sheltered regicides. He believed royal dominion should be imposed universally and that all charters—proprietary grants as well as company patents—should be revoked. His opinion was that of most Englishmen: New Englanders were anarchical, arrogant, self-righteous ingrates.[27]

Imperial supervision exacerbated grievances against England and its appointees. In the wake of the Virginia rebellion there was an uprising in Calvert County, Maryland, in defense of "immunities and freedoms" from unjust taxation. Marylanders also sent a petition championing Bacon and reminding the king that the colonies stimulated English trade. These petitioners wanted not independence, but royal control, so as to unseat Lord Baltimore, who, they said, "assum[e]s and attracts more Royall Power to himselfe over his Tenants then owr gratious King over his subjects in Engl[an]d." If Massachusetts was a self-declared republic, then Maryland was a sham-principality contemptuous of "the liberty of the freeborne subjects of England." Royal rule was thus criticized in the crown's choice of proprietor and *endorsed* through demands for its more direct application, in line with England's ancient constitution. Colonial anger about taxation and weak proprietary government was further evinced by a revolt in Carolina in 1677. The Lords Proprietor defended its instigator, John Culpeper, rather than risk losing their charter by advertising disorder and neglect of the Navigation Acts.[28]

The more interest Whitehall showed in colonists, the more it appeared to misunderstand them. Experience set the colonists apart, creating opposition internally and with England. And no experience was more estranging of one Englishman from another than war. While the Lords of Trade were scrutinizing New England behind desks, the conflict that might have destroyed it dragged on. Frontier-folk were too preoccupied to notice Edward Randolph's critique, even if they knew it existed. Desperation triggered occasional insanity. Increase Mather received a worrying letter from Stamford, a two days' ride away—a "pleasant Land [made] desolate" by the Indians—in the spring of 1677. A youth had set about his sister with an axe, "maulling & mashing her head to many pieces in a barbarous & bloudy maner." Here, then, was the Englishman indianized.[29]

Colonists were inured to bloodshed and the implosion of their world. A June 1677 battle with Indians at Scarborough, near Black Point in Maine, left half the hundred-strong English army dead or wounded. Boston, shaken by the news, ordered a day of prayer. The fact that the fighting had no obvious end, along with Anglo-Indian integration and intertribal conflict—a third of New England's natives supported the English—made the ongoing struggle resemble a civil war. Describing an attack in July, inhabitants of Amesbury, Massachusetts, told of a confrontation between a woman and her father's former Indian apprentice. "Why, s[ai]d he, goodwife Quimby . . . [why] doe you think th[a]t I will kill you? Said she, beccause you kill all english." He struck her on the head, "whereupon she called him rogue & threw a stone att him, & then he gave her two more [blows] & settled her for dead." In September, Indians took their captives from a raid in Hatfield and Deerfield into the mountains. Facing starvation, the Indians asked them to pray, and the next day three bears were caught. The shared meal was blessed by the captives at their captors' behest. These were people who understood each other's ways.[30]

Smallpox reached where Indians could not. More English people had died at Hadley, Massachusetts, in the winter of 1676–1677 than had been killed in the war, "the Lord hereby speaking aloud to us th[a]t [our] enemies had not done enough against us," their minister noted. Boston was hit north and south in an epidemic blamed on sin. By 1678, 15 percent of the city was infected, and over seven hundred people died. In April that year townsmen at Hatfield, which had lost its best men "by sword and sick-beds," together with half its houses and most of its food and livestock, requested protection from future miseries. Some of Hatfield's captives made it back; most did not. In May the Massachusetts authorities were informed about prisoners still being held at Albany, where "sufferings are great & their Crye for releife is loud." Towns contributed to a redemption fund—mostly a few pounds, Boston over a hundred—but there was only so much that could be done.[31]

Continued suffering bred English prejudice and fury. In Rhode Island, Indians were treated like traitors and tried by court-martial. At New London, Connecticut, an English youth who confessed to murdering a family with an axe was acquitted, and two Indians indicted instead. Natives were assaulted, and even lynched. The previous year, in retaliation for Wabanaki attacks on fishing shallops along the Maine coast, women at Marblehead had beaten two prisoners to death; an eyewitness reported "their heads off and gone, and flesh in a manner pulled from their bones." Brutality was normalized, and Indians were denied the civility and honor that, in theory, moderated European warfare. War souvenirs treasured by families included bones and scalps. Metacom's pickled hand was most prized.[32]

The England of 1678, meanwhile, was dealing with influenza and tense foreign affairs as Charles II allied himself to the Dutch against the French. Godly minds across the Atlantic world fixed on Protestant preservation. Increase Mather had received a letter from a stranger in Lancashire who implored God thus: "Let him make Old England new and renew new-Englands dayes as of old." These were sentiments shared by New England's ministers. Samuel Hooker prescribed "Faith, Holiness and Obedience." If only people had heeded warnings, preached the pastor of Dedham in November, "much of that sorrow and misery which we have felt, and do feel, in War, sickness and other shakings, might have been escaped." Nor was it over: God might yet forsake New England as he had abandoned Jerusalem to the Romans. The difficulty for the Puritan elite was that the war's dislocations had put even more folk beyond their reach: thus Massachusetts became more like Virginia. When councils and congregations *were* able to exert power over the peripheries, the outcome was an increase in quarrels over land and taxes. Massachusetts was now more like England, too: it was pushing law into dark corners of the land, only to have it ignored, selectively applied, or blithely adapted to local conditions.[33]

The Puritan grip was further weakened by popular desire for territory, trade, and manufacture. When William Hubbard told his Ipswich congregation that good Christians should desire only God's favor, not "lands and great farmes," one man burst out laughing. In the second half of the century, despite the war, New England's economic output increased. Some towns, such as Springfield, had seemingly risen from the dead. They were dynamic, stratified, and less introspectively communitarian than their forebears. Questions from England about Connecticut revealed a vibrant colony with prosperous market centers and healthy trade relations with Boston and the West Indies. Other towns, such as Wethersfield, were buying Indian land, which caused as much conflict between neighboring English communities as it did between rival tribes. Disputes festered along Connecticut's border with Rhode Island, the latter piously protesting how Connecticut's incursions dishonored the king. Like Springfield, Haverhill, a farming community on

Massachusetts's northern frontier, was evolving into a proto-industrial hub where wage laborers operated sawmills and gristmills. By the late 1670s, newcomers from England and other colonies were arriving in droves, putting pressure on land and triggering boundary disputes.[34]

Dissenters also caused friction. Charles II had twice failed to introduce religious toleration in England. The Test Acts of 1673 and 1678 restricted the rights of Catholics and nonconformists, such as Quakers, many of whom had fled to America. The minister at Ipswich, Massachusetts, William Hubbard, warned of Baptists, calling them "Wolves in Sheeps-cloathing, Devils in humane shape." A rumor circulated in London and Boston that Baptists had disemboweled a minister; later, Indians were blamed. When Quakers settled in New Jersey, territory between the Hudson and Delaware rivers first settled by the Dutch and the Swedish, it caused concern in Massachusetts and laughter in England. A ballad mocked their aim to banish Indian beliefs when Quakerism was just as daft and devilish. Not everyone was amused. So many nonconformists were leaving Yorkshire, Derbyshire, and Nottingham that a magistrate warned of "discouragement to thes[e] parts that suffer already for want of people." He urged the king to detain ships bound for New Jersey. Hundreds of migrants to the Delaware Valley came from the Midlands and Wales, and by 1678, 1,000 Irish people a year were settling along the Appalachian spine. Fears of "superfluous multitudes" who could be sent to the colonies were overtaken by fears of "draining the life-blood of the nation."[35]

In these new adventures were echoes of early Virginia and New England: overpraise, trepidation, the stark realities of starting over, reports both honest and false. Arriving at Burlington on the Delaware River in 1677, along with 230 others, John Crips wrote to a friend in London eulogizing everything from his family's health to the quiescence of the Indians (except when drunk). Then there was the plentiful venison, "full of Gravy, like Fat Young Beef." "Indeed," he wrote, "the Country is so likely that I do not see how it can reasonably be found fault with. As far as I perceive, all of the Things we heard of it in England are very true; and I wish that many People (that are in Straits in England) were Here. Here is good Land, enough lyes void, would serve many Thousands of Families; and we think if they cannot Live Here, they can hardly Live in any Place in the World." Another settler enthused about self-sufficiency: "In short, this is a rare place for any poor man." Promoters sold New Jersey as a happy medium and a fertile one.

"The Aire of this Province is very Serene, Sweet and Wholsome," John Scott told a London merchant, "which renders the Clime much more agreeable to European Bodies than the severe Colds of New-England or the sulphurous Heat in Virginia." Fish, fowl, and fruit were plentiful, and there were fine prospects for honey, silk, hops, potash, salt, and pitch. Furthermore, said another, they enjoyed "the most Ancient true English and best Christian Government in the World."[36]

People in England, it was said, spread rumors about wolves, foul water, and bad land distribution to prevent losing their countrymen and from sheer envy. New Jersey's houses were not, as alleged, two-room shacks with low ceilings and a single hearth, or inadequate in winter. The allocation of land had improved, even if chaos was succeeded by contention over property. As ever, calumnies upon America were frustrating to migrants who wanted their friends and family to join them. A Quaker insisted that his only interest in applauding the country was opposing "rash Censures of People that know it not." One colonist wept when he thought of the friend he longed to be with; others tried to persuade reluctant wives and parents to come to America. "It would be the joy of my heart to see thee and thy Husband and children here," a settler told her sister-in-law. "I long to see your faces if you be free to come."[37]

Arriving dissenters were as hungry for freedom as William Bradford or John Winthrop had been. "Here is liberty for the honest hearted that truly desire to fear the Lord," Esther Huckens, a Quaker, wrote to a friend. "Here is liberty from the cares and Bondage of this World." Another Quaker ended his letter with lines from George Herbert's "The Church Militant," a poem written in the 1630s: "Religion stands Tiptoe in Our Land, / Ready to pass to the American-Strand." Indeed, English pilgrims were still heading for the shores of the New World. In an age of burgeoning global commerce, these words still meant something. For as long as England's faiths remained in contention, America was a land of spiritual opportunity.[38]

Yet England and America were anything but opposites. The experience of colonization was transforming, in New England most acutely during King Philip's War. Affinities endured, however, even if they exercised greater or lesser influence depending on circumstance. Ties of blood and trade, the shared history and culture, a robust fraternity between coreligionists, and the way colonies were increasingly woven into imperial affairs ensured that in the next decade, amid intense paranoia about Catholics and an escalating succession crisis, the transatlantic, parallel lives in politics and religion would converge. The ideological battle lines would be fixed in England *and* America as much as *between* England and America. Questions of sovereignty and authority, and of loyalty and liberty, preoccupied people on both sides of the ocean as well as in the Caribbean, where slave economies created vast wealth, but compromised the political order by which Englishmen distinguished themselves from savages.

CHAPTER 18

Being a Constitution Within Themselves

"**T**here has now for diverse Years a design been carried on to change the Lawfull Government of England into an Absolute Tyranny, and to convert the established Protestant Religion into downright Popery." So began a pamphlet by Andrew Marvell in December 1677. Charles II, it seemed, could not be trusted to protect English interests, especially with his Catholic brother, James, duke of York, as heir presumptive. Marvell captured the public mood, implicit in which was the idea, current since the 1640s, that the authority of monarchs was not above that of the state.[1]

In May 1678, Samuel Petto, a nonconformist preacher in Suffolk, informed Increase Mather that Parliament was in vain pressuring the king to oppose France, and meanwhile, papists went unpunished. Matters reached a head in the autumn. The Popish Plot, a fantastical conspiracy to murder the king, touched off anti-Catholic hysteria, threatening constitutional crisis should Charles fail to act. In remembrance of the Gunpowder Plot of 1605 against James I, effigies of the pope were burnt on November 5. Early in 1679, Petto notified Mather of the "discovery of such a hellish plot, a designe of the Popish Jesuiticall party, as I think is not to be paralleled in any history." The typical reaction was an overreaction. Another of Mather's Suffolk friends called it a miracle that the first news of the year to reach America was not that "Engl[and] was drowned in a deluge of Protestant blood."[2]

Countervailing forces shaped American identity in the late 1670s and 1680s. These forces no longer included just a love of home set against the lure of adventure, but hostility to England against pressure, at least among Protestants, to align one's conscience and loyalties with dissidents in England. Even so, colonists of all faiths in Massachusetts, New Hampshire, Connecticut, and Virginia thought fondly of England and extolled its values, while at the same time feeling increasingly alienated from an absolutist state that was more interested in the servile future of its colonies than in their proud histories. As it had half a century earlier, New England reviled crypto-Catholicism in the English crown and aristocracy, but blamed itself, too: enemies, they believed, were chastisements from God. In the Chesapeake and in the Caribbean, the reasons to return to England had multiplied, or, for some, the reasons not to emigrate there in the first place. The Caribbean, in particular, was simmering with rebellion as the racial balance tipped and the imperial grip tightened. Some Virginians made it home; others were either too poor or had too much invested in the land to leave. Both the rich and the poor, then, found themselves caught between two worlds.

New England's Puritans were disquieted. The entire Atlantic Protestant world seemed in jeopardy. In Maryland, where Lord Baltimore symbolized "Absolute Tyranny" and "down-right Popery," fears were already being confirmed. In the winter of 1673, soldiers from Maryland had destroyed an Anglo-Dutch community at Whorekill, a strategic position on Delaware Bay claimed by Baltimore. Survivors reported that families were denied shelter and food; even the Indians wept "when they saw the spile [spoil] that the Inhabitents had suffered by there owne native Country men." Now the Whorekill atrocity made good propaganda in London, including the story of a naked woman and her child who were left to freeze by "inhumane Popish Souldiers." In Maryland, a rumor that Charles Calvert, Lord Baltimore since 1675, had been beheaded for the crime landed two women in jail. Others whispered that he was stockpiling arms for an American "popish plot," a whisper that in England became a shout. Maryland would soon be all Catholic, it was feared, "and Mary-Land lying in the Center of all the English Collonies in that part of America, may in a small time infect all the rest with their Damnable Doctrines."[3]

Boston went up in flames again in August 1679. The fire destroyed dozens of homes, warehouses, and ships. Suspicion fell on Catholics, as with other fires on either side of the Atlantic. New England was as paranoid as the old England. Rhode Island introduced an antipapal oath, and in Boston a Frenchman lost his ears for making "Rash Insulting speeches in the time of the late Conflagration," along with traitorously clipping silver coins. Learning of the Boston fire, a friend of Increase Mather's in Amsterdam wrote that England, Europe, and New England were suffering similar punishments, with the people "full of distractions & feares." The best defense, many New Englanders believed, was deference to Charles II as well as to God.[4]

However distracting the "exclusion crisis"—the duke of York's disputed heirdom—the English still desired to control the colonies. Whether England was a colossus in America or a pipsqueak is debatable. The ambition to rein in the colonists, combined with the domestic crisis, certainly highlighted the need for obedience. The king scorned Massachusetts' solipsistic oath, and he was angered by the arrival in London of an Indian who had been cheated out of land in Connecticut. Never, ordered Charles, should subjects "be forced to undertake so long and dangerous voyages for obtaining of justice." Good sense prevailed among colonial authorities. Connecticut showed its loyalty by trying a man for sedition: he had called the king a pretender and said the pope was inciting Catholics in England. Plymouth, meanwhile, was thanked for its deferential pledges and instructed to welcome Edward Randolph.[5]

Randolph had been appointed as a collector of his majesty's customs, a post that allowed critical observation of the colonies and so bred hatred. The incumbent of the position in Carolina had been imprisoned during Culpeper's Rebellion. Randolph's patch was New England, which he considered essentially decent and docile except for Massachusetts, where the "passions & little tricks of a misguided people" were a nuisance. Authorities there seemed to hate everyone: the king, his commissioners, Anglicans, Catholics, dissenters, Indians, and other colonies. Their world was one of obdurate self-righteousness and superstitious attachment of cosmic significance to mundane events. This mentality struck Englishmen of a more secular, rational outlook, such as Randolph, who was a Cambridge-educated lawyer, as ridiculous.[6]

"This year begins awfully," wrote Increase Mather early in 1681, after the latest comet sighting. John Russell, the minister at Hadley, was one of thousands who had stared at the night sky; it was, he said, "the most tremendous appearance th[a]t ever my eyes saw." Clearly, this was God trying to jolt New England out of its complacency lest it suffer the descent of what Mather called "the Cataracts of his wrath." Mather also connected the omen to the Popish Plot, agents of which had "resolved that the Protestant Name should no more be had in remembrance."

During that hot, rainless summer, he received a letter from a kinsman in London telling him of a suspicious fire and the nation's terror
of popery. In May, Boston's day of public prayer acknowledged not
just impending American apocalypse, but "the destruction of the lords
people in England, Scotland & Ireland." The heavens opened in time to
save part of the harvest, for which thanks were given.[7]

By then the author of the Popish Plot had been charged with sedition. The heat of the exclusion crisis had dissipated. The bill to deny
James the throne was defeated in the House of Lords in a victory of the
"Tories," the defenders of divine right and the established church, over
the "Whigs," the defenders of Protestantism and customary liberties.
The lesson was that Charles II, like his father, was willing to rule without Parliament—several Parliaments had in fact been dissolved since
1679—and that England might soon be ruled by a Catholic.[8]

Again nonconformists came under fire. Increase Mather heard that
many of them had been arrested, and that *quo warranto* proceedings
were under way to annul the charter of the City of London's Whig corporation. A fresh wave of emigration followed, pushing New England's
population to 70,000. Unlike in the 1630s, however, now neither side of
the Atlantic seemed like a haven for dissenters. Letters from Dedham,
Massachusetts, to Thomas Jollie, a preacher in Lancashire, were "full of
fears & sad thoughts of heart" for England: despite living "in a remote
corner of the world," his friends and colleagues in America could not
forget the "people in our nation & the place of our forefathers." At the
same time, they themselves were "in great distress . . . & many wayes
pincht"—that is, experiencing the misfortunes being presaged by the
comets. Moreover, legal proceedings against the City of London had
ominous implications for the Bay Colony, which depended on patented
privileges.[9]

The threat to Massachusetts occasioned more Puritan reflection. In
1682, John Dane of Ipswich, Massachusetts, wrote his life story. He had
left the Hertfordshire town of Bishop's Stortford in England in 1636,
with its markets, mills, tannery, and glassworks—a prosperous place
where tradesmen like Dane lived contentedly. But Bishop's Stortford
cradled an extraordinary idea: one that was idealistic and expansive and
courageous. A migrant named Thomas Emerson had left a few months
before Dane; Emerson's wife, Elizabeth, was the daughter of William
Brewster, who had sailed on the *Mayflower* in 1620. Without towns
like Bishop's Stortford, godly New England would never have existed,

something Dane's fellow pioneers now celebrated in the twilight of their lives. Their roots were in England; but from there the growth had been remarkable. Dane's son Francis, aged eleven when the family emigrated, was now a respectable divine at Andover, Massachusetts. Did the endangered state of the colony's charter now threaten to nullify such advances in faith and family fortune?[10]

The year 1682 also saw the publication of a book by Mary Rowlandson, who had been taken captive at Lancaster six years earlier. Under Increase Mather's mentorship, she had produced a best-seller, a book that melded spirit and experience in a way that spoke to New England's second and third generations. The literary seed was English: the Puritan trope of grace and redemption. The seed's germination, however, belonged to America. Mather wrote the preface: no one could, he said, understand what the frontier did to a person, not least exposure to the "diabolical" Indians, except one who "knows what it is to fight and pursue such an enemy." These trials might yet be wasted. In December, John Bailey, a dissenting minister in Ireland (and a product of Thomas Jollie's congregation in Lancashire), jotted on his almanac a prediction of New England's destruction. Earlier in the year he had written to Mather about the "wofull & sinking condition" of all Protestant nations; his pessimism had been brought on by the exclusion crisis. In the end, Bailey decided that America was the least of several evils and sailed to Boston.[11]

Not everyone was sunk in Puritan gloom. Boston harbor, bristling with masts and bustling with stevedores, exuded indifference to New England's woes. Prosperity came to the commercial elite, whose lives were directed not by Puritan inhibition and stasis but by movement and the love of pleasure. Salem, twenty miles north, was also thriving. Philip English, the port's richest trader, operating routes to Europe and the West Indies, had a keener eye for the balance sheet than for the Bible: for him, religion and profit still jumped together, but profit jumped higher. His wife, Mary, was herself the daughter of a Salem magnate (who was killed by Indians), and her mother had run a successful tavern. The extravagant house that the Englishes built in 1683—all gables, porches, and jutting storeys—earned admiration from visitors and contempt from the godly. Yet even merchants had reason to fear royal designs on New England, and this fear contributed to America's own Whig-Tory antagonism. This antagonism pitted the defense of colonial liberties against crown intrusion, and loyalism to the king against an overweening Puritan state. Charged with blasphemy in 1681, a loyalist named William King received twenty lashes for refusing to recognize the Boston court. "He would be tried by God & the King," he said, because "he owned [i.e., recognized] not the Country nor their lawes."[12]

Accusations of bad faith traversed the ocean. In 1682 a Boston preacher assailed European Protestants for their hypocrisy, while in the same year a report arrived in London alleging that New England's Puritans were "the very worst of your Enthusiasts and Hypocrites." Their critics in New England, said the report, felt that dissenters on the other side of the Atlantic would shun these insufferable saints if they saw their true nature. American Puritans, said one detractor, "continually [had] God in their mouths, but the Devil in their hearts and actions," and "fancy themselves unaccountable to any Power by being a Constitution within themselves." They ignored English laws, were addicted to the very sins they condemned, were "silly and extravagant in their Prayers and Ejaculations," and persecuted Quakers and Baptists in ways that were completely unacceptable. If the same types of persecution were attempted in England, the libertarian outcry would be deafening. "This sort of People," the report concluded, "are apt to say 'Stand off, for I am more holy than thou,' and under that cloud shall perpetuate the most horrid crime that ever Hell spawned."[13]

New Hampshire, a colony that divided from Massachusetts in 1679, demonstrated how adherence to England's liberties did not necessarily extend to obeying its laws. In 1683 a landowner named Edward Gove rebelled against the royal governor, Edward Cranfield, judging his commission invalid (because it was signed by the papist duke of York) and alleging that Cranfield ruled arbitrarily, especially in enforcing Anglicanism and the Navigation Acts. Gove's defiance was robust: "His sword was drawn and he would not lay it down till he knew who should hold the government." Cranfield, who had been sent to assess New England's loyalty and profitability, believed strongly that the Massachusetts charter should be revoked and colonists freed from clerical control. Bostonians had assured him that if *quo warranto* proceedings began, they would "cast themselves at his Maj[es]t[y]s feet and sue for pardon."[14]

Edward Randolph's authoritarianism as a customs surveyor had enraged New Hampshire, and by February 1683 he was asking Whitehall to suppress Gove's insurrection. Tired of surrendering to New England's "extravagancies" to keep the peace, he now feared for his life; yet without a frigate, he was forced to stay. He wrote, "T'is a mere mockery to thinck any thing here or in Boston Gov[ern]m[en]t can bee done." Writing from Boston in June, Governor Cranfield reported that colonists were as insolent as ever. He hoped for a speedy end to the royal patent by which they, like all colonies, asserted their autonomy. By October, word reached Cranfield that Puritan congregants were being told that "they may lawfully draw their Swords in ye defence of their Charter & ye liberties therin." Neighboring colonies, such as Rhode Island, also prepared to stand up for themselves. New York held its first assembly, something long forbidden by the duke of York, later that month, and subsequently published a defensive "charter of liber-tyes and priviledges." Gove was condemned for treason, having said the governor was the real traitor. He was deported and sent to the Tower of London, but later reprieved and returned to America. A friend gave him a silver-topped cane in recognition of his courage.[15]

Turbulence over sovereignty and authority, loyalty and liberty, de-fined later Stuart politics. Nor was this controversy confined to England and New England. Conflicting traditions and ambitions di-vided Englishmen in the Caribbean, too, but with less attention to Protestantism in danger, and with a pronounced social and racial slant. In November 1683, by which time blacks outnumbered whites seventeen to one in Barbados, a rumor spread in Bridgetown that slaves had risen up on the island's leeward side. Militiamen found nothing except for a few "insolent bold Negroes" and copies of a call to arms, of dubious authenticity, scattered in fields and alehouses. Suspects were whipped, and one who had criticized Englishmen for beating slaves—he said "the Negroes ere long would serve the Christians so"—was burned alive. The severity of the slaves' treatment reflected insecurity among the is-land's white inhabitants as well as their unique West Indian hierarchy.[16]

What happened at Bridgetown followed a series of alarms. Gold Coast slaves in Barbados had plotted to cut their masters' throats in 1675, but they had been betrayed, and seventeen of them had been sen-tenced to death. Chained to a post, faggots piled at his feet, a "sturdy Rogue" called Tony defied the jeering crowd with the words: "If you Roast me to day, you cannot Roast me tomorrow." Dozens more were arrested, a third of whom died: some were executed, and some com-mitted suicide. Islanders branded these men "ungrateful wretches" and traitors, thanking God for saving their liberty from a conspiracy that "had like in one Moment to have defaced the most Flourishing Colony the English have in the World." The backlash was more repression and more measures leveled against Quakers preaching equality.[17]

Almost a quarter of a million Africans were hauled to the sugar islands in the forty years after the Restoration, mostly to Barbados and Jamaica. The slave population of the former rose from 12,800 to 50,000 between 1661 and 1700, and that of the latter from 500 to 42,000 during the same period. In the mid-1670s, Barbados was racially balanced, but this quickly shifted to black predominance with the rising slave population; by 1680, slaves outnumbered colonists two to one. St. Kitts, England's first successful West Indian colony, had fewer than 700 white men, although this low number was mostly due to economic decline. Its Leeward neighbor, Nevis, managed the transition from tobacco to sugar better and its population grew, albeit lopsidedly, requiring "an Act for p[re]venting the Barbarism of Negros" in 1678, which imposed further controls on slaves. Whitehall worried that there were too few Englishmen in the Caribbean. The Lords of Trade proposed sending 300 convicted criminals to St. Kitts in 1684 "for the strengthening & security of the Island."[18]

Demand for slaves was insatiable, their further commodification inevitable. In his journal, George Kingston, a slaver operating between Guinea and Barbados, described them in the same terms merchants would use in describing barrels of cargo: his audit showed 175 men, 135 women, 9 boys, and 10 girls in the hold. One difference with barrels, of course, was that this cargo could perish, even though, as Kingston recorded, "wee . . . take the greatest Care wee can to preserve [them]." Slaves brought staggering profits: the big estate owners in Barbados were the richest men in English America. Henry Drax, son of the pioneer planter, owned 700 acres and most of the island's slaves. His annual income from sugar was £5,000, enabling him to live in sequestered splendor in "Little England." The "Sumptuous Houses, Cloaths and Liberal Entertainment" of these men, a visitor observed, "cannot be Exceeded by this their Mother Kingdom it self."[19]

The English state's love of the Caribbean grew. From the later 1660s, officials pored over facts and figures to decide which islands deserved the most attention. With characteristic understatement, a Whitehall report from 1673 described sugar exports as "no small help to the Balance of Trade of this Nation." Views about Jamaica were mixed: its

plantations seemed primitive, yet their potential was clear. The scope
for customs revenue from Barbados was also considered, though this
issue bred tension. In 1680, the governor, Sir Jonathan Atkins, sent
statistics to the Plantation Office, but he concealed his sympathy for
unsubmissive planters while withholding anything that might put Barbados's loyalty in question. Jamaican magnates, who also basked in
luxury, were similarly intractable. According to a pamphlet of 1683, they
believed they should be allowed "to enjoy their Property and Native
Right where they are under the King's Dominion"; the only new laws
that could affect them, they said, were ones to which they consented.
A greater difficulty with these colonists, however, was that there were
too few of them. From the 1670s, the Lords of Trade knew that the
West Indies stood, as one report put it, "in great neede of white men to
keep their vast number of negroes in subjection & defend their Islands
against forain Enemies." The Jamaican Assembly also warned "that the
proportion of Blacks might in a short tyme bee such that a Rebellion of
them would be easy."[20]

A Dutch engraving from about 1680 showing English Quakers on Barbados.
They used African slaves to scratch a living from growing tobacco, a cash crop
increasingly eclipsed by sugar. By 1700 there were some 50,000 unfree plantation workers toiling on the island.

Many English adventurers saw slaves as "unnatural merchandize"—expensive, fragile, unpredictable, and in need of civility and Christianity if Caribbean society was to become stable and increase in productivity. Naturally, the task of civilizing and Christianizing appealed to missionaries. Morgan Godwyn, an Anglican cleric in Barbados in the 1670s, complained to bishops in England that Africans were treated as "Creatures destitute of Souls, to be rank[e]d amongst brute beasts & treated accordingly." Quakers, he noted, reproached Barbadian preachers, asking: "Who made them Ministers of ye Gospell to ye white people only & not to ye Tawnies & Blacks." Touring English America in 1680, Joan Vokins, a Quaker from Berkshire, was drawn to Barbados, where illicitly she prayed with slaves, "so that my Soul was often melted."[21]

A few went beyond defending slaves' spiritual virtue and invited consideration of their human rights. In 1684, the vegetarian hatter Thomas Tryon, who had lived in Barbados two decades earlier, pitied slaves, who had been robbed of liberty, and condemned the masters, who treated their complaints as rebellion. He imagined a conversation between a slave and his enslaver, with the slave calling Christians hypocrites, and his master admitting his offense to religion and equity. Godwyn also put his opinions in print, suggesting that slaves be admitted to churches, like New England's Indians. Ancient Britons, he added, had painted their bodies and shared wives—"a greater Barbarity than I have at any time heard of amongst the Negro's." The benefit of concessions would exceed godliness and justice: it would make slaves "truer servants . . . wrought into a Compliance, and even the rest would become less sturdy in their Opposition." Skeptics stuck to the view that slaves were ignorant and the promotion of civility detrimental to the principle of owning them. Only forced subjection and a significant white presence would work.[22]

English men and women continued to go to the West Indies. In 1675 Edward Cranfield reported several hundred arriving annually. The town of Lyme Regis certificated apprenticeships throughout the 1680s, although the destination was more often Virginia or Maryland than the Caribbean. The number of white servants in Barbados—about 2,300—was constant between 1680 and 1684, as immigration was canceled out by high mortality. Disease deterred migrants and caused reverse migration, especially now that all the cultivable land was spoken for, which meant servants had no reason to stay beyond the expiry of their indentures.

Planters had decided that English youths were not the best laborers any-way. "Spirits" who sent unhappy children and work-shy adolescents were also a problem. John Wilmore, a London-based planter, granted a boy's wish to go to Jamaica in 1680 only to be prosecuted for abduction. Trans-porting such children, Wilmore protested, was an act of charity: they did a fraction of a slave's work. "I am sure the fewer white servants any Planter has," he added, "the more it would be for his profit."[23]

The old adventurer's lesson about labor quality over quantity still applied, but there were never enough industrious migrants for the social mechanisms of England (or New England) to be replicated in the Ca-ribbean. The problem grew worse as the motherland's demographic de-cline, combined with better agricultural yields, regional specialization, and a network of roads and waterways, boosted the economy and so reduced emigration. Scare stories didn't help, and the ranks from which England's parish and municipal officeholders were drawn—officehold-ers much needed in Barbados and Jamaica—were put off by perceptions of disorder. The difference between good and evil, complained Thomas Tryon, had dissolved in a torrent of rum. At New Providence in the Bahamas, a colonist noted, people "lived a lewd, licentious Sort of Life" and were "impatient under Government." In July 1679—about the time that the sugar magnate Henry Drax moved to London—the governor of Barbados was told to uphold the law exactly as the king would in any dominion. It was the height of the exclusion crisis, but Drax preferred seditious papists to rebellious Africans.[24]

Promotional writing sought to allay fears. A work of 1679 claimed that Jamaica's air was conducive to health and reproduction, and that illness was mostly caused by colonists failing to adjust their diets and other habits. The English moving to the colony had a tendency to "transport northern chilly propensities, and customs thereon depend-ing, into the southern hot Climes." Jamaican animals, fish, vegetables, and flowers were all admirable. A letter from Barbados received by John Evelyn at the Royal Society in 1680 praised "this fortunate cly-met where nature most industriously wayts upon every seed and plant even to the quickest production of any part of the univers[e]." Little attention was paid to slavery, either its morality or its dangers, or to the calamitous vicissitudes of the weather. Shortly after the 1675 revolt in Barbados, a hurricane flattened a thousand houses: "I never mett a more amazing sight," confessed the governor, "then in one nights difference to day." Distressed people vowed not to rebuild but to leave as soon as possible. Supply ships, their captains fearful of both rebellious slaves and high winds, stayed away for five months. In Nevis, the planters depended on African labor but were not rich enough to absent themselves. They endured the same anxieties, fearing their own laborers as well as the assault from nature: twelve hurricanes were recorded there between 1642 and 1669.[25]

Caribbean colonists were also menaced by French and Spanish invaders and feared that slaves would join forces with their liberators. French colonists had overrun the English half of St. Kitts in 1666–1667, and Nevis also suffered. Only whites could be relied upon as defenders, but their numbers were dwindling. New Providence, where half the population was enslaved, failed to resist Spanish invasion in 1684. Three English colonists were killed, many taken prisoner, and property worth £20,000 plundered. Alexander Gorges wrote to his stepbrother in Devon listing all the jewelry, plate, and other goods he had lost, and explaining that their plantation workers had been evacuated to Newfoundland. Gorges himself feared he would not see England again for many years.[26]

By 1685 panics about rebellion had become commonplace in Jamaica, where blacks now outnumbered whites six to one. An uprising that year started at Guanaboa when 150 of Widow Grey's slaves broke into her house and seized weapons; she fled to a neighbor's house, which was attacked next. Infantry and cavalry sent the rebels fleeing to the hills. There, they were hunted by Indian trackers—like beagles, it was said, following the scent of a hare. Two remote English families were slaughtered by the escaped slaves. The planters' only defenses were military readiness, draconian justice, and the practice of importing slaves from different parts of Africa to isolate them linguistically. Early in 1686, another Barbadian plot was uncovered. It involved an alliance with disgruntled Irish servants. A string of executions and a more thorough "act for the governing of negroes" followed. A rebellion on Antigua in 1687 led to at least one slave being burned. Another who had liaised with fugitives had a leg cut off. Englishmen who helped them, it was decreed, would be punished as traitors to the crown.[27]

M ost people in England were only dimly aware of Caribbean horrors, and in general, they were untroubled by contradictions between the ideals of empire and liberty. Trade enriched the nation; how it did so was a lesser concern. Still, the popular image of all the colonies was one of danger as well as opportunity, of incivility and irreligion, chaos and coercion. In official circles it was also apparent that colonial deference hid local desires to retain authority and assets as well as to defend Protestantism, in defiance of the state's economic interests and the Catholic and absolutist designs of Stuart kings. Asserted Englishness—loyalty to the crown and love of ancient rights—might even mask incriminating differences in identity that had evolved in America over three generations. These surfaced in public discourse—such as in protests, petitions, and sedition trials—but their subtleties also entered private diaries and correspondence. Many colonists were caught between two Atlantic worlds, resentful of English royal agents yet proud of England, often homesick but too poor or too rooted in America to leave.

Plantations continued to depend on England, especially for money, labor, and food. As ever, impressions of the colonies mattered, because, however selective, distorted, or false, they were all that potential migrants, commercial investors, and policymakers had to go on when making decisions. Take this scene from 1689: English men and women gaze upon an Indian king and queen before a temple. The music rises in intensity while the priests and priestesses begin a war dance with "ridiculous Postures and crying . . . Incantations." The setting is Virginia, but it is Virginia as imagined by the London stage. This was a performance of Aphra Behn's last play, a satire about Bacon's Rebellion of 1676 that was produced after Behn's death. Behn, a woman playwright, had lived in Surinam. She had also been a royalist, and beneath her mockery of Indian culture lay a ringing endorsement of kingship, hierarchy, loyalty, and honor. Many of the play's English characters, she explained, were transported criminals, and their political environment was topsy-turvy. "The Country wants nothing but to be People'd with a well-born Race," says a man in the first scene, "to make it one of the best Collonies in the World." The mixture of opinions in the audience, determining how such ideas were received, can only be imagined.[28]

A society where half the population—the half consisting of slaves and indentured servants—was unfree was perceived to be permanently on edge and in need of legal and military protection. Many saw the Chesapeake as a steamy faraway land where royal despots lorded it over a rabble, a view confirmed by tales of cruelty, madness, and murder. Thomas Hellier was a respectable apprentice from Dorset who ended up hanged in chains on the James River. "I was all on fire to set up in the world," he said, "to make a bustle abroad to and fro, and by doing that I might seem somebody." Set to work in Virginia as a tutor, he had tired of his mistress's nagging and felt separated from everything he knew and loved. So he snapped, killing the entire family with an axe. An account published in London in 1680 tried to balance the darkness with some light. Virginia was "a very ferti[le], good, pleasant Country abounding with the manifold Blessings of luxuriant Nature," it said, a place where men "(though Beggars in their Native soil) yet have by their drudging Industry . . . attained to something of Estate." But surely the blood dripping from Hellier's axe was this pamphlet's most memorable image.[29]

The Chesapeake attracted fewer and fewer English youths as time went by. The deterrent was not the Indians. At a meeting with the governors of Virginia and New York in 1684, local sachems admitted defeat; they now sought tutelage from "the Great Sachem Charles who liveth on the other side of the Great Lake." Yet, as in the Caribbean, the advance of slavery meant that white apprentices had to work alongside African slaves, with similar board and lodgings. Only one in ten apprentices eventually became a householder. Even their masters' lives were mostly unenviable. Virginia farmers, with neither slaves nor laborers, scratched a living from exhausted soils, constantly moving to new plantations; some just burned their houses and sifted the nails from the ashes. Indian dwellings were likened to pigsties; but many colonists didn't live much better. They ate primarily maize porridge and millet bread, and they were plagued by rattlesnakes and sickness. The high mortality rate did not bring them closer to God; instead, it hardened their hearts. By the 1680s, devotion was much as it had been thirty years earlier, when Virginians were said to be "the farthest from conscience and morall honesty of any such number together in the world." Between 1649 and 1680, only 15 percent of Charles Parish's babies were baptized. In Maryland's Kent County in the late 1650s and 1660s, the rate was 4 percent—5 out of 115 children.[30]

With the shortage of Anglican ministers in Maryland, papists and Quakers plugged the gap, causing the colony to become what one observer called "a Sodome of uncleanesses and a Pesthouse of Iniquity." One traveler found Marylanders so removed from English culture "that they scarcely knew how the Time passed, nor that they hardly knew the day of Rest or Lords Day." Falling tobacco prices left many unable to pay taxes. Michael Taney, mayor of Calvert County, pleaded for customs relief in 1685 in order to pay an orthodox preacher. His wife, Mary, shuddered to think "th[a]t for wont of the Gospell our Children & Posterity are in danger to be condemned to infidelity." She sought help from the archbishop of Canterbury, writing, "We ar[e] not i hope so foreign to your Jurisdiction but we may be owned your stray flock." The Taneys were loyal subjects. Lord Baltimore had revoked their tavern license for allowing sailors to have a bonfire one November. "It was Gun-powder Treason day in England," revelers had said, "and they would go and drink the King of England's Health."[31]

After Bacon's Rebellion, more and more Chesapeake planters began to see indentured servants, with their fixed terms and asserted rights, as a liability, and African slaves as the future. Others still preferred whites as laborers, but had difficulty finding them. In the 1680s, the number of slaves rose from 4,500 to 12,000, and the authorities moved to block their routes to emancipation. The days of black farmers winning freedom were numbered. The ossifying legal definition of slaves as movable chattels was illustrated in 1678, when a man known as "Black Tom" was sent as a gift from a woman in England to her brother, a farmer in Maryland.[32]

Owning slaves in Virginia offered the same boon as in the Caribbean, but not for everyone: modest planters could not compete with the grandees. One reaction was to plead, like Michael and Mary Taney. Another was to rebel. John Coode, a Cornishman, and Josias Fendall, a former governor of Maryland, incited an uprising in 1681, "telling the People that they were Fools to pay any Taxes," given the rift between crown and Parliament over the succession. "Now nothing was Treason," they claimed, "a man might say anything," though their sedition trials disproved this contention. Coode and Fendall, who were probably also the authors of the 1676 petition begging the king to seize Maryland, were condemned by Lord Baltimore as "rank Baconists."[33]

Such condemnation did not reduce the unrest. "All possible circumspection is used to keepe downe the spirit of Rebellion," noted the secretary of Virginia in August 1682, "to whic[h] too many Inhabitants have an Itching desier since the laste Rebellion." He was writing to Sir Leoline Jenkins in Whitehall, who also learned from this report that farmers, incensed by the tobacco slump (and drunk on cider), had cut down their crops on two hundred plantations—and would have cut down more had soldiers not intervened to stop them. Some said the sooner Virginia had a standing army, the better. The lieutenant governor, Sir Henry Chicheley, described the events to the king, writing of "a strange insurrection in the heart of this yo[u]r Ma[jes]ties Countrey." Chicheley's sympathies leaned toward the rebels, which embarrassed the absentee governor, Lord Thomas Culpeper, who was forced to return to Virginia, vowing to punish the riotous farmers. Culpeper's restoration of order was aided, in February 1683, by Chicheley's death, which, according to one report, saved the colony "from all future mal-administrations." In some ways, though, the instability and ineptness was illusory, for Virginia society rested on a bedrock of political order. During Bacon's Rebellion, courts had still met and taxes were collected, with barely a ripple in normal administration. The evolved structure of landowning families, men and women of the second and third generations, had real tensile strength, and it was made stronger by institutionalized slavery. The lives of the elite would not be disrupted by uppity plant-cutters; nor were their culture and identity entirely emulative of England, as it had been before. They had become a constitution within themselves.[34]

Following the brief acting governorship of one of his cousins, Lord Culpeper was succeeded by Baron Francis Howard of Effingham. In November 1683, soon after his fortieth birthday, Howard left Surrey, his wife (who was named Philadelphia), and four of his young children; his five-year-old daughter, Philly, accompanied him. As contrary winds held the ship at anchor off the Kent coast, Howard wrote to his wife: "I love you and yours with the tru[e]st cordiallest hart that ever man did any wife and children . . . and I assure you nothing in this voyage is grievous to me but my parting from you." He said he would never forget that moment, or his children's "wishfull lookes," though he half-wished he could. Howard arrived in Virginia on February 10, 1684, and sent another letter, which he had begun at sea. Philly had charmed the other passengers, he said, though she had been seasick and missed her mother. His family was constantly in his thoughts. Kiss the children, he told Philadelphia, and write soon. "I send thee a thousand kisses and embraces," he ended, "proceeding from the truest love and endirest affection that any hart is capable to receive."[35]

Disembarking at a plantation, Howard enjoyed a very English breakfast of bacon and eggs and was surprised to meet nice people in neat homes. He attended church, and the service exceeded his expectations. He felt that few English parishes could match it. An Indian king and his retinue, "Covered like the English Gyps[i]es," welcomed him as

Virginia's new governor. The land seemed so pleasant, wrote Howard, not "neere so sickly, nor that sicknesses so dangerous, as was represented in England." Philly was thriving, he assured his wife, and had sent a flying squirrel for little Peg. Howard asked for a portrait of her and their son Charles. He regretted not bringing a lock of her hair and missed her in his bed. He longed for letters, but received few. After a five-week silence, on June 8, one finally arrived: "This smale paper," began his reply, "is filled with more Joy than I can express." Howard was moved to hear that two-year-old Tommy would kiss a painting of his father; but such news also pained him, and he was desperate to be reunited with his wife. She arrived that autumn, bearing gifts of a punch bowl, cutlery, gold braid, and an inkhorn. The following summer was stiflingly hot, and fever spread to the governor's household. In August, Philadelphia Howard died, aged thirty. Philly, now ten, accompanied her mother's body back to Surrey, where it was interred with that of her daughter Peg, who had died three months earlier.[36]

Bacon's Rebellion had taught Virginia's aristocracy to beware of both Whitehall and the colonial lower orders; yet Howard managed better than any previous governor to align planters' political and economic aims with the will of the crown. The personal emotional cost, however, was crushing. The pleasures of colonial wealth for many transatlantic families were cut with separation and loss. The Mallorys of Lancashire served as deans of Chester Cathedral, but were also great Virginia landowners—physically distanced, but emotionally close. When the Reverend Philip Mallory died in 1671, he left his son Roger, a planter in Virginia's Kent County, twenty shillings to buy a ring as a memento. Colonists still experienced the frustrations of intercontinental business and property management. The Gloucestershire family of Samuel Griffin, a Virginia planter, were baffled by his mortgages and who owed what to whom. George Bond spent the last two decades of the century trying to acquire an estate in Virginia that had been bequeathed to him by his father, a Bristol merchant. And for all their self-confidence and grandeur, Virginia grandees shared Francis Howard's longing for reunion. William Fitzhugh was so homesick that he tried to swap his entire plantation—a thousand acres with twenty-nine slaves—for a townhouse in England. There were no takers. Throughout the 1680s, he begged his friends and relations to write, saying that "nothing would be more welcome or acceptable." He worried about his elderly mother and encouraged his sister to come over.[37]

William Byrd typified this state of cultural suspension. Born in London in 1652, he came to Virginia in his teens to live with his uncle, a trader at the falls of the James River. He inherited his uncle's estate, married the daughter of a cavalier, fought the Indians in the 1670s, and hedged his bets during Bacon's Rebellion. After his scheme to monopolize the fur trade failed, Byrd moved into tobacco and slaves. Like Howard and Fitzhugh, he was able and ambitious, yet craved news of home. His sister left England to join him in 1678, but she died at sea. Byrd visited England the same year, and upon his return he became the militia commander; in 1682, he became a member of the governor's council. Success impeded repatriation. He built a pleasant house with a garden planted in crocuses and tulips that he had imported from Oxford. He wrote often to his brother and his remaining sister, but they did not reply, which he took "very unkindly." In 1685, the worst floods in memory swamped his tobacco fields and washed away his English flowers. In November the following year, he bought slaves, but they were infected with smallpox. They in turn infected his agent, who infected Byrd's young daughter.[38]

A visitor to Virginia in the mid-1680s was struck by how ill everyone looked. There was a lack of qualified doctors, and the gap was being filled by "such as have been Surgeons or Apothecaries boys in England." Few settlers lived beyond the age of fifty. Everything was skewed. Hailstorms were staggering: "I saw Stones fall big as Pullets Eggs & in some places they were 9 or 10 inches about, & killed Calves & broke all ye Glass Windows to pieces," wrote one awed correspondent, describing a world of danger and discomfort. The English colonists believed they went to heaven after they died; Indians believed they would go to a temperate place of plenty; and slaves believed they would go back to their native countries. Everyone, it seemed, had to imagine a place better than Virginia for their souls' repose.[39]

Growing reliance upon slaves presented a new source of fear. By 1680 Virginia had begun formalizing their regulation. An act prescribed whipping for slaves who assembled in groups, fearing they might foment unrest, as well as for those who carried weapons or threatened their masters; runaways resisting arrest could be put to death. Baron Howard informed the council in 1687 that a "Negro Plott . . . for the Distroying and killing [of] his Majesties Subjects" had been foiled, and that conspirators would be severely punished. The council also noted with concern that, contrary to the law of 1680, masters allowed "great freedome and Libetty" to slaves on weekends and permitted them to assemble at funerals.[40]

Although the black-to-white ratio was changing, indentured servants and transported felons were prominent in the workforce until after 1700. They, too, resented their lot. In the same year as the "negro plot," servants in Middlesex County were charged with conspiracy to steal guns and abscond "to the greate disturbance of his Majesties Peace and the Terrour of his Leige People." The majority suffered quietly, counting the days. A ballad from the 1680s about a convict, James Revel, describes a tearful departure and stressful arrival in Virginia, where he is bought like a slave. "My Europian clothes were took from me," he says. Describing his work with Africans on a tobacco plantation, where punishments were harsh, he complains: "For by the Rigour of that very law / They're much kept under and to stand in awe." After fourteen years, Revel returns to England, where, according to the ballad, he is amazed to find his parents still alive: "My Mother over me did weep for Joy, / My Father cry'd once more to see my Boy."[41]

William Byrd arrived in England in the spring of 1687 and spent a year cramming in social visits. He was sorry to have to go back to Virginia. Even after "wee saw our owne American shore"—Byrd's real home now—and he had returned to his family, his thoughts strayed to those from whom he had recently departed. He drank to his brother's health with souvenir ale, but it had soured. He wrote a letter to a friend in England, wishing he could repay his hospitality with a gift, "but since wee have nothing but stinking Tobacco, & th[a]t not worth a farthing, I hope you will accept my thankes." As hostile Indians crept around the Falls, killing cattle and taking potshots, so Byrd began to "believe a private Gent[le] life in ye Country to bee (att this time) most eligible." Work commenced on his new house at Westover, which was twenty miles downriver, nearer the seat of government. Byrd requested furniture and fittings from England, "to bee Handsome & neat"; he also ordered claret (which arrived "utterly spoiled") and neck-cloths for riding. News from England came fragmented and late. "Wee are here att the end of ye World," Byrd lamented to his brother, "& Europe may be turned topsy turvy ere wee can hear a Word of itt."[42]

Suspension between two worlds meant being in America yet belonging emotionally to England. For Howard, Fitzhugh, and Byrd, preserving English identity involved maintaining a sense of themselves in relation to family and friends. As ever, not only was this an imperfect solution, but the very act of striving—for example, by making impassioned assertions of their ancient English rights—set the colonists apart from men at home whose cultural world was proximate and effortlessly accessible. Unattainable Englishness became absent Englishness, and American experience flowed into the void to make a hybrid colonial self. What sharpened this sensibility even more was the feeling that the England to which migrants were still attached was asserting a control that impinged upon cherished liberties. And nowhere was consternation keener than in New England, where the errand into the wilderness was in mortal danger.

CHAPTER 19

Strange Creatures in America

I N OCTOBER 1683, Increase Mather heard from Joshua Moodey, the minister at Portsmouth, New Hampshire, that a grotesquely deformed child had been born amid "sundry reports among us of new things th[a]t seem to bee matters of Witchcraft." Nearby, at the mouth of the Piscataqua River, lay Great Island. An elderly widow, Hannah Jones, had been accused as a witch, a suspicion that had also been leveled against her mother, the island's earliest English resident. Jones's crime was "lithobolia"—hurling stones supernaturally. Fear spread to Hartford, Connecticut, where Nicholas Desborough, the Pequot War veteran, was pelted, seemingly by an invisible hand, after quarreling with a neighbor. Mather was informed.[1]

These were not random outbursts of hysteria, but eruptions from a wellspring of social tension. To Puritans like Moodey, they were salutary signs of the times—a heavenly nudge to New England that it should rediscover its way in the wilderness. Two months earlier he had written to Mather about a demon troubling William Morse's house at Newbury, Massachusetts, for which Morse's wife was blamed. Mather updated his notes for a volume of "illustrious providences," a book intended to prove the folly of materialism and skepticism and to raise awareness of his colony's predicament. But he could not have foreseen the trials of the decade ahead, nor the part played by his vilification and vindication in those events.[2]

The years from 1683 to 1689 marked a watershed in how English America saw itself and how it was seen in England. Never had ideas about freedom and servitude, despotism and justice, toleration and persecution, been so eloquently articulated, not least in the new colony of Pennsylvania. At the same time, royal charters dating back to the

early Stuart monarchs—the legal and political basis of colonial life—
were threatened by kings who were indifferent to the liberties these
documents enshrined. Boston was proudly defiant, and strangers from
England were faced down and sometimes mocked. But New England's
Puritans were also anxious, sensing devils and Indians and royal agents
closing in. Resistance to imperial coercion was to achieve little in the
short term, but the feelings it unleashed galvanized colonial identity
and would yet be justified as England underwent a constitutional revolution that reverberated powerfully throughout the Atlantic and Caribbean worlds.

The catastrophes suffered by New England in the autumn of 1683
seemed to fit a pattern. The summer had brought floods, especially
to Connecticut, where crops were ruined, and to Virginia, Jamaica, and
Europe. "Thus doth the great God," wrote Mather in his book, "make
the World see how many wayes he hath to punish them." Elsewhere
there was drought. New Plymouth held a fast to mark both extremes,
as well as "the troubles of God's people in England." There, too, the
year 1683 saw weather portentously linked to human affairs: a plot to
murder Charles II, who was now ruling alone without Parliament, was
exposed; in Norfolk, toads fell from the sky—a symptom of a distem-
pered realm. Rumors of conspiracy lingered, focusing on the preten-
sions of the duke of Monmouth, the king's illegitimate son; and the
winter was the coldest in living memory. In Boston, the death of John
Hull, God's banker during King Philip's War, seemed to be another
omen. In his funeral sermon, Samuel Willard, confessor to the town
of Groton's demoniac, exalted Hull's generation of saints, calling their
passing a "sad prognostick of misery a coming."[3]

The loss of charters was the worst calamity. Once the corporation of
London's rights had been revoked, nothing could save Massachusetts
and Bermuda. And royal administrators like Edward Randolph and
Edward Cranfield had other colonies lined up, too, for assessment,
including Rhode Island, New Hampshire, Maryland, and Carolina.
The Bay Colony did not give up. In November 1683, its elders told the
king that revoking its charter would "be destructive to the interest
of religion and of Christ's kingdom in that colony"; it would offend
the basic principle of their settlement in America. They accepted the

crown's argument that Jews had submitted to Babylonian and Persian emperors, but they pointed out that those rulers had been *absolutists*, whereas the English monarchy was limited—wasn't it? In England such insolence just magnified the problem. The archbishop of Canterbury thought New Englanders "averse to ye Discipline of ye Church of England," their protestations notwithstanding. Obeying the Navigation Acts, claimed Randolph, was "wholly discountenanced and discouraged by them"—which was hardly surprising, he added, since they swore oaths to themselves and made repugnant laws.[4]

In vain, Increase Mather led a vanguard of opposition. He asked Thomas Gough, pastor at the English church in Amsterdam, to pray for New England, citing moribund privileges as well as the fevers and floods of a "sickly sumer." Gough replied with news of persecuted dissenters in England, causing Mather to respond, in December 1684, that "never was any age so farr gonn a whoreing after their owne Lusts and pleasures, yea from ye King that sitteth on the Throne to the Beggar." Randolph intercepted the letter (in which he was described as "a mortall Enemie to our Countrey") and had it copied. Six months earlier, the charter that had been brought to Boston by John Winthrop in 1630 had been vacated by a court at Westminster, and a provisional government had been set up by crown officials. Joseph Dudley, the son of Winthrop's successor, was made interim governor of Massachusetts, Maine, New Hampshire, and Rhode Island. Sent to London in 1682 to fight the *quo warranto* proceedings, Dudley had returned as a traitor to the colonies he represented. A tract by his royalist brother-in-law Daniel Denison shamed New England for its divisions and weaknesses. Now unity and uniformity would be imposed. The Royal Mint shut down its Boston counterpart—a blow that John Hull, mercifully, did not live to see—although the more pragmatic Treasury proposed an authorized New England mint.[5]

Defying Stuart absolutism failed to save the charter, but it did sharpen Puritan New England's identity, illustrating Francis Bacon's dictum that "a Mans disposition is never well knowen till hee be crossed, nor Proteus ever chaunged shapes till hee was straightened." This was not American exceptionalism: it was English tradition decrying modernity in the name of pan-national Protestantism. The closer England moved to Louis XIV's France, the more Increase Mather defended true religion and ancient freedoms. New England was part of the old, he argued, in that the *quo warranto* writs said it belonged to the manors of Westminster and Greenwich. He had a point: the colonies' relationship with London was similar to that of England's towns and counties. Although the aloof character of colonial councils owed something to distance from England, in some ways the effects resembled those caused by distance between the seat of government and, say, Cumberland or Cornwall. Regional boroughs were run by corporations, self-made oligarchies whose members were more like independent citizens than deferential subjects, their identity more local than national. And by the 1680s, those corporations faced the same pressures to surrender their charters as Massachusetts did. "American" resentment and resistance were not restricted to America, but united transatlantic champions of liberty. Puritans in New England took these freedoms seriously, likewise the unity required to defend them; they cherished an idealized vision of England and dreamed of its reification. This strange, vain aim showed, paradoxically, both how much their hearts and minds remained English and how much America had changed them.[6]

England's existence as a state of mind as well as a geographical entity is perfectly illustrated by one bizarre episode. On September 5, 1683, HMS *Rose* left England to find sunken Spanish treasure in the Bahamas. Her commander, William Phips, was thirty-two years old, thickset, it was said, with "a very Comely, though a very Manly Countenance." Born on the Maine frontier, where his father was a farmer and fur trader, Phips had become a shipwright and moved to Boston, where he learned to read. He was neither cultured nor pious, just fearless and tough, and his loyalty to the crown and transatlantic kinship advanced his career. On board the *Rose* was John Knepp, a government official who succeeded in making the unruly crew sign royal articles, but only after Phips gave the order: their contract, they said, was with the captain, not the king. A rattled Knepp tried to stop them from trading illegally, drinking, swearing, and smoking in the gunroom; they threatened to throw him overboard. Phips shrugged off Knepp's protests, warning of mutiny—or murder—if too heavy a hand were applied.[7]

By late October the *Rose* was anchored at Boston. It was frosty, and the harbor was choppy. On November 10, members of the crew were drinking at Scarlett's Wharf when constables ordered them to return to their ship. A brawl ensued. When Phips defended his men, the constables threatened to report him, to which the captain, it was later reported, replied that "he did not care a turd for the Governour for

Sir William Phips (1651–1695), the first royal governor of the Massachusetts Bay Colony. Born on the Maine frontier, he led an extraordinary life shaped not by privilege but by innate cunning and courage and luck. He was both a loyal agent of the English crown and a questing American.

he [Phips] had more power . . . and had orders to call the Governour and this country to an account and was sent to teach them better manners." A crowd gathered. Phips declared loyalty to his king and told the constables they could kiss his arse. The sailors called the Bostonians "rebels," adding that they would be as happy to fire on them as on Algiers. The parties were summoned by Governor Simon Bradstreet, who challenged Phips's authority. In any case, scoffed Bradstreet, Phips was hardly the man to teach Boston manners, for "every body in Boston knew very well what he was and from whence he came, therefore desired him not to carry it soe loftily amoung his country men." Phips threw his commission across the courtroom, to which the governor responded that it applied to the Bahamas, not New England. When Phips vowed to obtain justice in England, he was fined £5.[8]

Phips's allegiance was not like that of the king's officer, John Knepp; instead, he favored his crew and was faithful to no one except them. When they muttered about killing Knepp to stop him from taking their treasure, Phips did nothing, even after Knepp was assaulted ashore. Sensibly, Knepp decided not to rejoin the company when the *Rose* resumed its journey. The crew committed a final outrage, stealing livestock from local islands and raping a woman. In the weeks ahead, Phips managed to suppress mutiny and stop the *Rose* from becoming a pirate ship, but the shipwrecks were disappointing, the sunken treasures having been picked over by others. Phips returned to England with the Massachusetts governor's scorn burning his ears—but he would be back, immensely rich and able to exact revenge on these mocking Bostonians. His version of an England as an integrated and obedient empire, supremely commanded by the king, would supplant the England imagined by New Englanders. The American version was a geographically removed free state where men governed themselves, not in rebellion to England but precisely because they had been born in England, and found sovereignty in this. Charles II disagreed.[9]

Though not overtly religious, Phips was "very Zealous for all Men to enjoy such a Liberty of Conscience as he judged a Native Right of Mankind." In these words Cotton Mather, the son of Increase, would find common ground with this servant of the crown. Like his father (but unlike Phips), Mather, now a minister in his early twenties, mourned the loss of the charter and supported dissenters in England. Promises of toleration had followed the exclusion crisis, inhibiting a second "great migration." Yet suffering continued. The Suffolk Puritan Samuel Petto, describing the problems to Mather Sr., wrote: "I suppose you hear enough to put you in new England upon crying mightily to God for those in Old England wh[o] are of the same principles with y[ou]r fathers who first were planted in N.E.." In the summer of 1684, three suns reportedly appeared over East Anglia, one of them blood red. What, wondered Petto, did this portend?[10]

When Charles II died in February 1685, he was succeeded by his brother James. So momentous was the news that the *London Gazette* was reprinted in Boston. Governor Bradstreet and his council, recorded Samuel Sewall, were "very much startled." Feelings in Boston about James II were ambivalent: he was a Catholic, but perhaps that meant he would tolerate all faiths. So Cotton Mather rejoiced at the death of the "monster," Charles II, and applauded the new king. In September, however, news that the duke of Monmouth had mounted a rebellion caused Mather to leap out of bed. Hopes of a Protestant monarch were soon dashed, though: three weeks later, Boston heard that Monmouth's army had been crushed at Sedgemoor. This outcome pleased those who argued that revolution would destroy liberties that were protected by the crown. The Tory pamphleteer John Nalson warned that unrest in England could not easily be contained, but would "pass the Seas and discharter all the Forreign Plantations of Virginia, Maryland, Carolina &c which are holden by the Proprietors by vertue of Royal Grants."[11]

This "dischartering," of course, was already happening, and from above rather than from below; but Monmouth's Rebellion did stir turbulent spirits abroad. A New Hampshire colonist said no man could speak treason because there was no king; in Maryland, Protestants drank to Monmouth's health, and Bermudans hailed him as the rightful heir. In Barbados an argument about the English civil war led to a man being fined for calling royalists traitors. In New Hampshire the despised Edward Cranfield was replaced as governor by his deputy, Walter Barefoot, who was no less hated: in one altercation, he was pushed into a fireplace and broke some ribs and a tooth. In England, reactions to the rebellion were brutal. News of the developments traveled swiftly to Boston. Cotton Mather (who called England "home") informed his cousin John Cotton Jr. in New Plymouth about the scores of executions, including that of Monmouth himself. What impact, Mather wondered, would this bloodletting have in New England?[12]

Driven to do good, Cotton Mather was nonetheless crippled by contemplation of his own sinfulness; he never knelt before God when he could grind his face in the dust. At other times his spirits soared and he fancied himself heaven's favorite, but the vanity triggered self-disgust in a perpetual cycle of elation and despair. New England's past and future obsessed him: visiting Plymouth, he took the jawbone from Metacom's skull as a souvenir. Early in 1686 his morbid sensibility alighted on James Morgan, who had been sentenced to death for murder; Mather took the case as a lesson in how iniquity heaped God's anger on the Protestant world.[13]

It was bitterly cold that winter. Samuel Sewall, one of Morgan's judges, described bread rattling in the communion plate. The harbor froze, and icebergs lay beyond it. John Dunton, a Whig publisher fleeing Monmouth's Rebellion, arrived from London and walked a mile across the ice. He soon heard about Morgan's capital sentence, the first in Massachusetts for years. In March, people filled the meetinghouse to hear Cotton Mather deliver, before the prisoner, the first of three sermons. John Dunton was present. "The sharp Ax of Civil Justice

Cotton Mather (1663–1728) was one of New England's most influential Puritan thinkers. This portrait suggests serene self-satisfaction, but Mather was troubled by his own and his colony's moral failings, and styled himself a humble "American"—meaning "Indian"—to English correspondents.

will speedily cut you down," thundered Mather. "O for a little good Fruit before the Blow!" The "good fruit" was penitence, a sign of grace even in a wretch like Morgan. The final sermon, on execution day, was delivered by Cotton Mather's father, Increase; the weight of the spectators broke the gallery. In midafternoon, Morgan mounted the ladder and, wearing a noose, repudiated sin. A hood was pulled down, he announced his ascent to heaven, and his life was ended. Cotton Mather stood close by, praying earnestly. "I think during this Mournful Scene," Dunton wrote to a friend in London, "I never saw more serious nor greater Compassion."[14]

In general, Dunton saw Bostonians as "great Censors of other Men's Manners, but extremely careless of their own." He formed many impressions during his eight-month stay. The streets were cobbled, he reported, and the best houses "confirmable to our New Buildings in London since the fire." He visited the octogenarian John Eliot, "apostle to the Indians," who dismissed fears that England would return to Roman Catholicism. Dunton wrote to his wife, Iris, sounding homesick and lovesick. Perhaps he knew the old proverb that was cited by another visitor to New England: "Travail where thou canst, but dye where thou oughtest, that is in thine own Countrey." Dunton went home in the autumn of 1686. The seas were so calm, he wrote, it was "as if the Guardian Angel of my Iris had smooth'd the way for my Return to her." When he arrived in London, he and his wife were reunited at a tavern, where "our mutual Extasies of Joy swell'd to that mighty height . . . that Love lock'd up the Organs of our speech." Catholic king or no Catholic king, Dunton was back where he belonged. As with the confrontation between William Phips and Governor Bradstreet, one Englishman had met another in America, and found himself estranged.[15]

C ollisions between crown representatives and colonial authorities, such as the one that took place in the HMS *Rose* incident, revealed differences of transatlantic identity and interest as well as the relative importance of New England. Inevitably, the Mathers took New England more seriously than officials in London did. The latter demanded Boston's loyalty, but they hardly depended on it. For New England was just one province, a minor part of the wider empire-building project that commanded so much of the state's attention. Concepts of liberty and servitude, authority and allegiance, and true and false religion were at the heart of identity in the Atlantic and Caribbean and had never been more hotly contested, whether in old colonies like Virginia or new ones like Carolina.

In the mid-1680s, a memorandum entitled "An Essay on the Interest of the Crown in the American Plantations" appeared in Whitehall. Its author was William Blathwayt, a surveyor of colonial revenues who believed that Atlantic commerce was vital to England's future. "Trade and Negotiation," he observed, "has infected the whole Kingdom, and . . . by this means the very Genius of the people is alter'd"; the crown, he foresaw, must engage all its aims and powers with "this new nature come among us." Trade, however, had no boundaries, which, Blathwayt warned, bred disloyalty in migrants and merchants, filling their heads with republicanism. He estimated that the king had 200,000 subjects in America; most families of the English gentry and nobility had a cadet branch there. The West Indies had the smallest English population but the greatest potential; in northern plantations, the reverse was true. Blathwayt was convinced that New England, Maryland, New York, Carolina, and Bermuda should be made to pledge their allegiance to the king and obey his laws.[16]

England had to keep ahead of France and Holland, and it especially had to be sure not to repeat the "unaccountable stupidity & dullness in our Ancestors" that had allowed Spain free rein. A great debt was owed to the private enterprise—"a natural Emanation of the Minds freedom"—that nourished the state. Adventure counted as much as ever. The letters of Henry Ashurst, a London merchant, reveal interests across Anglo-America, from Caribbean slaves ("a good comoditie in Barbadoes") to cloth exports to New England, including, in 1685, flannel to make the evangelist John Eliot a suit. Ashurst was a friend to Massachusetts (and to the Mathers) and became its London agent. Blathwayt said New England had nothing to offer the motherland; but this was untrue. Alongside an array of imports stimulating to English industry, the Boston merchant Samuel Sewall listed exports of cod, pork, fish oil, tar, beaver, molasses, cranberries, and wooden shingles, and many of these goods went to the Caribbean plantations, whose sugar trade hugely benefited England. With traders went explorers and buccaneers. After his Bahamian fiasco, William Phips, in 1687, recovered treasure worth £250,000. According to Cotton Mather, when James II asked him to name his reward, Phips "prayed for nothing but this, That New-England might have its lost Priviledges Restored." The king replied, "Any Thing but that!" So Phips settled for a knighthood and booty that would be equivalent to more than £20 million today.[17]

And along with trade and adventure went scientific discovery— political economy intersecting with natural philosophy to support empire and sustain national vigor. Knowledge of the world in colonial times was advanced by transatlantic communication networks, for instance. In 1686, the Virginian planter William Byrd corresponded with John Clayton, a Yorkshire minister, and requested books on minerals; in return, Byrd sent Clayton's son an Indian costume. For two years Clayton had been rector at Jamestown, and there he had been an assiduous botanist, describing bald eagles and whirlwinds that caused showers of leaves. Indians he found "ye Sottishest people in ye world," implying they were drunks as well as fools, yet neither did he identify with white Virginians. He noted, "'Tis strange in how many things . . . they are remiss, which one would think Englishmen should not be guilty of." Clayton believed the American plantations could be more efficient, but his advice fell on deaf ears, despite some impressive experiments in land drainage. These folk, too, were "sottish," as well as "conceited of their old ways." John Banister, another clergyman in Virginia, collected plants, insects, and shells, which he sent to the bishop of London. Banister's friend William Byrd supplied seeds, crystals, and ores and oversaw a mining project. Among flora received by William Blathwayt were saplings of maple, cherry, and honeysuckle as well as gentian seeds and peach pits. Whitehall proposed that samples should be displayed in England, "to incourage p[er]sons of Estate . . . to adventure and undertake."[18]

Curiosity for its own sake remained important. Stories like that of Lionel Wafer, a Welsh explorer who in the 1680s lived among Indians in Panama while recovering from an injury, awed English audiences. So assimilated was he, with painted skin and nose-ring, that his former shipmates failed to recognize him. New World souvenirs were as fascinating as ever. In among Blathwayt's cuttings was a tomahawk, which he called simply "an Indian weapon." Samuel Sewall even sent Indian scalps to a physician in Bishopsgate. A survey of Carolina observed many strange things, including hummingbirds; in Barbados, it was noted, these were stuffed, perfumed, and exported "as pretty Delicacies for Ladies, who hang them at their Breasts and Girdles." Another commentator dubbed Carolina "this beautiful Aurora, or the Rising Sun of America"—a world of revelations. From Virginia in 1679 John Banister described to the professor of botany at Oxford a place of danger and beauty, where he studied possums and panthers and ate watermelons. Lord Thomas Culpeper went the following year and stayed with his cousin, Lady Frances Berkeley, Sir William's widow, at her Green Spring mansion. He was amazed and delighted. "We live frankly together," Culpeper wrote to his sister in Kent, referring to his host's household and the wider English community, "without any of your European selfishness or politick coveteousnesse to disturbe us." He promised to send her some keepsakes.[19]

Indian culture was dangerously alluring. Nathaniel Crouch's *The English Empire in America* (1685), for example, portrayed the colonies

An illustration of 1685 from Nathaniel Crouch's *The English Empire in America*. The pincers of the spider depicted (center right) were exported to the Old World to be used as exotic toothpicks. Among the many "strange creatures" are natives worshipping the devil.

as a lucrative "Land of Wonders." A woodcut captioned "Strange creatures in America" showed natives worshipping the devil among beasts, such as a monstrous black spider whose pincers, mounted in gold, were exported as luxury toothpicks. They were "esteemed to have a vertue of preserving from pain and corruption the places rubbed therewith." The New World was being pacified and commodified, but no one could neutralize its fierce magic.[20]

Expansion turned on an axis of freedom and bondage. By the 1680s, black slaves, universal in the Caribbean and the Chesapeake, were also common in New England. From a colonist's perspective buying slaves was a tempting, if risky, investment. In 1681, "Maria Negro" and "Jack Negro" were convicted of arson at Boston and burned—becoming a "Picture of Hell," said Cotton Mather. Peter Thacher, a New England clergyman, returned from Boston to find that his infant daughter had been dropped by an Indian servant, whom he beat severely. Three years later, after considerable vacillation, he bought an African for £20, whom he named "Ebed" after an Ethiopian slave in the Book of Jeremiah. Within a year Ebed had absconded, but he was later recaptured. When he fell sick that year, Thacher, an amateur physician, struggled to save his property. Slavery never took hold in New England as it did elsewhere. By 1700 slaves accounted for just 2 percent of the region's inhabitants, compared to 13 percent in Virginia and 78 percent in the West Indies.[21]

More *white* slaves also arrived in America—they were hauled from England's jails to meet demand. Convicted criminals pleaded to go to the New World. Sometimes their gratitude was misplaced. The lawyer Roger North described how in Bristol, "small rogues and pilferers were taken . . . [and] put under terror of being hanged . . . and some of the diligent officers attending instructed them to pray transportation as the only way to save them." Thus the mayor and aldermen lined their pockets, a scam exposed by Lord Chief Justice George Jeffreys. Merchants also complained that jailers charged extortionate fees to release prisoners, and called for regulation.[22]

By the 1680s, the transportation of felons to America was an unremarkable feature of English criminal justice. As usual, adventurers and planters complained about being lumped with the nation's dregs. Most transported felons were lazy. Some rose up; more just ran away. The best moment to escape was before leaving England: once, more than seventy prisoners bound for Jamaica seized control of their ship, went back to England, and disappeared into the Essex countryside. Escape from the Caribbean was harder. Once fleeing prisoners put to sea, they faced exposure, hunger, and thirst. Thirty of Monmouth's rebels broke free en route to the West Indies; but at least eight hundred others—working men from Somerset, Devon, and Dorset—were enslaved thousands of miles from home. Jeffreys had no qualms about enslaving Englishmen, but some, including William Blathwayt, were less certain. The ten-year terms inflicted upon the rebels, he believed, "makes them dispair of ever seeing an end of their slavery and obliges them to be ready for the contriving as well as executing any sort of Vilany that may occasion a publick Revolution." They should have been exiled as freeholders, he said, together with their families: liberty and property alone engendered loyalty. Scots prisoners from the civil wars who were promised freedom had thrived in New England and Barbados, learning skills and becoming planters.[23]

Another form of Anglo-American bondage was abduction by Barbary privateers. Thousands of sailors and colonists were seized at sea and sent to Algiers and Salé (in northwestern Morocco), causing paranoia and panic. John Dunton recalled that a "supposed Sally-Rover [Moroccan pirate ship] prov'd nothing else but a Virginia Merchant Man, as much afraid of us as we of them." Many of the English were put off emigration, especially in communities were ransoms had to be raised for those who had been taken by pirates. Mary Lynch of Plymouth saved £70 to redeem her husband, a mariner in Algiers who had "endured the utmost rigour of soule & body barbarity could inflict"; all she needed was £10, magistrates heard in 1683. Imperial competition in the Atlantic and Caribbean encouraged piracy; every power was happy when its enemies were harassed by African corsairs. When the Spanish took English prisoners, they often forced them to work in degrading occupations in Cuba and South America. Jonas Clough toiled in a Mexican tanning factory until, famished and crawling with lice, he escaped in 1681. With its growing naval strength, England got on top of piracy in the 1680s, but tales of incarceration, like captivity narratives from the New England frontier, haunted English folklore for decades.[24]

The rhetoric of slavery was used by colonists to describe compromised rights. But positive symbols of liberty became common in public discourse, too. The freedom of Carolina, said a promoter, "consists in the propriety of what God in his Wisdom intails upon Posterity, and intitles the inherent Birthright of every man born into the World." Even more promising was Pennsylvania on the Delaware River. This settlement came from a proprietary land grant of 45,000 acres in 1681 to William Penn, the Quaker son of the disgraced admiral, whose "holy experiment" to permit all religions conceived American freedom afresh. The grid-plan capital, Philadelphia—"city of brotherly love"— was to have fair government and no established church. Harried English Quakers bought plots from Penn, who issued deeds. In October 1681, Sarah Fuller of Chillington, five miles from Penn's Sussex home, bought 1,000 acres for £20. In advance of his departure for America, Penn wrote to settlers in the Delaware Valley, introducing himself as their governor and pledging that "you shall be govern'd by laws of y[ou]r own makeing & live a free, & if you will, a sober & industreous People. I shall not usurp the right of any or oppress his person." He set off for America in August 1682, leaving a pregnant wife and three young children in England, to whom he wrote: "Farewell to my thrice dearly belov'd wife and Children, yours as god pleaseth in that which no waters can quench, no time forget, nor Distance wear away."[25]

Patience and courage were as important for William Penn and those who bought into his new settlement as they had been for the earliest pioneers. By late 1681, James Claypoole, a Quaker merchant in London, decided to move to Pennsylvania. Preparing for the trip was so difficult (mainly because he had to call in debts) that he did not arrive until October 1683. Philadelphia was less than a year old at that time. It consisted of a few shoddy buildings among the trees, mostly bark-covered wigwams and cave dwellings dug into the banks of the Delaware. The house that Claypoole had ordered to be built disappointed him: it had a wine cellar (which he had specified), but no fireplaces (which he had forgotten). In a letter home he complained that his hands were almost too cold to write. Yet his prospects in his new home glittered. Desiring, as he said, only "to go on quietly and moderately," Claypoole nevertheless identified "divers ways to improve a stock of £1,000 or £2,000 to very great advantage."[26]

Penn, who had helped Claypoole get started, was enthusiastic. "I am mightily taken with this part of the World," he wrote to Lord Thomas Culpeper. "I like it so well that a plentiful Estate & a great Acquaintance on th'other side have no Charmes to remove. My family being once fixt w[i]th me, & if no other thing occur, I am like to be an adopted American." But his family never left England. By May 1684, divisions among settlers, criticism of taxes and land grants, and a boundary dispute with Lord Baltimore forced Penn to return to England. There he found he could not plead his case, because his secretary had not packed key documents. He was reunited with his family and stayed in England for fifteen years. The conflict that kept Penn at home arose from his most laudable aim: to connect, with English law and history, property and freedom of conscience as natural rights. The problem was the same as throughout English America. Leading colonists resented being bossed around, whether by crown, Parliament, or authoritarian proprietors.[27]

Pennsylvania was promoted not only as a haven of liberty but also as a place of middling prosperity. Pamphlets were published. One promised bumper crops to "such who by hard Labour here on Rack Rents are scarce able to maintain themselves." Tradesmen, too, were to be valued in Pennsylvania. And the landscape and soil were superior to that of New England. Thomas Budd, who arrived in 1668, praised the colonists for overcoming "the many Exercises and inward Combats" to leave their homes, and urged England to deliver their poor from slavery and poverty by sending them there. The vast country, a settler in New Jersey wrote, needs only people. Old arguments were aired: England's right to be in America; a generation's duty to go forth; the notion that godly migration was no drain on Protestantism. Men who derided the colonies, suggested William Loddington, a Baptist sympathetic to Quaker ambitions in the New World, should consider how poor England would be "if their Ancestors had not had Plantation Principles"—that is, the urge to emigrate and settle and grow. Albion was once "as rough and rugged as America, and the Inhabitants as blind and barbarous as the Indians," he said. Penn denied that his colony was a land of plenty: life was hard and plain, yet also blissful. "In vain do we admire the first and Simpler Ages of the World and stile them Golden," he observed, "while we object against America's Rusticity and Solitude."[28]

For people in England, America was forever a place more imagined than experienced; conversely, colonists of the second and third generations identified with England without necessarily ever going there. Thus far, the century had taught that life could be recast across the ocean, and waning values restored, but not without incurring familiar Old World problems. The stormy religious and political lives of the metropole and its colonies had increasingly run in parallel, and overlapped, since the 1650s. There was also an increase in economic integration between England and the colonies, for which imperial ideology provided the essential justifying commentary. England's constitutional instability, and its dramatic finale in 1688–1689, exposed colonial weaknesses, but it mostly exposed flaws at home, raising cries against tyranny and invoking the spirit of Magna Carta.

Religious liberty, which always found a place close to the hearts of colonists, mingled with thoughts of England. Samuel Sewall contemplated often the place he had left as a child. He once dreamed that his deceased father-in-law, John Hull, had returned there in a spiritual homecoming. In another dream, he saw Christ coming to Boston to lodge at Hull's house. Perhaps the dream reflected hopes for colonial redemption. In May 1687, Sewall visited Robert Walker, an old man who had been incapacitated by a stroke. An acquaintance of Sewall's grandfather, Walker had been a Manchester linen-weaver before emigrating in 1632. Recalling the maypole, a symbol of pagan idolatry, he explained to Sewall "what the manner was in England to dance about it with Musick, and 'twas to be feared such practices would be here." Walker died a few days later, and John Alden, the last surviving signatory to the Mayflower Compact, died shortly thereafter—another passing noted by Sewall. Witnesses to New England's birth were quickly vanishing. It was a summer of measles and blighted crops. Sewall's six-month-old son also died. In August, Sewall notified a cousin in England about the infant's death, adding that he had read James II's "declaration for the liberty of conscience," probably in the *London Gazette*, by which Sewall kept abreast of events at home.[29]

For New Englanders, toleration was attended by two fears: its extension to Catholics as well as dissenters, and dependence on the will of an absolutist king. Joseph Dudley's stint as governor of Massachusetts had not been happy: Boston's magistrates accused him of arbitrary rule; he retorted that they asserted their power arbitrarily. In May 1686, Governor Bradstreet grudgingly accepted Dudley's commission, "a thing contrived to abridge them of their Libertye & indeed against Magna Charta." Massachusetts, Maine, Plymouth, New Hampshire, and part of Rhode Island were to be ruled as the Dominion of New England by a royal appointee; representative assemblies were dissolved, Puritan magistrates and other officials removed. New York, New Jersey, and the rest of Rhode Island would soon be absorbed, likewise Connecticut, which openly deplored the abrogation of liberties and franchises granted by Charles I. Bermuda, too, became a royal colony.[30]

In December 1686, Sir Edmund Andros, who had suppressed Monmouth's Rebellion and who had been governor of New York, arrived in New England as governor-general of the dominion. His unilateral decrees, increase in levies, and trade regulations earned him special hatred. In August 1687, a tax strike at Ipswich, Massachusetts, declared Andros's revenues illegal, arguing "that it was not the town's duty any way to assist that ill method of raising money without a general assembly." Andros replied that upon leaving England, men gave up all rights except one: not to be sold as slaves. It was joked that if the devil was dead, as skeptics suggested, among Boston's excisemen he had left many fatherless offspring.[31]

Increase Mather had little faith in the king's Declaration of Indulgence—as feared, it promised religious freedom to Catholics and dissenters alike. Mather predicted in April 1687 that "our libertyes will not be long lived." He anticipated a new Puritan diaspora, as did Andros's official, Edward Randolph, who was ready to impose an oath of allegiance on the "multitudes of phannatticks" expected from England. One dissenter, Richard Lobb, writing to Mather for advice, said his brethren had "no inclinations to leave their native Country out of choice, yet they may be driven thence by force, or by the severitys of the Enemy of Godlines." Increase Mather's friends in New England also sought his reassurance. Meanwhile, Randolph prepared to unseat Mather. His weapon was the intercepted letter from Mather to Thomas Gough, which Randolph thought came "perilously close to sedition." When Mather finally saw the offending document and denounced it as a forgery, Randolph sued for slander. Mather was acquitted in January 1688, but a few weeks later, persuaded of God's will, he asked his church for a leave of absence and slipped away. The incendiary letter was published in the *Observator*, a Tory journal, with manuscript copies circulating throughout the Caribbean.[32]

In the summer of 1688, the agitations of the colony crystallized around the four children of a Boston mason named John Goodwin, who had all suffered, it was said, from the "stupendous Witchcraft" of Goody Glover, a Catholic Irishwoman. Cotton Mather prayed with the screaming, writing victims; magistrates sent Glover to prison, where she confessed and was hanged. As she had warned, her execution did not solve anything: other witches were at work. The children flushed hot and cold, saw specters, and levitated. Mather took in Martha, the eldest girl, who distracted him from his work and convulsed when he read her the story of a possessed girl from his father's book. Martha's last fit happened at Christmas, during which she said "something about the state of the Countrey" that astonished Mather. Writing up the episode for his own treatise, he decided there was nothing in his library to equal what her passions had taught him. The work was published in Boston and sent to Richard Baxter in England, who arranged a London edition to prove "the unreasonableness of Infidelity." Mather parried all Satan's blows, including Quakerism in Philadelphia and dancing, by which "the Devil will decoy us unto the utmost Edge of the Liberty that is Lawful for us."[33]

These were days of shaking on the public and private stages, as well as on the local and national and the English and American stages. Andros's regime in New England tottered; indeed, the execution of Goody Glover was a turning point. Before, judges had been reluctant to convict witches, but now the governor did not wish to appear to be soft on the likes of witches, or papists, either, for that matter. Leniency might have caused his downfall at a time of public sensitivity about the frontier war with the Wabenakis, and the mood was tense. A public fast to lift the colony's drought was followed by weeks of storms; a Boston woman was hurt when lightning splintered her roof. In England, James II had united all his enemies, and an Anglo-French agreement authorized an invasion of England by the Dutch Protestant *stadtholder*, Prince William of Orange-Nassau. By the autumn of 1688, rumors had spread that charters would be restored to corporations all over England, and by extension New England. William landed in England early in November, in what is known as the Glorious Revolution, putting the king to flight and sparking anti-Catholic disturbances in London and war with France. For over a decade, this war would be fought in America as well as Europe; it is remembered as King William's War.[34]

Winds of change blew in the fractious "middle colonies" of New York, New Jersey, Pennsylvania, and Delaware as well as in New England. In Boston a broadside was printed that hailed William as a "Second Constantine," an enemy to the despotic Andros and his henchman:

> *We were not treated by the insulting Knaves,*
> *As free-born English, but as poor French Slaves.*
> *Taxes were rais'd without Mercy or Measure,*
> *To keep us low and fill our Tyrant's Treasure,*
> *To Magna Charta, we could claim no Right,*
> *Neither our own nor English Laws would fit.*

Colonists, thrilled about the restoration of liberty, pledged their loyalty to William. Handwritten papers called on New England to rebel against papists and their French and Indian allies. But for now, Andros was still governor under the authority of James II. To suggest otherwise in word or deed was at best sedition, at worst treason. A hapless

Bostonian who found a copy of a tract entitled "New England Alarm'd" in the road was jailed after showing it to a friend. The same fate befell a man arriving at the harbor with William's declaration. Rumors of a Franco-Irish invasion rang through Boston's streets—"for that was the first place that was to be destroyed," an Indian had warned. In New York it was announced that natives spreading false news would be punished, or rewarded if the news proved to be true.[35]

On April 4, 1689, a merchant arrived from Nevis with news that William of Orange's invasion of England had caused a revolution— news that Andros had withheld. Handbills flew off the presses, and soon it was common knowledge. At eight in the morning on the 18th, word spread in the south of the city that the north had risen up; meanwhile, the north, where nothing was happening, reported rebellion in the south. Soon all points were on the move. Within an hour men who were associated with Andros's regime were in custody, and around noon a declaration, probably composed by Cotton Mather, was read from the gallery of the council house. It recalled the terrors of the Popish Plot in England and alleged cruel government in New England, with "multiplied contradictions to Magna Charta." By two o'clock, Boston was in ferment. Soon afterward, the captain of HMS *Rose* was detained for trying to rescue Andros. "The Rumour of it running like Lightning through the Town," an eyewitness reported, "all sorts of people were presently inspired with the most unanimous Resolution I believe that was ever seen." Drums sounded, and everywhere men were in arms. Andros, Randolph, and Dudley were arrested, and the Fort Hill garrison surrendered. The next day people from outlying towns swarmed into Boston, clamoring to reverse the "Treasonable Invasion of the Rights which the whole English Nation lays claim unto," and forcing recognition that "the vacating of our Charter was a most illegal and injurious thing."[36]

There was an uneasy pause as Boston calculated its next move. A man was reported for saying "God bless King James" and "Damn the Prince of Orange." The chief justice, seeking to quell disorder and manage expectations of the new regime, advised rebels that Magna Carta did not apply to dominions; nor were New England's towns formal corporations, and so had no rights. Massachusetts should submit *unconditionally*, he said, because it had neither legitimacy nor military strength to negotiate. Boston's elder statesman Edward Rawson replied that New England's loyalty was implicit, adding that its people enjoyed the constitutional freedoms of Englishmen anywhere. Andros was an enemy to liberty, he said, his commission "more Illegal and Arbitrary than that granted to Dudley and Empson by King Henry 7th"—courtiers who had been beheaded as traitors in 1510. At the end of May, reliable news arrived from England, and the new monarchs, William and Mary, were proclaimed. Andros was locked up at Castle Island. He allegedly tried to escape dressed as a woman, only to be halted by a guard who noticed his shoes. Randolph and Dudley were put in the common jail. Dudley paid £10,000 to be moved to house arrest, but as this caused rioting, he rejoined Randolph for his own safety.[37]

In Virginia, William Byrd was "heartily sorry to hear of ye destractions of my Native Country." He worried about unstable government, Indian hostility, and disrupted trade, and he craved word from England, complaining of being kept in the dark. As reports of the invasion of England spread, Virginia's secretary informed Whitehall that "it began to be in the mouths of the mobile that there was noe King in England and consequently noe Governm[en]t here." Acting on a rumor that papists in Maryland had joined Seneca Indians to destroy Protestants, armed bands sprang up "like Hydra's heads" in Virginia, until they heard of William and Mary's coronation, whereupon a loyal proclamation was rushed to all parts. Maryland saw uprisings for the new regime, and introduced an oath of fidelity repudiating Rome. Authorities in Connecticut congratulated the monarchs on their "happy access to the imperial throne of your kingdoms and territories." They sent an officer to Fort Albany, New York, where soldiers cheered the news. William and Mary were proclaimed there in July. The Caribbean colonies also came out for the king and queen. There was an uprising in the Leeward Islands, and Barbados celebrated with feasting and bonfires. Jamaican planters repatriated the widow of the duke of Albemarle, James II's governor, back to England. The duke had died the previous October, and his pitch-coated body went with her. A week later, a petition was sent to the king seeking restoration of the assembly and exoneration of a member who had been fined for saying: "Salus populi est Suprema Lex."[38]

This saying was Cicero's maxim—it meant "The good of the people is the supreme law"—and it was also heard elsewhere. It concluded a letter to London sent by a Bostonian on May 18, which argued that the charter had to be restored because it was New England's Magna Carta. "If we enjoy this, with the blessing of the Almighty, we are happy," the author said, "and that without this, we are wholly without Law—the Laws of England being made for England only, and in many things not suiting to us." Two days later, a letter from Simon Bradstreet to King William applauding his accession begged "our Share in that Universal Restoration of Charters and English Liberties. . . . That under the shadow of yor Imperial Crown wee may again bee made to flourish in the Enjoyment of our Ancient Rights and Priviledges." In Boston the sense of living in an interregnum, which had begun in 1684, had become acute. An account from late July described political chaos, with every man serving as his own governor, and lovers of order desperate for Increase Mather to return from London clutching a new patent. But the challenges were formidable, and in the last decade of the century, all of English America would endure providential punishments, including war and rebellion, witchcraft and disaster, that would speed its protean transformation.[39]

CHAPTER 20

These Dark Territories

WILLIAM OF ORANGE had saved true religion in England and America from Catholic absolutism. Yet, as King William III, he would uphold the imperial policies of James II and his predecessors. Disquiet, then, tempered the triumphalism of New England's elite; similarly, the Puritans' newfound loyalty to the crown was moderated by pride in having resisted England, even as they reached out to their Protestant brethren across the Atlantic. This sense of difference was intensified by the war with Franco-Indian forces resulting from the revolution. For England, this merely extended a European conflict, a logical move by an expansive and bellicose state. For New England, however, it relived the traumas of King Philip's War. At a time of remarkable commercial sophistication and change, life for many was as dangerous as ever, with scenes from hell played out before their eyes, both on the mainland and in the Caribbean. In Massachusetts, some believed the terrifying dramas of 1692, when colonists battled with witches, occurred not despite that sophistication and change, but rather because of it. If the century had taught them anything, it was that England's afflictions could not be cured by making a world that stood still. Conservative visions of a perfect Old World demanded energy and initiative, and ultimately a taste for radical reinvention and the courage to see it through.

One morning in June 1689, Samuel Sewall and Increase Mather were sitting in an Essex coffeehouse, en route from Cambridge to London, when they read in a newspaper that a revolution had occurred in Boston. "We were surpris'd with joy," recorded Sewall in his diary.[1]

As Americans abroad, Sewall and Mather met often, yet they felt differently about being in England. Mather had been there for over a year, having left Boston early in 1688, stoically rather than enthusiastically. Disguised, and with Edward Randolph snapping at his heels, he had boarded the *President* with his adolescent son Samuel, and then they sailed off into an Atlantic storm. As passengers retched, Mather read the Bible and prayed, nursing a toothache. After a month of icebergs, towering waves, and fog, they sighted land. Cornish fishermen were "very uncivil," refusing to confirm their location until Mather paid them. By May 16, he was in Weymouth, the port he had left twenty-seven years earlier and, by God's design (he perceived), the site of his repatriation. The Mathers left for London by coach, passing through Dorchester, Salisbury, and Basingstoke and stopping to preach and see friends.[2]

Sewall's visit to what he called "my Native Country" was for more self-indulgent reasons. Since his arrival in January 1689 he had spent his time visiting relatives (and their graves) and places of interest. At Winchester School, he donated a copy of John Eliot's Indian Bible. He admired Stonehenge and Canterbury Cathedral, and the universities of Oxford and Cambridge, enjoying Anglican services at the former, at the latter feeding sparrows in the hall of Trinity College. In London he swam in the Thames, soaked up the atmosphere of a royal wedding—"Ancients and Streamers of Ships flying, Bells Ringing, Guns roaring"—and saw eighteen felons hanged at Tyburn. Yet, like Mather, Sewall was homesick. He missed his wife, who hovered in his dreams. His distance from New England incubated his fears about America. A letter Mather received from Joshua Moodey at Portsmouth described the terrors of Indian warfare and "a strange th[ing] among us w[hi]ch we know not what to make of except it bee witchcraft." Learning that his son Nathaniel had died at Salem, Mather spent the winter of 1688–1689 grieving that "so hopeful a branch of my Family is gone." Moodey wrote again to report earthquakes and cannon-like thunder.[3]

Upon his arrival in London, Mather had liaised with the pro–New England merchant Henry Ashurst, and a meeting with James II was arranged. Mather made preparatory notes, defending freedom of worship and English privileges overseas. "No English men in their Wits," believed Mather, "will ever Venture their Lives and Estates to Enlarge the Kings Dominions abroad, and Enrich the whole English Nation, if their Reward after all must be to be deprived of their English

Liberties." Sir Edmund Andros's arbitrary rule had reduced a flourishing colony to a state of bondage; his removal was just, and the injunction from the Book of Samuel, "Rebellion is as the sin of witchcraft,"
did not apply. Mather's main argument was that loyal New England
supported imperial ambitions. Revoking the charter had been illegal;
it was also an insult to "the English born in New England," who "have
the true inherent Spirit of the Old."[4]

On the morning of May 30, 1688, Mather met the king in the Long
Gallery at Whitehall. He went to kneel but was pulled to his feet and
invited to speak. He read a letter of gratitude for toleration, to which
James replied: "I am glad my subjects in N[ew] E[ngland] are sensible
of any ease or benefit by my decl[aration]." At a second meeting in June,
this time in the privy chamber, Mather artfully suggested that New
England might accept Andros were he to abide by the Declaration of
Indulgence. The king was startled: "Does he *not* doe it?"—a response
that emboldened Mather to describe the continued persecutions. James
promised to help. This time, Mather did kneel, and kissed the royal
hand. He secured an aide's assurances that the king would understand
that New Englanders were not "such who have wronged his Majesty
in his customes & an odd humoured people." Yet there were crosscur-
rents. Edward Randolph warned the Plantation Office that Mather was
hiding "antimonarchicall principals." Mather bided his time. He spent
nine shillings having his tooth pulled, and more on outfits for Samuel
and himself. His greatest extravagance, in early summer, was sitting
for a life-size portrait, which so pleased him that he commissioned an
engraving.[5]

By the start of 1689, things had changed. This time, Mather's audience was with William of Orange, whom he met at St. James's Palace as
London lay muffled by snow, the Thames frozen. Mather requested the
restoration of the charter, which Parliament granted within a month.
Praying in his chilly chamber, Mather "was marvellously melted &
could not but w[i]th Tears say, God has saved New England." On May
14 he thanked William, now king, who promised to remove Andros
and asked that New England proclaim him. Mather assured him that
they would do so with "ye Joyfullest hearts in ye world."[6]

In this joyful heart grew a painful longing for home. But as Mather
prepared to leave that summer, his son Samuel developed smallpox.
He wrote to Lord Wharton, a courtier present at the meeting in May:
"I have little Hopes of seing N.E. again this winter." His ship, the

Increase Mather (1639–1723) was perhaps the most important intellectual in early New England. This portrait was painted in London in 1688 by the Dutch artist Jan van der Spriet. Mather was there seeking to negotiate royal concessions for his embattled colony—the home he missed dreadfully.

America, left in November, with Samuel Sewall aboard but not the Mathers. Increase Mather and Henry Ashurst were formally made agents for Massachusetts, stranding Mather in England for another two and a half years. He asked Wharton not to let "malicious Informations" poison the king's mind; but that effort proved to be in vain.[7]

The charges were that New England's governors had hesitated to proclaim William and Mary; their pledges were insincere, and their defense of liberty a smokescreen for independence. And all this despite most New Englanders preferring royal government. Like his son Cotton, Increase Mather conflated Anglicans with papists and called the Book of Common Prayer a tool of idolatry. In New Plymouth, news arrived that "the Torys Labour to fill mens eares & hearts with horror on the acco[un]t of ye pretended desolation and confusion of N.E., and say the Land will be ruined except a general Governor be sent." Mather had a defensive letter from New England turned into a pamphlet by the Whig publisher John Dunton. This was countered by another missive from New England defending Andros and alleging that "the late Subverters of the Government had no manner of regard to Their Majesty's Interest or Service."[8]

By spring 1691, Mather, contemplating a New England politically divided and drained by war, was fretting about his family, from whom he had heard nothing in ages. A diary entry for March 28 read: "Tis this day 3 years since I was in my own house." In public Mather remained composed. On April 9, he met Queen Mary to beg her favor. "I wish all would be of one mind and generally live peaceably with one another," she said. Later that month, weak from diarrhea, he rode to Kensington to convince the king that New England would expand his dominions in America, provided it could retain "Auncient priviledges."[9]

Mather took the waters at Epsom and Streatham, and weathered criticism. As ever, liberty and tyranny, civility and barbarism, were movable perspectives, easily reversed to make the righteous look perfidious. A tract satirized Mather's blandishments: "Who could ever imagine that a few Bankrupt Publicans and Vagabonds in New-England should send us over an Address of this nature, so doubtfully, ambiguously and cunningly penn'd." The rest of English America, it went on, was even more disordered, inhabited by runaways, slaves, and pirates, whose sorry plantations would, without discipline, become "a greater plague to England than ever were the Turks upon the Coast of Barbary." Similar comment was heard in official circles. A report to the archbishop of Canterbury condemned "waspish Creatures" who basked in a cornucopia but behaved like tyrants. Quakers who had been banished by the "inhumaine and barbarous" English were being saved by Indian "kindness." New Englanders were morose and vindictive, yet pious and censorious. They invented laws "so fantastic & childish that they will make a sober Man laugh." Restrictions on church membership and baptism threatened to paganize America, and in time "there will bee as much need of Evangelizing the English as there is now of the Indians." For them to call Andros's government "illegall & arbitrary" was deeply ironic.[10]

A pamphlet by Mather was, according to the Whitehall official William Blathwayt, "false, frivolous and hardly worth takeing notice of." The idea that New England should have its charters restored because planters had enlarged royal dominions gratis struck Blathwayt as impudent and disingenuous. The early colonists, he said, had behaved selfishly and would have served England better by staying at home. They had exploited the Interregnum of the 1650s to make a dependent corporation into "a free and absolute Commonwealth, separate and Independant." Why should England respect a patent from which New England had departed by arrogating power and mistreating royal subjects? Most colonists would happily throw off the Puritan yoke: "There is not one in a hundred but desire their Charter," Blathwayt believed. A letter filed at Whitehall in May 1691 condemned charter government, with all its libertarian bluster, as absolutist despotism requiring the crown's attention.[11]

Meanwhile, Henry Sloughter, governor of New York, informed Blathwayt that war was crushing New England. Without royal help, he advised, the empire in America might collapse. Sloughter had arrived in New York in March 1691. He had been ordered to regain control from Jacob Leisler, a German merchant who had rebelled after the Glorious Revolution. The city consisted of several hundred households, mostly Dutch or German, that were watched over by a fort housing the English governor and his garrison. It was not a colony that people in England knew much about. When the Virginian planter William Byrd visited New York, he was struck by how "ye people seem not concerned w[ha]t religion y[ou]r Neighbor is of, or whither hee hath any or none." They were, a minister conceived, "ignorant & conceited, fickle & regardless," their energies spent on trade, at which they were "cunning and crafty." As in most colonies, people in New York desired an assembly that could set taxes, but no sooner did they get one than James II abolished it. In 1689 imperial rule had been replaced with a new regime, which Leisler was defending in 1691. As Sloughter advanced, Leisler's men had held the fort, calling the invaders papists and Jacobites. But to no avail: the ringleaders were arrested for treason. Leisler, it was proclaimed at his execution, was no liberator but a "common Violater of our Laws and Liberties." His enmity to James II had not made him William III's friend: offense to the crown superseded that.[12]

Continuity in English policy shaped the settlement negotiated by Increase Mather. The Dominion of New England was to be disbanded, but the Lords of Trade would regulate colonies as before. The compensation was the charter. Mather sent word to his son Cotton, who from September 1691 spread the news in New England: Massachusetts would be a crown colony under a royal governor, except with better privileges.

They should rejoice. The new patent, published on October 7, authorized assemblies, but it replaced the religious qualification for participation with one based on property. Puritan wings had been clipped. A fortnight later Increase Mather met the master of the rolls, England's second most senior judge, who informed him that Massachusetts had no right to make money; nor could it impose taxes or death sentences. Yet the right to political representation had been established—it was now a basic safeguard for English subjects everywhere and a keystone of civil society. This development was accepted by the crown, whose colonial governors would go further; they would apply royal writ selectively and creatively. The distant pomp and ceremony of monarchy, they knew, was inferior to the reality of power in America.[13]

Pragmatism had defeated absolutism. Men must not tolerate arbitrary rule, wrote John Locke in 1690, unless they wished "to put themselves into a worse condition than the state of Nature wherein they had a Liberty to defend their Right against the Injuries of others." Across the Atlantic world, English Protestants closed ranks according to this principle. After a generation of rising tension—the result of royal interference and, in New England, a burgeoning sense of nationhood unique among colonies—William III's tact and compromise helped former dissidents to sound convincingly like loyalists. Many, mostly New Englanders, had publicly purged the historic ambiguity of their identity by exploiting England's constitutional crisis in the name of anti-popery and liberty, while privately forging an even more robust independent consciousness. The new king, meanwhile, quietly yet firmly adhered to the imperial policies of the Stuarts. At the same time, however, the colonial habit of assembly government preserved by the 1689 settlement became a way of life, with revolutionary consequences in the next century.[14]

Life as well as liberty was at stake in New England. King William's War had caused devastation in Maine and northern Massachusetts, revived memories of Metacom, and reprised the unifying experience of suffering and dread. Once more, it seemed, providence was turning colonists to account. Hostilities had begun in the summer of 1688—"a most mischievous thing th[a]t hath much of the angery hand of g[o]d in i[t]," a colonist named John Bailey told his brother in England. John

Eliot's mission to the Indians was in jeopardy again: "I feare its too much lost labour," opined Bailey. The following year brought border raids and skirmishes. In June, the fort at Saco was overrun, and Dover, New Hampshire, raided. People hid in garrisons. A woman at Cochecho was paralyzed by fear when, yelling to be let into her fort, she suddenly saw that it was full of Indians. In Massachusetts people also cowered. Governor Simon Bradstreet urged Connecticut to support Massachusetts or suffer when the conflict spread south. In Maryland, rumors of Indian insurrection caused panic; Virginia, too, braced itself. Boston was alarmed by the influx of poor refugees from the east.[15]

One morning in August 1689, people working in the fields at Pemaquid in Maine were cut off from their fort, among them ten-year-old John Gyles. He ran, but was caught by what he described as "a stout fellow, painted . . . with a gun and a cutlass glittering in his hand." The boy saw men casually butchered, then was joined by his brother and father, who had been shot. Thomas Gyles was allowed to pray with his sons, and then, "very pale by reason of the great loss of blood which boiled out of his shoes," was finished off with a hatchet. Led back toward the fort, which was now besieged, Gyles met his mother and two sisters, but they could hardly speak. Some hours later, the Indians sent a prisoner to the fort tied to a rope to make their demands—they wanted their country back—upon which the garrison surrendered. The prisoners watched as everything was burned. Beginning their journey to the coast, where canoes were waiting, Gyles's mother asked how he was, to which he lied: "Pretty well." "Oh my child!" she replied in tears, "how joyful and pleasant it would be if we were going to old England . . . [but] we are going into the wilderness, the Lord knows where." It was the last time they would see each other, and the start of eight years of captivity for John Gyles. He survived cold and disease, and also experienced firsthand what he guessed was Indian familiarity with Satan.[16]

Fifteen years of Indian rage erupted in such episodes. In September, a sagamore berated a captured colonist about "ye abuces ye Indians dayli Sufrad from ye English, in being cheated, beaten and put in ye Stockes, their Landes taken up." That year Maine lost three hundred people and property worth £40,000. Some colonists blamed the losses on the Glorious Revolution, which had caused soldiers to desert. Boston, meanwhile, prayed and heard sermons about godly soldiers opposing diabolical heathen. "At the first Appearance of the Tawny Pagans, then Courage!" Cotton Mather told his congregation. "Sacrifice

them to the Ghosts of the Christians whom they have Murdered." Cold
weather into 1690 offered colonists security. "They Dream't that while
the Deep Snow of the Winter continued," Mather wrote, "they were
Safe enough." But they were in for a shock: this was indeed a dream.[17]

In February 1690, a Franco-Indian force launched a night-raid at
Schenectady, twenty miles from Albany, killing sixty men, women, and
children. Some who fled froze to death. "The Cruelties Committed at
s[ai]d Place no Penn can write nor Tongue Expresse," it was reported.
The survivors claimed to have witnessed "women bigg with Childe
Rip'd up and ye Children alive throne into ye flames and there heads
Dash'd in Pieces." French prisoners revealed plans for the systematic
invasion of English settlements. Five weeks later, Salmon Falls, New
Hampshire—where some colonists swore they had seen the devil—was
attacked. A letter to Simon Bradstreet described "miserable and lamentable slaughter and havock": homes and mills burned, cattle destroyed,
inhabitants murdered. Troops pursued the attackers but were exhausted
by having to trudge through the snow. Seventy-nine colonists had been
captured or killed, including a boy who had been stabbed when he
cried for his parents. Militiamen also found a mutilated body tied to a
tree and children hiding in the woods. "The whole Country is so impoverished," read the letter, "that we are hardly able to Subsist." New
England and New York appealed to England. The bishop of London
received a plea from Portsmouth, Maine, informing him of "the destruction of many amongst us & the impoverishing of al[l]."[18]

The loss of Casco fort in May was described at Boston as "one of the
sorest blows." On the 17th, writing to his father in London, Cotton
Mather pitied "this distressed, Enfeebled ruined Countrey" and asked
when he would return. "I write with a most Ill-boding Jealousy," he
confessed tearfully, "that I shall never see you again in this Evil world."
Three days later, John Eliot died. "God hath made you to us and our
nation a spiritual father," was how native converts praised him. Cotton
Mather saluted not just a savior but New England's embodiment. Eliot's English birthplace he could not recall: "The Atlantick Ocean, like
a River of Lethe, may easily cause us to forget many of the things that
happened on the other side." He took his first breath in England, said
Mather, but his last and his *best* breath in America: "It is New-England
that with most right can call him hers." The Company for the Propagation of the Gospel continued to pay for preachers and Bibles in praying
towns. Now, however, the mission was as much political as spiritual.

New England had to resist the French army's Jesuit priests, who, it was said, sympathized with their Indian allies' demonic rituals.[19]

That summer, Whitehall received accounts of the dangerous position in which New England now found itself. "If we escape with our Lives," read one, "our Estates will in all probability be swallowed up"— they would be seized by the enemy, or spent on fighting them. Boston prayed for the divine and royal defense of England and New England: "ye whole English Israel." Indian cruelty, a Charlestown correspondent wrote, was compounded by political confusion: Where did power lie in the new state? God willing, "these Mists of Confusion and Darkness will soon be scatter'd by the clear Sun-shine of the King's Authority." Until then, New England would have to fend for itself, as it had during King Philip's War. But there was hope. Following the Schenectady massacre, and the despoiling of Maine and New Hampshire, representatives from Massachusetts, Plymouth, Connecticut, and New York had met to plan a combined assault. This included an eastern campaign led by Benjamin Church, hero of the previous war, and an invasion of Quebec by Sir William Phips, who was still puffed up with martial pride after capturing Port Royal in Acadia, New France.[20]

In August 1690, Phips left England with thirty-four ships and 2,000 men. After a terrible nine-week journey, the soldiers, many of whom had smallpox, landed at night on a freezing beach two miles from Quebec. The next morning, wading through a swamp, they were ambushed by the French, whom they fought all day until supplies ran low. The fleet had used up its ammunition on a chaotic coastal bombardment. The French rallied, forcing Phips to retreat. Three ships were sunk with all hands, another blown to an island, where the sixty-odd crew members built a few shacks using salvaged timbers. "This little Handful of Men," wrote Cotton Mather with a sort of rueful pride, "were now a sort of Commonwealth . . . separated from all the rest of Mankind." After four months, these survivors escaped in a ramshackle boat and, living on fish and seals, they made it to Boston in May 1691. Phips did not give up: like the port of Calais for Mary I in 1558, said Mather, Canada was written upon his heart.[21]

The expedition had cost Massachusetts over £50,000, and the colony had been forced to print paper money to pay the servicemen. The funds were underwritten by Phips. In spending it, soldiers spread smallpox, worsening Boston's epidemic; and their privations at the front, a minister noted, deterred new recruits. New England's defenses were faltering.

By the following summer everyone was desperate for England's assistance. In London, fears for New England's future exercised the minds of Englishmen and expatriated New Englanders alike: if French warships cut the Atlantic supply line, the consequences would be dire.[22]

On January 3, 1692, Increase Mather met the king one last time, then began to pack, reflecting that if God had not given his son smallpox, he might not have achieved anything. Nervous of enemy ships, he left Plymouth on March 29, accompanied by Sir William Phips, who had come to England the previous year. Mather had encouraged Phips's recent appointment as the first royal governor of Massachusetts, as had Henry Ashurst, who was also busy aligning Canada's commercial prospects with London's imperial interests.[23]

Mather and Phips arrived in Boston on May 14, 1692, a Saturday. Convening his governing council, Phips declared that God had sent him to serve his countrymen. He vowed that "he would not Abrige them of theire Ancient lawes and Customes, but all the privilliges and lawes and liberties as was prackticall in the dayes of ould should be as they were before." Seeing the sun setting, Phips interrupted a reading of the commission and letters patent, saying they should not dishonor the Sabbath. Outside, a gun salute boomed and the streets were noisy with celebration. Mather made his way home and was overjoyed to find his family well, a reunion tinged with sorrow because of his son Nathaniel's untimely death. The occasion was also clouded by war—not just fighting with the French and Indians, nor sparring between factions, but "a War from the Invisible World." Mather visited Nathaniel's grave in Salem, where people were "in a sad condition by reason of witchcrafts & possessed persons."[24]

In other colonies, optimism for the new order was muted. War-weary New York felt abandoned by everyone except Virginia and begged England's aid. The crisis-ridden government of Connecticut—"An house divided ag[ain]st itself"—was the same. Seventy-one years after the arrival of the *Mayflower*, New Plymouth's independence had gone, its territories ceded to Massachusetts Bay and its elders "brought exceeding low as to our civill Government." William Penn, fallen from grace, lost the right to govern Pennsylvania, although confidence among rich merchants in its assembly was undiminished, and the colony remained the migrant farmer's favorite destination, displacing New England. In Boston, Governor Phips tried to impose discipline upon a large, diverse, and wayward people.[25]

The transitions of the past thirty years had shaken New England, especially Puritans, who were steeped in virtue and history. The population now topped 75,000, of whom 5,000 were in Boston. Mercantile spirit was soaring, desire for land and trade routes insatiable. Most New Englanders, of course, were not Puritans, and lived lives of calendrical custom, rough justice, and alehouse sociability, like their cousins across the ocean. When magistrates tried to restrict their drinking, they resisted. Few were bothered about covenanted faith—the man who said "he did not care if the devil plucked the soul out of him" was perhaps typical—and the fight against Indian superstition was undermined by adherence to folk beliefs. Colonists brought with them every traditional totem and talisman: horseshoes, carved posts, salt-glazed hearth-bricks, and witch-bottles. The spiritual, verbal, and material were seamlessly joined, and no law or theology could have divided them. England's magic was America's now.[26]

The predicted punishment for this state of affairs came both slowly and suddenly. On the morning of August 4, 1692, Cotton Mather was writing a sermon—a diatribe against Satan, Indians, and France as well as against fellow Englishmen who were "perpetually aslaying to deprive us of . . . English Liberties"—when news came of an earthquake in Jamaica, where hundreds had been "pull'd into the Jaws of the Gaping and Groaning Earth." The next day Mather wrote to his uncle, John Cotton, about five witches who had been executed at Salem and the catastrophe at Port Royal, "a very Sodom for Wickedness." Apocalyptic storms in New England had also wrecked forty ships—"an Accident speaking to all our English America."[27]

Caribbean weather was the ideal metaphor for political turbulence. On St. Kitts, the revolution had triggered an Irish rebellion for King James, followed by a French bombardment preceding an invasion. The Leeward Islands were hit in April 1690 by tremors that wrecked plantations—they were "the severe Strokes of Celestial Indignation," said an eyewitness on Nevis. In July a Barbadian force liberated St. Kitts. There, the earthquake had been mild, but wartime disruption had prevented plantations from exporting sugar and had caused supply shortages. West Indian politics were based on the colonists' freedom to defend their economic fortunes. If taxes on sugar were neither curtailed nor passed on to consumers, they argued, trade would be undermined. Markets for English produce would be diminished, and the English-man's liberties abused.[28]

Still, Barbadian planters considered themselves part of the moth-erland. "By a kind of Magnetick Force England draws to it all that is good in the Plantations," wrote Edward Littleton, Barbados's agent in England. "Nothing but England can we relish or fancy: our Hearts are here, where ever our Bodies be." They needed slaves, Littleton added, but the Royal African Company's monopoly kept the price too high. Condemned to lives of degradation and toil, hundreds of slaves rebelled in Barbados; predictably, they failed, and scores of them were executed. The council then appealed to the king to provide a garrison. Jamaica followed the same avaricious, socially unhinged pattern. In January 1692, its council asked Whitehall for 3,000 Africans. English liveli-hoods, they said, depended "wholly upon the frail threat of the life of our negroes, the weakest of all freeholds."[29]

The Jamaican earthquake happened on June 7. Port Royal stood at the end of a thin spit dividing the Caribbean from the deep-water Kingston harbor. Except for merchants' wharfside houses, it was a sul-phurous jumble of multistory tenements, taverns, and warehouses. The area was infamous for drunks, thieves, and pirates—"unpleasant and uncommodious," was one visitor's opinion. Another visitor thought the people looked like fugitives or scarecrows, who "Fart and Sweat instead of Pissing"; the women were England's moral dregs, sporting nicknames like "Unconscionable Nan," "Salt-Beef Peg," and "Buttock-de-Clink Jenny." In previous days, the air had seemed thick, but the morning of the earthquake was clear. The council met at Port Royal to discuss the French occupation of the north of the island. Dr. Emman-uel Heath, the rector, read morning prayers "to keep up some shew of Religion amongst a most ungodly Debauched People," then repaired to an inn, where he met the council president, John White. Heath, already running late for a lunch appointment, reluctantly accepted an aperitif. He detested Port Royal's sinners, but he had learned to be realistic and to take pleasure in mercantile sociability.[30]

Then the ground began to move. "What's this?" Heath asked White, who replied: "It is an Earthquake, be not afraid, it will soon be over." But the shaking grew more violent until the church tower crashed down. People scattered. Heath ran to a clearing to escape falling ma-sonry, but there he "saw ye Earth open & Swallow up a Multitude

of People & ye Sea Mounting in upon us over ye Fortifications." The
initial quake lasted three minutes, during which time the earth seemed
to turn to quicksand. Buildings plunged vertically into the shifting
ground. After hurrying to his home (which was untouched), Heath
returned to the streets, where he persuaded a hysterical crowd to drop
to their knees. In sweltering heat, the earth roiling beneath them, they
prayed for nearly an hour. Heath, decrying their "haineous Provoca-
tions," was interrupted by merchants who led him to a boat. The harbor
was unrecognizable, the wharf having vanished into the sea "with all
those goodly Brick houses upon it, most . . . as fine as those in Cheapside." The two streets that lay behind the former wharf were visible but
submerged. Heath walked across roofs that were level with the water.[31]

The council applied itself vigorously "to the Restoreing of things"
and asked Whitehall for guidance and relief. There had been acts of
charity, but also looting. Returning ashore, Heath tended to the injured, helped bury the dead, and preached to the contrite. Perhaps
2,000 people had been lost, including Heath's lunch host, whose house
had sunk into the earth. The rector had been saved by John White's
aperitif. White also survived. Heath wrote to England describing the
destruction of buildings and bridges, and boats hurled into the town
by a tidal wave. He had seen people trapped in grinding crevices, their
corpses gnawed by dogs. Bodies floated in the sea.[32]

Massachusetts heard of the tragedy early in August, London a week
later. In September a broadside went on sale depicting Heath's ex-
temporaneous prayer circle. Earlier that month, tremors had alarmed
various parts of England. "We are only jogg'd that we may be awak-
en'd from our Security," a clergyman reflected. "Was there not in this
American Island a short representation of the great Day of Tryal?"
Another saw the earthquake as an indictment of infidelity and atheism.
In Boston, Edward Rawson, one of the city's oldest statesmen, received
news that his daughter Rebecca, whom he had, with much effort, persuaded to return to America from England, had been drowned just as
her ship, which had stopped off in Port Royal, had set sail.[33]

The earthquake occurred between the conviction and execution for
witchcraft of a sawyer's wife named Bridget Bishop, the first to
die in Salem's cyclone of affliction and accusation. After a four-year

The earthquake that laid waste to Port Royal on June 7, 1692, was, according to this broadside published in London, "a Dreadful Warning to the Sleepy World." The Reverend Emmanuel Heath can be seen (center right) leading a circle of people kneeling in prayer.

absence, Deodat Lawson, the son of a Puritan minister in England, returned there early in 1692, by which time three suspected witches had already been examined. Lawson had arrived in Boston at the start of King Philip's War, and in 1684 he was appointed pastor to Salem village—a scatter of farmsteads around the port of Salem that had developed a headstrong identity. Inhabitants wanted their own church and exemption from the levies for urban congregations: the first they got in 1672, the latter not until 1691.[34]

Conflict simmered between the town of Salem and the village, and within the village itself. Disagreements pivoted on traditionalist versus progressive views, principally over what kind of church to have and who should lead it. "Brother is against brother & neighbours against neighbours," it was said, "all quarrelling & smitting one another." Lawson's supporters clustered around the Putnams, his opponents around the Porters, both prosperous families who had left England in the 1640s. The faction lines, and the witch-trials they produced, followed participants' regional origins: accusers were more likely to hail from Puritan southeastern England, the accused from the West Country, Wales, and the north. The same was true at Andover, a town fifteen miles northwest of Salem, where witch accusations also emerged.[35]

Lawson finally gave up on a community consumed by what arbitrators called "settled prejudice and resolved animosity." He was replaced by Samuel Parris, who, as a Putnam nominee, proved no less controversial: he rejected the half-way covenant endorsed by Lawson, proposed moral reformation, and polarized opinion, thus increasing defaults on the rates that paid his salary. Lawson returned to Boston, where his wife and daughter died—"sent out of the World," an accused witch later confessed, "under the Malicious Operations of the Infernal Powers." This gave him a personal reason to revisit Salem.[36]

On March 19, 1692, Lawson took a room at a tavern situated between the meetinghouse and the parsonage. That evening he visited Samuel Parris, whose nine-year-old daughter and eleven-year-old niece were acting strangely. The niece, Abigail Williams, had been afflicted since January. As suspicions spread, arrest warrants had been issued, including for Parris's Indian slave Tituba. Lawson saw Abigail undergo "a grievous fit . . . sometimes makeing as if she would fly, stretching up her arms as high as she could, and crying 'Whish, Whish, Whish!'" The next day was Sunday. During Parris's sermon, Abigail cried out: "Look where Goodw[ife] C[orey] sits on the Beam suckling her Yellow bird betwixt her fingers!" Thomas Putnam's daughter Anne also saw this. On Monday at noon, by which time ten people were thought bewitched (including Putnam's wife), magistrates from the town of Salem arrived to examine Martha Corey, the first church member to be suspected. Standing in the packed meetinghouse, barn-like and dingy from its tiny windows, she denied the charges and was imprisoned.[37]

The villagers were in crisis. On March 24, Deodat Lawson preached to them that diabolical instigation was no longer the preserve of witches: "By giving way unto sinful and unruly Passions such as Envy, Malice or Hatred of our Neighbours and Brethren," he believed, everyone erred. Yet it was hard to distract minds from the effects of bewitchment. Samuel Sewall, who rode to Salem on April 11, noted in his diary that "'twas awfull to see how the afflicted persons were agitated." Cotton Mather spent the 29th praying for "the many continuing Iniquities and Calamities of the Countrey."³⁸

Prompt action was needed in Salem and Andover. Massachusetts had been in constitutional limbo since the ousting of Andros, hence the joy at Sir William Phips's arrival. The charter was published on May 16, 1692, and nine days later Phips convened a court of oyer and terminer at Salem, an emergency tribunal to investigate the disturbances, similar to the one that had been summoned in England in 1645 during another hot summer of witch-crammed jails. Powerless to legislate until after elections were held under the new charter, Phips decreed that previous laws should remain in force, provided they were consonant with English law. William Stoughton and his fellow judges—including Samuel Sewall—brushed up on legal procedure regarding witchcraft, and the trials began early in June. During pretrial hearings, English convention had been flouted: questions were leading, depositions embellished, and witnesses not bound, encouraging casual accusations. This irregularity continued in Salem's courtroom, notably when judges failed to declare conflicts of interest, and when confessing witches were spared execution, thereby perpetuating accusations; only the defiant were condemned. Little distinction was made between presumptions and proofs, and, most devastatingly, apparitions—as when the girls saw Martha Corey suckled by a bird-imp—were admitted as evidence.³⁹

How to explain the severity of the demonic attack? Increase Mather blamed popular magic, "an unhappy Omen that the Devil and Pagans will get these dark Territories into their Possession again." One witch confessed that his objective was "to set up Satans Kingdom, and then all will be well." It didn't help that four hundred Salem villagers were not church members, and thus unbaptized, or that Quakers abounded. Rather than natives being won for Christ, it seemed, the Christians had gone native. Inside these dark thoughts, demons and Indians became one. Many victims and witnesses had experienced the frontier terrors of King Philip's War—some, like Thomas Putnam, as combatants, most as children. Now King William's War resurrected that trauma. Mercy Short had survived the massacre at Salmon Falls in March 1690, but her parents had not. Along with six siblings she had been taken to Canada, where they were redeemed by Phips's expeditionary force. She then became a servant in Boston, where she suffered fits after offending a witch. The unconscious inspiration for the "Invisible Furies" in her mind may have been skulking Wabanakis. Cotton Mather, who linked events at Salem to Indian sorcery, and who elided temporal and celestial wars, wrote copiously about Mercy Short's "Intolerable Torments."[40]

Late that June, a report from New York described Salem as "infatuated"; Samuel Sewall said "perplexed." Within a month, eight women and two men had been tried, of whom six were hanged, including the "gospel witch" Rebecca Nurse. Her acquittal had raised such a "hideous outcry" that the verdict was reversed; Phips then ordered a reprieve, which he was forced to retract. The first week of August saw another six trials: four men, two women. George Burroughs, a veteran of the war in Maine and Sewall's Harvard contemporary, had been Salem village's minister in the early 1680s. Three things made him suspect: the abuse and premature death of his wife, his escape from massacres in which accusers' families had perished, and rumors that he was a Baptist. Some speculated that he ministered to devils and natives, disguised as God's servant. His case exercised Increase Mather, whose unease, especially about spectral evidence, was growing. Mather's son Cotton favored circumspection—"do not lay more stress upon pure Spectre-Testimony

The Salem witch-trials were less hysterical than posterity often assumes, but this nineteenth-century depiction of the trial of George Jacobs communicates an authentic sense of fear and pathos, as well as the magistrates' uncompromising demeanor.

than it will bear," he advised—yet also favored a purge. Like Parris, Cotton Mather painted infernal pictures in his sermons. "While You are Sleeping," he warned congregants, "the Divel is Busy, even to throw his Nets over You, and You are Hagridden by the most ugly things Imaginable."⁴¹

Fasting secretly, Cotton Mather visited incarcerated witches throughout the summer, "a very dolefull Time unto the whole Countrey." On August 5, he wrote to John Cotton that five Andover witches had named Burroughs as their ringleader, and that a vast crowd had seen him tried. Increase Mather had been present—it was the only trial he attended. Cotton Mather, though absent, deemed the evidence more damning than the testimony that had been leveled against the Lancashire witches in 1612. Burroughs's defense, during which he read from Thomas Ady's *A Candle in the Dark* (1656), a critique of the 1645 English witch-finding campaign, struck Cotton Mather as "Faltring, faulty, unconstant and contrary." Burroughs was convicted, a judgment endorsed by Mather senior, who said that no man could do what Burroughs had done, such as lifting heavy barrels, without Satan's help. A principal witness, however, had retracted her evidence. Margaret Jacobs claimed that only the magistrates' threats and her own wicked heart had made her confess and accuse Burroughs and others, including her own grandfather, George Jacobs. The retraction was not accepted; but she had now denied her guilt and so would be indicted.⁴²

The execution of George Burroughs, George Jacobs, and two others took place in Salem on the 19th, an unusually hot day. Cotton Mather was there, astride his horse. Spectators were restive at seeing their former minister climb the gallows, especially when he forgave his accusers and begged that no more innocent blood be shed. As Burroughs was turned off the ladder, Mather rode forward to steady the crowd. Owing to the heat, the bodies were hastily buried, leaving a chin and a hand protruding. Personal estates were forfeited; the sheriff had even taken clothes from George Jacobs's corpse and his wife's wedding ring.⁴³

Between September 6 and 17, 1692, there were trials almost every day—eleven in all—during which time Samuel Parris preached about war between Satan and the Lamb, lamenting the former's numerous allies. After her sentencing, Mary Easty petitioned Sir William Phips. She was resigned to death, but suggested, "By my own Innocencye I know you are in the wrong way." She was hanged a week later along with Martha Corey and six others, three days after Corey's husband

Giles had been crushed to death—in an antiquated punishment known as *peine forte et dure*—for refusing to be tried by jury. On October 3, Increase Mather completed a book about witches and gave Phips the manuscript. On the 12th, the worried governor banned further publications and wrote to William Blathwayt in Whitehall describing Salem's "strange ferment of dissatisfaction, which was increased by some hott Spiritts that blew up the flame." Phips now voiced Mather's opinion that the devil had conjured up specters of innocent people to pervert justice. Open to political attack, he lied to Blathwayt that he was in Maine during the trials, shifting blame to Chief Justice William Stoughton.[44]

The council in Boston debated how best to disperse the "Dismall Clouds of Darkness," and on the 29th, trials were suspended. By this time, Phips's letter and a copy of Cotton Mather's recently published *Wonders of the Invisible World* were halfway across the Atlantic. Worried that Phips would be sacked and the charter withdrawn, perhaps ushering in a new Andros, Mather backed the status quo. His decision also spared his book from censorship, and in London John Dunton had an edition in print by the year's end. The king approved the governor's report, and news rippled around England. In February 1693, the diarist John Evelyn noted "unheard-of stories of the universal increase of Witches in New England . . . so as to threaten the subversion of the government."[45]

By any measure, Salem had spun out of control. Witch-trials still happened in England, but they never led to executions; nor had there been a witch-hunt since the 1640s, when self-appointed witch-finders had roamed the land hunting for suspects—one of whom an elderly Salem man had seen at work in Berwick. On neither side of the Atlantic was the existence of witches doubted: the question was how to identify them. In America, the Salem trials had few precursors: between 1626 and 1705, just nineteen Virginians had been denounced as witches, ten of whom sued for defamation. From 1688 accusations in New England had begun to rise—Goody Glover was hanged that year—but most accusations fizzled out. A panic in Connecticut in 1692 involved six suspects, but only two were indicted, and one was convicted and then reprieved. At Salem, twenty had died, plus those who perished in jail, and another two hundred had been accused. These included John Alden, son of the *Mayflower* pioneer, who was imprisoned for fifteen weeks; the Reverend Samuel Willard, confessor to the possessed

Elizabeth Knapp; the wife of the Reverend John Hale, a supporter of the trials; and Ann Dolliver, the granddaughter of Francis Higginson, a stalwart of John Winthrop's fleet in the 1630s. Fingers even pointed at the governor's wife.[46]

The Puritan dream was not just over: it had become a nightmare. Extending the franchise to non-church members had first demoted the saints and then made diabolists of them. Also vulnerable were exponents of Salem's commercial worldliness. The merchant Philip English and his wife were arrested, their mansion ransacked, and their warehouses looted. Like other wealthy suspects, they escaped to New York, where the governor gave them sanctuary.[47]

Surely the devil was at work in Salem, but upon whom? Grappling with the problem, Sir William Phips had written to ministers in the English colonies seeking advice. The chaplain to the king's forces in New York replied that the suspects' guilt was indeterminable, and that apparently bewitched people were "deluded by the Devil to promote the misery of mankind." This opinion spread in Salem, where raw, conflicted villagers turned their attentions to surviving a hard winter. The trials resumed in January—fifty people by now had been detained in the icy prison—but on the attorney general's orders, Phips met convictions with reprieves, to Chief Justice Stoughton's fury. It became harder to believe that, as John Hale admitted, "so many in so small a compass of Land should so abominably leap into the Devils lap at once."[48]

On April 26, 1693, Phips instructed the sheriff to return Philip English's goods and try his wife's maidservant on a charge of making false accusations. Mary English had been incapacitated by the strain. The last trials came a fortnight later, as a letter from Queen Mary endorsing Phips's conduct was crossing the ocean. It was read by the council on July 31, by which time the witch-hunt had been over for ten weeks, and the dreadful, shameful, and protracted process of reckoning and restitution had begun.[49]

EPILOGUE

New Worlds

THANKFUL SMEAD HAD ENGLAND in her blood, but her heart belonged to the American frontier. She was descended from the Stoughtons of Essex, who had emigrated in 1632; her father's cousin was the Salem judge William Stoughton. One of nine children, Smead had been born in 1677 at Deerfield, in New England's extreme northwest, soon after its devastation in King Philip's War. Her oldest brother died at the Bloody Brook massacre. When she was four months old, Indians attacked again, dragging colonists from houses they had barely had time to rebuild. She married John Hawks Jr., the son of a carpenter who had been wounded in the fighting, and between 1696 and 1701 she had four children. In their home stood an intricately carved dowry chest, probably made by her father-in-law, a centerpiece of many colonial homes.[1]

After twenty years of peace, King William's War (from 1702, Queen Anne's War) had put Deerfield back on the front lines. In 1704, the Hawks family and their neighbors—269 of them—were protected by a garrison of twenty soldiers, but it was no match for the three-hundred-strong Franco-Indian army that arrived before dawn on February 29. Creeping across the snow, and seeing the English guards asleep, native scouts climbed the ten-foot palisade, helped by deep drifts. Inside they opened the north gate and signaled to raiders, who were lying low nearby. Shouts and bangs and flashes sent people scrambling from their beds, some of whom made it to the south gate or hid in cellars or under washtubs. By evening 56 lay dead, including John and Thankful Hawks, their children, and most of their relatives; of their immediate family members, only Thankful's brother Samuel and John Hawks Sr. survived. Over 100 others had vanished into the wilderness.[2]

A decorated Hadley chest made of oak and pine that once belonged to Thankful
Smead, born and raised in Deerfield, Massachusetts. It bears her initials, "T.S."

English colonists who endured such trials over three generations
developed a "split consciousness." Familiar with native ways, they were,
as ever, drawn to Indians from curiosity, commerce, and an urge to
save them. In 1693 William Stoughton and his fellow commissioners
in Boston still hoped "the Gospell may Spread it Self over all the Dark
American World." To this end, Samuel Sewall believed there should be
limits to English expansion. "It will be a vain Attempt for us to offer
Heaven to them if they take up prejudices against us," he said in 1700,
"as if we did grudge them a Living upon their own Earth." Many colonists agreed, but couldn't help themselves. Robert Beverley, a grasping
Virginian planter, admitted in 1705 that Englishmen had stolen the
Indians' land, felicity, and innocence and "introduce'd Drunkenness
and Luxury . . . which have multiply'd their Wants, and put them upon
desiring a thousand things they never dreamt of before." The European
gaze passed through different lenses, casting Indians as children or
devils or animals. The perpetrators of a massacre in Carolina in 1711
were, said the lieutenant governor of Virginia, "a People more like Wild

beasts than Men." A century after the first ships had arrived in Jamestown, a simple truth had emerged about American frontiers: settlers
wanted land and had to remove the Indians to get it.[3]

America was where English people learned about other worlds,
about the country they had left behind (seen with fresh and wistful
eyes), and about themselves, their capabilities, and their shortcomings.
The frontier was a mirror full of distorted images that obscured the
original. Traits loathed in Indians were what colonists most feared and
resisted in themselves. "Indianization" was the common complaint.
Ironically, given the comparisons between natives and beasts, Carolina reverted to something like a Hobbesian state of nature. Whites
had degenerated into savage hunters, thought an eighteenth-century
writer, governed by the wild beyond "the power of example and check
of shame." Robert Beverley's Virginia was seen by some "as ye best,
[by] others as ye worst Country in the world": it had attracted so many,
despite its reputation as a dead end where peasants ate corn porridge in
shingle houses. Beverley championed the land in which he considered
himself a white native. "I am an Indian," said Beverley, in admiration
of simple ethnic habits, and free from "the Curse of Labour." His
conceit was literally true, too. Eunice Williams, the daughter of Deerfield's minister, was seven years old when she was seized in the 1704
raid and taken to live with Catholic Mohawks in Canada. She was
renamed "Waongote," meaning "one who is planted like an ash tree,"
and within a decade had been completely assimilated, resisting all attempts at redemption.[4]

Historians prefer "zones of exchange" or "middle grounds" to divisive frontiers, but survivors of the Deerfield massacre saw things differently. They appreciated exchanges between natives and colonizers;
yet with harder hearts came feelings of separation and difference, especially from people leading urbane, comfortable lives in Boston or
London. The men and women of the frontier were combatants bonded
by fire, their experience and mentality impossible for outsiders to comprehend. Some tried to explain. The Reverend John Williams, Eunice's
father, was also taken prisoner in the Deerfield raid of 1704, after a desperate stand-off when his pistol misfired. After three years, he made it
home and wrote a book. If, with heaven's permission, he said, the devil
had used witches to chastise Salem, at Deerfield his instruments were
Indians and French papists. Unlike in shamed Salem, however, there
was nobility in captives' suffering, however just God's punishment.

Williams could not have imagined that his daughter would marry a Mohawk, or that when she returned to New England in 1741 she would have forgotten how to speak English.[5]

Even if the pride of men like John Williams was sometimes cloying, their adventures were awe-inspiring. They did seem special. The story of John Gyles of Pemaquid, who was captured by Indians in 1689 and wrenched from his family, is another example. In June 1698, now aged nineteen, he returned to Boston, where a boy boarded his sloop and quizzed him about Canada. "At length," recalled Gyles, "[he] gave me to understand that he was my little brother," who had made it to the fort just before John and their elder brother were captured and their father killed. Gyles was overwhelmed. But it got better: not only had his two little sisters survived, but the elder brother was waiting at the harbor. Their mother had died some years before, but against all odds, the five children were reunited. Gyles published his *Memoirs of Odd Adventures, Strange Deliverances* in 1736. The book was part of a burgeoning literature that conferred hallowed distinction upon veterans of the frontier.[6]

The Deerfield residents, like Jamestown's pioneers in 1607, knew what it felt like to be alone, exposed, and threatened from all sides. All the colonies were frontiers, however, and all posed adventurous challenges to selfhood. No one expressed these challenges better than Cotton Mather, who wrapped his generation in a comfort blanket of history and destiny. John Higginson's preface to Mather's *Magnalia Christi Americana* (1702) spoke of bequeathing sacred memories to the colonists who had been "born in the Country and may call New-England their Native Land." They were not American in the modern sense, but not quite English, either. Mather decried "creolian degeneracy"—the corruption of English culture—and bemoaned a world where breached walls let in demons, especially the "Shamefully Paganizing Villages in our Borders." It was still said, though, that the devil wanted New England more than anywhere else in English America. Long before anyone had heard of Eunice Williams, Mather described frontier folk, people who were descended not from idolatrous heathens but from Christians (albeit *Anglicans*); now, he noted, they "have almost forgotten even their Mother Tongue in their Vassalage among our own Wild Barbarians." Too many, he preached in 1696, had exchanged their ancestors' courage for "the Indian Vices of Lying, and Idleness and Sorcery, and a notorious want of all Family-Discipline."[7]

The heroes, by contrast, no longer belonged to England. In 1710, Cotton Mather wrote from "remote America" to Sir Basil Dixwell, the great-nephew of the regicide John Dixwell, in England. The letter attributed to Sir Basil's ancestor, a signatory to Charles I's death warrant, "a Genius elevated above the common level of the countrey where he had his Birth and Breeding." He was "*our* Dixwell," enthused Mather, echoing his eulogy for John Eliot, "ours in regard of his dying with us." Yet self-deprecation leavened chauvinism. When Mather referred to himself in such letters as "an American," the implication was creolization, not incipient nationhood. Like Robert Beverley, he meant that he was no better than an Indian.[8]

After 1692, Cotton Mather's sermons spoke of Sodom, but not Salem. He spoke of demons and lost souls, but few witches; the *Magnalia* mentioned the tragedy, yet only to distance Mather from it. His credibility and authority had suffered, like that of his father, Increase, who lived another thirty years haunted by the trials. Cotton's son, who was also named Increase, was born without a rectum and died, which Cotton blamed on a witch frightening his pregnant wife; but this kind of talk concealed guilt. For all his caution, Cotton Mather had deferred to the judges, and twenty people had died. Until his death in 1728, he dreamed of putting New England's Puritanism on the Protestant map, overcoming his American inferiority complex, and becoming as cultivated and confident as the men he admired in the Royal Society. It never happened. Asked in 1696 to list the sins for which Massachusetts might need atonement, he included "the late inexplicable storms from the Invisible World . . . whereby we were led unto errors and great hardships were brought upon innocent persons." The following year, he suggested anonymously that Salem "might have puzzled the Wisdom of the wisest Men on Earth." He was still troubled long after 1700, urging that reparations be made and reputations restored, and holding private vigils to contemplate events, and perhaps to beg forgiveness.[9]

Thomas Brattle, a Boston mathematician cited by Isaac Newton, *was* among the wisest men on earth. Yet the only thing that puzzled him about Salem was why no one had exploded it as nonsense. In July 1692, the first mass execution came, two days after an eclipse of the moon. Both events attracted Brattle's attention, though not because of any occult significance. In subsequent weeks, Brattle corresponded with the astronomer royal John Flamsteed about lunar matters and also visited the accused witches in prison. They were, he thought, "deluded, imposed upon, and under the influence of some evill spirit," and, as such, unfit to give evidence against anyone, themselves included. "What will be the issue of these troubles, God only knows," he wrote. "I am afraid that ages will not wear off that reproach and those stains which these things will leave behind them upon our land."[10]

Brattle was also a merchant, and he was a friend to both Anglicans and dissenters; there were many like him. Robert Calef, a Baptist cloth trader, shared Brattle's expansive outlook. Calef sent Cotton Mather appalled letters, which went unanswered until 1695. Even then, all Calef got were four self-justifying pages from Mather's writings. This answer led Calef to blame Mather directly for the colony's "dismal Convulsions." A fortnight later, church elders, including the Mathers, met in Salem village to discuss ongoing "unhappy differences." They agreed that Samuel Parris had taken "sundry unwarrantable and uncomfortable steps," albeit at a time of confusion. Parris was forced out in 1696. Calef published a book in London in 1700, followed by John Hale's *Modest Inquiry into the Nature of Witchcraft*. Hale, Calef archly observed, "had been very forward in these Prosecutions" until "it came so near himself"—namely, when his wife was accused of being a witch.[11]

In November 1697, Samuel Sewall spent an evening with Hale discussing witchcraft. Earlier that year, Sewall had publicly apologized for the trials (and, allegedly, began wearing a hair shirt), but he now feared that Hale might "go into the other extream" and deny witchcraft's reality. Yet the bitterness of the tragedy left little room for intellectual refinements: the persecuting spirit was already in full reverse. Shortly before Sewall began trying to atone for his sins, the jurors had apologized, and Parris's replacement at Salem had begun the delicate work of listening and mediating and healing. A Boston judge told the minister of Medfield that he hoped "no Body will [again] suffer as the Poor Innocents at Salem did in life or Limb."[12]

Massachusetts, in 1711, agreed to compensate families of the executed and incarcerated. Within a couple of years the courts were flooded with victims' petitions. Pardons were issued, attainders lifted, and spectral evidence invalidated. As a non-convict who had fled, Philip English fought to get compensation, only succeeding in 1718. Several of the dead were not exonerated because no one applied on their behalf; their names were finally cleared in 2001. Deodat Lawson returned to England and again justified his position. Within a decade, he was broke, and was writing letters to friends in America begging for help.[13]

The history of New England, it has been said, could be written as if Salem had never happened. Perhaps, but its importance lies not in how it affected church or state, despite dire local consequences, but in what it revealed about the wider changes taking place in Massachusetts. Boston's Brattle Street Church was founded in 1698 not upon scriptural literalism, the "New England way," or a covenant, but upon nature, reason, and inclusiveness. Membership did not hinge on conversion, and children were baptized freely. It was a poke in the eye for the Mathers, and a rebellion against three generations of American congregationalism. The world was changing. The following year, Mary Cushman, the last living *Mayflower* passenger, died, and with her went a physical link with the original godly vision. The myth of perfection gave way to the practical politics that had bedeviled it, leaving a religion neither pure nor exceptional but cobbled together from spares from England.[14]

Consolation lay in the nostalgic glorification epitomized by Cotton Mather's *Magnalia Christi Americana*. The contrasting styles of Mather and Calef, one bombastic, the other coolly analytical, represent the transition from Puritan to Yankee, from rule by divine right of magistrates to representative government, and from faith in a smuggled company charter to something like a workable constitution. After Andros's fall, differences between his enemies reemerged, especially over taxes and the prosecution of the war. Men, especially those in the younger generation, became more vocal in local politics, ending old habits of deference to Puritan oligarchs. Ties between church and state became looser, with the future trajectory of the former more spiritual, the latter more secular. Salem was the showdown between the Puritans' theatrical sense of cosmic dread and the requirement to prove it in specific cases. Their failure to do so only hastened the decline of the religious culture they had battled so hard to defend.[15]

Eighteenth-century English America drew closer to England economically and nurtured a middle-class ethos united in imperial Protestant pride and deferential in clothes, furniture, and books. "Puritan" writing became more belletristic, under the influence of journals like the *Spectator* and *Guardian*, and Boston printers aped the London press. Now there were reasons besides religion for "the Little Daughter of New

England in America," as John Higginson had put it, to "bow down herself to her Mother England." In 1699, the capital of Virginia was moved
from Jamestown to the more salubrious Middle Plantation, where, as in
Philadelphia, a town, Williamsburg, was laid out on a grid. In the same
year, the Reverend Hugh Jones described Maryland to an Oxford don
as a pristine world of forests that were dwindling under the planter's
axe and being replaced with industry, order, and reason. Towns were
compact, coherent, and organized, with public buildings of brick. Government conformed to English law, except "where ye lawes of England
doe not so aptly provide for some Circumstances under w[hi]ch our way
of living hath put"—an old proviso that, Whitehall knew, concealed a
multitude of sins. There were good Anglican churches, Jones could report, and congregations were strong. The few remaining Indians worked
for the English, but refused to "Imbrace our way of living or worshipp."
A vision of English provincial society shimmered off his letter.[16]

Settled colonists had a distinctive identity that was defined by the
world they inhabited—its land and community, laws and customs. They
did not see themselves as deracinated Englishmen. And yet their culture was derivative: it was Old World fantasy cut with New World
reality. America became more like England other ways, too. Over three
generations, an expanding population on the eastern seaboard had reduced the size of the landholdings there, which meant that many farmers were no better off than their equivalents across the Atlantic.[17]

Philadelphia, Williamsburg, and Annapolis were not all of English
America, and in most regions civility was absent. "Anglicization" competed with "creolization." A visit to Maryland by Thomas Bray, an
Anglican clergyman, in 1699 marked the start of the Society for Promoting Christian Knowledge. Bray appreciated Calvinism, Quakerism,
and even Catholicism in America: at least these faiths were Christian.
This was a very European wilderness—not a native paradise, but its
mutation. Bray raised funds for libraries, but more Englishmen poked
fun. "Bishops, Bailiffs and Bastards," opined the journalist Ned Ward,
"were the three Terrible Persecutions which chiefly drove our unhappy
Brethren to seek their Fortunes in our Forreign Colonies." Boston's
grandeur was amazing, he said, considering it had been built by tinkers
and peddlers. The women were handsome, but the men adopted "such
Puritanical postures that you would think they were always Praying
to them selves, or running melancholy Mad about some Mistery in

the *Revelations*." Piety masked profanity: New Englanders drank rum, smoked to excess, and were "as Subtile as Serpents." And they were obsessed with witches until they "Hang'd the best People in the Country," Ward scoffed. Ward never went to New England, but he did visit the Caribbean, where the white population plummeted from the 1690s, and about which he wrote a satire. Jamaica was, he concluded, "the Dunghill of the Universe." Since the earthquake, Port Royal's finest streets had been no better than "the Fag-end of [London's] Kent-street where the Broom-men Live." English America was only as good as its emigrants. Youthful Quakers arriving from Huntingdonshire in 1699 were awed by the stately beauty of Philadelphia, but "doe often take Extravagant Courses," it was noted at home, "spending th[ei]r money & Debauching themselves."[18]

Devotion to English culture in America extended to politics. A seam of royalism, accompanied by a hazy notion of who the monarch was, ran through the society. But inside lay a vein of something more dangerous: fierce devotion to representative institutions and a rhetoric of liberty drawn from Albion's constitutionalism and proclivity for local self-determination. It was the basis of a shared colonial culture. Devolutionary signs, evident in Virginia and Bermuda by 1620, were intensified by the Glorious Revolution, marking an ambition waxing in America as it waned in England. Colonists were loyal to sovereign law, but they preferred the customs of freeborn Englishmen. Among Thomas Brattle's charges against Salem was that the judges had stolen liberty, "evermore accounted the great priviledge of an Englishman." An early eighteenth-century lieutenant governor of New Hampshire, John Usher, "gott himself universally hated" by infringing colonists' "Just & antient rights."[19]

Without either official respect for these feelings or independent legislative control, especially over taxation, assemblies would always feel insecure and could never reproduce England in America as their instincts instructed. Conflict between the executive and legislative branches of government, an English hatchet from 1642 that had been buried in 1689, would persist in America, encouraged by England's assumption that acquiescence meant consent, and exacerbated to the point of revolution by the rapacity of the military-fiscal state. It was almost inevitable that a language of liberty created in England would one day be used against it.[20]

America's destiny, then, was shaped by an English political paradox. The motherland's predicament in the seventeenth century was that successive monarchs had been required to govern an increasingly large and intricate country. Negotiating between interests, balancing power between center and periphery, and containing dissent and disorder would have tested even a dynasty of unlimited energy and skill. The flawed Stuarts—and a Lord Protector, as much blinded by providential destiny as divine right had blinded kings—found it impossible. From the 1620s, through the years of the Interregnum and into the Whig-Tory battles of the Restoration era, the nation's future lay between a more authoritarian state—a repressive Leviathan of endless taxation—and the growth of devolved political bodies, self-guided and fiscally self-sufficient. Naturally, the American colonies inclined toward the latter, and from 1660 so did England as its country gentry shared in, and so limited, Charles II's power. Yet this was also a time of advancing imperial control and central management of taxes to fund a military and naval presence abroad, and the wars that were both cause and effect of this presence. As a model, England's monarchical republic, comprising many local and regional commonwealths, was not well suited to imperialism, and its extension and replication in America meant certain conflict with the crown.[21]

Writing to the governor of Barbados in 1700 to encourage trade with Pennsylvania, William Penn defined his service as an obligation "to nourish & preserve so very great an empire as is that of the Crown of England in America." As an engine of military and commercial might, the empire was indeed becoming great, an achievement driven by monarchs in London, migrants in America, and merchants in between. By the time Penn was writing, the population of English America was 250,000—91,000 in New England alone—compared to 15,000 in New France. The Deerfield massacre happened because of expansionist urges that aggravated France and made Indian neutrality impossible. Direct metropolitan control had never seemed more desirable or necessary. England realized that charters, whether private or proprietary, were obstructive, so by 1776 only Connecticut, Rhode Island, Pennsylvania, and Maryland had not become royal provinces. Yet one legacy of English America's private and piecemeal foundation was that colonies did not fit the dominion model well; nor did extensive intercolonial trade and coordinated militias help. In 1653, the Puritan Edward Johnson had boasted of "a Nation . . . borne in a day" with the arrival of the

This panorama of Bridgetown, Barbados, from 1695 exudes English mercantile vitality and self-confidence in the Caribbean, and only twenty years after the port and its warehouses were devastated by fire and hurricane. Slavery and sugar had made this possible.

Winthrop fleet. The statement was premature but prophetic. European America possessed huge demographic strength—in 1700 a population of 300,000, two-fifths of New English descent—and therefore tremendous economic and political vitality.[22]

The tragedy of 1704 made Deerfield special in American history. For decades it rippled through survivors' descendants, like other stories of suffering and courage that passed into folk legend and national myth. There are relics. Indians hacked at John Sheldon's front door, then fired guns through the hole, killing Sheldon's wife. The house was demolished in 1848, but the door resides in the Memorial Hall Museum in Deerfield. No less evocative is the richly decorated three-drawer pine-and-oak chest on loan to the Huntington American Art Gallery in California. Though exceptionally rare and valuable, its true historical importance lies in the initials "T.S." carved into a recessed panel, which identify its first owner: Thankful Smead. It is hard to stand in its presence and not imagine the horrific events unfolding around it in February 1704.[23]

Museums and galleries have many fragments of that world: a Massachusetts governor's blood-stained buff-coat; a christening shirt that belonged to William Bradford; a high-crowned hat supposedly worn on the *Mayflower*. There are mesmerising portraits, some of which were painted on visits to London: John Winthrop hanging at the American Antiquarian Society; Edward Rawson and his tragic daughter Rebecca, side-by-side at the New England Historic Genealogical Society; and in a corridor of the Massachusetts Historical Society, Anne Pollard, one hundred years old, venerable and impassive, both unrecognizable as the girl who led her elders ashore at Boston and yet the very same. Preeminent among sites memorialized for visitors is Plymouth Rock, a place idealized by Charles Upham in 1846 as "the point from which the ever-advancing and ever-expanding wave of Anglo-Saxon liberty and light began to flow over America." Each year the site attracts thousands of pilgrims, many of whom are disappointed; a journalist likened the rock itself to a fossilized potato. *Mayflower II*, an oceangoing copy, is staffed by reenactors and makes fewer demands on the imagination. On Cole's Hill, overlooking Plymouth Harbor, a plaque informs visitors that Thanksgiving Day reminds Indians "of the genocide of millions of their people, the theft of their lands and the relentless assault on their culture."[24]

Colonial cemeteries, most poignantly at Salem, are dotted with crisply inscribed slate gravestones. The house of Jonathan Corwin, a Salem judge, still stands, though it is heavily restored (and has been relocated). The Mather family tomb, high on a hill overlooking Boston harbor, was lidless in 2010, awaiting repair. One of the most evocative ways to touch things these people touched is through the letters they wrote and the books they read. The manuscript of William Bradford's "Of Plimoth Plantation" disappeared during the Revolutionary War and surfaced in 1856 in Fulham Palace Library, London. It was returned to Boston and today is treasured at the Massachusetts State House, before which, facing the common, stands a statue of Mary Dyer, the memorial her fellow Quakers had wanted there. An English pear tree that John Endecott planted in Salem flourished until 1964, when it was vandalized, but has since regrown. One can also hear echoes. On secluded Tangier Island in Virginia, people still speak seventeenth-century dialect.[25]

Relics come out of the ground, too. John Hull's pine-tree shillings fetch good money, although it is his silverware that commands astronomical prices: in 2001, a wine cup sold for $775,750. By 2006

Anne Pollard, painted in 1721 at the age of one hundred. As a girl, she was re-putedly the first colonist to set foot on the banks of the Charles River in 1630. She remembered a wilderness "very uneven, abounding in small hollows and swamps, and covered with blueberry and other bushes."

archaeologists had found more than 700,000 artifacts at Jamestown, a third of them from the period 1607–1610, and including everything from tobacco pipes to armor—although just twelve years earlier it was still assumed that the fort was lost underwater. At the southeastern bulwark, a brass signet ring was unearthed bearing the crest of William Strachey, who had spent a year at Jamestown after leaving Bermuda. In 2002, a swimmer at Roanoke stepped on a sixteenth-century axe-head, yet the colony's precise location remains unknown. Where Roa-noke's settlers went is a greater mystery, although the picture of a fort revealed in 2012, under a patch on John White's map, offers a clue. An archaeologist discovered the site of Sagadahoc in 2008, and went on to find glass buttons from Ralegh Gilbert's clothes. Thirteen acres of Port Royal lie beneath Kingston Harbour at depths of between a few inches and forty feet. Bones thought to belong to George Jacobs, who was be-trayed by his own granddaughter, were reinterred in 1992 beside Salem's memorial to Rebecca Nurse.[26]

English churches remember American adventurers, too. A marble slab at Boxley in Kent records how Haute Wyatt arrived in Virginia in 1621 with his brother, Sir Francis, the first royal governor. He came home four years later to become vicar of Boxley. How different Jamestown, where Wyatt had been the minister, was from this sleepy parish tucked beneath the North Downs. The embattled Virginia Company president, Edward Maria Wingfield, rests in peace at St. Andrew's, Kimbolton, near Huntingdon. Strange to think he had once been at England's first permanent colony, and, unlike so many, had made it back. Sir William Phips, son of Maine, died in London in 1695 after being summoned by the Privy Council for violating the Navigation Acts and thrashing a customs collector. He was buried at the church of St. Mary Woolnoth in the City, where the mystic Anne Hutchinson had been married in 1612. The *Mayflower* was probably broken up at Rotherhithe in 1624, although, by tradition, the "Mayflower Barn" at Jordans in Buckinghamshire contains its timbers. A trip on a pleasure boat from Plymouth's "Mayflower Steps" offers a chance to watch England shrink beyond the wake.[27]

England has many early American relics. What Martin Frobisher thought was gold—actually a mineral called hornblende—ended up at a royal manor house in Dartford, Kent, and was built into a wall; it is still there near the railway station. The ossified stump of a mulberry tree that John Rolfe may have brought from Virginia is set in cement on a Norfolk industrial estate. English record offices contain everything from reports of early native encounters in Virginia and Phips's letters about Salem (in the National Archives) to mere traces in parish registers, such as that of St. John de Sepulchre in Norwich, which says that on May 16, 1650, a youth named John Swadocke "took his Jorney to new England," or the 1647 entry for Margaret Chexill's baptism at Brenchley in Kent, noting the absence of her father, "he being th[e]n in new England." Who knows if Chexill ever returned, or if his family went to America. New World souvenirs include Wahunsonacock's mantle, passed from John Tradescant's collection to the Ashmolean Museum in Oxford, where it is displayed, though now as a wall hanging rather than a cloak. Metacom's gorget and belts, sent to Charles II, may have once been in Windsor Castle, although the Royal Collection cannot trace them.[28]

In 1624 Sir William Alexander believed that a man might make something of himself in America, predicting that his family would "claime unto him as the Author of their Nobilitie there." He was right.

Presidential hopefuls have long made capital of their English ancestry. In the 1630s, two sisters, Elizabeth and Margaret Reade, left a
village in Essex for New England, where Elizabeth married into the
Winthrops, Margaret into the Lakes. Some 370 years later, their descendants George W. Bush (on the Winthrop side) and John Kerry (on
the Lake side) were slugging it out at the hustings. Family heirlooms
help to focus memories: the sword used by John Endecott, it is said, to
cut the cross from the flag of St. George; a pair of Pocahontas's mus-
sel-shell earrings, passed down through generations of Rolfes; and a
cameo brooch bearing her likeness, thought to be a gift she received in
London. A replica was presented to Queen Elizabeth II by the chief of
the Pamunkey nation when the queen visited Jamestown in 2007, the
colony's four-hundredth anniversary. Thirty-five million US citizens
can claim ancestry to the *Mayflower* passengers of 1620, and links to the
victims of Salem (less often the accusers) are similarly cherished. There
is an almost mystical purity about the bloodline. Mark Twain was more
sensible and more skeptical, claiming descent not only from witches but
also from Quakers, Indians, and ruffians, all of whom, he told a Philadelphia audience in 1881, made him "an infinitely shaded and exquisite
Mongrel."[29]

Twain's targets were, of course, the Puritans: conceited, censorious,
and cruel, the persecutors of Hester Prynne in Nathaniel Hawthorne's
novel *The Scarlet Letter.* Their partial rehabilitation has been accompanied by a widening of the context of their lives, to include not just
Quakers, Indians, and ruffians, but also an array of settlers from around
the British Isles and Europe. Alexis de Tocqueville's vision of "the
whole destiny of America contained in the first Puritan who landed
on those shores" was a clouded one—clouded, in part, by Puritan elites
themselves, those who, despite being a fraction even of the minority
who migrated to New England, spoke the loudest in English America. Before historical exceptionalism, there was godly exceptionalism.
When Puritans fell from grace in the nineteenth century, the elevation
of the Pilgrim Fathers was assured: in them Abraham Lincoln saw the
upright forebears of a victorious Union. The providentialist, exceptionalist streak remains palpable in political rhetoric and academic discourse, although Atlantic history has helped to make Puritans variables
in a diverse process of change, rather than the colonial *non plus ultra.*[30]

Historians have also remade seventeenth-century America as part of
England, what one expatriated Englishman has called "the repatriation

of early American history." Atlantic history might even be misleading here, a distraction from the very Englishness of the story. This is why another scholar, this time an American, places England and America "in one analytic time frame, as separate histories that are deeply intertwined." Perspectives have shifted. No longer do colonies seem like wilderness worlds cut off from Europe, but outliers of a sprawling empire, distant yet reflexively alert.[31]

This book has argued that, rather than embracing new identities, English migrants to America strove to preserve Englishness, and when they did change, the causes were not exclusively American. Colonies presented opportunities, but did not break the mold quite as exceptionalist thinking supposes. Disputes and social problems were exported from a country in transformation, as were the hierarchy and discipline essential to achieve prosperity. This explains why adventurers—many of whom stayed at home—were less interested in building a new world than in nostalgically re-creating one they saw vanishing to the detriment of the state. Landowners wanted feudal estates, farmers smallholdings, Puritans the early church, Catholics pre-Reformation freedoms; everyone wanted a return to charity and "good fellowship." Many "new" conditions of American life, furthermore, existed in England before the migrants left or affected them later on—a tense religious pluralism (including Puritan disintegration), the defensive pride of chartered bodies, the self-hood of literacy, boundless ingenuity, migratory habits, not to mention debates about liberty and tyranny, freedom and bondage, sovereignty and authority. Even the language of American self-determination belongs to English common law and custom, and possibilities for political refashioning to the ambiguities of the "ancient constitution." The independent, even quasi-republican, spirit of colonial townships evolved from the self-reliance of England's urban elites and from amateur office-holding in its rural parishes.

The ways of the wilderness, then, were first those of the motherland, even if unique environmental conditions—landscape, climate, and a native presence—meant that the practical application of those ways put cultural distance between the English in America and their compatriots at home. A connected irony is that the colonists' struggle not to change was in itself a measure of difference: no Englishman in England had to try to be what he already was. The identity gap widened after 1660, with growing imperial intrusiveness and colonial self-confidence. By defending Protestantism and resisting absolutism, the Glorious

Revolution of 1689 encouraged expressions of cultural affinity between cousins across the sea. And yet for America, preserving colonial habits of assembly government would, in the next century, light the fuse for revolution.

Since 1776, the mentality of the first migrants has been up for grabs. Roger Williams of Rhode Island, who believed the "foundation of civil power lies in the people," is often pressed into service—his theocratic prejudices shorn to make a man ahead of his time. Thomas Jefferson recycled Williams's phrases for the Declaration of Independence. But Williams was no democrat, nor was the US Constitution any more democratic than the detested *ancien régime* against which it measured itself so favorably. John Winthrop would have agreed with George Washington that a party system encouraged the "unjust dominion" of "unprincipled men." Winthrop himself was called "an early freedom man" by Ronald Reagan in a televised address, and his sturdy migrants were hailed by John F. Kennedy in 1961 and Barack Obama in 2006.[32]

Yet these English men and women were, for the most part, deeply conservative, a people hankering for older, purer forms of hierarchy, discipline, and intolerance. And their new world was meant to be a haven from the restless innovation that so characterized life in seventeenth-century England. The true idea of a "city upon a hill"—a humble biblical exhortation, but full of doubt (and once applied to the unprepossessing English town of Colchester)—will never be reinstated, because the myth is too potent. What does survive of Williams and Winthrop and thousands of other migrants, and which must never be ignored or denigrated, is their extraordinary courage. This, above all else, resounds across the centuries and should inspire us. The best way to remember the Pilgrim Fathers, it has been said, is to look at Plymouth Rock, then turn around to gaze at the vastness of the ocean whence they came.[33]

ACKNOWLEDGMENTS

"In most of mankind," thought one seventeenth-century writer, "gratitude is merely a secret hope for greater favours." Let me declare myself in the minority. To the many who have helped me write this book I say: thank you, and you've done more than enough.

I would like to thank the School of History at the University of East Anglia for financing two trips to US archives, and the Faculty of Arts and Humanities for giving me leave in 2010–2011. The support of John Charmley and Cathie Carmichael was invaluable. The British Academy and Scouloudi Foundation also provided funds, and I was fortunate to be elected by the British Association for American Studies to an Eccles Fellowship at the British Library and to a Mayers Fellowship by the Huntington Library in San Marino, California. The Huntington is every scholar's dream of a haven in which to read and think, and I was made very welcome there. I am especially grateful to Mary Robertson, Olga Tsapina, and Jessica Smith.

On the East Coast, I'm indebted to the staffs at the Beinecke Library, the Connecticut State Library, the Virginia Historical Society, the Massachusetts Historical Society, the Massachusetts State Archives, the New England Historic Genealogical Society, the New York Public Library, and the American Antiquarian Society. At the Boston Public Library, Kim Reynolds was endlessly obliging. Mike McBride showed me Henry Whitfield's house in Guilford, Connecticut, and Danny Schmidt and his fellow archaeologists at Jamestown were fascinating guides to the world they are unearthing. In England, I received patient assistance at the British Library, the Bodleian Library, and the National Archives. Thanks go to Sara Rodger at Arundel Castle for supplying documents belonging to the duke of Norfolk; to Christopher Hunwick and the duke of Northumberland at Alnwick Castle; to David Wykes at Dr Williams's Library; and above all to Rupert Baker at the Royal Society and to Wendy Hawke at the London Metropolitan Archives—models of courteous assistance. Generous archivists in county record offices are too numerous to name. Many others advised me, including Kathryn Jones, who confirmed that Metacom's regalia are not in the Royal Collection.

This book began as a course at the University of East Anglia, where students have supplied me with many references and ideas, as have Simon Sandall, Beth Southard, Paul Warde, and Andy Wood. Jess Sharkey has been a true friend. I owe a great debt to Tad Baker and Frank Bremer, who commented on a first draft, and to others who read some or all of that draft: Catherine Armstrong, David Cressy, Mary Beth Norton, Sarah Pearsall, Roger Thompson, and Mike Zuckerman. I also benefited from reading a draft of Tad's *A Storm of Witchcraft*. Mary Beth exposed as a fake a letter that was framing my preface. John Demos and Keith Wrightson inspired me. I also thank Peter Thompson and John Walter, readers for Oxford University Press, and anonymous others, likewise OUP Delegates Chris Wickham and Paul Slack.

Lucky is the writer with two editors, especially ones as understanding and enthusiastic as Lara Heimert at Basic Books and Luciana O'Flaherty at OUP. Roger Labrie and Kathy Streckfus deserve thanks for whipping the manuscript into shape, as do Sandra Beris and Leah Stecher, who oversaw everything else in the final stages of production. Kathy is a peerless copyeditor. Thanks, too, go to everyone who helped with the illustrations, above all Stephen Tabor at the Huntington Library, Marilyn Meeker at ProQuest, and the book's designer, Jack Lenzo. My agent, Peter Robinson, has guided and encouraged me, and Mark A. Bradley dispensed wisdom and reassurance at a critical stage.

Friends and family have shown unflagging interest, above all Sheena Peirse, who has lived with this book, and its unreasonable author, longer than it was fair to expect. The unstinting support of Roger and Rosina Peirse makes life possible. My children—Kate, Tom, and Lily—have brought me immeasurable joy: Kate has asked many questions, including why I bother doing what I do, and even had a stab at the book jacket.

To my parents, Audrey and Ed Gaskill, I owe absolutely everything, and to them this book is dedicated with love.

ABBREVIATIONS

AAS	American Antiquarian Society, Worcester, Massachusetts
AHR	*American Historical Review*
Beinecke	Beinecke Library, Yale University
BL	British Library, London
Bodl.	Bodleian Library, Oxford University
BPL	Boston Public Library
CKS	Centre for Kentish Studies, Maidstone, United Kingdom
CO	Colonial Office
CSL	Connecticut State Library, Hartford
CSPC	W. Noel Sainsbury et al., eds., *Calendar of State Papers, Colonial, America and West Indies, 1574–1739*, 45 vols. (London, 1860–1969)
CUL	Cambridge University Library
CWF	Colonial Williamsburg Foundation, Virginia
DHC	Dorset History Centre, Dorchester, United Kingdom
DWL	Dr. Williams's Library, London
EIHC	*Essex Institute Historical Collections*
HEHL	Henry E. Huntington Library, San Marino, California
HMC	Historical Manuscripts Commission, United Kingdom
HUA	Harvard University Archives
JAH	*Journal of American History*
JBS	*Journal of British Studies*
LMA	London Metropolitan Archives
LPL	Lambeth Palace Library, London
Magd.	Magdalene College, Old Library, Cambridge University
MHS	Massachusetts Historical Society, Boston
MSA	Massachusetts State Archives, Dorchester, Massachusetts
NEHGR	*New England Historical and Genealogical Register*
NEHGS	New England Historic Genealogical Society
NEQ	*New England Quarterly*
NYPL	New York Public Library
ODNB	*Oxford Dictionary of National Biography*

Pepys   Pepys Library, Magdalene College, Cambridge University
Procs   *Proceedings*
RHS   Royal Historical Society, United Kingdom
RO   Record Office
RS   Royal Society, London
SP   State Papers
TNA   The National Archives, Kew, United Kingdom
VHS   Virginia Historical Society, Richmond, Virginia
VMHB   *Virginia Magazine of History and Biography*
WMQ   *William and Mary Quarterly*

NOTES

PREFACE

1. Only 21,000—under 6 percent—went to New England, more to the middle colonies (23,500), Chesapeake (116,000), and the West Indies (190,000): Nicholas Canny, "English migration into and across the Atlantic during the seventeenth and eighteenth centuries," in *idem*, ed., *Europeans on the Move: Studies on European Migration, 1500–1800* (Oxford, 1994), 64. Half migrated in 1630–1670: David Souden, "English indentured servants and the transatlantic colonial economy," in Shuka Marks and Peter Richardson, eds., *International Labour Migration: Historical Perspectives* (Hounslow, UK, 1984), 33. England's net migration loss, 1580–1780, including to Europe, was 1.3 million: James Horn and Philip D. Morgan, "Settlers and slaves: European and African migrations to early modern British America," in Elizabeth Mancke and Carole Shammas, eds., *The Creation of the British Atlantic World* (Baltimore, 2005), 23.

2. William Shakespeare, *The Taming of the Shrew*, Act 1, Sc. 2.

3. Catherine Armstrong, "The bookseller and the pedlar: the spread of knowledge of the New World in early modern England, 1580–1640," in John Hinks and Catherine Armstrong, eds., *Printing Places: Locations of Book Production and Distribution Since 1500* (New Castle, DE, 2005), 15–29; David Read, *New World, Known World: Shaping Knowledge in Early American Writing* (Columbia, MO, 2005), intro.

4. Bernard Bailyn, *The Peopling of British North America: An Introduction* (New York, 1986), 26 (quotation); Michael Zuckerman, "Identity in British America: unease in Eden," in Nicholas Canny and Anthony Pagden, eds., *Colonial Identity in the Atlantic World, 1500–1800* (Princeton, NJ, 1987), 115–159; David Grayson Allen, *In English Ways: The Movement of Societies . . . to Massachusetts Bay in the Seventeenth Century* (Chapel Hill, NC, 1981); Gloria L. Main, *Peoples of a Spacious Land: Families and Cultures in Colonial New England* (Cambridge, MA, 2001); David Hackett Fischer, *Albion's Seed: Four British Folkways in America* (Oxford, 1989); Francis J. Bremer, "The county of Massachusetts: the governance of John Winthrop's Suffolk and the shaping of the Massachusetts Bay Colony," in Francis J. Bremer and Lynn Botelho, eds., *The World of John Winthrop: Essays on England and New England, 1588–1649* (Charlottesville, VA, 2005), 187–236; John Canup, *Out of the Wilderness: The Emergence of an American Identity* (Middletown, CT, 1990), chs. 1–5. On the difficult semantics, see James H. Merrell, "Coming to terms with early America," *WMQ*, 69 (2012), 536–540.

5. Michael Zuckerman, "The fabrication of identity in early America," *WMQ*, 34 (1977), 183–214. For classic "exceptionalism," see Daniel J. Boorstin, *The Americans: The Colonial Experience* (New York, 1958). Exponents of "Americanization" include Sacvan Bercovitch, *The Puritan Origins of the American Self* (New Haven, CT, 1975), and Patricia Caldwell, *The Puritan Conversion Narrative: The Beginnings of American Expression* (Cambridge, UK, 1983). For critiques, see Norman Pettit, "God's Englishman in New England: his enduring ties to the motherland," *Procs of the MHS*, 101 (1989), 56–70; Daniel W. Howe, *American History in an Atlantic Context* (Oxford, 1993), 3–6, 21–22; Deborah L. Madsen, *American*

Exceptionalism (Edinburgh, 1998), ch. 1; and for partial restitution, Jack P. Greene, *The Intellectual Construction of America: Exceptionalism and Identity from 1492 to 1800* (Chapel Hill, NC, 1993), ch. 3; David S. Lovejoy, *Religious Enthusiasm in the New World: Heresy to Revolution* (Cambridge, MA, 1985), 2, 6–8, 20–21.

6. Richard Eburne, *A Plaine Path-Way to Plantations* (London, 1624), B2v; J. M. Bumsted, "'Things in the womb of time': ideas of American independence, 1633 to 1763," *WMQ*, 31 (1974), 533–564.

7. Christopher Tomlins, *Freedom Bound: Law, Labor and Civic Identity in Colonizing English America, 1580–1865* (Cambridge, UK, 2010); Glenn Burgess, *The Politics of the Ancient Constitution: An Introduction to English Political Thought, 1603–1642* (Basingstoke, UK, 1992), ch. 2; Mark Goldie, "The unacknowledged republic: officeholding in early modern England," in Tim Harris, ed., *The Politics of the Excluded, c. 1500–1850* (New York, 2001), 153–194; Patrick Collinson, *Elizabethan Essays* (London, 1994), ch. 2; Phil Withington, *The Politics of Commonwealth: Citizens and Freemen in Early Modern England* (Cambridge, UK, 2005), chs. 3–5. The "new" American history demands selectivity: David Reynolds, *America, Empire of Liberty: A New History* (London, 2009), xviii–xix. The colonial problem is that "unlike the American Revolution or the Civil War, there is no single tale to be told": Edward Countryman, "Postscript: large questions in a very large place," in Daniel Vickers, ed., *A Companion to Colonial America* (Oxford, 2003), 530. On exported "monarchical republicanism," see Richard D. Brown, *The Strength of a People: The Idea of an Informed Citizenry in America, 1650–1870* (Chapel Hill, NC, 1996), ch. 1.

8. Ethan H. Shagan, *The Rule of Moderation: Violence, Religion and the Politics of Restraint in Early Modern England* (Cambridge, UK, 2011), ch. 7.

9. Alan Taylor, *Colonial America: A Very Short Introduction* (Oxford, 2013), 6–7 (quotation); James Horn, *Adapting to a New World: English Society in the Seventeenth-Century Chesapeake* (Chapel Hill, NC, 1994), viii; Francis J. Bremer and Lynn Botelho, "Introduction: Atlantic history and the world of John Winthrop," in *idem*, eds., *World of John Winthrop*, 3–5, 10–11, 15–16; Joyce E. Chaplin, "Expansion and exceptionalism in early American history," *JAH*, 89 (2003), 1434–1435, 1438–1439; Hugh Kearney, "The problem of perspective in the history of colonial America," in K. R. Andrews, N. P. Canny, and P. E. H. Hair, eds., *The Westward Enterprise: English Activities in Ireland, the Atlantic, and America, 1480–1650* (Liverpool, 1978), 290–302; Michael Zuckerman, "Regionalism," in Vickers, ed., *Companion*, 311–333, esp. 310. See also Peter Laslett's call for English society to be studied "not only *in situ*, but . . . 3,000 miles across the sea": *The World We Have Lost* (London, 1965), 253. For a "developmental" colonial model embracing the Caribbean, see Jack P. Greene, *Pursuits of Happiness: The Social Development of Early Modern British Colonies and the Formation of American Culture* (Chapel Hill, NC, 1988), ch. 7. For American history reclaimed as English, see David Cressy, *Coming Over: Migration and Communication Between England and New England in the Seventeenth Century* (Cambridge, UK, 1987); Susan Dwyer Amussen, *Caribbean Exchanges: Slavery and the Transformation of English Society, 1640–1700* (Chapel Hill, NC, 2007).

10. Antoinette Sutto, "Lord Baltimore, the Society of Jesus, and Caroline absolutism in Maryland, 1630–1645," *JBS*, 48 (2009), 634; Nicholas Canny, "Writing Atlantic history; or, reconfiguring the history of colonial British America," *JAH*, 86 (2000), 1093–1114; David Armitage and Michael J. Braddick, eds., *The British Atlantic World, 1500–1800* (Basingstoke, UK, 2002); Bernard Bailyn, *Atlantic History: Concept and Contours* (Cambridge, MA, 2005); Peter A. Coclanis, "Atlantic world or Atlantic/world?" *WMQ*, 63 (2006), 725–742; Alison Games, "Atlantic history: definitions, challenges and opportunities," *AHR*, 111 (2006), 741–757; Nancy L. Rhoden, "Introduction: rewriting the English Atlantic in the context of Atlantic history," in *idem*, ed., *English Atlantics Revisited* (Montreal, 2007), xiii–xxviii; Jack P. Greene and Philip D. Morgan, eds., *Atlantic History: A Critical Appraisal* (Oxford, 2009); Jack P. Greene and J. R. Pole, "Reconstructing British American colonial history: an introduction," in *idem*, eds., *Colonial British America: Essays in the New History*

of the Early Modern Era (Baltimore, 1984), 1–17; Timothy H. Breen, "An empire of goods: the anglicization of colonial America, 1690–1776," *JBS*, 25 (1986), 468–470. For examples of this transatlantic reintegration: Stephen Foster, *The Long Argument: English Puritanism and the Shaping of New England Culture, 1570–1700* (Chapel Hill, NC, 1991); Carla Gardina Pestana, *The English Atlantic in an Age of Revolution, 1640–1661* (Cambridge, MA, 2004). Colonial diversity and unity formed "one side of a transoceanic system": D. W. Meinig, *The Shaping of America . . .*, vol. 1, *Atlantic America, 1492–1800* (New Haven, CT, 1986), 254.

11. John Locke, *Two Treatises of Government* (London, 1690), 268. An unreconstructed version of the epic story is Perry Miller, *The New England Mind: The Seventeenth Century* (Cambridge, MA, 1939). Critics include Darrett B. Rutman and Anita H. Rutman, *Small Worlds, Large Questions: Explorations in Early American Social History, 1600–1850* (Charlottesville, VA, 1994), ch. 4; Kearney, "Problem of perspective," 300–302.

12. J. H. Elliott, *Empires of the Atlantic World: Britain and Spain in America, 1492–1830* (New Haven, CT, 2006), xiii; Karl S. Bottigheimer, *English Money and Irish Land: The "Adventurers" in the Cromwellian Settlement of Ireland* (Oxford, 1971); Francis Jennings, *The Invasion of America: Indians, Colonialism and the Cant of Conquest* (Chapel Hill, NC, 1975). For an intellectual history shaped by emotion, see Andrew Delbanco, *The Puritan Ordeal* (Cambridge, MA, 1989). According to Marcus Lee Hansen, "What the son wishes to forget, the grandson wishes to remember," quoted in Peter Kivisto and Dag Blanck, eds., *American Immigrants and Their Generations* (Urbana, IL, 1990), 195.

PROLOGUE: WORLDS COLLIDE

1. Rory Rapple, "Sir Humphrey Gilbert," *ODNB*; David Beers Quinn, ed., *The Voyages and Colonising Enterprises of Sir Humphrey Gilbert*, 2 vols. (London, 1940). For the gory theatrics, see Thomas Churchyard, *A Generall Rehearsall of Warres* (London, 1579), Q3v.

2. Richard Hakluyt, *The Principall Navigations, Voiages and Discoveries of the English Nation* (London, 1589), 695; Carole Shammas, "English commercial development and American colonization, 1560–1620," in Andrews et al., eds., *Westward Enterprise*, 158–159.

3. John W. Shirley, *Thomas Harriot: A Biography* (Oxford, 1983); Peter C. Mancall, *Hakluyt's Promise: An Elizabethan's Obsession for an English America* (New Haven, CT, 2007), 126; William Camden, quoted in ibid., 103.

4. [George Peckham], *A True Reporte of the Late Discoveries and Possession . . . of the New-found Landes* (London, 1583), quotation B3v–B4; Peter C. Mancall, ed., *Envisioning America: English Plans for the Colonization of North America, 1580–1640* (Boston, 1995), 62–70; James McDermott, "Sir George Peckham," *ODNB*.

5. Kim Sloan, *A New World: England's First View of America* (London, 2007), 168.

6. Essex RO, D/DRh Z1; BL, Sloane MS 1447, 2v; David Beers Quinn, ed., *The Roanoke Voyages, 1584–1590* (London, 1955); Karen Ordahl Kupperman, *Roanoke: The Abandoned Colony*, 2nd ed. (Lanham, MD, 2007); Michael Foss, *Undreamed Shores: England's Wasted Empire in America* (London, 1974), ch. 6.

7. Jill Lepore, ed., *Encounters in the New World: A History in Documents* (New York, 2000), 107; William M. Hamlin, "Imagined apotheoses: Drake, Harriot and Ralegh in the Americas," *Journal of the History of Ideas*, 57 (1996), 405–428. Cf. Caliban asking Trinculo and Stephano, "Hast thou not dropped from heaven?": William Shakespeare, *The Tempest*, Act 2, Sc. 2.

8. For criticism of White: Joyce E. Chaplin, "Roanoke 'counterfeited according to the truth,'" in Sloan, *New World*, 51–63.

9. Peter Charles Hoffer, *Sensory Worlds in Early America* (Baltimore, 2003), 37–41; Francisco J. Borge, *A New World for a New Nation: The Promotion of America in Early Modern England* (Bern, 2007); Paul Hulton, *America, 1585: The Complete Drawings of John White* (Chapel Hill, NC, 1984); Anthony Grafton, *New Worlds, Ancient Texts: The Power of Tradition and the Shock of Discovery* (Cambridge, MA, 1992); Joyce E. Chaplin, *Subject Matter: Technology, the Body and Science on the Anglo-American Frontier, 1500–1676* (Cambridge,

MA, 2001); Susan Scott Parrish, *American Curiosity: Cultures of Natural History in the Co-lonial British Atlantic World* (Chapel Hill, NC, 2006). See also Sloan, *New World*. On mir-roring: Karen Ordahl Kupperman, *Facing Off in Early America* (Ithaca, NY, 2000), 39–43.

10. Nicholas Canny, "The ideology of English colonization: from Ireland to America," *WMQ*, 30 (1973), 575–598; Andrew Hadfield, "Irish colonies and the Americas," in Robert Appelbaum and John Wood Sweet, eds., *Envisioning an English Empire: Jamestown and the Making of the North Atlantic World* (Philadelphia, 2005), 172–191; John Patrick Montaño, *The Roots of English Colonialism in Ireland* (Cambridge, UK, 2011).

11. Warren M. Billings, "Sir Ralph Lane," *ODNB*.

12. James Horn, *A Kingdom Strange: The Brief and Tragic History of the Lost Colony of Ro-anoke* (New York, 2010), 95–100.

13. Thomas Harriot, *A Briefe and True Report of the New Found Land of Virginia* (Lon-don, 1588), E1v–E4v, quotation E4.

14. Ibid., A3–A4v, C3.

15. Inscribed stones, allegedly Eleanor Dare's diary, turned out to be fakes: David Stick, *Roanoke Island: The Beginnings of English America* (Chapel Hill, NC, 1983), 234–235, 237–239.

16. Mancall, *Hakluyt's Promise*, 195–207.

17. Thomas Harriot, *A Briefe and True Report of the New Found Land of Virginia* (Frank-furt, 1590), E1–F2; Theodor de Bry, quoted in Sloan, *New World*, 153. For Celtic compari-sons: Kupperman, *Indians and English*, 59–62.

CHAPTER 1: BRAVE HEROIC MINDS

1. William H. Tabor, "Maine's Popham colony," *Athena Review*, 3 (2002), 84–89; Rich-ard L. Pflederer, "Before New England: the Popham colony," *History Today*, 55 (2005), 10–17; Charles Edward Banks, "New documents relating to the Popham expedition, 1607," *Procs of the AAS*, 39 (1929), 307–334; David B. Quinn and Alison M. Quinn, eds., *The En-glish New England Voyages, 1602–1608* (London, 1983), ch. 12.

2. James Phinney Baxter, ed., *Sir Ferdinando Gorges and His Province of Maine*, 3 vols. (Boston, 1890), 3:158.

3. James Rosier, *A True Relation of the Most Prosperous Voyage . . . in the Discovery of the Land of Virginia* (London, 1605), B1–B2v.

4. LPL, MS 806.2, pt. 14, ff. 1–4v, 9–9v; Jeffrey P. Brain, "The John Hunt map of the first English colony in New England," *Northeast Historical Archaeology*, 37 (2008), 71.

5. Baxter, ed., *Gorges*, 3:154–164; Ferdinando Gorges, "A briefe narration of the original undertakings for the advancement of plantations in America," *Collections of the Maine His-torical Society*, 2 (1847), 22.

6. Christopher Carleill, *A Breef and Sommarie Discourse upon the Entended Voyage to the Hethermoste Partes of America* (London, 1583), B1. George Waymouth may have seeded Sagadahoc's failure: Neal Salisbury, *Manitou and Providence: Indians, Europeans and the Making of New England, 1500–1643* (New York, 1982), 90–98.

7. Gorges, "Briefe narration," 22–23.

8. William Alexander, *An Encouragement to Colonies* (London, 1624), 30; Ferdinando Gorges, *America Painted to the Life* (London, 1658), 19, 21–22; Beinecke, Osborn fb62, p. 25.

9. Keith Wrightson, *English Society, 1580–1680*, 2nd ed. (London, 2002); J. G. A. Po-cock, *The Ancient Constitution and the Feudal Law: A Study of English Historical Thought in the Seventeenth Century*, 2nd ed. (Cambridge, UK, 1987); Colin Kidd, *British Identities Before Nationalism: Ethnicity and Nationhood in the Atlantic World, 1600–1800* (Cambridge, UK, 1999), ch. 4.

10. Richard Hakluyt, *Divers Voyages Touching the Discoverie of America* (London, 1582), A3–A3v; Hakluyt's "Discourse," quoted in Edward C. Gray, ed., *Colonial America: A His-tory in Documents* (Oxford, 2003), 29; Carleill, *Breef and Sommarie Discourse*, B1v.

11. Cheshire RO, ZAB/1, ff. 191–191v; C. H. Firth, ed., *An American Garland, Being a Collection of Ballads Relating to America, 1563–1759* (Oxford, 1915), 7–8.

12. David Beers Quinn, *England and the Discovery of America, 1481–1620* (London, 1974), 307; Mancall, *Hakluyt's Promise*, 182–189.

13. BL, Add. MS 38823, ff. 1–5v, quotation 6v; Anthony Pagden, *Lords of All the World: Ideologies of Empire in Spain, Britain and France, c. 1500–c. 1800* (New Haven, CT, 1995), ch. 3; Ken MacMillan, *Sovereignty and Possession in the English New World: The Legal Foundations of Empire, 1576–1640* (Cambridge, UK, 2006); David Armitage, *The Ideological Origins of the British Empire* (Cambridge, UK, 2000), chs. 2–3, 5; Andrew Fitzmaurice, *Humanism and America: An Intellectual History of English Colonization, 1500–1625* (Cambridge, UK, 2003). On "civil conversation": Phillip H. Round, *By Nature and By Custom Cursed: Transatlantic Civil Discourse and New England Cultural Production, 1620–1660* (Hanover, NH, 1999).

14. John Brereton, *A Briefe and True Relation of the Discoverie of the North Part of Virginia* (London, 1602), 5–7, 19–21. For Hakluyt's influence on Gosnold, see Quinn, *England and the Discovery of America*, ch. 15.

15. BL, Harleian MS 1583, ff. 60–61v; Tim Harris, *Rebellion: Britain's First Stuart Kings* (Oxford, 2014), 63–65.

16. David Ibbetson, "Sir John Popham," *ODNB*; HMC, *Salisbury*, 18:84; Theodore K. Rabb, *Jacobean Gentleman: Sir Edwin Sandys, 1561–1629* (Princeton, NJ, 1998); Edwin Sandys, quoted in Conrad Russell, "James VI and I and rule over two kingdoms: an English view," *Historical Research*, 76 (2003), 163. See also Paul Warde, "The idea of improvement, c. 1520–1700," in Richard W. Hoyle, ed., *Custom, Improvement and the Landscape in Early Modern Britain* (Farnham, UK, 2011), 127–148; Jess Edwards, "Between 'plain wilderness' and 'goodly corn fields': representing land use in early Virginia," in Appelbaum and Sweet, eds., *Envisioning*, 217–235.

17. Elizabeth Mancke, "Chartered enterprises and the evolution of the British Atlantic world," in Mancke and Shammas, eds., *Creation*, 237–262.

18. Merrill Jensen, ed., *American Colonial Documents to 1776* (London, 1955), 61–62; W. Keith Kavenagh, ed., *Foundations of Colonial America: A Documentary History*, 3 vols. (New York, 1973), 1:5–10, 3:1673; Warren M. Billings, ed., *The Old Dominion in the Seventeenth Century: A Documentary History of Virginia, 1606–1700*, 2nd ed. (Chapel Hill, NC, 2007), 3–4.

19. Philip L. Barbour, ed., *The Jamestown Voyages Under the First Charter, 1606–1609*, 2 vols. (Cambridge, UK, 1969), 1:49–54, quotation 54.

20. West Devon RO, 1/132, f. 154; HMC, *Salisbury*, 18:133–134; Michael Drayton, *Poemes Lyrick and Pastorall* (London, n.d. [1606]), ode 11.

21. David R. Ransome, "Christopher Newport," *ODNB*; Benjamin Woolley, *Savage Kingdom: Virginia and the Founding of English America* (London, 2007), 24–25; Mark Nicholls, ed., "George Percy's 'Trewe Relacyon': a primary source for the Jamestown settlement," *VMHB*, 113 (2005), 214–215; John Smith, *The Generall Historie of Virginia, New-England and the Summer Isles* (London, 1624), 41–44.

22. Smith, *Generall Historie*, 22; Billings, ed., *Old Dominion*, 5; James Horn, *A Land as God Made It: Jamestown and the Birth of America* (New York, 2005), ch. 2.

23. John Smith, *Advertisements for the Unexperienced Planters of New-England* (London, 1631), 32–33.

24. TNA, CO 1/1, ff. 53–55.

25. Ibid., ff. 55–56v; Lepore, ed., *Encounters*, 107; Hoffer, *Sensory Worlds*, 47–48; Brereton, *Briefe and True Relation*, 10–11.

26. Sloan, *A New World*, 166–169; Alden T. Vaughan, *Transatlantic Encounters: American Indians in Britain, 1500–1776* (Cambridge, UK, 2006), 5–9, 58–63, 65; David Beers Quinn, ed., *The New American World: A Documentary History of North America to 1612*, 5 vols. (London, 1979), 5:166.

27. John Nicholl, *An Houre Glasse of Indian Newes* (London, 1607), D2v.

28. Harriot, *Briefe and True Report* (1588), E1–E2v; Samuel Purchas, *Purchas His Pilgrimage* (London, 1617), 613.

29. Jocelyn R. Wingfield, *Virginia's True Founder: Edward Maria Wingfield and His Times, 1560–1631*, 2nd ed. (North Charleston, SC, 2007), chs. 2–18; Samuel Purchas, *Hakluytus Posthumus*, 5 vols. (London, 1625–1626), 4:1753; Billings, ed., *Old Dominion*, 6.

30. TNA, CO 1/1, ff. 51–52; William M. Kelso, *Jamestown: The Buried Truth* (Charlottesville, VA, 2006), ch. 2; Patricia Seed, *Ceremonies of Possession in Europe's Conquest of the New World, 1492–1640* (Cambridge, UK, 1995), ch. 1.

31. Billings, ed., *Old Dominion*, 30–31; LPL, MS 250, pt. 23, f. 384.

32. BL, Harleian MS 7007, f. 139; Barbour, ed., *Jamestown Voyages*, 1:107–108; Alnwick Castle, Northumberland Papers, vol. 7, ff. 263–263v.

33. Robert Johnson, *The New Life of Virginia* (London, 1612), B3v–B4; Alnwick Castle, Northumberland Papers, vol. 7, f. 268; HMC, *Salisbury*, 14:417; TNA, SP 14/28; J. R. Smith, *Pilgrims and Adventurers: Essex (England) and the Making of the United States of America* (Chelmsford, UK, 1992), 5.

34. Smith, *Generall Historie*, 21; Barbour, ed., *Jamestown Voyages*, 1:158–163.

35. HEHL, EL 1683; Johnson, *New Life*, C1v; Martin H. Quitt, "Trade and acculturation at Jamestown, 1607–1609: the limits of understanding," *WMQ*, 52 (1995), 246–248.

36. John Smith, *A True Relation of Such Occurences and Accidents of Noate as Hapned in Virginia* (London, 1608), E4v; Barbour, ed., *Jamestown Voyages*, 1:5–7.

37. LPL, MS 250, pt. 23, ff. 382–392; Horn, *Land*, 58; Johnson, *New Life*, C2.

38. *For the Plantation in Virginia, or Nova Britannia* (London, 1609); Alexander Brown, ed., *The Genesis of the United States*, 2 vols. (London, 1890), 1:248–249; Robert Johnson, *Nova Britannia, Offring Most Excellent Fruites by Planting in Virginia* (London, 1609), B1–E1v; Robert Gray, *A Good Speed to Virginia* (London, 1609), A3v–D1v.

39. Brown, ed., *Genesis*, 1:252–254, 257–258, 277–282, 291–293, 302–310; HEHL, HM 960; West Devon RO, 1/359/54.

40. William Symonds, *Virginia, A Sermon Preached at White-Chappel* (London, 1609), A3v, 19, 21.

41. George Benson, *A Sermon Preached at Paules Crosse* (London, 1609); Daniel Price, *Saules Prohibition Staide* (London, 1609), quoted in Brown, ed., *Genesis*, 1:314.

CHAPTER 2: EARTH'S ONLY PARADISE

1. Natalie Zacek, "Sir Thomas Gates," *ODNB*.

2. BL, Harleian MS 7009, f. 58v.

3. Ibid., f. 60v; Horn, *Land*, 102–104; L. H. Roper, *The English Empire in America, 1602–1658: Beyond Jamestown* (London, 2009), ch. 2; Edmund S. Morgan, "The labor problem at Jamestown, 1607–18," *AHR*, 76 (1971), 608–611; John Gilbert McCurdy, "Gentlemen and soldiers: competing visions of manhood in early Jamestown," in Thomas A. Foster, ed., *New Men: Manliness in Early America* (New York, 2011), 9–30.

4. Nicholls, ed., "Percy's 'Trewe Relacyon,'" 246.

5. Smith, *Generall Historie*, 48; *idem, True Relation*, C1v.

6. Horn, *Land*, 68; Philip L. Barbour, ed., *The Complete Works of Captain John Smith*, 3 vols. (Chapel Hill, NC, 1986), 1:lx; Susan Castillo and Ivy Schweitzer, eds., *The Literatures of Colonial America: An Anthology* (Oxford, 2001), 198; Smith, *True Relation*, E3v. On the mixture of history and legend, see Robert S. Tilton, *Pocahontas: The Evolution of an American Narrative* (Cambridge, UK, 1994), esp. ch. 1.

7. Smith, *Generall Historie*, 30–31, 34–36, 38, 40.

8. Nicholls, ed., "Percy's 'Trewe Relacyon,'" 215–216, 228–230, 248–249; *CSPC, 1574–1660*, 10; Magd., FP 532, f. 3; Jane O'Brien, "'Proof' Jamestown settlers turned to cannibalism," BBC News, www.bbc.co.uk/news/world-us-canada-22362831/.

9. Smith, *Generall Historie*, 105–106; Nicholls, ed., "Percy's 'Trewe Relacyon,'" 249; *A True Declaration of the Estate of the Colonie of Virginia* (London, 1610), 38–39; Rachel B. Herrman, "The 'tragicall historie': cannibalism and abundance in colonial Jamestown," *WMQ*, 68 (2011), 47–74; Catherine Armstrong, "'Boiled and stewed with roots and herbs':

everyday tales of cannibalism in early modern Virginia," in Angela McShane and Garthine Walker, eds., *The Extraordinary and the Everyday in Early Modern England* (Basingstoke, UK, 2010), 161–176.

10. William Crashaw, *A Sermon Preached in London Before the Right Honorable the Lord Lawarre* (London, 1610), B4–C4v, D3v–D4, G1v, L1v.

11. *True Declaration . . . of Virginia*, 42–43, 49–50; BL, Harleian MS 7009, f. 59v.

12. Horn, *Land*, 187; Peter Heylyn, *Microcosmus, or a Little Description of the Great World* (Oxford, 1621), 403.

13. Firth, ed., *American Garland*, 17–20; Hakluyt, *Divers Voyages*, A4v; Robert C. Johnson, "The lotteries of the Virginia Company, 1612–1621," *VMHB*, 74 (1966), 259–292.

14. Purchas, *Pilgrimage*, 602; Alexander, *Encouragement*, 37, 40; Thomas Morton, *New English Canaan* (London, 1637), 18–19; William Strachey, *"The Historie of Travell into Virginia Britania" (1612)*, ed. Louis B. Wright and Virginia Freund (London, 1953), 53–55 (quotation); Johnson, *New Life*, B1–B1v; CUL, Dd.3.85, no. 4, f. 1v; Alexander Whitaker, *Good Newes from Virginia* (London, 1613), 24–25.

15. Bodl., Ashmole MS 1147, ff. 219–221; Johnson, *New Life*, D1; Magd., FP 30, ff. 1–2.

16. Magd., FP 40, f. 1; Whitaker, *Good Newes*, 24–26; Purchas, *Pilgrimage*, 637–639; George Abbot, *A Briefe Description of the Whole World* (London, 1656), 294. See also Edward L. Bond, "Source of knowledge, source of power: the supernatural world of English Virginia, 1607–1624," *VMHB*, 108 (2000), 105–138.

17. TNA, SP 89/3, ff. 160–174; BL, Stowe MS 173, ff. 222–223v; *CSPC, Addenda, 1574–1676*, 45–46, 48; Barbour, ed., *Jamestown Voyages*, 1:116–117, 158; Brain, "John Hunt map," 69–71, 73; Brown, ed., *Genesis*, 1:248–249; HMC, *Salisbury*, 20:58; 21:87, 288; BL, Add. MS 72268, ff. 44, 66; Add. MS 72248, ff. 137v, 139v–140.

18. Basil Morgan, "Sir Thomas Dale," *ODNB*; Bodl., Ashmole MS 1147, ff. 207–210; Johnson, *New Life*, C3v–C4; CUL, Dd.3.85, no. 4, ff. 4v–5.

19. Crashaw, *Sermon*, E1–E2, F4–G1v; Purchas, *Hakluytus Posthumus*, 4:1704 (after Harriot, *Briefe and True Report* [1588], A4v); Johnson, *New Life*, D4v, E2v–E3v, F1; Whitaker, *Good Newes*, 6–8, 18–21, 29–32, quotation 6; *True Declaration . . . of Virginia*, 61.

20. Purchas, *Hakluytus Posthumus*, 4:1753; Karen Ordahl Kupperman, "Fear of hot climates in the Anglo-American colonial experience," *WMQ*, 41 (1984), 213–240; *True Declaration . . . of Virginia*, 32; Purchas, *Hakluytus Posthumus*, 4:1704; *A Publication by the Counsell of Virginea Touching the Plantation There* (London, 1610); *A True and Sincere Declaration of the Purpose and Ends of the Plantation Begun in Virginia* (London, 1610), title-page. Alexander Whitaker thought English epidemics worse: *Good Newes*, 39–40.

21. HEHL, HM 961, HA 4117; East Kent Archives, Sa/ZB2/64–65, 66, 68; East Suffolk RO, C/2/2/2/1, p. 550.

22. HEHL, HA Americana Box 1 (1–2), HA 8510; HMC, *Hastings*, 1:374.

23. *The Relation of the Right Honourable the Lord De-La-Warr* (London, 1611), B1v–B2, B3v–C1; Johnson, *New Life*, C3; TNA, CO 1/1, ff. 94–95v; Jack P. Greene, ed., *Great Britain and the American Colonies, 1606–1763* (Columbia, SC, 1970), 11–20; Kavenagh, ed., *Foundations*, 3:1673.

24. Hyder E. Rollins, ed., *The Pepys Ballads*, 8 vols. (Cambridge, MA, 1929–1932), 1:24; Brown, ed., *Genesis*, 2:557–558, 560, 571–572.

25. John Stow, *Annales* (London, 1632), 1002; David A. Price, *Love and Hate in Jamestown: John Smith, Pocahontas and the Heart of a New Nation* (London, 2004), 146; BL, Add. MS 72268, f. 75v; Brown, ed., *Genesis*, 2:590–592.

26. W[illiam] S[ymonds], *The Proceedings of the English Colonie in Virginia* (Oxford, 1612), 77, in John Smith, *A Map of Virginia* (Oxford, 1612).

27. *True Declaration . . . of Virginia*, 21–22; S. G. Culliford, *William Strachey, 1572–1621* (Charlottesville, VA, 1965).

28. Purchas, *Hakluytus Posthumus*, 4:1734–1737.

29. Smith, *Generall Historie*, 174; Purchas, *Hakluytus Posthumus*, 4:1737–1738; Sylvester

Jourdain, *The Discovery of the Barmudas* (London, 1610), 8–10, 14; David B. Quinn, *European Approaches to North America, 1450–1640* (Aldershot, UK, 1998), ch. 9.

30. Purchas, *Hakluytus Posthumus*, iv: 1743–1745; Jourdain, *Discovery*, 17.

31. *CSPC, 1574–1660*, 9–10; Jourdain, *Discovery*, 22–23; Smith, *Generall Historie*, 176, 193; Brown, ed., *Genesis*, 2:1018–1019.

32. Firth, ed., *American Garland*, 9–16. There is controversy: Kenneth Muir, *The Sources of Shakespeare's Plays* (London, 2005), 280; Alden T. Vaughan, "William Strachey's 'True Reportory' and Shakespeare: a closer look at the evidence," *Shakespeare Quarterly*, 59 (2008), 245–273; Roger Stritmatter and Lynne Kositsky, "'O brave new world': *The Tempest* and Peter Martyr's *De Orbe Novo*," *Critical Survey*, 21, no. 2 (2009), 7–42. Ariel's song derives from a 1605 account: Kupperman, *Facing Off*, 111.

33. Whitaker, *Good Newes*, C1, 37. "America came . . . to be viewed as a place of cultural regress, for natives and immigrants alike": Greene, *Intellectual Construction*, 32. On dystopian visions: Michael D. Gordin, Helen Tilley, and Gyan Prakesh, eds., *Utopia/Dystopia: Conditions of Historical Possibility* (Princeton, NJ, 2010), 1–17.

34. Barbour, ed., *Jamestown Voyages*, 2:321–326; Strachey, *"Historie,"* xxi–xxiii; Quinn, ed., *New American World*, 5:309.

CHAPTER 3: EACH MAN SHALL HAVE HIS SHARE

1. E. K. Chambers, *The Elizabethan Stage*, 4 vols. (Oxford, 2009), 3:260–262; Norman Egbert McClure, ed., *The Letters of John Chamberlain*, 2 vols. (Philadelphia, 1939), 1:425. On imperial ideology in masques: Rebecca Ann Bach, *Colonial Transformations: The Cultural Production of the New Atlantic World, 1580–1640* (New York, 2000), ch. 4.

2. Ralph Hamor, *A True Discourse of the Present Estate of Virginia* (London, 1615), 30.

3. Ibid., 61–68, quotations 63, 64, 67.

4. Brown, ed., *Genesis*, 2:605.

5. James F. Hunnewell, ed., *Relation of Virginia by Henry Spelman* (London, 1872), 9–10, 30–43, 51, 57–58, quotations 57, 58. The boys earned distrust on both sides: J. Frederick Fausz, "Middlemen in peace and war: Virginia's earliest Indian interpreters, 1608–1632," *VMHB*, 95 (1987), 41–64.

6. Hamor, *True Discourse*, 11, 13–14, 55; Lepore, ed., *Encounters*, 115.

7. Strachey, *"Historie,"* 57; Magd., FP 40, f. 1.

8. Hamor, *True Discourse*, 37–46.

9. Billings, ed., *Old Dominion*, 209–210; Gary M. Walton and James F. Shepherd, *The Economic Rise of Early America* (Cambridge, UK, 1979), 42; James I, quoted in Horn, *Land*, 234; Harriot, *Briefe and True Report* (1588), C3–C3v; Edmund Gardiner, *The Triall of Tabacco* (London, 1610), 40, 52; James Walvin, *Fruits of Empire: Exotic Produce and British Trade, 1660–1800* (Basingstoke, UK, 1997), 76.

10. BL, Add. MS 72268, f. 79v; CKS, U269/1/Ov57; Beinecke, MS 567, f. 7.

11. Gustav Ungerer, "Mary Frith, alias Moll Cutpurse, in life and literature," *Shakespeare Studies*, 28 (2000), 42–84; J. L. Rayner and G. T. Crook, eds., *The Complete Newgate Calendar*, 5 vols. (London, 1926), 1:169–179; Edward Ditchfield, *Considerations Touching the New Contract for Tobacco* (London, 1625), 10.

12. Richard Rich, *Newes from Virginia* (London, 1610), B3; David W. Galenson, *White Servitude in Colonial America: An Economic Analysis* (Cambridge, UK, 1981).

13. John Smith, *A Description of New England* (London, 1616), 31, 35, 40; Nicholas Canny, "'To establish a common wealthe': Captain John Smith as New World colonist," *VMHB*, 96 (1988), 213–222.

14. Billings, ed., *Old Dominion*, 357; Bodl., Tanner MS 74, f. 49.

15. Brown, ed., *Genesis*, 1:440–442; Magd., FP 520; John Cordy Jeaffreson, ed., *Middlesex County Records*, 4 vols. (London, n.d.), 2:132.

16. Patrick Copland, *Virginia's God Be Thanked* (London, 1622), 31–34; *CSPC, 1574–1660*, 23; TNA, SP 14/103, f. 51; Don Jordan and Michael Walsh, *White Cargo: The Forgotten*

History of Britain's White Slaves in America (Edinburgh, 2007), ch. 8; Abbot Emerson Smith, *Colonists in Bondage: White Servitude and Convict Labor in America, 1607–1776* (Gloucester, MA, 1965), ch. 4.

17. East Kent Archives, Sa/ZB2/67; Jeaffreson, ed., *Middlesex*, 2:224.

18. Billings, ed., *Old Dominion*, 123–124; Smith, *Generall Historie*, 93–94, 124; *idem*, *Description*, 7.

19. CKS, U269/1/Ov63; Billings, ed., *Old Dominion*, 9; Magd., FP 85; Smith, *Generall Historie*, 39; Jeaffreson, ed., *Middlesex*, 2:225; Bodl., Ashmole MS 1147, ff. 220–221.

20. Roper, *English Empire*, 48.

21. Quinn, ed., *New American World*, 5:266; Smith, *Generall Historie*, 125; Hamor, *True Discourse*, A2, 19–23, 27, 32–33.

22. William Alexander, *The Mapp and Description of New-England* (London, 1630), 28; Ellen Chirelstein, "Lady Elizabeth Pope: the heraldic body," in Lucy Gent and Nigel Llewellyn, eds., *Renaissance Bodies: The Human Figure in English Culture, c.1540–1660* (London, 1990), 36–38, 41–44.

23. Susan Myra Kingsbury, ed., *The Records of the Virginia Company of London*, 4 vols. (Washington, DC, 1906–1935), 3:49–56; BL, Add. MS 39245, f. 20v; Norfolk RO, NCR Case 16a/15, f. 13v; Y/C 19/5, f. 147v; HMC, *Eleventh Report, Appendix Pt. VII*, 211; *CSPC, 1574–1660*, 17; HMC, *Fifth Report*, 559; Devon RO, ECA L&P 167.

24. *A Declaration for the Certaine Time of Drawing the Great Standing Lottery* (London, 1616); Vaughan, *Transatlantic Encounters*, 53–54; Horn, *Land*, 225–228; Smith, *Generall Historie*, 123; McClure, ed., *Letters*, 2:12.

25. Samuel Clarke, *A True and Faithful Account of the Four Chiefest Plantations of the English in America* (London, 1670), 15; Smith, *Generall Historie*, 121–123; McClure, ed., *Letters*, 2:50; Esmerelda Weatherwax, "Pocahontas in England," *New English Review*, October 2007, www.newenglishreview.org/custpage.cfm/frm/11100/sec_id/11100.

26. David R. Ransome, "Pocahontas and the mission to the Indians," *VMHB*, 99 (1991), 94; McClure, ed., *Letters*, 2:56–57, 66; Smith, *Generall Historie*, 123; Medway Archives and Local Studies Centre, P159/1/1; Magd., FP 76. Arriving in Virginia in 1635, Thomas Rolfe became a successful planter: Helen C. Rountree, *Pocahontas's People: The Powhatan Indians of Virginia Through Four Centuries* (Norman, OK, 1990), 84.

27. R. C. D. Baldwin, "Sir George Yeardley," *ODNB*; Magd., FP 93.

28. Smith, *Generall Historie*, 125; Kingsbury, ed., *Records*, 3:92; Kavanagh, ed., *Foundations*, 2:1674.

29. Magd., FP 134, 210; Cheshire RO, M/L/6/107; HMC, *Eighth Report, Pt. I*, 435; Norfolk RO, NCR Case 16a/15, ff. 17v–18, 164; CKS, U455/E21; TNA, E44/353; Smith, *Generall Historie*, 139.

30. Brown, ed., *Genesis*, 1:442; Robert Brenner, *Merchants and Revolution: Commercial Change, Political Conflict and London's Overseas Traders, 1550–1653* (Cambridge, UK, 1993), 93–99.

31. Magd., FP 106, f. 2v; John Ruston Pagan, *Anne Orthwood's Bastard: Sex and Law in Early Virginia* (Oxford, 2003), 150; *A Declaration of the State of the Colony and Affaires in Virginia* (London, 1620), 55–92; Kingsbury, ed., *Records*, 3:482–484; Billings, ed., *Old Dominion*, 10–12; Joseph H. Smith and Thomas G. Barnes, *The English Legal System: Carryover to the Colonies* (Los Angeles, 1975).

32. CKS, U269/1/Ov6, 41; Magd., FP 139; Peter Kolchin, *American Slavery, 1619–1877* (New York, 1993), ch. 1.

33. Lyon Gardiner Tyler, ed., *Narratives of Early Virginia, 1606–1625* (New York, 1907), 282–287, quotation 285.

34. NYPL, Mss. Col. 2799, SMYTH 3 (5–6, 8, 13–16, 34).

35. Ibid., SMYTH 3 (9), 13, 21–23; Edward Waterhouse, *A Declaration of the State of the Colony and Affaires in Virginia* (London, 1622), 21, 35.

CHAPTER 4: THE VAST AND FURIOUS OCEAN

1. *CSPC, 1574–1660*, 57; Charles E. Hatch Jr., *The First Seventeen Years: Virginia, 1607–1624* (Williamsburg, VA, 1957), 33–111; NYPL, Mss. Col. 2799, SMYTH 33.

2. *Declaration of . . . Virginia*, 2–5, 11–12.

3. HEHL, HA 10673; Magd., FP 158, 175, 177.

4. Smith, *Generall Historie*, 141–142; Magd., FP 247, ff. 1–2; Purchas, *Hakluytus Posthumus*, 4:1778–1779.

5. *Declaration of . . . Virginia*, 23–54; Waterhouse, *Declaration*, 6; *A Note of the Shipping, Men and Provisions Sent and Provided for Virginia* (London, 1622), 1–2.

6. Shammas, "English commercial development," 164–168, 171–174; Walton and Shepherd, *Economic Rise*, ch. 3; John Bonoeil, *Observations to Be Followed . . . to Keepe Silk-Wormes* (London, 1620), 18–19. For royal orders about tobacco and silk, see CKS, U269/1/Ov63.

7. Willie Graham et al., "Adaptation and innovation: archaeological and architectural perspectives on the seventeenth-century Chesapeake," *WMQ*, 64 (2007), 455, 465–467; Billings, ed., *Old Dominion*, 125–126, 358–360; Rutman and Rutman, *Small Worlds*, ch. 10; Hugh Amory and David D. Hall, eds., *A History of the Book in America*, vol. 1, *The Colonial Book in the Atlantic World* (Cambridge, UK, 2000), ch. 2. One farmer's estate included "1 old pillow, 1 old sheet, 1 old flock bed . . . 1 ould bible, 1 ould booke": Susie M. Ames, ed., *County Court Records of Accomack-Northampton, Virginia, 1632–1640* (Washington, DC, 1954), 112. On erstaz wine, see HMC, *Fifth Report*, 341.

8. Magd., FP 221; *CSPC, 1574–1660*, 35; CKS, U269/1/Ov10.

9. Magd., FP 93, f. 2.

10. Charles Deane, ed., *History of Plymouth Plantation by William Bradford* (Boston, 1856), 87–88. Nathaniel Philbrick, *Mayflower: A Voyage to War* (London, 2006), ch. 5, provides an evocative narrative.

11. John Cotton, *The Churches Resurrection* (London, 1642), 5–6, 13–15, 17–19.

12. A. W. Plumstead, ed., *The Wall and the Garden: Selected Massachusetts Election Sermons, 1670–1775* (Minneapolis, 1968), 25–27.

13. Edward Winslow, *Hypocrisie Unmasked* (London, 1647), 90–91; Deane, ed., *Plymouth*, 60.

14. William Bradford, *A Relation or Journall of . . . the English Plantation Setled at Plimoth in New England* (London, 1622), 1–3.

15. Greene, ed., *Great Britain*, 25–26; Kavenagh, ed., *Foundations*, 1:234; Jensen, ed., *Colonial Documents*, 167–168. Hugh Brogan is more sanguine: *The Penguin History of the USA*, 2nd ed. (London, 1999), 40–41. In 1822 the compact was celebrated as the moment a nation was born, "an event which has no parallel in the annals of the world": Terence Martin, *Parables of Possibility: The American Need for Beginnings* (New York, 1995), 34.

16. Deane, ed., *Plymouth*, 78; Bradford, *Relation*, 3–8, 21–24.

17. Bradford, *Relation*, 25, 28–30.

18. Ibid., 27–28; Philbrick, *Mayflower*, 76–77; Martha L. Finch, "'Civilized bodies' and the 'savage' environment of early New Plymouth," in Janet Moore Lindman and Michele Lise Tarter, eds., *A Centre of Wonders: The Body in Early America* (Ithaca, NY, 2001), 43–59. Colonists and investors quarreled: Ruth A. McIntyre, *Debts Hopeful and Desperate: Financing the Plymouth Colony* (Plymouth, MA, 1963).

19. Bradford, *Relation*, 15–20, 31–35.

20. Ibid., 35–46.

21. Edward Winslow, *Good Newes from New-England* (London, 1624), 28, 52–61 (quotation 52); John Smith, *New Englands Trials* (London, 1622), C1–C1v; Deane, ed., *Plymouth*, 101.

22. Robert Cushman, *A Sermon Preached at Plimmoth in New-England* (London, 1622), 3–6, 14–16; Bradford, *Relation*, 60–65.

23. Cushman, *Sermon*, A2–A2v, 8–9, 10–11; Roger Williams, *A Key into the Language*

of America, ed. John J. Teunissen and Evelyn J. Hinz (Detroit, 1973), 58; Richard Slotkin and James K. Folsom, eds., *So Dreadfull a Judgment: Puritan Responses to King Philip's War, 1676–1677* (Middletown, CT, 1978), 28; Robert Charles Anderson, *The Pilgrim Migration: Immigrants to Plymouth Colony, 1620–1633* (Boston, 2004).

24. Magd., FP 340; NYPL, Mss. Col. 2799, SMYTH 37; Catherine Armstrong, "Contesting the meaning of America: printed representations before 1630," in *idem*, Roger Fagge and Tim Lockley, eds., *America and the British Imagination* (Newcastle, UK, 2007), 8–26.

25. Magd., FP 251, 268, 293.

26. Magd., FP 280, 309, f. 1.

27. Magd., FP 255, 285, 313; Waterhouse, *Declaration*, 7–11.

28. Waterhouse, *Declaration*, 12–13, 15–16.

29. John Brinsley, *A Consolation for Our Grammar Schooles* (London, 1622), A2v–A3; Hertfordshire RO, ASA 5/4, nos. 219–221; AHH 8/1/141; AHH 5/89, ff. 18, 23; ASA 7/26, ff. 27v–28v; Kingsbury, ed., *Records*, 4:1–2; Peter Walne, "The collections for Henrico College, 1616–18," *VMHB*, 80 (1972), 259–266; CKS, U269/1/Ov41; Waterhouse, *Declaration*, 53–54; Alnwick Castle, Northumberland Papers, vol. 12, f. 113; Patrick Copland, *A Declaration . . . Towards the Building of a Free School in Virginia* (London, 1622), 1, 5–7; "Letters of Patrick Copland," *WMQ*, 9 (1929), 300.

30. Copland, *Virginia's God*, 8–10, 14–15, 24–29; Magd., FP 247, f. 1; Smith, *Generall Historie*, 139–140.

31. Waterhouse, *Declaration*, 14–17, 20–21, 35–43; Purchas, *Hakluytus Posthumus*, 4:1788–1790; Ivor Noël Hume, *Martin's Hundred* (London, 1982), ch. 13; Robert S. Tilton, "John Rolfe," *ODNB*.

32. Magd., FP 532, f. 9; FP 364, ff. 2–2v; CKS, U269/1/Ov37; Smith, *Generall Historie*, 155. Some farmers were still tracing property in 1631: CKS, U269/1/Ov15.

33. Kingsbury, ed., *Records*, 3:611–615; Waterhouse, *Declaration*, A3v, 20; Robert C. Johnson, "The Indian massacre of 1622: some correspondence of the Reverend Joseph Mead," *VMHB*, 71 (1963), 408; Shona MacLean Vance, "Patrick Copland," *ODNB*; Smith, *Generall Historie*, 157; Magd., FP 415, ff. 1–1v; FP 437, ff. 1–1v.

34. Smith, *Generall Historie*, 157; Magd., FP 532, f. 9; *Voyage of Anthony Chester to Virginia* (Leiden, 1707), 213; Kingsbury, ed., *Records*, 3:683; D. M. Loades, ed., *The Papers of George Wyatt Esquire* (London, 1968), 105–124, quotations 107, 112.

35. Alden T. Vaughan, "'Expulsion of the savages': English policy and the Virginia massacre of 1622," *WMQ*, 35 (1978), 57–84; Gary B. Nash, *Red, White, and Black: The Peoples of Early North America*, 4th ed. (Upper Saddle River, NJ, 2000), ch. 3; Waterhouse, *Declaration*, 17, 22–27; G[eorge] S[andys], *Ovid's Metamorphoses Englished* (London, 1626).

CHAPTER 5: FULL OF WILD BEASTS AND WILD MEN

1. Smith, *Generall Historie*, 157–160.

2. C. H. Firth, "The ballad history of the reign of James I," *Transactions of the RHS*, 5 (1911), 28; Robert C. Johnson, "A poem on the late massacre in Virginia by Christopher Brooke," *VMHB*, 72 (1964), 259–292; John Donne, *A Sermon upon the VIII Verse of the I Chapter of the Acts of the Apostles* (London, 1622), A3, 1–3, 44; G. E. Bentley, *The Jacobean and Caroline Stage*, 7 vols. (Oxford, 1956), 5:1396. In December 1622, Donne's sermon was sent to Bermuda's governor: Magd., FP 411.

3. Magd., FP 411; CKS, U269/1/Ov5; Smith, *Generall Historie*, 152; T. H. Breen, *Puritans and Adventurers: Change and Persistence in Early America* (New York, 1980), 123; BL, Add. MS 12496, ff. 456–457, 459–460.

4. D. R. Ransome, ed., *Sir Thomas Smith's Misgovernment of the Virginia Company by Nicholas Ferrar* (Cambridge, UK, 1990), xviii, 8, 14; TNA, SP 14/132, f. 51.

5. CKS, U269/1/Ov1; HEHL, HM 962, ff. 4–5, 8.

6. TNA, CO 1/2, ff. 113–114, 147–147v; Kingsbury, ed., *Records*, 4:41–42, 58–60; Smith, *Generall Historie*, 155–156.

7. TNA, CO 1/2, f. 171; Kingsbury, ed., *Records*, 4:93–94; *CSPC, 1574–1660*, 39–40; Magd., FP 497; CKS, U269/1/Ov26.

8. TNA, CO 1/2, f. 147; Kingsbury, ed., *Records*, 4:164, 166.

9. TNA, CO 1/3, ff. 1A–3; Magd., FP 556; Emily Rose, "The politics of pathos: Richard Frethorne's letters home," in Appelbaum and Sweet, eds., *Envisioning*, 105–108.

10. Magd., FP 503, 508, 527, ff. 1–3v; Tyler (ed.), *Narratives of Early Virginia*, 423; TNA, CO 1/2, f. 2v; CO 1/3, ff. 30–34; Kavanagh, ed., *Foundations*, 3:1674–1675.

11. Carl Bridenbaugh, *Jamestown, 1544–1699* (New York, 1980), ch. 10.

12. Barbour, ed., *Complete Works*, 2:28–30; Smith, *Generall Historie*, 94, 230; Alexander, *Encouragement*, 27.

13. Clarke, *True and Faithful Account*, 25–26; Michael J. Jarvis, "Lewis Hughes," *ODNB*; Lewis Hughes, *A Letter Sent into England from the Summer Islands* (London, 1615), A3, B1v–B2v, B3v.

14. Lewis Hughes, *A Plaine and True Relation of the Goodnes of God Towards the Sommer Ilands* (London, 1621), A4v–B1; *idem, Letter*, B3v.

15. Vernon A. Ives, ed., *Letters from Bermuda, 1615–1646* (Toronto, 1984), 3–4.

16. Ibid., 74; Hughes, *Plaine and True Relation*, A4.

17. J. Henry Lefroy, ed., *The Historye of the Bermudaes or Summer Islands* (London, 1882), chs. 3–5; A. C. Hollis Hallett, ed., *Bermuda Under the Sommer Islands Company, 1612–1684: Civil Records*, vol. 1, *1612–1669* (Bermuda, 2005), vii; Wesley Frank Craven and Walter B. Hayward, eds., *The Journal of Richard Norwood* (New York, 1945), xii–xiii, 14–15, 42, 59–63, 67–71.

18. Smith, *Generall Historie*, 183–184, 189; BL, Add. MS 12496, ff. 424–428v.

19. NYPL, Mss. Col. 2799, SMYTH 2; Clarke, *True and Faithful Account*, 22–24; Hughes, *Plaine and True Relation*, B4–B4v; HMC, *Eighth Report*, 32; BL, Add. MS 12496, f. 429; Ives, ed., *Letters*, 15–32, 37–42.

20. Lefroy, ed., *Historye of the Bermudaes*, ch. 6; Ives, ed., *Letters*, 9–11; HMC, *Eighth Report*, 32–33; Smith, *Generall Historie*, 193.

21. Ives, ed., *Letters*, 144, 156, 161–164, 184–199.

22. Hallett, ed., *Bermuda*, xviii–xv; Smith, *Generall Historie*, 198; Hughes, *Plaine and True Relation*, B4; BL, Add. MS 12496, ff. 431–437v.

23. Hughes, *Plaine and True Relation*, B3v; Magd., FP 406, 409, 458, 460, 466–468, 518; Smith, *Generall Historie*, 198.

24. BL, Add. MS 12496, ff. 437–437v.

25. C. E. Banks, "Thomas Morton of Merry Mount," *Procs of the MHS*, 63 (1924–1925), 147–193, quotation 171; Michael Zuckerman, "Pilgrims in the wilderness: community, modernity and the maypole at Merry Mount," *NEQ*, 50 (1977), 255–277; William Heath, "Thomas Morton: from merry old England to New England," *Journal of American Studies*, 41 (2007), 135–168.

26. Morton, *New English Canaan*, 116–117, 133–137; Deane, ed., *Plymouth*, 237.

27. John A. Doyle, ed., *History of the Plimoth Plantation* (London, 1896), 7–8. See also John Demos, *A Little Commonwealth: Family Life in Plymouth Colony* (New York, 1970); Helena M. Wall, *Fierce Communion: Family and Community in Early America* (Cambridge, MA, 1990).

28. Winslow, *Good Newes*, 9–12.

29. *A Briefe Relation of the Discovery and Plantation of New England* (London, 1622), B1, D2–D3v, E2; Winslow, *Good Newes*, 11, 64–65.

30. Winslow, *Good Newes*, 47–50.

31. Smith, *Advertisements*, 19–20; Alexander, *Encouragement*, 30–31; Bradford, *Relation*, B1–B1v, B2v, B4; *A Treatise of New England, Published in Anno Dom. 1637* (n.p. [London?], n.d. [1645?]), 8–10. On the importance of beavers, see Nick Bunker, *Making Haste from Babylon: The Mayflower Pilgrims and Their World* (London, 2010).

32. Cotton Mather, *Magnalia Christi Americana*, 7 vols. (London, 1702), 2:4; Deane, ed., *Plymouth*, 79–80; Winslow, *Good Newes*, A2v, 52.

33. Winslow, *Good Newes*, 20, 24; Morton, *New English Canaan*, 111–112.

34. Morton, *New English Canaan*, 17, 25–26, 43, 59–60, 68, 73, 90, 92–95, 113.

35. Deane, ed., *Plymouth*, 78; Winslow, *Good Newes*, 28–31, 33; Philbrick, *Mayflower*, 144–145.

36. Winslow, *Good Newes*, A3; *The True Travels, Adventures and Observations of Captaine John Smith* (London, 1630), 46; *idem*, *Advertisements*, 2, 17, 21; Morton, *New English Canaan*, 163–164; Alison Gilbert Olson, *Anglo-American Politics, 1660–1775: The Relationship Between Parties in England and Colonial America* (Oxford, 1973), 6.

37. West Devon RO, 1/48, f. 92; Bodl., Bankes Papers 7, ff. 2–3; Jensen, *Colonial Documents*, 184.

38. Arundel Castle, Duke of Norfolk, Autograph Letters no. 275.

CHAPTER 6: PROJECTS OF NO FANTASY

1. Faith Harrington, "Sea tenure in seventeenth-century New Hampshire: Native Americans and Englishmen in the sphere of coastal resources," *Historical New Hampshire*, 40 (1985), 24–29.

2. New England eels were the best eels that one London fishmonger ever saw: Morton, *New English Canaan*, 89.

3. University of Nottingham, Middleton MS, Mi x 1/15, 20, 23–24, 59–60, 66; Quinn, ed., *New American World*, 4:146–145, 152–158; LPL, MS 250, pt. 25, ff. 406–412v.

4. *CSPC, 1574–1660*, 26; HEHL, HM 2509; John Mason, *A Briefe Discourse of the New-found-land* (Edinburgh, 1620); Brenner, *Merchants*, 110. Devon and Cornwall lost one in five of their ships to corsairs in the 1610–1630s: Linda Colley, *Captives* (New York, 2002), 59.

5. *A Letter Written by Captaine Edward Winne to . . . Sir George Calvert* (London, 1621), 3; Greene, *Intellectual Construction*, 49; Richard Whitbourne, *A Discourse and Discovery of New-Found-Land* (London, 1623), 103–106, 108–110; Gillian T. Cell, ed., *Newfoundland Discovered: English Attempts at Colonization, 1610–1630* (London, 1982), 49, 258–269; Peter E. Pope, *Fish into Wine: The Newfoundland Plantation in the Seventeenth Century* (Chapel Hill, NC, 2004), 289.

6. Whitbourne, *Discourse*, 109; R. W. Dunning, ed., *A History of the County of Somerset*, vol. 7 (Oxford, 1999), 115; Eburne, *Plaine Path-Way*, 9–19, 28.

7. Bradford, *Relation*, 70; Michael Sparke, *Greevous Grones for the Poore* (London, 1621), A3v, 2–3, 6–11, 18–19; Thomas Scott, *The Belgicke Pismire, Stinging the Slothfull Sleeper* (London, 1623), 29–30, 37–40.

8. Whitbourne, *Discourse*, B1v, 100–101; Richard Eburne, *A Plain Pathway to Plantations (1624)*, ed. Louis B. Wright (Ithaca, NY, 1962), xii–xiii, xxvii; *CSPC, 1574–1660*, 35, 37, 50, 56. For parishes that owned copies of Whitbourne's book: Catherine Armstrong, *Writing North America in the Seventeenth Century: English Representations in Print and Manuscript* (Aldershot, UK, 2007), 191.

9. Eburne, *Plain Pathway*, ed. Wright, xxxi, xxxiii; Eburne, *Plaine Path-Way*, 116–117, 119; Somerset Heritage Centre, DD/PH/212/45, 219/63, 225/15; Scott, *Belgicke Pismire*, 39–41.

10. Alexander, *Encouragement*, A3v.

11. Harris, *Rebellion*, ch. 7.

12. [Thomas Scott], *Sir Walter Rawleighs Ghost, or Englands Forewarner* (Utrecht [London?], 1626), 3–4. 10–11, 15–17; John Hagthorpe, *Englands-Exchequer, Or a Discourse of the Sea and Navigation* (London, 1625), 6–7, 13–15, 24–28, 33–34; Purchas, *Hakluytus Posthumus*.

13. Smith, *Advertisements*, 12–13; Devon RO, ECA L&P 260–262, 361.

14. Christopher Levett, *A Voyage into New England* (London, 1624), 27–28; William Morrell, *New-England* (London, 1625), 24; James Phinney Baxter, *Christopher Levett of York: The Pioneer Colonist in Casco Bay* (Portland, ME, 1893); Levett, *Voyage*, 8–16, 18–19, 21.

15. Michael A. LaCombe, "Sir Thomas Warner," *ODNB*; Smith, *True Travels*, 51–52; Philip D. Morgan, "Virginia's other prototype: the Caribbean," in Peter C. Mancall, ed., *The Atlantic World and Virginia, 1550–1624* (Chapel Hill, NC, 2007), 342–380.

16. H. R. McIlwaine, ed., *Minutes of the Council and General Court of Colonial Virginia*, 2nd ed. (Richmond, VA, 1979), 111–114.

17. Ibid., 160–163; *The Parish Register of Christ Church . . . 1653 to 1812* (Richmond, VA, 1897), 31; Alexander, *Encouragement*, 5.

18. Smith, *True Travels*, 44; VHS, Mss 3, V8192 a 2, p. 471; Magd., FP 569; Ditchfield, *Considerations*, 1–2, 9–10; *CSPC, 1574–1660*, 86, 89–92, 124–125.

19. Smith, *True Travels*, 43; Graham et al., "Adaptation," 467, 470–484, 493–506; Lois Green Carr and Lorena S. Walsh, "The standard of living in the colonial Chesapeake," *WMQ*, 45 (1988), 135–136; Virginia Bernhard, "Poverty and the social order in seventeenth-century Virginia," *VMHB*, 85 (1977), 141–155; Clara Ann Bowler, "Carted whores and white shrouded apologies: slander in the county courts of seventeenth-century Virginia," *VMHB*, 85 (1977), 411–426; Darrett B. Rutman and Anita H. Rutman, *A Place in Time: Middlesex County, Virginia, 1650–1750* (New York, 1984), ch. 4; James R. Perry, *The Formation of a Society on Virginia's Eastern Shore, 1615–1655* (Chapel Hill, NC, 1990), esp. chs. 3–8; Karen Ordahl Kupperman, "The founding years of Virginia—and the United States," *VMHB*, 104 (1996), 107, 111–112, 275–298; Jon Kukla, "Order and chaos in early America: political and social stability in pre-Restoration Virginia," *AHR*, 90 (1985), 277. A 1634 census found 4,914 colonists: TNA, CO 1/8, f. 155.

20. Wesley Frank Craven, *White, Red and Black: The Seventeenth-Century Virginian* (Charlottesville, VA, 1971), 29–30; McIlwaine, ed., *Minutes*, 194–195; Kathleen M. Brown, "'Changed . . . into the fashion of a man': the politics of sexual difference in a seventeenth-century Anglo-American settlement," *Journal of the History of Sexuality*, 6 (1995), 17–93; Mary Beth Norton, *Founding Mothers and Fathers: Gendered Power and the Forming of American Society* (New York, 1996), 183–197.

21. Brenner, *Merchants*, 106–108, 111–112, 114; Edward Johnson, *A History of New-England* (London, 1653), 19; MHS, Ms. N-1182, Carton 36: SH 114M U, Folders 27 (1612–1628) and 29 (1629–1630). "Salem" came from Psalm 76:2.

22. Brenner, *Merchants*, 148–149, 153–156.

23. Walton and Shepherd, *Economic Rise*, 39–40; *The Winthrop Papers, 1498–1654*, 6 vols. (Boston, 1929–1992), 2:151–152; Richard S. Dunn, James Savage, and Laetitia Yeandle, eds., *The Journal of John Winthrop, 1630–1649* (Cambridge, MA, 1996), 649n; Beinecke, Osborn fb62, pp. 14–15, 21. On Winthrop's use of *vacuum domicilium*, see Tomlins, *Freedom Bound*, 149–150. For his formative years, see Francis J. Bremer, *John Winthrop: America's Forgotten Founding Father* (Oxford, 2003), chs. 5–8.

24. BPL, Ms. fAm. 2176, pp. 1–3, 8–11, 13–15; Essex RO, T/G 64/2 (original in HUA); Nicholas Canny, "The permissive frontier: the problem of social control in English settlements in Ireland and Virginia," in Andrews et al., eds., *Westward Enterprise*, 17–44; Warren M. Billings, John E. Selby, and Thad W. Tate, *Colonial Virginia: A History* (New York, 1986), ch. 2. See also Roger Thompson, *Mobility and Migration: East Anglian Founders of New England, 1629–1640* (Amherst, MA, 1994), esp. chs. 3–6; David W. Galenson, "'Middling people' or 'common sort'? The social origins of some early Americans re-examined," *WMQ*, 35 (1978), 499–524.

25. Bradford, *Relation*, 65–66; Alan Heimert and Andrew Delbanco, eds., *The Puritans in America: A Narrative Anthology* (Cambridge, MA, 1985), 70–74.

26. *Winthrop Papers*, 2:105–106, 153–154, 158.

27. Francis Higginson, *New-Englands Plantation* (London, 1630), B1v–C2v, C4v; Alexander Young, ed., *Chronicles of the First Planters of the Colony of Massachusetts Bay* (Boston, 1846), 232–235; Everett Emerson, ed., *Letters from New England: The Massachusetts Bay Colony, 1629–1638* (Amherst, MA, 1976), 25–27.

28. Young, ed., *Chronicles*, 230–231; Francis J. Bremer, *Congregational Communion: Clerical Friendship in the Anglo-American Puritan Community, 1610–1692* (Boston, 1994); David A. Weir, *Early New England: A Covenanted Society* (Grand Rapids, MI, 2005), chs. 2–3; Bremer, *Winthrop*, 166–167.

29. Johnson, *History*, 20.

30. James Savage, ed., *The History of New England from 1630 to 1649 by John Winthrop*, 2 vols. (Boston, 1853), 1:368–369; Johnson, *History*, 25–26.

31. John Winthrop, *The Humble Request of His Majesties Loyall Subjects . . . Late Gone for New-England* (London, 1630), 2–7, 9; Philip F. Gura, *A Glimpse of Sion's Glory: Puritan Radicalism in New England, 1620–1660* (Middletown, CT, 1984), 216; Heimert and Delbanco, eds., *Puritans*, 10–11; Castillo and Schweitzer, eds., *Literatures*, 109–111; Perry Miller and Thomas H. Johnson, eds., *The Puritans* (New York, 1938), 281; Dunn et al., eds., *Journal*, 72. See also Avihu Zakai, *Exile and Kingdom: History and Apocalypse in the Puritan Migration to America* (Cambridge, UK, 1992).

32. John Cotton, *Gods Promise to His Plantation* (London, 1630), 7–15; 2 Samuel 7:10; *Winthrop Papers*, 2:282–295; Theodore Dwight Bozeman, *To Live Ancient Lives: The Primitivist Dimension in Puritanism* (Chapel Hill, NC, 1988); Susan Hardman Moore, "Popery, purity and providence: deciphering the New England experiment," in Anthony Fletcher and Peter Roberts, eds., *Religion, Culture and Society in Early Modern Britain* (Cambridge, UK, 1994), 270–271, 273. The speech was neither "American" nor isolationist: Michael Warner, "What's colonial about colonial America?" in Robert Blair St. George, ed., *Possible Pasts: Becoming Colonial in Early America* (Ithaca, NY, 2000), 50–51; Robert Kagan, *Dangerous Nation: America and the World, 1600–1890* (London, 2006), ch. 1. Stephen Carl Arch sees Winthrop's aim as "restoring the Old World's misshapen forms—of man and society—to their original lineaments in the New": *Authorizing the Past: The Rhetoric of History in Seventeenth-Century New England* (DeKalb, IL, 1994), 14–15.

CHAPTER 7: TO CLEARER LIGHT AND MORE LIBERTY

1. Johnson, *History*, 30; Dunn et al., eds., *Journal*, 11–13.

2. Dunn et al., eds., *Journal*, 18–20; Smith, *Advertisements*, 26; Johnson, *History*, 34; Cressy, *Coming Over*, ch. 6.

3. Dunn et al., eds., *Journal*, 35–36; Bremer, *Winthrop*, 187; Smith, *Advertisements*, 29; Emerson, ed., *Letters*, 73; *Collections of the MHS*, 7 (1838), 291.

4. *Winthrop Papers*, 2:301–304.

5. BPL, Ms. fAm. 2176, pp. 42–43; Michael P. Winship, "Godly republicanism and the origins of the Massachusetts polity," *WMQ*, 63 (2006), 427–462; David Thomas Konig, *Law and Society in Puritan Massachusetts: Essex County, 1629–1692* (Chapel Hill, NC, 1979), ch. 1; Richard D. Pierce, ed., *The Records of the First Church in Boston, 1630–1868* (Boston, 1961), 12; Virginia DeJohn Anderson, *New England's Generation: The Great Migration and the Formation of Society and Culture in the Seventeenth Century* (Cambridge, UK, 1991), ch. 4. Jack P. Greene refers to "settler republics" in "'By their laws shall ye know them': law and identity in colonial British America," *Journal of Interdisciplinary History*, 33 (2002), 252.

6. DHC, DC/DOB 28/1; John White, *The Planters Plea* (London, 1630), 1, 5, 10–11, 17–22, 36, 55–59, 79; David Underdown, *Fire from Heaven: Life in an English Town in the Seventeenth Century* (New Haven, CT, 1992), ch. 4; Frances Rose-Troup, *John White: The Patriarch of Dorchester (Dorset) and Founder of Massachusetts, 1575–1648* (New York, 1930). Colonists respected White; see Winthrop's 1632 letter: TNA, CO 1/6, f. 63.

7. Johnson, *History*, 41–42; White, *Planters Plea*, 34.

8. *Winthrop Papers*, 2:312–313, 319–320; Emerson, ed., *Letters*, 73, 76; Dunn et al., eds., *Journal*, 43–44.

9. Dunn et al., eds., *Journal*, 69, 73–74, 81; Roger Thompson, *Divided We Stand: Watertown, Massachusetts, 1630–1680* (Amherst, MA, 2001), chs. 4–8; Robert E. Moody, ed., *The Saltonstall Papers, 1607–1815*, 2 vols. (Boston, 1972–1974), 1:117–118; BL, Egerton MS 2645, f. 245; *Winthrop Papers*, 3:17–19.

10. *Winthrop Papers*, 3:19; Smith, *Advertisements*, 29; BPL, Ms. fAm. 2176, pp. 46, 49–51, 58; BL, Sloane MS 922, ff. 92v–93. On reverse migration: Andrew Delbanco, "Looking homeward, going home: the lure of England for the founders of New England," *NEQ*, 59

(1986), 358–386; Susan Hardman Moore, *Pilgrims: New World Settlers and the Call of Home* (New Haven, CT, 2007).

11. MHS, Ms. N-1143, p. 43; BPL, Ms. fAm. 2176, pp. 59, 62, 69, 94; Carla Gardina Pestana, "The problem of land, status and authority: how early English governors negotiated the Atlantic world," *NEQ*, 78 (2005), 519–522, 534.

12. BL, Sloane MS 922, ff. 90–92; Keith Wrightson and David Levine, *Poverty and Piety in an English Village: Terling, 1525–1700*, 2nd ed. (Oxford, 2001), ch. 6.

13. Emerson, ed., *Letters*, 75, 93; Anderson, *New England's Generation*, chs. 1–3; Higginson, *New-Englands Plantation*, A2.

14. William Wood, *New Englands Prospect* (London, 1634), 5, 8–10, 47–48; Alden T. Vaughan, ed., *New England's Prospect by William Wood* (Amherst, MA, 1977), 1–3, 7–11; Armstrong, *Writing North America*, 177–180.

15. *Winthrop Papers*, 3:17; Johnson, *History*, 51–52; Gray, ed., *Colonial America*, 66; Cristobel Silva, "Miraculous plagues: epidemiology on New England's colonial landscape," *Early American Literature*, 43 (2008), 249–275. The motto was a Macedonian's plea to Paul in a vision: Acts 16:9.

16. Wood, *New Englands Prospect*, 56–65, 69–82, 86, 91–92; Dunn et al., eds., *Journal*, 43–44.

17. Wood, *New Englands Prospect*, 76–77, 79, 82–84; Dunn et al., eds., *Journal*, 105; NYPL, Mss. Col. 6404; David S. Lovejoy, "Satanizing the American Indian," *NEQ*, 67 (1994), 607–608.

18. *Winthrop Papers*, 3:176–178; Nathaniel Bouton et al., eds., *Documents and Records Relating to . . . New Hampshire*, 40 vols. (Concord, NH, 1867–1943), 1:81–82, 89, 91–93.

19. Anderson, *New England's Generation*, 23–24; Wood, *New Englands Prospect*, 37–38; BPL, Ms. fAm. 2176, pp. 99, 104, 109, 120; Darrett B. Rutman, *Winthrop's Boston: Portrait of a Puritan Town, 1630–1649* (Chapel Hill, NC, 1965), 279; Philip J. Greven Jr., *Four Generations: Population, Land and Family in Colonial Andover, Massachusetts* (Ithaca, NY, 1970), chs. 2–4; Linda Auwers Bissell, "From one generation to another: mobility in seventeenth-century Windsor, Connecticut," *WMQ*, 31 (1974), 79–110.

20. TNA, CO 1/6, f. 183; BPL, Ms. fAm. 2176, p. 89; Cressy, *Coming Over*, 87; Smith, *Advertisements*, 29; *The Legacy of a Dying Mother to Her Mourning Children* (London, 1673), 46–53; Dunn et al., eds., *Journal*, 111.

21. *Legacy of a Dying Mother*, 44–46; Ephesians 5:22; *CSPC, 1574–1660*, 154–155. On Susanna Bell's decision to emigrate: Moore, *Pilgrims*, 1–15.

22. Robert Fowler, *A Quakers Sea-Journal* (London, 1659), 3; *A True Relation of a Wonderfull Sea Fight* (London, 1621), C2; Wood, *New Englands Prospect*, 50; Smith, *Generall Historie*, 182; Copland, *Virginia's God*, 3; Coldham, ed., *English Adventurers*, 86; John Josselyn, *An Account of Two Voyages to New-England* (London, 1674), 214. For witches: William Hand Browne, ed., *Proceedings of the Council of Maryland, 1636–1667* (Baltimore, 1885), 306–308; George Lincoln Burr, ed., *Narratives of the Witchcraft Cases, 1648–1706* (New York, 1946), 81n. A near-mutiny occurred in 1634: Peter Wilson Coldham, ed., *English Adventurers and Emigrants, 1609–1660* (Baltimore, 1984), 45–52.

23. White, *Planters Plea*, 55; TNA, SP 16/267, f. 135; Castillo and Schweitzer, eds., *Literatures*, 105; Winslow, *Good News*, 25; BL, Sloane MS 922, ff. 101–102v.

24. Francis J. Bremer, "John Cotton," *ODNB*; Young, ed., *Chronicles*, 438–444; John Cotton, *The Answer to the Whole Set of Questions of the Celebrated Mr William Appolonius by John Norton*, ed. Douglas Horton (Cambridge, MA, 1958), 11; John Norton, *Abel Being Dead Yet Speaketh* (London, 1658), 18.

25. James Orchard Halliwell, ed., *The Autobiography and Correspondence of Sir Simonds D'Ewes*, 2 vols. (London, 1845), 2:117–118; *CSPC, 1574–1660*, 174; East Sussex RO, RYE/47/118/3; Dunn et al., eds., *Journal*, 157n.

26. Michael McGiffert, ed., *God's Plot: The Paradoxes of Puritan Piety* (Amherst, MA, 1972), 3–6, 12–17, 19–21; Heimert and Delbanco, eds., *Puritans*, 6; Thomas Shepard, *The Sound Beleever* (London, 1645); Thomas Shepard and John Allin, *A Defence of the Answer*

(London, 1648); Alison Games, *Migration and the Origins of the English Atlantic World* (Cambridge, MA, 1999), 62–63.

27. Dunn et al., eds., *Journal*, 151–152; BL, Sloane MS 922, ff. 109–115v. The story was immortalized in Increase Mather's *An Essay for the Recording of Illustrious Providences* (Boston, 1684), 3–14. See Julie Sievers, "Drowned pens and shaking hands: sea providence narratives in seventeenth-century New England," *WMQ*, 63 (2006), 743–744.

28. MSA, vol. 11/1; Robert G. Pope, ed., *The Notebook of the Reverend John Fiske, 1644–1675* (Boston, 1974), xxxviii; *Winthrop Papers*, 3:177–178; Norman C. P. Tyack, "English exports to New England, 1632–1640: some records in the port books," *NEHGR*, 135 (1981), 213–238; Carole Shammas, *The Pre-Industrial Consumer in England and America* (Oxford, 1990), ch. 3; MHS, Ms. N-1827, Box 161.A/013.2, no. 1. In 1635 Winthrop requested that his horse be sent over: West Suffolk RO, 613/909.

29. Louis Jordan, *John Hull, the Mint and the Economics of Massachusetts Coinage* (Lebanon, NH, 2002), ch. 1; MHS, Ms. N-791, p. 1; Hermann Frederick Clarke, *John Hull: A Builder of the Bay Colony* (Portland, ME, 1940), 3, 20–22, 48–49.

30. Anthony Salerno, "The social background of seventeenth-century emigration to America," *JBS*, 19 (1979), 32–33; Bodl., Tanner MS 68, f. 332; Allen, *In English Ways*, ch. 3; John J. Waters, "Hingham, Massachusetts, 1631–1681: an East Anglian oligarchy in the New World," *Journal of Social History*, 1 (1968), 351–370.

31. TNA, CO 1/6, f. 183; Emerson, ed., *Letters*, 79–81, 89–90; Ames, ed., *County Court Records*, 22–23; *Records of the Colony of Rhode Island and Providence Plantations in New England*, 10 vols. (Providence, RI, 1856–1865), 2:99–104; *Winthrop Papers*, 4:148–149; Games, *Migration*, 70, 80–81.

32. Josselyn, *Account*, 83–86, 92; Johnson, *History*, 49; Larry Burkhart, *The Good Fight: Medicine in Colonial Pennsylvania* (New York, 1989), 54; Bodl., Rawlinson MS A.185, f. 263.

33. Kenneth A. Lockridge, *A New England Town: The First Hundred Years, Dedham, Massachusetts, 1636–1736* (New York, 1970), 58; *CSPC, 1574–1660*, 155; R. E. Anderson and Anita McConnell, "Edward Howes," *ODNB*; Emerson, ed., *Letters*, 110–112, 199–200; Curtiss C. Gardiner, ed., *Lion Gardiner and His Descendants, 1599–1890* (St. Louis, MO, 1890), 22. A later colonist opened letters "as eagerly as a greedy heir tears open a father's will": Sarah M. S. Pearsall, *Atlantic Families: Lives and Letters in the Later Eighteenth Century* (Oxford, 2008), 36.

34. Wood, *New Englands Prospect*, 53–54; Morton, *New English Canaan*, 165–168; Bodl., Ashmole MS 38, ff. 104, 225v; Tanner MS 306, ff. 286–287; H. H. Hodson et al., eds., *A Nottinghamshire Miscellany*, Thoroton Society, 21 (1962), 37–39; Firth, ed., *American Garland*, 32–34.

35. Emerson, ed., *Letters*, 78–79; White, *Planters Plea*, 37–38, 59; *Winthrop Papers*, 3:54; DHC, DC/DOB 8/1; *CSPC, 1574–1660*, 157.

36. Savage, ed., *History*, 1:119; *Winthrop Papers*, 3:172; Emerson, ed., *Letters*, 176–177.

37. BL, Harleian MS 384, ff. 256–257; BL, Lansdowne MS 209, f. 107v; *Winthrop Papers*, 3:75–76, 94–95, 100–101; Elliott, *Empires of the Atlantic World*, 152; Bremer, *Winthrop*, 231–233; BPL, Ms. fAm. 2176, p. 50; Moody, ed., *Saltonstall Papers*, 1:118–119.

38. Dunn et al., eds., *Journal*, 131–132; TNA, CO 1/8, ff. 49–52v.

39. TNA, CO 1/8, ff. 110–111; Francis J. Bremer and Tom Webster, eds., *Puritans and Puritanism in Europe and America*, 2 vols. (Santa Barbara, CA, 2006), 1:265–266; *Winthrop Papers*, 3:233–234, 243–244, 288–289, 298–306, 376; Bodl., Bankes Papers 42, f. 74; *CSPC, 1574–1660*, 239.

40. TNA, CO 1/9, ff. 213–214; HMC, *Hastings*, 4:73, 75; East Sussex RO, RYE/47/123/8; *CSPC, 1574–1660*, 275; Norman C. P. Tyack, "The humbler Puritans of East Anglia and the New England movement: evidence for the court records of the 1630s," *NEHGR*, 138 (1984). 86, 90–91; Essex RO, D/ACA 40, ff. 95v–96; Stephen Foster, "English Puritanism and the progress of New England institutions, 1630–1660," in David D. Hall, John M. Murrin, and Thad W. Tate, eds., *Saints and Revolutionaries: Essays on Early American History* (New York, 1984), 16.

41. Josselyn, *Account*, 4–9, 20; Lancashire RO, DDKE/HMC/166; Heimert and Delbanco, eds., *Puritans*, 126–127.

CHAPTER 8: IN DARKNESS AND THE SHADOW OF DEATH

1. Games, *Migration*, 67.

2. Sandra W. Meditz and Dennis M. Hanratty, eds., *Caribbean Islands: A Country Study* (Washington, DC, 1987), http://countrystudies.us/caribbean-islands/7.htm; Miles Ogborn, *Global Lives: Britain and the World, 1550–1800* (Cambridge, UK, 2008), 230–231.

3. David Eltis, "The total product of Barbados, 1664–1701," *Journal of Economic History*, 55 (1995), 336; Brenner, *Merchants*, 92–93. On the West Indies in English culture, see Amussen, *Caribbean Exchanges*, esp. ch. 6.

4. [John Taylor], *Newes and Strange Newes from St Christophers of a Tempestuous Spirit* (London, 1638), 4–8.

5. Ibid., 1–3; Clayton Colman Hall, ed., *Narratives of Early Maryland, 1633–1684* (New York, 1910), 34; Smith, *True Travels*, 56; Kolchin, *American Slavery*, 21.

6. Gary A. Puckrein, *Little England: Plantation Society and Anglo-Barbadian Politics, 1627–1700* (New York, 1984), chs. 1–4; Larry Gragg, *Englishmen Transplanted: The English Colonization of Barbados, 1627–1660* (Oxford, 2003), chs. 2–4, 7–8; Richard S. Dunn, *Sugar and Slaves: The Rise of the Planter Class in the English West Indies, 1624–1713* (Chapel Hill, NC, 1972), 42; John Bruce, ed., *Letters and Papers of the Verney Family Down to the End of the Year 1639* (London, 1853), 194–195.

7. Karen Ordahl Kupperman, *Providence Island, 1630–1: The Other Puritan Colony* (Cambridge, UK, 1993), chs. 1–2, 8; Essex RO, D/DBa O2/8–8v.

8. BL, Egerton MS 2646, ff. 58, 76; *CSPC, 1574–1660*, 202, 226; Kupperman, *Providence Island*, 165–166.

9. *Treatise of New England*, 1–2.

10. Kupperman, *Providence Island*, 325–327; Leon E. Cranmer, *Cushnoc: The History and Archaeology of the Plymouth Colony Traders on the Kennebec* (Augusta, ME, 1990).

11. Johnson, *History*, 81–84; Dunn et al., eds., *Journal*, 158; Alan Heimert, "Puritanism, the wilderness and the frontier," *NEQ*, 26 (1953), 362–382; Mark Stoll, "Religion 'irradiates' the wilderness," in Michael Lewis, ed., *American Wilderness: A New History* (Oxford, 2007), 37–40.

12. N. N., *A Short Account of the Present State of New-England* (n.p., 1690), 3–4; LPL, MS 841, Pt. 7, f. 5; Sargent Bush Jr., ed., *The Writings of Thomas Hooker: Spiritual Adventure in Two Worlds* (Madison, WI, 1980).

13. Francis J. Bremer, "Roger Williams," *ODNB*; BPL, Ms. fAm. 2176, p. 115; John M. Barry, *Roger Williams and the Creation of the American Soul: Church, State and the Birth of Liberty* (New York, 2012); MHS, Ms. N-527, Misc. Docs., 1636–1717, pp. 5–16; Carl Bridenbaugh, *Fat Mutton and Liberty of Conscience: Society in Rhode Island, 1636–1690* (Providence, RI, 1974); Robert Middlekauff, *The Mathers: Three Generations of Puritan Intellectuals, 1596–1728* (New York, 1971).

14. Increase Mather, *The Life and Death of That Reverend Man of God, Mr Richard Mather* (Cambridge, MA, 1670), 20–22; Richard Mather and William Tompson, *An Heart-Melting Exhortation Together with a Cordiall Consolation* (London, 1650), 6; George H. Ellis, ed., *Records of the First Church at Dorchester in New England, 1636–1734* (Boston, 1891), intro.; B. R. Burg, *Richard Mather of Dorchester* (Lexington, KY, 1976), chs. 3–6.

15. Emerson, ed., *Letters*, 209; J. H. Adamson and H. F. Folland, *Sir Harry Vane: His Life and Times, 1613–1662* (Boston, 1973), 65–69; BPL, Ms. fAm. 2176, pp. 127, 151, 159; Dunn et al., eds., *Journal*, 221; Alan Macfarlane, ed., *The Diary of Ralph Josselin, 1616–1683* (London, 1976), 318.

16. John Cotton, *The Covenant of Gods Free Grace Most Sweetly Unfolded* (London, 1645), 38–39; Thomas Hooker, *A Survey of the Summe of Church-Discipline* (London, 1648), A4v; Thomas Lechford, *New-Englands Advice to Old-England* (London, 1644), A2–A4, 13.

17. BL, Add. MS 6394, f. 189; NYPL, Mss. Col. 731, no. 1; Savage, ed., *History*, 2:279–282.

18. CKS, U269/1/Ov16.

19. Billings, ed., *Old Dominion*, 50, 296–298; CKS, U269/1/Ov20.

20. *CSPC, 1574–1660*, 94; John D. Krugler, *English and Catholic: The Lords Baltimore in the Seventeenth Century* (Baltimore, 2004), 95–102, 104–108, 118; Luca Codignola, *The Coldest Harbour of the Land: Simon Stock and Lord Baltimore's Colony in Newfoundland, 1621–1649* (Kingston, Jamaica, 1988), 54.

21. Aubrey C. Land, *Colonial Maryland: A History* (New York, 1981), chs. 1–2; Greene, ed., *Great Britain*, 20–25; Jensen, ed., *Colonial Documents*, 63; Andrew White, *A Relation of the Successfull Beginnings of the Lord Baltemore's Plantation in Mary-land* (London, 1634), 1–3, 9.

22. Thomas Cecil, *A Relation of Maryland* (London, 1635), 4–16, 20–21, 61, 63 (HEHL copy).

23. Coldham, ed., *English Adventurers*, 101–105; Nathaniel C. Hale, *Virginia Venturer: A Historical Biography of William Claiborne, 1600–1677* (Richmond, VA, 1951); Cynthia J. Van Zandt, *Brothers Among Nations: The Pursuit of Intercultural Alliances in Early America, 1580–1660* (New York, 2008), ch. 5; William Hand Browne, *Maryland: The History of a Palatinate* (Boston, 1904), 33–34; Kavenagh, ed., *Foundations*, 2:97; David W. Jordan, *Foundations of Representative Government in Maryland, 1632–1715* (Cambridge, UK, 1987), chs. 1–2.

24. *CSPC, 1574–1660*, 193; Bodl., Bankes Papers 8, ff. 9, 13; "The mutiny in Virginia, 1635," *VMHB*, 1 (1893–1894), 416–430; Brenner, *Merchants*, 120–124, 140–148; Hall, ed., *Narratives*, 147–159; Kupperman, *Providence Island*, 213.

25. Gardiner, ed., *Lion Gardiner*, 8–12, 52; Dunn et al., eds., *Journal*, 157.

26. Philip Vincent, *A True Relation of the Late Batell Fought in New England* (London, 1638), B1–B2; Morton, *New English Canaan*, 55–58, quotation 57; *Treatise of New England*, 15; Charles T. Gehring and William A Starna, eds., *A Journey into Mohawk and Oneida Country, 1634–1635* (Syracuse, NY, 1988), 14; White, *Relation*, 12–13.

27. *Winthrop Papers*, 3:270–272, 298.

28. Dunn et al., eds., *Journal*, 189–190, 192–193; Virginia De John Anderson, *Creatures of Empire: How Domestic Animals Transformed Early America* (New York, 2004), 243; Increase Mather, *A Relation of the Troubles Which Have Hapned in New-England* (Boston, 1677), 43, 46.

29. Emerson W. Baker, *The Devil of Great Island: Witchcraft and Conflict in Early New England* (New York, 2007), 169–170; MHS, Ms. N-791, pp. 5–6; John Underhill, *Newes from America* (London, 1638), 2–3, 5, 17, 22. Another account claimed that soldiers were strangely unable to pierce Indian bodies: Johnson, *History*, 114–115.

30. Underhill, *Newes*, 36–44, quotations 37; Vincent, *True Relation*, C1v, C4–C4v; Laurence M. Hauptman and James D. Wherry, eds., *The Pequots in Southern New England: The Fall and Rise of an American Indian Nation* (Norman, OK, 1990), chs. 5–6.

31. William Bradford, quoted in Gray, ed., *Colonial America*, 71; Glenn W. LaFantasie, ed., *The Correspondence of Roger Williams*, 2 vols. (Hanover, PA, 1988), 1:117, 120n; Larzer Ziff, *Puritanism in America: A New Culture in a New World* (New York, 1973), 90–93; Michael Freeman, "Puritans and Pequots: the question of genocide," *NEQ*, 68 (1995), 278–279; Vincent, *True Relation*, C4; Mather, *Relation*, 46; Steven T. Katz, "The Pequot War reconsidered," *NEQ*, 64 (1991), 206–224; Ronald Dale Karr, "'Why should you be so furious?' The violence of the Pequot War," *JAH*, 85 (1998), 876–909.

32. Nash, *Red, White and Black*, ch. 4; Underhill, *Newes*, 40; [Henry Dunster], *New Englands First Fruits* (London, 1643), 5–7; Roger Williams, *A Key into the Language of America* (London, 1643), A6v–A7.

33. [Thomas Weld], *A Short Story of the Rise, Reign and Ruin of the Antinomians* (London, 1644), 31; Dunn et al., eds., *Journal*, 193; Heimert and Delbanco, eds., *Puritans*, 154–156. Michael P. Winship prefers "free grace controversy": *Making Heretics: Militant Protestantism*

and Free Grace in Massachusetts, 1636–1641 (Princeton, NJ, 2002); Stephen Foster, "New England and the challenge of heresy, 1630–1660: the Puritan crisis in transatlantic perspective," *WMQ*, 38 (1981), 624–660; David D. Hall, ed., *The Antinomian Controversy, 1636–1638: A Documentary History*, 2nd ed. (Durham, NC, 1990).

34. BPL, Ms. Am. 1506/2/7; Johnson, *History*, 101; Castillo and Schweitzer, eds., *Literatures*, 278; Weld, *Short Story*, B4; Marilyn J. Westerkamp, "Anne Hutchinson, sectarian mysticism, and the Puritan order," *Church History*, 59 (1990), 482–496; Jane Kamensky, *Governing the Tongue: The Politics of Speech in Early New England* (New York, 1997), 71–81, 88; Bethany Reid, "'Unfit for light': Anne Bradstreet's monstrous birth," *NEQ*, 71 (1998), 517–542; Hall, ed., *Antinomian Controversy*, 10–11, 20.

35. David R. Como, *Blown by the Spirit: Puritanism and the Emergence of an Antinomian Underground in Pre–Civil War England* (Stanford, CA, 2004), 24–27; Shagan, *Rule of Moderation*, ch. 4; Breen, *Puritans and Adventurers*, 16–18; Zuckerman, "Fabrication of identity," 194; Daniel K. Richter, *Before the Revolution: America's Ancient Pasts* (Cambridge, MA, 2011), ch. 8; Stephen Foster, *Their Solitary Way: The Puritan Social Ethic in the First Century of Settlement in New England* (New Haven, CT, 1971); Michal Rozbicki, *Transformation of the English Cultural Ethos in Colonial America: Maryland, 1634–1720* (Warsaw, 1985), 187.

36. Dunn et al., eds., *Journal*, 256; *Winthrop Papers*, 4:9–10; John Wheelwright, *Mercurius Americanus* (London, 1645), 5–8; Heimert and Delbanco, eds., *Puritans*, 192; Bouton et al., eds., *Documents*, 1:132–134.

37. Weld, *Short Story*, 33–41, 43–66, quotation 66; Josselyn, *Account*, 27–28; DWL, Baxter MSS, Letters vol. 5, f. 128; Valerie Pearl and Morris Pearl, "Governor John Winthrop on the birth of the Antinomians' 'monster,'" *Procs of MHS*, 102 (1990), 21–37. See also TNA, CO 1/9, f. 167; BL, Add. MS 35331, f. 131.

38. MHS, Ms. N-791, p. 6; Johnson, *History*, 131; Dunn et al., eds., *Journal*, 264–265; Weld, *Short Story*, B4, C1v; Michael P. Winship, *The Times and Trials of Anne Hutchinson: Puritans Divided* (Lawrence, KS, 2005), 145–146.

39. *Winthrop Papers*, 4:149–152, 159–160, 176–179; BPL, Ms. fAm 2176, p. 177; Pierce, ed., *Records*, 25; Timothy H. Breen and Stephen Foster, "The Puritans' greatest achievement: a study in social cohesion in seventeenth-century Massachusetts," *JAH*, 60 (1973), 5–22; James F. Cooper Jr., *Tenacious of Their Liberties: The Congregationalists in Colonial Massachusetts* (Oxford, 1999). Perry Miller's illusion is dispelled by: Robert Emmet Wall Jr., *Massachusetts Bay: The Crucial Decade, 1640–1650* (New Haven, CT, 1972); Janice Knight, *Orthodoxies in Massachusetts: Rereading American Puritanism* (Cambridge, MA, 1994); Louise A. Breen, *Transgressing the Bounds: Subversive Enterprises Among the Puritan Elite in Massachusetts, 1630–1692* (Oxford, 2001).

40. MHS, Ms. N-1182, Carton 36: SH 114M U, Folders 31–32, Endecott letters, July 28, 1640, and July 29, 1643.

41. Cressy, *Coming Over*, ch. 10; William Hooke, *New Englands Teares for Old Englands Feares* (London, 1641), 6–16, 20–21.

CHAPTER 9: THE DISTRACTED CONDITION OF MY DEAR NATIVE SOIL

1. BL, Loan MS 9, f. 16; Moore, *Pilgrims*, 61; F. D. A. Burns, "Robert Dover," *ODNB*.

2. Lechford, *New-Englands Advice*, 44.

3. Ibid., 44, 68–74, 78, quotation 78.

4. *Newes from New-England of a Most Strange and Prodigious Birth* (London, 1642); *Legacy of a Dying Mother*, 55–56.

5. Mather and Tompson, *Heart-Melting Exhortation*, 6; HEHL, HM 705; Joseph R. McElrath Jr. and Allan P. Robb, eds., *The Complete Works of Anne Bradstreet* (Boston, 1981), 141–148, quotation 146; BL, Sloane MS 922, ff. 104–107v.

6. Dunn et al., eds., *Journal*, 430; Dunster, *New Englands First Fruits*, 25–26.

7. Heimert and Delbanco, eds., *Puritans*, 7; [Nathaniel Ward], *The Simple Cobler of Aggawam in America* (London, 1647), B4.

8. [John Taylor], *The Devil Turn'd Round-Head* (London, 1642), A2v; Cressy, *Coming Over*, 205; Raymond Phineas Stearns, *The Strenuous Puritan: Hugh Peter, 1598–1660* (Urbana, IL, 1954), 234; Carla Gardina Pestana, "Hugh Peter," *ODNB*.

9. HMC, *Hastings*, 2:105–106; M. A. Stickney, "Notes on American currency," *EIHC*, 3 (1861), 33; Devon RO, 48/13/8/9/8, f. 10v.

10. Johnson, *History*, 171–174; John Davenport, *The Power of Congregational Churches Asserted and Vindicated* (London, 1672), 48; John Cotton, *The Keyes of the Kingdom of Heaven* (London, 1644), 9.

11. Pestana, *English Atlantic*, 58–60; Roger Williams, *Mr Cottons Letter Lately Printed, Examined and Answered* (London, 1644), 1, 9, 12, 46–47; idem, *The Bloudy Tenent of Persecution* (London, 1644); John Cotton, *The Bloudy Tenent, Washed and Made White in the Bloud of the Lambe* (London, 1647).

12. Kenneth W. Porter, "Samuell Gorton: New England firebrand," *NEQ*, 7 (1934), 405–444; Samuel Gorton, *Simplicities Defence Against Seven-Headed Policy* (London, 1646), A1, 2–3, quotation 3.

13. Winslow, *Hypocrisie Unmasked*, 28, 40–43; Gorton, *Simplicities Defence*, 33–41.

14. Gorton, *Simplicities Defence*, 45–65; Winslow, *Hypocrisie Unmasked*, 4, 5–7, 67.

15. Gorton, *Simplicities Defence*, 79–81.

16. Winslow, *Hypocrisie Unmasked*, 63–64; Lechford, *New-Englands Advice*, 70, 75–76; John Cotton, *Of the Holinesse of Church-Members* (London, 1650), 6, 8–9, 15.

17. Williams, *Key*, 49, 53, 107, 130, 135–137, 184 (see also John J. Teunissen and Evelyn J. Hinz's edition, 52); Karen Ordahl Kupperman, "Presentment of civility: English reading of American self-presentation in the early years of colonization," *WMQ*, 54 (1997), 193–228.

18. Thomas Shepard, *The Clear Sun-shine of the Gospel Breaking Forth upon the Indians in New-England* (London, 1648), 36–37; Dunster, *New Englands First Fruits*, 3–5; Richard W. Cogley, *John Eliot's Mission to the Indians Before King Philip's War* (Cambridge, MA, 1999), ch. 3; Edward Winslow, *The Glorious Progress of the Gospel Amongst the Indians* (London, 1649), C1v–C2.

19. Shepard, *New Englands Lamentation*, 6; BL, Egerton MS 2648, f. 1v; CSL, Colonial New England Records, Hartford, CT, vol. 52, p. 1.

20. *The Wyllys Papers . . . 1590–1796* (Hartford, CT, 1924), 61–63; Thomas Shepard, *New Englands Lamentation for Old Englands Present Errours and Divisions* (London, 1645), 1, 6; BL, Sloane MS 922, ff. 145v–146v; BL, Egerton MS 2648, f. 120.

21. MHS, Ms. N-1182, Carton 36: SH 114M U, Folder 33 (1644); Timothy B. Riordan, *The Plundering Time: Maryland and the English Civil War, 1645–1646* (Baltimore, 2004); HMC, *Sixth Report*, 101–102, 113.

22. Frederic W. Gleach, *Powhatan's World and Colonial Virginia: A Conflict of Cultures* (Lincoln, NE, 1997), chs. 6–8; *A Perfect Diurnall* (June 17–24, 1644); Rountree, *Pocahontas's People*, 84–88.

23. *Winthrop Papers*, 5:45–46; Williams, *Key*, 58.

24. BL, Ashmole MS 36, f. 100v; Dunn et al., eds., *Journal*, 500, 609–610.

25. Devon RO, 48/13/8/9/8, f. 7v; 48/13/8/9/9, ff. 7v, 8, 14; Keith Thomas, "The Puritans and adultery: the Act of 1650 reconsidered," in Donald Pennington and Keith Thomas, eds., *Puritans and Revolutionaries* (Oxford, 1978), 257–282; Moore, *Pilgrims*, 60, 61–62.

26. Ward, *Simple Cobler*, A4, B4v, E2v.

27. Dunn et al., eds., *Journal*, 370–376, 629; BPL, Ms. fAm. 2176, pp. 246, 279. For more ambivalent attitudes, see Richard Godbeer, "'The cry of Sodom': discourse, intercourse and desire in colonial New England," *WMQ*, 52 (1995), 259–286. In 1639–1640, Aaron Starke, convicted of buggery, was not executed: *Records of the Particular Court of Connecticut, 1639–1663* (Hartford, CT, 1928), 3–4, 13.

28. Pierce, ed., *Records*, 37; Dunn et al., eds., *Journal*, 209, 229–230, 271–272, 391–392, 469. On the gendered pressures of Puritanism: Elizabeth Reis, *Damned Women: Sinners and Witches in Puritan New England* (Ithaca, NY, 1997), chs. 1–3, 4.

29. Thomas Shepard, *Subjection to Christ in All His Ordinances and Appointments* (London, 1652), A4; Johnson, *History*, 64; McGiffert, ed., *God's Plot*, 16–17, 21–29, 70; Mary Rheinlander McCarl, "Thomas Shepard's record of religious experience, 1648–1649," *WMQ*, 48 (1991), 432–466.

30. NEHGS, MSS 553, no. 47; George Selement and Bruce C. Woolley, eds., *Thomas Shepard's Confessions* (Boston, 1981), 192–197.

31. Pope, ed., *Notebook*, 61; Dunster, *New Englands First Fruits*, 5; Winslow, *Glorious Progress*, D2.

32. Dunster, *New Englands First Fruits*, 3–4.

CHAPTER 10: MARCHING MANFULLY ON

1. *A General History of New England by the Rev. William Hubbard*, 2nd ed. (Boston, 1848), 327–328; Francis J. Bremer, "Henry Whitfield," *ODNB*.

2. Henry Whitfield, *The Light Appearing More and More Towards the Perfect Day* (London, 1651), 1–11; Winslow, *Glorious Progress*, B2; David J. Silverman, *Faith and Boundaries: Colonists, Christianity and Community Among the Wampanoag Indians of Martha's Vineyard, 1600–1871* (Cambridge, MA, 2005), ch. 1.

3. Whitfield, *Light Appearing*, 2; Shepard, *Clear Sunshine*, 29; Winslow, *Glorious Progress*, C1; John Wilson, *The Day-Breaking, if Not the Sun-Rising of the Gospell, with the Indians in New England* (London, 1647), 2–4, 7–14, 20–22; James Axtell, *The Invasion Within: The Contest of Cultures in Colonial North America* (New York, 1985), chs. 7, 9.

4. Whitfield, *Light Appearing*, 31, 46; George Gardyner, *A Description of the New World* (London, 1651), 92; Wilson, *Day-Breaking*, 5, 10, 15.

5. Wilson, *Day-Breaking*, 1–2, 24–25; Shepard, *Clear Sunshine*, A3–A3v, 6–7, 10–14.

6. [William Castell], *A Petition . . . for the Propagating of the Gospel in America* (London, 1641), 7; William Hooke, *New-Englands Sence of Old-England and Irelands Sorrowes* (London, 1645), 14–15, 30.

7. Winslow, *Glorious Progress*, A2–A3v; Whitfield, *Light Appearing*, 14, 24; Thomas Thorowgood, *Jewes in America* (London, 1650), A3; Richard W. Cogley, "'Some other kind of being and condition': the controversy in mid-seventeenth-century England over the peopling of ancient America," *Journal of History of Ideas*, 68 (2007), 35–56.

8. Macfarlane, ed., *Diary of Ralph Josselin*, 238; *Winthrop Papers*, 5:356; *To Our Reverend Brethren the Ministers of the Gospel in England and Wales* (London, 1649); William Kellaway, *The New England Company, 1649–1776: Missionary Society to the American Indians* (London, 1961), chs. 2–5.

9. Essex RO, D/P 50/12/1; CKS, P364/5/14; Fa/AC/4 Pt. 1, f. 5; Raymond P. Stearns, "The Weld-Peter mission to England," *Publications of the Colonial Society of Massachusetts*, 32 (1934), 188–246; Essex RO, D/DAy F4; Bodl., Rawlinson MS C.934, ff. 5–5v, 29v–30, 32; Macfarlane, ed., *Diary of Ralph Josselin*, 263, 291, 299; Whitfield, *Light Appearing*, 24; DHC, DC/DOB 1615, p. 154; DC/DOB 16/4, p. 193; DC/DOB 31/1/2; DC/DOB 31/1/3.

10. John Child, *New-Englands Jonas Cast Up at London* (London, 1647), 12–13.

11. Child, *New-Englands Jonas*, 3–4, 6–9; Edward Winslow, *New-Englands Salamander Discovered* (London, 1647), 14–17; Child, *New-Englands Jonas*, 12–13.

12. Winslow, *New-Englands Salamander*, 12, 14–21, 24.

13. Gura, *Glimpse of Sion's Glory*, ch. 10; Edward Symmons, *A Vindication of King Charles, or a Loyal Subjects Duty* (London, 1648), 109.

14. Winslow, *Hypocrisie Unmasked*, 1, 55–56; Roger Williams, quoted in Jensen, ed., *Colonial Documents*, 168. On agitation in England, see *A Manifestation from Lieutenant Col. John Lilburne* (London, 1649).

15. *Winthrop Papers*, 5:125–127, 144–145; BPL, Ms. Am. 1502/1/4; Thomas Shepard, quoted in McGiffert, ed., *God's Plot*, 70.

16. Austin Woolrych, *Britain in Revolution, 1625–1660* (Oxford, 2002), 433; MHS, Ms. N-791, p. 8.

17. Beinecke, Osborn fb62, p. 37; BL, Clarendon MS 74, f. 245; LaFantasie, ed., *Correspondence*, 288; Shepard, *Subjection to Christ*, A4.

18. Winslow, *Good News*, 24–25; *The British Bell-Man* (London, 1648), 3; Edward Johnson, *Wonder-Working Providence of Sions Saviour in New-England*, ed. Edward J. Gallagher (Delmar, NY, 1974), vii–viii; Child, *New-Englands Jonas*, 11.

19. C. H. Firth and R. S. Rait, eds., *Acts and Ordinances of the Interregnum, 1642–1660*, 3 vols. (London, 1911), 1:912–913; Billings, ed., *Old Dominion*, 300. For a Virginia letter of royal allegiance, c. 1649: Pepys, PL 2504, p. 789.

20. LPL, MS 754, pp. 1–2, 7, 9–10, 13–26, 41, 79–80, 108–111, 135–136.

21. William B. Trask, ed., "Samuel Danforth's records of the First Church in Roxbury, Mass.," *NEHGR*, 34 (1880), 85; MHS, Ms. N-1182, Carton 36: SH 114M U, Folder 35, Endecott letter, April 28, 1650; Whitfield, *Light Appearing*, 31; *Winthrop Papers*, 6:18–19.

22. Gardyner, *Description*, 92; John Clarke, *Ill Newes from New-England* (London, 1652), title page; Heimert and Delbanco, eds., *Puritans*, 208; *The Book of the General Lawes and Libertyes . . . of the Massachusets* (Cambridge, MA, 1648), 5–6.

23. *General Lawes and Libertyes*, 5; Malcolm Gaskill, *Witchfinders: A Seventeenth-Century English Tragedy* (London, 2005), 100; Dunn et al., eds., *Journal*, 711–713; Burr, ed., *Narratives*, 408.

24. Burr, ed., *Narratives*, 408–410; William Frederick Poole, "The witchcraft delusion of 1692, by Gov. Thomas Hutchinson," *NEHGR*, 24 (1870), 383–384. Cases are listed in John Putnam Demos, *Entertaining Satan: Witchcraft and the Culture of Early New England* (Oxford, 1982), 401–409.

25. Johnson, *History*, 199, 215–216; Carl Bridenbaugh, ed., *Letters of John Pynchon, 1654–1700* (Boston, 1982), xxv–xxi; Joseph H. Smith, ed., *Colonial Justice in Western Massachusetts (1639–1702): The Pynchon Court Record* (Cambridge, MA, 1961), 24; Stephen Innes, *Labor in a New Land: Economy and Society in Seventeenth-Century Springfield* (Princeton, NJ, 1983).

26. Samuel G. Drake, *Annals of Witchcraft in New England* (Boston, 1869), 219–258, quotation 244; David D. Hall, ed., *Witch-Hunting in Seventeenth-Century New England: A Documentary History, 1638–1692* (Boston, 1991), ch. 2; Smith, ed., *Colonial Justice*, 21–25; Jane Kamensky, "Talk like a man: speech, power and masculinity," *Gender and History*, 8 (1996), 36–37. On domestic roles, see Laurel Thatcher Ulrich, *Good Wives: Image and Reality in the Lives of Women in Northern New England, 1650–1750* (New York, 1982), ch. 2; Lisa Wilson, *Ye Heart of a Man: The Domestic Life of Men in Colonial New England* (New Haven, CT, 1999).

27. MHS, Ms. N-1182, Carton 36: SH 114M U, Folder 35, Arnold letter, September 1, 1651.

28. Clarke, *Ill Newes*, 1–7.

29. Ibid., 21–25.

30. Thomas Cobbett, *The Civil Magistrates Power in Matters of Religion Modestly Debated* (London, 1653), A2; Roger Williams, *The Bloody Tenent Yet More Bloody* (London, 1652), C3. Cf. John Norton, *A Discussion of That Great Point in Divinity, the Sufferings of Christ* (London, 1653).

31. Trask, ed., "Danforth's records," 85; Bremer, "Cotton"; Norton, *Abel Being Dead*, 45–46.

32. HEHL, HM 980, p. 418; Johnson, *History*, 84–85; Castillo and Schweitzer, eds., *Literatures*, 257; Heimert and Delbanco, eds., *Puritans*, 51.

33. Increase Mather, *Kometographia, or a Discourse Concerning Comets* (Boston, 1683), 111–112; *The Second Part of the Tragedy of Amboyna* (London, 1653), 4–5; Increase Mather, *A Relation of the Troubles . . . in New-England by Reason of the Indians There* (Boston, 1677), 67; HUA, UAI 15.850, Box 1, Folder 19, Cutter letter, May 19, 1654.

34. *The Humble Remonstrance and Petition of Certain Churches . . . in America* (London, 1653), 16; William Aspinwall, *A Premonition of Sundry Sad Calamities Yet to Come* (London, 1654), 14–15, 23–24, 37–39, quotation 39; *A Volume Relating to the Early History of Boston Containing the Aspinwall Notarial Records* (Boston, 1903), i–ix.

CHAPTER 11: DEVOURING CATERPILLARS AND GNAWING WORMS

1. Richard Ligon, *A True and Exact History of the Island of Barbados* (London, 1657), 1; Karen Ordahl Kupperman, "Richard Ligon," *ODNB.*

2. Ligon, *Barbados,* 1–2, 20–22, 25; *Certaine Inducements to Well Minded People* (London, n.d. [1643]), 5–6, 8, 9, 13.

3. Ligon, *Barbados,* 25, 27–29, 40–42.

4. Ibid., 30–34, 35, 37.

5. *Certaine Inducements,* 9, 13; Nicholas Foster, *A Briefe Relation of the Late Horrid Rebellion Acted in the Island Barbadas* (London, 1650), 1–3; *The Virginia Trade Stated* (London, 1647); Brenner, *Merchants,* 161; Nuala Zahedieh, "Sir Thomas Modyford," *ODNB.*

6. Ligon, *Barbados,* 43–53; Myra Jehlen, "History beside the fact: what we learn from *A True and Exact History of Barbadoes,*" in E. Ann Kaplan and George Levine, eds., *The Politics of Research* (Brunswick, NJ, 1997), 127–139.

7. Foster, *Briefe Relation,* 3–5, 16–17, 21–27, 31–34, 76, 102–104, 109; Matthew Parker, "Cavaliers of the Caribbean," *History Today,* 61 (2011), 28.

8. Firth and Rait, eds., *Acts and Ordinances,* 2:425–429; *CSPC, 1574–1660,* 345, 350, 364; A. B., *A Brief Relation of the Beginning and Ending of the Troubles of the Barbados* (London, 1653), 7; Bodl., Tanner MS 54, f. 153; Puckrein, *Little England,* chs. 6–7.

9. C. H. Josten, ed., *Elias Ashmole (1617–1692),* 5 vols. (Oxford, 1966), 2:562; TNA, CO 1/11, ff. 102–105v; Parker, "Cavaliers," 29–30.

10. T. H., *A True and Exact Narrative of the Proceedings of the Parliaments Fleet Against the Island of Barbadoes* (London, 1652), 10–12; Parker, "Cavaliers," 30–31; TNA, CO 1/11, f. 112; *Bloudy Newes from the Barbadaes* (London, 1652), 8; T. H., *True and Exact Narrative,* 8.

11. Arthur Woodnoth, *A Short Collection of the Most Remarkable Passages . . . of the Virginia Company* (London, 1651), A2; Billings, ed., *Old Dominion,* 300–301; *CSPC, 1574–1660,* 380–381, 408; BL, Egerton MS 2395, f. 175.

12. Ligon, *Barbados,* 35–37, 38–39.

13. Ibid., 85–92; *Winthrop Papers,* 5:220; Parker, "Cavaliers," 26–27.

14. *Winthrop Papers,* 5:96–97.

15. William Golding, *Servants on Horse-Back, or a Free-People Bestrided in Their Persons and Liberties by Worthlesse Men* (London, 1648), 1–2, 4, 7–8.

16. Josias Foster, *Copy of a Petition from the Governor and Company of the Sommer Islands* (London, 1651), 5–6, 12–15; Pestana, *English Atlantic,* 113–114; Hallett, ed., *Bermuda,* 311–324, 336, 340–344, 351; Craven and Hayward, eds., *Journal,* v, xlix; *CSPC, 1574–1660,* 449.

17. David Armitage, "The Cromwellian Protectorate and the languages of empire," *Historical Journal,* 35 (1992), 531–533; N. N., *America, or an Exact Description of the West-Indies* (London, 1655), A5–A5v (quotation); K. R. Andrews, "The English in the Caribbean, 1560–1620," in Andrews et al., eds., *Westward Enterprise,* 103–123.

18. Firth and Rait, eds., *Acts and Ordinances,* 2:403–406; John J. McCusker and Russell R. Menard, *The Economy of British America, 1607–1789* (Chapel Hill, NC, 1985), 48–50.

19. I. S., *A Brief and Perfect Journal of the Late Proceedings and Successe of the English Army in the West-Indies* (London, 1655), 5–6; *Winthrop Papers,* 4:263–267; Bernard Christian Steiner, *A History of the Plantation of Menunkatuck* (Baltimore, 1897), 74–75; BL, Egerton MS 2519, f. 10.

20. BL, Add. MS 11410, ff. 43v, 50; BL, Stowe MS 185, ff. 83–84; Thomas Gage, *The English-American, His Travail by Sea and Land* (London, 1648), A3v, A6v; Allen D. Boyer, "Thomas Gage," *ODNB.*

21. I. S., *Brief and Perfect Journal,* 11–15; BL, Egerton MS 2648, f. 247.

22. Nathaniel Morton, *New England's Memorial,* 6th ed. (Boston, 1855), 169; BL, Egerton MS 2648, ff. 242, 246v–247, 248v.

23. BL, Egerton MS 2648, f. 247; *CSPC, 1574–1660,* 176–177; *A Dialogue . . . Concerning the Present Designe in the West-Indies* (London, 1655), 5–6; Robert Latham and William Matthews, eds., *The Diary of Samuel Pepys,* 11 vols. (London, 1995), 4:376; I. S., *Brief and Perfect Journal,* 2–4; Boyer, "Gage"; HEHL, BL 312, ff. 1–1v.

24. BL, Egerton MS 2395, ff. 144–144v, 157–158; Daniel Gookin, *To All Persons . . . in the Several Townes and Plantations of the United Colonies in New England* ([Boston], 1656); Bodl., Rawlinson MS A.43, f. 125; Macfarlane, ed., *Diary*, 363.

25. *A True Description of Jamaica* (London, 1657), 4; *A Narrative of the Great Success . . . in Jamaica* (London, 1658), 2–4; Edward Doyley, *A Brief Relation of a Victory . . . Against the Forces of the King of Spain* (Edinburgh, 1659); Barry Coward, *The Cromwellian Protectorate* (Manchester, 2002), 134.

26. William Hand Browne, ed., *Judicial and Testamentary Business of the Provincial Court, 1649/50–1657* (Baltimore, 1891), 534–545, quotation 536; Alan Tully, *Forming American Politics: Ideals, Interests and Institutions in Colonial New York and Pennsylvania* (Baltimore, 1994), ch. 1.

27. Maryland State Archives, MSA S 977–971, ff. 354–359, quotations 354, 356; Edward C. Papenfuse et al., eds., *A Biographical Dictionary of the Maryland Legislature, 1635–1789*, 2 vols. (Baltimore, 1979, 1985), 1:374.

28. Bodl., Rawlinson MS A.43, ff. 93, 107; *The Lord Baltemores Case Concerning the Province of Maryland* (London, 1653), 2, 10–11, 14, quotations 10, 14; *Virginia and Maryland, or the Lord Baltamore's Printed Case Uncased and Answered* (London, 1655), 1–5, 10–12, quotations 5, 10; William E. Nelson, *The Common Law in Colonial America*, vol. 1, *The Chesapeake and New England, 1607–1660* (Oxford, 2008), ch. 6.

29. William Gouge, *Strength Out of Weakness* (London, 1652), A4v, 27–29, 38–39; John Cotton, *An Exposition upon the Thirteenth Chapter of the Revelation* (London, 1655), 93, 111. Cf. idem, *The Saints Support & Comfort in the Time of Distress and Danger* (London, 1657).

30. *Virginia and Maryland*, 33–38, 40–42, 46–49, quotations 34, 37; Roger Heaman, *An Additional Brief Narrative of a Late Bloody Design* (London, 1655), 2–4.

31. Heaman, *Additional Brief Narrative*, 3; Bodl., Rawlinson MS A.43, f. 96; Leonard Strong, *Babylon's Fall in Maryland: A Fair Warning to Lord Baltamore* (London, 1655), 7–11, quotation 10; *Virginia and Maryland*, 67.

32. John Langford, *A Just and Cleer Refutaton of a False and Scandalous Pamphlet* (London, 1655), 15–20; Strong, *Babylon's Fall*, 11; Cotton, *Exposition*; John Hammond, *Leah and Rachel, or the Two Fruitfull Sisters Virginia and Mary-land* (London, 1656), 23–25, 30.

CHAPTER 12: A HEAP OF TROUBLES AND CONFUSION

1. George Alsop, *A Character of the Province of Mary-Land* (London, 1666), 73–80, quotation 74.

2. Ibid., 80–85, quotations 83, 85.

3. Firth, ed., *American Garland*, 35–38; Hammond, *Leah and Rachel*, 1, 5, 14–15, 19.

4. Hammond, *Leah and Rachel*, 2–14, 15–16.

5. HMC, *Seventh Report*, 45.

6. *A Perfect Description of Virginia* (London, 1649), 5–6; William Bullock, *Virginia Impartially Examined* (London, 1649), A4v, 2–9, 12–14, 31, 40, 54–55, 66; Peter Thompson, "William Bullock's 'strange adventure': a plan to transform seventeenth-century Virginia," *WMQ*, 61 (2004), 114–115.

7. Edward Williams, *Virginia: More Especially the South Part Thereof Richly and Truly Valued*, 2nd ed. (London, 1650), B2–B4, 4–5, 13, 39; idem, *Virginia's Discovery of Silke-Wormes* (London, 1650), 32.

8. BL, Egerton MS 1238, f. 2; Gloucestershire Archives, GBR/H/2/3, pp. 177–178; *Harry Hangman's Honour* (London, 1655); Williams, *Virginia*, 46, 51–52, 60–71, 76–78.

9. Bodl., Rawlinson MS A.14, ff. 84–85; Nora Miller Turman and Mark C. Lewis, eds., "The will of Ann Littleton of Northampton County, Virginia, 1656," *VMHB*, 75 (1967), 11–21; Billings, ed., *Old Dominion*, 126–129, 135–143.

10. Alsop, *Mary-land*, 86–96, quotations 86–87, 94; Castillo and Schweitzer, eds., *Literatures*, 108; Bullock, *Virginia*, 29; O. L., *A Despised Virgin Beautified, or Virginia Benefited* (London, 1653), 3; *CSPC, 1574–1660*, 98.

11. Sheila D. Thompson, ed., *The Book of Examinations and Depositions Before the Mayor*

and Justices of Southampton, 1648–1663 (Southampton, UK, 1994), 113–117; E. H. Bates Harbin, ed., *Quarter Sessions Records for the County of Somerset*, 4 vols. (London, 1907–1919), 3:358–359; Lionel Gatford, *Publick Good Without Private Interest* (London, 1657), A2v, B3–B4, 3–4, 5–7, 9–12; Jason McElligott, "Lionel Gatford," *ODNB*.

12. Gatford, *Publick Good*, 4–5, 19, quotation 5; Hammond, *Leah and Rachel*, 16; Peter Wilson Coldham, "The 'spiriting' of London children to Virginia, 1648–1685," *VMHB*, 83 (1975), 280–282; Jeaffreson, ed., *Middlesex*, 3:239, 253, 259, 271, 274; Bullock, *Virginia*, 14.

13. *CSPC, 1574–1660*, 220–221; Peter Wilson Coldham, ed., *The Bristol Registers of Servants Sent to Foreign Plantations, 1654–1686* (Baltimore, 1988), v. See Gloucestershire Archives, GBR/C/10/2, pp. 371–378, for apprentices to Virginia and Barbados, 1659–1660.

14. *Strange Newes from Virginia, Being a True Relation of a Great Tempest* (London, 1667), 6; MHS, Ms. N-791, p. 23; MHS, Ms. N-1182, Carton 36: SH 114M U, Folder 35, Arnold letter, 1651.

15. Johnson, *History*, 42–43, 174–175; Gardyner, *Description*, 91; John Josselyn, *New-Englands Rarities Discovered* (London, 1672), 1; *idem, Account*, 162, 172–173. Cf. the 1660s survey, which said, "Their houses are generally wooden; their streets crooked; with little decency and no uniformity": Kavenagh, ed., *Foundations*, 1:138.

16. Clarke, *John Hull*, 39–44, 53–57; Jensen, ed., *Colonial Documents*, 424–426; Mark Peterson, "Big money comes to Boston: the curious history of the pine tree shilling," *Common-Place*, 6 (2006), www.common-place.org/vol-06/no-03/peterson/; Williams, *Key*, 144–146, 153–156, esp. 146.

17. Gragg, *Englishmen Transplanted*, 179; Josselyn, *Account*, 185; Kavenagh, ed., *Foundations*, 1:981; James M. O'Toole, "New England reactions to the English civil wars," *NEHGR*, 129 (1975), 240; Margaret Ellen Newell, *From Dependency to Independence: Economic Revolution in Colonial New England* (Ithaca, NY, 1998). In the 1630s, Lord Maltravers was licensed to mint plantation farthings to inhibit barter: *CSPC, 1574–1660*, 285.

18. Olson, *Anglo-American Politics*, 16–22, 30–37; Clarke, *John Hull*, 85–90; Kavenagh, ed., *Foundations*, 1:455, 2:1270; Gatford, *Publick Good*, 20.

19. Johnson, *History*, 208–210; James E. McWilliams, "Beyond declension: economic adaptation and the pursuit of export markets in the Massachusetts Bay region, 1630–1700," in Robert Olwell and Alan Tully, eds., *Cultures and Identities in Colonial British America* (Baltimore, 2006), 123; Brian Donahue, *The Great Meadow: Farmers and Land in Colonial Concord* (New Haven, CT, 2004), 79; Sarah F. MacMahon, "'A comfortable subsistence': the changing composition of diet in rural New England, 1620–1840," *WMQ*, 42 (1985), 35; Sumner Chilton Powell, *Puritan Village: The Formation of a New England Town* (Middlebrook, CT, 1963); William Cronon, *Changes in the Land: Indians, Colonists and the Ecology of New England* (New York, 1983), ch. 7.

20. Daniel Vickers, "Competency and competition: economic culture in early America," *WMQ*, 47 (1990), 3–29; Lockridge, *New England Town*, 55; Winslow, *Good Newes*, 64; Richard P. Gildrie, *Salem, Massachusetts, 1626–1683: A Covenant Community* (Charlottesville, VA, 1975), chs. 5–8; Mark Valeri, "Puritans in the marketplace," in Bremer and Botelho, eds., *World of John Winthrop*, 147–186; Stephen Innes, *Creating the Commonwealth: The Economic Culture of Puritan New England* (New York, 1995), ch. 3.

21. General court quoted in Miller, *New England Mind*, 28; Bouton et al., eds., *Documents*, 1:191n; MSA, vol. 38B/185–189; Pope, ed., *Notebook*, 193.

22. Samuel Abbott Green, ed., *Note-Book Kept by Capt. Robert Keayne* (Cambridge, MA, 1889), 5–7; Pierce, ed., *Records*, 32–33; MHS, Ms. N-791, p. 16; CSL, Hartford County Court Minutes, vol. 2, p. 113; BL, Lansdowne MS 93, ff. 185, 187, 189–215, quotation 193v.

23. John Eliot, *A Late and Further Manifestation of the Progress of the Gospel Amongst the Indians in New-England* (London, 1655), 11; *The Banners of Grace and Love Displayed* (London, 1657), 18–19; Gouge, *Strength Out of Weakness*, 34; *A Further Accompt of the Progresse of the Gospel Amongst the Indians in New-England* (London, 1659), A2v.

24. LMA, MS 7947, ff. 3, 5, 6–7, 14, 18; LMA, MS 7943; Essex RO, D/P 95/1/1, January 8, 1653; Norfolk RO, PD 209/167.

25. Bodl., Rawlinson C.934, ff. 10–11v; Eliot, *Late and Further Manifestation*, 3–4; *Further Accompt*, 2–3; John Eliot, *Tears of Repentance* (London, 1653), B3v; *Banners of Grace*, 22–23.

26. DWL, Baxter MSS, Letters, vol. 3, f. 9; LMA, MS 7936, f. 2; LMA, MS 7947, ff. 23, 27, 29; CSL, Connecticut Archives, Indians, series I, vol. 1, nos. 4a–4b.

27. DWL, Baxter MSS, Letters, vol. 4, ff. 6–7v; John Eliot, *The Christian Commonwealth* (London, 1659), A3–A3v, B1–2, C1–4, quotations C1v, C3–C4v.

28. Bodl., Ashmole MS 240, f. 276. The colonial population was 109,209 in 1660; in 1651 that of England was 5,228,000: Greene, *Pursuits of Happiness*, 178; E. A. Wrigley and R. S. Schofield, *The Population History of England, 1541–1871: A Reconstruction* (Cambridge, UK, 1981), 208–209; Robert V. Wells, "The population of England's colonies in America: old English or new Americans?" *Population Studies*, 46 (1992), 85–102.

29. Martha W. Hiden and Henry M. Dargan, eds., "John Gibbon's manuscript notes concerning Virginia," *VMHB*, 74 (1966), 10, 12–13, 15; Alsop, *Mary-land*, 100–101.

30. Henry Jessey, *The Lords Loud Call to England* (London, 1660), 17–18, 20–23, quotations 18, 22; Thomas Clark, *The Voice of Truth Uttered Forth Against . . . the Island of Barbados* (London, 1661), 4–6; Robert Maylins, *A Letter . . . from the Barbadoes* (London, 1661).

31. Elizabeth Donnan, ed., *Documents Illustrative of the History of the Slave Trade to America*, 4 vols. (Washington, DC, 1930–1950), 1:125–126; McCusker and Menard, *Economy of British America*, 153; K. G. Davies, *The North Atlantic World in the Seventeenth Century* (Minneapolis, 1974), 74; Jordan and Walsh, *White Cargo*, chs. 9–12; Sean O'Callaghan, *To Hell or Barbados: The Ethnic Cleansing of Ireland* (Dingle, 2001); Charles Edward Banks, "Scotch prisoners deported to New England by Cromwell," *Procs of the MHS*, 61 (1927–1928), 4–29; Laurence William Towner, *A Good Master Well Served: Masters and Servants in Colonial Massachusetts, 1620–1750* (New York, 1998); Bodl., Rawlinson MS A.14, f. 92; Peter Wilson Coldham, ed., *Lord Mayor's Court of London Depositions Relating to Americans, 1641–1736* (Washington, DC, 1980), 80.

32. *Englands Slavery, or Barbados Merchandize* (London, 1659), 4–5.

33. Ibid., 8–10; BL, Egerton MS 2395, ff. 182–183. On the extension of Cromwellian policy: Pestana, *English Atlantic*, 213–226.

34. MHS, Ms. N-791, pp. 31, 33; Ms. N-1182, Carton 36: SH 114M U, Folder 39, Leverett letter, 1660; *CSPC, 1574–1660*, 495; Isabel MacBeath Calder, ed., *Letters of John Davenport, Puritan Divine* (New Haven, CT, 1937), 184–189.

35. Clarke, *John Hull*, 96; Greene, ed., *Great Britain*, xiii–xiv; Jensen, ed., *Colonial Documents*, 233–234; Kavenagh, ed., *Foundations*, 2:1344–1345.

36. Henry Gardiner, *New-Englands Vindication* (London, 1660), title page, 4–8; Charles Edward Banks, ed., *New-England's Vindication by Henry Gardiner* (Portland, ME, 1884), 7–8.

CHAPTER 13: HOW IS YOUR BEAUTY BECOME ASHES?

1. MHS, Ms. N-791, p. 30; Carla Gardina Pestana, "The city upon a hill under siege: the Puritan perception of the Quaker threat to Massachusetts Bay, 1656–1661," *NEQ*, 56 (1983), 323–353; Jonathan M. Chu, *Neighbors, Friends or Madmen: The Puritan Adjustment to Quakerism in Seventeenth-Century Massachusetts Bay* (Westport, CT, 1985); Edward Burrough, *A Declaration of the Sad and Great Persecution and Martyrdom of the People of God Called Quakers* (London, 1661), 29–30.

2. *A Call from Death to Life* (London, 1660), 32; Kenneth L. Carroll, "Maryland Quakers in England, 1659–1720," *Maryland Historical Magazine*, 91 (1996), 453–454; George Bishop, *New England Judged* (London, 1661), 107; *An Answer to a Scandalous Paper* (London, 1656), A4v; John Norton, *The Heart of New-England Rent at the Blasphemies of the Present Generation* (London, 1659), 3–4, 32.

3. Kavenagh, ed., *Foundations*, 1:480; Catie Gill, "Edward Burrough," *ODNB*; Several Epistles Given Forth by Two of the Lords Faithful Servants Whom He Sent to New-England* (London, 1669), 9–11, quotation 11. Burrough died in prison in 1663 at the age of

twenty-nine. See also Adrian Davies, *The Quakers in English Society, 1655–1725* (Oxford, 2000), ch. 13.

4. BPL, Ms. Ch.F.7.4; *CSPC, 1661–1668*, 32; Bishop, *New England Judged*, 170–171.

5. *A Declaration of the General Court of the Massachusets . . . Concerning the Execution of Two Quakers* (London, 1659); Edward Rawson, *A True Relation of the Proceedings Against Certain Quakers* (London, 1660); Francis Howgill, *The Popish Inquisition Newly Erected in New-England* (London, 1659), 63–70; Laurence Claxton, *The Quakers Downfal* (London, 1659), 42, 50–51; Humphrey Smith, *New-Englands Pretended Christians* (London, 1660); Joseph Nicholson, *The Standard of the Lord Lifted Up in New-England* (London, 1660), 9, 20.

6. George Fox, *Secret Workes of a Cruel People Made Manifest* (London, 1659), 2–3, quotation 2; TNA, CO 1/15, f. 60.

7. Bishop, *New England Judged*, 29–31, quotation 30; Fox, *Secret Workes*, 17.

8. DWL, Baxter MSS, Letters, vol. 4, ff. 6–7v; Hooke, *New Englands Teares*, 21; Joseph Rowlandson, *The Possibility of Gods Forsaking a People* (Boston, 1678), 18; BL, Egerton MS 2395, f. 418; N. N., *Short Account*, 6–7; Fischer, *Albion's Seed*, 130.

9. N. N., *Short Account*, 7; Gatford, *Publick Good*, 10; Alsop, *Mary-land*, 96; S[amuel] G[orton], *A Glass for the People of New-England* (London, 1676), 16; Josselyn, *Account*, 173; George Fox, *Cain Against Abel, Representing New-England's Church-Hirarchy in Opposition* (London, 1675), 31–32; John Noble, ed., *Records of the Court of Assistants of the Colony of the Massachusetts Bay, 1630–1692*, 3 vols. (Boston, 1901–1928), 3:34–38.

10. TNA, CO 1/15, ff. 56–57v.

11. Ogborn, *Global Lives*, 132–134.

12. HMC, *Seventh Report*, 115–116; Pepys, PL 2504, p. 697; Pestana, "Hugh Peter."

13. TNA, CO 1/15, ff. 165–165v, 167; *The Humble Petition and Address of the General Court Sitting at Boston* ([Cambridge, MA], 1660), 3–5; *CSPC, 1661–1668*, 12.

14. Bodl., Clarendon MS 74, ff. 228–229; *CSPC, 1574–1660*, 24–27.

15. TNA, CO 1/15, f. 121; Mather, *Magnalia*, 6:38–39.

16. Joan Brooksop, *An Invitation of Love unto the Seed of God Throughout the World* (London, 1662), 13–15; Robert G. Pope, *The Half-Way Covenant: Church Membership in Puritan New England* (Princeton, NJ, 1969); Darren Staloff, *The Making of an American Thinking Class: Intellectuals and Intelligensia in Puritan Massachusetts* (New York, 1998), chs. 5–7; John Allyn, *Animadversions upon the Antisynodalia Americana, a Treatise Printed in Old England* (Cambridge, MA, 1664), 15–16.

17. *Monthly Magazine*, 7 (1799), 30; Clarke, *John Hull*, 97–99; HEHL, Goodspeed Collection, Folder 2, Charles II to Endecott, 1662; TNA, SP 14/13, pp. 356–357; Bodl., Clarendon MS 74, ff. 238, 245–249v, 259–261.

18. Shagan, *Rule of Moderation*, ch. 5; Elliott, *Empires of the Atlantic World*, chs. 5–8.

19. Trask, ed., "Roxbury," 88–89; Samuel Danforth, *An Astronomical Description of the Late Comet or Blazing-Star as It Appeared in New England* (London, 1666), 23–24; CSL, Hartford County Court Minutes, vol. 2, pp. 160, 174–175, 182–184; Helen Schatvet Ullmann, ed., *Hartford County, Connecticut, Court Minutes, Vols. 3 and 4* (Boston, 2005), 7, 48–49, 50, 61–62; John Higginson, *The Cause of God and His People in New-England* (Cambridge, MA, 1663), 10–12.

20. Harrison T. Meserole, ed., *Seventeenth-Century American Poetry* (New York, 1968), 37–38; Edmund S. Morgan, ed., *The Diary of Michael Wigglesworth, 1653–1657: The Conscience of a Puritan* (New York, 1965), v–viii, x–xi; NYPL, Mss Col. 731, no. 39; NEHGS, MSS 71, Folder 6, Wigglesworth's notebook, December 20–21, 1659.

21. NEHGS, MSS 71, Folder 1 (Middlebrook letter, 1657), Folder 6 (Wigglesworth's notebook, 1663–1664); BL, Egerton MS 2543, f. 127; Richard Blome, *A Description of the Island of Jamaica with Other Isles and Territories in America* (London, 1672), 123–124.

22. Pepys, PL 2504, p. 697; George Francis Dow, ed., *Records and Files of the Quarterly Courts of Essex County, Massachusetts*, 8 vols. (Salem, MA, 1911–1921), 3:142–143.

23. Bodl., Clarendon MS 103, ff. 28, 51; Bouton et al., eds., *Documents*, 1:265–270, quotation 269; Danforth, *Astronomical Description*, 19.

24. BL, Egerton MS 2395, ff. 426–435.

25. New Haven Historical Society, MSS 8, Box I, Folders C–D.

26. *CSPC, 1661–1668*, 332–333.

27. Taylor, *Colonial America*, 40, 41, 92–93; *CSPC, 1661–1668*, 385–387, 390–391, 616–617.

28. BL, Egerton MS 2543, f. 123v; Egerton MS 2395, f. 24; *CSPC, 1675–1676*, 125; Thomas W. Krise, ed., *Caribbeana: An Anthology of English Literature of the West Indies, 1657–1777* (Chicago, 1999), 31–32; Edmund Hickeringill, *Jamaica Viewed*, 2nd ed. (London, 1661), 1–3, 80–81; *CSPC, 1661–1668*, 63; LPL, Fulham Papers, vol. 17, f. 93.

29. BL, Add. Ms 11410, f. 34; TNA, CO 1/19, ff. 187–190v; John Gadbury, *The West India or Jamaica Almanack* (London, 1673), A3, B1; Blome, *Description*, 8–14, 59; William Hughes, *The American Physitian* (London, 1672), 111–112, 127–131, 142–143, 147.

30. TNA, SP 44/14/46; David Souden, "'Rogues, whores and vagabonds'? Indentured servant emigrants to North America, and the case of mid-seventeenth-century Bristol," *Social History*, 3 (1978), 36–37; Joseph E. Inikori, *Africans and the Industrial Revolution in England* (Cambridge, UK, 2002), 219–220; Donnan, ed., *Documents*, 1:174; Puckrein, *Little England*, ch. 5.

31. BL, Egerton MS 2543, f. 123; Taylor, *Colonial America*, 78; *CSPC, 1661–1668*, 317; J. Horsfall Turner, ed., *The Rev. Oliver Heywood, B.A., 1630–1702: His Autobiography*, 3 vols. (Brighouse, UK, 1882–1885), 1:3–5, 35, 101; Jack P. Greene, *Imperatives, Behaviors and Identities: Essays in Early American Cultural History* (Charlottesville, VA, 1992), ch. 2; Franklin W. Knight, *The Caribbean: The Genesis of a Fragmented Nationalism*, 2nd ed. (New York, 1990), ch. 5; Dunn, *Sugar and Slaves*, 238–246; Amussen, *Caribbean Exchanges*, 129–135; David Barry Gaspar, "'Rigid and inclement': origins of the Jamaica slave laws of the seventeenth century," in Christopher L. Tomlins and Bruce H. Mann, eds., *The Many Legalities of Early America* (Chapel Hill, NC, 2001), 78–96; Kathleen M. Brown, *Good Wives, Nasty Wenches, and Anxious Patriarchs: Gender, Race, and Power in Colonial Virginia* (Chapel Hill, NC, 1996), ch. 4.

32. Essex RO, D/DRg 1/157; CKS, U840/T223; *CSPC, 1661–1668*, 194, 196.

33. Thomas Tryon, *Friendly Advice to the Gentlemen-Planters of the East and West Indies* (London, 1684), 81–82, 85; Blome, *Description*, 84–86, 88. The Quakers' leader said white Barbadians and Jamaicans would find slavery "hard Measure": George Fox, *Gospel Family-ly-Order* (London, 1676), 18.

34. Michael A. LaCombe, "Francis Willoughby," *ODNB*; *CSPC, 1661–1668*, 167–168; George Warren, *An Impartial Description of Surinam* (London, 1667), 19; LaCombe, "Willoughby"; *CSPC, 1661–1668*, 325, 364–366.

35. *CSPC, 1661–1668*, 207–208; BL, Add. MS 27382, f. 193v; TNA, CO 1/19, ff. 211–212, quotation 211; LaCombe, "Willoughby."

36. Latham and Matthews, eds., *Diary*, 7:390–391.

CHAPTER 14: REMEMBRANCE OF AN EXILE IN A REMOTE WILDERNESS

1. Quinn, ed., *New American World*, 266; Cornwall RO, DD/CN/3478; Samuel Eliot Morison et al., eds., *Records of the Suffolk County Court, 1671–1680*, 2 vols. (Boston, 1933), 1:128, 149–150, 185–186, 189; Borthwick Institute, York, CP.H.3497; Ian K. Steele, *The English Atlantic, 1675–1740: An Exploration of Communication and Community* (New York, 1986), 10–11.

2. Josten, ed., *Ashmole*, 2:598; Bernard Capp, "Nehemiah Bourne," *ODNB*; *Winthrop Papers*, 5:243–245; *CSPC, 1675–1676*, 83; *CSPC, 1681–1685*, 77–78. In 1647 a Barbadian was ordered to support a child in Somerset: Harbin, ed., *Quarter Sessions*, 3:46, 337.

3. Dow, ed., *Records*, 3:70; Jeaffreson, ed., *Middlesex*, 3:220–221. For transatlantic bequests: Ullmann, ed., *Hartford*, 142; HUA, UAI 15.850, Box 4, Folder 1, Dunster petition (1652) and another (1654) in Box 1, Folder 20; HEHL, HM 9747; East Suffolk RO, T4/19/3 (Ives); HMC, *Twelfth Report*, 362.

4. HEHL, BR Box 217 (1); HM 9736; Ullmann, ed., *Hartford*, 117, 277; Nuala Zahedieh, "Making mercantilism work: London merchants and Atlantic trade in the seventeenth

century," *Transactions of the RHS*, 9 (1999), 152–154; Bodl., Add. MS C.267, ff. 3v, 16–16v, 17v–18v; HMC, *Seventh Report*, 87; Coldham, ed., *Lord Mayor's Court*, 3; TNA, C 2/ChasI/B86/3, B93–94; Cressy, *Coming Over*, 179.

5. TNA, C 10/18/3, ff. 1–2.

6. Jordan and Walsh, *White Cargo*, 13; Edward Holyoke, *The Doctrine of Life, or of Mans Redemtion* (London, 1658), A2; Coldham, ed., *Lord Mayor's Court*, 35; BPL, Ms. Am. 1502/2/2; Susan J. Matt, *Homesickness: An American History* (Oxford, 2011), ch. 1; Cotton Mather, *The Wonders of the Invisible World* (London, 1693), 53–55.

7. A. Rupert Hall and Marie Boas Hall, eds., *The Correspondence of Henry Oldenburg*, 12 vols. (London and Philadelphia, 1965–1986), 5:158–161.

8. Richard S. Dunn, *Puritans and Yankees: The Winthrop Dynasty of New England, 1630–1717* (Princeton, NJ, 1962), 169.

9. Sarah Irving, "An empire restored: America and the Royal Society of London in the Restoration," in Armstrong et al., eds., *America and the British Imagination*, 27–47; Walter W. Woodward, *Prospero's America: John Winthrop Jr., Alchemy, and the Creation of New England Culture, 1606–1676* (Chapel Hill, NC, 2010), ch. 8; Hall and Hall, eds., *Correspondence*, 4:525; 5:156.

10. RS, Cl.P/3i/23, ff. 1–1v; RBO/2i/19, 81–92; EL/W3/20, p. 2 (quotation); Hall and Hall, eds., *Correspondence*, 2:105, 149, 241; 5:422–425; RS, RBO/1, ff. 205–207.

11. Hall and Hall, eds., *Correspondence*, 6:253–257, 528–530, 594–596; 7:142–145, 568; 8:265–268, 305–306, 594–595; 9:256; Raymond Phineas Stearns, *Science in the British Colonies in America* (Urbana, IL, 1970), 131–138.

12. *CSPC, 1574–1660*, 75; Purchas, *Pilgrimage*, 621; Vaughan, *Transatlantic Encounters*, 43; Arthur MacGregor, "John Tradescant, the younger," *ODNB*; Marjorie Swann, *Curiosities and Texts: The Culture of Collecting in Early Modern England* (Philadelphia, 2001), 28; Hall and Hall, eds., *Correspondence*, 2:149–150; BL, Add. MS 11411, ff. 7v–8.

13. Hickeringill, *Jamaica*, 24–25; Krise, ed., *Caribbeana*, 89; Tryon, *Friendly Advice*, 11; Hughes, *American Physitian*, 60; *Certaine Inducements*, 8; Bruce, ed., *Verney*, 194; Walvin, *Fruits of Empire*, 95–96.

14. Ogborn, *Global Lives*, 118; John Ogilby, *America: Being the Latest and Most Accurate Description of the New World* (London, 1671), 151; HEHL, Rare Books 47507P, "Geographical playing cards," c. 1675; Catherine Perry Hargrave, "The playing cards of Puritan New England," *Old Time New England*, 18 (1927), 167–181.

15. MHS, Ms. N-522, Folder 1, pp. 1–3, 12 (original at AAS); Michael G. Hall, *The Last American Puritan: The Life of Increase Mather, 1639–1723* (Middletown, CT, 1988), chs. 1–2; AAS, MSS Boxes "M," Box 3, Folder 1, March 28, October 5, and November 5, 1664; July 17, 1666 (original at MHS).

16. Bodl., Ashmole MS 423, ff. 244–244v; Calder, ed., *Letters*, 256–257; MHS, Ms. N-791, p. 55; Dow, ed., *Records*, 3:298; Trask, ed., "Danforth's records," 164.

17. MHS, Ms. N-791, p. 54; Josselyn, *Account*, 273; Anne Bradstreet, *Several Poems*, 2nd ed. (Boston, 1678), 248; AAS, MSS Boxes "M," Box 3, Folder 1, December 1, 1664; August 28, 1666; January 1, 1667.

18. LaFantasie, ed., *Correspondence*, 2:539; Trask, ed., "Danforth's records," 165; Josselyn, *Account*, 274–275; MHS, Ms. N-791, p. 57; NYPL, Mss. Col. 731, no. 27; Trask, ed., "Danforth's records," 166.

19. Mather, *Kometographia*, 117–118; Thomas Vincent, *Gods Terrible Voice in the City* (Cambridge, MA, 1668), 30, 32–33, 69–70, 154, 194, quotations 30, 69; Coldham, ed., *Lord Mayor's Court*, 16; LMA, MS 7936, f. 7.

20. CSL, Crimes & Misdemeanors, series I, 1662–1789, vol. 1, p. 18a; Kavenagh, ed., *Foundations*, 1:143–144; Samuel Coddington, *A Demonstration of True Love unto . . . Massachusets in New-England* (n.p., 1674), 7–8; Robert M. Bliss, *Revolution and Empire: English Politics and the American Colonies in the Seventeenth Century* (Manchester, 1990), 157–159; Dow, ed., *Records*, 3:431.

21. Bodl., Ashmole MS 423, f. 268; *CSPC, 1661–1668*, 465, 619; Norfolk RO, AYL 535/6/3, ff. 1–2v; 535/6/4; 831/4.

22. TNA, CO 1/24, f. 164.

23. Norfolk RO, AYL 535/6/5, f. 1v; *CSPC, 1661–1668*, 561, 563; *A True and Perfect Narrative of the Late Dreadful Fire . . . in the Barbadoes* (London, 1668); Latham and Mathews, eds., *Diary*, 9:243; TNA, CO 1/24, ff. 164v, 165v.

24. CKS, Fa/FAm 4–5; Norfolk RO, Y/PP 27; *CSPC, 1661–1668*, 284; MHS, Ms. N-791, p. 60; Lydia Fell, *A Testimony and Warning Given Forth in the Love of Truth* (London, 1676), 1–3, 7.

25. Samuel Hartlib, *A Rare and New Discovery of a Speedy Way and Easy Means . . . for the Feeding of Silk-Worms* (London, 1652); *idem, The Reformed Virginian Silk-Worm* (London, 1655), esp. 19–20, 23–29; BL, Add. MS 11411, f. 24; Egerton MS 2395, ff. 296–298; RS, Cl.P/19/48, ff. 1, 92–93; Hall and Hall, eds., *Correspondence*, 8:595; RS, RBC/2, p. 91; Hartlib, *Reformed Virginian Silk-Worm*, 27.

26. Warren M. Billings, *Sir William Berkeley and the Forging of Colonial Virginia* (Baton Rouge, LA, 2004), 272; William Berkeley, *A Discourse and View of Virginia* (London, 1663), 4–5; BL, Egerton MS 2395, ff. 363, 365–366.

27. BL, Egerton MS 2395, ff. 362–362v, 366–367, 666; Johnson, *History*, 227–228.

28. Morgan Godwyn, *The Negro's and Indians Advocate* (London, 1680), 168; RS, RB/1/3, ff. 128–130; Gatford, *Publick Good*, B4; Robert C. Winthrop, ed., *Life and Letters of John Winthrop*, 2 vols. (Boston, 1864–1867), 2:430. On popular religion in Virginia: Rutman and Rutman, *Small Worlds*, ch. 8.

29. R[obert] G[reene], *Virginia's Cure, or an Advisive Narrative Concerning Virginia* (London, 1662), 6–9, 18–21, quotations 6, 7.

30. CKS, U120/C8/14; RS, EL/M1/36a, 37; Edward L. Bond, *Damned Souls in a Tobacco Colony: Religion in Seventeenth-Century Virginia* (Macon, GA, 2000), 214n; HEHL, Goodspeed Collection, Folder 5, Rogers letter, July 10, 1671.

31. Warren M. Billings, "The transfer of English law to Virginia, 1606–50," in Andrews et al., eds., *Westward Enterprise*, 243–244; Steven Sarson, *British America, 1500–1800: Creating Colonies, Imagining an Empire* (London, 2005), 192; McIlwaine, ed., *Minutes*, 488; Alan Taylor, *American Colonies: The Settling of North America* (London, 2002), 136; Bodl., Clarendon MS 84, ff. 230–231.

32. Berkeley, *Discourse*, 3; VHS, Mss 1 B4678/b1; Mss 1 T2118 d 4, 9–10; Jeaffreson, ed., *Middlesex*, 3:336–337, 381; *CSPC, 1661–1668*, 555; *CSPC, 1675–1676*, 521; *Calendar of State Papers, Domestic, 1667*, 250; Joseph Glanvill, *Some Philosophical Considerations Touching the Being of Witches* (London, 1668), 38; *The Kid-napper Trapan'd, or the Treacherous Husband Caught in His Own Trap* (London, 1675).

33. *CSPC, 1661–1668*, 273; MHS, Ms. N-1182, Carton 36: SH 114M U, Folder 33, Berkeley letter, June 12, 1644; HEHL, BL 82 (New York, 1665); Virginia Center for Digital History, University of Virginia, York Co. Deeds, Orders & Wills, vol. 3, ff. 66, 79, 85, 176; vol. 4, ff. 61, 111, 119, 126a, 178, 301; Billings, ed., *Old Dominion*, 167–172; McIlwaine, ed., *Minutes*, 209–210; *CSPC, 1669–1674*, 63–64.

34. Ogilby, *America*, 197; Berkeley, *Discourse*, 1, 10; HMC, *Hastings*, 2:317; Billings, ed., *Old Dominion*, 133; Warren M. Billings, "Sir William Berkeley," *ODNB*.

35. Peter Thompson, "The thief, the householder and the commons: languages of class in seventeenth-century Virginia," *WMQ*, 63 (2006), 257–258, 276–279; Billings, ed., *Old Dominion*, 296, 319–329. Edward Bond sees these colonists as "ambiguous Englishmen": *Damned Souls*, ch. 4.

CHAPTER 15: THE DAY OF TROUBLE IS NEAR

1. BPL, Ms. Am. 1502/2/16; Randall Balmer, *A Perfect Babel of Confusion: Dutch Religion and English Culture in the Middle Colonies* (New York, 1989), ch. 1; Joyce D. Goodfriend, *Before the Melting Pot: Society and Culture in Colonial New York City, 1664–1730* (Princeton, NJ,

1992); Donna Merwick, "Becoming English: Anglo-Dutch conflict in the 1670s in Albany, New York," *New York History*, 62 (1981), 389–414.

2. John Evelyn, *Navigation and Commerce, Their Original and Progress* (London, 1674), 15; Carew Reynell, *The True English Interest, or an Account of the Chief National Improvements* (London, 1674), 85, 90–91; V. E. Chancellor, "Carew Reynell," *ODNB*.

3. Hall and Hall, eds., *Correspondence*, 5:425.

4. William Talbot, *The Discoveries of John Lederer* (London, 1672), 6–11, 16, 22–25. Believed to be a trip of a few days, it was actually 10,000 miles across the Pacific.

5. RS, RB/1/44/16, ff. 117–126; TNA, PRO 30/24/48, ff. 196–196v, 308–309, 313; *CSPC, 1669–1674*, 270–271.

6. AAS, MSS Boxes "C," Box 1, Folder 1, undated notes, c. 1650; Josselyn, *New-Englands Rarities*, 2–3, 9, 13, 18, 37, 43, 93–94; Josselyn, *Account*, 143, 178–179, 180.

7. Fredson Bowers, ed., *The Dramatic Works in the Beaumont and Fletcher Canon*, 10 vols. (Cambridge, UK, 2008), 9:1–94; Latham and Matthews, ed., *Diary*, 8:450–451; Warren, *Impartial Description*, 7, 9, 12–13, 16–17, 22–27. Cf. an enthusiastic Dutch account from 1663: TNA, CO 1/17, ff. 226–227.

8. John Forster, *Englands Happiness Increased* (London, 1664), 18–19; Hughes, *American Physitian*, 14–15; Thomas Trapham, *A Discourse of the State of Health in the Island of Jamaica* (London, 1679), 56, 58.

9. Geoffrey F. Nuttall, ed., *The Journal of George Fox* (Cambridge, UK, 1952), 579–588; Bodl., Add. MS A.95, ff. 2–5, 8–10, 13v–14; *The Life & Death, Travels and Sufferings of Robert Widders* (London, 1688), 10, 16, 26–28.

10. William Hilton, *A Relation of a Discovery Lately Made on the Coast of Florida* (London, 1664), 10, 18–19, 22; Jensen, ed., *Colonial Documents*, 64, 233; Kavenagh, ed., *Foundations*, 3:1676–1677; BL, Add. MS 70009, ff. 270–270v.

11. *A Brief Description of the Province of Carolina on the Coasts of Floreda* (London, 1666), 1–9; Taylor, *Colonial America*, 82.

12. *CSPC, 1669–74*, 89–90, 254–255, 260–261, 296–297, quotation 297; Richard Waterhouse, "England, the Caribbean, and the settlement of Carolina," *Journal of American Studies*, 9 (1975), 259–281; Daniel C. Littlefield, *Rice and Slaves: Ethnicity and the Slave Trade in Colonial South Carolina* (Baton Rouge, LA, 1981), ch. 1.

13. Samuel Wilson, *An Account of the Province of Carolina in America* (London, 1682), 7–8, 10–11; Blome, *Description*, 127; R. F., *The Present State of Carolina with Advice to the Setlers* (London, 1682), 18, 28; *Carolina Described More Fully Then Heretofore* (Dublin, 1684), 3–19; Kavenagh, ed., *Foundations*, 3:1677–1678; Richard Waterhouse, *A New World Gentry: The Making of a Merchant and Planter Class in South Carolina, 1670–1770* (New York, 1989), chs. 1–2; Peter A. Coclanis, *The Shadow of a Dream: Economic Life and Death in the South Carolina Low Country, 1670–1920* (New York, 1989), ch. 1.

14. NYPL, Mss. Col. 6404, Pratt letter, 1668; "A declaration of the affairs of the English people that first inhabited New England, by Phineas Pratt," *Collections of the MHS*, 4 (1858), 474–491; Josselyn, *Account*, 183.

15. *CSPC, 1669–1674*, 43; Increase Mather, *The First Principles of New-England Concerning the Subject of Baptism & Communion of Churches* (Cambridge, MA, 1675), A3, A4; idem, *Life and Death*, A2v, 25–26; Nathaniel Morton, *New-Englands Memoriall* (Cambridge, MA, 1669), A2v–A3v; Roger Clap, quoted in Roderick Frazier Nash, *Wilderness and the American Mind*, 4th ed. (New Haven, CT, 2001), 38; Richard Mather, *A Farewell Exhortation to the Church and People of Dorchester in New-England* (Cambridge, MA, 1657), 10–11. See also David M. Scobey, "Revising the errand: New England's ways and the Puritan sense of the past," *WMQ*, 41 (1984), 3–31, esp. 24; David D. Hall, "The world of print and collective mentality in seventeenth-century New England," in John Higham and Paul K. Conkin, eds., *New Directions in American Intellectual History* (Baltimore, 1979), 166–180.

16. Sacvan Bercovitch, *The American Jeremiad* (Madison, WI, 1978); Bozeman, *To Live Ancient Lives*, chs. 9–10; Robert G. Pope, "New England versus the New England mind:

the myth of declension," *Journal of Social History*, 3 (1969), 99; David D. Hall, *The Faithful Shepherd: A History of the New England Ministry in the Seventeenth Century* (Chapel Hill, NC, 1972), ch. 10.

17. John Davenport, *A Sermon Preach'd at the Election of the Governour of Boston* (Cambridge, MA, 1670), 15–16; William Stoughton, *New Englands True Interest Not to Lie* (Cambridge, MA, 1670), 27; Samuel Danforth, *A Brief Recognition of New-Englands Errand into the Wilderness* (London, 1671), 5, 10, 13, 18–19; Plumstead, ed., *Wall and the Garden*, 24; Eleazer Mather, *A Serious Exhortation to the Present and Succeeding Generation in New-England* (Cambridge, MA, 1671), 21.

18. Josselyn, *Account*, 182; Carla Gardina Pestana, "The Quaker executions as myth and history," *JAH*, 80 (1993), 441–469; *A Representation to King and Parliament of Some of the Unparalleld Sufferings of the People of the Lord Called Quakers* (London, 1669).

19. Roger Williams, *George Fox Digg'd Out of His Burrowes* (London, 1676), A2–A3; David Lovejoy, "Roger Williams and George Fox: the arrogance of self-righteousness," *NEQ*, 66 (1993), 199–225; George Fox, *A New-England Fire-Brand Quenched* (London, 1678), title page; idem, *Cain Against Abel*, 5–6, 14, 30, 35, quotation 35; idem, *An Epistle to All My Dear Friends Elect and Precious in America* (London, 1675).

20. John Oxenbridge, *New-England Freemen Warned and Warmed* (Cambridge, MA, 1673), 21–22, 28; Coddington, *Demonstration*, A2, 5–6, 8–20, quotations A2, 16.

21. Moody, ed., *Saltonstall Papers*, 1:161–162; Urian Oakes, *New-England Pleaded With* (Cambridge, MA, 1673), 18–19, 61–64, quotation 61; Samuel Torrey, *An Exhortation unto Reformation Amplified* (Cambridge, MA, 1674), 21–23, 26; Joshua Moodey, *Souldiery Spiritualized* (Cambridge, MA, 1674), 26; Samuel Arnold, *David Serving His Generation* (Cambridge, MA, 1674); Increase Mather, *The Day of Trouble Is Near* (Cambridge, MA, 1674), 5, 30. Thomas Shepard Jr. linked toleration and idolatry: *Eye-Salve, or a Watch-Word from Our Lord Jesus Christ unto His Churches* (Cambridge, MA, 1673), 38.

22. CSL, Crimes & Misdemeanors, series I, 1662–1789, vol. 3, pp. 211–214; Thomas Walley, *Balm in Gilead to Heal Sions Wounds* (Cambridge, MA, 1670), 9; Mather, *Illustrious Providences*, 140–142.

23. Noble, ed., *Records*, 1:10–11; Samuel Danforth, *The Cry of Sodom Enquired Into* (Cambridge, MA, 1674), 1–3, 5–6, 9, 13; Ronald A. Bosco, "Lectures at the pillory: the early American execution sermon," *American Quarterly*, 30 (1978), 156–176; John M. Murrin, "'Things fearful to name': bestiality in early America," in Elizabeth Reis, ed., *American Sexual Histories* (Malden, MA, 2001), 29. Cf. Robert F. Oaks, "'Things fearful to name': sodomy and buggery in seventeenth-century New England," *Journal of Social History*, 12 (1978), 268–281.

24. Mather, *Day of Trouble*, 21–26, quotations 23, 26; idem, *Essay*, 140; MHS, Adams Papers, vol. 4, Massachusetts proclamation, March 11, 1674.

25. Increase Mather, quoted in Jennifer L. Hochschild, *Facing Up to the American Dream: Race, Class and the Soul of the Nation* (Princeton, NJ, 1995), 257; Slotkin and Folsom, eds., *So Dreadfull*, 371–373; T[homas] C[hurch], *Entertaining Passages Relating to Philip's War* (Boston, 1716), reproduced in ibid., 395. See also Bruce C. Daniels, *Dissent and Conformity on Narragansett Bay: The Colonial Rhode Island Town* (Middletown, CT, 1983).

26. Church, *Entertaining Passages*, 373; Joshua Micah Marshall, "'A melancholy people': Anglo-Indian relations in early Warwick, RI, 1642–1675," *NEQ*, 68 (1995), 402–428.

27. *CSPC, 1661–1668*, 95; RS, RB/1/4/21, f. 122; Josselyn, *Account*, 149; Bodl., Add. MS A.95, f. 9; Fox, *Gospel Family-Order*, 13–14; James Axtell, "The white Indians of colonial America," *WMQ*, 32 (1975), 55–88; Increase Mather, *A Brief History of the Warr with the Indians in New-England* (Boston, 1676), 12–13.

28. LMA, MS 7936, f. 12; Jean M. O'Brien, *Dispossession by Degrees: Indian Land and Identity in Natick, Massachusetts, 1650–1790* (New York, 1997), chs. 2–3; DWL, Baxter MSS, Letters, vol. 2, f. 229; LMA, MS 7936, f. 15; John Eliot, *Indian Dialogues* (Cambridge, MA, 1671), 44; *A Brief Narrative of the Progress of the Gospel Amongst the Indians*

in New-England (London, 1671), 8; *Brief Narrative*, 5; Neal Salisbury, "Red Puritans: the 'praying Indians' of Massachusetts Bay and John Eliot," *WMQ*, 31 (1974), 27–54; James P. Ronda, "'We are well as we are': an Indian critique of seventeenth-century Christian missions," *WMQ*, 34 (1977), 66–82.

29. Len Travers, ed., "The missionary journal of John Cotton Jnr, 1666–1678," *Procs of the MHS*, 109 (1997), 95; Dunster, *New Englands First Fruits*, 8; Gardiner, ed., *Lion Gardiner*, 18.

30. Church, *Entertaining Passages*, 397.

31. Noble, ed., *Records*, 1:30, 32–33; Increase Mather, *The Wicked Mans Portion* (Boston, 1675), 9–10, 16–17, 21–22, quotation 17; AAS, MSS Boxes "M," Box 3, Folder 2, March 25, April 7, and April 10, 1675 (original at MHS); Mather, *Wicked Mans Portion*, A2v; *idem*, *The Times of Men Are in the Hand of God* (Boston, 1675), A2, 13.

32. Mather, *Relation*, 74–75; Church, *Entertaining Passages*, 397–400. Sassamon "had not been able to stay alive between two worlds that were colliding": Ogborn, *Global Lives*, 67.

33. Bruce C. Daniels, *The Connecticut Town: Growth and Development, 1635–1790* (Middletown, CT, 1979), 9–17; TNA, CO 1/34, f. 141; BL, Add. MS 72867, f. 48; Sidney H. Miner and George D. Stanton Jr., eds., *The Diary of Thomas Minor, Stonington, Connecticut* (New London, CT, 1899), 108–115; Ulrich, *Good Wives*, 19–21.

34. Luke 17:28–29.

CHAPTER 16: EXQUISITE TORMENTS

1. *A Brief and True Narration of the Late Wars Risen in New-England* (London, 1675), 5; Church, *Entertaining Passages*, 400–401. Church kept notes, which were later written up by his son, Thomas.

2. BPL, Ms. Am. 1506/6/24; CSL, Connecticut Archives, Colonial Wars, series I, vol. 1, 1675–1676, nos. 2a–2c, 3a; Sheila McIntyre and Len Travers, eds., *The Correspondence of John Cotton Junior* (Boston, 2009), 109; *Brief and True Narration*, 6; LaFantasie, ed., *Correspondence*, 1:xliii.

3. Thomas Wheeler, *A Thankefull Remembrance of Gods Mercy* (Cambridge, MA, 1676), 5–9; *Brief and True Narration*, 7; Bridenbaugh, ed., *Letters*, 138.

4. Bridenbaugh, ed., *Letters*, 147; CSL, Connecticut Archives, Colonial Wars, series I, vol. 1, 1675–1676, no. 16a; George Sheldon, *A History of Deerfield, Massachusetts*, 2 vols. (Deerfield, MA, 1895–1896), 1:93–96, 99; BPL, Ms. Am. 1506/6/27–27v.

5. Mather, *Brief History*, 4, 12–13; MHS, Adams Papers, vol. 4, order against sin, September 17, 1675. Cf. earlier, more hopeful, prayers: AAS, MSS Boxes "M," Box 3, Folder 2, June 29 and August 12, 1675 (original at MHS).

6. Mather, *Brief History*, 14; Wheeler, *Thankefull Remembrance*, 9; Beinecke, Osborn b 161, pp. 302–303; Bouton et al., ed., *Documents*, 1:355; Bridenbaugh, ed., *Letters*, 154–155; Patrick M. Malone, *The Skulking Way of War: Technology and Tactics Among the New England Indians* (Lanham, MD, 1991).

7. John Pynchon, quoted in Sheldon, *Deerfield*, 115; MSA, vol. 67/285, 288; Bridenbaugh, ed., *Letters*, 157–159, 160–161.

8. *London Gazette*, August 16–19, 1675; *CSPC, 1675–1676*, 251–253, 441–444; Bridenbaugh, ed., *Letters*, 164–165. Many colonists had been in England's civil wars, e.g., Edward Denison, a Connecticut militia captain, wounded at Naseby in 1645: Hertfordshire RO, D/P21 29/36, Belknap letter, December 22, 1911.

9. *Brief and True Narration*, 5; N[athaniel] S[altonstall], *The Present State of New-England with Respect to the Indian War* (London, 1675), 5–6; *New England's Present Sufferings Under Their Cruel Neighbouring Indians* (London, 1675), 3–4, 6, quotation 4.

10. Slotkin and Folsom, eds., *So Dreadfull*, 256; Saltonstall, *Present State*, 12–13, 19.

11. *New England's Present Sufferings*, 8.

12. N[athaniel] S[altonstall], *A Continuation of the State of New-England, Being a Farther Account of the Indian Warr* (London, 1676), 5, 8; CSL, Connecticut Archives, Colonial Wars, series I, vol. 1, 1675–1676, no. 27a; Thomas Franklin Waters, *Ipswich in the Massachusetts Bay Colony*, 2 vols. (Ipswich, MA, 1905–1907), 1:190–191.

13. CSL, Connecticut Archives, Colonial Wars, series I, vol. 1, 1675–1676, no. 29b; AAS, MSS Boxes "M," Box 3, Folder 2, December 2, 1675 (original at MHS); Mather, *Brief History*, 18. The narrative here relies on Douglas Edward Leach, *Flintlock and Tomahawk: New England in King Philip's War* (New York, 1958), 123–135.

14. Slotkin and Folsom, eds., *So Dreadfull*, 49; Saltonstall, *Continuation*, 5; Jill Lepore, *The Name of War: King Philip's War and the Origin of American Identity* (New York, 1998), 88; Saltonstall, *Continuation*, 6; *A Farther Brief and True Narration of the Late Wars Risen in New-England* (London, 1676), 9–10.

15. *CSPC, 1675–1676*, 317–319; *Farther Brief and True Narration*, 3–4, 9–10; BPL, Ms. Am. 1506/7/3.

16. Saltonstall, *Continuation*, 7; *News from New-England . . . of the Present Bloody Wars* (London, 1676), 3; W[ait] W[inthrop], *Some Meditations Concerning Our Honourable Gentlemen and Fellow-Souldiers* (New London, CT, 1721); McIntyre and Travers, eds., *Correspondence*, 119, 125.

17. Lepore, ed., *Encounters*, 153–154; LMA, MS 7936, f. 22.

18. *News from New-England*, 2; AAS, MSS Boxes "M," Box 3, Folder 2, January 13, 1676 (original at MHS); Saltonstall, *Continuation*, 14; *News from New-England*, 2–3.

19. Beinecke, Osborn b 161, p. 358; Saltonstall, *Continuation*, 14; Lepore, *Name of War*, 131–136.

20. Beinecke, Osborn b 161, pp. 339, 359.

21. [Increase Mather], *A Brief Relation of the State of New England* (London, 1689), 6; *Farther Brief and True Narration*, 4; *A True Account of the Most Considerable Occurrences . . . in the Warre Between the English and the Indians* (London, 1676), 2–3; Saltonstall, *Continuation*, 15; C. Alice Baker, *True Stories of New England Captives Carried to Canada During the Old French and Indian Wars* (Cambridge, MA, 1897), 107. On fear for children: BPL, Ms. Am. 1502/2/24.

22. [Mary Rowlandson], *A True History of the Captivity & Restoration of Mrs Mary Rowlandson* (London, 1682), A2, 1–3, quotations 1.

23. AAS, MSS Boxes "M," Box 3, Folder 2, February 24, 1676 (original at MHS); "C," Box 1, Folder 3, Newman letter, March 14, 1676; McIntyre and Travers, eds., *Correspondence*, 136; BPL, Ms. Am. 1506/7/7; N[athaniel] S[altonstall], *A New and Further Narrative of the State of New-England* (London, 1676), 1.

24. CSL, Connecticut Archives, Colonial Wars, series I, vol. 1, 1675–1676, nos. 44a–44c; AAS, MSS Boxes "C," Box 1, Folder 3, Newman letter (March 14, 1676) and Dummer letter (May 24, 1676); Saltonstall, *New and Further Narrative*, 4–5, 14, quotation 14.

25. Daniel Gookin, "An historical account of . . . the Christian Indians in New England," *Collections of the AAS*, 2 (1836), 456–457; BPL, Ms. Am. 1506/7/4v; *Brief and True Narration*, 5; James Axtell and William C. Sturtevant, "The unkindest cut, or who invented scalping?" *WMQ*, 37 (1980), 470; MSA, vol. 30/207a.

26. LaFantasie, ed., *Correspondence*, 1:xliii–xliv; CSL, Connecticut Archives, Colonial Wars, series I, vol. 1, 1675–1676, no. 55; *CSPC, 1675–1676*, 366, 371–373.

27. AAS, MSS Boxes "M," Box 3, Folder 2, April 28, 1676 (original at MHS); Benjamin Tompson, quoted in Neil Kamil, *Fortress of the Soul: Violence, Metaphysics, and Material Life in the Huguenots' New World, 1517–1751* (Baltimore, 2005), 473; [Benjamin Tompson], *New-Englands Tears* (London, 1676), 7–8; Mather, *Brief History*, 27; Slotkin and Folsom, eds., *So Dreadfull*, 50–51.

28. Mather, *Brief History*, 32; *Wyllys Papers*, 242–244; Slotkin and Folsom, eds., *So Dreadfull*, 51; William Hubbard, *The Happiness of a People in the Wisdome of Their Rulers*

(Boston, 1676), 49–50; [Benjamin Tompson], *New Englands Crisis* (Boston, 1676), 8. Rage led to atrocities, such as the murders of Indian women and children near Concord in August 1676: Noble, ed., *Records*, 1:72–73.

29. CSL, Connecticut Archives, Colonial Wars, series I, vol. 1, 1675–1676, nos. 75b, 78a; Ullmann, ed., *Hartford*, 199–200; HEHL, HM 8411; Mather, *Brief History*, 34, 42.

30. Slotkin and Folsom, eds., *So Dreadfull*, 51–52, 381–382, 418–433; M. Halsey Thomas, ed., *The Diary of Samuel Sewall, 1674–1729*, 2 vols. (New York, 1973), 1:18; BPL, Ms. Am. 1506/7/10; Church, *Entertaining Passages*, 443–447, quotation 447.

31. Church, *Entertaining Passages*, 449–452, quotation 451; Thomas, ed., *Diary . . . Sewall*, 1:19; Mather, *Relation*, preface.

32. Church, *Entertaining Passages*, 457–460, 462, quotation 460; *CSPC, 1677–1680*, 109.

CHAPTER 17: A PEOPLE BRED UP IN THIS COUNTRY

1. Lepore, *Name of War*, 175; Slotkin and Folsom, eds., *So Dreadfull*, 38–39.

2. Saltonstall, *New and Further Narrative*, 13–14; James D. Drake, *King Philip's War: Civil War in New England, 1675–1676* (Boston, 1999), 4; Stephen Saunders Webb, *1676: The End of American Independence* (New York, 1984), 221–244, esp. 243. For a rosier view: Terry L. Anderson, "Economic growth in colonial New England: 'statistical renaissance,'" *Journal of Economic History*, 39 (1979), 243–257.

3. BPL, Ms. Am. 1502/2/23; Clarke, *John Hull*, 35, 101, 110, 163, 173–174; NEHGS, MSS 60, vol. 3 (1675–1677), *passim*; CSL, Connecticut Archives, Colonial Wars, series I, vol. 1, 1675–1676, no. 72a. For Hull's trade interests and pursuit of debtors: AAS, MSS Folio vols. "H": John Hull Papers, vol. 1, letterbook, 1670–1685.

4. HEHL, HM 8407; J. H. Temple, *History of Framingham* (Framingham, MA, 1887), 71–79; CSL, Connecticut Archives, Colonial Wars, series I, vol. 1, 1675–1676, no. 68. On losses, see: Heimert and Delbanco, eds., *Puritans*, 275; Clarke, *John Hull*, 174. According to Daniel R. Mandell, a combined population of 80,000 fell by 9,000; the proportion of Indians in southern New England fell from 25 percent to 10 percent: *King Philip's War: The Conflict over New England* (New York, 2007), 117.

5. *CSPC, 1675–1676*, 441; BPL, Ms. Am. 1506/7/11; Plymouth Colony Wills, vol. 3, pt. 2, f. 11 (transcription by James Deetz, Plimoth Plantation, Plymouth, MA); CSL, Connecticut Archives, Colonial Wars, series I, vol. 1, 1675–1676, no. 70; MSA, vol. 69/48; NYPL, Mss. Col. 6404 (petitions of Philip Cashman, September 6, 1676, and Johanna Williams, August 24, 1676); Dow, ed., *Records*, 7:377; MSA, vols. 11/13, 69/143; NYPL, Mss. Col. 6404 (petition of Richard Wait, 1680); Temple, *History*, 75.

6. Temple, *History*, 72–74; Mather, *Brief History*, 3; Rowlandson, *True History*, 3–8, quotation 3, 8.

7. Rowlandson, *True History*, 10; Slotkin and Folsom, eds., *So Dreadfull*, 36–37; Noble, ed., *Records*, 1:102–103; William Hubbard, *The Present State of New-England* (London, 1677), 115.

8. [Richard Hutchinson], *The Warr in New-England Visibly Ended* (London, 1677), 2; Ignatius Thomson, *A Genealogy of John Thomson* (Taunton, UK, 1841), 10.

9. Bouton et al., eds., *Documents*, 1:360–361; MSA, vol. 69/86; MHS, Adams Papers, vol. 4, Massachusetts order, October 11, 1676. On the war as the *start* of a troubled era, as opposed to its climax, see Michael J. Puglisi, *Puritans Besieged: The Legacies of King Philip's War in the Massachusetts Bay Colony* (Lanham, MD, 1991).

10. Colin G. Calloway, ed., *After King Philip's War: Presence and Persistence in Indian New England* (Hanover, NH, 1997), 2–7; S[amuel] N[owell], *Abraham in Arms* (Boston, 1678), 17; Slotkin and Folsom, eds., *So Dreadfull*, 268.

11. Mather, *Brief History*, 49; *idem*, *A Call from Heaven to the Present and Succeeding Generations* (Boston, 1679), 27; McIntyre and Travers, eds., *Correspondence*, 112; Hubbard, *Happiness*, 54–56; Mather, *Necessity*, 2–3; Dow, ed., *Records*, 6:72–73, 135; *Plymouth Church Records, 1620–1859, Part I* (Boston, 1920), 149–151; MHS, Adams Papers, vol. 4, order against sin, September 17, 1675.

12. BPL, Ms. Am. 1502/2/27; Increase Mather, *An Earnest Exhortation to the Inhabitants of New-England* (Boston, 1676), preface; *idem, The Necessity of Reformation* (Boston, 1679), 2–7; Heimert and Delbanco, eds., *Puritans*, 275–276; AAS, MSS Boxes "M," Box 2, Folder 9, Mather letter, December 13, 1676; Hall, *Last American Puritan*, 127–128; Thomas Hutchinson, *The History of the Colony of Massachusetts Bay*, 2nd ed. (London, 1765), 349.

13. BPL, Ms. Am. 1502/1/48, 50, 55, 60, 67, 75 (Westgate at 60).

14. Hutchinson, *Warr*, 1; Mather, *Necessity*, 3; *New England's Present Sufferings*, 4–5, 7–8; John Browne, *A Lamentation over New England* (London, 1678); HEHL, HM 986, f. 1; Gorton, *Glass*, 14–17, 30–31. A minister blamed for the war by a Quaker said its true cause was tolerating "false worship": McIntyre and Travers, eds., *Correspondence*, 111–112.

15. Gorton, *Glass*, 17; MHS, Adams Papers, vol. 4, Massachusetts order, June 25, 1675; RS, RB/1/4/21, f. 121v; LMA, MS 07955/1, ff. 1–1v; BPL, Ms. Am. 1502/2/24; MSA, vol. 69/51; Mather, *Relation*, 75–76.

16. Thomas Mathew, "The beginning, progress and conclusion of Bacon's Rebellion, 1675 and 1676," in Charles M. Andrews, ed., *Narratives of the Insurrections, 1675–1690* (New York, 1915), 15–18, quotation 18.

17. William Hand Browne, ed., *Proceedings and Acts of the General Assembly of Maryland, 1666–1676* (Baltimore, 1884), 478, 480; Billings, ed., *Old Dominion*, 260–261.

18. BL, Egerton MS 2395, ff. 542–543v; Warren M. Billings, "Nathaniel Bacon," *ODNB*; Pepys, PL 2582, p. 125.

19. TNA, CO 1/36, ff. 67–67v; Greene, ed., *Great Britain*, 85; Pepys, PL 2582, pp. 164–200; Nathaniel Bacon, quoted in Peter Charles Hoffer, *The Brave New World: A History of Early America* (Boston, 2000), 259; VHS, Mss 3 V8192 a 3, pp. 361–362.

20. Hoffer, *Brave New World*, 260; Kavenagh, ed., *Foundations*, 3:1777–1778; TNA, CO 1/36, f. 139; BL, Egerton MS 2395, ff. 541, 545–546, 551; "Petition and proposals respecting Nathaniel Bacon," *VMHB*, 1 (1893–1894), 430–435, quotation 431.

21. HEHL, BL 85, f. 1–3; HEHL, HM 21810 (2), f. 1; BL, Egerton MS 2395, ff. 555–555v; *CSPC, 1675–1676*, 386–387, 550–550v.

22. HEHL, HM 1716; Kavenagh, ed., *Foundations*, 3:1780–1781; VHS, Mss 3 V8192 a 3, pp. 363–364; Mathew, "Bacon's Rebellion," 37–39.

23. HEHL, BR Box 256 (4); Pepys, PL 2582, pp. 209, 216, quotation 216; *CSPC, 1677–1680*, 51–52, 114, 162–163, 180, 258; Mary Beth Norton, *Separated by Their Sex: Women in Public and Private in the Colonial Atlantic World* (Ithaca, NY, 2011), 22; Pepys, PL 2582, pp. 8, 20–21, 23; TNA, CO 1/39, f. 244.

24. Pepys, PL 2582, pp. 55–56; *Strange News from Virginia, Being a Full and True Account of the Life and Death of Nathanael Bacon* (London, 1677), 7.

25. Billings, "Berkeley," *ODNB*. "As both a Virginia planter and a Restoration imperialist, he embodied the dual fountainheads of a flood that nearly swept the colony away": Richter, *Before the Revolution*, 270–271.

26. Webb, *1676*, Book 2; BL, Add. MS 72867, ff. 48–52; HEHL, HM 32266; BL, Egerton MS 2650, f. 27.

27. Greene, ed., *Great Britain*, xiv, 68–70; Jensen, ed., *Colonial Documents*, 233–234; Michael Garibaldi Hall, *Edward Randolph and the American Colonies, 1676–1703* (Chapel Hill, NC, 1960); Philip S. Haffenden, *New England in the English Nation, 1689–1713* (Oxford, 1974), 68–69.

28. TNA, CO 1/36, ff. 213–218; David S. Lovejoy, *The Glorious Revolution in America*, 2nd ed. (Hanover, NH, 1987), 78–84, quotation 82; Hugh F. Rankin, *Upheaval in Albemarle: The Story of Culpeper's Rebellion, 1675–1689* (Raleigh, NC, 1962).

29. BPL, Ms. Am. 1502/1/48; CSL, Crimes & Misdemeanors, series I, 1662–1789, vol. 1, pp. 80–84.

30. Sumner Hunnewell, "'A doleful slaughter near Black Point': the battle at Moore's Brook . . . 1677," *Maine Genealogist* (May 2003), 51–72; (August 2003), 99–120; Russell Bourne, *The Red King's Rebellion: Racial Politics in New England, 1675–1678* (New York,

1990), chs. 3–6; Jenny Hale Pulsipher, *Subjects unto the Same King: Indians, English and the Contest for Authority in Colonial New England* (Philadelphia, 2005), ch. 9; Drake, *King Philip's War*, 2; NYPL, Mss. Col. 834, pp. 65–67; BPL, Ms. Am. 1502/1/79. On the merging of Anglo-Indian experiences: Ian K. Steele, "Exploding colonial American history: Amerindian, Atlantic and global perspectives," *Reviews in American History*, 26 (1998), 70–95; Kupperman, *Facing Off*, ch. 7. Francis Jennings talks of "symbiotic interdependence": *Invasion of America*, ix.

31. BPL, Ms. Am. 1502/1/59, 1506/8/1; MHS, Adams Papers, vol. 4, order of January 3, 1678; Heimert and Delbanco, eds., *Puritans*, 276; MSA, vol. 69/193–194, 206–206a.

32. *Records of . . . Rhode Island*, 3:5; CSL, Crimes & Misdemeanors, series I, 1662–1789, vol. 1, pp. 110–112b; James Axtell, "The vengeful women of Marblehead: Robert Roules's deposition of 1677," *WMQ*, 31 (1974), 647–652, quotation 652; Jennings, *Invasion of America*, 212–213; Lepore, *Name of War*, 177–178.

33. BPL, Ms. Am. 1502/1/53; Samuel Hooker, *Righteousness Rained from Heaven* (Cambridge, MA, 1677), title page; William Adams, *The Necessity of the Pouring Out of the Spirit from on High* (Boston, 1679), 2; Thomas Thacher, *A Fast of Gods Chusing Plainly Opened* (Boston, 1678), 23; Rowlandson, *Possibility of Gods Forsaking a People*, 10–11; Harry S. Stout, *The New England Soul: Preaching and Religious Culture in Colonial New England* (Oxford, 1986), 106–108; Breen, *Puritans and Adventurers*, ch. 5.

34. Dow, ed., *Records*, 6:425; Sarson, *British America*, 143–145; J. Hammond Trumbull and Charles J. Hoadly, eds., *The Public Records of the Colony of Connecticut, 1636–1776*, 15 vols. (Hartford, CT, 1850–1890), 3:294–300; BL, Lansdowne MS 1052, ff. 1–4; *Records of . . . Rhode Island*, 2:343–346, 439–442; Robert E. Moody, ed., "Records of the magistrates' court at Haverhill, Massachusetts, kept by Nathaniel Saltonstall, 1682–5," *Procs of the MHS*, 79 (1967), 152. On tension between introversion and expansionism: Peter N. Carroll, *Puritanism and the Wilderness: The Intellectual Significance of the New England Frontier, 1629–1700* (New York, 1969).

35. Hubbard, *Happiness*, 39; *Mr Baxter Baptiz'd in Bloud* (London, 1673); *Forgery Detected and Innocency Vindicated* (London, 1673); Worthington C. Ford, "The case of the Rev. Josiah Baxter," *Transactions of the Colonial Society of Massachusetts*, 25 (1922–1924), 348–355; *The Quakers Farewel to England* (London, 1675); Wesley Frank Craven, *New Jersey and the English Colonization of North America* (Princeton, NJ, 1964), ch. 3; Bodl., Rawlinson MS D.204, ff. 63v–65; Andrew Browning, ed., *Memoirs of Sir John Reresby* (Glasgow, 1936), 127; Nuala Zahedieh, "London and the colonial consumer in the later seventeenth century," *Economic History Review*, 47 (1994), 239–261.

36. *An Abstract or Abbreviation of Some . . . Testimonys from the Inhabitants of New Jersey* (London, 1681), 11–12; *A Further Account of New Jersey* (London, 1676), 3; *Abstract . . . of New Jersey*, 8–10, 29, quotation 29.

37. *Abstract . . . of New Jersey*, 3, 13–16, 21; James Drummond, *An Advertisement Concerning the Province of East-New-Jersey in America* (Edinburgh, 1685), 1–2; Brendan McConville, *These Daring Disturbers of the Public Peace: The Struggle for Property and Power in Early New Jersey* (Philadelphia, 2003), ch. 1; *Further Account*, 1, 4–7, 10–11, quotation 4–5.

38. *Further Account*, 8; *Abstract . . . of New Jersey*, 10.

CHAPTER 18: BEING A CONSTITUTION WITHIN THEMSELVES

1. [Andrew Marvell], *An Account of the Growth of Popery and Arbitrary Government in England* (Amsterdam, 1677), 3.

2. BPL, Ms. Am. 1502/2/48; 1502/3/1, 4. The regicide John Dixwell was warned of "great feares and troubles that are in England": New Haven Historical Society, MSS 8, Box I, Folder B, Prince letter, June 5, 1679.

3. Leon de Valinger Jr., "The burning of the Whorekill, 1673," *Pennsylvania Magazine of History and Biography*, 74 (1950), 473–487, quotation 477; *To the Parliament of England, the Case of the Poor English Protestants in Mary-Land* (London, 1681), 2–4, quotation 3.

4. John Danforth, *An Almanack or Register of Coelestial Configurations* (Cambridge, MA, 1679); Hutchinson, *History of . . . Massachusetts*, 349; BPL, Ms. Am. 1502/4/5; 1506/7/8; *Records of . . . Rhode Island*, 3:69–70; Noble, ed., *Records*, 1:145–146; BL, Add. MS 25120, ff. 132–133. In 1677 a man was arrested for "suspicious speeches . . . of a fire likely to happen in the town of Boston": Morison et al., eds., *Suffolk County Court*, 2:785.

5. *CSPC, 1677–1680*, 250, 340, quotation 340; CSL, Crimes & Misdemeanors, series I, 1662–1789, vol. 1, pp. 133–139; BL, Add. MS 25120, f. 145. For contrasting views on England's status in America, see: Robert C. Ritchie, "Will the real empire please stand up?" *Reviews in American History*, 10 (1982), 24; Stephen Saunders Webb, *The Governors-General: The English Army and the Definition of Empire, 1569–1681* (Chapel Hill, NC, 1979); J. M. Sosin, *English America and the Restoration Monarchy of Charles II: Transatlantic Politics, Commerce, and Kinship* (Lincoln, NE, 1980).

6. Richard R. Johnson, "Edward Randolph," *ODNB*; *CSPC, 1677–80*, 460, 473–474; HEHL, BL 227, f. 1.

7. Carroll, *Puritanism and the Wilderness*, 213–214; BPL, Ms. Am. 1502/4/6; Increase Mather, *Heavens Alarm to the World* (Boston, 1682), A2–A2v, 6–7, 9, 12–16, quotation 12; idem, *Kometographia*, 122; AAS, MSS Boxes "C," Box 1, Folder 3, Tuckney letter, March 5, 1681; MSA, vol. 11/8a, 21a.

8. See John Miller, *Popery and Politics in England, 1660–1688* (Cambridge, UK, 1973), ch. 8.

9. BPL, Ms. Am. 1502/4/64; Cressy, *Coming Over*, 70; DWL, MSS 12.78, pp. 195–198; LMA, COL/CH/03/024; Gary S. De Krey, *London and the Restoration, 1659–1683* (Cambridge, UK, 2005), ch. 7.

10. *A Declaration of Remarkable Providences in the Course of My Life by John Dane* (Boston, 1854); Hertfordshire RO, D/P21 29/36, Thomas letter, February 28, 1961, and "Stortford Emigrants to New England"; Frederick Adams Virkus, ed., *The Compendium of American Genealogy*, 7 vols. (Chicago, 1925–1942), 6:146.

11. Rowlandson, *True History*, A3; Kathryn Zabelle Derounian-Stodola, ed., *Women's Indian Captivity Narratives* (London, 1998), 4–5; Alden T. Vaughan and Edward W. Clark, eds., *Puritans Among the Indians: Accounts of Captivity and Redemption, 1676–1724* (Cambridge, MA, 1981), 2–4, 10, 13; Richard Slotkin, *Regeneration Through Violence: The Mythology of the American Frontier, 1600–1860* (Middletown, CT, 1973), chs. 4–5; MHS, Ms. SBd-61, December 10, 1682; Richard L. Greaves, *God's Other Children: Protestant Nonconformists and the Emergence of Denominational Churches in Ireland, 1660–1700* (Stanford, CA, 1997), 256; Stephen Wright, "John Bailey," *ODNB*.

12. Bernard Bailyn, *The New England Merchants in the Seventeenth Century* (Cambridge, MA, 1955), 139; George F. Chever, "A sketch of Philip English: a merchant in Salem, c.1670–c.1734," *EIHC*, 1 (1859), 157–160; Frances Hill, *A Delusion of Satan: The Full Story of the Salem Witch Trials* (London, 1995), 123; Bailyn, *New England Merchants*, 144–145; Noble, ed., *Records*, 1:201; Christine Leigh Heyrman, *Commerce and Culture: The Maritime Communities of Colonial Massachusetts, 1690–1750*, 2nd ed. (New York, 1986).

13. Samuel Willard, *The Fiery Trial No Strange Thing* (Boston, 1682), 8–9, 13–15; *A Letter from New-England Concerning Their Customs, Manners and Religion* (London, 1682), 1–9, quotations 2, 7, 8–9.

14. Lucy E. Dow, ed., *History of the Town of Hampton, New Hampshire . . . by Joseph Dow*, 2 vols. (Salem, MA, 1893), 1:103–105; William Henry Gove, *The Gove Book: History and Genealogy of the American Family of Gove* (Salem, MA, 1922), 13–49; Dow, ed., *Hampton*, 103; *CSPC, 1675–6*, 181–182; CWF, MS 46.02, Cranfield letter, January 10, 1683.

15. CWF, MS 46.02, Cranfield letters, February 20, June 19, and October 5, 1683; Greene, ed., *Great Britain*, 90–96; Dow, ed., *Hampton*, 105; Gove, *Gove Book*, 49.

16. TNA, CO 1/53, ff. 264–266; Sally E. Hadden, *Slave Patrols: Law and Violence in Virginia and the Carolinas* (Cambridge, MA, 2001), 230.

17. *Great Newes from the Barbadoes* (London, 1676), 3, 11, 9–12, quotation 12; TNA CO 1/35, f. 231; Hilary Beckles, *Black Rebellion in Barbados: The Struggle Against Slavery,*

1627–1838 (Bridgetown, Barbados, 1984), 37–41. In 1673 Barbadian grand jurors complained that Quakers encouraged civil and political disobedience: *CSPC, 1669–1674*, 506.

18. Amussen, *Caribbean Exchanges*, 94; *CSPC, 1675–6*, 349; Richard S. Dunn, "The Barbados census of 1680: profile of the richest colony in America," *WMQ*, 26 (1969), 8; Natalie A. Zacek, *Settler Society in the English Leeward Islands, 1670–1776* (Cambridge, UK, 2010), 48–49; TNA, PC 5/1, f. 38; HEHL, HM 32268. Between 1640 and 1700, 85,000 slaves were shipped to Jamaica, 134,000 to Barbados, and 44,000 to the Leewards: Thomas Benjamin, *The Atlantic World: Europeans, Africans, Indians and Their Shared History, 1400–1900* (Cambridge, UK, 2009), 394.

19. Donnan, ed., *Documents*, 1:226–233; Dunn, "Barbados census," 4; *Great Newes*, 7.

20. BL, Egerton MS 2395, f. 490–490v; *CSPC, 1675–6*, 314–315, 348–349; TNA, CO 1/44, ff. 142–379; Dunn, "Barbados census," 3, 5–6; *The Present State of Jamaica* (London, 1683), 45–46; Donnan, ed., *Documents*, 1:173–174.

21. Alexander, *Encouragement*, 7; Bodl., Tanner MS 447, ff. 53–54; RS, RB/1/4/21, ff. 127–128; RB/1/3, ff. 130, 132; *God's Mighty Power Magnified . . . in His Faithful Handmaid John Vokins* (London, 1691), 43; *CSPC, 1677–80*, 231.

22. Tryon, *Friendly Advice*, 75–77, 146, 221; Krise, ed., *Caribbeana*, 51; Godwyn, *Negro's and Indians Advocate*, 7, 34–35, 155–156, 161, quotations 34, 156.

23. *CSPC, 1675–6*, 314; DHC, DC/LR/M/9/1–28; Dunn, "Barbados census," 7–8; T. M., *A Letter from Jamaica to a Friend in London Concerning Kid-Napping* (London, 1682); *The Case of John Wilmore Truly and Impartially Related* (London, 1682), 3.

24. Thomas Tryon, *The Planter's Speech to His Neighbours & Country-Men of Pennsylvania, East & West-Jersey* (London, 1684), 14–15; Michael Craton and Gail Saunders, *Islanders in the Stream: A History of the Bahamian People*, vol. 1 (Athens, GA, 1992), 97; BL, Add. MS 25120, f. 143 (see ff. 120–121 on disrespect for royal officers); Peter Thompson, "Henry Drax's instructions on the management of a seventeenth-century Barbadian sugar plantation," *WMQ*, 66 (2009), 569.

25. Trapham, *Discourse*, 13–17, 20–22, 70–71, quotations 17, 50; *Present State of Jamaica*, 2–6, 12–22; RS, EL/L5/114, p. 1; TNA, CO 1/35, f. 231; *CSPC, 1675–6*, 368; Zacek, *Settler Society*, 49.

26. Zacek, *Settler Society*, 48–49; HEHL, HM 32272; *CSPC, 1681–5*, 607–608; Devon RO, 48/13/8/9/16–17.

27. *CSPC, 1685–8*, 82–83, 343, 348–349; James Robertson, "'Stories' and 'histories' in late-seventeenth-century Jamaica," in Kathleen E. A. Monteith and Glen Richards, eds., *Jamaica in Slavery and Freedom: History, Heritage and Culture* (Kingston, Jamaica, 2002), 42–43; Jerome S. Handler, "Slave revolts and conspiracies in seventeenth-century Barbados," *Nieuwe West-Indische Gids—New West Indian Guide*, 56 (1982), 20–21.

28. Aphra Behn, *The Widdow Ranter, or the History of Bacon in Virginia* (London, 1690), A2v, 3, 36; Jenny Hale Pulsipher, "The *Widow Ranter* and royalist culture in colonial Virginia," *Early American Literature*, 39 (2004), 41–66; Peter C. Herman, "'We all smoke here': Behn's *The Widow Ranter* and the invention of American identity," in Appelbaum and Sweet, eds., *Envisioning*, 254–274.

29. Billings, ed., *Old Dominion*, 149; *The Vain Prodigal Life and Tragical Pentient Death of Thomas Hellier* (London, 1680), 7, 10–13, 26–28.

30. Peter Wraxall, *An Abridgment of the Indian Affairs . . . in the Colony of New York, 1678–1751*, ed. Charles Howard McIlwain (Cambridge, MA, 1915), 11–12; Kenneth Morgan, *Slavery and Servitude in North America, 1607–1800* (Edinburgh, 2000), 22–24; Gloria L. Main, *Tobacco Colony: Life in Early Maryland, 1650–1720* (Princeton, NJ, 1982), chs. 4–5; David Freeman Hawke, *Everyday Life in Early America* (New York, 1988), 48; Blome, *Description*, 156; Gardyner, *Description*, 99–101, quotation 101; Jon Butler, *New World Faiths: Religion in Colonial America* (Oxford, 2008), 66. On the growth of mainland slavery, see also Winthrop D. Jordan, *White over Black: American Attitudes Towards the Negro, 1550–1812* (Chapel Hill, NC, 1968), chs. 1–2; Ira Berlin, *Many Thousands Gone: The First Two Centuries*

of Slavery in North America (Cambridge, MA, 1998), ch. 1; John Thornton, *Africa and Africans in the Making of the Atlantic World, 1400–1800*, 2nd ed. (Cambridge, UK, 1998), chs. 5–6.

31. Bodl., Tanner MS 114, f. 79; Tanner MS 31, ff. 137, 139–140; Samuel Atkins, *Kalendarium Pennsilvaniense* (Philadelphia, 1686), A2v; *Case of the Poor English Protestants in Mary-Land*, 3; Patricia U. Bonomi, *Under the Cope of Heaven: Religion, Society and Politics in Colonial America*, 2nd ed. (Oxford, 2003), 21–24.

32. Edmund S. Morgan, *American Slavery, American Freedom: The Ordeal of Colonial Virginia* (New York, 1975), chs. 13–16; Allan Kulikoff, *Tobacco and Slaves: The Development of Southern Cultures in the Chesapeake, 1680–1800* (Chapel Hill, NC, 1986), 37–43; Anthony S. Parent Jr., *Foul Means: The Formation of a Slave Society in Virginia, 1660–1740* (Chapel Hill, NC, 2003), chs. 2–5; T. H. Breen and Stephen Innes, *"Myne Owne Ground": Race and Freedom on Virginia's Eastern Shore, 1640–1676*, 2nd ed. (Oxford, 2005), ch. 4; Tim Hashaw, *The Birth of Black America: The First African Americans and the Pursuit of Freedom at Jamestown* (New York, 2007); Coldham, ed., *Lord Mayor's Court*, 40.

33. *A Letter from the Chancellour of Mary-Land to Col. Henry Meese* (London, 1682), 1–2; William Hand Browne, ed., *Proceedings of the Council of Maryland, 1667–1687/8* (Baltimore, 1887), 281.

34. TNA, CO 1/49, f. 106; CO 5/1356, ff. 66–69, 155–160; HEHL, BL 86; HMC, *Eleventh Report, Appendix Pt. V*, 80–81; Billings, ed., *Old Dominion*, 308–309.

35. Warren M. Billings, ed., *The Papers of Francis Howard, Baron Howard of Effingham, 1643–1695* (Richmond, VA, 1989), 38–39, 46–49.

36. Ibid., 51, 55, 58–59, 67–69, 89–91, 102–109, 113–114, 124–125, 133–136, 140–141; *idem, Virginia's Viceroy: Their Majesties' Governor General, Francis Howard, Baron Howard of Effingham* (Fairfax, VA, 1991), ch. 5. A Huguenot found houses plain but neat and comfortable: Billings, ed., *Old Dominion*, 306.

37. Elliott, *Empires of the Atlantic World*, 167–168; Billings, *Virginia's Viceroy*, ch. 10; VHS, Mss 1 M2976 a 28; Gloucestershire Archives, D149/F210, D2026/E24; Richard Beale Davis, ed., *William Fitzhugh and His Chesapeake World, 1676–1701* (Chapel Hill, NC, 1963), 169–170, 171–174, 187–188, 192–193, quotation 169; John Demos, ed., *Remarkable Providences: Readings on Early American History*, 2nd ed. (Boston, 1991), 135–136.

38. Marion Tinling, ed., *The Correspondence of the Three William Byrds of Westover, Virginia, 1684–1776*, 2 vols. (Charlottesville, VA, 1977), 1:3–7; Pierre Marambaud, "Col. William Byrd I," *VMHB*, 82 (1974), 430–457. The original source was used: VHS, Mss 5:2 B9965:1, ff. 5v, 6v, 15–15v, 28–29v.

39. RS, RB/1/39, ff. 182–183v; *Great Newes from the Barbadoes*, 12.

40. Billings, ed., *Old Dominion*, 178, 185–186, 205.

41. Ibid., 172, 178; Castillo and Schweitzer, eds., *Literatures*, 230–235.

42. VHS, Mss 5:2 B9965:1, ff. 32v–34, 46v, 48, 51v, 57v, 58v, 59, quotations 33, 34.

CHAPTER 19: STRANGE CREATURES IN AMERICA

1. BPL, Ms. Am. 1502/5/29, 39; Bouton et al., eds., *Documents*, 1:217–219. In general, see Baker, *Devil of Great Island*.

2. Burr, ed., *Narratives*, 31n; Noble, ed., *Records*, 1:159; Mather, *Illustrious Providences*, 155–156, 158–164.

3. Mather, *Illustrious Providences*, 329–333, quotation 331; *Plymouth Church Records*, 158–159; HMC, *Marquess of Lothian*, 132; BPL, Ms. Am. 1502/5/78; Samuel Willard, *The High Esteem Which God Hath of the Death of His Saints* (Boston, 1683), 13–14, 18, quotation 18.

4. Barbara C. Murison, "The talented Mr Blathwayt, his empire revisited," in Rhoden, ed., *English Atlantics Revisited*, 45–46; Kavenagh, ed., *Foundations*, 1:155–159, quotation 155; Bodl., Tanner MS 35, f. 140; HEHL, BL 228, ff. 1–2v.

5. TNA, MINT 13/223; *CSPC, 1685–8*, 266–267; John Craig, *The Mint: A History of the London Mint from A.D. 287 to 1948* (Cambridge, UK, 1953), 377; *A Model for Erecting a Bank*

of Credit (London, 1688), 34–38. See Dudley's ostracism on election day: BL, Stowe MS 746, f. 89v.

6. Francis Bacon, *Of the Proficience and Advancement of Learning* (London, 1605), second book, 10; Olson, *Anglo-American Politics*, 103; J. R. Pole, *The Gift of Government: Political Responsibility from the English Restoration to American Independence* (Athens, GA, 1983), 13; Zuckerman, "Identity in British America," 116–117.

7. Mark Van Doren, ed., *The Life of Sir William Phips by Cotton Mather* (New York, 1929), 165; Emerson W. Baker and John G. Reid, *The New England Knight: Sir William Phips, 1651–1695* (Toronto, 1998), ch. 2; BL, Egerton MS 2526, ff. 1–5v, 24–25.

8. BL, Egerton MS 2526, ff. 8v–11, 13, 18–18v, quotation 9v.

9. Ibid, ff. 18v–22, 25–26v.

10. Van Doren, ed., *Phips*, 170; BPL, Ms. Am. 1502/5/78.

11. Cressy, *Coming Over*, 260–261; *Letter-Book . . . Sewall, 1686–1729*, 2 vols. (Boston, 1886–1888), 1:2; Worthington Chauncey Ford, ed., *Diary of Cotton Mather, 1681–1708* (Boston, 1911), 113; John Nalson, *The Character of a Rebellion and What England May Expect from One* (London, 1681), 14.

12. *CSPC, 1685–8*, 41–42, 114, 240, 289–290, 401; *Collections of the New Hampshire Historical Society*, vol. 1 (Concord, MA, 1824), 197; AAS, MSS Boxes "C," Box 1, Folder 4, Mather letters, September 25, 1685, February 5, 1686.

13. Cotton Mather, *Magnalia Christi Americana*, ed. Kenneth B. Murdock and Elizabeth W. Miller (Cambridge, MA, 1977), 3–4, 23; Kenneth Silverman, ed., *Selected Letters of Cotton Mather* (Baton Rouge, LA, 1971), ix–xii; Ford, ed., *Diary of Cotton Mather*, 15, 80–81, 83, 109–110; David Levin, *Cotton Mather: The Young Life of the Lord's Remembrancer, 1663–1703* (Cambridge, MA, 1978), 310; Lepore, *Name of War*, 174–175; Noble, ed., *Records*, 1:287.

14. Thomas, ed., *Diary . . . Sewall*, 1:94–95, 97, 99; W. H. Whitmore, ed., *Letters Written from New-England A.D. 1686 by John Dunton* (Boston, 1867), 54, 121–124, 135–136, quotations 123, 136.

15. Whitmore, ed., *Letters*, 66–70, 192–193, 246–299, 302–305, quotations 67, 69, 302, 304; Josselyn, *Account*, 215.

16. BL, Add. MS 47131, ff. 22–28, quotations 24v–25; Barbara C. Murison, "William Blathwayt," *ODNB*. England and the West Indies "draw one Breath, live and dye together": *The Interest of the Nation As It Respects All the Sugar-plantations Abroad* (London, 1691), 4.

17. BL, Add. MS 47131, ff. 22, 24–25; Bodl., MS Don. C. 169, ff. 39v–40; Gary S. De Krey, "Sir Henry Ashurst," *ODNB*; Perry Gauci, *The Politics of Trade: The Overseas Merchant in State and Society, 1660–1720* (Oxford, 2001), ch. 3; *Letter-Book . . . Sewall*, 1:4n; Baker and Reid, *New England Knight*, ch. 3; Van Doren, ed., *Phips*, 39. For a ballad applauding Sir William Phips: Rollins, ed., *Pepys Ballads*, 3:281–286.

18. Parrish, *American Curiosity*, ch. 3; VHS, Mss 5:2 B9965:1, f. 26; RS, RB/1/39, ff. 99–100, 118, 133; Demos, ed., *Remarkable Providences*, xxxvi; RS, EL/C2/21, pp. 2–4, quotation 3; BL, Sloane MS 3321, ff. 8–8v; VHS, Mss 5:2 B9965:1, ff. 35, 55; Gloucestershire Archives, D1799/X5 (list of plants 1693); BL, Sloane MS 3962, f. 51; Edmund Berkeley and Dorothy Smith Berkeley, eds., *The Reverend John Clayton: A Parson with a Scientific Mind* (Charlottesville, VA, 1965).

19. Lionel Wafer, *A New Voyage and Description of the Isthmus of America* (London, 1699), 42; Gloucestershire Archives, D1799/X5; George Lyman Kittredge, ed., *Letters of Samuel Lee and Samuel Sewall Relating to New England and the Indians* (Cambridge, UK, 1912), 153; Thomas Amy, *Carolina, Or a Description of the Present State of That Country* (London, 1682), 23–24; R. F., *Carolina*, 18; LPL, Fulham Papers, vol. 11, ff. 7–10v; CKS, U23/C1/11. A servant of the earl of Huntingdon apologized for a lack of "rarities" in Massachusetts but sent Eliot's Bible: HEHL, HA 6245.

20. R. B. [Nathaniel Crouch], *The English Empire in America* (London, 1685), 166, illustration at 188–189. See also his *Miracles of Art and Nature* (London, 1678), 26–29, describing fabulous American creatures.

21. Berlin, *Many Thousands Gone*, ch. 2; Noble, ed., *Records*, 1:198–199; Mather, *Magnalia*, 6:40; MHS, N-1649, August 18, 1679, August 24, 1682, June 18, 1683, November 1683; Edward Pierce Hamilton, "The diary of a colonial clergyman, Peter Thacher of Milton," *Procs of the MHS*, 71 (1957), 50–63; Taylor, *Colonial America*, 70.

22. *CSPC, 1574–1660*, 447; *CSPC, 1661–8*, 221; Coldham, ed., *Bristol Registers*, vi; HEHL, BL 363, f. 3. For felons' pleas: LMA, MJ/SPT/2/1 (Mary Harris, 1682); *CSPC, 1661–8*, 158, 463; *CSPC, 1669–74*, 6.

23. *A Great Plot Discovered* (London, 1661); Josselyn, *Account*, 37; *CSPC, 1685–8*, 109–110, 147–149, 651–652; BL, Add. MS 47131, f. 26; Bridenbaugh, ed., *Letters*, 21; *A Brief Account of the Province of East New Jersey in America* (Edinburgh, 1683), 4–5. Transportation was not institutionalized until after 1700: Gwenda Morgan and Peter Rushton, *Eighteenth-Century Criminal Transportation: The Formation of the Criminal Atlantic* (Basingstoke, UK, 2004).

24. Robert C. Davis, *Christian Slaves, Muslim Masters: White Slavery in the Mediterranean, the Barbary Coast and Italy, 1500–1800* (Basingstoke, UK, 2004), chs. 1–4; Colley, *Captives*, ch. 2; Whitmore, ed., *Letters*, 29–30; Devon RO, QS/128/199/2; Coldham, ed., *English Adventurers*, 15–16, 25–26; *Sad and Dreadful News from New-England* (London, 1684); *CSPC, 1681–5*, 143–144; Daniel J. Vitkus, ed., *Piracy, Slavery, and Redemption: Barbary Captivity Narratives from Early Modern England* (New York, 2001). A Lyme Regis man, taken by "the Piratts of Algeire" in 1678, arrived home four years later thanks to the town's generosity: DHC, DC/LR/A/4/3.

25. R. F., *Carolina*, 28; TNA, SP 44/55, p. 80; HEHL, HM 782; Mary Maples Dunn et al., eds., *The Papers of William Penn*, 5 vols. (Philadelphia, 1981–1986), 2:84, 269–275, 280–281, quotation 275. Penn's grant was "a remarkable achievement in the English political climate of 1680–1681": ibid., 23; Edwin B. Bronner, *William Penn's "Holy Experiment": The Founding of Pennsylvania, 1681–1701* (New York, 1962).

26. Marion Balderston, ed., *James Claypoole's Letter Book: London and Philadelphia, 1681–1684* (San Marino, CA, 1967), 11–14; William Chauncy Langdon, *Everyday Things in American Life, 1607–1776* (New York, 1937), 4–5, 236.

27. Dunn et al., eds., *Papers*, 2:350, 375, 381, 509–510, 569–578, 581–582; J. William Frost, *A Perfect Freedom: Religious Liberty in Pennsylvania* (Cambridge, UK, 1990), 11–12. On political strain: Gary B. Nash, *Quakers and Politics: Pennsylvania, 1681–1726* (Princeton, NJ, 1968).

28. James T. Lemon, *The Best Poor Man's Country: A Geographical Study of Early Southeastern Pennsylvania* (Baltimore, 1972), ch. 1; *A Brief Account of the Province of East-Jersey in America* (London, 1682), 4; Thomas Budd, *Good Order Established in Pennsilvania & New-Jersey in America* (Philadelphia, 1685), 2–11, 37–39, quotations 2, 37; *Proposals by the Proprietors of East-Jersey in America for the Building of a Town on Ambo-Point* (London, 1682); George Lockhart, *A Further Account of East-New-Jersey* (Edinburgh, 1683), quotation 4; [William Loddington], *Plantation Work, Generation Work* (London, 1682), 1–8, quotations 1, 3; [William Penn], *Information and Direction to Such Persons as Are Inclined to America*, 2nd ed. (London, 1686), 8; idem, *Letter from Doctor More . . . Relating to the Province of Pennsilvania* (London, 1687).

29. Thomas, ed., *Diary . . . Sewall*, 1:65n, 141, 150; *NEHGR*, vii (1853), 46; Edward Tompson, *An Elegiack Tribute to the Sacred Dust of . . . Mr Seaborn Cotton* (Boston, 1686); MHS, Ms. SBd-98, March 9, 1688; *Letter-Book . . . Sewall*, 1:52; Increase Mather, *A Testimony Against Several Prophane and Superstitious Customs* (London, 1687), A4. For Sewall's mentality: David D. Hall, *Worlds of Wonder, Days of Judgment: Popular Religious Belief in Early New England* (New York, 1989), ch. 5.

30. Viola F. Barnes, *The Dominion of New England: A Study in British Colonial Policy* (New Haven, CT, 1923), 53; CWF, MS46.02, Randolph letter, May 29, 1686; Kavenagh, ed., *Foundations*, 1:177–179. One man repudiated the Boston court because there was no governor: Noble, ed., *Records*, 1:297–298.

31. Isaac Appleton Jewett, ed., *Memorial of Samuel Appleton of Ipswich, Massachusetts* (Boston, 1850), 153; Taylor, *American Colonies*, 277; George Allan Cook, *John Wise: Early American Democrat* (New York, 1952), 43–58; MHS, Ms. SBd-98, notes on J. Broadbent.

32. BPL, Ms. Am. 1502/6/4, 34, 40, 52, quotations 4, 40; CWF, MS46.02, Randolph letter, July 1, 1686; MHS, Ms. N-522, Folder 1, p. 49 (original at AAS); Thomas, ed., *Diary . . . Sewall*, 1:155, 155n–156n; Hall, *Last American Puritan*, 193.

33. Cotton Mather, *Memorable Providences Relating to Witchcrafts and Possessions* (Boston, 1689), 1–23, 32–37, 39–40, quotation 40; *idem*, *Little Flocks Guarded Against Grievous Wolves* (Boston, 1691), 1–4, 23, 29–30, 101–103, 106; *idem*, *Late Memorable Providences*, 2nd ed. (London, 1691), B1v; [*idem*], *The Principles of the Protestant Religion Maintained* (Boston, 1690); Mather, *Wonders*, 95; Mather, *Illustrious Providences*, 135–139; BPL, Ms. Am. 1502/1/28. See also Increase Mather, *An Arrow Against Profane and Promiscuous Dancing* (Boston, 1684).

34. MHS, Ms. SBd-98, June 1, 1688; BPL, Ms. Am. 1502/7/47, 80.

35. *The Plain Case Stated of Old but Especially New-England in an Address to His Highness the Prince of Orange* (Boston, 1688); MSA, vol. 35/166; *An Account of the Late Revolutions in New-England in a Letter* (Boston, 1689), 3; [Edward Rawson], *The Revolution in New England Justified* (Boston, 1691), 27; CSL, Connecticut Archives, Colonial Wars, series I, vol. 2, 1688–1694, no. 4.

36. Thomas, ed., *Diary . . . Sewall*, 1:222; Ian K. Steele, "Communicating an English revolution to the colonies, 1688–1689," *JBS*, 24 (1985), 347–352; Lovejoy, *Glorious Revolution*, ch. 12; Nathaniel Byfield, *An Account of the Late Revolution in New-England* (London, 1689), A2–A3, A4–C1v, quotation B2v; Robert Earle Moody and Richard Clive Simmons, eds., *The Glorious Revolution in Massachusetts: Selected Documents, 1689–1692* (Boston, 1988), 45–51; *Account . . . in a Letter*, 1–6, quotation 4.

37. *CSPC, 1689–92*, 55, 111, 169–170; [John Palmer], *The Present State of New-England Impartially Considered* (London, 1689), 8–9, 11, 17, 42–43; Rawson, *Revolution*, 1–2, 6, 23–24, 42–47, quotation 1; *Account . . . in a Letter*, 7.

38. VHS, Mss 5:2 B9965:1, ff. 38v, 46v, 48; TNA, CO 5/1305, ff. 30–31; CO 137/2, f. 14; Kavenagh, ed., *Foundations*, 1:99; 2:877–878; *CSPC, Addenda 1688–96*, 1–3, 7–8; *CSPC, 1689–92*, 56; Lovejoy, *Glorious Revolution*, ch. 14; Lois Green Carr and David William Jordan, *Maryland's Revolution of Government, 1689–1692* (Ithaca, NY, 1974); *A Relation of Captain Bull Concerning the Mohawks at Fort-Albany* (Boston, 1689); Michael Pawson and David Buisseret, *Port Royal, Jamaica* (Kingston, Jamaica, 1974), 79–80.

39. TNA, CO 5/855, ff. 5, 9; *CSPC, 1689–92*, 111; Bruce Tucker, "The reinvention of New England, 1691–1770," *NEQ*, 59 (1986), 315–340; Richard R. Johnson, "The revolution of 1688–9 in the American colonies," in Jonathan I. Israel, ed., *The Anglo-Dutch Moment: Essays on the Glorious Revolution and Its World Impact* (Cambridge, UK, 1991), 215–240; Owen Stanwood, *The Empire Reformed: English America in the Age of the Glorious Revolution* (Philadelphia, 2011), chs. 2–5.

CHAPTER 20: THESE DARK TERRITORIES

1. Thomas, ed., *Diary . . . Sewall*, 1:222.

2. AAS, MSS Boxes "M," Box 3, Folder 2, April 4–5 and 17, May 10–16, 1688.

3. BPL, Ms. Am. 1502/7/44–45, 53; MHS, Special Collections, Sewall Box 2, Folder 2 (E187); Thomas, ed., *Diary . . . Sewall*, 1:185–186, 192–221, quotation 195; AAS, MSS Boxes "M," Box 3, Folder 2, December 3, 1688; Richard Francis, *Judge Sewall's Apology: The Salem Witch-Trials and the Forming of a Conscience* (London, 2005), ch. 3. His was "the earliest diary to give a substantial account of sight-seeing in London by an American": William L. Sachse, *The Colonial American in Britain* (Madison, WI, 1956), 24.

4. BPL, Ms. Am. 1502/7/12; [Increase Mather], *A Narrative of the Miseries of New-England by Reason of an Arbitrary Government* (Boston, 1688), 1–2, 4, 6; [*idem*], *A Vindication of New-England from the Vile Aspersions Cast upon that Country* (Boston, n.d. [1688?]), 1, 3, 26–27, quotation 26; 1 Samuel 15:23; Mather, *Brief Relation*, 6, 8–9, quotation 9.

5. AAS, MSS Boxes "M," Box 3, Folder 2, May 3, June 1, 1688; BPL, Ms. Am. 1502/7/17; TNA, CO 1/65, ff. 322–322v; Hall, *Last American Puritan*, 215, 217–218. On Mather's negotiations: Moody and Simmons, eds., *Glorious Revolution*, 1–41.

6. AAS, MSS Boxes "M," Box 3, Folder 2, January 9, February 2 and 17, March 12 and 14, 1689; Hall, *Last American Puritan*, 221–222.

7. Bodl., Rawlinson Letters 51, f. 139; Francis, *Judge Sewall's Apology*, 170–171. Mather begged for financial help: Charles J. Hoadly, ed., *Early Letters and Documents Relating to Connecticut, 1643–1709* (Hartford, CT, 1932), 46–47.

8. *New-England's Faction Discovered* (London, 1690), 3, 8; *CSPC, 1689–92*, 40; Bodl., Tanner MS 27, f. 29v; *New-England's Faction Discovered*, 4; AAS, MSS Boxes "C," Box 1, Folder 4, letter to John Cotton, October 17, 1690; *News from New-England: In a Letter Written to a Person of Quality* (London, 1690).

9. MHS, Ms. N-528, February 28, March 28, April 9 and 28, 1691.

10. *The Humble Address of the Publicans of New-England* (London, 1691), 5, 13–14; LPL, MS 841, Pt. 7, quotations ff. 3v, 9, 11v, 13.

11. [Increase Mather], *Reasons for the Confirmation of the Charters . . . in New-England* (n.p. [London?], n.d. [1691?]), 1; Moody and Simmons, eds., *Glorious Revolution*, 491–508, quotations 492, 495, 501; *CSPC, 1689–92*, 456–457.

12. *CSPC, 1689–92*, 514; Daniel Denton, *A Brief Description of New-York* (London, 1670), 19–21; VHS, Mss 5:2 B9965:1, f. 22v; John Miller, *New York Considered and Improved, 1695*, ed. Victor Hugo Paltsits (Cleveland, OH, 1903), 40; Robert C. Ritchie, *The Duke's Province: A Study of New York Politics and Society, 1664–1691* (Chapel Hill, NC, 1977), chs. 7–9; *A Model and Impartial Narrative of Several Grievances and Great Oppressions . . . of New-York* (London 1690), A1v. See also Patricia U. Bonomi, *A Factious People: Politics and Society in Colonial New York* (New York, 1971), 75–81.

13. Greene, ed., *Great Britain*, xvii, 115–120; AAS, MSS Boxes "M," Box 5, Folder 2, Mather to Cotton, September 1, 1691; MHS, Ms. N-528, April 9, 1691. See also [Increase Mather], *New-England Vindicated* (London, 1689), 2–3; Edmund S. Morgan, *Inventing the People: The Rise of Popular Sovereignty in England and America* (New York, 1988), chs. 1–4.

14. Locke, *Two Treatises of Government*, 358–359; Haffenden, *New England in the English Nation*, chs. 1–2.

15. DWL, MS 12.78, p. 206; MSA, vol. 11/48; Cotton Mather, *Decennium Luctuosum* (Boston, 1699), 33–34; CSL, Connecticut Archives, Colonial Wars, series I, vol. 2, 1688–1694, nos. 10a–b, 12a, 13a, 17a; TNA, CO 5/855, f. 73; Bridenbaugh, ed., *Letters*, 203.

16. *CSPC, 1689–92*, 114–115; Vaughan and Clark, eds., *Puritans*, 96–115, quotations 97, 99.

17. CSL, Connecticut Archives, Colonial Wars, series I, vol. 2, 1688–1694, no. 19b; *CSPC, 1689–92*, 212; N. N., *Short Account*, 5; Cotton Mather, *Souldiers Counselled and Comforted* (Boston, 1689), 18–19, 23–28, 37–38, quotation 28; MSA, vol. 11/47; Mather, *Decennium Luctuosum*, 45.

18. MSA, vol. 35/239–240, quotation 239; Thomas, ed., *Diary . . . Sewall*, 1:251; HEHL, BL 239; CSL, Connecticut Archives, Colonial Wars, series I, vol. 2, 1688–1694, no. 40a; Mather, *Illustrious Providences*, 160–167; Moody, ed., *Saltonstall Papers*, 1:195–198; Mather, *Decennium Luctuosum*, 47–49, 51–52; MSA, vol. 35/319; TNA, CO 5/713, f. 16. Cf. Jacob Leisler's letter to the bishop of Salisbury, March 31, 1690: *CSPC, 1689–92*, 385.

19. CSL, Connecticut Archives, Colonial Wars, series I, vol. 2, 1688–1694, no. 61a; AAS, MSS Boxes "M," Box 5, Folder 2, May 17, 1690 (original at MHS); Cotton Mather, *The Life and Death of the Renown'd Mr John Eliot* (London, 1691), 3–5, quotation 5; LMA, MS 7936, f. 29; MS 7927B, p. 8; MS 7956/1, f. 26. In 1691, praying Indians sent William and Mary a porcupine-quill pouch: LMA, MS 7957, ff. 3–4v.

20. HEHL, BL 240, 242; MSA, vol. 11/48, 50, 54, quotation 11/54; L[aurence] H[ammond], *To the King's Most Excellent Majesty* (London, 1691), 1, 7–8; *Letter-Book . . . Sewall*, 1:126n–127n.

21. Thomas Savage, *An Account of the Late Action of the New-Englanders* (London, 1691), 3–4, 11–12; *CSPC, 1689–92*, 384–386; Van Doren, ed., *Phips*, 92–103, quotations 93–94.

22. *CSPC, 1689–92*, 385, 368–369; Savage, *Account*, 12–13; MHS, Ms. N-1649, October 26, 1690; *Letter-Book . . . Sewall*, 1:120; BL, Add. MS 70015, f. 144v.

23. MHS, Ms. N-522, Folder 1, pp. 65–66, 72 (original at AAS).

24. TNA, CO 5/1037, f. 227; Van Doren, ed., *Phips*, 153; MHS, Ms. N-522, Folder 1, p. 72 (original at AAS). Nathaniel Mather's epitaph was, "The Ashes of an Hard Student, a Good Scholar, and a Great Christian": [Cotton Mather], *A Token for the Children of New-England* (Boston, 1700), 15.

25. *CSPC*, *1689–92*, 643–644, 753; Hoadly, ed., *Early Letters*, 49–52, quotation 51; *Plymouth Church Records*, 167–168; Sarson, *British America*, 162; MSA, vol. 40/275.

26. Terry Lee Anderson, *The Economic Growth of Seventeenth-Century New England* (New York, 1972), 60; Richard P. Gildrie, *The Profane, the Civil, and the Godly: The Reformation of Manners in Orthodox New England, 1679–1749* (University Park, PA, 1994), chs. 3, 5–6; Bruce C. Daniels, *Puritans at Play: Leisure and Recreation in Colonial New England* (Basingstoke, UK, 1995), chs. 4–5, 8; William Pencak, Matthew Dennis, and Simon P. Newman, eds., *Riot and Revelry in Early America* (University Park, PA, 2002), chs. 3–5; David W. Conroy, *In Public Houses: Drink and the Revolution of Authority in Colonial Massachusetts* (Chapel Hill, NC, 1995), chs. 1–3; Hall, *Worlds of Wonder*, 162; Alfred A. Cave, "Indian shamans and English witches in seventeenth-century New England," *EIHC*, 128 (1992), 239–254; Richard Weisman, *Witchcraft, Magic, and Religion in 17th-Century Massachusetts* (Amherst, MA, 1984), chs. 3–5; Richard Godbeer, *The Devil's Dominion: Magic and Religion in Early New England* (Cambridge, UK, 1992); Richard P. Gildrie, "Visions of evil: popular culture, Puritanism and the Massachusetts witchcraft crisis of 1692," *Journal of American Culture*, 8, no. 4 (1985), 17–33; Robert Blair St. George, *Conversing by Signs: Poetics of Implication in Colonial New England Culture* (Chapel Hill, NC, 1998), 188–195. See also John Demos, *Circles and Lines: The Shape of Life in Early America* (Cambridge, MA, 2004). Increase Mather's estimate of the population was 200,000: *Brief Relation*, 5.

27. Mather, *Wonders*, 15–16, 37–38; AAS, MSS Boxes "M," Box 5, Folder 2, letter to John Cotton, August 5, 1692.

28. *CSPC*, *1689–92*, 83–84, 137–138, 249–250; *An Account of the Late Dreadful Earth-Quake* (London, 1690), 2; *A True and Faithful Account of . . . Victory over the French Fleet in the West-Indies* (London, 1690); *A True and Faithful Relation of the Proceeedings . . . Against the French in the Caribby Islands* (London, 1691); *The Case of the Planters and Traders Belonging to the English Sugar Plantations* (London, 1690); Thomas Dalby, *An Historical Account of the Rise and Growth of the West-Indian Collonies* (London, 1690), 10–11.

29. Edward Littleton, *The Groans of the Plantations* (London, 1689), 2–3, 6–7, 14–15, 26–30, 34, quotation 34; *A Brief but Most True Relation of the Late Barbarous and Bloody Plot of the Negro's in the Island of Barbados* (London, 1693); Beckles, *Black Rebellion*, 42–48; *CSPC*, *1689–92*, 730; TNA, CO 140/2, p. 141. On hazardous slave existence: BL, Sloane MS 3861, f. 67; Littleton, *Groans*, 19–20.

30. Larry Gragg, "The Port Royal earthquake," *History Today*, 50 (2000), 29–30; *CSPC*, *1681–5*, 464; Trapham, *Discourse*, 20–22; *Present State of Jamaica*, 11–12; BL, Sloane MS 3861, f. 67v; Blome, *Description*, 31; Krise, ed., *Caribbeana*, 90–91; *A Sad and Terrible Relation of the Dreadful Earth-quake That Happened at Jamaco* (London, 1692), 6–7; TNA, CO 140/5, p. 184; BL, Harleian MS 6922, f. 19.

31. BL, Harleian MS 6922, ff. 19–19v; Gragg, "Port Royal earthquake," 30.

32. TNA, CO 137/44, f. 51; *CSPC*, *1689–92*, 685, 690, 711–712; *A Full Account of the Late Dreadful Earthquake at Port Royal in Jamaica* (London, 1692). A poem by John Tutchin evoked Judgement Day: *The Earth-Quake of Jamaica* (London, 1692).

33. MHS, Ms. SBd.98, August 3, 1692; Narcissus Luttrell, *A Brief Historical Relation of State Affairs from September 1678 to April 1714*, 6 vols. (Oxford, 1857), 2:533–534, 539; *A True and Perfect Relation of That Most Sad and Terrible Earthquake at Port-Royal* (London, 1692); *A Sad and Terrible Relation of Two Dreadful Earth-quakes That Happened in England and at Jamaca* (London, 1692), 5–8; *The Truest and Largest Account of the Late Earthquake in Jamaica* (London, 1693), A2v, 20; John Shower, *Practical Reflections on the Late Earthquakes* (London, 1693); Glenn Tilley Morse, "Edward Rawson . . . and his unfortunate daughter Rebecca," *Old Time New England*, 11 (1920), 129.

34. MSA, vol. 11/57a (petition, 1690). Cf. complaint at Concord in 1686: HEHL, HM 8403. My account relies on Mary Beth Norton, *In the Devil's Snare: The Salem Witchcraft Crisis of 1692* (New York, 2002); John Demos, *The Enemy Within: 2,000 Years of Witch-Hunting in the Western World* (New York, 2008), chs. 7–9; Larry Gragg, *The Salem Witchcraft Crisis* (New York, 1992), ch. 10; Emerson W. Baker, *A Storm of Witchcraft: The Trials of Salem and a Nation* (New York, 2014).

35. Gildrie, *Salem*, chs. 8–10; Paul Boyer and Stephen Nissenbaum, *Salem Possessed: The Social Origins of Witchcraft* (Cambridge, MA, 1974), ch. 5; "Forum: Salem repossessed," *WMQ*, 65 (2008); Dow, ed., *Records*, 8:294; Cedric B. Cowing, *The Saving Remnant: Religion and the Settling of New England* (Urbana, IL, 1995), ch. 3; Elinor Abbot, *Our Company Increases Apace: History, Language and Social Identity in Early Andover, Massachusetts* (Dallas, TX, 2007), esp. 129–149; cf. Greven, *Four Generations*.

36. Frances Hill, *The Salem Witch Trials Reader* (New York, 2000), 252; Larry Gragg, *A Quest for Security: The Life of Samuel Parris, 1653–1720* (New York, 1990), chs. 3–5; Richard Latner, "'Here are no newters': witchcraft and religious discord in Salem village and Andover," *NEQ*, 79 (2006), 92–122; Burr, ed., *Narratives*, 148.

37. Deodat Lawson, *A Brief and True Narrative of . . . Witchcraft* (Boston, 1692), in Burr, ed., *Narratives*, 152–164; Burr, ed., *Narratives*, 153–157, quotation 154; James F. Cooper Jr. and Kenneth P. Minkema, eds., *The Sermon Notebook of Samuel Parris, 1689–1694* (Boston, 1993), 194–207; Gragg, *Quest for Security*, chs. 6–7. Tituba was probably a South American slave whom Parris had bought in Barbados: Elaine G. Breslaw, *Tituba, Reluctant Witch of Salem: Devilish Indians and Puritan Fantasies* (New York, 1996), ch. 2.

38. Deodat Lawson, *Christ's Fidelity the Only Shield Against Satans Malignity* (Boston, 1693), 61; Thomas, ed., *Diary . . . Sewall*, 1:289; Ford, ed., *Diary of Cotton Mather*, 146–147.

39. Poole, "Witchcraft delusion," 382–383; Gaskill, *Witchfinders*, 150–151; Bernard Rosenthal, ed., *Records of the Salem Witch-Hunt* (Cambridge, UK, 2009), 19, 22, 23–24, 33–34, 36–38, 46–52, 85. The judges used Joseph Keble, *An Assistance to Justices of the Peace* (London, 1683), which cited older law books: Norton, *Devil's Snare*, 200; Burr, ed., *Narratives*, 163; Rosenthal, ed., *Records*, 18n.

40. Increase Mather, *A Further Account of the Tryals of the New-England Witches* (London, 1693), 30; Burr, ed., *Narratives*, 420; Benjamin C. Ray, "Salem's war against the covenant in Salem village, 1692," *NEQ*, 80 (2007), 75; Christine Leigh Heyrman, "Specters of subversion, societies of Friends: dissent and the devil in provincial Essex Country, Massachusetts," in Hall et al., eds., *Saints and Revolutionaries*, 38–74; James E. Kences, "Some unexplored relationships of Essex County witchcraft to the Indian wars of 1675 and 1689," *EIHC*, 120 (1984), 181–186, 203–204, 208; Norton, *Devil's Snare*, esp. ch. 3; Baker and Reid, *New England Knight*, ch. 7; Cotton Mather, "A brand pluck'd out of the burning," in Burr, ed., *Narratives*, 255–287, quotation 275; idem, *Decennium Luctuosum*, 102–103.

41. TNA, CO 5/1037, f. 227; *Letter-Book . . . Sewall*, 1:132; Demos, *Enemy Within*, 152–153; Norton, *Devil's Snare*, 123–125, 128–132; AAS, MSS Boxes "M," Box 5, Folder 2, Mather letter, May 31, 1692; Cotton Mather, *A Midnight Cry* (Boston, 1692), 53–54. Increase Mather read the Elizabethan theologian William Perkins, who thought spectral evidence a mere presumption: Rosenthal, ed., *Records*, 32–34.

42. Ford, cd., *Diary of Cotton Mather*, 150–152, quotation 150; AAS, MSS Boxes "M," Box 5, Folder 2, Cotton letter, August 5, 1692; Mather, *Further Account*, 41–42; Mather, *Wonders*, 63–65; Thomas Ady, *A Candle in the Dark* (London, 1656); Robert Calef, *More Wonders of the Invisible World* (London, 1700), 105–106.

43. Calef, *More Wonders*, 104.

44. Cooper and Minkema, eds., *Sermon Notebook*, 204; Rosenthal, ed., *Records*, 658; Mather, *Magnalia*, ed. Murdock and Miller, 10; TNA, CO 5/905, ff. 202–203v, quotation 202; Baker and Reid, *New England Knight*, 155; Norton, *Devil's Snare*, 286.

45. MSA, vol.11/69–70; vol. 47/98; Burr, ed., *Narratives*, 206–207; TNA, CO 5/905, ff. 203v–204; Baker, *Storm of Witchcraft*, ch. 7; William Bray, ed., *Memoirs Illustrative of the*

Life and Writings of John Evelyn (London, 1871), 552. Other publications included *A True Account of . . . Divers Witches at Salem* (London, 1692).

46. Mather, *Wonders*, 15; Rutman and Rutman, *Small Worlds*, 140; Demos, *Enemy Within*, ch. 5; CSL, Crimes & Misdemeanors, Series I, 1662–1789, vol. 1, pp. 185–187; CSL, Samuel Wyllys Papers, ff. 1–5, 18–41; Richard Godbeer, *Escaping Salem: The Other Witch-Hunt of 1692* (Oxford, 2005); Norton, *Devil's Snare*, 224–225, 229, 238, 279, 385; Burr, ed., *Narratives*, 397; Baker and Reid, *New England Knight*, 147–151; [Samuel Willard], *Some Miscellany Observations on Our Present Debates Respecting Witchcrafts* (Philadelphia, 1692). England experienced a small witch-panic in Kent in 1692: C. L'Estrange Ewen, ed., *Witch Hunting and Witch Trials* (London, 1929), 263.

47. Bryan Le Beau, "Philip English and the witchcraft hysteria," *Historical Journal of Massachusetts*, 15 (1987), 1–20; Chever, "Sketch," 163–165.

48. Miller, *New York Considered*, 124; Owen Manning and William Bray, *The History and Antiquities of the County of Surrey*, 3 vols. (London, 1804–1814), 2:714n; *CSPC, Jan. 1693–14 May 1696*, 29–30; John Hale, *A Modest Enquiry into the Nature of Witchcraft* (Boston, 1702), 35.

49. Rosenthal, ed., *Records*, 813–814, 830; TNA, CO 5/905, ff. 204–204v; Chever, "Sketch," 166–167.

EPILOGUE: NEW WORLDS

1. Mather, *Illustrious Providences*, 39–40; Vaughan and Clark, eds., *Puritans*, ch. 2; Clair Franklin Luther, *The Hadley Chest* (Hartford, CT, 1935), ch. 6; Wallace Nutting, *Furniture Treasury*, 3 vols. (New York, 1948–1949), 38–39, 42–43; MSA, vol. 69/230a; Laurel Thatcher Ulrich, *The Age of Homespun: Objects and Stories in the Creation of an American Myth* (New York, 2001), ch. 3. Details of Smead's background come from the Huntington American Art Gallery and Ancestry.com. See also Thompson, *Mobility and Migration*, 195. A relative, possibly her brother, was taken in an earlier raid: *Wyllys Papers*, 239.

2. Evan Haefeli and Kevin Sweeney, *Captors and Captives: The 1704 French and Indian Raid on Deerfield* (Amherst, MA, 2003), ch. 6; "The destruction at Deerfield, February 29, 1703–4," *Procs of the MHS*, 9 (1866–1867), 478–482.

3. Demos, ed., *Remarkable Providences*, xxii; LMA, MS 07955/1, ff. 5–5v, 8; Robert Beverley, *The History and Present State of Virginia*, ed. Louis B. Wright (Chapel Hill, NC, 1947), 233; HEHL, HM 59962, f. 2; Michael Leroy Oberg, *Dominion and Civility: English Imperialism and Native America, 1585–1685* (Ithaca, NY, 1999), 227.

4. Roy Harvey Pearce, *Savagism and Civilization: A Study of the Indian and the American Mind* (Baltimore, 1965), ch. 1; Bailyn, *Peopling*, 110; Nash, *Wilderness*, 30; BL, Add. MS 27382, f. 196; Billings et al., *Colonial Virginia*, 125–128, 131–132; Beverley, *History . . . of Virginia*, ed. Wright, 233; John Demos, *The Unredeemed Captive: A Family Story from Early America* (New York, 1994), 141–142, 146. In the 1690s, one Virginian parish stopped recording communicants' English origins: *Parish Register of Christ Church*.

5. Richard I. Melvoin, *New England Outpost: War and Society in Colonial Deerfield* (New York, 1989), 282–284; Richard White, *The Middle Ground: Indians, Empires, and Republics in the Great Lakes Region, 1650–1815*, 2nd ed. (Cambridge, UK, 2011); Haefeli and Sweeney, *Captors and Captives*, 3–6; John Williams, *The Redeemed Captive Returning to Zion*, ed. Stephen W. Williams (Northampton, MA, 1853), 10–11; Demos, *Unredeemed Captive*, 104–105, 110–111, 146–147. The classic "frontier" thesis is Frederick Jackson Turner, *The Frontier in American History* (New York, 1921), chs. 1–2. For a critique: Ray Allen Billington, "The American frontier," in Paul Bohannen and Fred Plog, eds., *Beyond the Frontier: Social Process and Cultural Change* (Garden City, NY, 1967), 3–24.

6. Vaughan and Clark, eds., *Puritans*, 130; John Gyles, *Memoirs of Odd Adventures, Strange Deliverances etc.* (Boston, 1736).

7. Mather, *Magnalia*, 1:A2; Cotton Mather, *The Short History of New-England* (Boston, 1694), 4–5, 18–20, 32–33, 37–38, quotations 20, 37; *idem, Things for a Distress'd People to Think*

Upon (Boston, 1696), 11–15, quotation 11; *idem, Midnight Cry,* 48–49; *idem, New-England's Faction Discovered,* 5; John Canup, "Cotton Mather and 'creolian degeneracy,'" *Early American Literature,* 24 (1989), 20–34.

8. New Haven Historical Society, MSS 8, Box I, Folder F, Mather letter, November 13, 1710; Canup, *Out of the Wilderness,* 225.

9. Kathleen M. Brown, "Murderous uncleanness: the body of the female infanticide in Puritan New England," in Lindman and Tarter, eds., *Centre of Wonders,* 90–91; Silverman, ed., *Selected Letters,* xvi–xvii, 30–35; Parrish, *American Curiosity,* 127–128; Marilynne K. Roach, *The Salem Witch Trials: A Day-by-Day Chronicle of a Community Under Siege* (Lanham, MD, 2002), 548; Van Doren, ed., *Phips,* 151; Demos, *Enemy Within,* 228; Michael P. Winship, *Seers of God: Puritan Providentialism in the Restoration and Early Enlightenment* (Baltimore, 1996), chs. 4–8.

10. Conrad Edick Wright, "Thomas Brattle," *ODNB;* CUL, RGO/1/36, f. 106; Burr, ed., *Narratives,* 173; Burr, ed., *Narratives,* 190. A diary records the eclipse on July 17 and executions on the 19th: MHS, SBd-98.

11. Calef, *More Wonders,* 26–30, 33, 59–60, 63–64, 108, quotations 33, 59, 108; Gragg, *Quest for Security,* ch. 8; Sarah Rivett, *The Science of the Soul in Colonial New England* (Chapel Hill, NC, 2011), ch. 5.

12. Burr, ed., *Narratives,* 398; Calef, *More Wonders,* 144–145; Demos, *Enemy Within,* 186–187; NEHGS, MSS 78, Folder 11, Baxter letter, n.d. [c. 1710].

13. Rosenthal, ed., *Records,* 844–885, 888–889, 912–915; Chever, "Sketch," 160n; Bodl., Rawlinson MSS C.128, f. 12.

14. Miller, *New England Mind,* 191; Foster, *Long Argument,* 281–283; Plumstead, ed., *Wall and the Garden,* 27.

15. Heimert and Delbanco, eds., *Puritans,* 347–348; Richard R. Johnson, *Adjustment to Empire: The New England Colonies, 1675–1715* (Leicester, UK, 1981), 417; Robin Briggs, *Witches and Neighbours: The Social and Cultural Context of European Witchcraft* (London, 1996), 311, 315. In general, see Richard L. Bushman, *From Puritan to Yankee: Character and the Social Order in Connecticut, 1690–1765* (Cambridge, MA, 1967).

16. Richard L. Bushman, *The Refinement of America: Persons, Houses, Cities* (New York, 1992); David S. Shields, *Civil Tongues and Polite Letters in British America* (Chapel Hill, NC, 1997); Ned C. Landsman, *From Colonials to Provincials: American Thought and Culture, 1680–1760* (Ithaca, NY, 2000); Miller and Johnson, eds., *Puritans,* 76; Charles E. Clark, *The Public Prints: The Newspaper in Anglo-American Culture, 1665–1740* (Oxford, 1994); Mather, *Magnalia,* 1:A3v; RS, EL/I1/182, ff. 331–332v.

17. Catherine Armstrong, *Landscape and Identity in North America's Southern Colonies from 1660 to 1745* (Farnham, UK, 2013); Demos, ed., *Remarkable Providences,* xxvii–xxix, xxxvii–xxxviii; Castillo and Schweitzer, eds., *Literatures,* 105; Kenneth Lockridge, "Land, population and the evolution of New England society, 1630–1790," *Past & Present,* 39 (1968), 62–80; Jackson Turner Main, *Society and Economy in Colonial Connecticut* (Princeton, NJ, 1985), ch. 3.

18. Thomas Bray, *A Memorial Representing the Present State of Religion on the Continent of North-America* (London, 1700); Edward Ward, *A Trip to New-England* (London, 1699), 3–12, quotations 3, 7, 12; Krise, ed., *Caribbeana,* 88, 90; Trevor Burnard, "European migration to Jamaica, 1655–1780," *WMQ,* 53 (1996), 771–772; Cambridgeshire RO, P59/25/7/4–4v; Gabriel Thomas, *An Historical and Geographical Account of . . . Pensilvania* (London, 1698), 5–7; Olwell and Tully, eds., *Cultures and Identities,* intro. For a New Englander regarded with fascination in England in 1696: Charles Jackson, ed., *The Diary of Abraham de la Pryme* (Durham, UK, 1870), 99.

19. Brendan McConville, *The King's Three Faces: The Rise and Fall of Royal America, 1688–1776* (Chapel Hill, NC, 2006); Michael Warner, *The Letters of the Republic: Publication and the Public Sphere in Eighteenth-Century America* (Cambridge, MA, 1990); T. H. Breen, *The Marketplace of Revolution: How Consumer Politics Shaped American Independence* (Oxford,

2004); James S. Hart and Richard J. Ross, "The ancient constitution in the old world and the new," in Bremer and Botelho, eds., *World of John Winthrop*, 237–289; Burr, ed., *Narratives*, 182; Bodl., Rawlinson MSS C.128, f. iv.

20. Greene, ed., *Great Britain*, xxxi; Jack P. Greene, *The Quest for Power: The Lower Houses of Assembly in the Southern Royal Colonies, 1689–1776* (Chapel Hill, NC, 1963), 14–17; Kevin Phillips, *The Cousins' Wars: Religion, Politics and the Triumph of Anglo-America* (New York, 1999); Michal Jan Rozbicki, "Between private and public spheres: liberty as cultural property in eighteenth-century British America," in Olwell and Tully, eds., *Cultures and Identities*, 293–318; J. C. D. Clark, *The Language of Liberty, 1660–1832: Political Discourse and Social Dynamics in the Anglo-American World* (Cambridge, UK, 1994).

21. John Morrill, *Stuart Britain: A Very Short Introduction* (Oxford, 2000), esp. 76.

22. Essex RO, D/DBy O25/2; Taylor, *Colonial America*, 42, 69; Haefeli and Sweeney, *Captors and Captives*, 1–2; Jensen, ed., *Colonial Documents*, 64; "An Act for re-uniting to the Crown the Government of several Colonies" (1701), *Journals of the House of Lords*, 16:659; Johnson, *History*, 34; Joseph A. Conforti, *Saints and Strangers: New England in British North America* (Baltimore, 2006), 44. By 1770 the population exceeded 2 million: Breen, "Empire of goods," 485.

23. Haefeli and Sweeney, *Captors and Captives*, 1; Sheldon, *Deerfield*, 2:291–293; Evan Haefeli and Kevin Sweeney, eds., *Captive Histories: English, French, and Native Narratives of the 1704 Deerfield Raid* (Amherst, MA, 2006), 276n.

24. Hawke, *Everyday Life*, at 52–53; Gray, ed., *Colonial America*, 53; Charles Upham, quoted in Michael Kammen, *Mystic Chords of Memory: The Transformation of Tradition in American Culture* (New York, 1991), 64; Robert D. Arner, "Plymouth Rock revisited: the landing of the Pilgrim Fathers," *Journal of American Culture*, 6, no. 4 (1983), 25–35; Tony Horwitz, *A Voyage Long and Strange: Rediscovering the New World* (London, 2008), 2; Warwick Charlton, *The Voyage of the Mayflower II* (London, 1957); Horwitz, *Voyage*, 382; James W. Loewen, *Lies My Teacher Told Me: Everything Your American History Textbook Got Wrong* (New York, 1995), 88. "If Plymouth Rock is our oldest monument, it is also our most ridiculous icon": John Seelye, *Memory's Nation: The Place of Plymouth Rock* (Chapel Hill, NC, 1998), 5.

25. David C. Brown, *A Guide to the Salem Witchcraft Hysteria of 1692* (n.p., 1984); Castillo and Schweitzer, eds., *Literatures*, 257; "335-year-old tree felled, apparently by vandals," *New York Times*, July 28, 1964, 31; David L. Shores, *Tangier Island: Place, People and Talk* (Cranbury, NJ, 2000). Dyer's statue, commissioned in 1959 by the Boston general court for the three-hundredth anniversary of her execution, was created by Sylvia Shaw Judson, a Quaker.

26. Archaeologists believe Roanoke may be underwater: Willie Drye, "America's lost colony: can new dig solve mystery?" *National Geographic News* (March 2, 2004); www .firstcolonyfoundation.org/news/2012_white_map.aspx; Tabor, "Maine's Popham colony"; Jeffrey Phipps Brain, *Fort St George: Archaeological Investigation of the 1607–1608 Popham Colony on the Kennebec River in Maine* (Augusta, ME, 2007); D. L. Hamilton and Robyn Woodward, "A sunken 17th-century city: Port Royal, Jamaica," *Archaeology*, 37 (1984), 38–45; Marion Gibson, *Witchcraft Myths in American Culture* (New York, 2007), 67.

27. Barbara Ritter Dailey, "Sir William Phips," *ODNB*; Kate Caffrey, *The Mayflower* (New York, 1974), 324, 330–331.

28. Robert Ruby, *Unknown Shore: The Lost History of England's Arctic Colony* (New York, 2001), 257–259; Weatherwax, "Pocahontas"; Savage, ed., *History*, 1:30; Norfolk RO, PD 90/1; CKS, P45/1/1A; R. H. Ovenell, *The Ashmolean Museum, 1683–1894* (Oxford, 1986), 5; Lepore, *Name of War*, 174. Russell Bourne doubts that Metacom's regalia ever reached the king: *Red King's Rebellion*, 205.

29. Alexander, *Encouragement*, 42; Julian Borger, "Candidates have same Essex ancestor," *Guardian* (September 21, 2004), 15; MHS, MS. N-1182, Carton 36: SH 114M U, Folder 30, note re. William Crowninshield in 1900; Kathy Flood, *Warman's Jewelry: Identification*

and Price Guide, 4th ed. (Iola, WI, 2010), 76; Philbrick, *Mayflower*, 356; Ann Uhry Abrams, *The Pilgrims and Pocahontas: Rival Myths of American Origin* (Boulder, CO, 1999), 258.

30. Nathaniel Hawthorne, *The Scarlet Letter* (Boston, 1850) (No one did more than Hawthorne to establish the negative image of "these stern and black-browed Puritans": Penguin ed. [1994], 9); Richard Archer, *Fissures in the Rock: New England in the Seventeenth Century* (Hanover, NH, 2001); Charles E. Clark, *The Eastern Frontier: The Settlement of Northern New England, 1610–1763* (New York, 1970), chs. 2–4; Greene, *Pursuits of Happiness*, chs. 1, 3, 4; Alexis de Tocqueville, quoted in Robert N. Bellah et al., *Habits of the Heart: Individualism and Commitment in American Life*, 3rd ed. (Berkeley, CA, 2008), 28; Peter J. Gomes, "Pilgrims and Puritans: 'heroes' and 'villains' in the creation of the American past," *Procs of the MHS*, 94 (1982), 1–16; Abrams, *Pilgrims*, 4–14; Nicholas Guyatt, *Providence and the Invention of the United States, 1607–1876* (Cambridge, UK, 2007), esp. ch. 1; Andrew Preston, *Sword of the Spirit, Shield of Faith: Religion in American War and Diplomacy* (New York, 2012), ch. 1. Perhaps 1 percent of English migrants were justified members of a New England congregation.

31. Cressy, *Coming Over*, viii; Amussen, *Caribbean Exchanges*, 11; Alan Taylor, "An Atlantic people," *JBS*, 29 (1990), 402. The colonies were "a marchland of the metropolitan European culture system": Bailyn, *Peopling*, 112.

32. Jensen, ed., *Colonial Documents*, 167–168, 174; Williams, *Key*, ed. Teunissen and Hinz, 13; Timothy L. Hall, *Separating Church and State: Roger Williams and Religious Liberty* (Urbana, IL, 1998), ch. 6; Frank Prochaska, "Flaws across the pond," *History Today*, 62 (2012), 42; James G. Moseley, *John Winthrop's World: History as a Story, the Story as History* (Madison, WI, 1992), 7; John F. Kennedy, Massachusetts General Court, January 9, 1961; Barack Obama, University of Massachusetts commencement address, June 2, 2006.

33. Bremer, *Winthrop*, 179–181; Theodore Dwight Bozeman, "The Puritans' 'errand into the wilderness' reconsidered," *NEQ*, 59 (1986), 231–251; Delbanco, *Puritan Ordeal*, 72–76; Matthew 5:14–16; Seelye, *Memory's Nation*, 636.

FURTHER READING

Students coming to this subject for the first time, as I did some years ago, risk overload. Colonies that were once covered by a single book, or events by an article, have produced their own subfields, and, like all burrowing creatures, historians can lose perspective. My impression was that many textbooks and lecture courses dealt cursorily with the early colonial period, and that the national stories of England and America in this era had been sundered, despite sharing so much. It was almost as if they were, to misquote George Bernard Shaw, two countries divided by a common history. I found much recent research that was sensitive to the original "special relationship"; but the two sides still didn't pay each other enough attention: historians of early modern England, my own tribe, certainly neglect America. I became curious about the mentality of English people beyond England, living between two worlds when the old was solid and certain, the new wild and unknown. This book is the result.

In England, there are major manuscript collections at the National Archives at Kew (especially the CO series), the British Library in London (e.g., Egerton MS 2395), and the Bodleian Library in Oxford (e.g., Clarendon MS 74). Smaller holdings exist in the Metropolitan Archives, Lambeth Palace Library, Dr. Williams's Library, and the Royal Society—all in London. In Cambridge, the University Library has relevant documents, but a richer crop can be found at Magdalene College, including the Ferrar Papers on Virginia. County record offices have fragments relating to America, such as letters, parish accounts, share certificates, and so on; I used those at Kent, Essex, Suffolk, Norfolk, Cambridgeshire, Hertfordshire, Gloucestershire, Somerset, Devon, Dorset, Cornwall, Sussex, Cheshire, and Lancashire. Other archives I consulted included the Borthwick Institute at York; the University of Nottingham's Manuscripts and Special Collections; and the libraries of Arundel Castle, Sussex, and Alnwick Castle, Northumberland.

In the United States, I spent most of my time in Boston at the Massachusetts Historical Society; Boston Public Library's Rare Books Department; and the New England Historic Genealogical Society. Outside the city, the Harvard University Archives, the Massachusetts State Archives at Dorchester, and the American Antiquarian Society at Worcester are gold mines. There are rich seams in Connecticut at the State Library in Hartford as well as at Yale University's Beinecke Library (e.g., Osborn fb62: "Lord Aylmer's New England Affairs"); the New Haven Historical Society contains hidden gems. The New York Public Library's Manuscripts and Archives Division preserves the papers of John Davenport, Samuel Gardner Drake, and John Smyth of Nibley. Worthwhile destinations farther south include the Virginia Historical Society at Richmond, the Colonial Williamsburg Foundation, and the Maryland State Archives at Annapolis. In California, the Huntington Library at San Marino is a treasure house, containing the Mather, Shattuck, and Blathwayt papers; the Hastings, Kane, and Stowe Americana; and much besides.

A number of colonial manuscripts are available in printed editions. Jill Lepore, ed., *Encounters in the New World: A History in Documents* (New York, 2000), and Edward C. Gray, *Colonial America: A History in Documents* (Oxford, 2003), provide introductions. More advanced are Merrill Jensen, ed., *American Colonial Documents to 1776* (London, 1955); Jack P. Greene, ed., *Great Britain and the American Colonies, 1606–1763* (Columbia, SC, 1970); and W. Keith Kavenagh, ed., *Foundations of Colonial America: A Documentary History*, 3 vols. (New York, 1973).

Published sources for Virginia include Susan Myra Kingsbury, ed., *The Records of the Virginia Company of London*, 4 vols. (Washington, DC, 1906–1935), and Warren M. Billings, ed., *The Old Dominion in the Seventeenth Century: A Documentary History of Virginia, 1606–1700*, 2nd ed. (Chapel Hill, NC, 2007). For other colonies: John Noble, ed., *Records of the Court of Assistants of the Colony of the Massachusetts Bay, 1630–1692*, 3 vols. (Boston, 1901–1928); J. Hammond Trumbull and Charles J. Hoadly, eds., *The Public Records of the Colony of Connecticut, 1636–1776*, 15 vols. (Hartford, CT, 1850–1890); *Records of the Colony of Rhode Island and Providence Plantations in New England*, 10 vols. (Providence, RI, 1856–1865); Nathaniel Bouton et al., eds., *Documents and Records Relating to the Province of New Hampshire*, 40 vols. (Concord, NH, 1867–1943); William Hand Browne, ed., *Proceedings and Acts of the General Assembly of Maryland, 1666–1676* (Baltimore, 1884); A. C. Hollis Hallett, ed., *Bermuda Under the Sommer Islands Company, 1612–1684: Civil Records*, vol. 1, *1612–1669* (Bermuda, 2005).

Among documentary histories of specific episodes are David D. Hall, ed., *The Antinomian Controversy, 1636–1638*, 2nd ed. (Durham, NC, 1990); idem, ed., *Witch-Hunting in Seventeenth-Century New England . . . 1638–1692* (Boston, 1991); Bernard Rosenthal, ed., *Records of the Salem Witch-Hunt* (Cambridge, UK, 2009); Richard Slotkin and James K. Folsom, eds., *So Dreadfull a Judgment: Puritan Responses to King Philip's War, 1676–1677* (Middletown, CT, 1978); and Robert E. Moody and Richard Clive Simmons, eds., *The Glorious Revolution in Massachusetts: Selected Documents, 1689–1692* (Boston, 1988).

Legal records from colonial America are revealing, including Susie M. Ames, ed., *County Court Records of Accomack-Northampton, Virginia, 1632–1640*

(Washington, DC, 1954); George Francis Dow, ed., *Records and Files of the Quarterly Courts of Essex County*, 8 vols. (Salem, MA, 1911–1921); Samuel Eliot Morison et al., eds., *Records of the Suffolk County Court, 1671–1680*, 2 vols. (Boston, 1933); Joseph H. Smith, ed., *Colonial Justice in Western Massachusetts (1639–1702): The Pynchon Court Record* (Cambridge, MA, 1961); and Helen Schatvet Ullmann, ed., *Hartford County, Connecticut, Court Minutes, Vols. 3 and 4* (Boston, 2005).

For the view from England, the following are helpful resources: W. Noel Sainsbury et al., eds., *Calendar of State Papers, Colonial*, 46 vols. (London, 1860–1969); various *Reports* of the Historical Manuscripts Commission; Peter Wilson Coldham, ed., *Lord Mayor's Court of London Depositions Relating to Americans, 1641–1736* (Washington, DC, 1980). Slavery is covered by Elizabeth Donnan, ed., *Documents Illustrative of the History of the Slave Trade to America*, 4 vols. (Washington, DC, 1930–1950).

Correspondence between many different colonial actors has been preserved and is invaluable. Printed collections include Everett Emerson, ed., *Letters from New England: The Massachusetts Bay Colony, 1629–1638* (Amherst, MA, 1976); *The Winthrop Papers, 1498–1654*, 6 vols. (Boston, 1929–1992); Robert E. Moody, ed., *The Saltonstall Papers, 1607–1815*, 2 vols. (Boston, 1972–1974); Carl Bridenbaugh, ed., *Letters of John Pynchon, 1654–1700* (Boston, 1982); and Vernon A. Ives, ed., *Letters from Bermuda, 1615–1646* (Toronto, 1984). For correspondence involving people suspended between two worlds, the following editions are useful: Marion Tinling, ed., *The Correspondence of the Three William Byrds of Westover, Virginia, 1684–1776*, 2 vols. (Charlottesville, VA, 1977); Richard Beale Davis, ed., *William Fitzhugh and His Chesapeake World, 1676–1701* (Chapel Hill, NC, 1963); Warren M. Billings, ed., *The Papers of Francis Howard . . . 1643–1695* (Richmond, VA, 1989); Mary Maples Dunn et al., eds., *The Papers of William Penn*, 5 vols. (Philadelphia, 1981–1986); Marion Balderston, ed., *James Claypoole's Letter Book: London and Philadelphia, 1681–1684* (San Marino, CA, 1967). Puritan correspondence can be sampled in Isabel MacBeath Calder, ed., *Letters of John Davenport, Puritan Divine* (New Haven, CT, 1937); Kenneth Silverman, ed., *Selected Letters of Cotton Mather* (Baton Rouge, LA, 1971); Glenn W. LaFantasie, ed., *The Correspondence of Roger Williams*, 2 vols. (Hanover, PA, 1988); and Sheila McIntyre and Len Travers, eds., *The Correspondence of John Cotton Junior* (Boston, 2009).

Diaries are also a rich source of information. Some that have been edited and printed include Worthington Chauncey Ford, ed., *Diary of Cotton Mather, 1681–1708* (Boston, 1911); M. Halsey Thomas, ed., *The Diary of Samuel Sewall, 1674–1729*, 2 vols. (New York, 1973); Richard S. Dunn, James Savage, and Laetitia Yeandle, eds., *The Journal of John Winthrop, 1630–1649* (Cambridge, MA, 1996); Edmund S. Morgan, ed., *The Diary of Michael Wigglesworth, 1653–1657: The Conscience of a Puritan* (New York, 1965); and Sidney H. Miner and George D. Stanton Jr., eds., *The Diary of Thomas Minor, Stonington, Connecticut*

(New London, CT, 1899). Some colonial actors wrote autobiographies that exist in published editions, including Charles Deane, ed., *History of Plymouth Plantation by William Bradford* (Boston, 1856); *A Declaration of Remarkable Providences in the Course of My Life by John Dane* (Boston, 1854); "A declaration of the affairs of the English people that first inhabited New England, by Phineas Pratt," *Collections of the MHS*, 4 (1858), 474–491; and Isaac Appleton Jewett, ed., *Memorial of Samuel Appleton of Ipswich, Massachusetts* (Boston, 1850). See also George Selement and Bruce C. Woolley, eds., *Thomas Shepard's Confessions* (Boston, 1981).

The seventeenth century saw the expansion of writing and printing, developments reciprocally beneficial to colonization. I read several hundred treatises, tracts, pamphlets, ballads, sermons, newspapers, petitions, and proclamations (see endnotes). Almost all of these can be accessed at the web resource Early English Books Online (http://eebo.chadwyck.com/home), and many in modern editions, some of which are also online, such as at the Internet Archive (https://archive.org).

For early Virginia, a good beginning is Philip L. Barbour, ed., *The Complete Works of Captain John Smith*, 3 vols. (Chapel Hill, NC, 1986), and two unpublished accounts: Mark Nicholls, ed., "George Percy's 'Trewe Relacyon': a primary source for the Jamestown settlement," *VMHB*, 113 (2005), 212–275, and William Strachey, *The Historie of Travell into Virginia Britania (1612)*, ed. Louis B. Wright and Virginia Freund (London, 1953). Richard Eburne, *A Plain Pathway to Plantations (1624)*, ed. Louis B. Wright (Ithaca, NY, 1962), describes the colonial solution to England's crisis. On New England: Edward Johnson, *Wonder-Working Providence of Sions Saviour in New-England*, ed. Edward J. Gallagher (Delmar, NY, 1974); Alden T. Vaughan, ed., *New England's Prospect by William Wood* (Amherst, MA, 1977); Roger Williams, *A Key into the Language of America*, ed. John J. Teunissen and Evelyn J. Hinz (Detroit, 1973). The condition of America in 1700 is captured by Robert Beverley, *The History and Present State of Virginia*, ed. Louis B. Wright (Chapel Hill, NC, 1947); and Cotton Mather, *Magnalia Christi Americana*, ed. Kenneth B. Murdock and Elizabeth W. Miller (Cambridge, MA, 1977).

Useful anthologies include John Demos, ed., *Remarkable Providences: Readings on Early American History*, 2nd ed. (Boston, 1991); Susan Castillo and Ivy Schweitzer, eds., *The Literatures of Colonial America: An Anthology* (Oxford, 2001); and C. H. Firth, ed., *An American Garland, Being a Collection of Ballads Relating to America, 1563–1759* (Oxford, 1915). On Puritanism: Alan Heimert and Andrew Delbanco, eds., *The Puritans in America: A Narrative Anthology* (Cambridge, MA, 1985); A. W. Plumstead, ed., *The Wall and the Garden: Selected Massachusetts Election Sermons, 1670–1775* (Minneapolis, 1968); Sargent Bush Jr., ed., *The Writings of Thomas Hooker: Spiritual Adventure in Two Worlds* (Madison, WI, 1980). On captivity: Alden T. Vaughan and Edward W. Clark, eds., *Puritans Among the Indians: Accounts of Captivity and Redemption,*

1676–1724 (Cambridge, MA, 1981). For the West Indies: Thomas W. Krise, ed., *Caribbeana: An Anthology of English Literature of the West Indies, 1657–1777* (Chicago, 1999).

Good editions of contemporary histories include James Savage, ed., *The History of New England from 1630 to 1649 by John Winthrop*, 2 vols. (Boston, 1853); *A General History of New England by the Rev. William Hubbard*, 2nd ed. (Boston, 1848); Nathaniel Morton, *New England's Memorial*, 6th ed. (Boston, 1855); and J. Henry Lefroy, ed., *The Historye of the Bermudaes or Summer Islands* (London, 1882).

Moving to secondary sources, for an introduction to England in this era see John Morrill, *Stuart Britain: A Very Short Introduction* (Oxford, 2000), and, for detail, Tim Harris's trilogy: *Rebellion: Britain's First Stuart Kings* (Oxford, 2014); *Restoration: Charles II and His Kingdoms* (London, 2005); and *Revolution: The Great Crisis of the British Monarchy, 1685–1720* (London, 2006). Also see Michael Braddick, *God's Fury, England's Fire: A New History of the English Civil Wars* (London, 2008); and Barry Coward, *The Cromwellian Protectorate* (Manchester, 2002). On social change: Keith Wrightson, *English Society, 1580–1680*, 2nd ed. (London, 2002); Keith Thomas, *Religion and the Decline of Magic* (London, 1971).

For the imperial dimension: David Armitage, *The Ideological Origins of the British Empire* (Cambridge, UK, 2000); Steven Sarson, *British America, 1500–1800: Creating Colonies, Imagining an Empire* (London, 2005); Miles Ogborn, *Global Lives: Britain and the World, 1550–1800* (Cambridge, UK, 2008). See also John Patrick Montaño, *The Roots of English Colonialism in Ireland* (Cambridge, UK, 2011). On justifications: Andrew Fitzmaurice, *Humanism and America: An Intellectual History of English Colonization, 1500–1625* (Cambridge, UK, 2003); Ken MacMillan, *Sovereignty and Possession in the English New World: The Legal Foundations of Empire, 1576–1640* (Cambridge, UK, 2006); Francisco J. Borge, *A New World for a New Nation: The Promotion of America in Early Modern England* (Bern, 2007); Peter C. Mancall, *Hakluyt's Promise: An Elizabethan's Obsession for an English America* (New Haven, CT, 2007).

Brief overviews of early America include Mary K. Geiter and W. A. Speck, *Colonial America: From Jamestown to Yorktown* (Basingstoke, UK, 2002); and Alan Taylor, *Colonial America: A Very Short Introduction* (Oxford, 2013). Among fuller treatments are D. W. Meinig, *The Shaping of America . . .* vol. 1, *Atlantic America, 1492–1800* (New Haven, CT, 1986); Alan Taylor, *American Colonies: The Settling of North America* (London, 2002); T. H. Breen and Timothy D. Hall, *Colonial America in an Atlantic World* (New York, 2004); J. H. Elliott, *Empires of the Atlantic World: Britain and Spain in America, 1492–1830* (New Haven, CT, 2006); Daniel K. Richter, *Before the Revolution: America's Ancient Pasts* (Cambridge, MA, 2011); and Richard Middleton and Anne Lombard, *Colonial America: A History to 1763*, 4th ed. (Oxford, 2011). See also the essays in T. H. Breen, *Puritans and Adventurers: Change and Persistence in*

Early America (New York, 1980); David Armitage and Michael J. Braddick, eds., *The British Atlantic World, 1500–1800* (Basingstoke, UK, 2002); and Daniel Vickers, ed., *A Companion to Colonial America* (Oxford, 2003).

On early ventures, see Anthony Grafton, *New Worlds, Ancient Texts: The Power of Tradition and the Shock of Discovery* (Cambridge, MA, 1992). Anthony Pagden, *Lords of All the World: Ideologies of Empire in Spain, Britain and France, c. 1500–c.1800* (New Haven, CT, 1995); and Patricia Seed, *Ceremonies of Possession in Europe's Conquest of the New World, 1492–1640* (Cambridge, UK, 1995). For England: David B. Quinn, *England and the Discovery of America, 1481–1620* (London, 1974); Michael Foss, *Undreamed Shores: England's Wasted Empire in America* (New York, 1974); K. R. Andrews, N. P. Canny, and P. E. H. Hair, eds., *The Westward Enterprise: English Activities in Ireland, the Atlantic and America, 1480–1650* (Liverpool, 1978); Mary C. Fuller, *Voyages in Print: English Travel to America, 1576-1624* (Cambridge, UK, 1995); William M. Hamlin, "Imagined apotheoses: Drake, Harriot, and Ralegh in the Americas," *Journal of the History of Ideas*, 57 (1996), 405–428. On Roanoke: Karen Ordahl Kupperman, *Roanoke: The Abandoned Colony*, 2nd ed. (Lanham, MD, 2007); James Horn, *A Kingdom Strange: The Brief and Tragic History of the Lost Colony of Roanoke* (New York, 2010). See also Kim Sloan, *A New World: England's First View of America* (London, 2007).

On Newfoundland: Gillian T. Cell, ed., *Newfoundland Discovered: English Attempts at Colonization, 1610–1630* (London, 1982); Luca Codignola, *The Coldest Harbour of the Land: Simon Stock and Lord Baltimore's Colony in Newfoundland, 1621–1649* (Kingston, Jamaica, 1988); Peter E. Pope, *Fish into Wine: The Newfoundland Plantation in the Seventeenth Century* (Chapel Hill, NC, 2004). Early Maine is covered by Jeffrey Phipps Brain, *Fort St George: Archaeological Investigation of the 1607–1608 Popham Colony* (Augusta, ME, 2007); and William H. Tabor, "Maine's Popham colony," *Athena Review*, 3 (2002), 84–89. New Hampshire is the focus of David E. Van Deventer, *The Emergence of Provincial New Hampshire, 1623–1741* (Baltimore, 1976); and Jere R. Daniell, *Colonial New Hampshire: A History* (Millwood, NY, 1981).

Works on New England include Jonathan L. Fairbanks and Robert F. Trent, eds., *New England Begins: The Seventeenth Century*, 3 vols. (Boston, 1982); Charles E. Clark, *The Eastern Frontier: The Settlement of Northern New England, 1610–1763* (Hanover, NH, 1983); David D. Hall, John H. Murrin, and Thad W. Tate, eds., *Saints and Revolutionaries: Essays on Early American History* (New York, 1984); Richard Archer, *Fissures in the Rock: New England in the Seventeenth Century* (Hanover, NH, 2001); Gloria L. Main, *Peoples of a Spacious Land: Families and Cultures in Colonial New England* (Cambridge, MA, 2001); Francis J. Bremer and Lynn A. Botelho, eds., *The World of John Winthrop: Essays on England and New England* (Boston, 2005); and Joseph A. Conforti, *Saints and Strangers: New England in British North America* (Baltimore, 2006).

For Massachusetts, see case-studies of its townships in Darrett B. Rutman,

Winthrop's Boston: Portrait of a Puritan Town, 1630–1649 (Chapel Hill, NC, 1965); Kenneth A. Lockridge, *A New England Town: The First Hundred Years, Dedham, Massachusetts, 1636–1736* (New York, 1970); Richard P. Gildrie, *Salem, Massachusetts, 1626–1683: A Covenant Community* (Charlottesville, VA, 1975); Stephen Innes, *Labor in a New Land: Economy and Society in Seventeenth-Century Springfield* (Princeton, NJ, 1983); Roger Thompson, *Divided We Stand: Watertown, Massachusetts, 1630–1680* (Amherst, MA, 2001); and Brian Donahue, *The Great Meadow: Farmers and the Land in Colonial Concord* (New Haven, CT, 2004). For contrasting views: Philip J. Greven Jr., *Four Generations: Population, Land and Family in Colonial Andover, Massachusetts* (Ithaca, NY, 1970); Elinor Abbot, *Our Company Increases Apace: History, Language and Social Identity in Early Andover, Massachusetts* (Dallas, TX, 2007). See also Robert Emmet Wall Jr., *Massachusetts Bay: The Crucial Decade, 1640–1650* (New Haven, CT, 1972); Timothy J. Sehr, *Colony and Commonwealth: Massachusetts Bay, 1649–1660* (New York, 1989); Michael P. Winship, "Godly republicanism and the origins of the Massachusetts polity," *WMQ*, 13 (2006), 427–462.

New Plymouth is the subject of the following: H. Roger King, *Cape Cod and Plymouth Colony in the Seventeenth Century* (Lanham, MD, 1994); Robert Charles Anderson, *The Pilgrim Migration: Immigrants to Plymouth Colony, 1620–1633* (Boston, 2004); Nathaniel Philbrick, *Mayflower: A Voyage to War* (London, 2006); Nick Bunker, *Making Haste from Babylon: The Mayflower Pilgrims and Their World* (London, 2010). See also Michael Zuckerman, "Pilgrims in the wilderness: community, modernity and the maypole at Merry Mount," *NEQ*, 50 (1977), 255–277.

On Connecticut: Bruce C. Daniels, *The Connecticut Town: Growth and Development, 1635–1790* (Middletown, CT, 1979); Jackson Turner Main, *Society and Economy in Colonial Connecticut* (Princeton, NJ, 1985). For later developments: Richard L. Bushman, *From Puritan to Yankee: Character and the Social Order in Connecticut, 1690–1765* (Cambridge, MA, 1967); Bruce H. Mann, *Neighbors and Strangers: Law and Community in Early Connecticut* (Chapel Hill, NC, 1987). On Rhode Island: Carl Bridenbaugh, *Fat Mutton and Liberty of Conscience: Society in Rhode Island, 1636–1690* (Providence, RI, 1974); Bruce C. Daniels, *Dissent and Conformity on Narragansett Bay: The Colonial Rhode Island Town* (Middletown, CT, 1983); Sydney V. James, *John Clarke and His Legacies: Religion and Law in Colonial Rhode Island, 1638–1750* (University Park, PA, 1999).

Works on Virginia include Warren M. Billings, John E. Selby, and Thad W. Tate, *Colonial Virginia: A History* (New York, 1986); Allan Kulikoff, *Tobacco and Slaves: The Development of Southern Cultures in the Chesapeake, 1680–1800* (Chapel Hill, NC, 1986); James R. Perry, *The Formation of a Society on Virginia's Eastern Shore, 1615–1655* (Chapel Hill, NC, 1990); James Horn, *Adapting to a New World: English Society in the Seventeenth-Century Chesapeake* (Chapel Hill, NC, 1994); Warren M. Billings, *Sir William Berkeley and the Forging of Colonial Virginia* (Baton Rouge, LA, 2004); and April Lee Hatfield, *Atlantic*

Virginia: Intercolonial Relations in the Seventeenth Century (Philadelphia, 2004). See also Wesley Frank Craven, *White, Red and Black: The Seventeenth-Century Virginian* (Charlottesville, VA, 1971); Darrett B. Rutman and Anita H. Rutman, *A Place in Time: Middlesex County, Virginia, 1650–1750* (New York, 1984); Jon Kukla, "Order and chaos in early America: political and social stability in pre-Restoration Virginia," *AHR*, 90 (1985), 275–298, and the essays in Robert Appelbaum and John Wood Sweet, eds., *Envisioning an English Empire: Jamestown and the Making of the North Atlantic World* (Philadelphia, 2005); and Peter C. Mancall, ed., *The Atlantic World and Virginia, 1550–1624* (Chapel Hill, NC, 2007).

On Jamestown: Edmund S. Morgan, "The labor problem at Jamestown, 1607–1618," *AHR*, 76 (1971), 595–611; Carl Bridenbaugh, *Jamestown, 1544–1699* (New York, 1980); Martin H. Quitt, "Trade and acculturation at Jamestown, 1607–1609: the limits of understanding," *WMQ*, 52 (1995), 227–258; James Horn, *A Land as God Made It: Jamestown and the Birth of America* (New York, 2005); Rachel B. Herrmann, "The 'tragical historie': cannibalism and abundance in colonial Jamestown," *WMQ*, 68 (2011), 47–74.

For Maryland: Paul G. E. Clemens, *The Atlantic Economy and Colonial Maryland's Eastern Shore: From Tobacco to Grain* (Ithaca, NY, 1980); Aubrey C. Land, *Colonial Maryland: A History* (New York, 1981); Gloria L. Main, *Tobacco Colony: Life in Early Maryland, 1650–1720* (Princeton, NJ, 1982); David W. Jordan, *Foundations of Representative Government in Maryland, 1632–1715* (Cambridge, UK, 1987).

New York is the subject of Frank Craven, *New Jersey and the English Colonization of North America* (Princeton, NJ, 1964); Patricia U. Bonomi, *A Factious People: Politics and Society in Colonial New York* (New York, 1971); Robert C. Ritchie, *The Duke's Province: A Study of New York Politics and Society, 1664–1691* (Chapel Hill, NC, 1977); Randall H. Balmer, *A Perfect Babel of Confusion: Dutch Religion and English Culture in the Middle Colonies* (New York, 1989); David G. Hackett, *The Rude Hand of Innovation: Religion and Social Order in Albany, New York, 1652–1836* (New York, 1990); and Joyce D. Goodfriend, *Before the Melting Pot: Society and Culture in Colonial New York City, 1664–1730* (Princeton, NJ, 1992). For Pennsylvania: Edwin B. Bronner, *William Penn's "Holy Experiment": The Founding of Pennsylvania, 1681–1701* (New York, 1962); Gary B. Nash, *Quakers and Politics: Pennsylvania, 1681–1726* (Princeton, NJ, 1968); James T. Lemon, *The Best Poor Man's Country: A Geographical Study of Early Southeastern Pennsylvania* (Baltimore, 1972); J. William Frost, *A Perfect Freedom: Religious Liberty in Pennsylvania* (Cambridge, UK, 1990).

Carolina is covered by Peter A. Coclanis, *The Shadow of a Dream: Economic Life and Death in the South Carolina Low Country, 1670–1920* (New York, 1989); Richard Waterhouse, *A New World Gentry: The Making of a Merchant and Planter Class in South Carolina, 1670–1770* (New York, 1989); and L. H. Roper, *Conceiving Carolina: Proprietors, Planters, and Plots, 1662–1729* (Basingstoke,

UK, 2004). For links between southern colonies and the West Indies: Richard Waterhouse, "England, the Caribbean, and the settlement of Carolina," *Journal of American Studies*, 9 (1975), 259–281; Philip D. Morgan, "Virginia's other prototype: the Caribbean," in Mancall, ed., *Atlantic World*, 342–380.

On the Caribbean generally: Carl Bridenbaugh and Roberta Bridenbaugh, *No Peace Beyond the Line: The English in the Caribbean, 1624–1690* (Oxford, 1972); Richard S. Dunn, *Sugar and Slaves: The Rise of the Planter Class in the English West Indies, 1624–1713* (Chapel Hill, NC, 1972); K. R. Andrews, "The English in the Caribbean, 1560–1620," in *idem* et al., eds., *Westward Enterprise*, 103–123; Gary A. Puckrein, *Little England: Plantation Society and Anglo-Barbadian Politics, 1627–1700* (New York, 1984); Franklin W. Knight, *The Caribbean: The Genesis of a Fragmented Nationalism*, 2nd ed. (New York, 1990); Trevor Burnard, "European migration to Jamaica, 1655–1780," *WMQ*, 53 (1996), 769–796; James Robertson, "'Stories' and 'histories' in late-seventeenth-century Jamaica," in Kathleen E. A. Monteith and Glen Richards, eds., *Jamaica in Slavery and Freedom: History, Heritage and Culture* (Kingston, Jamaica, 2002), 25–51; Larry Gragg, *Englishmen Transplanted: The English Colonization of Barbados, 1627–1660* (Oxford, 2003). See also Karen Ordahl Kupperman, *Providence Island, 1630–1: The Other Puritan Colony* (Cambridge, UK, 1993).

The history of the Caribbean is indivisible from that of slavery. Books on this theme include Hilary Beckles, *Black Rebellion in Barbados: The Struggle Against Slavery, 1627–1838* (Bridgetown, Barbados, 1984); Betty Wood, *The Origins of American Slavery: Freedom and Bondage in the English Colonies* (New York, 1997); John Thornton, *Africa and Africans in the Making of the Atlantic World, 1400–1800*, 2nd ed. (Cambridge, UK, 1998); James Horn and Philip D. Morgan, "Settlers and slaves: European and African migrations to early modern British America," in Elizabeth Mancke and Carole Shammas, eds., *The Creation of the British Atlantic World* (Baltimore, 2005), 19–44; and Thomas Benjamin, *The Atlantic World: Europeans, Africans, Indians and Their Shared History, 1400–1900* (Cambridge, UK, 2009). On the Caribbean in English culture: Susan Dwyer Amussen, *Caribbean Exchanges: Slavery and the Transformation of English Society, 1640–1700* (Chapel Hill, NC, 2007); James Walvin, *Fruits of Empire: Exotic Produce and British Trade, 1660–1800* (Basingstoke, UK, 1997).

For mainland slavery: Edmund S. Morgan, *American Slavery, American Freedom: The Ordeal of Colonial Virginia* (New York, 1975); Daniel C. Littlefield, *Rice and Slaves: Ethnicity and the Slave Trade in Colonial South Carolina* (Baton Rouge, LA, 1981); Peter Kolchin, *American Slavery, 1619–1877* (New York, 1993); Ira Berlin, *Many Thousands Gone: The First Two Centuries of Slavery in North America* (Cambridge, MA, 1998); Kenneth Morgan, *Slavery and Servitude in North America, 1607–1800* (Edinburgh, 2000); Anthony S. Parent Jr., *Foul Means: The Formation of a Slave Society in Virginia, 1660–1740* (Chapel Hill, NC, 2003); T. H. Breen and Stephen Innes, *"Myne Owne Ground": Race and Freedom on Virginia's Eastern Shore, 1640–1676*, 2nd ed. (Oxford, 2005); Tim Hashaw, *The Birth of Black America: The First African Americans and the Pursuit of Freedom at Jamestown* (New York, 2007). See also Abbot Emerson Smith, *Colonists in Bondage: White Servitude and Convict Labor in America, 1607–1776* (Gloucester, MA, 1965).

Colonial economies are described in Gary M. Walton and James F. Shepherd, *The Economic Rise of Early America* (Cambridge, UK, 1979); John J. McCusker and Russell R. Menard, *The Economy of British North America, 1607–1789* (Chapel Hill, NC, 1985); Stephen Innes, *Creating the Commonwealth: The Economic Culture of New England* (New York, 1995); and Margaret Ellen Newell, *From Dependency to Independence: Economic Revolution in Colonial New England* (Ithaca, NY, 1998). For society: Lois Green Carr and Lorena S. Walsh, "The standard of living in the colonial Chesapeake," *WMQ*, 45 (1988), 135–159; Daniel Vickers, "Competency and competition: economic culture in early America," *WMQ*, 47 (1990), 3–29; Darrett B. Rutman and Anita H. Rutman, *Small Worlds, Large Questions: Explorations in Early American Social History, 1600–1850* (Charlottesville, VA, 1994); Peter Thompson, "The thief, the householder and the commons: languages of class in seventeenth-century Virginia," *WMQ*, 63 (2006), 253–280.

On colonial households: John Demos, *A Little Commonwealth: Family Life in Plymouth Colony* (New York, 1970); Melvin Yazawa, *From Colonies to Commonwealth: Familial Ideology and the Beginnings of the American Republic* (Baltimore, 1985); Sharon V. Salinger, *"To Serve Well and Faithfully": Labour and Indentured Servants in Pennsylvania, 1682–1800* (Cambridge, UK, 1987); Helena M. Wall, *Fierce Communion: Family and Community in Early America* (Cambridge, MA, 1990); Lawrence Towner, *A Good Master Well Served: Masters and Servants in Colonial Massachusetts, 1620–1750* (New York, 1998).

On Puritanism (and its domination of colonial religion): Stephen Foster, *Their Solitary Way: The Puritan Social Ethic in the First Century of Settlement in New England* (New Haven, CT, 1971); Philip A. Gura, *A Glimpse of Sion's Glory: Puritan Radicalism in New England, 1620–1640* (Middletown, CT, 1984); Theodore Dwight Bozeman, *To Live Ancient Lives: The Primitivist Dimension in Puritanism* (Chapel Hill, NC, 1988); Avihu Zakai, *Exile and Kingdom: History and Apocalypse in the Puritan Migration to America* (Cambridge, UK, 1992); Michael P. Winship, *Seers of God: Puritan Providentialism in the Restoration and Early Enlightenment* (Baltimore, 1996); James F. Cooper Jr., *Tenacious of Their Liberties: The Congregationalists in Colonial Massachusetts* (Oxford, 1999). For a sample of personalities: Robert Middlekauff, *The Mathers: Three Generations of Puritan Intellectuals, 1596–1728* (New York, 1971); Michael McGiffert, ed., *God's Plot: The Paradoxes of Puritan Piety* (Amherst, MA, 1972); Francis J. Bremer, *John Winthrop: America's Forgotten Founding Father* (Oxford, 2003).

On the Antinomian controversy: Stephen Foster, "New England and the challenge of heresy, 1630–1660: the Puritan crisis in trans-Atlantic perspective," *WMQ*, 38 (1981), 624–660; Michael P. Winship, *Making Heretics: Militant Protestantism and Free Grace in Massachusetts, 1636–1641* (Princeton, NJ, 2002). On Quakers: Jonathan M. Chu, *Neighbors, Friends or Madmen: The Puritan Adjustment to Quakerism in Seventeenth-Century Massachusetts Bay* (Westport, CT, 1985); Carla Gardina Pestana, "The Quaker executions as myth and history," *JAH*, 80 (1993), 441–469.

For religion elsewhere: Edward L. Bond, *Damned Souls in a Tobacco Colony: Religion in Seventeenth-Century Virginia* (Macon, GA, 2001); Patricia U. Bonomi, *Under the Cope of Heaven: Religion, Society and Politics in Colonial America*, 2nd ed. (Oxford, 2003); Jon Butler, *New World Faiths: Religion in Colonial America* (New York, 2008). On popular beliefs: David D. Hall, *Worlds of Wonder, Days of Judgment: Popular Religious Belief in Early New England* (New York, 1989); Richard Godbeer, *The Devil's Dominion: Magic and Religion in Early New England* (Cambridge, UK, 1992); Edward L. Bond, "Source of knowledge, source of power: the supernatural world of English Virginia, 1607–1624," *VMHB*, 108 (2000), 105–138.

For popular culture: Bruce C. Daniels, *Puritans at Play: Leisure and Recreation in Colonial New England* (Basingstoke, UK, 1995); David W. Conroy, *In Public Houses: Drink and the Revolution of Authority in Colonial Massachusetts* (Chapel Hill, NC, 1995); John Demos, *Circles and Lines: The Shape of Life in Early America* (Cambridge, MA, 2004); William Pencak, Matthew Dennis and Simon P. Newman, eds., *Riot and Revelry in Early America* (University Park, PA, 2002). On deeper meanings: Robert Blair St George, *Conversing by Signs: Poetics of Implication in Colonial New England* (Chapel Hill, NC, 1998); Peter Charles Hoffer, *Sensory Worlds in Early America* (Baltimore, 2003).

On home life: James Deetz, *In Small Things Forgotten: The Archaeology of Early American Life* (New York, 1977); Abbott Lowell Cummings, *The Framed Houses of Massachusetts Bay, 1625–1725* (Cambridge, MA, 1979); David Freeman Hawke, *Everyday Life in Early America* (New York, 1988); Laurel Thatcher Ulrich, *The Age of Homespun: Objects and Stories in the Creation of an American Myth* (New York, 2001). On food: Sarah F. MacMahon, "'A comfortable subsistence': the changing composition of diet in rural New England, 1620–1840," *WMQ*, 42 (1985), 26–65; Virginia DeJohn Anderson, *Creatures of Empire: How Domesticated Animals Transformed Early America* (New York, 2004). See also Carole Shammas, *The Pre-Industrial Consumer in England and America* (Oxford, 1990); and Nuala Zahedieh, "London and the colonial consumer in the late seventeenth century," *Economic History Review*, 47 (1994), 239–261.

Print is covered by David D. Hall, *Cultures of Print: Essays in the History of the Book* (Amherst, MA, 1996); Hugh Amory and David D. Hall, eds., *A History of the Book in America*, vol. 1 (Cambridge, UK, 2000); Charles E. Clark, *The Public Prints: The Newspaper in Anglo-American Culture, 1665–1740* (New York, 1994); David Read, *New World, Known World: Shaping Knowledge in Early Anglo-American Writing* (Columbia, MO, 2005). In England: Nicholas

Canny, "'To establish a common wealthe': Captain John Smith as New World colonist," *VMHB*, 96 (1988), 213–222; Catherine Armstrong, *Writing North America in the Seventeenth Century: English Representations in Print and Manuscript* (Abingdon, UK, 2007). See also Rebecca Ann Bach, *Colonial Transformations: The Cultural Production of the New Atlantic World, 1580–1640* (New York, 2000).

On growing colonial knowledge: Philip H. Round, *By Nature and by Custom Cursed: Transatlantic Civil Discourse and New England Cultural Production, 1620–1660* (Hanover, NH, 1999); Richard D. Brown, *The Strength of a People: The Idea of an Informed Citizenry in America, 1650–1870* (Chapel Hill, NC, 1996); Darren Staloff, *The Making of an American Thinking Class: Intellectuals and Intelligence in Puritan Massachusetts* (New York, 1998). See also Raymond Phineas Stearns, *Science in the British Colonies in America* (Urbana, IL, 1970); Joyce E. Chaplin, *Subject Matter: Technology, the Body, and Science on the Anglo-American Frontier, 1500–1676* (Cambridge, MA, 2001); and Sarah Scott Parrish, *American Curiosity: Cultures of Natural History in the Colonial British Atlantic World* (Chapel Hill, NC, 2006).

For the law: Christopher L. Tomlins and Bruce H. Mann, eds., *The Many Legalities of Early America* (Chapel Hill, NC, 2001); William Edward Nelson, *The Common Law in Colonial America*, vol. 1, *The Chesapeake and New England, 1607–1660* (Oxford, 2008). On the English heritage: Joseph H. Smith and Thomas G. Barnes, *The English Legal System: Carryover to the Colonies* (Los Angeles, 1975); Richard J. Ross, "The legal past of early New England: notes for the study of law, legal culture and intellectual history," *WMQ*, 50 (1993), 28–41; Jack P. Greene, "'By their laws shall ye know them': law and identity in colonial British America," *Journal of Interdisciplinary History*, 33 (2002), 247–260.

For crime and deviance: Richard P. Gildrie, *The Profane, the Civil and the Godly: The Reformation of Manners in Orthodox New England, 1679–1749* (University Park, PA, 1994); Richard Godbeer, "The cry of Sodom: discourse, intercourse, and desire in colonial New England," *WMQ*, 52 (1995), 259–286; John M. Murrin, "'Things fearful to name': bestiality in early America," in Elizabeth Reis, ed., *American Sexual Histories* (Oxford, 2001), 14–34. On defamation: Clara Ann Bouler, "Carted whores and white shrouded apologies: slander and the county courts of seventeenth-century Virginia," *VMHB*, 85 (1977), 411–426; Mary Beth Norton, "Gender and defamation in seventeenth-century Maryland," *WMQ*, 44 (1987), 3–39.

On witchcraft: John Putnam Demos, *Entertaining Satan: Witchcraft and the Culture of Early New England* (Oxford, 1982); Richard Weisman, *Witchcraft, Magic, and Religion in 17th-Century Massachusetts* (Amherst, MA, 1984); Elizabeth Reis, *Damned Women: Sinners and Witches in Puritan New England* (Ithaca, NY, 1997); Emerson W. Baker, *The Devil of Great Island: Witchcraft and Conflict in Early New England* (New York, 2007). On Salem: Paul Boyer and Stephen Nissenbaum, *Salem Possessed: The Social Origins of Witchcraft* (Cambridge, MA, 1974); Larry Gragg, *The Salem Witch Crisis* (New York, 1992); Mary Beth Norton, *In the Devil's Snare: The Salem Witchcraft Crisis of 1692* (New York, 2002); Emerson W. Baker, *A Storm of Witchcraft: The Trials of Salem and a Nation* (New York, 2014). For some transatlantic connections: George Lyman Kittredge, *Witchcraft in Old and New England* (New York, 1929); Marion Gibson, *Witchcraft and Society in England and America, 1550–1750* (London, 2003).

For gender: Laurel Thatcher Ulrich, *Good Wives: Image and Reality in the Lives of Women in Northern New England, 1650–1750* (New York, 1982); Mary Beth Norton, *Founding Mothers and Fathers: Gendered Power and the Forming of American Society* (New York, 1996); Kathleen Brown, *Good Wives, Nasty Wenches and Anxious Patriarchs: Gender, Race, and Power in Colonial Virginia* (Chapel Hill, NC, 1996); Jane Kamensky, *Governing the Tongue: The Politics of Speech in Early New England* (New York, 1997); Karin Wulf, *Not All Wives: Women of Colonial Philadelphia* (Ithaca, NY, 2000). On men: Lisa Wilson, *Ye Heart of a Man: The Domestic Life of Men in Colonial New England* (New Haven, CT, 1999); Anne S. Lombard, *Making Manhood: Growing Up Male in Colonial New England* (Cambridge, MA, 2003); Thomas A. Foster, ed., *New Men: Manliness in Early America* (New York, 2011). See also James Marten, ed., *Children in Colonial America* (New York, 2007).

Indians suffused the colonial experience. For works on this topic, see Francis Jennings, *The Invasion of America: Indians, Colonialism and the Cant of Conquest* (Chapel Hill, NC, 1975); James Axtell, *The Invasion Within: The Contest of Cultures in Colonial North America* (New York, 1985); Helen C. Rountree, *Pocahontas's People: The Powhatan Indians of Virginia Through Four Centuries* (Norman, OK, 1990); Frederic W. Gleach, *Powhatan's World and Colonial Virginia: A Conflict of Cultures* (Lincoln, NE, 1997); Michael Leroy Oberg, *Dominion and Civility: English Imperialism and Native America, 1585–1685* (Ithaca, NY, 1999); Gary B. Nash, *Red, White, and Black: The Peoples of Early North America*, 4th ed. (Upper Saddle River, NJ, 2000); Karen Ordahl Kupperman, *Indians and English: Facing Off in Early America* (Ithaca, NY, 2000); and Jenny Hale Pulsipher, *Subjects unto the Same King: Indians, English, and the Contest for Authority in Colonial New England* (Philadelphia, 2005). See also William Cronon, *Changes in the Land: Indians, Colonists, and the Ecology of New England* (New York, 1983). On conversions: Neal Salisbury, "Red Puritans: the 'praying Indians' of Massachusetts Bay and John Eliot," *WMQ*, 31 (1974), 27–54; Richard W. Cogley, *John Eliot's Mission to the Indians Before King Philip's War* (Cambridge, MA, 1999).

On the Indian uprising of 1622: Alden T. Vaughan, "'Expulsion of the savages': English policy and the Virginia massacre of 1622," *WMQ*, 35 (1978), 57–84. For the Pequot War: Steven T. Katz, "The Pequot War reconsidered," *NEQ*, 64 (1991), 206–224; Michael Freeman, "Puritans and Pequots: the question of genocide," *NEQ*, 68 (1995), 278–293; Ronald Dale Karr, "'Why should you be so furious?' The violence of the Pequot War," *JAH*, 85 (1998), 876–909. On King Philip's War: Russell Bourne, *The Red King's Rebellion: Racial Politics in New England, 1675–1678* (New York, 1990); Michael J. Puglisi, *Puritans Besieged: Legacies of King Philip's War in the Massachusetts Bay Colony* (Lanham, MD, 1991); Jill Lepore, *The Name of War: King Philip's War and the Origin of American Identity* (New York, 1998); James D. Drake, *King Philip's War: Civil War in New England, 1675–1676* (Boston, 1999). See also Guy Chet, *Conquering the American Wilderness: The Triumph of European Warfare in the Colonial Northeast* (Amherst, MA, 2003).

The following works deal with American identity and its English origins. On emigration: Timothy H. Breen and Stephen Foster, "Moving to the New World: the character of early Massachusetts immigration," *WMQ*, 30 (1973), 189–222; David Grayson Allen, *In English Ways: The Movement of Societies . . . to Massachusetts Bay in the Seventeenth Century* (Chapel Hill, NC, 1981); Bernard Bailyn, *The Peopling of British North America: An Introduction* (New York, 1986); David Hackett Fischer, *Albion's Seed: Four British Folkways in America* (Oxford, 1989); Virginia DeJohn Anderson, *New England's Generation: The Great Migration and the Formation of Society and Culture in the Seventeenth Century* (Cambridge, UK, 1991); Nicholas Canny, "English migration into and across the Atlantic during the seventeenth and eighteenth centuries," in *idem*, ed., *Europeans on the Move: Studies on European Migration, 1500–1800* (Oxford, 1994), 39–75; Roger Thompson, *Mobility and Migration: East Anglian Founders of New England, 1629–1640* (Amherst, MA, 1994). On trade links: Robert Brenner, *Merchants and Revolution: Commercial Change, Political Conflict and London's Overseas Traders, 1550–1653* (Cambridge, UK, 1993); Perry Gauci, *The Politics of Trade: The Overseas Merchant in State and Society, 1600–1720* (Oxford, 2001).

Communication with England was vital to colonization. See David Cressy, *Coming Over: Migration and Communication Between England and New England in the Seventeenth Century* (Cambridge, UK, 1987); Stephen Foster, *The Long Argument: English Puritanism and the Shaping of New England Culture* (Chapel Hill, NC, 1991); and Francis J. Bremer, *Congregational Communion: Clerical Friendship in the Anglo-American Puritan Community, 1610–1692* (Boston, 1994). On the civil war period: Francis J. Bremer, *Puritan Crisis: New England and the English Civil Wars, 1630–1670* (New York, 1989); Carla Gardina Pestana, *The English Atlantic in an Age of Revolution, 1640–1661* (Cambridge, MA, 2004); Timothy B. Riordan, *The Plundering Time: Maryland and the English Civil War, 1645–1646* (Baltimore, 2004). On reverse migration: Andrew Delbanco, "Looking homeward, going home: the lure of England for the founders of New England," *NEQ*, 59 (1986), 358–386; Susan Hardman Moore, *Pilgrims: New World Settlers and the Call of Home* (New Haven, CT, 2007).

For later connections: Alison Gilbert Olsen, *Anglo-American Politics, 1660–1775: The Relationship Between Parties in England and Colonial America* (Oxford,

1973); Philip S. Haffenden, *New England in the English Nation, 1689–1713* (Oxford, 1974); J. M. Sosin, *English America and the Restoration Monarchy of Charles II: Transatlantic Politics, Commerce and Kinship* (Lincoln, NE, 1981); Richard R. Johnson, *Adjustment to Empire: The New England Colonies, 1675–1715* (Leicester, UK, 1981); Ian K. Steele, *The English Atlantic, 1675–1740: An Exploration of Communication and Community* (New York, 1986); Robert M. Bliss, *Revolution and Empire: English Politics and the American Colonies in the Seventeenth Century* (Manchester, 1990); Warren M. Billings, *Virginia's Viceroy: Their Majesties' Governor General, Francis Howard* (Fairfax, VA, 1991); Stephen Saunders Webb, *1676: The End of American Independence* (Syracuse, NY, 1995); Emerson W. Baker and John G. Reid, *The New England Knight: Sir William Phips, 1651–1695* (Toronto, 1998); Owen Stanwood, *The Empire Reformed: English America in the Age of the Glorious Revolution* (Philadelphia, 2011).

On the Glorious Revolution: Richard R. Johnson, "The Revolution of 1688–9 in the American colonies," in Jonathan I. Israel, ed., *The Anglo-Dutch Moment: Essays on the Glorious Revolution and Its World Impact* (Cambridge, UK, 1991), 215–240; Ian K. Steele, "Communicating an English revolution to the colonies, 1688–1689," *JBS*, 24 (1985), 333–357; Lois Green Carr and David William Jordan, *Maryland's Revolution of Government, 1689–1692* (Ithaca, NY, 1974).

For the evolution of colonial character: Jack P. Greene, *Pursuits of Happiness: The Social Development of Early Modern British Colonies and the Formation of American Culture* (Chapel Hill, NC, 1988); idem, *The Intellectual Construction of America: Exceptionalism and Identity from 1492 to 1800* (Chapel Hill, NC, 1993); William Leach, *Land of Desire: Merchants, Power and the Rise of a New American Culture* (New York, 1993); Andrew Delbanco, *The Real American Dream: A Meditation on Hope* (Cambridge, MA, 1999); Robert Blair St George, *Possible Pasts: Becoming Colonial in Early America* (Ithaca, NY, 2000); Ned C. Landsman, *From Colonials to Provincials: American Thought and Culture, 1680–1760* (Ithaca, NY, 2000); Christopher Tomlins, *Freedom Bound: Law, Labor and Civic Identity in Colonizing English America, 1580–1865* (Cambridge, UK, 2010); Catherine Armstrong, *Landscape and Identity in North America's Southern Colonies from 1660 to 1745* (Farnham, UK, 2013).

On the wilderness as a cultural motif: John Canup, *Out of the Wilderness: The Emergence of an American Identity* (Middletown, CT, 1990); Roderick Frazier Nash, *Wilderness and the American Mind*, 4th ed. (New Haven, CT, 2001); Michael Lewis, ed., *American Wilderness: A New History* (Oxford, 2007). On frontiers: Frederick Jackson Turner, *The Frontier in American History* (New York, 1921); Peter N. Carroll, *Puritanism and the Wilderness: The Intellectual Significance of the New England Frontier, 1629–1700* (New York, 1969); Richard Slotkin, *Regeneration Through Violence: The Mythology of the American Frontier, 1600–1860* (Middletown, CT, 1973).

On "Americanization": Sacvan Bercovitch, *The Puritan Origins of the American Self* (New Haven, CT, 1975); Patricia Caldwell, *The Puritan Conversion*

Narrative: The Beginnings of American Expression (Cambridge, UK, 1983); David D. Hall, *The Faithful Shepherd: A History of the New England Ministry in the Seventeenth Century* (Chapel Hill, NC, 1972). For skepticism: Norman Pettit, "God's Englishman in New England: his enduring ties to the motherland," *Procs of the MHS*, 101 (1989), 56–70; Michael Zuckerman, "Identity in British America: unease in Eden," in Nicholas Canny and Anthony Pagden, eds., *Colonial Identity in the Atlantic World, 1500–1800* (Princeton, NJ, 1987), 115–157.

On political autonomy: Jack P. Greene, *The Quest for Power: The Lower Houses of Assembly in the Southern Royal Colonies, 1689–1776* (Chapel Hill, NC, 1963); J. M. Bumsted, "'Things in the womb of time': ideas of American independence, 1633 to 1763," *WMQ*, 31 (1974), 533–564; Kenneth A. Lockridge, *Settlement and Unsettlement in Early America: The Crisis of Political Legitimacy Before the Revolution* (Cambridge, UK, 1981); J. R. Pole, *The Gift of Government: Political Responsibility from the English Restoration to American Independence* (Athens, GA, 1983); Alan Tully, *Forming American Politics: Ideals, Interests and Institutions in Colonial New York and Pennsylvania* (Baltimore, 1994); Esmond Wright, *The Search for Liberty: From Origins to Independence* (Oxford, 1994). For some cultural perspectives: Timothy H. Breen, "An empire of goods: the anglicization of colonial America, 1690–1776," *JBS*, 25 (1986), 467–499; Richard L. Bushman, *The Refinement of America: Persons, Houses, Cities* (New York, 1992); David S. Shields, *Civil Tongues and Polite Letters in British America* (Chapel Hill, NC, 1997); Robert Olwell and Alan Tully, eds., *Cultures and Identities in Colonial British America* (Baltimore, 2006).

Historical legacies are legion. See Michael Kammen, *Mystic Chords of Memory: The Transformation of Tradition in American Culture* (New York, 1991); John Bodnar, *Remaking America: Public Memory, Commemoration, and Patriotism in the Twentieth Century* (Princeton, NJ, 1992); Terence Martin, *Parables of Possibility: The American Need for Beginnings* (New York, 1995); and Nicholas Guyatt, *Providence and the Invention of the United States, 1607–1876* (Cambridge, UK, 2007). The classic take on Puritanism is Perry Miller, *The New England Mind: The Seventeenth Century* (Cambridge, MA, 1939), but also see David A. Hall, "On common ground: the coherence of American Puritan studies," *WMQ*, 44 (1987), 193–229; Janice Knight, *Orthodoxies in Massachusetts: Rereading American Puritanism* (Cambridge, MA, 1994); and Louise A. Breen, *Transgressing the Bounds: Subversive Enterprises Among the Puritan Elite in Massachusetts, 1630–1692* (Oxford, 2001).

Plymouth's myths endure. See Peter J. Gomes, "Pilgrims and Puritans: 'heroes' and 'villains' in the creation of the American past," *Procs of the MHS*, 94 (1982), 1–16; and Robert D. Arner, "Plymouth Rock revisited: the landing of the Pilgrim Fathers," *Journal of American Culture*, 6 (1983), 25–35. On Pocahontas: Robert S. Tilton, *Pocahontas: The Evolution of an American Narrative* (Cambridge, UK, 1994); Ann Uhry Abrams, *The Pilgrims and Pocahontas: Rival Myths of American Origin* (Boulder, CO, 1999).

The defining statement of "exceptionalism" is Daniel J. Boorstin, *The Americans: The Colonial Experience* (New York, 1958). But see also Joyce Appleby, "Recovering America's historic diversity: beyond exceptionalism," *JAH*, 79 (1992), 419–431; Jack P. Greene, *Interpreting Early America: Historiographical Essays* (Charlottesville, VA, 1996); Deborah L. Madsen, *American Exceptionalism* (Edinburgh, 1998); and Joyce E. Chaplin, "Expansion and exceptionalism in early American history," *JAH*, 89 (2003), 1431–1455.

On Atlantic history as an antidote to exceptionalism: Daniel W. Howe, *American History in an Atlantic Context* (Oxford, 1993); Ian K. Steele, "Exploding colonial American history: Amerindian, Atlantic and global perspectives," *Reviews in American History*, 26 (1998), 70–95; David Armitage, *Greater Britain, 1516–1776: Essays in Atlantic History* (Aldershot, UK, 2004); Stephen J. Hornsby, *British Atlantic, American Frontier: Spaces of Power in Early Modern British America* (Lebanon, NH, 2005); Bernard Bailyn, *Atlantic History: Concept and Contours* (Cambridge, MA, 2005); Alison Games, "Atlantic history: definitions, challenges and opportunities," *AHR*, III (2006), 741–757; Nancy L. Rhoden, ed., *English Atlantics Revisited* (Montreal, 2007); Jack P. Greene and Philip D. Morgan, eds., *Atlantic History: A Critical Appraisal* (Oxford, 2009). L. H. Roper, *The English Empire in America, 1602–1658: Beyond Jamestown* (London, 2009), is "a different sort of attempt to bridge the histories of early modern England and 'colonial British America'" (p. 7).

The key work of anti-exceptionalism, and for me a seminal source of inspiration, is Charles M. Andrews, *The Colonial Period of American History*, 4 vols. (New Haven, CT, 1934–1938), which predated the more insular postwar work of Perry Miller, Daniel Boorstin, and others. Though rather dated now in its neglect of social history, Andrews's work first established the idea that "the seventeenth century shows us an English world in America, with but little in it that can strictly be called American." See also Richard Johnson, "Charles McLean Andrews and the invention of American colonial history," *WMQ*, 43 (1986), 519–541.

ILLUSTRATION CREDITS

xix. John White, *An Indian Woman and Her Daughter of Pomeiooc*, watercolor, c. 1585. Courtesy of the Trustees of the British Museum.

xxii. Theodor de Bry, *A Weroan or Great Lorde of Virginia* and *The True Picture of One Picte*, from Thomas Harriot, *A Briefe and True Report of the New Found Land of Virginia* (London, 1590). Courtesy of The Huntington Library, San Marino, California. (Images supplied by and published with permission of ProQuest.)

13. Captain John Smith, engraving, c. 1624. Courtesy of The Huntington Library, San Marino, California.

17. Sidney E. King, Jamestown fort, painting, c. 1956. Courtesy of Peter Newark American Pictures/Bridgeman Images.

25. The mock execution of Captain John Smith at the court of Wahunsonacock, from Smith's *Generall Historie of Virginia, New-England and the Summer Isles* (London, 1624). Courtesy of The Huntington Library, San Marino, California.

42. Ralph Hamor visiting the Powhatan Indians, from Theodor de Bry, *America* (Frankfurt, 1628). Courtesy of The Huntington Library, San Marino, California.

48. Robert Peake, *Lady Elizabeth Pope*, oil portrait, c. 1615. Courtesy of the Tate Gallery, London.

49. Illustration from *A Declaration for the Certaine Time of Drawing the Great Standing Lottery* (London, 1616). Courtesy of the Society of Antiquaries, London.

51. Simon van de Passe, *Matoaka Alias Rebecca*, engraving, 1616. Courtesy of the Library of Congress, Washington, DC.

63. Charles Lucy, *The Departure of the Pilgrims from Delft Haven*, 1847. Courtesy of the Pilgrim Hall Museum, Plymouth, Massachusetts.

71. Indian rebellion in Virginia, 1622, engraving by Matthäus Merian, from Theodor de Bry, *America* (Frankfurt, 1628). Courtesy of The Huntington Library, San Marino, California.

85. *The Summer Isles* (Bermuda), from John Smith's *Generall Historie of Virginia, New-England and the Summer Isles* (London, 1624). Courtesy of The Huntington Library, San Marino, California.

94. John Guy in Newfoundland, 1612, engraving by Matthäus Merian, from Theodor de Bry, *America* (Frankfurt, 1628). Courtesy of The Huntington Library, San Marino, California.

104. John Winthrop, oil portrait, unknown artist, c. 1630. Courtesy of the American Antiquarian Society, Worcester, Massachusetts.

110. Wenceslaus Hollar, *Three Ships in a Rough Sea*, c. 1665. Courtesy of the Thomas Fisher Rare Book Library, University of Toronto.

116. Massachusetts Bay Colony seal. Courtesy of the Library of Congress, Washington, DC.

137. Ralph Hall, *Virginia*, engraving, 1636. Courtesy of The Huntington Library, San Marino, California.

143. [R]alph [H]all (?), *The Figure of the Indians' Fort or Palizado in New England*, from John

Underhill, *Newes from America* (London, 1638). Courtesy of the Library of Congress, Washington, DC.

163. Wenceslaus Hollar, *Unus Americanus ex Virginia, Aetat 23*. Courtesy of the Library of Congress, Washington, DC.

174. Edward Winslow, oil portrait, unknown artist (school of Robert Walker), London, 1651. Courtesy of the Pilgrim Hall Museum, Plymouth, Massachusetts.

201. *The Battle at the Mouth of the Severn*, engraving from William Cullen Bryant and Sydney Howard Gay, *A Popular History of the United States*, 3 vols. (New York, 1881). Courtesy of The Huntington Library, San Marino, California.

205. Title page to *Virginia's Discovery of Silke-Wormes* (London, 1650). Courtesy of The Huntington Library, San Marino, California. (Image supplied by and published with permission of ProQuest.)

221. Howard Pyle, *Mary Dyer on the Way to Her Execution, 1660* (c. 1905). Courtesy of the Newport Historical Society, Newport, Rhode Island.

235. Engraving from Charles de Rochefort, *Histoire Naturelle et Morale des Iles Antilles de l'Amerique* (Rotterdam, 1665). Courtesy of The Huntington Library, San Marino, California.

245. Henry Winstanley, geographical playing cards, c. 1675. Courtesy of The Huntington Library, San Marino, California.

253. Sir Peter Lely, *Sir William Berkeley*, oil portrait, c. 1663. Courtesy of the National Gallery of Art, Washington, DC / The Art Archive / Superstock, London.

262. *America*, frontispiece to Ferdinando Gorges, *America Painted to the Life* (London, 1658). Courtesy of The Huntington Library, San Marino, California.

272. Paul Revere, *Philip, King of Mount Hope*, from Benjamin Church, *The Entertaining History of King Philip's War*, 2nd ed. (Boston, 1772). Courtesy of the Library of Congress, Washington, DC.

287. Mary Rowlandson defends her home against the Indians, 1676, from *A Narrative of the Captivity, Sufferings and Removes of Mrs Mary Rowlandson* (Boston, 1791). Courtesy of the American Antiquarian Society, Worcester, Massachusetts.

294. Inventory of Thomas Eames's losses, Framingham Massachusetts, 1676 (manuscript HM 8407). Courtesy of The Huntington Library, San Marino, California.

318. *Engelse Quakers en Tabak aende Barbados, c. 1680*. Courtesy of the British Museum / Robana Picture Library.

334. Thomas Child, *Sir William Phips*, oil portrait, Boston, c. 1690. Copyright Cory Gardiner.

337. *Cottonus Matherus S. theologiae doctor regia societatis Londonensis*, engraving, 1727. Courtesy of the Library of Congress, Washington, DC.

341. *Strange Creatures in America*, woodcut, from R. B. [Nathaniel Crouch], *The English Empire in America* (London, 1685). Courtesy of The Huntington Library, San Marino, California.

355. Jan van der Spriet, *Increase Mather*, oil portrait, 1688. Courtesy of the Massachusetts Historical Society, Boston.

366. *A True and Perfect Relation of That Most Sad and Terrible Earthquake at Port-Royal in Jamaica* (London, 1692). Courtesy of the British Library / Robana Picture Library.

369. Tompkins H. Matteson, *The Trial of George Jacobs, August 5, 1692* (1855). Courtesy of the Peabody-Essex Museum, Salem, Massachusetts / Art Resource.

374. Hadley chest, oak and pine, Massachusetts, c. 1695. Courtesy of The Dietrich American Foundation. Photograph: Will Brown.

383. Johannes Kip, *A Prospect of Bridge Town in Barbados*, engraving after Samuel Copen, 1695. Courtesy of the Library of Congress, Washington, DC.

385. *Anne Pollard at One Hundred Years of Age*, oil portrait, unknown artist, 1721. Courtesy of the Massachusetts Historical Society, Boston.

INDEX

ML   12-14